THE HOME
BOOK OF
CHRISTMAS

The
Home Book
of
Christmas

Edited by

May Lamberton Becker

Dodd, Mead & Company

New York

Published by Dodd, Mead & Company, Inc.
79 Madison Avenue, New York, N.Y. 10016
Distributed in Canada by
McClelland and Stewart Limited, Toronto
Manufactured in the United States of America

Library of Congress Cataloging in Publication Data
Main entry under title:

The Home book of Christmas.

Originally published in 1941.
1. Christmas—Literary collections.   I. Becker, May
Lamberton, 1873-1958.
PN6071.C6H58   1984   808.8'033   84-6115
ISBN 0-396-08478-8

TO MY FREQUENT PARDNER

RAYMOND T. BOND

PRINCE OF COLLABORATORS

—TO WHOM THIS BOOK OWES SO MUCH—

IT IS DEDICATED

WITH THANKS AND ADMIRATION

Acknowledgments

Acknowledgments are made to the following authors and publishers for kind permission to use selections from their copyrighted publications:

D. Appleton–Century Company for selections from *The Lone Winter* by Anne Bosworth Greene, copyright, 1923; and from *Social Life in Old New Orleans* by Eliza Ripley, copyright, 1912; *Sonny, A Christmas Guest* by Ruth McEnery Stuart, copyright, 1894, 1895, 1896.

Faith Baldwin and *Liberty* Magazine for *Still Is the Night*, copyright, 1941.

Emma Bugbee for "Christmas in Our Town."

The Columbia Broadcasting System for "A Broadcast from the Trenches, Finland," by William L. White.

Merrill Denison for "Christmas Calories."

Dodd, Mead & Company, Inc. for "The Sending of the Magi" by Bliss Carman, copyright, 1931; poems by G. K. Chesterton, copyright, 1911, 1923, 1932; *The Errors of Santa Claus* by Stephen Leacock, copyright, 1931.

Doubleday, Doran and Company, Inc. for "Frankincense and Myrrh" from *Pieces of Hate* by Heywood Broun, copyright, 1922; "The Blossoming Rod" from *Refractory Husbands* by Mary Stewart Cutting, copyright, 1913; "Gift of the Magi" from *The Four Million* by O. Henry, copyright, 1905, 1933.

Charles J. Finger for *The Affair at the Inn*, copyright, 1930.

Good Housekeeping Magazine for "Hoofbeats on a Bridge" by Alexander Woollcott, copyright, 1940.

Geraldine Gordon for *The Christmas Tree*.

Harcourt, Brace and Company, Inc. for selections from *The Collected Edition of Heywood Broun*, copyright, 1941; "Three Stockings" from *Mrs. Miniver*, copyright, 1940; *The Donkey of God*, copyright, 1932.

Harper and Brothers for "A Christmas Spectacle" from *Love Conquers All* by Robert Benchley, copyright, 1922; *How Come Christmas* by Roark Bradford, copyright, 1930; "How the Good Gifts Were Used" from *The Wonder Clock* by Howard Pyle, copyright, 1887, 1915; "Why Santa Claus Chose the Reindeer" from *The Giant Who Liked Chocolate Cake* by Estella Hitchcock Lane, copyright, 1939.

Henry Holt and Company for "The Holy Night" from *Christ Legends* by Selma Lagerlof, copyright, 1908, 1936.

Houghton, Mifflin Company for "The Shepherds in Judea" from *The Children Sing in the Far West* by Mary Austin, copyright, 1928; "The Christmas Tree" from *The Book of the Little Past* by Josephine Preston Peabody, copyright, 1908, 1936; *A Plantation Christmas* by Julia Peterkin, copyright, 1929, 1934.

J. B. Lippincott Company for "Old Thoughts for Christmas" and "The Tree That Didn't Get Trimmed" from *Essays* by Christopher Morley, copyright, 1918, 1919, 1920, 1921, 1923, 1925, 1926, 1927.

Little, Brown and Company for "Christmas on Bee Tree" from Lucy Furman's *The Glass Window,* copyright, 1925; "Master Jack's Song" from *Sundown Songs* by Laura E. Richards, copyright, 1899, 1927; "Crisp New Bills for Mr. Teagle" from *A Pearl in Every Oyster* by Frank Sullivan, copyright, 1933, 1934, 1935, 1936, 1937, 1938.

Liveright Publishing Corporation for "If Christmas Comes" from *How to Be a Hermit* by Will Cuppy, copyright, 1929.

McFarlane, Warde, McFarlane, Inc. for "Centerpiece" from *Tryptich of the Three Kings* by Felix Timmermans, copyright, 1936.

Lee McNeely for "In the Storm Country" by Marian Hurd McNeely.

The Macmillan Company for "One Thousand Aves" from *Maria Chapdelaine* by Louis Hémon, copyright, 1921; "In Clean Hay" from *The Christmas Nightingale* by Eric P. Kelly, copyright, 1932; and a selection from *Maud* by I. M. Rittenhouse, copyright, 1939.

G. P. Putnam's Sons for two selections, "Balsam" and "Mistletoe," from *An Almanac for Moderns* by Donald Culross Peattie, copyright, 1935.

P. E. G. Quercus for "Christmas Poem for Motorists."

Fleming H. Revell Company for "Christmas Eve at Topmost Tickle" from *Doctor Luke of the Labrador* by Norman Duncan, copyright, 1904.

Charles Scribner's Sons for "The Facts" and "Old Folks' Christmas" from *Round Up* by Ring Lardner, copyright, 1924, 1926, 1929; "Jest 'Fore Christmas," "The First Christmas Tree" and "The Mouse and the Moonbeam" from *The Collected Works of Eugene Field,* copyright, 1889; "The Shepherd Who Watched by Night" from *The Land of the Spirit* by Thomas Nelson Page, copyright, 1913, 1941.

Sheed and Ward, Inc. for Act I of *The Journey of the Three Kings* by Henri Gheon.

Henry A. Shute for a selection from *Plupy, "The Real Boy,"* copyright, 1910.

Peter Smith for "A Christmas Present for a Lady" from *Little Citizens* by Myra Kelly, copyright, 1904, 1932.

Frederick A. Stokes Company for a selection from *First Adventures in Reading* by May Lamberton Becker, copyright, 1936.

The New York *Sun* for *Is There a Santa Claus?*

The Viking Press, Inc. for "About Three Kings, Uncle Herman's Uniform and Christmas Night" from *Hansi* by Ludwig Bemelmans, copyright, 1934.

Beatrice Warde (Paul Beaujon) for *Peace Under Earth*.

Contents

xi

THE SHEPHERDS

THE MAGI

THE PREPARATIONS

THE GREAT DAY

THE STOCKINGS

THE TREE

SANTA CLAUS

READING ALOUD TO YOUNG PEOPLE

FOOD AND FUN

SONGS AND VERSES

CAROLS

HOW THEY SPENT CHRISTMAS

THERE'LL ALWAYS BE A CHRISTMAS

"WHOSOEVER on ye nighte of ye nativity of ye younge Lord Jesus, in ye greate snows, shall fare forth bearing a succulent bone for ye lost and lamenting hounde, a whisp of hay for ye shivering horse, a cloak of warm raiment for ye stranded wayfarer, a bundle of fagots for ye twittering crone, a flagon of red wine for him whose marrow withers, a garland of bright berries for one who has worn chains, a dish of crumbs with a song of love for all huddled birds who thought that song was dead, and divers lush sweetmeats for such babes' faces as peer from lonely windows,

TO HIM shall be proffered and returned gifts of such an astonishment as will rival the hues of the peacock and the harmonies of heaven, so that though he live to ye greate age when man goes stooping and querulous because of the nothing that is left in him, yet shall he walk upright and remembering, as one whose hearte shines like a greate star in his breaste."

—Anon

THE BIBLE STORY

AND it came to pass in those days, that there went out a decree from Caesar Augustus, that all the world should be taxed. . . . And all went to be taxed, every one into his own city.

And Joseph also went up from Galilee, out of the city of Nazareth, into Judaea, unto the city of David which is called Bethlehem, (because he was of the house and lineage of David), to be taxed with Mary his espoused wife, being great with child. And so it was that, while they were there, the days were accomplished that she should be delivered. And she brought forth her firstborn son; and wrapped him in swaddling clothes, and laid him in a manger; because there was no room for them in the inn.

And there were in the same country shepherds abiding in the field, keeping watch over their flock by night. And, lo, the angel of the Lord came upon them, and the glory of the Lord shone round about them: and they were sore afraid.

And the angel said unto them, Fear not; for, behold, I bring you good tidings of great joy, which shall be to all people. For unto you is born this day in the city of David a Saviour, which is Christ the Lord. And this shall be a sign unto you; ye shall find the babe wrapped in swaddling clothes, lying in a manger.

And suddenly there was with the angel a multitude of the heavenly host praising God, and saying, Glory to God in the highest, and on earth peace, goodwill toward men.

And it came to pass, as the angels were gone away from them into heaven, the shepherds said one to another, Let us now go even unto Bethlehem, and see this thing which is come to pass, which the Lord hath made known unto us.

And they came with haste, and found Mary, and Joseph, and the babe lying in a manger. And when they had seen it, they made known abroad the saying which was told them concerning this child. And all they that heard it wondered at those things which were told them by the shepherds. But Mary kept all these things, and pondered them in her heart. And the shepherds returned, glorifying and praising God for all the things that they had heard and seen, as it was told unto them.

The Gospel according to ST. LUKE.

Now when Jesus was born in Bethlehem of Judaea in the days of Herod the king, behold, there came wise men from the east to Jerusalem, saying, Where is he that is born King of the Jews? for we have seen his star in the east, and are come to worship him.

When Herod the king had heard these things, he was troubled, and all Jerusalem with him. And when he had gathered all the chief priests and scribes of the people together, he demanded of them where Christ should be born.

And they said unto him, In Bethlehem of Judaea: for thus it is written by the prophet:

And thou Bethlehem, in the land of Juda,

Art not the least among the princes of Juda:

For out of thee shall come a Governor,

That shall rule my people Israel.

Then Herod, when he had privily called the wise men, inquired of them diligently what time the star appeared. And he sent them to Bethlehem, and said, Go and search diligently for the young child; and when ye have found him, bring me word again, that I may come and worship him also.

When they had heard the king, they departed; and, lo, the star, which they saw in the east, went before them, till it came and stood over where the young child was. When they saw the star, they rejoiced with exceeding great joy. And when they were come into the house, they saw the young child with Mary his mother, and fell down, and worshipped him: and when they had opened their treasures, they presented unto him gifts; gold, and frankincense, and myrrh. And being warned of God in a dream that they should not return to Herod, they departed into their own country another way.

The Gospel according to ST. MATTHEW.

For unto us a child is born, unto us a son is given, and the government shall be upon his shoulder; and his name shall be called Wonderful, Counsellor, The mighty God, The everlasting Father, The Prince of Peace.

Isaiah.

CHRISTMAS EVE

THE HOLY NIGHT

By Selma Lagerlöf

IT was a Christmas Day and all the folks had driven to church except grandmother and I. I believe we were all alone in the house. We had not been permitted to go along, because one of us was too old and the other was too young. And we were sad, both of us, because we had not been taken to early mass to hear the singing and to see the Christmas candles.

But as we sat there in our loneliness, grandmother began to tell a story.

"There was a man," said she, "who went out in the dark night to borrow live coals to kindle a fire. He went from hut to hut and knocked. 'Dear friends, help me!' said he. 'My wife has just given birth to a child, and I must make a fire to warm her and the little one.'

"But it was way in the night, and all the people were asleep. No one replied.

"The man walked and walked. At last he saw the gleam of a fire a long way off. Then he went in that direction, and saw that the fire was burning in the open. A lot of sheep were sleeping around the fire, and an old shepherd sat and watched over the flock.

"When the man who wanted to borrow fire came up to the sheep, he saw that three big dogs lay asleep at the shepherd's feet. All three awoke when the man approached and opened their great jaws, as though they wanted to bark; but not a sound was heard. The man noticed that the hair on their backs stood up and that their sharp, white teeth glistened in the firelight. They dashed toward him. He felt that one of them bit at his leg and one at his hand and that one clung to his throat. But their jaws and teeth wouldn't obey them, and the man didn't suffer the least harm.

"Now the man wished to go farther, to get what he needed. But the sheep lay back to back and so close to one another that he couldn't pass them. Then the man stepped upon their backs and walked over them and up to the fire. And not one of the animals awoke or moved."

Thus far, grandmother had been allowed to narrate without interruption. But at this point I couldn't help breaking in. "Why didn't they do it, grandma?" I asked.

"That you shall hear in a moment," said grandmother—and went on with her story.

"When the man had almost reached the fire, the shepherd looked up. He was a surly old man, who was unfriendly and harsh toward human beings. And when he saw the strange man coming, he seized the long spiked staff, which he always held in his hand when he tended his flock, and threw it at him. The staff came right toward the man, but, before it reached him, it turned off to one side and whizzed past him, far out in the meadow."

When grandmother had got this far, I interrupted her again. "Grandma, why wouldn't the stick hurt the man?" Grandmother did not bother about answering me, but continued her story.

"Now the man came up to the shepherd and said to him: 'Good man, help me, and lend me a little fire! My wife has just given birth to a child, and I must make a fire to warm her and the little one.'

"The shepherd would rather have said no, but when he pondered that the dogs couldn't hurt the man, and the sheep had not run from him, and that the staff had not wished to strike him, he was a little afraid, and dared not deny the man that which he asked.

" 'Take as much as you need!' he said to the man.

"But then the fire was nearly burnt out. There were no logs or branches left, only a big heap of live coals; and the stranger had neither spade nor shovel, wherein he could carry the red-hot coals.

"When the shepherd saw this, he said again: 'Take as much as you need!' And he was glad that the man wouldn't be able to take away any coals.

"But the man stooped and picked coals from the ashes with his bare hands, and laid them in his mantle. And he didn't burn his hands when he touched them, nor did the coals scorch his mantle; but he carried them away as if they had been nuts or apples."

But here the story-teller was interrupted for the third time. "Grandma, why wouldn't the coals burn the man?"

"That you shall hear," said grandmother, and went on:

"And when the shepherd, who was such a cruel and hard-hearted man, saw all this, he began to wonder to himself: 'What kind of a night is this, when the dogs do not bite, the sheep are not scared, the staff does not kill, or the fire scorch?' He called the stranger back, and said to him: 'What kind of a night is this? And how does it happen that all things show you compassion?'

"Then said the man: 'I cannot tell you if you yourself do not see it.' And he wished to go his way, that he might soon make a fire and warm his wife and child.

"But the shepherd did not wish to lose sight of the man before he had found out what all this might portend. He got up and followed the man till they came to the place where he lived.

"Then the shepherd saw that the man didn't have so much as a hut to dwell in, but that his wife and babe were lying in a mountain grotto, where there was nothing except the cold and naked stone walls.

"But the shepherd thought that perhaps the poor innocent child might freeze to death there in the grotto; and, although he was a hard man, he was touched, and thought he would like to help it. And he loosened his knapsack from his shoulder, took from it a soft white sheepskin, gave it to the strange man, and said that he should let the child sleep on it.

"But just as soon as he showed that he, too, could be merciful, his eyes were opened, and he saw what he had not been able to see before and heard what he could not have heard before.

"He saw that all around him stood a ring of little silver-winged angels, and each held a stringed instrument, and all sang in loud tones that to-night the Saviour was born who should redeem the world from its sins.

"Then he understood how all things were so happy this night that they didn't want to do anything wrong.

"And it was not only around the shepherd that there were angels, but he saw them everywhere. They sat inside the grotto, they sat outside on the mountain, and they flew under the heavens. They came marching in great companies, and, as they passed, they paused and cast a glance at the child.

"There were such jubilation and such gladness and songs and play! And all this he saw in the dark night, whereas before he could not have made out anything. He was so happy because his eyes had been opened that he fell upon his knees and thanked God."

Here grandmother sighed and said: "What that shepherd saw we might also see, for the angels fly down from heaven every Christmas Eve, if we could only see them."

Then grandmother laid her hand on my head, and said: "You must remember this, for it is as true, as true as that I see you and you see me. It is not revealed by the light of lamps or candles, and it does not depend upon sun and moon; but that which is needful is, that we have such eyes as can see God's glory."

INASMUCH

By Heywood Broun

ONCE there lived near Bethlehem a man named Simon and his wife Deborah. And Deborah dreamed a curious dream, a dream so vivid that it might better be called a vision. It was not yet daybreak, but she roused her husband and told him that an angel had come to her in the vision and had said, as she remembered it, "Tomorrow night in Bethlehem the King of the World will be born." The rest was not so vivid in Deborah's mind, but she told Simon that wise men and kings were already on their way to Bethlehem, bringing gifts for the wonder child.

"When he is born," she said, "the wise men and the kings who bring these gifts will see the stars dance in the heavens and hear the voices of angels. You and I must send presents, too, for this child will be the greatest man in all the world."

Simon objected that there was nothing of enough value in the house to take to such a child, but Deborah replied, "The King of the World will understand." Then, although it was not yet light, she got up and began to bake a cake, and Simon went beyond the town to the hills and got holly and made a wreath. Later in the day husband and wife looked over all their belongings, but the only suitable gift they could find was one old toy, a somewhat battered wooden duck that had belonged to their eldest son, who had grown up and married and gone away to live in Galilee. Simon painted the toy duck as well as he could, and Deborah told him to take it and the cake and the wreath of holly and go to Bethlehem. "It's not much," she said, "but the King will understand."

It was almost sunset when Simon started down the winding road that led to Bethlehem. Deborah watched him round the first turn and would have watched longer except that he was walking straight toward the sun and the light hurt her eyes. She went back into the house and an hour had hardly passed when she heard Simon whistling in the garden. He was walking very slowly. At the door he hesitated for almost a minute. She looked up when he came in. He was empty handed.

"You haven't been to Bethlehem," said Deborah.

"No," said Simon.

"Then, where is the cake, and the holly wreath, and the toy duck?"

"I'm sorry," said Simon, "I couldn't help it somehow. It just happened."

"What happened?" asked Deborah sharply.

"Well," said Simon, "just after I went around the first turn in the road I found a child sitting on that big white rock, crying. He was about two or three years old, and I stopped and asked him why he was crying. He didn't answer. Then I told him not to cry like that, and I patted his head, but that didn't do any good. I hung around, trying to think up something, and I decided to put the cake down and take him up in my arms for a minute. But the cake slipped out of my hands and hit the rock, and a piece of the icing chipped off. Well, I thought, that baby in Bethlehem won't miss a little piece of icing, and

I gave it to the child and he stopped crying. But when he finished he began to cry again. I just sort of squeezed another little piece of icing off, and that was all right, for a little while; but then I had to give him another piece, and things went on that way, and all of a sudden I found that there wasn't any cake left. After that he looked as if he might cry again, and I didn't have any more cake and so I showed him the duck and he said 'Ta-ta.' I just meant to lend him the duck for a minute, but he wouldn't give it up. I coaxed him a good while, but he wouldn't let go. And then a woman came out of that little house and she began to scold him for staying out so late, and so I told her it was my fault and I gave her the holly wreath just so she wouldn't be mad at the child. And after that, you see, I didn't have anything to take to Bethlehem, and so I came back here."

Deborah had begun to cry long before Simon finished his story, but when he had done she lifted up her head and said, "How could you do it, Simon? Those presents were meant for the King of the World, and you gave them to the first crying child you met on the road."

Then she began to cry again, and Simon didn't know what to say or do, and it grew darker and darker in the room and the fire on the hearth faded to a few embers. And that little red glow was all there was in the room. Now, Simon could not even see Deborah across the room, but he could still hear her sobbing. But suddenly the room was flooded with light and Deborah's sobbing broke into a great gulp and she rushed to the window and looked out. The stars danced in the sky and from high above the house came the voice of angels saying, "Glory to God in the highest, and on earth peace, good will toward men."

Deborah dropped to her knees in a panic of joy and fear. Simon knelt beside her, but first he said, "I thought maybe that the baby in Bethlehem wouldn't mind so very much."

THE DONKEY OF GOD

By Louis Untermeyer

YOU must know that, at the time of this story, Italy was not one country as she is today. Italy was divided into many provinces, each of them jealous of the other. There was not even a united feeling within the provinces themselves. In the Middle Ages very city had its own government, and every city hated its neighbor. Milan fought with Mantua; Florence despised Siena and spoke of its citizens as "the treacherous Sienese"; Pisa sneered at Florence, there being continual conflict between the proud Pisans "already powerful when the ancient Greeks struggled beneath the walls of Troy" and "the upstart Florentines"; Assisi and Perugia always had been at war with each other.

Assisi claimed to be the oldest of the hill-towns. It boasted of tombs that were even older than the temple-ruins; its vine-terraced slopes grew the richest grapes and the juiciest olives. More important from the point of view of the generals of Assisi, those slopes commanded a view of the Umbrian valley and no enemy could approach without being seen from a great distance. Thus prepared and fortified, Assisi was a happy place. It was even a merry one. Its merchants were wealthy, its churches were richly decorated, its young people were dressed as though life were one long carnival.

Of all the gay youths none was as richly costumed as Francis. His father was a cloth-merchant and Francis was his favorite son. No wonder his horse was the swiftest, his cap-feather the longest, his armor the handsomest, and his eyes the most impudent in Assisi. No one danced more wildly in the festival masquerades; no one swung a lute so gallantly or composed a livelier serenade; no one shook his fist more patriotically than Francis at the towers of Perugia. When, after an uncomfortable peace, the neighboring cities threatened a new war, no one was quicker to call for action than the bold son of the cloth-merchant.

"Let us not wait until Perugia comes out against us," cried Francis. "Let us carry the war into her own fields, against her own gates. Let our swords break down her pride; let torches lay waste the old enemy. On to Perugia!"

A little past midnight, after the moon had gone down, the army from Assisi set out to surprise the foe. But the Perugians must have had the same idea, for that night the Umbrian plain held two armies marching against each other. It was still dark when they met. The surprise was complete and all plans of orderly battle vanished with the first blow. They fought recklessly in a blackness lit only by torches suddenly lifted, suddenly dashed out. The quiet plain was shocked from its nightly peace to a hideous awaking. Arrows and spear-throwing machines were useless; it was short range fighting. Shield and sword, mace and dagger rang against each other in utter confusion.

With the first streak of dawn the fight came to an end. The scene was horrible beyond description. Each army had killed more of its own men than the enemy's. What was left of the Perugians was a battered remnant of soldiers; the champions of Assisi were too worn to continue. Without another blow, without a word of hate, the remainder of the two armies turned toward their towns. No one had a boast left to utter. It was a broken army that returned to Assisi in a dull, red dawn. The stoutest of the old horsemen felt sick.

None felt sicker than Francis. He had seen things that turned his ideas upside down. He had seen a man lying dead—not beautifully dead like an image on a stone-coffin, but deformedly, unspeakably dead—dead at his feet. His encrusted armor was foul with blood—blood that, a few hours ago, had flowed in veins as happy as his—there was blood on his hands. His heart felt as though an unseen dagger had run through it. With the dawn something new had dawned in Francis, something that would not die.

For weeks he lay tossing in a high fever. The doctors could do nothing to make him rest. Francis would start from a short sleep, call out, and lie awake the rest of the night, crying things that no one could understand. He was wasting away; his condition seemed hopeless. On the fortieth day, after the doctors had shaken their heads and gone,

Francis got up. No one saw him go. He walked out of the house at dawn as softly as the light that showed him the way. Assisi was just awaking as he passed through the crooked streets and out of the town.

It was a different Francis that wandered, silently and alone, past the Umbrian plain. The rich suit had been exchanged for a coarse brown frock; instead of a sword he carried a wooden staff; there were no ornaments on his sleeves, no feathers on his hat—even the hat was gone. The impudent look had vanished from his eyes, the lines of boastfulness had left his lips. The face of Francis had grown long and finely cut; the eyes looked *through* things, not merely at them; a light seemed to be upon his brow.

Forty more days Francis wandered. He crossed valleys and climbed mountains; now in shaded woods, now in sun-baked marshes, making his way without a chart. He journeyed through Orvieto and Rome as in a dream. At the end of the fortieth day he came to the sea. Still following some inner guide, he took passage on a boat and landed on the island of Sardinia. He had no plan, but somehow he knew that he must work out his cure in this primitive place.

Here, far from the frivolous life of his past, he learned to live. Poorer than the poorest peasant, he was grateful for the common *frue,* or sour milk, and he who had been used to the rarest and most delicate dishes considered an occasional bowl of fresh cheese, which the natives called *ricotta,* a great treat. He did not indulge himself often in this, nor, for that matter, in anything else; his little hut was the humblest on an island where everything was scanty.

Little by little Francis' health returned; his step grew more vigorous, and he became himself again. But it was another self that now saw grandeur in the lowly and good in everything. He preferred the simple customs and dignity of the poor Sardinians to the hot carelessness of his one-time companions. But, though he visited the peasants every evening, he spent most of his time alone. He learned to know the animals of the island and was trusted by them. He became so familiar a sight that even the shy mouflon, a sort of wild sheep, let him walk among them, stroking their long coats. He understood their ways; he began to understand their speech.

One day as he was walking among the ruins of monuments as old as the stone-age, he noticed he had gone farther than usual and was straying in a circle of queer structures that the natives called "Fairy Houses." He smiled as he thought of the fear the peasants had of these stone-chambers and the superstition that any one resting within the circle would "dream true." He noticed a donkey standing in the shade of a stunted tree, but it did not appear in the least astonished to see him. Now that he observed it closer, he could not remember ever having seen a donkey so small. It was no larger than a large dog, a sheep-dog with unusually long ears. Its ankles were more delicate than a deer's and the eyes had a speaking softness. But the most peculiar feature was revealed to Francis only when he stood close. The color was a soft pigeon-gray without a spot except for one distinguishing mark: a pattern made by two intersecting lines of black, one line running down the back from head to tail, the other line running across the shoulders. Presently, Francis noticed that the animal was speaking to him and he was aware that he understood it.

"Tell me, my good man," it was saying, "for I can see you are good, is there no justice in creation? Isn't it bad enough that we donkeys have to carry every sort of burden—twice as much as the much larger horse —without also being a joke among men and animals? Is that just? And if that were not enough, why should we be made still more foolish by having to wear such a disfiguring pattern on our back? Can you answer that?"

To his surprise, Francis heard himself replying to the little donkey as if he were a priest and it were one of his flock.

"Yes, my daughter, I think I can. There is a justice in all things, though we cannot see it at once. We must wait until the pattern is completed before we judge any of its parts. In your case the answer is easier than most, for you are the donkey of God."

"The donkey of God?" asked the little animal.

"Surely," replied Francis, amazed at the way he was talking, but keeping on in an even voice. "If you do not know your own story, I will tell it to you."

And Francis, who had never seen the creature before, and who certainly had never thought of its origin, heard himself telling this strange legend:

It was the morning of the Sixth Day. God had spent the First Day inventing Light. Then, seeing that continual light would be too cruel on the eyes, He made Darkness for relief. On the Second Day God had designed the seas and had put a clear border of sky about them to prevent the waters from overflowing. On the Third Day, being dissatisfied with the emptiness of a world of water, He had gathered the waters in one place and had put dry land carefully among the seas. He called the dry land Earth and liked it much better, especially after He had caused green things to grow and had planned fruit to come after the flower. He had told Himself it was good. On the Fourth Day God had looked at the widespread Heaven and realized it needed something. So He had put lights in it: a great gold light to rule the day, and a soft silver one to rule the night, and a lot of lesser lights to decorate the evening. And once more He had been pleased. On the Fifth Day He decided He wanted more motion and sound in the universe. So He had filled the waters with whales and minnows and the air with insects and eagles. He had smiled when the first whale, that island afloat, had blown his first spout, and His great heart had tightened when the lark, hoping to reach heaven, sang his first song.

And now it was the Sixth Day. The earth, God saw, needed life no less than the sea and sky. So early in the morning He began making animals. First He made small simple ones: the snake and the snail, the mouse and the mole, rat and rabbit, cat and dog, lamb and wolf, goat, mink, fox, hedge-hog, beaver, woodchuck and a hundred others, each after his kind. Then, watching them leap or crawl or dig or prowl, He tried the same design on an ever-growing scale. It was then He made donkey and deer, horse and cattle, lion and tiger, bear, buffalo, elk, the great apes, the giant lizards, the mammoths like mountains on the move. Then God, out of the humor of His heart, indulged Himself in a few experiments. He made the giraffe with his feet in the mud, his long neck lost in the leaves, and his silly head trying to scrape the stars. He tied a bird and a snake together and made the ostrich.

He took a lump of clay, shaped it, unshaped it, dug His thumb twice into it and threw it away—and that was the camel. He thought of a hill-side with a tiny tail and nose-arm-fingers in one long trunk—and thus the elephant was made. He took some river-mud, breathed on it, changed His mind, saying, "No animal that looked like that would want to live"—and it was the hippopotamus. When He saw these absurd shapes strut about, He laughed so long that the stars began to fall from their places—some of them are still so loose that they tremble in the sky—and, for a while, He did nothing at all.

But since He was God, He could not stop creating. So in the afternoon He looked at everything and said, "It is good." After a little while He added, "But it could be better. It lacks something."

All afternoon He sat pondering among the clouds. At last toward evening, He said, "It is not enough like Me. I will take the very best soil from the earth, for this will be an earth-creature. I will mix it with water so he need not be afraid of the sea. I will knead it with air so he can trust himself in any element and even fly if he wishes. I will then put a spark of Myself deep in him so he may be God-like. And it will be Man."

When the animals heard this they began arguing with God.

"Consider, O Lord," said the lion in his gentlest, most persuasive roar. He was already known as the king of beasts, so he spoke first. "Consider, O Lord, before You breathe life into the creature. If You make him of the elements, he will be master not only of them, but of us all."

"Yes," said the elephant with a gruff simplicity, "such an animal as Man will do no labor at all. He'll say he's not made for it, and we'll have to do his work for him."

"Not that we mind, Lord," hissed the serpent with false meekness. "But if You put Your spark in him, he'll think he's divine. And after he's mastered us—not that *we* mind—he'll try to master what created him. And then—"

"And then," said God in the still small voice which was more terrible than thunder, "he will be part of Me again. Meanwhile, I have no need of advice from My own creations."

And so He made Man.

You are wondering, I see, what had become of the donkey. Up to now he had done nothing but listen and mind his own affairs. While the others were arguing with God or grumbling among themselves, the donkey calmly went on eating rose-leaves and lettuces and growing lovelier every minute. Perhaps I should have told you that he had been born the most perfect of four-footed creatures. He was very much like the donkeys of today except that his color was softer, his eyes more tender, his ankles even more graceful—and, at that time, the long ears of his great-great-grandchildren did not disfigure his head. Instead of the grotesque flapping sails of the donkey of today, the original donkey had two of the finest, most perfectly shaped ears you can imagine. They were like those of a dainty fox, only smaller, and so wax-like that you could half see through them. Everything satisfied him; he feared nothing; the world was good. So he continued to munch lettuces and rose-leaves.

The donkey was so busy eating—it was at the beautiful beginning of things when there were no worms in the lettuces nor thorns on the roses—that he did not see God make the first man. Nor did he see Him, late in the night, creating the first woman. The next morning —it was Sunday—the other animals told him about it and said the man-animal was called Adam and the woman-animal was called Eve. A little tired of doing nothing but eating, the donkey joined the other beasts and peered into the garden where the two newest-born creatures were sitting. When he saw them he burst into the loudest and most ridiculous laugh on earth. It was like no sound that had ever been made; it was the first wild, weird, astonishing bray. Today only the smallest echoes are in the throat of all the donkeys, but then it rang so fiercely against the skies that it almost threw the fixed stars out of their courses.

"Ho-hee-haw!" screamed the donkey. "It is *too* funny! *Such* animals! They're made all wrong! No hide! No hoofs! Not even a tail! And so pink—so *naked!* God must have meant to put a coat of fleece on them and forgot it! Ho-hee-*haw!*"

Eve, frightened by the screaming and screeching, ran into the woods. Adam sprang to his feet.

."And look!" the donkey brayed in a still ruder laugh, while the other beasts roared and cackled and barked. "Look! The she-man runs on her hind legs! She doesn't even know how to walk! Ho-ho—hee—haw—hee—HAW!"

This was too much for Adam. He ran over to the donkey and grasped him by the ears. The donkey tried to pull himself free, but Adam held fast. As he tugged and Adam tightened, his ears began to stretch, grow long, longer. . . . And while they were pulling, God suddenly appeared.

Said the Lord, "Because you have spoiled My day of rest and because you have made fun of My creation you shall be punished. Because you saw fit to laugh at your betters, you shall never cease from laughing. But no one will listen with joy; your voice will be a mockery by day and a horror by night. The louder you laugh, the longer will you be despised. You shall serve man and be subject to him all the days of your life. Other animals shall serve him, also: the horse, the cow, the elephant and the dog. But, unlike them, you shall work for man without winning his love. Unlike them, you shall resist him foolishly, and he shall beat you for it. You who are the most comely of My creatures shall be the most comic. Instead of roses you shall feed on thorns and thistles. You shall have a rope for a tail. And your ears shall remain long."

So it was decreed. And so it turned out. When Adam and Eve were forced to leave the Garden and go to work, the donkey went with them. Adam rode on the horse, the dog trotted at Eve's side, but it was the donkey who carried the tools, the spinning-wheel and all the household machinery. Throughout Adam's life the donkey was reminded of the saying about laughing last instead of first. Sometimes he was ashamed and dropped his long ears like a lop-eared rabbit; sometimes his pride came back and he refused to take another step. At such times Adam beat him and the donkey remembered the Lord's prophecy. He wondered how long the burdens would be piled upon him.

After Adam died the donkey thought things would go easier, but he soon realized his hardships were only beginning. He belonged, he discovered, not to one man but to all men. Cain, the brutal son of Adam, broke him to harness and made him drag a heavy plow. When Noah built the ark the donkey carried more timber than the elephant, but no one praised him for it. Forty days and forty nights the floating menagerie breasted the flood, and every day and most of the nights the other animals jeered and mocked him. He knew now what it was to be laughed at. And when the windows of heaven were closed and the fountains of the flood went back into the heart of the sea, the donkey walked the earth again with meek eyes and bowed head. From that time on he swore to serve man faithfully and ask no reward.

At the building of Babel, the donkey was there, working willingly, although he knew no tower built by hands would ever reach Heaven. After the city was deserted, the donkey helped Abraham with his flocks, and carried for Isaac, and wandered with Jacob. So, through Bible times, the donkey remained loyal to his masters. He brought Joseph and his twelve brothers together; he dragged bricks for the Hebrews during their long slavery in Egypt; he crossed the Red Sea with Moses; he was beaten for trying to save the wizard Balaam; he entered Canaan with Joshua.

He worked; he wandered; he did not die.

Years passed; centuries vanished. The donkey was in Palestine. His master was a carpenter in the little town of Nazareth, a good master by the name of Joseph, though far different from the Joseph who had become a ruler in the land of Egypt. He had worked for him a long time, and he had served his owner well. A few years ago, when Joseph and his wife Mary were on their wanderings, the little donkey carried them everywhere without complaining. They were terribly poor and innkeepers had no room for them. The donkey trudged on, carrying his load that seemed to grow heavier with each step. For a long day and a longer night, he plodded toward the distant haven, never stopping or stumbling till he brought them to the little town of Bethlehem. That night, in a cattle-stall, Mary's child had been born.

The donkey obeyed his master, but he worshiped his master's small son. The child was not only beautiful, but even as perfect as he seemed to his mother. Goodness shone from his eyes; miracles, they said, flowed from his hands. The donkey believed it, for he had seen one performed.

Once, when playing with some other children in the streets of Nazareth, the carpenter's son picked up some clay from the gutter and kneaded it into a shape. His companions gathered around to watch him.

"Good," said Simon, "let's all do it. What shall we model?"

"Let's make horses," cried Zadoc, the son of the priest. "When I grow up I'm going to have six horses of my own—two white ones, two black ones and two horses with many-colored coats."

"Stupid!" said Azor, the broom-maker's child. "There are no horses with many-colored coats. Besides, horses are too hard to model. Let's make pigeons."

So they started to make pigeons of clay. After a while Zadoc called out, "I've made seven. How many have the rest of you?"

"Five," said Zithri, the beggar's boy.

"Four," said Simon.

"Three," said Azor.

"Two," said Jesus, who was the carpenter's son.

"Only two!" sneered Zadoc. "And not even good ones. Mine look much more like pigeons than yours!"

"You are right," said Jesus and he tossed his aside. But though the clay pigeons were thrown, they did not fall to the ground. Instead, they hung in the air, spread wings and flew away.

The other children stared for a moment and then grew angry. "He's playing tricks on us!" cried Zadoc, son of the priest. "Let's play a trick on him!" The others joined Zadoc and soon they had tied the little Jesus tightly. The cord bit deep into his wrists but he did not cry.

"He's just making believe he's brave," said Zadoc. "He acts as if he were a king."

"All right," jeered Azor. "Let him be king."

"I'll get him a crown," shouted Zithri.

They pulled down part of a withered rose-tree and twisted two small branches into a crown. They pressed this upon his forehead and cried, "King Jesus! Hail to King Jesus!" Then they ran away laughing, while tears stood in the eyes of the carpenter's son.

The donkey had seen it all, had seen that the hands of Jesus were still tied and that the child could not remove the crown of thorns. Then he nuzzled his soft nose along the child's shoulder, raised his head and, though the thorns stabbed his lips, lifted the piercing weight from Jesus' forehead. He tugged at the cords till he freed the child's hands; then he carried him home.

More years passed. Jesus had gone away. Though the donkey did not know it, the carpenter's son had grown from childhood to manhood, had traveled and studied, had healed the sick, restored eyesight to the blind, cast out devils, had suffered untold hardships. But now the moment had come; Jesus was to enter Jerusalem in triumph.

It was a tremendous moment; one that must be celebrated in the proper manner. Naturally, Jesus could not enter the queen-city of Palestine on foot; he must ride, they said, on a charger worthy of the event. So the Archangel Michael called all the animals before Jesus that they might plead their case.

"Choose me," said the lion. "I am king of the beasts; you are a king among men. Men respect royalty—but only when they recognize it! When the people of Jerusalem see you riding on my back, they will know you are of noble blood and they will bow down and fear you. With me as your mascot, they will never dare oppose, but follow you in terror."

"Choose me," said the eagle. "I am lord of the upper air. Choose me and you will have power to leave the earth and fly on the very back of the wind. I will take you to borders of the sky; there, from heights unknown to man, you shall see everything that happens below. When you enter Jerusalem flying between my strong wings, the people will believe you are a god and they will worship."

"Choose me," said the mole. "I go where the eagle is helpless and the lion cannot follow. Choose me and I will give you the keys of earth. I will guide you to the roots of power, to secrets buried beneath the stones. I know where every vein of gold is hidden; my home is among caves of rubies, hills of emerald, ledges of pure diamond. Choose me and you will be greater than the greatest; you will be able to buy empires; you will not only be a king, but King of kings."

"The great ones laugh at treasures," whispered the fox. "Who but a fool desires gold and glittering pebbles that turn men against each other with greed and jealousy. Choose me and I will give you cunning. I will show you how to outwit all men and overcome your enemies with shrewdness. Choose me and I will teach you cleverness that is better than wealth and craft that is stronger than strength."

"Craft!" trumpeted the elephant. "Craft and cunning are for knaves who will never be wise. Choose me and I will give you true wisdom. I am the oldest of living creatures; my years span a century and I have watched the comings and goings of all the races. Choose me and you will rule the changing mind of the unchanging world."

"Choose me," lowed the cow. "I am sacred. India and Egypt worship me. I feed the world."

"Choose me," bellowed the dragon. "I will spread fire before you and magic wherever you go."

"Choose me!" neighed the horse. "I am swift as rage. The glory of my nostrils is terrible to the enemy. I swallow the ground; I laugh at fear."

"Choose me!" screamed the camel. "Choose me! Choose me!" cried the animals separately and in chorus. Only the donkey was silent.

"And what can you give?" asked Jesus, speaking for the first time and turning to the dusty little fellow. "What have you to promise?"

"Nothing," murmured the donkey. "Nothing. I am the lowest of all God's creatures and the least."

But Jesus remembered. "The lowest shall be lifted up," he said, "And the last shall be first."

And so the meekest of men chose the meekest of animals. And they entered Jerusalem together.

But the great moment passed. Proud Jerusalem sneered at the carpenter's son even as it had stoned the prophets before him, and only a handful of poor folk listened to his words. He was despised and rejected. The people turned against him. He was imprisoned on a false charge and condemned to death. They put a crown of thorns upon his head, mocked him and made him carry his own cross.

It was while Jesus was struggling up the hill that the donkey saw him for the last time. Their sad eyes met.

"No," said Jesus. "You cannot help me now. Yet, since you have done more for me than have most men, you shall be rewarded. I cannot undo what God has done; what He has ordained must be carried out. But I can soften His decree. True, you will have to fetch and carry and feed on thorns. Yet these things will never again be hard for you. Because you carried me three times, so shall you be able to carry three times as much as animals thrice your size—and your load will seem lighter than theirs. You suffered thorns for my sake; so shall you be nourished when others can find nothing to feed on. You shall eat the thorns and nettles of the field—and they shall taste like sweet salads. You bore me when I grew to manhood, when I was a child, and even my mother before I was born. So shall you bear my cross—but you shall bear it without pain. Here—!" And as Jesus touched the shoulders of the donkey, a velvet-black cross appeared on the back of the kneeling animal.

And Jesus shouldering his burden, climbed up Calvary . . .

Francis heard the last syllable leave his lips in a kind of wonder. His tiredness had gone: everything in him was full of strength. He was surprised to see that the sun had set and that a little horned moon had come into the sky, one horn pointing to Assisi. He thought he understood the sign. When he turned back, the donkey had disappeared. The field was dark. But a light greater than the moon's was on Francis' face.

IN CLEAN HAY

By Eric P. Kelly

Hetman: In all your lands there are tidings about a new-born child. Unknown in what family, yet still a kingly son. People find in him a miracle—that he shall be king of the whole world. Ignorant peasant folk are collecting and seek him everywhere in the kingdom, and then too, some of the nobles are even seeking to honor him and put their trust in him.

Herod: I heard all that from Three Kings who were here, but I don't know where the child is.

Hetman: King, in Bethlehem City, he is born, and lies in a stable in clean hay.

From the Szopka Krakowska, the "Krakow Stable," a miracle play performed these seven hundred years in the streets of Krakow.

IN a little village on the outskirts of the Polish city of Krakow there stands a happy farmhouse whose owner is Pan Jan. In the early spring the fields about the house are dark and rich, awaiting the planting of seed; and in the summer they are green with ripened grain. In the fall they turn to russet brown; and in the winter they lie deep beneath the shining snow. From earliest morning until sundown the house is astir with action, but at sundown everything ceases and peace descends, for did the Lord not ordain that all work should cease with the sun? Then the lamp is lighted in the large room and the newspaper which has come from Krakow will be read to all the family by the father or the eldest boy, Antek. The others sit about and listen. Antek is fifteen and goes every day to the high school in the city; it is a walk of about three miles, but the road is good and there is often company on the way.

Antek reads from the gazette: "To-morrow is the day before Christmas and there will be many visitors who come to the city to attend services at night in the churches. The Christmas trees will be on sale in the Rynek (market place) and the booths full of candy and toys will be opened directly after dark. In the homes, the children will await the sight of the first star; when the first star shines, then an angel will come and knock at the door, and the rejoicing at the birth of Christ will begin. This year there will be a special treat for Krakow people, for a very famous performer will give his puppet play, the Szopka Krakowska, at the Falcon Hall on Grodska Street. With him will be his wife, who will sing the hymns."

Antek put down the paper. "Our puppet show is all made."

The father: "Don't stay out too late."

Antek answered quickly: "No, little Father, we won't. We will give our show several times between five and seven o'clock and then we will start on the road home."

In one corner of the little farmhouse stood a small, wooden two-towered church in miniature; between the towers at the base, large doors stood wide open, revealing a stage. And on this stage were piled a number of little wooden figures, like dolls, dressed in various jaunty colors, and in the background was the figure of a woman with a baby in her arms. This was a stage in miniature—a Szopka Krakowska with its little wooden puppets. When set up for the entertainment of lookers-on, Antek would crawl beneath it and operate the puppets from little sticks that went through a slot in the floor. This slot extended the whole length of the stage, so that a puppet could be brought upon the scene from one side, made to perform, and then be taken away on the farther side. During the performance of a puppet play the figures moved in constant succession across this stage.

The mother entered from the stove room with a huge pot of steaming soup and poured it out into wooden bowls before each of the children.

"Well, to-morrow will be Christmas Eve," she said, "and you will go out with the Szopka."

"Yes. And make a lot of money." This was from Stefan, the second in age. He was a more practical boy than his brother, although younger—yet he had less of the vivid imagination which made Antek the better showman of the puppet show.

The mother sighed. "I wish we could give it to you; but what we have is being laid by against the days when you go up to the university. How much did you make last year?"

"Fifty zlotys (about five dollars)," answered Antek proudly.

"We'll make a hundred this year," said Stefan.

"And what will you do with it?" asked the mother.

A clamor went up. Antek was saying something about a book, Stefan about a chest of tools, and Anusia, the "baby" of ten years, said something that sounded like "shoes." Christopher, who played all the songs for the Szopka on his violin, tried to make known his want for new strings and a bow. However, the whole pandemonium was such that anyone might see that at least *something* was wanted rather eagerly: it was true, as the mother had said, that the scanty profits from the farm were going into the children's educations: Antek for the university, Stefan for the school of commerce and trade, Christopher for the academy of music, and Anusia—for—well, that would come later. The child had a clear and appealing voice, and might become a great singer if placed with the proper teachers. Who knows?

Therefore this chance of making a little money on the night before Christmas meant a great deal to them all. The boys, working with the father, had built the little theater themselves. It stood upon little folding legs which Stefan had devised. The mother had dressed the dolls, and on the night before Christmas it was all in readiness to carry to Krakow. Now, since the very earliest days of the city, boys have gone about in Krakow giving this show on Christmas Eve, most of them poor or needy boys to whom the gift of money was a veritable godsend. And on Christmas Eve there descends over the earth, each year, that spirit of gladness and kindness that makes people eager and anxious to relieve suffering and soften the hard ways of life with the cheer that the Christ Child brought to men.

The day before Christmas dawned bright. It was crisp but not so cold as usual. There was not a cloud in the sky, and the children knew that they could not have selected a better day for their puppet show. At about one o'clock in the afternoon they started for Krakow.

Antek walked in front with the Szopka strapped to his shoulders. Stefan, carrying the sticks on which the Szopka was to rest, walked by his side. Christopher on the left side, carrying his violin and bow in a case in one hand, had extended the other hand to Anusia, who walked just beyond. A happy company it was, and all along the way people greeted them and shouted out "Wesolych Swiat (Merry Christmas)!" or else "Niech bendzie pochwalony Jesus Christ." (May Jesus Christ be praised.) As they neared the city the sun was sinking, for they had walked slowly and, too, the sun sinks early in the Christmas season. Lights were coming on everywhere, and as they stood at the Florian Gate, Anusia turning about screamed with delight and pointed at the sky.

For there, hanging like a little candle, was the first star. The Christmas season had begun.

In the market place they selected a corner by one path and mounted the puppet theater on its legs. "It was here that we stood last year," said Antek.

Candles were lighted before the little theater; a crowd gathered. Then Anusia stepped out before the people, and bravely sang a little carol, while Christopher played on the violin. The crowd increased.

"Oh, what a crowd!" cried Stefan, rubbing his hands. "Here at least for the first performance is a good twenty-five zlotys." His words were correct. The first performance netted exactly that amount. It was a splendid performance too: Anusia sang the carols beautifully, Antek made the puppets dance as if they were alive, and everybody reached for handkerchiefs when King Herod ordered that all the babies in the kingdom should be put to death.

They had begun again when suddenly there came a rude end to their performance, and to all their hopes.

A dignitary wearing a huge star stepped into the circle before the little theater and ordered the play to be stopped.

"We can't! We can't!" shrieked Stefan, who was reading the lines for the puppets. "Don't bother us. The show must go on."

The dignitary grinned. "Where is your license?" he asked.

"License?" Antek crept out from beneath the theater where he was operating the puppets and faced the officer.

"Yes. Don't you know that you must buy a license to give public performances in this city?"

"No. It was not so last year."

"But it is so this year. It is a new ordinance that no shows may be given on the streets without a license."

"How much is the license?" asked Antek.

"One hundred zlotys," said the man.

"But I haven't got one hundred zlotys!" groaned Antek.

"Then you must move along or I will report you to the police." He motioned to a police officer on the corner.

"Come quick," ordered Antek, snatching up the theater to his back. "Take the stool, Stefan, and you, Anusia, hang on to Christopher."

They emerged in a quiet place behind the Cloth Hall to take counsel.

"We can't do anything. We've got to go home," Antek announced. Every face fell. Anusia began to cry. "It can't be helped. We must obey the law and we haven't one hundred zlotys in the world."

"Let's give the show in some private street," suggested Stefan.

"Can't be done. We'd be arrested."

They marched out into the street. Two men engaged in a spirited conversation almost ran them down.

"Look out there," said one, sidestepping the Szopka. "The street doesn't belong to you boys."

"No, but we have our rights," answered Antek.

"That you have," answered the second man suddenly striking Antek in friendly fashion upon the back. "A Szopka, as I live!"

"A Szopka—" the second man fell back in amazement.

"Yes, and a good one," said the first man examining the show quickly. "Here is an answer to our prayers sent from Heaven. Do you people operate the Szopka?"

"We do," answered Antek wonderingly.

"Do you want an engagement?"

"Yes!" shouted Antek, Stefan and Christopher at the tops of their voices.

"Then come with us. You see, we were to have had a very famous Szopka with us to-night—Pan Kowalski and his wife were to entertain us. The crowd is all there—has been for half an hour—waiting for the show to begin. And there is no Pan Kowalski. We have looked up and down the town; we have hunted all through the villages, we have inquired everywhere that he might have been, and yet we cannot find him. We must have the show or send the people home."

"How much do we get?" asked Stefan, characteristically, for he had recovered from his astonishment at this quick turn of affairs.

"We will take a collection. We can at least guarantee you one hundred zlotys. You will probably make much more than that."

As they spoke the two men hustled the children along Grodska Street and stopped in front of a building on which there was a coat of arms bearing the figure of a falcon.

"In here," said one of the men.

"Why this is the Falcon Hall we read of in the newspaper," said Stefan. "This is the best place in Krakow in which to give the Szopka. Antek, do you realize"—he turned to his brother, "that we will make lots of money out of this?"

"We must give a good performance first," admonished Antek.

One of the men made a speech to the people, while the children prepared the show. He was sorry, he said, that Pan Kowalski had not been able to come. But in his place there had come a very fine Szopka operated by young men who were quite experienced—at this the crowd laughed, for the youth of the performers was quite evident. "It is Christmas Eve," the man went on. "And it is not the time to show any displeasure. We have come here to see acted the old story of the wonderful evening so many centuries ago when Christ was born to earth to bring peace and good will to all men."

It was a Christmas crowd at that, and if it felt any ill will at this substitution on the program, it did not show it. The lamp in front of the stage was lighted. Antek stepped out in front and played on his little bugle the Heynal, or little trumpet song that the trumpeter in the tower of the Church of Our Lady had played every hour of the day and night since Christianity in Krakow began. Then lights appeared in the two towers, and Christopher and Anusia stepped out to play and sing the old hymn, "Amid the Silence." The curtains were swept back by Stefan, and there on the stage were two shepherds sleeping. Red fire is burned, an angel descends, and again Christopher and Anusia step forward. This time the song is "Gloria in Excelsis," the song sung by the angels when Christ was born. The curtain is closed. It opens again on Bethlehem, whither the shepherds have come to greet the Christ Child, who lies there with the Mother, asleep on the clean hay. From the back of the manger a sheep and a cow look over the wall.

Then the scene changes. We are now in the court of Herod, the king, and Three Kings come in from the East to ask their way to the newborn King; Herod cannot tell them, and so they go out again and follow a star that is gleaming in the heavens; here Stefan lifts into the air a great gold star which shines with brilliance when the light falls upon it. They come to the Christ Child and they too worship. Then the shepherds dance, and the soldiers sing, and the violin makes merry music for all the company. It is truly a splendid sight; the children shout, the babies crow, and the men and women clap their hands in applause.

O thou cruel Herod! For now he commands his Hetman to send out the soldiers and destroy the Christ Child; but because they do not know who the Christ Child is, they must destroy every child in the kingdom. Cruel King Herod, for this thou shalt pay—for the floor of the stage opens and the Devil dances out; how the children scream as he cuts off Herod's head, and the head goes rolling out of the little theater and onto the floor. Then there comes more dancing and singing; little Anusia sings like an angel—the men and women take her up and the children kiss her and stroke her hands.

And when the collection is taken the bowl is heaped high with paper and silver and copper. There are at least five hundred zlotys upon the plate (about fifty dollars) the best day's work that any Szopka has ever done in Krakow. The crowd leaves slowly; the men come and take their leave of the children; the show is packed up, and the four, now beaming with happiness and delight, take again the road for the village three miles away. It is a lovely night, not over cold, but just comfortably cold, and though there is no moon, the stars are as bright as the little pin points of light in the Szopka walls. As they pass the Church of Our Lady they hear the trumpet playing the Heynal, and it makes them feel suddenly that over all the world has come this happiness at the birth of Christ.

Two hours later, on the road still, they put into the home of neighbor Kolesza for a rest. He meets them at the door with a Christmas greeting and then tells them to come to the stable for there they will find a surprise.

"I had no room for them in the house," he said. "The hay of the stable is much warmer than my floor and I have a stove here where I have heat for the animals in winter. Come and you shall see."

They entered the stable. He flashed his lantern high above his head —they looked—they drew their breaths—and then with one accord fell upon their knees.

For there in the manger was a young woman. She had been sleeping but was now awake; and in her arms, nestled close to her body, was a little baby, wrapped in a blue coat.

"It is the Christ Child," whispered Stefan. "See, there is the cow and the sheep looking over the back of the manger; and there is the place where the Wise Men knelt." He pointed—indeed a dark figure arose there and looked about; it was a man, and he put his fingers to his lips lest they should talk and disturb the mother and child.

"It is Pan Kowalski the puppet-show man," said Pan Kolesza in an undertone. "He was on his way to Krakow to-night to give a performance in the hall of the Falcons. He and his wife stopped here; and while they were here this child was born."

The children looked at one another strangely. Then they looked at Pan Kowalski, and then at the mother and the child.

"They have no money," went on Pan Kolesza; "they were to have received much money for their performance in Krakow to-night, but they were not able to go, and therefore they lose it. I do not know what they will do when they leave here, though the good God knows I will let them stay as long as they like. They have only this show which they give at Christmas; it is not given at any other time of the year."

"And it was on this night that Christ was born. . . ." said Antek. "Stefan . . ." he added after a long pause.

"I know what you are going to say," retorted Stefan. They went out into the air again, not even taking leave of either of the men, so engrossed were they in their own thoughts.

"It means that we lose what we wanted," said Antek. "I think I'll go back."

"No," said Stefan. "Let me."

Antek squeezed something into his hand. Stefan ran back to the stable and entered. Pan Kowalski had sunk into a stupor again and heeded nothing; Stefan crept up to the manger and listened to the deep breathing of the mother. Then he slipped his hand over the edge of the manger and dropped all the silver and notes that had been collected in Krakow; then he fell upon his knees for a moment and said a little prayer. But as he staggered after his companions down the long dark road, something of the most infinite happiness seized upon his heart, and when he reached Antek he was sobbing like a baby. Whereupon Antek fell to sobbing likewise, and out there upon the Krakow road Christ was born again in the hearts of four happy children.

BETHLEHEM, DEC. 25

BY HEYWOOD BROUN

WHEN we first came into the office it looked like a dreary Christmas afternoon. To us there is something mournful in the sight of a scantily staffed city room. Just two men were at work typing away at stories of small moment. The telegraph instruments appeared to be meditating. One continued to chatter along, but there was nobody to set down what it said.

Its shrill, staccato insistence seemed momentous. But telegraph instruments are always like that. Their tone is just as excited whether the message tells of mighty tremors in the earth or baby parades at Asbury Park. Probably a job in a newspaper office is rather unhealthy for a telegraph instrument. The contrivance is too emotional and excitable to live calmly under the strain. Even an old instrument seldom learns enough about news values to pick and choose suitable moments in which to grow panicky. As soon as a story begins to move along a wire the little key screams and dances. It is devoid of reticence. Every distant whisper which comes to it must be rattled out at top voice and at once. Words are its very blood stream and for all the telegraph instrument knows one word is just as good and just as important as another.

And so the one restless key in the telegraph room shrieked, and whined, and implored listeners. We tried to help by coming close and paying strict attention, but we could not get even the gist of the message. It seemed to us as if the key were trying to say, with clicking tumult, that some great one, a King perhaps, was dead or dying. Or, maybe, it was a war and each dash and dot stood for some contending soldier moving forward under heavy fire. And again, it might be that a volcano had stirred and spit. Or great waves had swept a coast. And we thought of sinking steamers and trains up-ended.

Certainly it was an affair of great moment. Even though we discounted the passion and vehemence of the machine there was something almost awe-inspiring in its sincerity and insistence. After a time it seemed to us as if this was in fact no long running narrative, but one announcement repeated over and over again. And suddenly we wondered why we had assumed from the beginning that only catastrophes were important and epoch-making. By now we realized that though the tongue was alien we did recognize the color of its clamor. These dots and dashes were seeking to convey something of triumph. That was not to be doubted.

And in a flash we knew what the machine said. It was nothing more than, "A child is born." And of course nobody paid any attention to that. It is an old story.

EVEN TO JUDAS

By Heywood Broun

WE were sitting in a high room above the chapel and although it was Christmas Eve my good friend the dominie seemed curiously troubled. And that was strange, for he was a man extremely sensitive to the festivities of his faith.

The joys and sorrows of Jesus were not to him events of a remote past but more current and living happenings than the headlines in the newspapers. At Christmas he seems actually to hear the voice of the herald angels.

My friend is an old man, and I have known him for many years, but this was the first time the Nativity failed to rouse him to an ecstasy. He admitted to me something was wrong. "Tomorrow," he said, "I must go down into that chapel and preach a Christmas sermon. And I must speak of peace and good-will toward men. I know you think of me as a man too cloistered to be of any use to my community. And I know that our world is one of war and hate and enmity. And you, my young friend, and others keep insisting that before there can be brotherhood there must be the bashing of heads. You are all for good-will to men, but you want to note very many exceptions. And I am still hoping and praying that in the great love of God the final seal of interdiction must not be put on even one. You may laugh at me, but right now I am wondering about how Christmas came to Judas Iscariot."

It is the habit of my friend, when he is troubled by doubts, to reach for the Book, and he did so now. He smiled and said, "Will you assist me in a little experiment? I will close my eyes and you hold out the Bible to me. I will open it at random and run my fingers down a page. You read me the text which I blindly select."

I did as he told me and he happened on the twenty-sixth chapter of St. Matthew and the twenty-fourth verse. I felt sorry for him, for this was no part of the story of the birth of Christ but instead an account of the great betrayal.

"Read what it says," commanded the dominie. And I read: "Then Judas, which betrayed Him, answered and said, 'Master, is it I?' He said unto him, 'Thou hast said.'"

My friend frowned, but then he looked at me in triumph. "My hand is not as steady as it used to be. You should have taken the lower part of my finger and not the top. Read the twenty-seventh verse. It is not an eighth of an inch away. Read what it says." And I read, "And He took the cup and gave thanks and gave it to them, saying, 'Drink ye all of it.'"

"Mark that," cried the old man exultantly. "Not even to Judas, the betrayer, was the wine of life denied. I can preach my Christmas sermon now, and my text will be 'Drink ye all of it.' Good-will toward men means good-will to every last son of God. Peace on earth means peace to Pilate, peace to the thieves on the cross, and peace to poor Iscariot."

I was glad, for he had found Christmas and I saw by his face that once more he heard the voice of the herald angels.

THE AFFAIR AT THE INN

AS SEEN BY PHILO THE INNKEEPER AND THE TAXGATHERER OF ROME; AND NOW WRITTEN DOWN

BY CHARLES J. FINGER

PHILO the innkeeper was in an overwrought mood. He was worried, although his aspect was outwardly calm. He was snappish, too. Yet he was a man worthy enough when things were going well, and one not without lightness and humor, and a measure of good nature was in his composition. But the keeping of an inn is a trying business at the best of times, the more so when an unexpected press of people comes, and when demands are made without thought and without courtesy, and when guests, because of the money they pay, make of a host a safety valve for their own ill humors.

Not only the inn, but the town itself was crowded; so much that a laden camel, or an ass with its bales, or slaves with a palanquin could with difficulty pass down the narrow cobblestone lanes which were streets. Even the wide place at the fountain, where Philo loved to sit, half-dreaming of an afternoon, while he dabbled his fingers in the water and watched the pigeons—even that place was noisy, what with Phoenicians and Syrians, with Arabs and Byzantines and Greeks, many of them with trade affairs to push.

So the innkeeper pondered on the folly of Quirinius, the Roman consul, and cursed his mad freak by which he sought to number the people, commanding that each should go to his own town where he had been born. For that folly had made for all the press of brown and hard-looking men from the desert; of whining beggars, often blind and diseased, who showed their sores for alms; of women famine-wasted; and other women with bold eyes and glossy hair hung with gold coins, who looked from courtyard windows. There were some who had opened packs and set things out for sale; others loud and fierce who bullied and threatened; others again who threw dice, play-ing for stakes. There were fellows with their ears clipped and their noses slit, or with an eye thrust out, or with hands from which fingers had been lopped for thievery, Roman law being swift and sharp. Aged men and old crones, and shepherd lads with shapely limbs were there, also children who danced with joy because all was new, and because life was flowing full and free. And there were water carriers with their bulging goatskins; and men from the mountains, from Carmel and Shechem and the hills of Gilboa, and from the high plains of Peraea; and from Tabor and Endor and Shunem. These made much of their shaggy horses, looking to their comfort as if they had been chil-dren. Sometimes slaves carrying a palanquin passed, when lesser folk, to avoid a beating for being in the way, squeezed themselves up steps, into doorways, or under the arches of houses. So Philo the innkeeper was in an overwrought mood, the more because his house and the courtyard were so crowded that what had commenced as triumph because of business was turned into something very much like colossal failure because of great revenues turned away. Therefore, in his dull way, he thought of the misery and futility of existence.

His inn had been filled before the rich man came; that rich man who was a dignified someone, who had something to do with Rome, and who talked so provokingly and masterfully and overbearingly. Philo knew, as soon as he clapped eyes on him, that there would be active collisions and unpleasant scenes. He knew him to be one who would regard other men as base vessels to be shattered, if he regarded them at all. For those who acted for Augustus were hard in their pride of place at all times and in all places, cutting across men's speech when they told of sickness or sorrow or age, taking for Rome the widow's goat and the herder's last penny, talking all the while of laws and activities and forces not understood by simpler men. And sometimes they hinted at terrifying things which might take place, of fierce and strong powers to be loosed among the people, of the slaying of infants, besides other fearful things which would affect the lives and the happiness of a thousand households. And when those who were the mouthpieces of Augustus spoke thus and so, threatening and browbeating, then the high priests took it upon themselves to become the mouthpieces of the mouthpieces, threatening still further those who were threatened.

The rich man had ridden into the inn-yard ahead of his train, his steward with him, their horses fine with silk and silver. Then came the camels, one especially bright dressed in barbaric and confused gorgeousness and led by a black glossy negro in a cloak of gaudy colors, for it carried the rich man's infant son.

When Philo spoke of his crowded inn the lord seemed amused, and, with a couple of words and a lofty gesture, as though sweeping away difficulties, lightly turned the matter over to his hawk-eyed and hawk-nosed steward. Then he dismounted and walked to a stone seat in the narrow garden ground, for the day was warm although it was winter, and a pleasant breeze was in that place. Two women who had been seated there moved away. So the rich man was all dignity and preeminence, watching the people being ordered out of the inn to make room for him much as he might have watched the passing of a muddy stream.

For in the manner of those days, his steward was active and boisterously coarse, thundering and vituperating, ordering·men and horses and asses away so that there might be ample space for the stalling of the camels and their unlading, his master being a taxgatherer with riches in his charge, to whom great wealth belonged because of his office. Therefore even the harried and robbed people spoke in hushed voices of his dignity and influence, saying that he stood for Rome and the rulers, doing what he did for Caesar in the interests of the empire. But none dared oppose, even with a word.

Now when some of the rich man's camels were unladen and while the most precious of the goods were being carried into the inn, some of those who were looking on crowded close, elbowing and pushing, finding it good to be there and to see the wonders and rare things, they being from the uplands and people whose affairs were simple. Whereupon the steward gave a word of command to some of the slaves, and they fell to laying about them with their whips, slashing those who were slow in moving. That was to clear a way for the passage of bearers with the cradle of gold and ivory in which slept the rich man's infant son.

One about whose shoulders the lash fell was a shepherd youth, brown-eyed and firm-lipped, straight and tall, Johannes by name. Swiftly he swung round, his nostrils dilated and his eyes ablaze like points of fire. But never a foot did he budge, not being in the path of the slaves who bore the cradle.

"Make way, beggar! cried the steward. "You stand there like a dreamer, or a fool, when you should be on your knees to your betters." He lifted a hand to threaten or strike as he spoke.

Then Philo interfered, for he was close by, having been walking by the side of the cradle as testimony to the rich man's wealth and influence. "Nay, nay," he said to the steward. "Strike him not. It is enough. There's no harm in Johannes." He said the rest half whispering and with his curved hand at his mouth. "The lad may be half mad, we think. He is one of those who takes the prophets seriously, babbling of the Messiah. Not more than two days ago he came from Jerusalem where he had been listening to Anna, the daughter of Phanuel, and she, it is said, is not in her right mind."

"No harm indeed!" said the steward with a furious visage, and loudly, with an eye on his master who sat as if seeing a dull show. He added, "Get thee gone and dream of Messiahs out in the desert! Or be off and away with those we saw a little while ago, shepherding sheep. This is no place for dreamers, and Messiahs are not likely to be here, in a common inn."

Suddenly the steward clipped his own speech, for the lad Johannes moved a step toward him instead of away as bidden, and the youth overtopped the man by many inches.

"It is no matter to me where I stand," said the shepherd lad. "But I dream no dreams. Or if you choose to hold me as a dreamer, then I tell you that this day may be the end of my dreaming, and from now on the world shall not be the same."

At that out shot Johannes' hand, taking the steward by the shoulder and gripping him like steel. And when the man tried to free himself and lifted his hand, the lad deftly caught him by the wrist and held him, bearded man and stout built though he was. Yet the youth spoke softly, saying: "Lord, indeed! One who sells honor for gold! One who grinds the faces of the poor because they are poor! Know that a man's greatness comes not from his possessions, but rather lies in how he sets his face against the wrongful doings of men. Know that a man is nothing except as he does and dares for the right. Also know that your law of mastery shall soon be set aside for the law of love. Know also that the master of your master, even the master of your master's master, and a king of kings, shall soon come. Know that long before the one you serve pays his debts to Caesar, men wiser than the wisest you know shall stand before your master's master, shall do homage to the lowliest who shall yet be the greatest. Even Gaspar, and Melchior, and Balthasar shall come bearing gifts, not to your lord but to mine. Go, tell all that to your master! Say too that a new law, the law of the love of men, the law of good fellowship and of fair dealing, shall fill the minds of men."

Johannes, having ended, stood with dark eyes fixed on space, strangely abstracted as though he saw a vision. And the onlookers wondered at him because of the splendor of courage. As for the steward, being loosed he looked at the youth a little while, wondering at his daring and the speech he had made; then turned away, not proudly as was his habit, but somewhat in the manner of one beaten, or suddenly grown old. For never before in his life had he been ordered, except by his master; while the laying of a masterful hand upon him was a thing altogether new. Yet that day he had been ruled and chidden by a nobody, while other nobodies looked on, and his authority in a moment had become like a hill of sliding sand. So the flame of pride in his heart went low because someone had stood out against his insolence.

Like a broken man he went into the house, following the slaves who carried the cradle; then fell to ordering the servants to make a large room rich and wonderful with carpets and hangings and ornaments of gold and silver, but he commanded in a spiritless manner. And as he watched the work going on, it came to him to wonder how a meek lad had been suddenly exalted while he was thrust down; also to wonder at the daring of the youth, then at the narrowness of life because this Johannes might have killed him had he so chosen. Then his mind ran on to dwell upon the short space of time given to a man, and how a life was bounded by mystery and darkness. So he remembered his own loneliness, and how he was friendless, none having spoken a word in his defense. Fawners and flatterers he knew, but not friends; wherefore he was sad at heart, and ill-content with things, and with the way his life had gone.

In the evening time, though the wind had grown chill, the steward went outside, for he could not rest within the house. Wrapped in his Persian cloak of silk he paced the courtyard. Others were there, a dozen or more of men and women, some of those who had been turned out of the inn to make room for the rich man's train, making shift to pass the night as well as they could. Some of them sat silent about a little fire. Some huddled on benches. And as the steward walked up and down, a lonely man full of heavy thought and hungering for companionship, he heard the sound of hoofs in the street and at the noise a little warmth came into his heart. For, he thought, with the newcomer, whoever he might be, there was the shadow of companionship, if only for a moment. But that spark of hope died almost immediately, for the sound resolved itself into a dainty and rapid clattering which was not horse hoofs, whereas those of his own sort and rank rode horses.

Soon there appeared out of the light mist a man with a damsel, he leading, she riding an ass. The steward made out a tall man clad in a long, dark brown robe; the woman white-skinned and dark-haired, neatly dressed in spun lamb's wool, but without adornment such as women love to wear. The man led the ass to the middle of the yard, then advanced to the house and struck his hand on the doorpost, calling softly.

At the alarm, an upper window was opened, and Philo thrust out his head crying: "If ye seek lodging, ye must go elsewhere"; then fell to grumbling and calling upon the gods to witness how he was pestered.

The steward was not so far off but that he could see the woman weeping softly. And when the man started to lead the ass away out of the courtyard, suddenly there was a kind of anger in the steward's heart, and anger against Philo for his roughness, and anger against his master the tax gatherer for his selfishness and greed, an anger against himself because he was what he was. Somehow he remembered his own youth when he was full of the joy of life, a boy eager for companionship, one offering and receiving friendship. Like fleeting ghosts, memories thronged on him, as how in time of need and stress such a one had done this and such another that. Old voices, looks and deeds, came back in sudden glimpses; a dash of sorrow dismissed by a good-natured parent; a shadow dispelled by a youthful friend; an indignity softened by a brother; some good-natured tolerance at a thoughtless deed. So he was angered that one should cast the shadow of grief upon others, the while he stood like an image, giving no light of fellowship. All those words spoken by the lad Johannes rang strangely through his mind: "Know that a man's greatness comes not from his possessions, but rather how he sets his face against the wrongful doings of men." Yet all the while something whispered that the matter was not his affair and that he would do well to let things go as they would without meddling. So the steward stood, wishful to do, but not daring.

Then, like lightning, the questioning thought came: "Am I then an imitation of the man I serve, and no master of myself?" At once, half ashamed yet defiant, he went across the inn-yard to the two. Even while he told himself that what he did was whimsical and childish, he took the rich cloak from his own shoulders and gave it to the man, bidding him wrap the woman in it, strangely excusing himself to himself by the lie that he was too warm and had no need for the garment. Yet he wondered in his heart, now and then, finding himself doing humble things in a courteous manner, and he was amazed to see the man accept the gift, not humbly or deferentially, but as a friend accepts from a friend and an equal from an equal. Also the light in the woman's face warmed him.

"Ye shall do ill to go further, friend," said the steward, and, as he spoke the words, he felt as if he had tasted a new pleasure, or had known a fresh strength and sweetness.

"But how shall I stay here where there is no room?" asked the man. "Yet any corner would serve, could we but pass the night in peace."

"Now neither frightened, wearied nor anxious shall the woman be," answered the steward. "Wait but a short while, for I go to make a place for you."

So, much wondering at himself, yet radiant in service, he ran into the stable and took his own and his master's horses where they were stalled; then led them outside. After that, with his own hands he did things which at other times he might have thought petty and unworthy and which at a word would have been done by slaves, such as cleaning the place where the horses had stood, dragging new hay from the loft and spreading it upon the floor, filling a large earthen pot with water and making the stable everywhere sweet and clean. Then, being satisfied with the seemliness of the place, he went out, and led the ass into the stable and helped the man, doing what he could for the woman's comfort. Nor when he heard those outside saying hurtful things, was he either ashamed or insulted. Indeed he was happy and singing softly, feeling the rightness and justice of what he did. And when he again stood in the inn-yard the world seemed to be a kinder and easier place, as if the placid peace of the silver-sprinkled velvet sky had entered his soul.

He was not aware that he slept, sitting on the stone bench in the inn-yard, but when he awoke, in a dawn of opal beauty, he seemed to remember visions, and music like a concert of sweet stringed instruments, and voices and answering voices, and a coming and going of persons, and a great star that hung effulgent. If it was a dream, he told himself, then it was one to be laid away in memory. But it did not seem to be of the nature of a dream. It was more as though he had learned some bewildering and gracious secret. It was as if he had been lifted into some glowing and shining realm, and from a hill-top had seen far horizons. Further, some new thing to awaken interest and energies seemed to be in him so that he was anxious for the day and its activities, eager to grapple with things in a new way and to do what his hand found to do. And the secret hope was in his heart that he would find, in some way, rich and true fellowship in manhood, even as he had known it in his childhood.

And in the manger he saw the new-born Child.

And there were the wise men, Gaspar, and Melchior, and Balthasar. Johannes, too, was there with his brother shepherds. So they talked, all of them, the steward, too, without disdain, not hiding themselves behind a screen of words, but freely and frankly, so that the man's heart was delivered from the depths of his loneliness. Nor was their talk of mystical things, but of everyday matters; of the mightiness of true fellowship and how one may so love another that he will lay down his life for his friend; of how a strange pride prevents the un-acted good within men; of how mercy is given to the merciful; of how men hunger and thirst for that bread and wine of life which is friend-ship; of how none are pure and undefiled, wherefore none may judge another; of a world exquisite and fine with men striving for well do-ing; of high and heavenly things about which men long to talk but rarely dare.

So when the steward left that place he was full of happiness and hope, for a secret seemed to have been made plain, though he could find no words to tell what was in his heart.

The next morning as they rode toward Jerusalem, both the rich man and his steward were silent, not sulkily, nor in any unfriendly way, but with that shyness which often keeps two sympathetic men from talking of their feelings and experiences. Yet there were glimpses and hints of what was passing in their minds, as when, noting the barbaric splendor of the trappings on the camel which carried his son's litter, the rich man said something about the costliness of it, almost as if he had seen it for the first time, or as if he had experienced a new sensation in seeing it. After that they went on mile after mile, and it was not until they passed through the gap between the mountains of Shunem and Tabor, which broadened into the valley of the Jordan and the plain of Peraea, that anything further was said.

Then the rich man spoke, thoughtfully and with something like hesitation. He said: "A miserable piece of business, that at the inn last night. Things ought not to be so; a world with no place for a newborn child. I heard all through the open window and could not sleep for thinking of it. And I, with all that space and room, no whit better than other men when stripped, when you come to consider. Yet I and mine had place for a score or more." He mused for awhile, then added, "But I suppose things must be so. I suppose some are born into the world to be as weeds and rejected things. Outcasts there must be. And slaves too. And those born to rule, as is my son. Thus it is willed. But it is strange, nevertheless, and I wondered last night, though I had not thought of it in that way before."

When the steward spoke, after a time of thought, weighing matters, it was with a curious zeal. Said he: "Now as to your son, tell me this. Suppose you could have a wish gratified. Or suppose you could ask the giver of gifts to give him a gift. What is it that you would ask?" The rich man pondered long; then said:

"Money he will have. But what is money? It brings no joy, and, as the sage said, 'Whoso seeks wealth is like a child who eats honey with a knife, for scarcely has he tasted the sweetness, when he finds he has cut his tongue.' A true man's wealth is the good he does in the world. So I would not ask for riches. Then there is power. But last night as I lay sleepless, I remembered how, for a man in high place, there is little but vexation, a hundred hands being stretched forth to drag him down, another hundred digging pitfalls. So rather than have him rule, I would have him know that men are born for the sake of men, perhaps that they might benefit one another. Nor would I have him a conquering captain, for such a one must needs wade through innocent blood, fighting those with whom they have no quarrel. You see, there are princes of war, but never yet has the world seen a prince of peace. As for a life of ease, I would not ask that for him. For a man softens to his fall in luxury, and it is not idleness but work which ennobles a man. But I think that I would have my son faithful in all things. I would have him speak the truth with his fellow, not being a lying tongue as so many of us are who seek our gain and that only. And I would have him brave and steadfast. And I would that he had a friend, also that he was a friend, each true to the other in adversity as in prosperity."

The steward answered: "Something of that hope has been in the hearts of many. But no philosopher or priest yet has held forth such a vision. I thought, last night, that perchance some day there would be in the world one who taught that the joy of life lay in love and friendship. And it was a pleasing fancy that the child born last night was a kind of peace-bringer and a welder of the hearts of men. Certainly the soul of man does cry out for the companionship of one with understanding. In this world, all moil and toil, all of us need to commence again, to be reborn, as it might be, shaking off these ancient creeds and dogmas, and all these sorceries of custom. So strong was my dream that the whole world seemed clothed with light and strange beauty, the very stars singing as they swam about the world."

He passed his hand across his forehead as he ended, like a man very anxious about a great business.

"If such a one came, I would be his follower, giving up all this," said the rich man, indicating his caravan. "And when my son came to years of understanding I would send him to such a teacher, to the end that he might be saved from himself and his cares. Indeed, it would seem that the whole world would leap with gladness to follow such a peace-bringer, one who carried a message of good will to men. Does it not?"

"Indeed it does," replied the steward. "And, after all, the purpose would be the making of oneself a man. It is common sense. For there is no good but good will. Then this life, which all of us hold to be a useless burden, would have a meaning and an end."

The steward's eyes were bright as he talked, and his voice had a new quality, as if he felt the onrush of something within him.

"A fair picture," said the rich man. "A wonderful one, too, though simple. Think of it! That a child rejected and born in a stable should be a bringer of tidings of great joy to the world. A fountainhead of truth and love. A something to turn earth's roughness smooth; the One whose coming was foretold by the Hebrew prophet many centuries before, to regenerate the world."

"Indeed," agreed the steward, "it would be a fair dream, that of a world with good will between man and man."

TRYSTE NOËL

The Ox he openeth wide the Doore,
   And from the Snowe he calls her inne,
And he hath seen her Smile therefor,
   Our Ladye without Sinne.
     Now soone from Sleep
     A Starre shall leap,
And soone arrive both King and Hinde:
     Amen, Amen:
But O, the Place co'd I but finde!

The Ox hath hushed his voyce and bent
   Trewe eyes of Pitty ore the Mow,

And on his lovelie Neck, forspent,
  The Blessed layes her Browe.
    Around her feet
    Full Warme and Sweete
His bowerie Breath doth meeklie dwell:
    Amen, Amen:
But sore am I with Vaine Travèl!

The Ox is host in Judah stall
  And Host of more than onelie one,
For close she gathereth withal
  · Our Lorde her littel Sonne.
    Glad Hinde and King
    Their Gyfte may bring,
But wo'd to-night my Teares were there,
    Amèn, Amen:
Between her Bosom and His hayre!
           LOUISE IMOGEN GUINEY

THE HOUSE OF CHRISTMAS

There fared a mother driven forth
Out of an inn to roam;
In the place where she was homeless
All men are at home.
The crazy stable close at hand,
With shaking timber and shifting sand,
Grew a stronger thing to abide and stand
Than the square stones of Rome.

For men are homesick in their homes,
And strangers under the sun,
And they lay their heads in a foreign land
Whenever the day is done.

Here we have battle and blazing eyes,
And chance and honor and high surprise,
But our homes are under miraculous skies
Where the yule tale was begun.

A Child in a foul stable,
Where the beasts feed and foam,
Only where He was homeless
Are you and I at home;
We have hands that fashion and heads that know,
But our hearts we lost—how long ago!
In a place no chart nor ship can show
Under the sky's dome.

This world is wild as an old wives' tale,
And strange the plain things are,
The earth is enough and the air is enough
For our wonder and our war;
But our rest is as far as the fire-drake swings
And our peace is put in impossible things
Where clashed and thundered unthinkable wings
Round an incredible star.

To an open house in the evening
Home shall men come,
To an older place than Eden
And a taller town than Rome.
To the end of the way of the wandering star,
To the things that cannot be and that are,
To the place where God was homeless
And all men are at home.

Gilbert Keith Chesterton

SILENT NIGHT!

Silent night! Holy night!
All is calm, all is bright;
Round yon Virgin Mother and Child!
Holy Infant, so tender and mild,
Sleep in heavenly peace,
Sleep in heavenly peace.

Silent night! Holy night!
Shepherds quake at the sight!
Glories stream from heaven afar,
Heavenly hosts sing Alleluia.
Christ, the Saviour, is born!
Christ, the Saviour, is born!

Silent night! Holy night!
Son of God, love's pure light
Radiant beams from Thy Holy face,
With the dawn of redeeming grace,
Jesus, Lord, at Thy birth,
Jesus, Lord, at Thy birth.

JOSEPH MOHR

IT CAME UPON THE MIDNIGHT CLEAR

It came upon the midnight clear,
  That glorious song of old,
From angels bending near the earth
  To touch their harps of gold:
"Peace on the earth, good will to men
  From heaven's all-gracious King"—
The world in solemn stillness lay
  To hear the angels sing.

Still through the cloven skies they come
  With peaceful wings unfurled,
And still their heavenly music floats
  O'er all the weary world;
Above its sad and lowly plains
  They bend on hovering wing,
And ever o'er its Babel-sounds
  The blessèd angels sing.

But with the woes of sin and strife
  The world has suffered long;
Beneath the angel-strain have rolled
  Two thousand years of wrong;
And man, at war with man, hears not
  The love-song which they bring;—
Oh, hush the noise, ye men of strife,
  And hear the angels sing!

And ye, beneath life's crushing load,
  Whose forms are bending low,
Who toil along the climbing way
  With painful steps and slow,
Look now! for glad and golden hours
  Come swiftly on the wing;—
Oh, rest beside the weary road
  And hear the angels sing!

For lo! the days are hastening on
  By prophet bards foretold,
When with the ever circling years
  Comes round the age of gold;
When Peace shall over all the earth
  Its ancient splendors fling,
And the whole world give back the song
  Which now the angels sing.

Edmund Hamilton Sears

HARK! THE HERALD ANGELS SING

Hark! the herald angels sing,
Glory to the new-born King;
Peace on earth and mercy mild;
God and sinners reconciled.
Joyful all ye nations rise;
Join the triumph of the skies;
With th' angelic host proclaim,
Christ is born in Bethlehem.
  Hark! the herald angels sing,
  Glory to the new-born King.

Christ, by highest heaven adored,
Christ, the everlasting Lord,
Late in time behold Him come,
Offspring of a virgin's womb.
Veiled in flesh the Godhead see;
Hail th' incarnate Deity,
Pleased as man with man to dwell,
Jesus, our Emmanuel!

Hail the heaven-born Prince of Peace!
Hail the Sun of Righteousness!
Light and life to all He brings,
Risen with healing in His wings.
Mild He lays His glory by;
Born that man no more may die;
Born to raise the sons of earth;
Born to give them second birth.

CHARLES WESLEY

THERE'S A SONG IN THE AIR

There's a song in the air!
   There's a star in the sky!
There's a Mother's deep prayer,
   And a Baby's low cry!
And the star rains its fire while the beautiful sing,
For the manger of Bethlehem cradles a King.

There's a tumult of joy
   O'er the wonderful birth,
For the Virgin's sweet Boy
   Is the Lord of the earth.
Ay! the star rains its fire while the beautiful sing,
For the manger of Bethlehem cradles a King!

In the light of that star
   Lie the ages impearled;
And that song from afar
   Has swept over the world.
Every hearth is aflame, and the beautiful sing
In the homes of the nations that Jesus is King!

We rejoice in the light,
   And we echo the song
That comes down through the night
   From the heavenly throng.
Ay! we shout to the lovely evangel they bring,
And we greet in His cradle our Saviour and King!

JOSIAH G. HOLLAND

JOY TO THE WORLD! THE LORD IS COME!

Joy to the world! the Lord is come;
Let earth receive her King;
Let every heart prepare Him room,
And heaven and nature sing.

Joy to the world! the Saviour reigns;
Let men their song employ;
While fields and floods, rocks, hills and plains;
Repeat the sounding joy.

No more let sin and sorrow grow,
Nor thorns infest the ground;
He comes to make His blessings flow
Far as the curse is found.

He rules the world with truth and grace,
And makes the nations prove
The glories of His righteousness,
And wonders of His love.

                                    ISAAC WATTS

O LITTLE TOWN OF BETHLEHEM

O little town of Bethlehem,
  How still we see thee lie!
Above thy deep and dreamless sleep
  The silent stars go by;
Yet in thy dark streets shineth
  The everlasting Light;
The hopes and fears of all the years
  Are met in thee to-night.

For Christ is born of Mary,
  And, gathered all above,
While mortals sleep, the angels keep
  Their watch of wondering love.
O morning stars, together
  Proclaim the holy birth!
And praises sing to God the King,
  And peace to men on earth.

How silently, how silently,
  The wondrous gift is given!
So God imparts to human hearts
  The blessings of His heaven.
No ear may hear His coming,
  But in this world of sin,
Where meek souls will receive Him still,
  The dear Christ enters in.

O holy Child of Bethlehem!
  Descend to us, we pray;
Cast out our sin, and enter in,
  Be born in us to-day.
We hear the Christmas angels
  The great glad tidings tell;
Oh come to us, abide with us,
  Our Lord Emmanuel!

                      PHILLIPS BROOKS

AWAY IN A MANGER

Away in a manger,
  No crib for His bed,
The little Lord Jesus
  Laid down His sweet head.

The stars in the bright sky
   Look'd down where He lay,
The little Lord Jesus
   Asleep in the hay.

The cattle are lowing,
   The poor Baby wakes,
But little Lord Jesus,
   No crying He makes.

I love Thee, Lord Jesus;
   Look down from the sky,
And stay by my crib,
   Watching my lullaby.
                MARTIN LUTHER

ONCE IN ROYAL DAVID'S CITY

Once in royal David's city
   Stood a lowly cattle shed,
Where a mother laid her Baby
   In a manger for His bed.
Mary was that mother mild,
Jesus Christ that little Child.

He came down to earth from Heaven,
   Who is God and Lord of all.
And His shelter was a stable,
   And His cradle was a stall.
With the poor and mean and lowly,
Lived on earth our Saviour Holy.

And our eyes at last shall see Him
   Through His own redeeming love,

For that Child so dear and gentle
   Is our Lord in Heaven above;
And He leads His children on
To the place where He is gone.

Not in that poor, lowly stable,
   With the oxen standing by,
We shall see Him; but in Heaven,
   Set at God's right hand on high,
When, like stars, His children crowned
All in white, shall wait around.

             C. FRANCES ALEXANDER

ANGELS, FROM THE REALMS OF GLORY

Angels, from the realms of glory,
   Wing your flight o'er all the earth;
Ye who sang creation's story
   Now proclaim Messiah's birth:
      Come and worship, Come and worship,
Worship Christ, the newborn King.

Shepherds, in the field abiding,
   Watching o'er your flocks by night,
God with man is now residing;
   Yonder shines the infant light:
      Come and worship,
Worship Christ, the newborn King.

Sages, leave your contemplations,
   Brighter visions beam afar;
Seek the great Desire of nations;
   Ye have seen his natal star:
      Come and worship,
Worship Christ, the newborn King.

Saints, before the altar bending,
  Watching long in hope and fear,
Suddenly the Lord, descending,
  In His temple shall appear:
    Come and worship,
Worship Christ, the newborn King.

Sinners, wrung with true repentance,
  Doomed for guilt to endless pains,
Justice now revokes the sentence,
  Mercy calls you, break your chains:
    Come and worship,
Worship Christ, the newborn King.

JAMES MONTGOMERY

GOOD CHRISTIAN MEN, REJOICE

Good Christian men, rejoice
With heart, and soul, and voice;
Give ye heed to what we say: News! News!
Jesus Christ is born today:
Ox and ass before Him bow,
And He is in the manger now.
Christ is born today!
Christ is born today!

Good Christian men, rejoice
With heart, and soul, and voice;
Now ye hear of endless bliss: Joy! Joy!
Jesus Christ was born for this!
He hath oped the heav'nly door,
And man is blessed ever more.
Christ was born for this!
Christ was born for this!

Good Christian men, rejoice
With heart, and soul, and voice;
Now ye need not fear the grave: Peace! Peace!
Jesus Christ was born to save!
Calls you one and calls you all,
To gain His everlasting hall.
Christ was born to save!
Christ was born to save!

J. M. NEALE

CHRISTMAS EVERYWHERE

Everywhere, everywhere, Christmas tonight!
Christmas in lands of the fir-tree and pine,
Christmas in lands of the palm-tree and vine,
Christmas where snow peaks stand solemn and white,
Christmas where cornfields stand sunny and bright.
Christmas where old men are patient and gray,.
Christmas where peace, like a dove in his flight,
Broods o'er brave men in the thick of the fight;
Everywhere, everywhere, Christmas tonight!
For the Christ-child who comes is the Master of all;
No Palace too great, no cottage too small.

PHILLIPS BROOKS

O COME, ALL YE FAITHFUL

ADESTE FIDELES

O come, all ye faithful,
Joyful and triumphant,
O come ye, O come ye to Bethlehem;
Come and behold Him,

Born the King of angels:
O come, let us adore Him,
O come, let us adore Him,
O come, let us adore Him,
   Christ the Lord.

Sing, choirs of angels,
Sing in exultation,
Sing, all ye citizens of heaven above;
"Glory to God
In the highest":

Yea, Lord, we greet Thee,
Born this happy morning;
Jesu, to Thee be glory given;
Word of the Father,
Now in flesh appearing:
   O come, let us adore Him,
   O come, let us adore Him,
   O come, let us adore Him,
    Christ the Lord.

          FROM THE LATIN

THE SHEPHERDS

THE NATIVITY

From the Pageant of the Shearmen and Tailors in Coventry,
Transcribed in 1534

Pastor I

Now God that art in Trinity
Save Thou my fellows and me;
For I know not where my sheep nor they be,
This night it is so cold.
Now it is nigh the midst of night,
These weathers are dark and dim of light,
So that of them I can have no sight,
Standing here on this wold.
Now will I cry with all my might
—Full well my voice they know—
What ho! fellows! Ho! ho! ho!

Pastor II

Hark, Sym, hark; I hear our brother on the lea;
This is his voice, right well I know,
Therefore toward him let us go
And follow his voice aright.
See, Sym, see where he doth stand!
I am right glad we have him found.
Brother! where hast thou been so long
And this night it is so cold!

Pastor I

Eh, friends! there came a gust of wind with a mist suddenly,
So that far off my way went I,

And was full sore afraid.
For to go, wist I not whither,
But travelled on this lea hither and thither.
I was so ware of this cold weather
That near spent was my might.

Pastor III

Brothers, now are we past that fright
And it is far within the night:
Full soon will spring the day light;
It draweth full near the tide.
Here a while let us rest
And repast us of the best;
Till that the sun rise in the east
Let us all here abide.

> *There the Shepherds draw forth their meat, and do eat and drink,
> and as they drink, they find the star and say thus:*

Pastor III

Brother, look up and behold,
What thing is yonder that shineth so bright?
As long as ever I have watched my fold,
Yet saw I never such a sight in the field.
Aha! now cometh the time our fathers foretold,
That in the winter's night so cold
A child of maiden born would be
In whom all prophecies shall be fulfilled—

Pastor I

Truth it is without nay,
So said the prophet I saye,
That a child should be born of a maid so bright

In winter, near the shortest day,
Or else in the middle of the night.

> *There the Angels sing Gloria in excelsis Deo.*

Pastor III

Hark, they sing above in the clouds so clear—
Heard I never so merry a choir!
Now gentle brothers, shall we draw near
To hear their harmony?

Pastor I

Brothers, mirth and solace is come us among:
For by the sweetness of their song,
God's son is come, whom we have looked for long—

Pastor II

Glory, glory in the highest—that was their song—
How say ye, fellows, said they not thus?

Pastor I

That is well said; now go we hence
To worship that child of high magnificence
And that we may sing in his presence
Sit in terra pax hominibus.

> *They come to the manger.*

Pastor I

Hail, maid, mother and wife so mild!
As the Angel said, so have we found.
I have nothing to give to the child
But my pipe. There! take it in thy hand!

Wherein much pleasure have I found;
And now to honor thy glorious birth
Thou shalt have it to make thee mirth.

Pastor II

Now hail to thee, child, and thy dame,
For in poor lodgings here art thou lain.
See, the Angel said, and told us thy name—
Hold, take thou here my hat on thy head—
And now of one thing thou are well sped:
For weather thou hast no need to complain,
For wind, nor sun, hail, snow and rain.

Pastor III

Hail, be thou lord over water and land,
For thy coming we all make mirth.
Have here my mittens to put on thy hands
Other treasure have I none to present thee with.

Mary

Now kind herdsmen, for your coming,
To my child shall I pray,
As he is heaven's King, to grant you his blessing,
And to his bliss that you may come at your last day.

The shepherds go forth out of that place.

THE SHEPHERD WHO WATCHED BY NIGHT

By Thomas Nelson Page

THE place had nothing distinguished or even perhaps distinctive about it except its trees and the tapering spire of a church lifting above them. It was not unlike a hundred other places that one sees as one travels through the country. It called itself a town but it was hardly more than a village. One long street, now paved on both sides, climbed the hill, where the old post-road used to run in from the country on one side and out again on the other, passing a dingy, large house with whitewashed pillars, formerly known as the tavern, but now calling itself "The Inn." This, with two or three built-up cross streets and a short street or two on either side of the main street, constituted "the town." A number of good houses, and a few very good indeed, sat back in yards dignified by fine trees. Three or four churches stood on corners, as far apart apparently as possible. Several of them were much newer and fresher painted than the one with the spire and cross; but this was the only old one and was generally spoken of as "The Church," as the rector was meant when the people spoke of "The Preacher." It sat back from the street, and near it, yet more retired, was an old dwelling, also dilapidated, with a wide porch, much decayed, and an out-building or two to the side and a little behind it, one of which was also occupied as a dwelling. The former was the rectory and the smaller dwelling was where the old woman lived who took care of the rectory, cleaned up the two rooms which the rector used since his wife's death, and furnished him his meals. It had begun only as a temporary arrangement, but it had seemed to work well enough and had gone on now for years and no one thought of changing it. If an idea of change ever entered the mind of any one, it was only when the old woman's grumbling floated out into the town as to the tramps who would come and whom the preacher would try to take care of. Then, indeed, discussion would take place as to the utter impracticability of the old preacher and the possibility of getting a younger and liver man in his place. For the rest of the time the people were hopeless. The old preacher was past his prime; no one else wanted him, and they could not turn him out. He was saddled on them for life. They ran simply by the old propulsion; but the church was going down, they said, and they were helpless. This had been the case for years. And now as the year neared its close it was the same.

Such was the talk as they finished dressing the church for Christmas and made their way homeward, the few who still took interest enough to help in this way. They felt sorry for the old man, who had been much in their way during the dressing, but sorrier for themselves. This had been a few days before Christmas and now it was Christmas eve.

The old rector sat at his table trying to write his Christmas sermon. He was hopelessly behindhand with it. The table was drawn up close to the worn stove, but the little bare room was cold, and now and then the old man blew on his fingers to warm them, and pushed his feet closer to the black hearth. Again and again he took up his pen as if to write, and as often laid it down again. The weather was bitter and the coal would not burn. There was little to burn. Before him on the table, amid a litter of other books and papers, lay a worn bible and prayer-book—open, and beside them a folded letter on which his eye often rested. Outside, the wind roared, shaking the doors, rattling the windows, and whistling at the key-holes. Now and then the sound of a passing vehicle was borne in on the wind, and at intervals came the voices of boys shouting to each other as they ran by. The old man did not hear the former, but when the boys shouted he listened till they had ceased and his thoughts turned to the past and to the two boys whom God had given him and had then taken back to Himself. His gray face wore a look of deep concern, and, indeed, of dejection, and his eye wandered once more to the folded letter on the table. It was signed "A Friend," and it was this which was responsible for the unwritten Christmas sermon. It was what the world calls an anonymous letter and, though couched in kindly terms, it had struck a dagger into the old man's heart. And yet he could not but say that in tone and manner it was a kind act. Certainly it had told the truth and if in tearing a veil from his eyes it had stunned him, why should he not face the truth!

He took up the letter again and reread it, not that he needed to read it, for he knew it by heart.

He reread it hoping to find some answer to its plain, blunt, true statements, but he found none. It was all true, every word, from the ominous beginning which stated that the writer felt that he had "a clear duty to perform," down to the close when with a protestation of good-will he signed himself the old man's "friend."

"You must see, unless you are blind," ran the letter, "that your church is running down, and unless you get out and let the congregation secure a new and younger man, there will soon be no congregation at all left. No men come to church any longer and many women who used to come now stay away. You are a good man, but you are a failure. Your usefulness is past."

Yes, it was true, he was a failure. His usefulness was past. This was the reason no Christmas things had come this year—they wanted to let him know. It pained him to think it, and he sighed.

"You spend your time fooling about a lot of useless things, visiting people who do not come to church, and you have turned the rectory into a harbor for tramps," continued the anonymous friend.

"You cannot preach any longer. You are hopelessly behind the times. People nowadays want no more doctrinal points discussed; they want to hear live, up-to-date, practical discourses on the vital problems of the day—such as the Rev. Dr. —— delivers. His church is full." This also was true. He was no longer able to preach. He had felt something of this himself. Now it came home to him like a blow on the head, and a deeper pain was the conviction which, long hovering about his heart, now settled and took definite shape, that he ought to get out. But where could he go? He would have gone long since if he had known where to go. He could not go out and graze like an old horse on the roadside. There was no provision made for those like him. No pensions were provided by his church for old and disabled clergymen and the suggestion made in the letter had no foundation in his case. It ran, "You must or, at least, you should have saved something in all this time."

This sounded almost humorous and a wintry little smile flickered for a moment about the old man's wrinkled mouth. His salary had never been a thousand dollars, and there were so many to give to. Of late, it had been less than two-thirds of this amount and not all of this had been paid. The smile died out and the old man's face grew grave again as he tried to figure out what he could do. He thought of one or two old friends to whom he could write. Possibly, they might know of some country parish that would be willing to take him, though it was a forlorn hope. If he could but hold on till they invited him, it would be easier, for he knew how difficult it was for a clergyman out of a place to get a call. People were so suspicious. Once out, he was lost.

At the thought, a picture of a little plot amid the trees in the small cemetery on the hill near the town slipped into his mind. Three little slabs stood there above three mounds, one longer than the others. They covered all that was mortal of what he had loved best on earth. The old man sighed and his face in the dim light took on an expression very far away. He drifted off into a reverie. Ah, if they had only been left to him, the two boys that God had sent him and had then taken back to Himself, and the good wife who had borne up so bravely till she had sunk by the wayside! If he were only with them! He used to be rebellious at the neglect that left the drains so deadly, but that was gone now. He leant forward on his elbows and gradually slipped slowly to his knees. He was on them a long time, and when he tried to rise he was quite stiff; but his face had grown tranquil. He had been in high converse with the blessed of God and his mind had cleared. He had placed everything in God's hands, and He had given him light. He would wait until after Christmas and then he would resign. But he would announce it next day. The flock there should have a new and younger and abler shepherd. This would be glad tidings to them.

He folded up the letter and put it away. He no longer felt wounded by it. It was of God's ordaining and was to be received as a kindness, a ray of light to show him the path of duty. He drew his paper toward him and, taking up his pen, began to write rapidly and firmly. The doubt was gone, the way was clear. His text had come to his mind.

"And there were in the same country, shepherds abiding in the field, keeping watch over their flock by night, and lo, the angel of the Lord came upon them, and the glory of the Lord shone round about them. And they were sore afraid. And the angel said unto them: Fear not, for behold, I bring unto you good tidings of great joy, which shall be to all people. For unto you is born this day in the City of David a Saviour which is Christ the Lord. And this shall be a sign unto you. You shall find the Babe wrapped in swaddling clothes lying in a manger."

Unfolding the story, he told of the darkness that had settled over Israel under the Roman sway and the formalism of the Jewish hierarchy at the time of Christ's coming, drawing from it the lesson that God still had shepherds watching over His flocks in the night to whom He vouchsafed to send His heavenly messengers. On and on he wrote, picturing the divine mission of the Redeemer and His power to save souls, and dwelling on Christmas as the ever-recurrent reminder of "the tender mercy of our God whereby the Day Spring from on High hath visited us."

Suddenly he came to a pause. Something troubled him. It flashed over him that he had heard that a woman in the town was very sick and he had intended going to see her. She had had a bad reputation; but he had heard that she had reformed. At any rate she was ill. He paused and deliberated. At the moment the wind rattled the shutters. She did not belong to his flock or, so far as he knew, to any flock, and once when he had stopped her on the street and spoken to her of her evil life, she had insulted him.

He turned back to his paper, pen in hand; but it was borne in on him that he was writing of watching over the flock by night and here he was neglecting one of his Father's sheep. He laid aside his pen and, rising, took down his old overcoat and hat and stick, lit his lantern, turned down his lamp, and shuffling through the bare, narrow passage, let himself out at the door.

As he came out on to the little porch to step down to the walk, the wind struck him fiercely and he had some difficulty in fastening the door with its loose lock; but this done he pushed forward. The black trees swayed and creaked above him in the high night wind, and fine particles of snow stung his withered cheeks. He wondered if the shepherds in the fields ever had such a night as this for their watch. He remembered to have read that snow fell on the mountains of Judæa.

At length he reached the little house on a back street where he had heard the sick woman lived. A light glimmered dimly in an upper window and his knocking finally brought to the door a woman who looked after her. She was not in a good humor at being disturbed at that hour, for her rest had been much broken of late; but she was civil and invited him in.

In answer to his question of how her patient was, she replied gloomily: "No better; the doctor says she can't last much longer. Do you want to see her?" she added presently.

The old rector said he did and she waved toward the stair. "You can walk up."

As they climbed the stair she added: "She said you'd come if you knew." The words made the old man warmer. And when she opened the door of the sick room and said, "Here's the preacher, as you said," the faint voice of the invalid murmuring, "I hoped you'd come," made him feel yet warmer.

He was still of some use even in this parish.

Whatever her face had been in the past, illness and suffering had refined it. He stayed there long, for he found that she needed him. She unburdened herself to him. She was sorry she had been rude to him that time. She had been a sinful woman. She said she had tried of late to live a good life, since that day he had spoken to her, but she now found that she had not. She had wanted to be a believer and she had gone to hear him preach one day after that, but now she did not seem to believe anything. She wanted to repent, but she could not feel. She was in the dark and she feared she was lost.

The old man had taken his seat by her side, and he now held her hand and soothed her tenderly.

"Once, perhaps," he said doubtfully, "though God only knows that, but certainly no longer. Christ died for you. You say you wanted to change, that you tried to ask God's pardon and to live a better life even before you fell ill. Do you think you could want this as much as God wanted it? He put the wish into your heart. Do you think He would now let you remain lost? Why, He sent His Son into the world to seek and to save the lost. He has sent me to you to-night to tell you that He has come to save you. It is not you that can save yourself, but He, and if you feel that it is dark about you, never mind—the path is still there. One of the old Fathers has said that God sometimes puts His children to sleep in the dark. He not only forgave the Magdalen for her love of Him, but He vouchsafed to her the first sight of His face after His resurrection."

"I see," she said simply.

A little later she dozed off, but presently roused up again. A bell was ringing somewhere in the distance. It was the ushering in of the Christmas morn.

"What is that?" she asked feebly.

He told her.

"I think if I were well, if I could ever be good enough, I should like to join the church," she said. "I remember being baptized—long ago."

"You have joined it," he replied.

Just then the nurse brought her a glass.

"What is that?" she asked feebly.

"A little wine." She held up a bottle in which a small quantity remained.

It seemed to the old preacher a sort of answer to his thought. "Have you bread here?" he asked the young woman. She went out and a moment later brought him a piece of bread.

He had often administered the early communion on Christmas morning, but never remembered a celebration that had seemed to him so real and satisfying. As he thought of the saints departed this life in the faith and fear of the Lord, they appeared to throng about him as never before, and among them were the faces he had known and loved best on earth.

It was toward morning when he left. As he bade her good-by he knew he should see her no more this side of heaven.

As he came out into the night the snow was falling softly, but the wind had died down and he no longer felt cold. The street was empty, but he no longer felt lonely. He seemed to have got nearer to God's throne.

Suddenly, as he neared his house, a sound fell on his ears. He stopped short and listened. Could he have been mistaken? Could that have been a baby's cry? There was no dwelling near but his own, and on that side only the old and unoccupied stable in the yard whence the sound had seemed to come. A glance at it showed that it was dark and he was moving on again to the house when the sound was repeated. This time there was no doubt of it. A baby's wail came clear on the silence of the night from the unused stable. A thought that it might be some poor foundling flashed into his mind. The old man turned and, stumbling across the yard, went to the door.

"Who is here?" he asked of the dark. There was no answer, but the child wailed again, and he entered the dark building, asking again, "Who is here?" as he groped his way forward. This time a voice almost inarticulate answered. Holding his dim little lantern above his head, he made his way inside, peering into the darkness, and presently, in a stall, on a lot of old litter, he descried a dark and shapeless mass from which the sound came. Moving forward, he bent down, with the lantern held low, and the dark mass gradually took shape as a woman's form seated on the straw. A patch of white, from which a pair of eyes gazed up at him, became a face, and below, a small bundle clasped to her breast took on the lines of a babe.

"What are you doing here?" he asked, breathless with astonishment. She shook her head wearily and her lips moved as if to say: "I didn't mean any harm." But no sound came. She only tried to fold the babe more warmly in her shawl. He took off his overcoat and wrapped it around her. "Come," he said firmly. "You must come with me," he added kindly; then, as she did not rise, he put out his hand to lift her, but, instead, suddenly set down the lantern and took the babe gently in his arms. She let him take the child, and rose slowly, her eyes still on him. He motioned for her to take the lantern and she did so. And they came to the door. He turned up the walk, the babe in his arms, and she going before him with the lantern. The ground was softly carpeted with snow; the wind had died down, but the clouds had disappeared and the trees were all white, softly gleaming, like dream-trees in a dreamland. The old man shivered slightly, but not now with cold. He felt as if he had gone back and held once more in his arms one of those babes he had given back to God. He thought of the shepherds who watched by night on the Judæan hills. "It must have been such a night as this," he thought, as his eyes caught the morning star which appeared to rest just over his home.

When they reached his door he saw that some one had been there in his absence. A large box stood on the little porch and beside it a basket filled with things. So he had not been forgotten after all. The milkman also had called and for his customary small bottle of milk had left one of double the ·usual size. When he let himself in at the door, he took the milk with him. So the shepherds might have done, he thought.

It was long before he could get the fire to burn; but in time this was done; the room was warm and the milk was warmed also. The baby was quieted and was soon asleep in its mother's lap, where she sat still hooded, before the stove. And as the firelight fell from the open stove on the child, in its mother's arms, the old man thought of a little picture he had once seen in a shop window. He had wanted to buy it, but he had never felt that he could gratify such a taste. There were too many calls on him. Then, as the young woman appeared overcome with fatigue, the old man put her with the child in the only bed in the house that was ready for an occupant and, returning to the little living-room, ensconced himself in his arm-chair by the stove. He had meant to finish his sermon, but he was conscious for the first time that he was very tired; but he was also very happy. When he awoke he found that it was quite late. He had overslept and though his breakfast had been set out for him, he had time only to make his toilet and to go to church. The mother and child were still asleep in his room, the babe folded in her arm, and he stopped only to gaze on them a moment and to set the rest of the milk and his breakfast where the young mother could find it on awaking. Then he went to church, taking his half-finished sermon in his worn case. He thought with some dismay that it was unfinished, but the memory of the poor woman and the midnight communion, and of the young mother and her babe, comforted him; so he plodded on bravely. When he reached the church it was nearly full. He had not had such a congregation in a long time. And they were all cheerful and happy. The pang he had had as he remembered that he was to announce his resignation that day was renewed, but only for a second. The thought of the babe and its mother, warmed and fed in his little home, drove it away. And soon he began the service.

He had never had such a service. It all appeared to him to have a new meaning. He felt nearer to the people in the pews than he ever remembered to have felt. They were more than ever his flock and he more than ever their shepherd. More, he felt nearer to mankind, and yet more near to those who had gone before—the innumerable company of the redeemed. They were all about him, clad all in white, glistening like the sun. The heavens seemed full of them. When he turned his eyes to the window, the whole earth seemed white with them. The singing sounded in his ears like the choiring of angels. He was now in a maze. He forgot the notice he had meant to give and went straight into his sermon, stumbling a little as he climbed the steps to the pulpit. He repeated the text and kept straight on. He told the story of the shepherds in the fields watching their flocks when the Angel of the Lord came upon them and told of the Babe in the manger who was Christ the Lord. He spoke for the shepherds. He pictured the shepherds watching through the night and made a plea for their loneliness and the hardship of their lives. They were very poor and ignorant. But they had to watch the flock and God had chosen them to be His messengers. The wise men would come later, but now it was the shepherds who first knew of the birth of Christ the Lord. He was not reading as was his wont. It was all out of his heart and the eyes of all seemed to be on him—of all in pews and of all that innumerable white-clad host about him.

He was not altogether coherent, for he at times appeared to confuse himself with the shepherds. He spoke as if the message had come to him, and after a while he talked of some experiences he had had in finding a child in a stable. He spoke as though he had really seen it. "And now," he said, "this old shepherd must leave his flock, the message has come for him."

He paused and looked down at his sermon and turned the leaves slowly, at first carefully and then almost aimlessly. A breath of wind blew in and a few leaves slid off the desk and fluttered down to the floor.

"I have been in some fear lately," he said, "but God has appeared to make the way plain. A friend has helped me, and I thank him." He looked around and lost himself. "I seem to have come to the end," he said, smiling simply with a soft, childish expression stealing over and lighting up his wan face. "I had something more I wanted to say, but I can't find it and—I can't remember. I seem too tired to remember it. I am a very old man and you must bear with me, please, while I try." He quietly turned and walked down the steps, holding on to the railing.

As he stooped to pick up a loose sheet from the floor, he sank to his knees, but he picked it up. "Here it is," he said with a tone of relief. "I remember now. It is that there were shepherds abiding in the fields, keeping watch over their flocks by night, and the light came upon them and the glory of the Lord shone round about them and they were sore afraid, and the angel said unto them: 'Fear not, for behold, I bring unto you good tidings of great joy which shall be unto all people; for unto you is born this day in the city of David a Saviour which is Christ the Lord.'"

They reached him as he sank down and, lifting him, placed him on a cushion taken from a pew. He was babbling softly of a babe in a stable and of the glory of the Lord that shone round about them. "Don't you hear them singing?" he said. "You must sing too; we must all join them."

At the suggestion of some one, a woman's clear voice struck up,

"While shepherds watched their flocks by night,"

and they sang it through as well as they could for sobbing. But before the hymn was ended the old shepherd had joined the heavenly choir and had gone away up into heaven.

As they laid him in the little chamber on the hill opening to the sunrise, the look on his face showed that the name of that chamber was Peace.

They talk of him still in his old parish—of the good he did, and of his peaceful death on the day that of all the year signified Birth and Life.

Nothing was ever known of the mother and babe. Only there was a rumor that one had been seen leaving the house during the morning and passing out into the white-clad country. And at the little inn in the town there was vague wonder what had become of the woman and her baby who had applied for shelter there the night before and had been told that there was no place for her there, and that she had better go to the old preacher, as he took in all the tramps. But in heaven it is known that there was that Christmas eve a shepherd who kept watch over his flock by night.

WHILE SHEPHERDS WATCH'D

While shepherds watch'd their flocks by night,
    All seated on the ground,
The angel of the Lord came down,
    And glory shone around.

"Fear not," said he (for mighty dread
    Had seized their troubled mind);
"Glad tidings of great joy I bring
    To you and all mankind.

"To you, in David's town, this day
   Is born of David's line
The Saviour who is Christ the Lord;
   And this shall be the sign:

"The heavenly Babe you there shall find
   To human view display'd,
All meanly wrapt in swathing bands,
   And in a manger laid."

Thus spake the Seraph; and forthwith
   Appear'd a shining throng
Of angels, praising God, and thus
   Address'd their joyful song:

"All glory be to God on high,
   And to the earth be peace;
Good-will henceforth from heaven to men
   Begin, and never cease!"

NAHUM TATE

AND SHALL I SILENT BE?

All after pleasures as I rid one day,
   My horse and I, both tir'd, body and mind,
   With full cry of affections, quite astray;
I took up in the next inn I could find.

There when I came, whom found I but my dear,
   My dearest Lord, expecting till the grief
   Of pleasures brought me to Him, ready there
To be all passengers' most sweet relief?

O Thou, whose glorious, yet contracted light,
    Wrapt in night's mantle, stole into a manger;
    Since my dark soul and brutish is Thy right,
To man of all beasts be not Thou a stranger:
    Furnish and deck my soul, that Thou mayst have
    A better lodging, then a rack, or grave.

The shepherds sing; and shall I silent be?
    My God, no hymn for Thee?
My soul's a shepherd too; a flock it feeds
    Of thoughts, and words, and deeds.
The pasture is Thy word: the streams, Thy grace
    Enriching all the place.
Shepherd and flock shall sing, and all my powers
    Out-sing the day-light hours.
Then we will chide the sun for letting night
    Take up his place and right:
We sing one common Lord; wherefore He should
    Himself the candle hold.
I will go searching, till I find a sun
    Shall stay, till we have done;
A willing shiner, that shall shine as gladly,
    As frost-nipt suns look sadly,
Then we will sing, and shine all our own day,
    And one another pay:
His beams shall cheer my breast, and both so twine,
Till ev'n His beams sing, and my music shine.

                    GEORGE HERBERT

HEAVEN CANNOT HOLD HIM

In the bleak mid-winter
  Frosty wind made moan,
Earth stood hard as iron,
  Water like a stone;
Snow had fallen, snow on snow,
  Snow on snow,
In the bleak mid-winter
  Long ago.

Our God, Heaven cannot hold Him
  Nor earth sustain;
Heaven and earth shall flee away,
  When He comes to reign.
In the bleak mid-winter
  A stable-place sufficed
The Lord God Almighty,
  Jesus Christ.

Angels and archangels
  May have gathered there;
Cherubim and seraphim
  Thronged the air.
But only His Mother,
  In her maiden bliss,
Worshipped her Beloved
  With a kiss.

What can I give Him,
  Poor as I am?
If I were a shepherd
  I would bring a lamb;

> If I were a wise man,
>   I would do my part,—
> Yet what I can I give Him,
>   Give my heart.
>
> CHRISTINA G. ROSSETTI

A CHRISTMAS CAROL

> The Christ-child lay on Mary's lap,
>   His hair was like a light.
> (O weary, weary were the world,
>   But here is all aright.)
>
> The Christ-child lay on Mary's breast,
>   His hair was like a star.
> (O stern and cunning are the kings,
>   But here the true hearts are.)
>
> The Christ-child lay on Mary's heart,
>   His hair was like a fire.
> (O weary, weary is the world,
>   But here the world's desire.)
>
> The Christ-child stood at Mary's knee,
>   His hair was like a crown,
> And all the flowers looked up at Him,
>   And all the stars looked down.
>
> GILBERT K. CHESTERTON

A MAIDEN THAT IS MAKELESS

I sing of a maiden
  That is makeless.*
King of all kinges
  To her son she chose.

He came all so stille
  There his mother was
As dew in Aprille
  That falleth on the grass.

He came all so stille
  To his mother's bower,
As dew in Aprille
  That falleth on the flower.

He came all so stille
  There his mother lay,
As dew in Aprille
  That falleth on the spray.

Mother and maiden
  Was never none but she;
Well may such a lady
  Godes mother be.
          FROM THE FIFTEENTH CENTURY

* Matchless.

THE LAMB

Little Lamb, who made thee?
Dost thou know who made thee,
Gave thee life, and bade thee feed
By the stream and o'er the mead;
Gave thee clothing of delight,
Softest clothing, wooly, bright;
Gave thee such a tender voice,
Making all the vales rejoice?
    Little Lamb, who made thee?
    Dost thou know who made thee?

Little Lamb, I'll tell thee,
Little Lamb, I'll tell thee;
He is callèd by thy name,
For He calls Himself a Lamb.
He is meek, and He is mild;
He became a little child.
I a child, and thou a lamb,
We are callèd by His name.
    Little Lamb, God bless thee!
    Little Lamb, God bless thee.
        WILLIAM BLAKE

A CHRISTMAS CAROL

"What means this glory round our feet,"
  The Magi mused, "more bright than morn?"
And voices chanted clear and sweet,
  "To-day the Prince of Peace is born!"

"What means that star," the Shepherds said,
  "That brightens through the rocky glen?"
And angels, answering overhead,
  Sang, "Peace on earth, good-will to men!"

'Tis eighteen hundred years and more
  Since those sweet oracles were dumb;
We wait for Him, like them of yore;
  Alas, He seems so slow to come!

But it was said, in words of gold,
  No time or sorrow e'er shall dim,
That little children might be bold
  In perfect trust to come to Him.

All round about our feet shall shine
  A light like that the wise men saw,
If we our loving wills incline
  To that sweet Life which is the Law.

So shall we learn to understand
  The simple faith of shepherds then,
And, clasping kindly hand in hand,
  Sing, "Peace on earth, good-will to men!"

But they who do their souls no wrong,
  But keep at eve the faith of morn,
Shall daily hear the angel-song,
  "To-day the Prince of Peace is born!"

JAMES RUSSELL LOWELL

THE SHEPHERDS IN JUDEA

Oh, the Shepherds in Judea,
　　They are pacing to and fro,
For the air grows chill at twilight
　　And the weanling lambs are slow!

Leave, O lambs, the dripping sedges, quit the bramble and the brier,
Leave the fields of barley stubble, for we light the watching fire;
Twinkling fires across the twilight, and a bitter watch to keep,
Lest the prowlers come a-thieving where the flocks unguarded sleep.

Oh, the Shepherds in Judea,
　　They are singing soft and low—
Song the blessed angels taught them
　　All the centuries ago!

There was never roof to hide them, there were never walls to bind;
Stark they lie beneath the star-beams, whom the blessed angels find,
With the huddled flocks upstarting, wondering if they hear aright,
While the Kings come riding, riding, solemn shadows in the night.

Oh, the Shepherds in Judea,
　　They are thinking, as they go,
Of the light that broke their watching
　　On the hillside in the snow!—

Scattered snow along the hillside, white as springtime fleeces are,
With the whiter wings above them and the glory-streaming star—
Guiding-star across the housetops; never fear the Shepherds felt
Till they found the Babe in manger where the kindly cattle knelt.

Oh, the shepherds in Judea!—
Do you think the Shepherds know
How the whole round earth is brightened
In the ruddy Christmas glow?

How the sighs are lost in laughter, and the laughter brings the tears,
As the thoughts of men go seeking back across the darkling years
Till they find the wayside stable that the star-led Wise Men found,
With the Shepherds, mute, adoring, and the glory shining round!

MARY AUSTIN

CHRISTMAS SONG

Why do bells for Christmas ring?
Why do little children sing?

Once a lovely, shining star,
Seen by shepherds from afar,
Gently moved until its light
Made a manger-cradle bright.

There a darling Baby lay
Pillowed soft upon the hay.
And his mother sang and smiled,
"This is Christ, the Holy Child."

So the bells for Christmas ring,
So the little children sing.

LYDIA A. C. WARD

CRADLE HYMN

Hush, my dear, lie still and slumber;
   Holy angels guard thy bed;
Heavenly blessings without number
   Gently falling on thy head.

Sleep, my babe, thy food and raiment,
   House and home, thy friends provide;
All without thy care, or payment,
   All thy wants are well supplied.

How much better thou'rt attended
   Than the Son of God could be,
When from heaven He descended,
   And became a child like thee!

Soft and easy is thy cradle;
   Coarse and hard thy Saviour lay,
When His birthplace was a stable,
   And His softest bed was hay.

See the kindly shepherds round Him,
   Telling wonders from the sky!
When they sought Him, there they found Him,
   With His Virgin-Mother by.

See the lovely babe a-dressing;
   Lovely infant, how He smiled!
When He wept, the mother's blessing
   Soothed and hushed the holy child.

Lo, He slumbers in His manger,
   Where the honest oxen fed;
Peace, my darling! here's no danger!
   Here's no ox a-near thy bed!

Mayst thou live to know and fear Him,
   Trust and love Him all thy days;
Then go dwell forever near Him,
   See His face, and sing His praise!

I could give thee thousand kisses,
   Hoping what I most desire;
Not a mother's fondest wishes
   Can to greater joys aspire.
                  ISAAC WATTS

A HYMN
ON THE NATIVITY OF MY SAVIOUR

I sing the Birth was born to-night,
The Author both of life and light;
   The angels so did sound it.
And like the ravished shepherds said,
Who saw the light, and were afraid,
   Yet searched, and true they found it.

The Son of God, th' eternal King,
That did us all salvation bring,
   And freed the soul from danger;
He whom the whole world could not take,
The Word, which heaven and earth did make,
   Was now laid in a manger.

The Father's wisdom willed it so,
The Son's obedience knew no No,
   Both wills were in one stature;
And as that Wisdom had decreed,
The Word was now made flesh indeed,
   And took on Him our nature.

What comfort by Him do we win,
Who made Himself the price of sin,
   To make us heirs of glory!
To see this Babe all innocence;
A martyr born in our defence:
   Can man forget the story?

BEN JONSON

HYMN ON THE NATIVITY

It was the winter wild,
While the heaven-born Child
   All meanly wrapt in the rude manger lies;
Nature, in awe of Him,
Had doffed her gaudy trim,
   With her great Master so to sympathize:
It was no season then for her
To wanton with the sun, her lusty paramour.

Only with speeches fair
She wooes the gentle air,
   To hide her guilty front with innocent snow;
And on her naked shame,
Pollute with sinful blame,
   The saintly veil of maiden-white to throw;
Confounded, that her Maker's eyes
Should look so near upon her foul deformities.

But He, her fears to cease,
Sent down the meek-eyed Peace;
   She, crowned with olive green, came softly sliding
Down through the turning sphere,
His ready harbinger,
   With turtle wing the amorous clouds dividing;
And, waving wide her myrtle wand,
She strikes a universal peace through sea and land.

No war or battle's sound
Was heard the world around:
   The idle spear and shield were high uphung;
The hookèd chariot stood
Unstained with hostile blood;
   The trumpet spake not to the armèd throng;
And kings sat still with awful eye,
As if they surely knew their Sovereign Lord was by.

But peaceful was the night,
Wherein the Prince of Light
   His reign of peace upon the earth began:
The winds, with wonder whist,
Smoothly the waters kissed,
   Whispering new joys to the mild ocean,
Who now hath quite forgot to rave,
While birds of calm sit brooding on the charmèd wave.

The stars, with deep amaze,
Stand fixed in steadfast gaze,
   Bending one way their precious influence;
And will not take their flight,
For all the morning light,
   Or Lucifer had often warned them thence:
But in their glimmering orbs did glow,
Until their Lord himself bespake, and bid them go.

And, though the shady gloom
Had given day her room,
   The sun himself withheld his wonted speed,
And hid his head for shame,
As his inferior flame
   The new-enlightened world no more should need;
He saw a greater sun appear
Than his bright throne, or burning axletree, could bear.

The shepherds on the lawn,
Or ere the point of dawn,
   Sat simply chatting in a rustic row;
Full little thought they then
That the mighty Pan
   Was kindly come to live with them below;
Perhaps their loves, or else their sheep,
Was all that did their silly thoughts so busy keep.

When such music sweet
Their hearts and ears did greet,
   As never was by mortal fingers strook,
Divinely warbled voice
Answering the stringèd noise,
   As all their souls in blissful rapture took:
The air, such pleasure loath to lose,
With thousand echoes still prolongs each heavenly close.

Nature, that heard such sound,
Beneath the hollow round
   Of Cynthia's seat, the airy region thrilling,
Now was almost won,
To think her part was done,
   And that her reign had here its last fulfilling;
She knew such harmony alone
Could hold all heaven and earth in happier union.

At last surrounds their sight
A globe of circular light,
　　That with long beams the shame-faced night arrayed;
The helmèd cherubim,
And sworded seraphim,
　　Are seen in glittering ranks with wings displayed,
Harping in loud and solemn quire,
With unexpressive notes, to Heaven's new-born Heir.

Such music as 'tis said
Before was never made,
　　But when of old the sons of morning sung,
While the Creator great
His constellations set,
　　And the well-balanced world on hinges hung,
And cast the dark foundations deep,
And bid the weltering waves their oozy channel keep.

Ring out, ye crystal spheres,
Once bless our human ears,
　　If ye have power to touch our senses so;
And let your silver chime
Move in melodious time;
　　And let the bass of Heaven's deep organ blow;
And, with your ninefold harmony,
Make up full concert to the angelic symphony.

For, if such holy song
Enwrap our fancy long,
　　Time will run back, and fetch the age of gold;
And speckled Vanity
Will sicken soon and die,
　　And leprous Sin will melt from earthly mould;
And Hell itself will pass away,
And leave her dolorous mansions to the peering day.

Yea, Truth and Justice then
Will down return to men,
   Orbed in a rainbow; and, like glories wearing,
Mercy will sit between,
Throned in celestial sheen,
   With radiant feet the tissued clouds down steering;
And Heaven, as at some festival,
Will open wide the gates of her high palace hall.

But wisest Fate says no,
This must not yet be so;
   The Babe yet lies in smiling infancy,
That on the bitter cross
Must redeem our loss,
   So both Himself and us to glorify:
Yet first, to those chained in sleep,
The wakeful trump of doom must thunder through the deep,

With such a horrid clang
As on Mount Sinai rang,
   While the red fire and smouldering clouds outbrake;
The aged earth aghast,
With terror of that blast,
   Shall from the surface to the centre shake;
When, at the world's last session,
The dreadful Judge in middle air shall spread His throne.

And then at last our bliss,
Full and perfect is,
   But now begins; for, from this happy day,
The old dragon, underground,
In straiter limits bound,
   Not half so far casts his usurpèd sway;
And, wroth to see his kingdom fail,
Swinges the scaly horror of his folded tail.

The oracles are dumb;
No voice or hideous hum
   Runs through the archèd roof in words deceiving.
Apollo from his shrine
Can no more divine,
   With hollow shriek the steep of Delphos leaving.
No nightly trance, or breathèd spell,
Inspires the pale-eyed priest from the prophetic cell.

The lonely mountains o'er,
And the resounding shore,
   A voice of weeping heard and loud lament;
From haunted spring and dale,
Edged with poplar pale,
   The parting Genius is with sighing sent;
With flower-inwoven tresses torn,
The nymphs in twilight shade of tangled thickets mourn.

In consecrated earth,
And on the holy hearth,
   The Lars and Lemures mourn with midnight plaint.
In urns and altars round,
A drear and dying sound
   Affrights the Flamens at their service quaint;
And the chill marble seems to sweat,
While each peculiar power foregoes his wonted seat.

Peor and Baälim
Forsake their temples dim
   With that twice-battered God of Palestine;
And moonèd Ashtaroth
Heaven's queen and mother both,
   Now sits not girt with tapers' holy shine;
The Libyac Hammon shrinks his horn;
In vain the Tyrian maids their wounded Thammuz mourn.

And sullen Moloch, fled,
Hath left in shadows dread
　　His burning idol of all blackest hue:
In vain with cymbals' ring
They call the grisly king,
　　In dismal dance about the furnace blue:
The brutish gods of Nile as fast,
Isis, and Orus, and the dog Anubis, haste.

Nor is Osiris seen
In Memphian grove or green,
　　Trampling the unshowered grass with lowings loud;
Nor can he be at rest
Within his sacred chest,
　　Naught but profoundest hell can be his shroud;
In vain with timbrelled anthems dark
The sable-stolèd sorcerers bear his worshipped ark.

He feels from Judah's land
The dreaded Infant's hand,
　　The rays of Bethlehem blind his dusky eyne;
Nor all the gods beside
Longer dare abide,
　　Not Typhon huge ending in snaky twine;
Our babe, to show his Godhead true,
Can in his swaddling bands control the damnèd crew.

So, when the sun in bed,
Curtained with cloudy red,
　　Pillows his chin upon an orient wave,
The flocking shadows pale
Troop to the infernal jail,
　　Each fettered ghost slips to his several grave;
And the yellow-skirted fays
Fly after the night-steeds, leaving their moon-loved maze.

But see, the Virgin blest
Hath laid her Babe to rest;
    Time is our tedious song should here have ending:
Heaven's youngest-teemèd star
Hath fixed her polished car,
    Her sleeping Lord with handmaid lamp attending;
And all about the courtly stable
Bright-harnessed angels sit in order serviceable.

JOHN MILTON

THE MAGI

THE JOURNEY OF THE THREE KINGS

By Henri Ghéon

Night. Nothing is seen save an enormous sky glittering with stars. A long sand-bank closes in the horizon. The Three Wise Kings appear all at the same time, standing on the sand-bank, one exactly in the middle, the others away at the right and left. A moment's music. Then they all speak together—

THE THREE MAGI.

The Magi from the East are we;
The Three Wise Kings you always see
When Christmas turns to Epiphany!
    Look at our elephants, clumpety-clump!
    Look at our camels, humpety-hump!
    Look at our turbans, wrappety-wrap;
    Hark how our shoes go tappety-tap!
O silver shoes, and silken dress—
And in our eyes, what happiness!

They come down one after the other towards the audience.

1ST MAGUS.

I am the King of Chaldea.

2ND MAGUS.

I am the King of Arabia.

3RD MAGUS.

I am the King of Ethiopia—that is why I am coal-black!

THE MAGI (*in turn*).

Balthazar!—Melchior!—And Caspar!

BALTHAZAR.

Every night, when the sky is fine, we pull our telescopes out of their covers—

MELCHIOR.

And we turn them on the sky at night, to watch the movements of the stars.

CASPAR.

For all knowledge lives in the heavens and it is a mistake to look for it anywhere else.

They sit down cross-legged, take out their telescopes, and turn them skywards. Pause.

BALTHAZAR.

Nothing new?

MELCHIOR.

Nothing new.

CASPAR.

Absolutely nothing.

BALTHAZAR.

Saturn, Jupiter and Mars.

MELCHIOR.

Saturn, Mars and Jupiter.

CASPAR.

Jupiter, Mars and Saturn.

BALTHAZAR.

The sky doesn't change as quick as all that.

MELCHIOR.

Still it is so lovely that one never gets tired of it.

CASPAR.

Let us thank the Maker of the sky . . . (*They bow low.*)

BALTHAZAR.

And yet . . .

MELCHIOR.

And yet . . .

CASPAR.

What do you mean, my lords?

BALTHAZAR.

We mean, that if the sky is beautiful, He who made it must be far fairer still.

MELCHIOR.

And that—perhaps this is foolish—one might also like . . . just a glimpse of Him . . .

> *Caspar laughs.*

BALTHAZAR.

Don't laugh, Caspar. Don't you remember the prophecy? If my calculations are correct, it cannot be far from its fulfilment.

CASPAR.

Oh—nonsense!

BALTHAZAR.

But you know it, Melchior?

MELCHIOR (*opening his book*).

I've made a mark in my book. (*Reading*) "Arise and shine, Jerusalem, for thy light is come to thee, and the glory of the Lord is risen upon thee. The darkness covers the earth, and thick darkness the peoples; but the Lord shall be born, and His glory shall appear unto thee!"

BALTHAZAR.

So speaks Isaias. But you remember too the words of Balaam: "There shall rise up a Star out of Jacob; a King shall arise from the midst of Israel." The King of the Jews!

CASPAR.

What have we to do with them? That's the business of the Israelites.

MELCHIOR.

It's the business of every nation, of all the sons of Adam, and yours too, black as you are. For Isaias adds: "The Nations shall walk in thy light, and Kings in the glory of thy dawning"; and long ago, before he died, Jacob foretold, as he lay there: "The One who shall be sent," and he named Him: "Him whom the world awaits."

CASPAR.

Indeed, we await Him! I too have let myself dream of a star that should be lovelier than any other; of a star greater than all stars, and of how that star should move and march, and lead us towards happiness.

BALTHAZAR.

And what is happiness?

MELCHIOR.

God.

CASPAR.

Yes, God Himself. But alas, our first parents were turned out of God's Garden. Along with all the beasts—not one was savage then— why, they say that all of them, even tigers, lived on honey. And now, tigers live on flesh—and nearly every man is a tiger. Ah! God is far away, and the age of happiness is gone by.

BALTHAZAR.

It is to come back again, Caspar.

MELCHIOR.

We shall see God! He will send us His star.

BALTHAZAR.

If we have faith enough in Him.

MELCHIOR.

If we pray hard to Him.

CASPAR.

Is that really true?

BALTHAZAR.

The prophets have declared it.

MELCHIOR.

God never lies to His prophets.

CASPAR.

If that is so, let us pray—pray hard!

MELCHIOR.

Let us pray ever so hard!

BALTHAZAR.

He *must* answer us.

CASPAR.

We will wait, prostrate on the ground, till He does answer.

MELCHIOR and BALTHAZAR.

Yes! yes!

CASPAR.

Each close to the others, please, so that our prayers may be the stronger.

MELCHIOR.

Head touching head.

BALTHAZAR.

And heart to heart. (*They come close together, R., and prostrate themselves side by side.*)
Then, a lovely child—an Angel—passes along the sand-bank. He has a wand in his hand, long and flexible like a fishing-rod, and a great star at its end.

ANGEL.

I am the shepherd of the stars. I urge them forward with my wand, like a flock of white sheep, day and night. Each of them knows me; each of them obeys me. They move step by step, never halting, never hesitating, cropping the blue sky like sweet fresh grass. (*Pause.*)

When evening comes, I milk them, and, like milk, their spiritual light falls on the poor, the wanderer, on sailors who have no beacon, on children with no parents, on all who are seeking for their path. I am a shepherd, and it is God who sends me. (*Pause.*)

I am a shepherd, and God said to me: "Join your two hands, and then open them wide, my child. I am going to place between them the loveliest star of all. I have kept it hidden ever since the first day of all days, keeping it in store for the Day of Love. Now that Day has come; and it is time to start." (*Pause.*)

And God said to me: "Let the star loose, if you will, and urge it forward with your wand. Gently, slowly, from the dawning towards the dusk. They who watch the sky shall see it, and love it, and, maybe, follow it. The others look too low down—so much the worse for them! They shall not see it come to rest upon the stable where My Son is born." (*Pause.*)

"Go, Shepherd of Stars! My Son is born. I promised Him, and I have given Him, to suffering and to poverty, for the Redemption of mankind. At this very moment He is asleep for the first time, wrapped up in swaddling-clothes, under a roof of rock. Go; when you see Him, you must stop, and I shall take back the star!" (*Pause.*)

God has spoken, and I obey. Go forth, dear star, my lamb! (*He moves slowly forward from R. to L., with the star at the end of his wand.*)

Adapted from *The Journey of the Three Kings*

FRANKINCENSE AND MYRRH

By Heywood Broun

ONCE there were three kings in the East and they were wise men. They read the heavens and they saw a certain strange star by which they knew that in a distant land the King of the world was to be born. The star beckoned to them and they made preparations for a long journey.

From their palaces they gathered rich gifts, gold and frankincense and myrrh. Great sacks of precious stuffs were loaded upon the backs of the camels which were to bear them on their journey. Everything was in readiness, but one of the wise men seemed perplexed and would not come at once to join his two companions, who were eager and impatient to be on their way in the direction indicated by the star.

They were old, these two kings, and the other wise man was young. When they asked him he could not tell why he waited. He knew that his treasuries had been ransacked for rich gifts for the King of Kings. It seemed that there was nothing more which he could give, and yet he was not content.

He made no answer to the old men who shouted to him that the time had come. The camels were impatient and swayed and snarled. The shadows across the desert grew longer. And still the young king sat and thought deeply.

At length he smiled, and he ordered his servants to open the great treasure sack upon the back of the first of his camels. Then he went into a high chamber to which he had not been since he was a child. He rummaged about and presently came out and approached the caravan. In his hand he carried something which glinted in the sun.

The kings thought that he bore some new gift more rare and precious than any which they had been able to find in all their treasure rooms. They bent down to see, and even the camel drivers peered from the backs of the great beasts to find out what it was which gleamed in the sun. They were curious about this last gift for which all the caravan had waited.

And the young king took a toy from his hand and placed it upon the sand. It was a dog of tin, painted white and speckled with black spots. Great patches of paint had worn away and left the metal clear, and that was why the toy shone in the sun as if it had been silver.

The youngest of the wise men turned a key in the side of the little black and white dog and then he stepped aside so that the kings and the camel drivers could see. The dog leaped high in the air and turned a somersault. He turned another and another and then fell over upon his side and lay there with a set and painted grin upon his face.

A child, the son of a camel driver, laughed and clapped his hands, but the kings were stern. They rebuked the youngest of the wise men and he paid no attention but called to his chief servant to make the first of all the camels kneel. Then he picked up the toy of tin and, opening the treasure sack, placed his last gift with his own hands in the mouth of the sack so that it rested safely upon the soft bags of incense.

"What folly has seized you?" cried the eldest of the wise men. "Is this a gift to bear to the King of Kings in the far country?"

And the young man answered and said: "For the King of Kings there are gifts of great richness, gold and frankincense and myrrh.

"But this," he said, "is for the child in Bethlehem!"

THE TRIPTYCH OF THE THREE KINGS

By Felix Timmermans

CENTERPIECE

THE day before, towards dusk, a creaky little kermis wagon passed down the street. It was drawn through the falling snow by an old man and a dog. Through the window pane, one saw the pale face of a young, slender woman. Her eyes were large and troubled. They had gone by, and those who had seen them thought no more about it.

The day after was Christmas and the air stood frozen crystal clear, pale blue over the wide world bedecked with white fur.

The lame shepherd Suskewiet, the eel-fisher Pitjevogel with his bald head, and the blear-eyed beggar Schrobberbeeck went from house to house dressed as the three Holy Kings. With them they carried a cardboard star which turned on a wooden pole, a stocking to hold the money they collected and a double-sack for food. They had turned their shabby coats inside out. The shepherd had on a high hat, Schrobberbeeck wore a crown of flowers left over from the last procession, and Pitjevogel, who turned the star, had smeared his face with shoe blacking.

It had been a good year with a fat harvest. Every peasant had a pig in brine, and now they sat puffing at their pipes with their paunches before the warm stoves, and, care-free, awaited the coming of spring.

Suskewiet, the shepherd, knew such lovely pious songs of olden days, Pitjevogel turned the star with such regularity, and the beggar made such pitiful, convincing beggar's eyes, that when the red moon came up, the foot of the stocking was filled with money and the sack was blown up like a bellows. It was full of bread, ham bones, apples, pears, and sausage.

They were in the best of spirits and nudged each other with their elbows. They could already taste the long swigs of "vitriol" they would enjoy later in the evening in the Water Nymph. They would round out their empty bellies with the good tasty food and make them so taut that one could squash a flea on them.

It was not until the peasants had put out their lamps and had gone yawning to bed, that they stopped their singing and began to count their money in the clear moonlight. Boy, O boy! Gin for a whole week! And they could even buy some fresh meat and tobacco as well.

With the star on his shoulder, the black Pitjevogel stamped quickly ahead and the other two followed, their mouths watering. Gradually a strange feeling of oppression came over their rough souls. They were silent. Was it because of all the white snow on which the pale moon stared down so fixedly? Or was it the mighty, ghost-like shadows of the trees? Or was it because of their own shadows? Or was it this silence, the silence of moonlit snow, in which not even an owl was heard nor a dog's bark from near or far?

But these lovers and loafers of out-of-the-way streets and unfrequented river banks and fields were not easily frightened. They had seen much that was wonderful in their life. Will-o'-the-wisps, spooks, and even real ghosts. But this was something different. Something like the choking fear at the approach of some great happiness. It closed in around their hearts.

The beggar took courage and said, "I am not afraid."

"I'm not either," said each of the others at the same time. Their voices trembled.

"Today is Christmas," comforted Pitjevogel.

"And God will be born anew," added the shepherd with childish piety.

"Is it true that the sheep will then stand with their heads turned toward the East?" asked Schrobberbeeck.

"Yes, and the bees will sing and fly."

"And you will be able to see right through the water," said Pitjevogel, "but I have never done it."

Again there was this silence, which was different from silence. It was as if one could feel a soul trembling in the moonlight.

"Do you believe that God will really come to earth again?" the beggar asked timidly, thinking of his sins.

"Yes," said the shepherd, "but where, no one knows. . . . He only comes for one night."

Their hard shadows now ran before them and increased their fear. Suddenly they noticed that they had lost their way. It was the fault of the endless snow which had covered over the frozen streams, the roads, and the entire countryside. They stood still and looked around; all about was snow and moonlight, and here and there trees, but no house, and even the familiar mill was nowhere to be seen. They had gone astray, and in the moonlight they could see the fear in each other's eyes.

"Let us pray," begged Suskewiet, the shepherd, "then no evil can happen to us."

The beggar and the shepherd mumbled a Hail Mary. Pitjevogel began to mutter, for since his First Communion he had forgotten how to pray.

They went around a clump of bushes and it was then that Pitjevogel saw a stream of friendly light in the distance. Without saying a word, but breathing more easily, they went toward it. And suddenly a miracle happened. All three saw and heard it but they did not dare to speak of it. They heard the humming of bees and under the snow, where the ditches were, it was as light as if lamps were burning there.

And against a row of dreaming willows there stood a lame kermis wagon and candle-light shone from its window.

Pitjevogel climbed up the small steps and knocked. A friendly old man with a beard opened the door. He did not seem astonished at their strange dress, the star, or the black face.

"We have come to ask you the way," Pitjevogel stammered.

"The way is here," said the man, "come in."

Amazed at this answer they followed obediently and in the corner of the cold empty wagon they saw a young woman. She wore a blue hooded mantle and held a very small, new-born babe at her breast. A large, yellow dog lay at her side with his faithful head on her lean knees. Her eyes were dreaming in sadness, but, as she saw the men, they filled with friendliness and confidence. Even the little child, whose head was still covered with down and whose eyes were like little slits, laughed at them and seemed particularly pleased with the black face of Pitjevogel.

Schrobberbeeck saw the shepherd kneel down and take off his high hat. He too knelt down and took the procession crown from his head and suddenly began to regret the many sins that were on his conscience. And then Pitjevogel bent his knee as well. And as they knelt, sweet voices swelled about them and a heavenly happiness, greater than any joy, filled them. And none of them knew why.

In the meantime the old man tried to start a fire in the small iron stove. Pitjevogel seeing that it would not work, asked eagerly: "May I help you?"

"It is no use, the wood is wet," the man replied.

"But you have no coals?"

"We have no money," said the old man sadly.

"What do you eat then?" asked the shepherd.

"We have nothing to eat."

Filled with confusion and compassion, the Kings looked at the old man and the young woman, at the child and the bony dog. Then they looked at each other. Their thoughts were as one and lo, the stocking with its money was emptied into the lap of the woman, and the sack of food was turned inside out and all that was in it was laid on the shaky little table. Eagerly the old man reached for the bread and gave the young woman a rosy apple. She turned it before the laughing eyes of the child before she bit into it.

"We thank you," said the old man. "God will reward you."

Once again they were under way on the road which they now knew so well and which led direct to the Water Nymph. But the stocking was rolled up in Suskewiet's pocket and the sack was empty. They hadn't a cent or a crumb.

"Do you know why we gave all of our earnings to these poor people?" asked Pitjevogel.

"No," said the others.

"I don't either," Pitjevogel replied.

A little later the shepherd said, "I think I know why. Couldn't the child have been God?"

"What are you thinking of?" laughed the eel-fisher. "God wears a white mantle with borders of gold, and He has a beard and wears a crown, as in Church."

"But formerly He was born in a stable at Christmas," asserted the shepherd.

"Yes, formerly," said Pitjevogel, "but that was a hundred years ago and even longer."

"But why did we give everything away then?"

"I'm breaking my head about that, too," said the beggar whose stomach began to rumble.

Silently, with lips that thirsted for a generous swallow of gin and longed for meat thickly spread with mustard, they passed by the Water Nymph. It was still lighted and they heard singing and the sounds of a harmonica.

Pitjevogel gave the star to the shepherd, whose task it was to keep it, and without saying a single word, but with contentment in their hearts, they parted at the crossroads, each one going to his bed. The shepherd went to his sheep, the beggar to his hut of straw, and Pitjevogel to his garret into which the snow drifted.

THE THREE KINGS

Three Kings came riding from far away,
　　Melchior and Gaspar and Baltasar;
Three Wise Men out of the East were they,
And they traveled by night and they slept by day,
　　For their guide was a beautiful, wonderful star.

The star was so beautiful, large and clear,
　　That all the other stars of the sky
Became a white mist in the atmosphere;
And by this they knew that the coming was near
　　Of the Prince foretold in the prophecy.

Three caskets they bore on their saddle-bows,
　　Three caskets of gold with golden keys;
Their robes were of crimson silk, with rows
Of bells and pomegranates and furbelows,
　　Their turbans like blossoming almond-trees.

And so the Three Kings rode into the West,
　　Through the dusk of night over hill and dell,
And sometimes they nodded with beard on breast,
And sometimes talked, as they paused to rest,
　　With the people they met at some wayside well.

"Of the Child that is born," said Baltasar,
　　"Good people, I pray you, tell us the news;
For we in the East have seen His star,
And have ridden fast, and have ridden far,
　　To find and worship the King of the Jews."

And the people answered, "You ask in vain;
  We know of no king but Herod the Great!"
They thought the Wise Men were men insane,
As they spurred their horses across the plain
  Like riders in haste who cannot wait.

And when they came to Jerusalem,
  Herod the Great, who had heard this thing,
Sent for the Wise Men and questioned them:
And said, "Go down unto Bethlehem,
  And bring me tidings of this new king."

So they rode away, and the star stood still,
  The only one in the gray of morn;
Yes, it stopped, it stood still of its own free will,
Right over Bethlehem on the hill,
  The city of David where Christ was born.

And the Three Kings rode through the gate and the guard,
  Through the silent street, till their horses turned
And neighed as they entered the great inn-yard;
But the windows were closed, and the doors were barred,
  And only a light in the stable burned.

And cradled there in the scented hay,
  In the air made sweet by the breath of kine,
The little Child in the manger lay,
The Child that would be King one day
  Of a kingdom not human, but divine.

His mother, Mary of Nazareth,
  Sat watching beside his place of rest,
Watching the even flow of his breath,
For the joy of life and the terror of death
  Were mingled together in her breast.

They laid their offerings at his feet:
 The gold was their tribute to a King;
The frankincense, with its odor sweet,
Was for the Priest, the Paraclete;
 The myrrh for the body's burying.

And the mother wondered and bowed her head,
 And sat as still as a statue of stone;
Her heart was troubled yet comforted,
Remembering what the angel had said
 Of an endless reign and of David's throne.

Then the Kings rode out of the city gate,
 With a clatter of hoofs in proud array;
But they went not back to Herod the Great,
For they knew his malice and feared his hate,
 And returned to their homes by another way.

      HENRY WADSWORTH LONGFELLOW

A CHILD'S SONG OF CHRISTMAS

My counterpane is soft as silk,
My blankets white as creamy milk.
 The hay was soft to Him, I know,
 Our little Lord of long ago.

Above the roofs the pigeons fly
In silver wheels across the sky.
 The stable-doves they cooed to them,
 Mary and Christ in Bethlehem.

Bright shines the sun across the drifts,
And bright upon my Christmas gifts.
 They brought Him incense, myrrh, and gold,
 Our little Lord who lived of old.

Oh, soft and clear our mother sings
Of Christmas joys and Christmas things.
  God's holy angels sang to them,
  Mary and Christ in Bethlehem.

Our hearts they hold all Christmas dear,
And earth seems sweet and heaven seems near,
  Oh, heaven was in His sight, I know,
  That little Child of long ago.

MARJORIE L. C. PICKTHALL

PEACE

My soul, there is a country
  Afar beyond the stars,
Where stands a wingèd sentry
  All skilful in the wars:
There, above noise and danger,
  Sweet Peace sits crowned with smiles,
And One born in a manger
  Commands the beauteous files.
He is thy gracious Friend,
  And—O my soul, awake!—
Did in pure love descend
  To die here for thy sake.
If thou canst get but thither,
  There grows the flower of Peace,
The Rose that cannot wither,
  Thy fortress, and thy ease.
Leave then thy foolish ranges;
  For none can thee secure
But One who never changes—
  Thy God, thy Life, thy Cure.

HENRY VAUGHAN

THE SENDING OF THE MAGI

In a far Eastern country
It happened long of yore,
Where a lone and level sunrise
Flushes the desert floor,
That three kings sat together
And a spearman kept the door.

Gaspar, whose wealth was counted
By city and caravan;
With Melchior, the seer
Who read the starry plan;
And Balthasar, the blameless,
Who loved his fellow man.

There while they talked, a sudden
Strange rushing sound arose,
And as with startled faces
They thought upon their foes,
Three figures stood before them
In imperial repose.

One in flame-gold and one in blue
And one in scarlet clear,
With the almighty portent
Of sunrise they drew near!
And the kings made obeisance
With hand on breast, in fear.

"Arise," said they, "we bring you
Good tidings of great peace!
Today a power is wakened

Whose working must increase,
Till fear and greed and malice
And violence shall cease."

The messengers were Michael,
By whom all things were wrought
To shape and hue; and Gabriel
Who is the lord of thought;
And Rafael without whose love
All toil must come to nought.

Then Rafael said to Balthasar,
"In a country west from here
A Lord is born in lowliness,
In love without a peer.
Take grievances and gifts to him
And prove his Kingship clear!

"By this sign ye shall know him;
Within his Mother's arm
Among the sweet-breathed cattle
He slumbers without harm,
While wicked hearts are troubled
And tyrants take alarm."

And Gabriel said to Melchior,
"My comrade, I will send
My star to go before you,
That ye may comprehend
Where leads your mystic learning
In a humaner trend."

And Michael said to Gaspar,
"Thou royal builder, go
With tribute to thy riches!

Though time shall overthrow
Thy kingdom, no undoing
His gentle might shall know."

Then while the kings' hearts greatened
And all the chamber shone,
As when the hills at sundown
Take a new glory on
And the air thrills with purple,
Their visitors were gone.

Then straightway up rose Gaspar,
Melchior and Balthasar,
And passed out through the murmur
Of palace and bazar,
To make without misgiving
The journey of the Star.

BLISS CARMAN

THE PREPARATIONS

OLD THOUGHTS FOR CHRISTMAS

By Christopher Morley

A NEW thought for Christmas? Who ever wanted a new thought for Christmas? That man should be shot who would try to think one. It is an impertinence even to write about Christmas. Christmas is a matter that humanity has taken so deeply to heart that we will not have our festival meddled with by bungling hands. No efficiency expert would dare tell us that Christmas is inefficient; that the clock-work toys will soon be broken; that no one can eat a peppermint cane a yard long; that the curves on our chart of kindness should be ironed out so that the "peak load" of December would be evenly distributed through the year. No sour-face dare tell us that we drive postmen and shopgirls into Bolshevism by overtaxing them with our frenzied purchasing or that it is absurd to send to a friend in a steam-heated apartment in a prohibition republic a bright little picture card of a gentleman in Georgian costume drinking ale by a roaring fire of logs. None in his senses, I say, would emit such sophistries, for Christmas is a law unto itself and is not conducted by card-index. Even the postmen and shopgirls, severe though their labours, would not have matters altered. There is none of us who does not enjoy hardship and bustle that contribute to the happiness of others.

There is an efficiency of the heart that transcends and contradicts that of the head. Things of the spirit differ from things material in that the more you give the more you have. The comedian has an immensely better time than the audience. To modernize the adage, to give is more fun than to receive. Especially if you have wit enough to give to those who don't expect it. Surprise is the most primitive joy of humanity. Surprise is the first reason for a baby's laughter. And at Christmas time, when we are all a little childish I hope, surprise is the flavour of our keenest joys. We all remember the thrill with which we once heard, behind some closed door, the rustle and crackle of paper parcels being tied up. We knew that we were going to be surprised—a delicious refinement and luxuriant seasoning of the emotion!

Christmas, then, conforms to this deeper efficiency of the heart. We are not methodical in kindness; we do not "fill orders" for consignments of affection. We let our kindness ramble and explore; old forgotten friendships pop up in our minds and we mail a card to Harry Hunt, of Minneapolis (from whom we have not heard for half a dozen years), "just to surprise him." A business man who shipped a carload of goods to a customer, just to surprise him, would soon perish of abuse. But no one ever refuses a shipment of kindness, because no one ever feels overstocked with it. It is coin of the realm, current everywhere. And we do not try to measure our kindnesses to the capacity of our friends. Friendship is not measurable in calories. How many times this year have you "turned" your stock of kindness?

It is the gradual approach to the Great Surprise that lends full savour to the experience. It has been thought by some that Christmas would gain in excitement if no one knew when it was to be; if (keeping the festival within the winter months) some public functionary were to announce some unexpected morning, "A week from to-day will be Christmas!" Then what a scurrying and joyful frenzy—what a festooning of shops and mad purchasing of presents! But it would not be half the fun of the slow approach of the familiar date. All through November and December we watch it drawing nearer; we see the shop windows begin to glow with red and green and lively colours; we note the altered demeanour of bellboys and janitors as the Date flows quietly toward us; we pass through the haggard perplexity of "Only Four Days More" when we suddenly realize it is too late to make our shopping the display of lucid affectionate reasoning we had contemplated, and clutch wildly at grotesque tokens—and then (sweetest of all) comes the quiet calmness of Christmas Eve. Then, while we decorate the tree or carry parcels of tissue paper and red ribbon to a carefully prepared list of aunts and godmothers, or reckon up a little pile of bright quarters on the dining-room table in preparation for to-morrow's largesse—then it is that the brief, poignant and precious sweetness of the experience claims us at the full. Then we can see that all our careful wisdom and shrewdness were folly and stupidity; and we can understand the meaning of that Great Surprise —that where we planned wealth we found ourselves poor; that where we thought to be impoverished we were enriched. The world is built upon a lovely plan if we take time to study the blue-prints of the heart.

Humanity must be forgiven much for having invented Christmas. What does it matter that a great poet and philosopher urges "the abandonment of the masculine pronoun in allusions to the First or Fundamental Energy?" Theology is not saddled upon pronouns; the best doctrine is but three words, God is Love. Love, or kindness, is fundamental energy enough to satisfy any brooder. And Christmas Day means the birth of a child; that is to say, the triumph of life and hope over suffering.

Just for a few hours on Christmas Eve and Christmas Day the stupid, harsh mechanism of the world runs down and we permit ourselves to live according to untrammelled common sense, the unconquerable efficiency of good will. We grant ourselves the complete and selfish pleasure of loving others better than ourselves. How odd it seems, how unnaturally happy we are! We feel there must be some mistake, and rather yearn for the familiar frictions and distresses. Just for a few hours we "purge out of every heart the lurking grudge." We know then that hatred is a form of illness; that suspicion and pride are only fear; that the rascally acts of others are perhaps, in the queer webwork of human relations, due to some callousness of our own. Who knows? Some man may have robbed a bank in Nashville or fired a gun in Louvain because we looked so intolerably smug in Philadelphia!

So at Christmas we tap that vast reservoir of wisdom and strength— call it efficiency or the fundamental energy if you will—Kindness. And our kindness, thank heaven, is not the placid kindness of angels; it is veined with human blood; it is full of absurdities, irritations, frustrations. A man 100 per cent. kind would be intolerable. As a wise teacher said, the milk of human kindness easily curdles into cheese. We like our friends' affections because we know the tincture of mortal acid is in them. We remember the satirist who remarked that to love one's self is the beginning of a lifelong romance. We know this lifelong romance will resume its sway; we shall lose our tempers, be obstinate, peevish and crank. We shall fidget and fume while waiting our turn in the barber's chair; we shall argue and muddle and mope. And yet, for a few hours, what a happy vision that was! And we turn, on Christmas Eve, to pages which those who speak our tongue immortally associate with the season—the pages of Charles Dickens. Love of humanity endures as long as the thing it loves, and those pages are packed as full of it as a pound cake is full of fruit. A pound cake will keep moist three years; a sponge cake is dry in three days.

And now humanity has its most beautiful and most appropriate Christmas gift—Peace. The Magi of Versailles and Washington having unwound for us the tissue paper and red ribbon (or red tape) from this greatest of all gifts, let us in days to come measure up to what has been born through such anguish and horror. If war is illness and peace is health, let us remember also that health is not merely a blessing to be received intact once and for all. It is not a substance but a condition, to be maintained only by sound régime, self-discipline and simplicity. Let the Wise Men not be too wise; let them remember those other Wise Men who, after their long journey and their sage surmisings, found only a Child. On this evening it serves us nothing to pile up filing cases and rolltop desks toward the stars, for in our city square the Star itself has fallen, and shines upon the Tree.

CHRISTMAS SHOPPING

FROM A LETTER

By WILLIAM BOLITHO

London.—Christmas in England is fundamental. Russia, Spain, keep Easter. France has New Year. In mysterious, sentimental Germany, they have a Christmas of their own, but I suspect birthdays and marriage anniversaries are bigger feasts. Here we have only Christmas.

London is as seasonably changed, waiting for it, as Rome in the Orgies. The old sober things for sale have been put away, and all the superfluities of earth in their season have taken their place and leap to sight in the shop windows. Oxford Street, from end to end, is an exhibition of what life has to offer to taste and fancy at "lowest possible prices." Bond Street has thrown off exclusion and marks its goods in plain figures. Every material want of the imagination to decorate the body, or satisfy it, is arranged in Christmas allegories round Piccadilly and Regent Street, with tinsel snow behind plate glass. There is a snow man of cotton, hemstitched handkerchiefs in a storm of sheets and dressing cases. There is an Eastern Palace of gingerbread. Food for the most extravagant desires; strange fancies; brass coal scuttles embossed with lilies; wrought iron art penholders; marble headed walking sticks.

One window, like a crystal dream, in the Haymarket, reveals packed hampers of all possible dainties for a cold banquet. There is the "Oxford" hamper, a dozen bottles of special port; the "Heather," with an iced greeting cake, two pounds of ham and a basket of Alsatian plums; or the "Surprise" with nuts. The workmen from the skeleton of a new cinema over the way spend their hour in front of this pane, smoking at the bottles in the English way, unfathomably. Rank above rank of varied liqueur flasks present their fat labeled bodies for inspection, with promises of a queer, new taste after the Christmas dinner.

In every poulterer's are curtains of imperial turkeys hanging by the feet, tasseled with purple heads over fences of yellow chickens, waiting. Like flowers, outrageously colored crackers, those naïve luxuries, are scattered over the good things for sale, and all the hams are tied with red ribbons. For everything at Christmas must look like a toy, romantic and desirable to children. All else is subsidiary to them, and tributary. The most important and dressed windows are filled with miniature worlds, which the biggest crowds stare at, day long, where nothing moves and everything is small; houses of miniature furniture, jungles of tiny animals, populations of dwarfs. Clockwork spiders climb from cardboard boxes, tin policemen straddle over waxen babies; battalions of lead soldiers stand guard in straw lined boxes. For five pounds one can play with a world that never gets out of hand and gentle children could make it last a year. But even the smallest doll has a price ticket attached. Ragged watchers may join the crush at the next window, where there is a new advertising game. Five tortoises, each with a white letter on his back,—an A, two S's, an H and an E—budge by inches on the sawdust, tiring lesser patiences. When they range up and form the word ASHES, all who see may call the commissaire and have ten shillings worth of dolls free. But these living pebbles stand for hours misspelt.

Outside the next door is the spirit of the time: Father Christmas, with a small green pine tree in his hand. He is old and redfaced, well fed on rich food, and his gown is flaked with white cotton wool. This is Northern generosity and good times impersonated: the family socialism that rules in England once a year; the inwardness of Christmas, which religion adapted, not altered. For one day the affairs of the nation run smooth; one dinner a year is a banquet. Apples drop roasted into every mouth that wants them, fulfilling the prophecy. The good things of the earth appear suddenly overnight beside every bedside without being earned. The most obstinate factors of life, even tigers and Zulus and policemen, shrink in size and become manageable and amusing toys, which children can play with without debate. Thousands of children have houses of their own, and well-stored shops, and pudding and holidays, so weeks before coming into power Mr. Ramsay MacDonald sees his prophecies fulfilled.

It is not only a coincidence. All social reformers take their ultimate dream from Christmas, though Communists and revolutionaries may deny it, in hate of religion. Dickens, before Karl Marx, discovered the capitalist Scrooge, and the right way of dealing with him. Indeed, under the hard statistical talk of the economic reconstruction of the world, the Socialist program is nothing more than to make Christmas last all the year; put pudding and roast turkey with sausages and port from the wood into every meal. In those days, the world will go by clockwork, as the toys do, and instead of hard competition the free spirit of giving, the social spirit, will prevail. Only it will not be called by the old-fashioned name. Perhaps the real symbolic image of Lenin himself to his followers is not a wild head with a knife in its teeth, but good old Santa Claus, with red coat, face hearty with good feeling and living. Even the rod with which he chastises the bad bourgeois boys is in the character of the orthodox legend.

In those days of Christmas all the year round, there will be no more price tickets on the good things, no different sizes for the generous hampers; snow, the most evanescent beauty of all, will no longer be the symbol of the Socialist Christmas, when it lasts through four seasons. And like the sleepy tortoises, economic laws will arrange themselves and spell out the proper word, which will not be ASHES. Every one will enjoy himself, with high living on earth, for there is plenty for all.

If it is all true, then the wish of all children for Christmas to last forever is a very proper one, and soundly based on the hard principles of rational economic distribution, and the imminent Labor Cabinet is the best gift in the stocking of the British nation. They have not long to wait now, to see if Heine's great summary of Socialist theory is correct, or if, as a man grown up, and moreover a Jew, he was a little ironical about this Christmas theory of life—

> Es wächst hinieder Brod genug
> Für alle Menschenkinder,
> Auch Rosen und Myrthen, Schönheit und Lust—
> Und Zuckererbsen nicht minder.
> From *The New York World.* (1924)

PLUPY GOES TO SUNDAY SCHOOL

BY HENRY A. SHUTE

THE Christmas holidays were now nearly at hand. It had been a snowless fall; skating had been good, so good indeed that the boys had almost tired of it. Indeed the hockey games played in the school yard were fully as interesting as and much more prolific in scrimmages than ice hockey.

But Christmas was in the near future and that particular holiday was the burden of their thoughts by day and dreams by night. How to make the most of that holiday was the scheme to which all the ingenuity of their active minds turned.

One morning shortly after Thanksgiving, the elder Shute, father of our friend Plupy, slowly descended the steps of his modest habitation, pulling thoughtfully on a cigar, which showed an irritating propensity to burn up on one side. It was a crisp and quiet Sabbath morning, and that gentleman, having seen his numerous family troop off to church, wended his way meditatively towards one of his favorite Sunday retreats, the paint shop of his neighbor, "Brad" Purinton, father of a certain co-miscreant of Plupy, known as Pewt.

As he entered that warm and cosy retreat he found the worthy Bradbury sitting in a rush-bottomed chair and smoking a most virulent clay pipe. His coat, laid aside, disclosed the sleeves of his snowy Sunday shirt, while his feet, ordinarily encased in stout leather boots with much wrinkled legs, were now ornate in gaudy-colored carpet slippers. Opposite him sat the trim looking gentleman who boasted the distinguished paternity of the sinful Beany, smoking a meerschaum with silver trimmings and flecking the dust from polished boots with a snowy handkerchief.

The room contained the assortment of articles peculiar to a paint shop. The walls and doors, on which painters had tried their brushes, were daubed with many colored paints and presented the red, orange, yellow, green, blue, indigo and violet of the rainbow, while colored lithographs of Dolly Bidwell, Morris Brothers' Minstrels, Comical Brown, and Washburn's Grand Sensation, were pasted thereon. Scattered around the room were wooden buckets of paint and oil, with half submerged brushes and stirring sticks projecting from them, greasy papers of putty and casks of white lead, while across one side of the shop appeared a long board supported on barrels, covered with rolls of wall paper and broad brushes, under which board stood a pail of flour paste.

By the window stood a carpenter's bench with a wooden vise clamped at its side, while in a wall-rack were bit and bitstock, spokeshaves, chisels, screwdrivers, hand and whipsaws, sandpaper, calipers and paint brushes, dry and stiff with ancient dust and lead.

Evidences of a flourishing business were in sight. On a rack in front of the stove stood a long and very brilliant sign of bright blue sanded ground, and golden letters which informed the public that "W. I. Goods, and Groceries" were to be had at lowest prices.

In the back of the shop a pair of wheels in sober garb of dull blue priming, patiently awaited the bright paint, gaudy stripes and dazzling gold leaf destined for them.

In the place of honor on the wall hung a most patriotic and soul stirring creation, the *chef d'oeuvre* of the artist, in which a most astonishingly pigeon-breasted young lady, clad in little but the hectic flush of crimson lake, held aloft with powerful and ruddy-tinted hand a glowing banner of red, white and blue, with folds admirably even and measured as if by calipers, while at her side, with out-stretched wings, a glorious and jointless eagle, holding jagged lightning in his claws, shrieked aloud, but whether in defiance or horror the artist had neglected to state.

"Hullo, George," slowly drawled Pewt's father, pushing forward an old chair with board bottom and wire bound legs, "you look glum, what's wrong? Don't your cigar suit you?"

"Hullo, Brad. Hullo, Wat," replied the father of Plupy. "Cigar's all right. No worse than any of old Si's," he added as he sat down and crossed his legs. "I'm bothered about my little boy," replied Plupy's father thoughtfully.

"Which one, George?" inquired Beany's father with interest. "Frank or the baby?"

"Frankie," replied Plupy's father.

"Whacher call it, George, croup, chicken pox, measles, scarlet fever or what?" asked Brad, opening the stove door and putting in a stick of wood.

"Got an abscess on his back," replied the elder Shute, "mighty bad one, too," he added.

"Whacher do for it?" asked Brad, puffing a cloud of smoke.

"Poultices," replied the elder Shute concisely.

"Too bad," said Brad.

"That's so," said Wat.

For a while they smoked in silence, then Plupy's father threw his cigar away, leaned back and said, "But what bothers me is what my oldest boy is up to now?"

"What signals is he flying?" asked Wat, who had contracted nautical expressions from his position in the Portsmouth navy yard. "Can't you make 'em out?"

"No, I can't, hang me if I can," George replied emphatically. "It ain't anything so bad that he's doing, only I like to be on my guard, for it may be a case that will require a course at the reform school to cure."

"What d'ye mean? What does he do?" they demanded, leaning forward and removing their pipes in their absorbing interest.

"What do you think of his going to three Sunday schools at once?" demanded Plupy's father, leaning back on the bench and tilting his cigar towards the brim of his hat.

To his surprise, both fathers nodded wisely and said in concert, "Just what my boy is doing," and Wat added, "Don't you understand it, George, three Christmas trees and three presents for good behavior."

"Of course I understand what they are after well enough," replied Plupy's father, "but what I am thinking about is the almighty relapse they will have after the thing is over. You know just how it is, every time those little devils are good for a week, they keep us in hot water for a month to even up things. Ain't that so, Wat? Ain't that so, Brad?"

"Um-m-huh," replied Wat, as he puffed comfortably at his pipe.

"P'tu," replied Brad, as he made a startlingly accurate shot at the front damper in the stove.

"And then," continued Plupy's father, "think what a combination! Methodist, Congregational and Unitarian. You might as well put a bull-dog, a tom-cat and a parrot in the same box and expect them to agree."

"Um-m-huh," replied Wat, letting the blue smoke curl upwards.

"P'tu," remarked Brad, sending a hissing shot into the crackling flames.

"Well," disgustedly continued Plupy's father, "if that's all you can say about it, there ain't much use for me to say any more. You remind one of a caucus of paralytics," and he rose to depart.

"Um-m-huh," said Wat, thoughtfully.

"P'tu," replied Brad, meditatively.

"Beats all," said Beany's father, after a pause, "how much trouble the oldest boy of Shute's makes in the neighborhood. Before he came here to live, my boy was as good a boy as I ever saw. But get him with that infernal Shute boy, he is most as bad as he is."

"That's right," said Pewt's father, "never had any trouble with Clarence 'fore that brat of Shute's came here. 'Pears to put the devil into all the boys."

"Takes after his father a good deal," said Beany's father.

"That's so," said Pewt's father.

"Beats all how much George thinks of that little Frankie," said Beany's father.

"Well, you know he thinks more of him since he got that bile on his back, because 'Abscess makes the heart grow fonder.' "

"Um-m-huh," assented Beany's father thoughtfully.

"P'tu," replied Pewt's father, meditatively, and they relapsed into silence.

Now while this brilliant and instructive conference was being held, a few rods away three boys with freshly soaped faces and hair plastered over their foreheads, sat in the vestry of the Unitarian church, singing vigorously and restraining themselves with difficulty from jabbing pins into each other, while they cast frequent glances at the old clock which seemed to them to tick the seconds with dragging slowness.

An hour later the same boys might have been seen vigorously tuning their lusty pipes to the more fervent hymns of the Methodist Sabbath school, while still later in the day their shrill and vociferous singing was the wonder and admiration of their associates in the Sunday school of the Congregational church.

The reason for all this, Wat had sententiously given. "Three Sunday schools and three presents for good behavior."

When a short time before Christmas they had ascertained that the Methodist church would probably hold their Christmas festival on Christmas night, the First Congregational on the night before, and the Unitarian the night after Christmas, they decided at once to become members of the Sunday schools of all three organizations. True enough, they already were more or less discredited members of the Unitarian Sunday school, but as they were exceedingly liberal in their religious views, they thought that great good would come from their relations with several churches at once, especially in the Christmas season.

As Beany's family were members of the Congregational parish, Beany occupying a position as blow-boy of the Unitarian church from financial and utilitarian reasons solely, it was easy to secure admission to the first named Sunday school through the kind invitation extended by that pious youth.

Admission to the Methodist school was not so easy. Several young Methodists, to whom they applied, were proof against their blandishments, but one day, having artfully enticed one Diddly Colcord, an enthusiastic Christmas Methodist, into Pewt's back yard, they solicited his good offices; but fearful of too liberally watering the stock of Christmas presents by the admission of new members, he rudely refused, whereupon they jointly set upon him and soundly mauled him until he became converted to their views, and loudly and wailingly consented.

And Diddly was as good as his word, and the next Sabbath, with a black eye and damaged nose he ushered them, somewhat abashed, into a class of small, tough looking gamins, evidently new converts.

That three Sunday schools only were joined by the trio was due solely to the fact that the hours of service in other schools conflicted with these, while these three did not conflict in the least with each other.

The Unitarian held their school directly after the morning service, and any benefit that children might have derived from the instruction was effectually prevented by the fact that before the end of the school service they were nearly starved from their unaccustomed fasting, the dinner hour in that good old town being at sharp noon.

The Methodist held their Sunday school just after the dinner hour, and pupils after the hearty Sunday dinner were generally in such a condition of turgidity, as to gain little, if any, spiritual uplifting from their instruction.

Again, the First Congregational deferred their Sunday school until after the regular afternoon service, when the pupils who had attended the two prior services were in a state of mental and physical exhaustion that ill-fitted them for their soul's improvement. In the case of our three friends, by the time the afternoon services began, they were in the most irresponsible condition of semi-idiocy.

Indeed, after the last service they were accustomed to tone up their shattered nerves by snow-balling, wrestling and fighting with their school-mates, and secretly doing many other things not warranted by their bringing up, and which upon ordinary Sundays we trust that even they would not have done.

As Christmas approached their fervor increased, and they even went so far as to study with some care their Sunday school lesson, and apart from their ludicrous mispronunciation of unfamiliar words and four syllabled names, they acquitted themselves creditably. While the strain on them was great, they consoled themselves with the assurance that it would not last much longer, and the goal of their ambition was already in sight. As it was, the safety valve was under very great pressure.

The Sunday before Christmas, the superintendent of the Unitarian Sunday school made the expected announcement that the usual Christmas festival and tree exercises would be held in the Town Hall on Thursday evening, the day after Christmas, at which the three boys grinned broadly and winked expansively at each other, and when their voices rang out blithely in the school songs, they were most favorably looked upon by their teachers, who knew some particulars of their daily life, as brands plucked from the burning.

To rush gleefully home and gobble their dinner and repair expectantly to the Methodist Sunday school required but a short time. But once there, a most astonishing and unlooked for facer awaited them. At the close of the lesson the superintendent, a portly and bulging man in black and shiny broadcloth, ponderously arose and rubbing his hands informed his "De-a-a-r-r-r hea-r-r-rer-r-s" that the teachers of the school and trustees of the church had decided to use the money ordinarily devoted to the Christmas tree festival, for the relief of the heathen, and that to reward the "Dear-r-r" pupils who had so generously given up their enjoyment, a Sunday school concert would be held next Sunday evening, at which all pupils were expected to commit and recite at least four verses of Scripture. At the close of this announcement, the school was dismissed amid a horrified silence, which was broken as the scholars dashed noisily down the stairs, when Plupy, Beany and Pewt, each giving the amazed and innocent Diddly Colcord a prodigious punch, fled for home.

But despite their discomfiture, they were promptly on hand at the late service of the Congregational Sunday school, only to have their breath taken away by the harrowing announcement that, owing to the unavoidable absence of the good pastor on the evening usually appointed for the Christmas festival, it would be held in the large vestry on the evening after Christmas.

The disgust and disappointment of our three friends was pitiful. For this they had given the best of their young energies, the best of their fresh voices, the best of their religious attainments. During the long and dreary hour of that session they were dangerously near the verge of mutiny, but restrained their feelings until after singing that harmonious morceau, "We all love one another," they were dismissed, when Beany, conscious from their sullen looks that something was in store for him, although he was entirely innocent and as much chagrined as Pewt and Plupy, prudently took to his heels and was pursued to the door of his father's house by his disappointed fellow-conspirators, burning to wreak upon his plump person, the vengeance their disappointed ambition demanded.

And when on Christmas morning instead of the usual knife, or bowgun or book of animals or birds, they each received a New Testament from their amused and admiring relatives, their disgust knew no bounds.

IF CHRISTMAS COMES

By WILL CUPPY

HERE it is almost Christmas, and not even a list made out yet. No, that's hardly true. I did prepare my usual schedule of the presents I want, but I'm not going to send it around—and you can be the judge who's to blame for it all. It looks very very much as though there would be an empty sock in a certain hermit's shanty this Yuletide, and just when I was trying for a banner year.

Maybe I tried too hard. Anyway, all it got me to go flinging gifts right, left and sideways most of last spring and summer and part of this fall was the name of angling for return parcels this Christmas, an aspersion the more unfortunate in that I already had a slight reputation as a hinter; though I don't call it hinting to tell people to whom I have been properly introduced that I am fond of blue neckties. I repeat that I am fond of blue neckties, and blue neckties I will have, one way or the other.

Those heavy suitcases, huge cardboard boxes and mysterious packages wrapped in old newspapers which I kept lugging ashore all year were presents to friends in New York. That much is perfectly true. For these same friends I risked chronic lumbago and permanently weakened the rowing muscles of Portygee Pete. For them I weathered a blizzard, two cloudbursts and several fights with Long Island railway conductors who tried to put me in the baggage car. At the cost of a pretty penny, as pennies go at Jones's Island, I employed every means of efficient distribution of presents known to modern science, short of calling out Dasher, Dancer, Prancer and Vixen, only to discover—with Christmas at my very door!—that my friends weren't much thrilled, if at all, by those boatloads of beach pebbles I took them. No matter how I found out. I can put two and two together when I am notified by a lot of people upon whom I have been lavishing beach pebbles that they have just started on a trip around the world and will be gone quite some time.

Well, I accomplished one thing. I did bring on a sudden and sensational epidemic of Chinese lilies in dozens of homes where all they had ever known about botany was a pot of verbenas. These verbena fans were particularly hard to manage. There seems to be something about that unassuming little plant that makes housewives positively stubborn, or perhaps the verbenas are the effect rather than the cause. Yet I beat down all opposition, terrorized the cowering verbenas and saw to it that those housewives had Chinese lilies, willy-nilly; since, after all, about the only thing you can do with a large consignment of pebbles, after the goldfish bowl is full and the children have taken their pick, is to put them in a shallow bowl and go buy a bulb. And when my generosity was at its height, it took a lot of bulbs to come out even. It was fun while it lasted, but I might have known there was bound to be a reaction.

To be sure, the Jones's Island pebbles are only small stones, not very expertly colored. Yet, on their native beach, as the Atlantic surf swirls coolly over them, they are translucent, opaline, iridescent and all that sort of thing. The pity is that in captivity they lose much of their wild, free spirit. A pebble on the seashore is really a wonderful phenomenon, but a pebble in a rolled oats container looks like nothing so much as a pebble in a rolled oats container. By the time it gets to town it is utterly disillusioned. It has lost its joy of living and most of its looks. All the more reason, say I, to give it a helping hand, a warm, old-fashioned welcome in the home and some assurance of a better and brighter to-morrow in a shallow bowl with a bulb. Mere outward beauty isn't everything, though I must admit it's a great deal.

Then look what happened to the tons of bayberries I gave away, not to mention the stone paper weights, the empty quart bottles suitable for lamps and candlesticks, the little glass jugs to be used as vinegar cruets and the skimmer shells for the kiddies. I expected the bay-berries to make more of a hit, seems like they used to. With all their faults I love bayberries. The gray, waxen pellets, when denuded of their leafage make delightful decorations and will last forever if you are careful to glue, sew or tack each berry to the stem; otherwise you will put in a lot of time sweeping them up. The blighted specimens, of course, are not so pretty, and many persons object to the little red worms that come with them. So my bayberry clients have started around the world, too. They seem to have forgotten that I never gave them any umbrella stands full of pampas grass.

Whatever happens Christmas morning—and I'll be up at dawn— my conscience is clear. My motives were good, as motives go; if I happened to think of Christmas once or twice while delivering my beach products, it was in a perfectly nice way and not what they say. I hold no malice. I make no secret of the fact that I love my friends and should like something to remember them by, and if they see eye to eye with me on this proposition, I can do nothing to prevent them. I'll even include the ones who called me a hinter trying to acquire Christmas merit and blue neckties by unloading useless Jones's Island junk all over their rugs. All I want this year, though, is for my friends ashore to have a gorgeous time and give marvelous presents to each other and never think of the lonely hermit in his hut. In this connection I am reminded of a favorite quotation from Wordsworth, immortalized by Mr. Bartlett:

"Give all thou canst; high Heaven rejects the lore
  Of nicely calculated less or more."

Good old Wordsworth!

Although I am not officially releasing my list this year, I may state in a general way that hermits as a class, or sub-species, are not very particular what they get for Christmas, so long as it's something. One hermit, whose identity must not be disclosed, is always tickled to receive shoes in fairly good condition, sizes 8½ to 10, inclusive; dungarees, 34 waist; chest, unexpanded, 38 inches; height, 5 feet 10½ inches; blue eyes and mild disposition unless riled. He's on the prowl all the year round, and nothing makes his eyes glisten with sheer mischief like diverting from its proper source a missionary box intended for the Patagonians, the Uap Islanders, the Binbinga of Northern Australia or the Wagogo of East Africa, unless it's obtaining access to a barrel of odds and ends addressed to some community stricken by flood, earthquake or famine—he's forever asking people if they have heard of an earthquake lately and who is going to send a box.

Since it happens to be extremely fashionable this season to provide for hermits, I will add that presents need not be confined to cut flowers, sheet music and picture postcards of Anne Hathaway's cottage. Why not a beribboned carton of peanut brittle or a gayly painted tin of glacéd prunes, both acceptable combinations of art and nourishment and much more tactful than a great crate of bread and butter. A safe rule to go by is that hermits need about two of everything, and if I were rich I'd see that they got it. So far I have received but one Christmas present from a millionaire. It came in a grand envelope that must have cost a quarter all by itself, and when I opened it, out popped—what do you think?—a wonderful paragraph just bursting with love, best wishes and good advice.

Meanwhile, Christmas is coming! And I, for one, shall be on my best behavior until the last returns are in. I suspect that a great many people are secretly rejoicing in the fact that pebbles and bayberries are out of season. But who knows what a hermit may do when the Yuletide spirit seizes him like a frenzy and the joy of giving rouses all that is worst in his nature? I still have a few pebbles left. I wonder!

THE FACTS

By Ring Lardner

I

THE engagement was broken off before it was announced. So only a thousand or so of the intimate friends and relatives of the parties knew anything about it. What they knew was that there had been an engagement and that there was one no longer. The cause of the breach they merely guessed, and most of the guesses were, in most particulars, wrong.

Each intimate and relative had a fragment of the truth. It remained for me to piece the fragments together. It was a difficult job, but I did it. Part of my evidence is hearsay; the major portion is fully corroborated. And not one of my witnesses had anything to gain through perjury.

So I am positive that I have at my tongue's end the facts, and I believe that in justice to everybody concerned I should make them public.

Ellen McDonald had lived on the North Side of Chicago for twenty-one years. Billy Bowen had been a South-Sider for seven years longer. But neither knew of the other's existence until they met in New York, the night before the Army-Navy game.

Billy, sitting with a business acquaintance at a neighboring table in Tonio's, was spotted by a male member of Ellen's party, a Chicagoan, too. He was urged to come on over. He did, and was introduced. The business acquaintance was also urged, came, was introduced and forgotten; forgotten, that is, by every one but the waiter, who observed that he danced not nor told stories, and figured that his function must be to pay. The business acquaintance had been Billy's guest. Now he became host, and without seeking the office.

It was not that Billy and Miss McDonald's male friends were niggards. But unfortunately for the b. a., the checks always happened to arrive when everybody else was dancing or so hysterical over Billy's repartee as to be potentially insolvent.

Billy was somewhere between his fourteenth and twenty-first high-ball; in other words, at his best, from the audience's standpoint. His dialogue was simply screaming and his dancing just heavenly. He was Frank Tinney doubling as Vernon Castle. On the floor he tried and accomplished twinkles that would have spelled catastrophe if attempted under the fourteen mark, or over the twenty-one. And he said the cutest things—one right after the other.

II

You can be charmed by a man's dancing, but you can't fall in love with his funniness. If you're going to fall in love with him at all, you'll do it when you catch him in a serious mood.

Miss McDonald caught Billy Bowen in one at the game next day. Entirely by accident or a decree of fate, her party and his sat in adjoining boxes. Not by accident, Miss McDonald sat in the chair that was nearest Billy's. She sat there first to be amused; she stayed to be conquered.

Here was a different Billy from the Billy of Tonio's. Here was a Billy who trained his gun on your heart and let your risibles alone. Here was a dreamy Billy, a Billy of romance.

How calm he remained through the excitement! How indifferent to the thrills of the game! There was depth to him. He was a man. Her escort and the others round her were children, screaming with delight at the puerile deeds of pseudo heroes. Football was a great sport, but a sport. It wasn't Life. Would the world be better or worse for that nine-yard gain that Elephant or Oliphant, or whatever his name was, had just made? She knew it wouldn't. Billy knew, too, for Billy was deep. He was thinking man's thoughts. She could tell by his silence, by his inattention to the scene before him. She scarcely could believe that here was the same person who, last night, had kept his own, yes, and the neighboring tables, roaring with laughter. What a complex character his!

In sooth, Mr. Bowen was thinking man's thoughts. He was thinking that if this pretty Miss McDowell, or Donnelly, were elsewhere, he could go to sleep. And that if he could remember which team he had bet on and could tell which team was which, he would have a better idea of whether he was likely to win or lose.

When, after the game, they parted, Billy rallied to the extent of asking permission to call. Ellen, it seemed, would be very glad to have him, but she couldn't tell exactly when she would have to be back in Chicago; she still had three more places to visit in the East. Could she possibly let him know when she did get back? Yes, she could and would; if he really wanted her to, she would drop him a note. He certainly wanted her to.

This, thought Billy, was the best possible arrangement. Her note would tell him her name and address, and save him the trouble of 'phoning to all the McConnells, McDowells, and Donnellys on the North Side. He did want to see her again; she was pretty, and, judging from last night, full of pep. And she had fallen for him; he knew it from that look.

He watched her until she was lost in the crowd. Then he hunted round for his pals and the car that had brought them up. At length he gave up the search and wearily climbed the elevated stairs. His hotel was on Broadway, near Forty-fourth. He left the train at Forty-second, the third time it stopped there.

"I guess you've rode far enough," said the guard. "Fifteen cents' worth for a nickel. I guess we ought to have a Pullman on these here trains."

"I guess," said Billy, "I guess—"

But the repartee well was dry. He stumbled down-stairs and hurried toward Broadway to replenish it.

III

Ellen McDonald's three more places to visit in the East must have been deadly dull. Anyway, on the sixth of December, scarcely more than a week after his parting with her in New York, Billy Bowen received the promised note. It informed him merely that her name was Ellen McDonald, that she lived at so-and-so Walton Place, and that she was back in Chicago.

That day, if you'll remember, was Monday. Miss McDonald's parents had tickets for the opera. But Ellen was honestly just worn out, and would they be mad at her if she stayed home and went to bed? They wouldn't. They would take Aunt Mary in her place.

On Tuesday morning, Paul Potter called up and wanted to know if she would go with him that night to "The Follies." She was horribly sorry, but she'd made an engagement. The engagement, evidently, was to study, and the subject was harmony, with Berlin, Kern, and Van Alstyne as instructors. She sat on the piano-bench from half-past seven till quarter after nine, and then went to her room vowing that she would accept any and all invitations for the following evening.

Fortunately, no invitations arrived, for at a quarter of nine Wednesday night, Mr. Bowen did. And in a brand-new mood. He was a bit shy and listened more than he talked. But when he talked, he talked well, though the sparkling wit of the night at Tonio's was lacking. Lacking, too, was the preoccupied air of the day at the football game. There was no problem to keep his mind busy, but even if the Army and Navy had been playing football in this very room, he could have told at a glance which was which. Vision and brain was perfectly clear. And he had been getting his old eight hours, and, like the railroad hen, sometimes nine and sometimes ten, every night since his arrival home from Gotham, N. Y. Mr. Bowen was on the wagon.

They talked of the East, of Tonio's, of the game (this was where Billy did most of his listening), of the war, of theatres, of books, of college, of automobiles, of the market. They talked, too, of their immediate families. Billy's, consisting of one married sister in South Bend, was soon exhausted. He had two cousins here in town whom he saw frequently, two cousins and their wives, but they were people who simply couldn't stay home nights. As for himself, he preferred his rooms and a good book to the so-called gay life. Ellen should think that a man who danced so well would want to be doing it all the time. It was nice of her to say that he danced well, but really he didn't, you know. Oh, yes, he did. She guessed she could tell. Well, anyway, the giddy whirl made no appeal to him, unless, of course, he was in particularly charming company. His avowed love for home and quiet surprised Ellen a little. It surprised Mr. Bowen a great deal. Only last night, he remembered, he had been driven almost desperate by that quiet of which he was now so fond; he had been on the point of busting loose, but had checked himself in time. He had played Canfield till ten, though the book-shelves were groaning with their load.

Ellen's family kept them busy for an hour and a half. It was a dear family and she wished he could meet it. Mother and father were out playing bridge somewhere to-night. Aunt Mary had gone to bed. Aunts Louise and Harriet lived in the next block. Sisters Edith and Wilma would be home from Northampton for the holidays about the twentieth. Brother Bob and his wife had built the cutest house; in Evanston. Her younger brother, Walter, was a case! He was away to-night, had gone out right after dinner. He'd better be in before mother and father came. He had a new love-affair every week, and sixteen years old last August. Mother and father really didn't care how many girls he was interested in, so long as they kept him too busy to run round with those crazy schoolmates of his. The latter were older than he; just at the age when it seems smart to drink beer and play cards for money. Father said if he ever found out that Walter was doing those things, he'd take him out of school and lock him up somewhere.

Aunts Louise and Mary and Harriet did a lot of settlement work. They met all sorts of queer people, people you'd never believe existed. The three aunts were unmarried.

Brother Bob's wife was dear, but absolutely without a sense of humor. Bob was full of fun, but they got along just beautifully together. You never saw a couple so much in love.

Edith was on the basket-ball team at college and terribly popular. Wilma was horribly clever and everybody said she'd make Phi Beta Kappa.

Ellen, so she averred, had been just nothing in school; not bright; not athletic, and, of course, not popular.

"Oh, of course not," said Billy, smiling.

"Honestly," fibbed Ellen.

"You never could make me believe it," said Billy.

Whereat Ellen blushed, and Billy's unbelief strengthened.

At this crisis, the Case burst into the room with his hat on. He removed it at sight of the caller and awkwardly advanced to be introduced.

"I'm going to bed," he announced, after the formality.

"I hoped," said Ellen, "you'd tell us about the latest. Who is it now? Beth?"

"Beth nothing!" scoffed the Case. "We split up the day of the Keewatin game."

"What was the matter?" asked his sister.

"I'm going to bed," said the Case. "It's pretty near midnight."

"By George, it is!" exclaimed Billy. "I didn't dream it was that late!"

"No," said Walter. "That's what I tell dad—the clock goes along some when you're having a good time."

Billy and Ellen looked shyly at each other, and then laughed; laughed harder, it seemed to Walter, than the joke warranted. In fact, he hadn't thought of it as a joke. If it was that good, he'd spring it on Kathryn to-morrow night. It would just about clinch her.

The Case, carrying out his repeated threat, went to bed and dreamed of Kathryn. Fifteen minutes later Ellen retired to dream of Billy. And an hour later than that, Billy was dreaming of Ellen, who had become suddenly popular with him, even if she hadn't been so at Northampton, which he didn't believe.

IV

They saw "The Follies" Friday night. A criticism of the show by either would have been the greatest folly of all. It is doubtful that they could have told what theatre they'd been to ten minutes after they'd left it. From wherever it was, they walked to a dancing place and danced. Ellen was so far gone that she failed to note the change in Billy's trotting. Foxes would have blushed for shame at its awkwardness and lack of variety. If Billy was a splendid dancer, he certainly did not prove it this night. All he knew or cared to know was that he was. with the girl he wanted. And she knew only that she was with Billy, and happy.

On the drive home, the usual superfluous words were spoken. They were repeated inside the storm-door at Ellen's father's house, while the taxi driver, waiting, wondered audibly why them suckers of explorers beat it to the Pole to freeze when the North Side was so damn handy.

Ellen's father was out of town. So in the morning she broke the news to mother and Aunt Mary, and then sat down and wrote it to Edith and Wilma. Next she called up Bob's wife in Evanston, and after that she hurried to the next block and sprang it on Aunts Louise and Harriet. It was decided that Walter had better not be told. He didn't know how to keep a secret. Walter, therefore, was in ignorance till he got home from school. The only person he confided in the same evening was Kathryn, who was the only person he saw.

Bob and his wife and Aunts Louise and Harriet came to Sunday dinner, but were chased home early in the afternoon. Mr. McDonald was back and Billy was coming to talk to him. It would embarrass Billy to death to find such a crowd in the house. They'd all meet him soon, never fear, and when they met him, they'd be crazy about him. Bob and Aunt Mary and mother would like him because he was so bright and said such screaming things, and the rest would like him because he was so well-read and sensible, and so horribly good-looking.

Billy, I said, was coming to talk to Mr. McDonald. When he came, he did very little of the talking. He stated the purpose of his visit, told what business he was in and affirmed his ability to support a wife. Then he assumed the rôle of audience while Ellen's father delivered an hour's lecture. The speaker did not express his opinion of Tyrus Cobb or the Kaiser, but they were the only subjects he overlooked. Sobriety and industry were words frequently used.

"I don't care," he prevaricated, in conclusion, "how much money a man is making if he is sober and industrious. You attended college, and I presume you did all the fool things college boys do. Some men recover from their college education, others don't. I hope you're one of the former."

The Sunday-night supper, just cold scraps you might say, was partaken of by the happy but embarrassed pair, the trying-to-look happy but unembarrassed parents, and Aunt Mary. Walter, the Case, was out. He had stayed home the previous evening.

"He'll be here to-morrow night and the rest of the week, or I'll know the reason why," said Mr. McDonald.

"He won't, and I'll tell you the reason why," said Ellen.

"He's a real boy, Sam," put in the real boy's mother. "You can't expect him to stay home every minute."

"I can't expect anything of him," said the father. "You and the girls and Mary here have let him have his own way so long that he's past managing. When I was his age, I was in my bed at nine o'clock."

"Morning or night?" asked Ellen.

Her father scowled. It was evident he could not take a joke, not even a good one.

After the cold scraps had been ruined, Mr. McDonald drew Billy into the smoking-room and offered him a cigar. The prospective son-in-law was about to refuse and express a preference for cigarettes when something told him not to. A moment later he was deeply grateful to the something.

"I smoke three cigars a day," said the oracle, "one after each meal. That amount of smoking will hurt nobody. More than that is too much. I used to smoke to excess, four or five cigars per day, and maybe a pipe or two. I found it was affecting my health, and I cut down. Thank heaven, no one in my family ever got the cigarette habit; disease, rather. How any sane, clean-minded man can start on those things is beyond me."

"Me, too," agreed Billy, taking the proffered cigar with one hand and making sure with the other that his silver pill-case was as deep down in his pocket as it would go.

"Cigarettes, gambling, and drinking go hand in hand," continued the man of the house. "I couldn't trust a cigarette fiend with a nickel."

"There are only two or three kinds he could get for that," said Billy.

"What say?" demanded Mr. McDonald, but before Billy was obliged to wriggle out of it, Aunt Mary came in and reminded her brother-in-law that it was nearly church time.

Mr. McDonald and Aunt Mary went to church. Mrs. McDonald, pleading weariness, stayed home with "the children." She wanted a chance to get acquainted with this pleasant-faced boy who was going to rob her of one of her five dearest treasures.

The three were no sooner settled in front of the fireplace than Ellen adroitly brought up the subject of auction bridge, knowing that it would relieve Billy of the conversational burden.

"Mother is really quite a shark, aren't you, mother?" she said.

"I don't fancy being called a fish," said the mother.

"She's written two books on it, and she and father have won so many prizes that they may have to lease a warehouse. If they'd only play for money, just think how rich we'd all be!"

"The game is fascinating enough without adding to it the excitements and evils of gambling," said Mrs. McDonald.

"It is a fascinating game," agreed Billy.

"It is," said Mrs. McDonald, and away she went.

Before father and Aunt Mary got home from church, Mr. Bowen was a strong disciple of conservativeness in bidding and thoroughly convinced that all the rules that had been taught were dead wrong. He saw the shark's points so quickly and agreed so whole-heartedly with her arguments that he impressed her as one of the most intelligent young men she had ever talked to. It was too bad it was Sunday night, but some evening soon he must come over for a game.

"I'd like awfully well to read your books," said Billy.

"The first one's usefulness died with the changes in the rules," replied Mrs. McDonald. "But I think I have one of the new ones in the house, and I'll be glad to have you take it."

"I don't like to have you give me your only copy."

"Oh, I believe we have two."

She knew perfectly well she had two dozen.

Aunt Mary announced that Walter had been seen in church with Kathryn. He had made it his business to be seen. He and the lady had come early and had manœuvred into the third row from the back, on the aisle leading to the McDonald family pew. He had nudged his aunt as she passed on the way to her seat, and she had turned and spoken to him. She could not know that he and Kathryn had "ducked" before the end of the processional.

After reporting favorably on the Case, Aunt Mary launched into a description of the service. About seventy had turned out. The music had been good, but not quite as good as in the morning. Mr. Pratt had sung "Fear Ye Not, O Israel!" for the offertory. Dr. Gish was still sick and a lay reader had served. She had heard from Allie French that Dr. Gish expected to be out by the middle of the week and certainly would be able to preach next Sunday morning. The church had been cold at first, but very comfortable finally.

Ellen rose and said she and Billy would go out in the kitchen and make some fudge.

"I was afraid Aunt Mary would bore you to death," she told Billy, when they had kissed for the first time since five o'clock. "She just lives for the church and can talk on no other subject."

"I wouldn't hold that against her," said Billy charitably.

The fudge was a failure, as it was bound to be. But the Case, who came in just as it was being passed round, was the only one rude enough to say so.

"Is this a new stunt?" he inquired, when he had tested it.

"Is what a new stunt?" asked Ellen.

"Using cheese instead of chocolate."

"That will do, Walter," said his father. "You can go to bed."

Walter got up and started for the hall. At the threshold he stopped.

"I don't suppose there'll be any of that fudge left," he said. "But if there should be, you'd better put it in the mouse trap."

Billy called a taxi and departed soon after Walter's exit. When he got out at his South Side abode, the floor of the tonneau was littered with recent cigarettes.

And that night he dreamed that he was president of the anti-cigarette league; that Dr. Gish was vice-president, and that the motto of the organization was "No trump."

Billy Bowen's business took him out of town the second week in

December, and it was not until the twentieth that he returned. He had been East and had ridden home from Buffalo on the same train with Wilma and Edith McDonald. But he didn't know it and neither did they. They could not be expected to recognize him from Ellen's description—that he was horribly good-looking. The dining-car conductor was all of that.

Ellen had further written them that he (not the dining-car conductor) was a man of many moods; that sometimes he was just nice and deep, and sometimes he was screamingly funny, and sometimes so serious and silent that she was almost afraid of him.

They were wild to see him and the journey through Ohio and Indiana would not have been half so long in his company. Edith, the athletic, would have revelled in his wit. Wilma would gleefully have fathomed his depths. They would both have been proud to flaunt his looks before the hundreds of their kind aboard the train. Their loss was greater than Billy's, for he, smoking cigarettes as fast as he could light them and playing bridge·that would have brought tears of compassion to the shark's eyes, enjoyed the trip, every minute of it.

Ellen and her father were at the station to meet the girls. His arrival on this train had not been heralded, and it added greatly to the hysterics of the occasion.

Wilma and Edith upbraided him for not knowing by instinct who they were. He accused them of recognizing him and purposely avoiding him. Much more of it was pulled in the same light vein, pro and con.

He was permitted at length to depart for his office. On the way he congratulated himself on the improbability of his ever being obliged to play basket-ball versus Edith. She must be a whizz in condition. Chances were she'd train down to a hundred and ninety-five before the big games. The other one, Wilma, was a splinter if he ever saw one. You had to keep your eyes peeled or you'd miss her entirely. But suppose you did miss her; what then! If she won her Phi Beta Kappa pin, he thought, it would make her a dandy belt.

These two, he thought, were a misdeal. They should be reshuffled and cut nearer the middle of the deck. Lots of other funny things he thought about these two.

Just before he had left Chicago on this trip, his stenographer had quit him to marry an elevator-starter named Felix Bond. He had 'phoned one of his cousins and asked him to be on the lookout for a live stenographer who wasn't likely to take the eye of an elevator-starter. The cousin had had one in mind.

Here was her card on Billy's desk when he reached the office. It was not a business-card visiting-card, at $3 per hundred. "Miss Violet Moore," the engraved part said. Above was written: "Mr. Bowen— Call me up any night after seven. Calumet 2678."

Billy stowed the card in his pocket and plunged into a pile of uninteresting letters.

On the night of the twenty-second there was a family dinner at McDonald's, and Billy was in on it. At the function he met the rest of them—Bob and his wife, and Aunt Harriet and Aunt Louise.

Bob and his wife, despite the former's alleged sense of humor, spooned every time they were contiguous. That they were in love with each other, as Ellen had said, was easy to see. The wherefore was more of a puzzle.

Bob's hirsute adornment having been disturbed by his spouse's digits during one of the orgies, he went up-stairs ten minutes before dinner time to effect repairs. Mrs. Bob was left alone on the davenport. In performance of his social duties, Billy went over and sat down beside her. She was not, like Miss Muffet, frightened away, but terror or some other fiend rendered her temporarily dumb. The game Mr. Bowen was making his fifth attempt to pry open a conversation when Bob came back.

To the impartial observer the scene on the davenport appeared heartless enough. There was a generous neutral zone between Billy and Flo, that being an abbreviation of Mrs. Bob's given name, which, as a few may suspect, was Florence. Billy was working hard and his face was flushed with the effort. The flush may have aroused Bob's suspicions. At any rate, he strode across the room, scowling almost audibly, shot a glance at Billy that would have made the Kaiser wince, halted magnificently in front of his wife, and commanded her to accompany him to the hall.

Billy's flush became ace high. He was about to get up and break a chair when a look from Ellen stopped him. She was at his side before the pair of Bobs had skidded out of the room.

"Please don't mind," she begged. "He's crazy. I forgot to tell you that he's insanely jealous."

"Did I understand you to say he had a sense of humor?"

"It doesn't work where Flo's concerned. If he sees her talking to a man he goes wild."

"With astonishment, probably," said Billy.

"You're a nice boy," said Ellen irrelevantly.

Dinner was announced and Mr. Bowen was glad to observe that Flo's terrestrial body was still intact. He was glad, too, to note that Bob was no longer frothing. He learned for the first time that the Case and Kathryn were of the party. Mrs. McDonald had wanted to make sure of Walter's presence; hence the presence of his crush.

Kathryn giggled when she was presented to Billy. It made him uncomfortable and he thought for a moment that a couple of studs had fallen out. He soon discovered, however, that the giggle was permanent, just as much a part of Kathryn as her fraction of a nose. He looked forward with new interest to the soup course, but was disappointed to find that she could negotiate it without disturbing the giggle or the linen.

He next centred his attention on Wilma and Edith. Another disappointment was in store. There were as many and as large oysters in Wilma's soup as in any one's. She ate them all, and, so far as appearances went, was the same Wilma. He had expected that Edith would either diet or plunge. But Edith was as prosaic in her consumption of victuals as Ellen, for instance, or Aunt Louise.

He must content himself for the present with Aunt Louise. She was sitting directly opposite and he had an unobstructed view of the widest part he had ever seen in woman's hair.

"Ogden Avenue," he said to himself.

Aunt Louise was telling about her experiences and Aunt Harriet's among the heathen of Peoria Street.

"You never would dream there were such people!" said she.

"I suppose most of them are foreign born," supposed her brother, who was Mr. McDonald.

"Practically all of them," said Aunt Louise.

Billy wanted to ask her whether she had ever missionaried among the Indians. He thought possibly an attempt to scalp her had failed by a narrow margin.

Between courses Edith worked hard to draw out his predicated comicality and Wilma worked as hard to make him sound his low notes. Their labors were in vain. He was not sleepy enough to be deep, and he was fourteen highballs shy of comedy.

In disgust, perhaps, at her failure to be amused, the major portion of the misdeal capsized her cocoa just before the close of the meal and drew a frown from her father, whom she could have thrown in ten minutes, straight falls, any style.

"She'll never miss that ounce," thought Billy.

When they got up from the table and started for the living-room, Mr. Bowen found himself walking beside Aunt Harriet, who had been so silent during dinner that he had all but forgotten her.

"Well, Miss McDonald," he said, "it's certainly a big family, isn't it?"

"Well, young man," said Aunt Harriet, "it ain't no small family, that's sure."

"I should say not," repeated Billy.

Walter and his giggling crush intercepted him.

"What do you think of Aunt Harriet's grammar?" demanded Walter.

"I didn't notice it," lied Billy.

"No, I s'pose not. 'Ain't no small family.' I s'pose you didn't notice it. She isn't a real aunt like Aunt Louise and Aunt Mary. She's just an adopted aunt. She kept house for dad and Aunt Louise after their mother died, and when dad got married, she just kept on living with Aunt Louise."

"Oh," was Billy's fresh comment, and it brought forth a fresh supply of giggles from Kathryn.

Ellen had already been made aware of Billy's disgusting plans. He had to catch a night train for St. Louis, and he would be there all day to-morrow, and he'd be back Friday, but he wouldn't have time to see her, and he'd surely call her up. And Friday afternoon he was going to South Bend to spend Christmas Day with his married sister, because it was probably the last Christmas he'd be able to spend with her.

"But I'll hustle home from South Bend Sunday morning," he said. "And don't you dare make any engagement for the afternoon."

"I do wish you could be with us Christmas Eve. The tree won't be a bit of fun without you."

"You know I wish I could. But you see how it is."

"I think your sister's mean."

Billy didn't deny it.

"Who's going to be here Christmas Eve?"

"Just the people we had to-night, except Kathryn and you. Why?"

"Oh, nothing," said Billy.

"Look here, sir," said his betrothed. "Don't you do anything foolish. You're not supposed to buy presents for the whole family. Just a little, tiny one for me, if you want to, but you mustn't spend much on it. And if you get anything for any one else in this house, I'll be mad."

"I'd like to see you mad," said Billy.

"You'd wish you hadn't," Ellen retorted.

When Billy had gone, Ellen returned to the living-room and faced the assembled company.

"Well," she said, "now that you've all seen him, what's the verdict?"

The verdict seemed to be unanimously in his favor.

"But," said Bob, "I thought you said he was so screamingly funny."

"Yes," said Edith, "you told me that, too."

"Give him a chance," said Ellen. "Wait till he's in a funny mood. You'll simply die laughing!"

v

It is a compound fracture of the rules to have so important a character as Tommy Richards appear in only one chapter. But remember, this isn't a regular story, but a simple statement of what occurred when it occurred. During Chapter Four, Tommy had been on his way home from the Pacific Coast, where business had kept him all fall. His business out there and what he said en route to Chicago are collateral.

Tommy had been Billy's pal at college. Tommy's home was in Minnesota, and Billy was his most intimate, practically his only friend in the so-called metropolis of the Middle West. So Tommy, not knowing that Billy had gone to St. Louis, looked forward to a few pleasant hours with him between the time of the coast train's arrival and the Minnesota train's departure.

The coast train reached Chicago about noon. It was Thursday noon, the twenty-third. Tommy hustled from the station to Billy's office, and there learned of the St. Louis trip. Disappointed, he roamed the streets a while and at length dropped into the downtown ticket office of his favorite Minnesota road. He was told that everything for the night was sold out. Big Christmas business. Tommy pondered.

The coast train reached Chicago about noon. It was Thursday noon, the twenty-third.

"How about to-morrow night?" he inquired.

"I can give you a lower to-morrow night on the six-thirty," replied Leslie Painter, that being the clerk's name.

"I'll take it," said Tommy.

He did so, and the clerk took $10.05.

"I'll see old Bill after all," said Tommy.

Leslie Painter made no reply.

In the afternoon Tommy sat through a vaudeville show, and at night he looped the loop. He retired early, for the next day promised to be a big one.

Billy got in from St. Louis at seven Friday morning and had been in his office an hour when Tommy appeared. I have no details of the meeting.

At half-past eight Tommy suggested that they'd better go out and h'ist one.

"Still on it, eh?" said Billy.

"What do you mean?"

"I mean that I'm off of it."

"Good Lord! For how long?"

"The last day of November."

"Too long! You look sick already."

"I feel great," averred Billy.

"Well, I don't. So come along and bathe in vichy."

On the way "along" Billy told Tommy about Ellen. Tommy's congratulations were physical and jarred Billy from head to heels.

"Good stuff!" cried Tommy so loudly that three pedestrians jumped sideways. "Old Bill hooked! And do you think you're going to celebrate this occasion with water?"

"I think I am," was Billy's firm reply.

"You think you are! What odds?"

"A good lunch against a red hot."

"You're on!" said Tommy. "And I'm going to be mighty hungry at one o'clock."

"You'll be hungry and alone."

"What's the idea? If you've got a lunch date with the future, I'm in on it."

"I haven't," said Billy. "But I'm going to South Bend on the one-forty, and between now and then I have nothing to do but clean up my mail and buy a dozen Christmas presents."

They turned in somewhere.

"Don't you see the girl at all to-day?" asked Tommy.

"Not to-day. All I do is call her up."

"Well, then, if you get outside of a couple, who'll be hurt? Just for old time's sake."

"If you need lunch money, I'll give it to you."

"No, no. That bet's off."

"It's not off. I won't call it off."

"Suit yourself," said Tommy graciously.

At half-past nine, it was officially decided that Billy had lost the bet. At half-past twelve, Billy said it was time to pay it.

"I'm not hungry enough," said Tommy.

"Hungry or no hungry," said Billy, "I buy your lunch now or I don't buy it. See? Hungry or no hungry."

"What's the hurry?" asked Tommy.

"I guess you know what's the hurry. Me for South Bend on the one-forty, and I got to go to the office first. Hurry or no hurry."

"Listen to reason, Bill. How are you going to eat lunch, go to the office, buy a dozen Christmas presents and catch the one-forty?"

"Christmas presents! I forgot 'em! What do you think of that? I forgot 'em. Good night!"

"What are you going to do?"

"Do! What can I do? You got me into this mess. Get me out!"

"Sure, I'll get you out if you'll listen to reason!" said Tommy. "Has this one-forty train got anything on you? Are you under obligations to it? Is the engineer your girl's uncle?"

"I guess you know better than that. I guess you know I'm not engaged to a girl who's got an uncle for an engineer."

"Well, then, what's the next train?"

"That's the boy, Tommy! That fixes it! I'll go on the next train."

"You're sure there is one?" asked Tommy.

"Is one! Say, where do you think South Bend is? In Europe?"

"I wouldn't mind," said Tommy.

"South Bend's only a two-hour run. Where did you think it was? Europe?"

"I don't care where it is. The question is, what's the next train after one-forty?"

"Maybe you think I don't know," said Billy. He called the gentleman with the apron. "What do you know about this, Charley? Here's an old pal of mine who thinks I don't know the time-table to South Bend."

"He's mistaken, isn't he?" said Charley.

"Is he mistaken? Say, Charley, if you knew as much as I do about the time-table to South Bend, you wouldn't be here."

"No, sir," said Charley. "I'd be an announcer over in the station."

"There!" said Billy triumphantly. "How's that, Tommy? Do I know the time-table or don't I?"

"I guess you do," said Tommy. "But I don't think you ought to have secrets from an old friend."

"There's no secrets about it, Charley."

"My name is Tommy," corrected his friend.

"I know that. I know your name as well as my own, better'n my own. I know your name as well as I know the time-table."

"If you'd just tell me the time of that train, we'd all be better off."

"I'll tell you, Tommy. I wouldn't hold out anything on you, old boy. It's five twenty-five."

"You're sure?"

"Sure! Say, I've taken it a hundred times if I've taken it once."

"All right," said Tommy. "That fixes it. We'll go in and have lunch and be through by half-past one. That'll give you four hours to do your shopping, get to your office and make your train."

"Where you going while I shop?"

"Don't bother about me."

"You go along with me."

"Nothing doing."

"Yes, you do."

"No, I don't."

But this argument was won by Mr. Bowen. At ten minutes of three, when they at last called for the check, Mr. Richards looked on the shopping expedition in an entirely different light. Two hours before, it had not appealed to him at all. Now he could think of nothing that would afford more real entertainment. Mr. Richards was at a stage corresponding to Billy's twenty-one. Billy was far past it.

"What we better do," said Tommy, "is write down a list of all the people so we won't forget anybody."

"That's the stuff!" said Billy. "I'll name 'em, you write 'em."

So Tommy produced a pencil and took dictation on the back of a menu-card.

"First, girl's father, Sam'l McDonald."

"Samuel McDonald," repeated Tommy. "Maybe you'd better give me some dope on each one, so if we're shy of time, we can both be buying at once."

"All right," said Billy. "First, Sam'l McDonal'. He's an ol' crab. Raves about cig'rettes."

"Like 'em?"

"No. Hates 'em."

"Sam'l McDonald, cigarettes," wrote Tommy. "Old crab," he added.

When the important preliminary arrangement had at last been completed, the two old college chums went out into the air.

"Where do we shop?" asked Tommy.

"Marsh's," said Billy. " 'S only place I got charge account."

"Maybe we better take a taxi and save time," suggested Tommy.

So they waited five minutes for a taxi and were driven to Marsh's, two blocks away.

"We'll start on the first floor and work up," said Tommy, who had evidently appointed himself captain.

They found themselves among the jewelry and silverware.

"You might get something for the girl here," suggested Tommy.

"Don't worry 'bout her," said Billy. "Leave her till las'."

"What's the limit on the others?"

"I don't care," said Billy. "Dollar, two dollars, three dollars."

"Well, come on," said Tommy. "We got to make it snappy."

But Billy hung back.

"Say, ol' boy," he wheedled. "You're my ol'st frien'. Is that right?"

"That's right," agreed Tommy.

"Well, say, ol' frien', I'm pretty near all in."

"Go home, then, if you want to. I can pull this all right alone."

"Nothin' doin'. But if I could jus' li'l nap, ten, fifteen minutes—you could get couple things here on fir' floor and then come get me."

"Where?"

"Third floor waitin'-room."

"Go ahead. But wait a minute. Give me some of your cards. And will I have any trouble charging things?"

"Not a bit. Tell 'em you're me."

It was thus that Tommy Richards was left alone in a large store, with Billy Bowen's charge account, Billy Bowen's list, and Billy Bowen's cards.

He glanced at the list.

" 'Samuel McDonald, cigarettes. Old crab,' " he read.

He approached a floor-walker.

"Say, old pal," he said. "I'm doing some shopping and I'm in a big hurry. Where'd I find something for an old cigarette fiend?"

"Cigarette-cases, two aisles down and an aisle to your left," said Old Pal.

Tommy raised the limit on the cigarette-case he picked out for Samuel McDonald. It was $3.75.

"I'll cut down somewhere else," he thought. "The father-in-law ought to be favored a little."

"Charge," he said in response to a query. "William Bowen, Bowen and Company, 18 South La Salle. And here's a card for it. That go out to-night sure?"

He looked again at the list.

"Mrs. Samuel McDonald, bridge bug. Miss Harriet McDonald, reverse English. Miss Louise McDonald, thin hair. Miss Mary Carey, church stuff. Bob and Wife, 'The Man Who Married a Dumb Wife' and gets mysteriously jealous. Walter McDonald, real kid. Edith, fat lady. Wilma, a splinter."

He consulted Old Pal once more. Old Pal's advice was to go to the third floor and look over the books. The advice proved sound. On the third floor Tommy found for Mother "The First Principles of Auction Bridge," and for Aunt Harriet an English grammar. He also bumped into a counter laden with hymnals, chant books, and Books of Common Prayer.

"Aunt Mary!" he exclaimed. And to the clerk: "How much are your medium prayer-books?"

"What denomination?" asked the clerk, whose name was Freda Swanson.

"One or two dollars," said Tommy.

"What church, I mean?" inquired Freda.

"How would I know?" said Tommy. "Are there different books for different churches?"

"Sure. Catholic, Presbyterian, Episcopal, Lutheran—"

"Let's see. McDonald, Carey. How much are the Catholic?"

"Here's one at a dollar and a half. In Latin, too."

"That's it. That'll give her something to work on."

Tommy figured on the back of his list.

"Good work, Tommy!" he thought. "Four and a half under the top limit for those three. Walter's next."

He plunged on Walter. A nice poker set, discovered on the fourth floor, came to five even. Tommy wished he could keep it for himself. He also wished constantly that the women shoppers had taken a course in dodging. He was almost as badly battered as the day he played guard against the Indians.

"Three left besides the queen herself," he observed. "Lord, no. I forgot Bob and his missus."

He moved down-stairs again to the books.

"Have you got 'The Man Who Married a Dumb Wife'? he queried.

Anna Henderson looked, but could not find it.

"Never mind!" said Tommy. "Here's one that'll do."

And he ordered "The Green-Eyed Monster" for the cooing doves in Evanston.

"Now," he figured, "there's just Wilma and Edith and Aunt Louise." Once more he started away from the books, but a title caught his eye: "Eat and Grow Thin."

"Great!" exclaimed Tommy. "It'll do for Edith. By George! It'll do for both of them. 'Eat' for Wilma, and the 'Grow Thin' for Edith. I guess that's doubling up some! And now for Aunt Louise."

The nearest floor-walker told him, in response to his query, that switches would be found on the second floor.

"I ought to have a switch-engine to take me round," said Tommy, who never had felt better in his life. But the floor-walker did not laugh, possibly because he was tired.

"Have you anything to match it with?" asked the lady in the switch-yard.

"No, I haven't."

"Can you give me an idea of the color?"

"What colors have you got?" demanded Tommy.

"Everything there is. I'll show them all to you, if you've got the time."

"Never mind," said Tommy. "What's your favorite color in hair?"

The girl laughed.

"Golden," she said.

"You're satisfied, aren't you?" said Tommy, for the girl had chosen the shade of her own shaggy mane. "All right, make it golden. And a merry Christmas to you."

He forgot to ask the price of switches. He added up the rest and found that the total was $16.25.

"About seventy-five cents for the hair," he guessed. "That will make it seventeen even. I'm some shopper. And all done in an hour and thirteen minutes."

He discovered Billy asleep in the waiting-room and it took him three precious minutes to bring him to.

"Everybody's fixed but the girl herself," he boasted. "I got books for most of 'em."

"Where you been?" asked Billy. "What time is it?"

"You've got about thirty-three minutes to get a present for your lady love and grab your train. You'll have to pass up the office."

"What time is it? Where you been?"

"Don't bother about that. Come on."

On the ride down, Billy begged every one in the elevator to tell him the time, but no one seemed to know. Tommy hurried him out of the store and into a taxi.

"There's a flock of stores round the station," said Tommy. "You can find something there for the dame."

But the progress of the cab through the packed down-town streets was painfully slow and the station clock, when at last they got in sight of it, registered 5.17.

"You can't wait!" said Tommy. "Give me some money and tell me what to get."

Billy fumbled clumsily in seven pockets before he located his pocketbook. In it were two fives and a ten.

"I gotta have a feevee," he said.

"All right. I'll get something for fifteen. What'll it be?"

"Make it a wrist-watch."

"Sure she has none?"

"She's got one. That's for other wris'."

"I used your last card. Have you got another?"

"Pocketbook," said Billy.

Tommy hastily searched and found a card. He pushed Billy toward the station entrance.

"Good-by and merry Christmas," said Tommy.

"Goo'-by and God bless you!" said Billy, but he was talking to a large policeman.

"Where are you trying to go?" asked the latter.

"Souse Ben'," said Billy.

"Hurry up, then. You've only got a minute."

The minute and six more were spent in the purchase of a ticket. And when Billy reached the gate, the 5.25 had gone and the 5.30 was about to chase it.

"Where to?" inquired the gateman.

"Souse Ben'," said Billy.

"Run then," said the gateman.

Billy ran. He ran to the first open vestibule of the Rock Island train, bound for St. Joe, Missouri.

"Where to?" asked a porter.

"Souse," said Billy.

"Ah can see that," said the porter. "But where you goin'?"

The train began to move and Billy, one foot dragging on the station platform, moved with it. The porter dexterously pulled him aboard. And he was allowed to ride to Englewood.

Walking down Van Buren Street, it suddenly occurred to the genial Mr. Richards that he would have to go some himself to get his baggage and catch the 6.30 for the northwest. He thought of it in front of a Van Buren jewelry shop. He stopped and went in.

Three-quarters of an hour later, a messenger-boy delivered a particularly ugly and frankly inexpensive wrist-watch at the McDonald home. The parcel was addressed to Miss McDonald and the accompanying card read:

"Mr. Bowen: Call me up any night after seven. Calumet 2678. Miss Violet Moore."

There was no good-will toward men in the McDonald home this Christmas. Ellen spent the day in bed and the orders were that she must not be disturbed.

Down-stairs, one person smiled. It was Walter. He smiled in spite of the fact that his father had tossed his brand-new five-dollar poker set into the open fireplace. He smiled in spite of the fact that he was not allowed to leave the house, not even to take Kathryn to church.

"Gee!" he thought, between smiles, "Billy sure had nerve!"

Bob walked round among his relatives seeking to dispel the gloom with a remark that he thought apt and nifty:

"Be grateful," was the remark, "that he had one of his screamingly funny moods before it was too late."

But no one but Bob seemed to think much of the remark, and no one seemed grateful.

Those are the facts, and it was quite a job to dig them up. But I did it.

A CHRISTMAS SPECTACLE

FOR USE IN CHRISTMAS EVE ENTERTAINMENTS IN THE VESTRY

By ROBERT BENCHLEY

AT the opening of the entertainment the Superintendent will step into the footlights, recover his balance apologetically, and say:

"Boys and girls of the Intermediate Department, parents and friends: I suppose you all know why we are here tonight. (At this point the audience will titter apprehensively). Mrs. Drury and her class of little girls have been working very hard to make this entertainment a success, and I am sure that everyone here to-night is going to have what

I overheard one of my boys the other day calling 'some good time.' (Indulgent laughter from the little boys). And may I add before the curtain goes up that immediately after the entertainment we want you all to file out into the Christian Endeavor room, where there will be a Christmas tree, 'with all the fixin's,' as the boys say." (Shrill whistling from the little boys and immoderate applause from everyone).

There will then be a wait of twenty-five minutes, while sounds of hammering and dropping may be heard from behind the curtains. The Boys' Club orchestra will render the "Poet and Peasant Overture" four times in succession, each time differently.

At last one side of the curtains will be drawn back; the other will catch on something and have to be released by hand; someone will whisper loudly, "Put out the lights," following which the entire house will be plunged into darkness. Amid catcalls from the little boys, the footlights will at last go on, disclosing:

The windows in the rear of the vestry rather ineffectively concealed by a group of small fir trees on standards, one of which has already fallen over, leaving exposed a corner of the map of Palestine and the list of gold-star classes for November. In the center of the stage is a larger tree, undecorated, while at the extreme left, invisible to everyone in the audience except those sitting at the extreme right, is an imitation fireplace, leaning against the wall.

Twenty-five seconds too early little Flora Rochester will prance out from the wings, uttering the first shrill notes of a song, and will have to be grabbed by eager hands and pulled back. Twenty-four seconds later the piano will begin "The Return of the Reindeer" with a powerful accent on the first note of each bar, and Flora Rochester, Lillian McNulty, Gertrude Hamingham and Martha Wrist will swirl on, dressed in white, and advance heavily into the footlights, which will go out.

There will then be an interlude while Mr. Neff, the sexton, adjusts the connection, during which the four little girls stand undecided whether to brave it out or cry. As a compromise they giggle and are herded back into the wings by Mrs. Drury, amid applause. When the lights go on again, the applause becomes deafening, and as Mr. Neff walks triumphantly away, the little boys in the audience will whistle: "There she goes, there she goes, all dressed up in her Sunday clothes!"

"The Return of the Reindeer" will be started again and the show-girls will reappear, this time more gingerly and somewhat dispirited. They will, however, sing the following, to the music of the "Ballet Pizzicato" from "Sylvia":

> "We greet you, we greet you,
> On this Christmas Eve so fine.
> We greet you, we greet you,
> And wish you a good time."

They will then turn toward the tree and Flora Rochester will advance, hanging a silver star on one of the branches, meanwhile reciting a verse, the only distinguishable words of which are:*"I am Faith so strong and pure—"*

At the conclusion of her recitation, the star will fall off.

Lillian McNulty will then step forward and hang her star on a branch, reading her lines in clear tones:

> *"And I am Hope, a virtue great,*
> *My gift to Christmas now I make,*
> *That children and grown-ups may hope today*
> *That tomorrow will be a merry Christmas Day."*

The hanging of the third star will be consummated by Gertrude Hamingham, who will get as far as *"Sweet Charity I bring to place upon the tree—"* at which point the strain will become too great and she will forget the remainder. After several frantic glances toward the wings, from which Mrs. Drury is sending out whispered messages to the effect that the next line begins, *"My message bright—"* Gertrude will disappear, crying softly.

After the morale of the cast has been in some measure restored by the pianist, who, with great presence of mind, plays a few bars of "Will There Be Any Stars In My Crown?" to cover up Gertrude's exit,

Martha Wrist will unleash a rope of silver tinsel from the foot of the tree, and, stringing it over the boughs as she skips around in a circle, will say, with great assurance:

> " *'Round and 'round the tree I go,*
> *Through the holly and the snow*
> *Bringing love and Christmas cheer*
> *Through the happy year to come.*"

At this point there will be a great commotion and the jangling of sleigh-bells off-stage, and Mr. Creamer, rather poorly disguised as Santa Claus, will emerge from the opening in the imitation fireplace. A great popular demonstration for Mr. Creamer will follow. He will then advance to the footlights, and, rubbing his pillow and ducking his knees to denote joviality, will say thickly through his false beard:

"Well, well, well, what have we here? A lot of bad little boys and girls who aren't going to get any Christmas presents this year? (Nervous laughter from the little boys and girls). Let me see, let me see! I have a note here from Dr. Whidden. Let's see what it says. (Reads from a paper on which there is obviously nothing written). 'If you and the young people of the Intermediate Department will come into the Christian Endeavor room, I think we may have a little surprise for you. . . .' Well, well, well! What do you suppose it can be? (Cries of "I know, I know!" from sophisticated ones in the audience). Maybe it is a bottle of castor-oil! (Raucous jeers from the little boys and elaborately simulated disgust on the part of the little girls.) Well, anyway, suppose we go out and see? Now if Miss Liftnagle will oblige us with a little march on the piano, we will all form in single file—"

At this point there will ensue a stampede toward the Christian Endeavor room, in which chairs will be broken, decorations demolished, and the protesting Mr. Creamer badly hurt.

This will bring to a close the first part of the entertainment.

CHRISTMAS WAITS IN BOSTON

By Edward Everett Hale

I

I ALWAYS give myself a Christmas present. And on this particular year the present was a Carol party,—which is about as good fun, all things consenting kindly, as a man can have.

Many things must consent, as will appear. First of all there must be good sleighing,—and second, a fine night for Christmas Eve. Ours are not the carollings of your poor shivering little East Angles or South Mercians, where they have to plod around afoot in countries where they do not know what a sleigh-ride is.

I had asked Harry to have sixteen of the best voices in the chapel school to be trained to eight or ten good carols without knowing why. We did not care to disappoint them if a February thaw setting in on the twenty-fourth of December should break up the spree before it began. Then I had told Howland that he must reserve for me a span of good horses and a sleigh that I could pack sixteen small children into, tight-stowed. Howland is always good about such things, knew what the sleigh was for, having done the same in other years, and doubled the span of horses of his own accord, because the children would like it better, and "it would be no difference to him." Sunday night, as the weather nymphs ordered, the wind hauled round to the northwest and everything froze hard. Monday night things moderated, and the snow began to fall steadily,—so steadily; —and so Tuesday night the Metropolitan people gave up their unequal contest, all good men and angels rejoicing at their discomfiture, and only a few of the people in the very lowest *Bolgie* being ill-natured enough to grieve. And thus it was, that by Thursday evening there was one hard compact roadway from Copp's Hill to the Bone-burner's Gehenna, fit for good men and angels to ride over, without jar, without noise, and without fatigue to horse or man. So it was that when I came down with Lycidas to the chapel at seven o'clock, I found Harry had gathered there his eight pretty girls and his eight jolly boys, and had them practising for the last time:

> "Carol, carol, Christians,
> Carol joyfully;
> Carol for the coming
> Of Christ's nativity."

I think the children had got inkling of what was coming, or perhaps Harry had hinted it to their mothers. Certainly they were warmly dressed, and when, fifteen minutes afterwards, Howland came round himself with the sleigh, he had put in as many rugs and bearskins as if he thought the children were to be taken new-born from their respective cradles. Great was the rejoicing as the bells of the horses rang beneath the chapel windows, and Harry did not get his last *du capo* for his last carol, not much matter indeed, for they were perfect enough in it before midnight.

Lycidas and I tumbled in on the back seat, each with a child on his lap to keep us warm; I was flanked by Sam Perry, and he by John Rich, both of the mercurial age, and therefore good to do errands. Harry was in front somewhere, flanked in likewise, and the twelve other children lay in miscellaneously between, like sardines when you have first opened the box. I had invited Lycidas, because, besides being my best friend, he is the best fellow in the world, and so deserves the best Christmas Eve can give him. Under the full moon, on the snow still white, with sixteen children at the happiest, and with the blessed memories of the best the world has ever had, there can be nothing better than two or three such hours.

"First, driver, out on Commonwealth Avenue. That will tone down the horses. Stop on the left after you have passed Fairfield Street." So we dashed up to the front of Haliburton's palace, where he was keeping his first Christmastide. And the children, whom Harry had hushed down for a square or two, broke forth with good full voice under his strong lead in

"Shepherd of tender sheep,"

singing with all that unconscious pathos with which children do sing, and starting the tears in your eyes in the midst of your gladness. The instant the horses' bells stopped, their voices began. In an instant more we saw Haliburton and Anna run to the window and pull up the shades, and, in a minute more, faces at all the windows. And so the children sung through Clement's old hymn. Little did Clement think of bells and snow, as he taught it in his Sunday school there in Alexandria. But perhaps to-day, as they pin up the laurels and the palm in the chapel at Alexandria, they are humming the words, not thinking of Clement more than he thought of us. As the children closed with

> "Swell the triumphant song
> To Christ, our King,"

Haliburton came running out, and begged me to bring them in. But I told him, "No," as soon as I could hush their shouts of "Merry Christmas;" that we had a long journey before us, and must not alight by the way. And the children broke out with

> "Hail to the night,
> Hail to the day,"

rather a favorite,—quicker and more to the childish taste, perhaps, than the other,—and with another "Merry Christmas" we were off again.

Off, the length of Commonwealth Avenue, to where it crosses the Brookline branch of the Mill-Dam,—dashing along with the gayest of sleighing-parties as we came back into town, up Chestnut Street, through Louisburg Square,—we ran the sleigh into a bank on the slope of Pinckney Street in front of Walter's house,—and before they suspected there that any one had come, the children were singing

> "Carol, carol, Christians,
> Carol joyfully."

Kisses flung from the window; kisses flung back from the street. "Merry Christmas" again and a good-will, and then one of the girls began

> "When Anna took the baby,
> And pressed his lips to hers"—

and all of them fell in so cheerily. O dear me! it is a scrap of old Ephrem the Syrian, if they did but know it! And when, after this, Harry would fain have driven on, how the little witches begged that they might sing just one song more there, because Mrs. Alexander had been so kind to them, when she showed them about the German stitches. And then up the hill and over to the North End, and as far as we could get the horses up into Moon Court, that they might sing to the Italian image-man who gave Lucy the boy and dog in plaster, when she was sick in the spring. For the children had, you know, the choice of where they would go; and they select their best friends, and will be more apt to remember the Italian image-man than Chrysostom himself, though Chrysostom should have "made a few remarks" to them seventeen times in the chapel. Then the Italian image-man heard for the first time in his life:

> "Now is the time of Christmas come,"

and

> "Jesus in his babes abiding."

And then we came up Hanover Street and stopped under Mr. Gerry's chapel, where they were dressing the walls with their evergreens, and gave them

> "Hail to the night,
> Hail to the day:"

And so down State Street and stopped at the *Advertiser* office, because when the boys gave their Literary Entertainment, Mr. Hale put in their advertisement for nothing, and up in the old attic there the compositors were relieved to hear

"No war nor battle sound,"

and

"The waiting world was still."

Even the leading editor relaxed from his gravity and the "In General" man from his more serious views, and the *Daily* the next morning wished everybody a "Merry Christmas" with even more unction, and resolved that in coming years it would have a supplement, large enough to contain all the good wishes. So away again to the houses of confectioners who had given the children candy,—to Miss Simonds' house, because she had been so good to them in school,—to the palaces of millionaires who had prayed for these children with tears if the children only knew it,—to Dr. Frothingham in Summer Street, I remember, where we stopped because the Boston Association of Ministers met there,—and out on Dover Street Bridge, that the poor chair mender might hear our carols sung once more before he heard them better sung in another world where nothing needs mending. . . . O, we went to twenty places that night, I suppose; we went to the grandest places in Boston, and we went to the meanest. At nine we brought up at my house, D Street, three doors from the corner, and the children picked out their very best for Polly and my six little girls to hear, and then for the first time we let them jump out and run in. Polly had some hot oysters for them, so that the frolic was crowned with a treat. There was a Christmas cake cut into sixteen pieces, which they took home to dream upon; and then hoods and mufflers on again, and by ten o'clock or a little after, we had all the girls and all the little ones at their homes. . . .

II

Lycidas and I both thought that the welcome of these homes was perhaps the best part of it all, as we went into these modest houses, to leave the children, to say they had been good, and to wish a "Merry Christmas" ourselves to fathers, mothers, and to guardian aunts. . . . Here was brave Mrs. Masury. I had not seen her since her mother died.

"Indeed, Mr. Ingham, I got so used to watching then, that I cannot sleep well yet o'nights; I wish you knew some poor creature that wanted me to-night, if it were only in memory of Bethlehem" . . . "What can I send to your children," said Dalton, who was finishing sword-blades. (Ill wind was Fort Sumter, but it blew good to poor Dalton, whom it set up in the world with his sword-factory.) "Here's an old-fashioned tape-measure for the girl, and a Sheffield wimble for the boy. What, there is no boy? Let one of the girls have it, then; it will count one more present for her." And so he pressed his brown-paper parcel into my hand. From every house, though it were the humblest, a word of love, as sweet, in truth, as if we could have heard the voice of angels singing in the sky.

I bade Harry good-night; took Lycidas to his house, and gave his wife my Christmas wishes and good-night; and, coming down to the sleigh again, gave way to the feeling which I think you will all understand, that this was not the time to stop, but just the time to begin. For the streets were stiller now, and the moon brighter than ever, and the blessings of these simple people and of the proud people, and of the very angels in heaven, who are not bound to the misery of using words when they have anything worth saying,—all these wishes and blessings were round me, all the purity of the still winter night, and I didn't want to lose it all by going to bed to sleep. So I put the boys all together, where they could chatter, and then, passing through Charles Street . . . I noticed the lights in Woodhull's house, and, seeing they were up, thought I would make Fanny a midnight call. She came to the door herself. I asked if she were waiting for Santa Claus, but I saw in a moment that I must not joke with her. She said she had hoped I was her husband. In a minute was one of those contrasts which make life, life . . . Poor Fanny's mother had been blocked up in the Springfield train as she was coming on for Christmas. The old lady had been chilled through, and was here in bed now with pneumonia. Both Fanny's children had been ailing when she came, and this morning the doctor had pronounced it scarlet fever. Fanny had not undressed herself since Monday, nor slept, I thought, in the same time. So while we had been singing carols and wishing

Merry Christmas, the poor child had been waiting, hoping that her husband or Edward, both of whom were on the tramp, would find for her and bring to her the model nurse, who had not yet arrived, nor had either of the men returned. Professional paragons, dear reader, are shy of scarlet fever. I told the poor child that it was better as it was. I wrote a line for Sam Perry to take to his aunt, Mrs. Masury, in which I simply said: "Dear mamma, I have found the poor creature who wants you to-night. Come back in this carriage." I bade him take a hack at Barnard's, where they were all up waiting for the assembly to be done at Papanti's. I sent him over to Albany Street; and really as I sat there trying to soothe Fanny, it seemed to me less time than it has taken me to dictate this little story about her, before Mrs. Masury rang gently, and I left them, having made Fanny promise that she would consecrate the day, which at that moment was born, by trusting God, by going to bed and going to sleep, knowing that her children were in much better hands than hers. . . .

And so I walked home. Better so, perhaps, after all, than in the lively sleigh with the tinkling bells. What an eternity it seemed since I started with those children singing carols!

> "Within that province far away
>   Went plodding home a weary boor;
> A streak of light before him lay,
>   Fallen through a half-shut stable door
> Across his path. He passed, for naught
>   Told what was going on within:
> How keen the stars, his only thought,
>   The air how calm and cold and thin,
>   In the solemn midnight,
>   Centuries ago!"

"Streak of light"—Is there a light in Lycidas's room? They are not in bed? That is making a night of it! Well, there are few hours of the day or night when I have not been in Lycidas's room, so I let myself in by the night-key he gave me, and ran up the stairs,—it is a horrid seven-storied first-class, apartment-house. For my part, I had as lief live in a steeple. Two flights I ran up, two steps at a time,—I was younger then than I am now,—pushed open the door which was ajar, and saw such a scene of confusion as I never saw in Mary's over-nice parlor before. Queer! I remember the first thing that I saw was wrong was a great ball of white German worsted on the floor. Her basket was upset. A great Christmas tree lay across the rug, quite too high for the room; a large, sharp-pointed Spanish clasp-knife was by it, with which they had been lopping it; there were two immense baskets of white papered presents, both upset; but what frightened me most was the centre-table. Three or four handkerchiefs on it,—towels, napkins, I know not what,—all brown and red and almost black with blood! I turned, heart-sick, to look into the bedroom,—and I really had a sense of relief when I saw somebody . . . Lycidas, but just now so strong and well, lay pale and exhausted . . . while over him bent Mary and Morton. I learned afterwards that poor Lycidas, while trimming the Christmas tree and talking merrily with Mary and Morton,—who, by good luck, had brought round his presents late, and was staying to tie on glass balls and apples,—had given himself a deep and dangerous wound with the point of the unlucky knife, and had lost a great deal of blood before the hemorrhage could be controlled. Just before I entered, the stick tourniquet which Morton had temporised had slipped in poor Mary's unpractised hand, at the moment he was about to secure the artery . . .

"O Fred," said Morton, without looking up, "I am glad you are here."

"And what can I do for you?"

"Some whiskey,—first of all."

"There are two bottles," said Mary, "in the cupboard behind his dressing-glass."

I took Bridget with me, struck a light in the dressing-room (how she blundered about the match) and found the cupboard door locked! Key doubtless in Mary's pocket,—probably in pocket of "another dress." I did not ask. Took my own bunch, willed tremendously that my account-book drawer key should govern the lock, and it did. If it had not, I should have put my fist through the panels. Bottle marked "bay rum;" another bottle with no mark; two bottles of Saratoga water. "Set them all on the floor, Bridget." A tall bottle of cologne. Bottle marked in manuscript. What in the world is it? "Bring that candle, Bridget." "Eau distillée, Marron, Montreal." What in the world did Lycidas bring distilled water from Montreal for? And then Morton's clear voice from the other room, "As quick as you can, Fred." "Yes! in one moment. Put all these on the floor, Bridget." Here they are at last. "Corkscrew, Bridget."

"Indade, sir, and where is it?" "Where? I don't know. Run as quick as you can, and bring it. His wife cannot leave him." So Bridget ran, and I meanwhile am driving a silver pronged fork into the Bourbon corks, and the blade of my own penknife for the other side.

"Now, Fred," from Morton, within. "Yes, in one moment," I replied. Penknife blade breaks off, fork pulls right out, two crumbs of cork with it. Will that girl never come?

I turned round; I found a goblet on the wash-stand; I took Lycidas's heavy clothes-brush and knocked off the neck of the bottle. . . . It smashed like a Prince Rupert's drop in my hand, crumbled into seventy pieces,—a nasty smell of whiskey on the floor,—and I, holding just the hard bottom of the thing with two large spikes running worthless up into the air. But I seized the goblet, poured into it what was left in the bottom, and carried it into Morton as quietly as I could. He bade me give Lycidas as much as he could swallow; then showed me how to compress the great artery. When he was satisfied that he could trust me, he began his work again, silently. . . . When all was secure, he glanced at the ghostly white face, with beads of perspiration on the forehead and upper lip, laid his finger on the pulse and said, "We will have a little more whiskey. No, Mary, you are overdone already; let Fred bring it." The truth was that poor Mary was almost as white as Lycidas. She would not faint,—that was the only reason she did not,—and at the moment I wondered that she did not fall. Bridget, you see, was still nowhere.

So I retired again, to attack that other bottle. Would that Kelt ever come? I passed the bell-rope as I went into the dressing-room, and rang as hard as I could ring. I took the other bottle and bit steadily with my teeth at the cork, only, of course, to wrench the end of it off. Morton called me, and I stepped back. "No," said he, "bring your whiskey."

Mary had just rolled gently back on the floor. I went again in despair. But I heard Bridget's step this time. She ran in, in triumph, with a *screw-driver!*

"No!" I whispered,—"no. The crooked thing you draw corks with," and I showed her the bottle again. "Find one somewhere and don't come back without it."

"Frederic!" said Morton. I think he never called me so before . . . "Frederic!" "Yes," I said. But why did I say "Yes"? "Father of Mercy, tell me what to do."

And my mazed eyes, dim with tears,—did you ever shed tears from excitement?—fell on an old razor-strop of those days of shaving, made by *C. Whittaker*, SHEFFIELD. The Sheffield stood in black letters out from the rest like a vision. They made corkscrews in Sheffield too. If this Whittaker had only made a corkscrew! And what is a "Sheffield wimble?"

Hand in my pocket—brown paper parcel.

"Where are you, Frederic?" "Yes," said I for the last time. Twine off! brown paper off! And I learned that the "Sheffield wimble" was one of those things whose name you never heard before, which people sell you in Thames Tunnel, where a hoof-cleaner, a gimlet, a screw-driver and a *corkscrew* fold into one handle. "Yes," said I again. "Pop," said the cork. "Bubble, bubble, bubble," said the whiskey. Bottle in one hand, full tumbler in the other, I walked in. Morton poured half a tumblerful down Lycidas's throat that time. . . . I found that there was need of it, from what he said of the pulse when it was all over. . . .

This was the turning-point. He was exceedingly weak, and we sat by him through the night, . . . but there was no real danger after that.

As we turned away from the house on Christmas morning,—I to preach and he to visit his patients,—he said to me, "Did you *make* that whiskey?"

"No," said I, "but poor Dod Dalton had to furnish the corkscrew."

And I went down to the chapel to preach. The sermon had been lying ready at home on my desk, and Polly had brought it round to me, for there had been no time for me to go from Lycidas's home to D Street and to return. There was the text, all as it was the day before:

They helped every one his neighbor, and every one said to his brother, Be of good courage. So the carpenter encouraged the gold-smith, and he that smootheth with the hammer him that smote the anvil.

And there were the pat illustrations, as I had finished them yes-terday. . . . And I said to them all, "O, if I could tell you, my friends, what every twelve hours of my life tells me,—of the way in which woman helps woman, and man helps man, when only the ice is broken, —how we are all rich as soon as we find out that we are all brothers, and how we are all in want, unless we can call at any moment for a brother's hand,—then I could make you understand something, in the lives you lead every day, of what the New Covenant, the New Com-monwealth, the New Kingdom, is to be . . ."

But when we had our tree in the evening at home, I did tell all this story to Polly and the bairns, and I gave Alice her measuring-tape,— precious with a spot of Lycidas's blood,—and Bertha her Sheffield wimble. "Papa," said old Clara, who is the next child, "all the people gave presents, did not they, as they did in the picture in your study?"

"Yes," said I, "though they did not all know they were giving them."

"Why do they not give such presents every day?" said Clara.

"O child," I said, "it is only for thirty-six hours of the three hun-dred and sixty-five days that all people remember that they are all brothers and sisters, and those are the hours that we call, therefore, Christmas Eve and Christmas Day."

JEST 'FORE CHRISTMAS

Father calls me William, sister calls me Will,
Mother calls me Willie, but the fellers call me Bill!
Mighty glad I ain't a girl—ruther be a boy,
Without them sashes, curls, an' things that's worn by Fauntleroy!
Love to chawnk green apples an' go swimmin' in the lake—
Hate to take the castor-ile they give for belly-ache!
'Most all the time, the whole year round, there ain't no flies on me,
But jest 'fore Christmas I'm good as I kin be!

Got a yeller dog named Sport, sick him on the cat;
First thing she knows she doesn't know where she is at!
Got a clipper sled, an' when us kids goes out to slide,
'Long comes the grocery cart, an' we all hook a ride!
But sometimes when the grocery man is worried an' cross,
He reaches at us with his whip, an' larrups up his hoss,
An' then I laff an' holler, "Oh, ye never teched *me!*"
But jest 'fore Christmas I'm good as I kin be!

Gran'ma says she hopes that when I git to be a man,
I'll be a missionarer like her oldest brother, Dan,
As was et up by the cannibuls that lives in Ceylon's Isle,
Where every prospeck pleases, an' only man is vile!
But gran'ma she has never been to see a Wild West show,
Nor read the Life of Daniel Boone, or else I guess she'd know
That Buff'lo Bill and cow-boys is good enough for me!
Except' jest 'fore Christmas, when I'm good as I kin be!

And when old Sport he hangs around, so solemn-like an' still,
His eyes they keep a-sayin': "What's the matter, little Bill?"
The old cat sneaks down off her perch an' wonders what's become
Of them two enemies of hern that used to make things hum!
But I am so perlite an' tend so earnestly to biz,

That mother says to father: "How improved our Willie is!"
But father, havin' been a boy hisself, suspicions me
When jest 'fore Christmas, I'm as good as I kin be!

For Christmas, with its lots an' lots of candies, cakes an' toys,
Was made, they say, for proper kids an' not for naughty boys;
So wash yer face an' bresh yer hair, an' mind yer p's and q's,
An' don't bust out yer pantaloons, an' don't wear out yer shoes;
Say "Yessum" to the ladies, an' "Yessur" to the men,
An' when they's company, don't pass yer plate for pie again;
But, thinking of the things yer'd like to see upon that tree,
Jest 'fore Christmas be as good as yer kin be!

Eugene Field

THE BIRTH OF CHRIST

The time draws near the birth of Christ;
  The moon is hid—the night is still;
  The Christmas bells from hill to hill
Answer each other in the mist.

Four voices of four hamlets round,
  From far and near, on mead and moor,
  Swell out and fail, as if a door
Were shut between me and the sound.

Each voice four changes on the wind,
  That now dilate and now decrease,
  Peace and good-will, good-will and peace,
Peace and good-will to all mankind.

Rise, happy morn! rise, holy morn!
  Draw forth the cheerful day from night;
  O Father! touch the east, and light
The light that shone when hope was born!

Alfred Tennyson

THE GREAT DAY

A PLANTATION CHRISTMAS

By Julia Peterkin

I HEAR that in many places something has happened to Christmas; that it is changing from a time of merriment and carefree gaiety to a holiday which is filled with tedium; that many people dread the day and the obligation to give Christmas presents is a nightmare to weary, bored souls; that the children of enlightened parents no longer believe in Santa Claus; that all in all, the effort to be happy and have pleasure makes many honest hearts grow dark with despair instead of beaming with good will and cheerfulness.

These dark rumors make me thank the kind fate which placed me in a home which is removed from the beaten track of that thing which, for want of a better name, we call progress. Here, where time moves slowly and few changes come in, we remain faithful to the old-fashioned ways which were a part of our childhood and of the childhood of those who were here before us, and we delight in defending them against anything which tends to destroy them or to lessen their brightness.

Every manner of life has its compensations, but nowhere is life more generous in compensating for its lacks than on this old plantation.

Individuals are few, so each one counts for much. Hours are long and quiet and time is abundant. Since loneliness is one of the evils which threaten us, our holidays are important occasions. Birthdays, anniversaries, old church festivals, long forgotten by most of the outside world, make reasons for us to gather our friends together and make merry. But among all these gala days Christmas comes first. Our Christmas preparations begin as soon as Thanksgiving is over, when the Christmas cakes are baked and put away to ripen, with oiled paper wrapped carefully around them to hold the delicious flavor of the scuppernong wine which has been carefully poured all over their dark brown crusts.

The house servants begin to bestir themselves industriously in order to have every piece of glass and silver bright and shining, every piece of furniture and every floor polished and looking its best.

The pantry shelves already hold rows of jars filled with jellies and jams and pickles and preserves made of figs and peaches and apples and watermelon rinds, and every other fruit and vegetable the garden and orchard yield. Bottles of red and white juices made of berries and grapes stand in colorful and tempting array until they are ready to be used.

In the kitchen, the cook moves about with much dignity and importance among his pots and pans and measuring-cups and scales, pausing now and then to ponder over some old recipe stored away in his mind or to boast of how much better he can cook out of his head than most people can cook out of books.

Long strands of red peppers hang to nails outside the kitchen door, ready to season the Christmas turkey dressing. Store-bought pepper is hot enough, but it lacks the flavor which these home-grown peppers give, not only to the turkey dressing and the game which the hunters bring in, but to the links of sausage which will soon be strung across the smokehouse and the piles of rich liver pudding in which rice and corn meal both furnish such a large share.

The shoats are growing fatter each day on the sweet acorns falling from the live-oak trees, and on the peanuts and potatoes, peas and ears of corn which were left in the fields when those crops were gathered.

In the wild-crabapple thickets fruit is covering the ground, for the nights are cool and frosty; enough must be gathered for the clear yellow bitter-sweet jelly which is perfect with roasted pork hams.

The sugar-cane mills scattered over the place cannot finish all their work by daylight and their bright fires make shining red stars at night, while the fragrance of the boiling sirup steams up from the brown gallons which simmer and thicken in the wood-lined vats, promising molasses cake and delicious candy and the best sirup that was ever poured over hot waffles.

The sweet potatoes are in banks, the hay is in stacks, the corn is in the barns, most of the cotton has been picked. Still, the cotton-pickers sing and laugh and talk happily as they pick the last scattering white locks out of belated bolls, for every extra pound of cotton means extra coins for Christmas, and at Christmas-time money is needed, not only for necessities, but for pleasuring.

The cotton gins run at full tilt, packing this last cotton into bales while the plantation foreman, big, black, muscular, keen-eyed, walks about among the belts and pulleys and running gear, watching the soft white downy stream pour out from the gin rolls into the press to be packed and then labeled with the owner's mark.

Axes swing and ring in the woods nearby as their sharp steel is driven into the hearts of trees. As the fresh logs are cut, they are hauled in, and woodpiles grow high in every back yard. A clean hickory backlog for the Christmas fire lies waiting on every pile beside the sturdy lengths of pine and oak and ash, and the fat rosiny pine knots and bits of pine hearts are split up into small kindling wood which can rouse the sleepiest blaze into bright burning.

The wild broom grass, with its tall strong growth, is ripe enough to gather, and the year's supply of brooms must be wrung before a hard frost comes and scorches the straw and makes it lifeless and brittle. Bound into neat bundles with withes of split hickory so that they make a comfortable handful, these brooms make welcome Christmas presents. No store-bought broom can sweep dust out of corners half so well.

Partridges like the broom fields, and it is not uncommon for fine coveys to flutter up and away with startling whirs, or for rabbits to go bouncing through the sedge at the sight of the broom-gatherers who wring the straw.

The old houses in the Quarters have been weathered by long years of rain and wind and sunshine into a soft gray, but underneath this gentle color their yellow wood stands as solid and steadfast as it was a hundred years ago.

Before Christmas Eve the old cypress floors must be scoured white, the inside walls repapered with newspapers pasted on tight, the mantel-shelves and bare rafters decorated with papers cut into fringes and scallops. The front doors and window blinds must be white-washed with lime or with the white clay which lines the big gully near the spring. The yards must be raked clear of fallen leaves and swept clean, for everything must be spick-and-span and neat for Christmas.

The store at the crossroads is kept open until long after dark, for the buying for Christmas must be carefully done, and those who come to buy like to linger and talk awhile. Printed words are scarce and so spoken words are all the more precious. News has to be passed on, old tales retold, present problems discussed and measured by old-fashioned wisdom. For old fashions are still in style here. Age has precedence, children are trained to be seen and not heard, and they are expected to listen quietly while their elders repeat their tales of days which are forever gone, but which have left so many fine old beliefs and traditions.

Everybody goes dressed in his Sunday best, and merry laughter rises above the serious words of buying. Friendly hands are shaken and held. Treats are offered and accepted graciously.

Glass bottles with strings tied around their necks for handles gurgle as they are filled with kerosene. Paper bags threaten to burst and spill the loads of fruit and candy and cakes they are given to hold. The scent of coffee newly parched and ground smothers the pleasant smell of the bunches of bananas which swing from the ceiling and the rank scent of the dried herrings in their stained slatted boxes.

The gristmill across the road clatters noisily as it grinds hoppers full of corn into meal and hominy, and the miller's black hands and eyebrows are whitened with the soft dust as he rubs the crushed grain between his fingers to see if its fineness is right.

The restaurant next door flaps its red-and-white calico curtains and sends out inviting odors of catfish and rice.

In a pit at one side of the restaurant's yard, a barbecued pig drips sizzling fat on the coals which have cooked it so done and brown. Barbecue sandwiches made of pork and slices of store-bought bread rival the catfish and rice as a welcome change from the food eaten every day. Gallant beaus escort their ladies about and feed them well.

Banjos and guitars plucked by work-hardened fingers add music and encourage the singing and dancing.

Many strange styles of dress are seen. The middle-aged and elderly women keep to their old-time full, long skirts, which are usually half-hidden by wide white aprons, and their heads are neatly tied with bandanna headkerchiefs, large squares of white cambric or black calico which are bound gracefully around their heads and tied with a deft knot in the back. No head covering could be more dignified or becoming than these kerchiefs, especially when another square of the same material is folded around the wearer's neck and pinned across her bosom.

Bright hoop earrings twinkle in many ears, for they make the wearer's eyesight better; strings of gay beads tinkle around many necks, setting off the holiday costumes.

Christmas is no holiday gotten up for the amusement of children, but a season which is enjoyed by the grown people with the utmost enthusiasm. People who have always loved one another are bound closer by the fun they have together. Old pain and old strain are forgotten in the good time which is come. There is a sudden new joy in just being alive.

Important journeys are made to town, where the matter of choosing Christmas presents becomes so absorbing that traffic lights are overlooked and remembered only when indignant traffic cops shout severe reprimands.

If we lived nearer to many stores and were used to getting packages, then the pleasure of sending and receiving gifts might be less. If the circle of our friends was larger, the sheer fun of deciding what each one would like might not be so great. But here the mere sight of an acquaintance warms our hearts, and just knowing that the sight of ourselves makes other hearts glad is one of life's richest experiences.

Fine mornings are spent getting Christmas trees from the woods, in making holly wreaths and hanging up mistletoe boughs. The days are golden with sunshine, the forests glowing with color. Everywhere there is fulfillment of last spring's promise. Black walnuts and hickory nuts drop with emphatic thuds; chinquapins fall from dry burs and hide under their own fallen leaves; under live-oaks, water-oaks, Spanish oaks, the earth is covered with acorns, yet the chestnut-oaks drop their loads of big over-cups in a steady patter. The magnolias are green and glossy, mock oranges glisten in the sunlight, Cherokee-rose apples shine among the glossy leaves.

Sometimes Autumn is generous and lets some of its blossoms stay until Christmas. Roses bloom, chrysanthemums are bewilderingly brilliant in a few protected places, Cape jasmines linger to help the tea olives keep the air perfumed, and vagrant butterflies hover over the frost-tinged zinnias and marigolds.

A festival without feasting would be an empty thing, and the hunters all go out for game. Doves and partridges are plentiful, the big wild ducks have come to spend the winter in the swamps where the sweet gums, drunk on the warmth of the mild winter sunshine, scatter leaves in bright showers of purple and gold with every stir of the wind, hiding the deer tracks which mingle with those of turkeys and wildcats and foxes and raccoons.

The mazes of the swamp are treacherous, but one glimpse of a wild gobbler's shining, burnished feathers is enough to induce any hunter to go slipping stealthily between the great trunks of cypresses and sweet gums, climbing over fallen logs, tramping through mud, side-stepping bogs, stooping under the low-swung nooses of wild grape-vines and thorny bamboos.

Christmas Eve finds the plantation rich with unexpected things. Unusual sounds and colors are everywhere. Happy voices rise above the whispering and rustling of paper wrappings, fires crackle and heighten and shed a rosy glow over the Christmas decorations and warn the outside darkness to keep away. As the first stars twinkle out, the whole world becomes radiant with a light which does not come from the sky, because once, long ago, the Star of Bethlehem shone just so above the manger where Christ Jesus was born. The fields lie quiet, the hills away over the river are folded with hazy blue, and the hearts of human beings beat softly because He who could heal the sick and raise the dead and make the sinful sinless was born on just such a night.

Suppers are eaten early so that the fires can be covered and the houses closed by the time the old cowbell starts ringing to·tell the people that the time for watch-night meeting in the Quarters is near. Nobody wants to be late, although the meeting lasts until dawn.

The cows are left unmilked with their calves, for all creatures are alike on Christmas Eve night, and mothers, whether they are beasts or women, whether they pray in churches or in stables and stalls, want their children close beside them when they kneel at midnight to pray to the great Father of us all.

Wheels creak along the roads that lead through the fields toward the Quarters, for they carry heavy loads of people. The old meeting benches sag with the weight of so many who have come to worship. Heads are bowed and glad tears are shed as the story of the first Christmas is read from the Book, and Christians are reminded that the sky holds a resting-place for them, that in Heaven many mansions have room for all who need peace and comfort.

Solemn, soul-stirring old hymns, lined out two lines at a time in the deep, booming voice of the prayer leader, are sung until midnight, and prayers lifted high by earnest, reverent voices pleading with the Most High for His blessing and protection rise and fall like breakers on the beach. But as soon as the cocks crow to announce that middle-night, the holy hour, has come, then the prayers change into rejoicing. The old meeting-house walls ring with exultant voices, the old floor boards give with the beating of so many shouting feet. All night long singing voices float out into the darkness and join the blurred songs of the wind in the trees until the morning star rides high in the sky and the Christmas sun rises shouting in the east. Then the benediction is said.

The cock crowing for sunrise is scarcely over when the servants steal into the Big House on tiptoe so they can catch everybody there with a shouted "Christmas Gift!" before the kitchen fire is even started or the water put on to boil for the early morning coffee.

This is an old game. Everybody tries to catch everybody else and win an extra Christmas gift. Kind old maumas arrive before breakfast is over, fetching presents of new-laid eggs or fat pullet chickens tied by the legs, and their thanks for their gifts—aprons or sweets or fruits, or whatever else has been prepared for them—are expressed in the most charming, gracious words accompanied by the most graceful curtsies. Gentle old men fetch bags of peanuts or ears of popcorn or bottles of home-made sirup.

The cook forgets the heavy day's work ahead of him and joins heartily in the singing of Christmas spirituals out in the yard. The words of the beautiful songs are few, but their refrains repeated over and over in a thundering swirl unite us all in voice and faith and joy and help us to know that Christmas Day is the best day of our year.

And Christmas Week is our best week. Every night the big drum booms out with an invitation to a Christmas-tree party at some cabin. The Big Houses at the neighboring plantations are filled with fun until New Year's Day comes and ends the glad holiday season.

When nothing is left of the merry-making but withered holly and faded mistletoe and the few red embers that still shine among the hickory ashes of the Christmas backlog, we rejoice that we are spared to pause and wonder over that strange miracle we call life.

HOW COME CHRISTMAS?

A MODERN MORALITY

BY ROARK BRADFORD

SCENE: *Corner in rural Negro church by the stove. The stove is old, and the pipe is held approximately erect by guywires, but a cheerful fire is evident through cracks in the stove, and the woodbox is well filled. Six children sit on a bench which has been shifted to face the stove, and the Reverend stands between them and the stove. A hat-rack on the wall supports sprigs of holly and one "plug" hat. A win-*

dow is festooned with holly, long strips of red paper, and strings of popcorn. A small Christmas bell and a tiny American flag are the only "store bought" decorations.

REVEREND—Well, hyar we is, chilluns, and hyar hit is Christmas. Now we all knows we's hyar 'cause hit's Christmas, don't we? But what I want to know is, who gonter tell me how come hit's Christmas?

WILLIE—'Cause old Sandy Claus come around about dis time er de year, clawin' all de good chilluns wid presents.

CHRISTINE—Dat ain't right, is hit, Revund? Hit's Christmas 'cause de Poor Little Jesus was bawned on Christmas, ain't hit, Revund?

REVEREND—Well, bofe er dem is mighty good answers. Old Sandy Claus do happen around about dis time er de year wid presents, and de Poor Little Jesus sho was bawned on Christmas Day. Now, de question is, did old Sandy Claus start clawin' chillun wid presents before de Poor Little Jesus got bawned, or did de Little Jesus git bawned before old Sandy Claus started gittin' around?

WILLIE—I bet old Sandy Claus was clawin' chilluns before de Poor Little Jesus started studdin' about gittin' bawned.

CHRISTINE—Naw, suh. De Little Jesus comed first, didn't he, Revund?

WILLIE—Old Sandy Claus is de oldest. I seed his pitchers and I seed Jesus' pitchers and old Sandy Claus is a heap de oldest. His whiskers mighty nigh tetch de ground.

DELIA—Dat ain't right. Old Methuselah is de oldest, ain't he, Revund? Cause de Bible say

> *Methuselah was de oldest man of his time.*
> *He lived nine hund'ed and sixty-nine.*
> *And he died and went to heaven in due time.*

REVEREND—Methuselah was powerful old, all right.

WILLIE—He wa'n't no older den old Sandy Claus, I bet. Old Sandy Claus got a heap er whiskers.

CHRISTINE—But de Poor Little Jesus come first. He was hyar before old man Methuselah, wa'n't he, Revund?

REVEREND—He been hyar a powerful long time, all right.

WILLIE—So has old Sandy Claus. He got powerful long whiskers.

DELIA—Moses got a heap er whiskers too.

REVEREND—Yeah, Moses was a mighty old man, too, but de p'int is, how come Christmas git started bein' Christmas? Now who gonter tell me? 'Cause hyar hit is Christmas Day, wid ev'ybody happy and rejoicin' about, and hyar is us, settin' by de stove in de wa'm churchhouse, tawkin' about hit. But ain't nobody got no idee how come hit start bein' Christmas?

WILLIE—You can't fool old Sandy Claus about Christmas. He know, don't he, Revund? He jest lay around and watch and see how de chilluns mind dey maw, and den de fust thing you know he got his mind make up about who been good and who been bad, and den he just hauls off and has hisse'f a Christmas.

CHRISTINE—Yeah, but how come he know hit's time to haul off and have hisse'f a Christmas?

WILLIE—'Cause any time old Sandy Claus make up his mind to have Christmas, well, who gonter stop him?

CHRISTINE—Den how come he don't never make up his mind ontwell de middle er winter? How come he don't make up his mind on de Fou'th er July? Ev'ybody git good around de Fou'th er July, jest like Christmas, so's dey kin go to de picnic. But Sandy Claus ain't payin' no mind to dat cause hit ain't time for Christmas, is hit, Revund?

WILLIE—Cou'se he don't have Christmas on de Fou'th er July. 'Cause hit ain't no p'int in Sandy Claus clawin' ev'ybody when ev'ybody's goin' to de picnic, anyhow. Sandy Claus b'lieve in scatterin' de good stuff out, don't he, Revund? He say, "Well, hit ain't no p'int in me clawin' fo'ks when dey already havin' a good time goin' to de picnic. Maybe I better wait to de dead er winter when hit's too cold for de picnic." Ain't dat right, Revund?

REVEREND—Sandy Claus do b'lieve in scatterin' de good stuff about de seasons, Willie, and hit sho ain't no p'int in havin' Christmas on de Fou'th er July. 'Cause de Fou'th er July is got hit's own p'int. And who gonter tell me what de p'int er de Fou'th er July is?

CHORUS—

> Old Gawge Wash'n'ton whupped de kaing,
> And de eagle squalled, Let Freedom raing.

REVEREND—Dat's right. And dat was in de summertime, so ev'ybody went out and had a picnic 'cause dey was so glad dat Gawge Wash'n'ton whupped dat kaing. Now what's de p'int er Christmas?

WILLIE—Old Sandy Claus . . .

CHRISTINE—De Poor Little Jesus . . .

REVEREND—Well, hit seem like old Sandy Claus and de Poor Little Jesus bofe is mixed up in dis thing, f'm de way y'all chilluns looks at hit. And I reckon y'all is just about zackly right too. 'Cause dat's how hit is. Bofe of 'em is so mixed up in hit I can't tell which is which, hardly.

DELIA—Was dat before de Fou'th er July?

CHRISTINE—Cou'se hit was. Don't Christmas always come before de Fou'th er July?

WILLIE—Naw, suh. Hit's de Fou'th er July fust, and den hit's Christmas. Ain't dat right, Revund?

REVEREND—I b'lieve Christine got you dat time, Willie. Christmas do come before de Fou'th er July. 'Cause you see hit was at Christmas when old Gawge Wash'n'ton got mad at de kaing 'cause de kaing was gonter kill de Poor Little Jesus. And him and de kaing fit f'm Christmas to de Fou'th er July before old Gawge Wash'n'ton finally done dat kaing up.

WILLIE—And Gawge Wash'n'ton whupped dat kaing, didn't he?

REVEREND—He whupped de stuffin' outn him. He whupped him f'm Balmoral to Belial and den back again. He jest done dat kaing up so bad dat he jest natchally put kaingin' outn style, and ev'y since den, hit ain't been no more kaings to 'mount to much.

You see, kaings was bad fo'ks. Dey was mean. Dey'd druther kill you den leave you alone. You see a kaing wawkin' down de road, and you better light out across de field, 'cause de kaing would wawk up and chop yo' haid off. And de law couldn't tech him, cause he was de kaing.

So all de fo'ks got skeered er de kaing, 'cause dey didn't know how to do nothin' about hit. So ev'ybody went around, tryin' to stay on de good side of him. And all er dat is how come de Poor Little Jesus and Old Sandy Claus got mixed up wid gittin' Christmas goin'.

You see, one time hit was a little baby bawned name' de Poor Little Jesus, but didn't nobody know dat was his name yit. Dey knew he was a powerful smart and powerful purty little baby, but dey didn't know his name was de Poor Little Jesus. So, 'cause he was so smart and so purty, ev'ybody thought he was gonter grow up and be de kaing. So quick as dat news got spread around, ev'ybody jest about bust to git on de good side er de baby, 'cause dey figure efn dey start soon enough he'd grow up likin' 'em and not chop dey haids off.

So old Moses went over and give him a hund'ed dollars in gold. And old Methuselah went over and give him a diamond ring. And old Peter give him a fine white silk robe. And ev'ybody was runnin' in wid fine presents so de Poor Little Jesus wouldn't grow up and chop de haids off.

Ev'ybody but old Sandy Claus. Old Sandy Claus was kind er old and didn't git around much, and he didn't hyar de news dat de Poor Little Jesus was gonter grow up and be de kaing. So him and de old lady was settin' back by de fire one night, toastin' dey shins and tawkin' about dis and dat, when old Miz Sandy Claus up and remark, she say, "Sandy, I hyars Miss Mary got a brand new baby over at her house."

"Is dat a fack?" says Sandy Claus. "Well, well, hit's a mighty cold night to do anything like dat, ain't hit? But on de yuther hand, he'll be a heap er pleasure and fun for her next summer I reckon."

So de tawk went on, and finally old Sandy Claus remark dat hit was powerful lonesome around de house since all er de chilluns growed up and married off.

"Dey all married well," say Miz Sandy Claus, "and so I say, 'Good ruddance.' You ain't never had to git up and cyore dey colic and mend dey clothes, so you gittin' lonesome. Me, I love 'em all, but I'm glad dey's married and doin' well."

So de tawk run on like dat for a while, and den old Sandy Claus got up and got his hat. "I b'lieve," he say, "I'll drap over and see how dat baby's gittin' along. I ain't seed no chillun in so long I'm pyore hongry to lean my eyes up agin a baby."

"You ain't goin' out on a night like dis, is you?" say Miz Sandy Claus.

"Sho I'm goin' out on a night like dis," say Sandy Claus. "I'm pyore cravin' to see some chilluns."

"But hit's snowin' and goin' on," say Miz Sandy Claus. "You know yo' phthisic been develin' you, anyhow, and you'll git de chawley maw-buses sloppin' around in dis weather."

"No mind de tawk," say Sandy Claus. "Git me my umbrella and my overshoes. And you better git me a little somethin' to take along for a cradle gift, too, I reckon."

"You know hit ain't nothin' in de house for no cradle gift," say Miz Sandy Claus.

"Git somethin'," say Sandy Claus. "You got to give a new baby somethin', or else you got bad luck. Get me one er dem big red apples outn de kitchen."

"What kind er cradle gift is an apple?" say Miz Sandy Claus. "Don't you reckon dat baby git all de apples he want?"

"Git me de apple," say Sandy Claus. "Hit ain't much, one way you looks at hit. But f'm de way dat baby gonter look at de apple, hit'll be a heap."

So Sandy Claus got de apple and he lit out.

Well, when he got to Miss Mary's house ev'ybody was standin' around givin' de Poor Little Jesus presents. Fine presents. Made outn gold and silver and diamonds and silk, and all like dat. Dey had de presents stacked around dat baby so high you couldn't hardly see over 'em. So when ev'ybody seed old Sandy Claus come in dey looked to see what he brang. And when dey seed he didn't brang nothin' but a red apple, dey all laughed.

"Quick as dat boy grows up and gits to be de kaing," dey told him, "he gonter chop yo' haid off."

"No mind dat," say Sandy Claus. "Y'all jest stand back." And so he went up to de crib and he pushed away a handful er gold and silver and diamonds and stuff, and handed de Poor Little Jesus dat red apple. "Hyar, son," he say, "take dis old apple. See how she shines?"

And de Poor Little Jesus reached up and grabbed dat apple in bofe hands, and laughed jest as brash as you please!

Den Sandy Claus tuck and tickled him under de chin wid his before finger, and say, "Goodly-goodly-goodly." And de Poor Little Jesus laughed some more and he reached up and grabbed a fist full er old Sandy Claus' whiskers, and him and old Sandy Claus went round and round!

So about dat time, up stepped de Lawd. "I swear, old Sandy Claus," say de Lawd. "Betwixt dat apple and dem whiskers, de Poor Little Jesus ain't had so much fun since he been bawn."

So Sandy Claus stepped back and bowed low and give de Lawd hy-dy, and say, "I didn't know ev'ybody was chiv-areein', or else I'd a stayed at home. I didn't had nothin' much to bring dis time, 'cause you see how hit's been dis year. De dry weather and de bull weevils got mighty nigh all de cotton, and de old lady been kind er puny—"

"Dat's all right, Sandy," say de Lawd. "Gold and silver have I a heap of. But verily you sho do know how to handle yo'se'f around de chilluns."

"Well, Lawd," say Sandy Claus, "I don't know much about chilluns. Me and de old lady raised up fou'teen. But she done most er de work. Me, I jest likes 'em and I manages to git along wid 'em."

"You sho do git along wid 'em good," say de Lawd.

"Hit's easy to do what you likes to do," say Sandy Claus.

"Well," say de Lawd, "hit might be somethin' in dat, too. But de trouble wid my world is, hit ain't enough people which likes to do de right thing. But you likes to do wid chilluns, and dat's what I needs. So stand still and shet yo' eyes whilst I passes a miracle on you."

So Sandy Claus stood still and shet his eyes, and de Lawd r'ared back and passed a miracle on him and say, "Old Sandy Claus, live forever, and make my chilluns happy."

So Sandy Claus opened his eyes and say, "Thank you kindly, Lawd. But do I got to keep 'em happy all de time? Dat's a purty big job. Hit'd be a heap er fun, but still and at de same time—"

"Yeah, I knows about chilluns, too," say de Lawd. "Chilluns got to fret and git in devilment ev'y now and den and git a whuppin' f'm dey maw, or else dey skin won't git loose so's dey kin grow. But you jest keep yo' eyes on 'em and make 'em all happy about once a year. How's dat?"

"Dat's fine," say Sandy Claus. "Hit'll be a heap er fun, too. What time er de year you speck I better make 'em happy, Lawd?"

"Christmas suit me," say de Lawd, "efn hit's all o.k. wid you."

"Hit's jest about right for me," say old Sandy Claus.

So ev'y since dat day and time old Sandy Claus been clawin' de chilluns on Christmas, and dat's on de same day dat de Poor Little Jesus got bawned. 'Cause dat's de way de Lawd runs things. O' cou'se de Lawd knowed hit wa'n't gonter be long before de Poor Little Jesus growed up and got to be a man. And when he done dat, all de grown fo'ks had him so's dey c'd moan they sins away and lay they burdens down on him, and git happy in they hearts. De Lawd made Jesus for de grown fo'ks. But de Lawd know de chilluns got to have some fun, too, so dat's how come hit's Sandy Claus and Christmas and all.

THE GIFT OF THE MAGI

By O. Henry

ONE dollar and eighty-seven cents. That was àll. And sixty cents of it was in pennies. Pennies saved one and two at a time by bulldozing the grocer and the vegetable man and the butcher until one's cheeks burned with the silent imputation of parsimony that such close dealing implied. Three times Della counted it. One dollar and eighty-seven cents. And the next day would be Christmas.

There was clearly nothing to do but flop down on the shabby little couch and howl. So Della did it. Which instigates the moral reflection that life is made up of sobs, sniffles, and smiles, with sniffles predominating.

While the mistress of the home is gradually subsiding from the first stage to the second, take a look at the home. A furnished flat at eight dollars per week. It did not exactly beggar description, but it certainly had that word on the lookout for the mendicancy squad.

In the vestibule below was a letter-box into which no letter would go, and an electric button from which no mortal finger could coax a ring. Also appertaining thereunto was a card bearing the name "Mr. James Dillingham Young."

The "Dillingham" had been flung to the breeze during a former period of prosperity when its possessor was being paid thirty dollars per week. Now, when the income was shrunk to twenty dollars, the letters of "Dillingham" looked blurred, as though they were thinking seriously of contracting to a modest and unassuming D. But whenever Mr. James Dillingham Young came home and reached his flat above he was called "Jim" and greatly hugged by Mrs. James Dillingham Young, already introduced to you as Della. Which is all very good.

Della finished her cry and attended to her cheeks with a powderpuff. She stood by the window and looked out dully at a gray cat walking a gray fence in a gray back yard. Tomorrow would be Christmas Day, and she had only $1.87 with which to buy Jim a present. She had been saving every penny she could for months, with this result. Twenty dollars a week doesn't go far. Expenses had been greater than she had calculated. They always are. Only $1.87 to buy a present for Jim. Her Jim. Many a happy hour she had spent planning for something nice for him. Something fine and rare and sterling—something just a little bit near to being worthy of the honor of being owned by Jim.

There was a pier-glass between the windows of the room. Perhaps you have seen a pier-glass in an eight-dollar flat. A very thin and very agile person may, by observing his reflection in a rapid sequence of longitudinal strips, obtain a fairly accurate conception of his looks. Della, being slender, had mastered the art.

Suddenly she whirled from the window and stood before the glass. Her eyes were shining brilliantly, but her face had lost its color within twenty seconds. Rapidly she pulled down her hair and let it fall to its full length.

Now, there were two possessions of the James Dillingham Youngs in which they both took a mighty pride. One was Jim's gold watch that had been his father's and his grandfather's. The other was Della's hair. Had the Queen of Sheba lived in the flat across the airshaft, Della would have let her hair hang out the window some day to dry just to depreciate Her Majesty's jewels and gifts. Had King Solomon been the janitor, with all his treasures piled up in the basement, Jim would have pulled out his watch every time he passed, just to see him pluck at his beard from envy.

So now Della's beautiful hair fell about her, rippling and shining like a cascade of brown waters. She did it up again nervously and quickly. Once she faltered for a minute and stood still while a tear or two splashed on the worn red carpet.

On went her old brown jacket; on went her old brown hat. With a whirl of skirts and with the brilliant sparkle still in her eyes, she fluttered out the door and down the stairs to the street.

Where she stopped the sign read: "Mme. Sofronie. Hair Goods of All Kinds." One flight up Della ran, and collected herself, panting. Madame, large, too white, chilly, hardly looked the "Sofronie."

"Will you buy my hair?" asked Della.

"I buy hair," said Madame. "Take yer hat off and let's have a sight at the looks of it."

Down rippled the brown cascade.

"Twenty dollars," said Madame, lifting the mass with a practiced hand.

"Give it to me quick," said Della.

Oh, and the next two hours tripped by on rosy wings. Forget the hashed metaphor. She was ransacking the stores for Jim's present.

She found it at last. It surely had been made for Jim and no one

else. There was no other like it in any of the stores, and she had turned
all of them inside out. It was a platinum watch-chain, simple and
chaste in design, properly proclaiming its value by substance alone
and not by meretricious ornamentation—as all good things should
do. It was even worthy of The Watch. As soon as she saw it she knew
that it must be Jim's. It was like him. Quietness and value—the description applied to both. Twenty-one dollars they took from her for
it, and she hurried home with the eighty-seven cents. With that chain
on his watch Jim might be properly anxious about the time in any
company. Grand as the watch was, he sometimes looked at it on the
sly on account of the old leather strap that he used in place of a chain.

When Della reached home her intoxication gave way a little to
prudence and reason. She got out her curling-irons and lighted the
gas and went to work repairing the ravages made by generosity added
to love. Which is always a tremendous task, dear friends—a mammoth
task.

Within forty minutes her head was covered with tiny close-lying
curls that made her look wonderfully like a truant schoolboy. She
looked at her reflection in the mirror long, carefully, and critically.

"If Jim doesn't kill me," she said to herself, "before he takes a second look at me, he'll say I look like a Coney Island chorus girl. But
what could I do—oh! what could I do with a dollar and eighty-seven
cents?"

At seven o'clock the coffee was made and the frying-pan was on
the back of the stove, hot and ready to cook the chops.

Jim was never late. Della doubled the watch chain in her hand
and sat on the corner of the table near the door that he always entered. Then she heard his step on the stair away down on the first
flight, and she turned white for just a moment. She had a habit of
saying little silent prayers about the simplest everyday things, and
now she whispered: "Please, God, make him think I am still pretty."

The door opened and Jim stepped in and closed it. He looked
thin and very serious. Poor fellow, he was only twenty-two—and to
be burdened with a family! He needed a new overcoat and he was
without gloves.

Jim stepped inside the door, as immovable as a setter at the scent of quail. His eyes were fixed upon Della, and there was an expression in them that she could not read, and it terrified her. It was not anger, nor surprise, nor disapproval, nor horror, nor any of the sentiments that she had been prepared for. He simply stared at her fixedly with that peculiar expression on his face.

Della wriggled off the table and went for him.

"Jim, darling," she cried, "don't look at me that way. I had my hair cut off and sold it because I couldn't have lived through Christmas without giving you a present. It'll grow out again—you won't mind, will you? I just had to do it. My hair grows awfully fast. Say 'Merry Christmas!' Jim, and let's be happy. You don't know what a nice— what a beautiful, nice gift I've got for you."

"You've cut off your hair?" asked Jim, laboriously, as if he had not arrived at that patent fact yet even after the hardest mental labor.

"Cut it off and sold it," said Della. "Don't you like me just as well, anyhow? I'm me without my hair, ain't I?"

Jim looked about the room curiously.

"You say your hair is gone?" he said, with an air almost of idiocy.

"You needn't look for it," said Della. "It's sold, I tell you—sold and gone, too. It's Christmas Eve, boy. Be good to me, for it went for you. Maybe the hairs of my head were numbered," she went on with a sudden serious sweetness, "but nobody could ever count my love for you. Shall I put the chops on, Jim?"

Out of his trance Jim seemed to quickly wake. He enfolded his Della. For ten seconds let us regard with discreet scrutiny some inconsequential object in the other direction. Eight dollars a week or a million a year—what is the difference? A mathematician or a wit would give you the wrong answer. The Magi brought valuable gifts, but that was not among them. This dark assertion will be illuminated later on.

Jim drew a package from his overcoat pocket and threw it upon the table.

"Don't make any mistake, Dell," he said, "about me. I don't think there's anything in the way of a haircut or a shave or a shampoo that could make me like my girl any less. But if you'll unwrap that package you may see why you had me going awhile at first."

White fingers and nimble tore at the string and paper. And then an ecstatic scream of joy; and then, alas! a quick feminine change to hysterical tears and wails, necessitating the immediate employment of all the comforting powers of the lord of the flat.

For there lay The Combs—the set of combs that Della had worshiped for long in a Broadway window. Beautiful combs, pure tortoise shell, with jeweled rims—just the shade to wear in the beautiful vanished hair. They were expensive combs, she knew, and her heart had simply craved and yearned over them without the least hope of possession. And now they were hers, but the tresses that should have adorned the coveted adornments were gone.

But she hugged them to her bosom, and at length she was able to look up with dim eyes and a smile and say: "My hair grows so fast, Jim!"

And then Della leaped up like a little singed cat and cried, "Oh, oh!"

Jim had not yet seen his beautiful present. She held it out to him eagerly upon her open palm. The dull precious metal seemed to flash with a reflection of her bright and ardent spirit.

"Isn't it a dandy, Jim? I hunted all over town to find it. You'll have to look at the time a hundred times a day now. Give me your watch. I want to see how it looks on it."

Instead of obeying, Jim tumbled down on the couch and put his hands under the back of his head and smiled.

"Dell," said he, "let's put our Christmas presents away and keep 'em awhile. They're too nice to use just at present. I sold the watch to get the money to buy your combs. And now suppose you put the chops on."

The Magi, as you know, were wise men—wonderfully wise men—who brought gifts to the Babe in the manger. They invented the art of giving Christmas presents. Being wise, their gifts were no doubt wise ones, possibly bearing the privilege of exchange in case of duplication. And here I have lamely related to you the uneventful chronicle of two foolish children in a flat who most unwisely sacrificed for each other the greatest treasures of their house. But in a last word to the wise of these days let it be said that of all who give gifts these two were the wisest. Of all who give and receive gifts, such as they are wisest. Everywhere they are wisest. They are the Magi.

GOING THE ROUNDS ON CHRISTMAS EVE WITH THE MELLSTOCK CHOIR

BY THOMAS HARDY

SHORTLY after ten o'clock the singing-boys arrived at the tranter's house, which was invariably the place of meeting, and preparations were made for the start. The older men and musicians wore thick coats, with stiff perpendicular collars, and coloured handkerchiefs wound round and round the neck till the end came to hand, over all which they just showed their ears and noses, like people looking over a wall. The remainder, stalwart ruddy men and boys, were dressed mainly in snow-white smock-frocks, embroidered upon the shoulders and breasts in ornamental forms of hearts, diamonds, and zigzags. The cider-mug was emptied for the ninth time, the music-books were arranged, and the pieces finally decided upon. The boys in the meantime put the old horn-lanterns in order, cut candles into short lengths to fit the lanterns; and, a thin fleece of snow having fallen since the early part of the evening, those who had no leggings went to the stable and wound wisps of hay round their ankles to keep the insidious flakes from the interior of their boots.

Mellstock was a parish of considerable acreage, the hamlets composing it lying at a much greater distance from each other than is ordinarily the case. Hence several hours were consumed in playing and singing within hearing of every family, even if but a single air were bestowed on each. . . .

Old William Dewy, with the violoncello, played the bass; his grandson Dick the treble violin; and Reuben and Michael Mail the tenor and second violins respectively. The singers consisted of four men and seven boys, upon whom devolved the task of carrying and attending to the lanterns, and holding the books open for the players. Directly music was the theme old William ever and instinctively came to the front.

"Now mind, neighbours," he said, as they all went out one by one at the door, he himself holding it ajar and regarding them with a critical face as they passed, like a shepherd counting out his sheep. "You two counter-boys, keep your ears open to Michael's fingering, and don't ye go straying into the treble part along o' Dick and his set, as ye did last year; and mind this especially when we be in 'Arise, and hail.' Billy Chimlen, don't you sing quite so raving mad as you fain would; and, all o' ye, whatever ye do, keep from making a great scuffle on the ground when we go in at people's gates; but go quietly, so as to strike up all of a sudden, like spirits."

Just before the clock struck twelve they lighted the lanterns and started. . . . Most of the outlying homesteads and hamlets had been visited by about two o'clock. . . .

"Times have changed from the times they used to be," said Mail, regarding nobody can tell what interesting old panoramas with an inward eye, and letting his outward glance rest on the ground because it was as convenient a position as any. "People don't care much about us now! I've been thinking we must be almost the last left in the county of the old string players? Barrel-organs, and the things next door to 'em that you blow wi' your foot, have come in terribly of late years."

"Ay!" said Bowman shaking his head; and old William on seeing him did the same thing.

"More's the pity," replied another. "Time was—long and merry ago now!—when not one of the varmits was to be heard of; but it served some of the quires right. They should have stuck to strings as we did, and kept out clarinets, and done away with serpents. If you'd thrive in musical religion, stick to strings says I."

"Strings be safe soul-lifters, as far as that do go," said Mr. Spinks.

"Yet there's worse things than serpents," said Mr. Penny. "Old things pass away, 'tis true; but a serpent was a good old note: a deep rich note was the serpent."

"Clar'nets, however, be bad at all times," said Michael Mail. "One Christmas—years agone now, years—I went the rounds wi' the Weatherbury quire. 'Twas a hard frosty night, and the keys of all the clar'nets froze—ah, they did freeze!—so that 'twas like drawing a cork every time a key was opened; and the players o' 'em had to go into a hedger-and-ditcher's chimley-corner, and thaw their clar'nets every now and then. An icicle o' spet hung down from the end of every man's clar'net a span long; and as to fingers—well, there, if ye'll believe me, we had no fingers at all, to our knowing."

"I can well bring back to my mind," said Mr. Penny, "what I said to poor Joseph Ryme (who took the treble part in Chalk-Newton Church for two-and-forty year) when they thought of having clar'nets there. 'Joseph,' I said says I, 'depend upon't, if so be you have them tooting clar'nets you'll spoil the whole set-out. Clar'nets were not made for the service of the Lard; you can see it by looking at 'em,' I said. And what came o't? Why, souls, the parson set up a barrel-organ on his own account within two years o' the time I spoke, and the old quire went to nothing.'

"As far as look is concerned," said the tranter, "I don't for my part see that a fiddle is much nearer heaven than a clar'net. 'Tis further off. There's always a rakish, scampish twist about a fiddle's looks that seems to say the Wicked One had a hand in making o'en; while angels be supposed to play clar'nets in heaven, or som'at like 'em, if ye may believe picters."

"Robert Penny, you was in the right," broke in the oldest Dewy. "They should ha' stuck to strings. Your brass-man is a rafting dog—well and good; your reed-man is a dab at stirring ye—well and good; your drum-man is a rare bowel-shaker—good again. But I don't care who hears me say it, nothing will spak to your heart wi' the sweetness o' the man of strings!"

"Strings for ever!" said little Jimmy.

"Strings alone would have held their ground against all the new comers in creation." ("True, true!" said Bowman.) "But clarinets was death." ("Death they was!" said Mr. Penny.) "And harmonions," William continued in a louder voice, and getting excited by these signs of approval, "harmonions and barrel-organs" ("Ah!" and groans from Spinks) "be miserable—what shall I call 'em?—miserable—"

"Sinners," suggested Jimmy, who made large strides like the men and did not lag behind with the other little boys.

"Miserable dumbledores!"

"Right, William, and so they be—miserable dumbledores!" said the choir with unanimity.

By this time they were crossing to a gate in the direction of the school which, standing on a slight eminence at the junction of three ways, now rose in unvarying and dark flatness against the sky. The instruments were retuned, and all the band entered the school enclosure, enjoined by old William to keep upon the grass.

"Number seventy-eight," he softly gave out as they formed round in a semicircle, the boys opening the lanterns to get a clearer light, and directing their rays on the books.

Then passed forth into the quiet night an ancient and time-worn hymn, embodying a quaint Christianity in words orally transmitted from father to son through several generations down to the present characters, who sang them out right earnestly:

> "Remember Adam's fall,
> 　O thou Man:
> Remember Adam's fall
> 　From Heaven to Hell.
> Remember Adam's fall;
> How he hath condemn'd all
> In Hell perpetual
> 　There for to dwell.
>
> Remember God's goodnesse,
> 　O thou Man:
> Remember God's goodnesse,
> 　His promise made.

Remember God's goodnesse;
He sent His Son sinlesse
Our ails for to redress;
    Be not afraid!

In Bethlehem He was born,
    O thou Man:
In Bethlehem He was born,
    For mankind's sake.
In Bethlehem He was born,
Christmas-day i' the morn:
Our Saviour thought no scorn
    Our faults to take.

Give thanks to God alway,
    O thou Man:
Give thanks to God alway
    With heart-most joy.
Give thanks to God alway
On this our joyful day:
Let all men sing and say,
    Holy, Holy!"

Having concluded the last note they listened for a minute or two. but found that no sound issued from the schoolhouse.

"Four breaths, and then, 'O, what unbounded goodness!' number fifty-nine," said William.

This was duly gone through, and no notice whatever seemed to be taken of the performance.

"Good guide us, surely 'tisn't a' empty house, as befell us in the year thirty-nine and forty-three!" said old Dewy.

"Perhaps she's jist come from some musical city, and sneers at our doings?" the tranter whispered.

"Od rabbit her!" said Mr. Penny, with an annihilating look at a corner of the school chimney, "I don't quite stomach her, if this is it. Your plain music well done is as worthy as your other sort done bad, a' b'lieve, souls; so say I."

"Four breaths, and then the last," said the leader authoritatively.

" 'Rejoice, ye Tenants of the Earth,' number sixty-four."

At the close, waiting yet another minute, he said in a clear loud voice, as he had said in the village at that hour and season for the previous forty years, "A Merry Christmas to ye!"

When the expectant stillness consequent upon the exclamation had nearly died out of them all, an increasing light made itself visible in one of the windows of the upper floor. It came so close to the blind that the exact position of the flame could be perceived from the outside. Remaining steady for an instant, the blind went upward from before it, revealing to thirty concentrated eyes a young girl framed as a picture by the window architrave, and unconsciously illuminating her countenance to a vivid brightness by a candle she held in her left hand, close to her face, her right hand being extended to the side of the window.

Opening the window, she said lightly and warmly—

"Thank you, singers, thank you!"

Together went the window quickly and quietly, and the blind started downward on its return to its place. Her fair forehead and eyes vanished; her little mouth; her neck and shoulders; all of her. Then the spot of candlelight shone nebulously as before; then it moved away.

"How pretty!" exclaimed Dick Dewy.

"If she'd been rale wexwork she couldn't ha' been comelier," said Michael Mail.

"As near a thing to a spiritual vision as ever *I* wish to see!" said tranter Dewy.

"O, sich I never, never see!" said Leaf fervently.

All the rest, after clearing their throats and adjusting their hats, agreed that such a sight was worth singing for.

"Now to Farmer Shiner's, and then replenish our insides, father?" said the tranter.

"Wi' all my heart," said old William, shouldering his bass-viol.

From *Under the Greenwood Tree*

CHRISTMAS MORNING IN MELLSTOCK CHURCH

By Thomas Hardy

THE gallery of Mellstock Church had a status and sentiment of its own. A stranger there was regarded with a feeling altogether differing from that of the congregation below towards him. Banished from the nave as an intruder whom no originality could make interesting, he was received above as a curiosity that no unfitness could render dull. The gallery, too, looked down upon and knew the habits of the nave to its remotest peculiarity, and had an extensive stock of exclusive information about it; whilst the nave knew nothing of the gallery folk, as gallery folk, beyond their loud-sounding minims and chest notes. . . .

Old William sat in the centre of the front row, his violoncello between his knees and two singers on each hand. Behind him, on the left, came the treble singers and Dick; and on the right the tranter and the tenors. Further back was old Mail with the altos and supernumeraries. . . .

The music on Christmas mornings was frequently below the standard of church-performances at other times. The boys were sleepy from the heavy exertions of the night; the men were slightly wearied; and now, in addition to these constant reasons, there was a dampness in the atmosphere that still further aggravated the evil. Their strings, from the recent long exposure to the night air, rose whole semitones, and snapped with a loud twang at the most silent moment; which necessitated more retiring than ever to the back of the gallery, and made the gallery throats quite husky with the quantity of coughing and hemming required for tuning in. The vicar looked cross.

When the singing was in progress there was suddenly discovered to be a strong and shrill reinforcement from some point, ultimately found to be the school-girls' aisle. At every attempt it grew bolder

and more distinct. At the third time of singing, these intrusive feminine voices were as mighty as those of the regular singers; in fact, the
flood of sound from this quarter assumed such an individuality, that
it had a time, a key, almost a tune of its own, surging upwards when
the gallery plunged downwards, and the reverse.

Now this had never happened before within the memory of man.
The girls, like the rest of the congregation, had always been humble
and respectful followers of the gallery; singing at sixes and sevens
if without gallery leaders; never interfering with the ordinances of
these practised artists—having no will, union, power, or proclivity
except it was given them from the established choir enthroned above
them.

A good deal of desperation became noticeable in the gallery
throats and strings, which continued throughout the musical portion
of the service. Directly the fiddles were laid down, Mr. Penny's
spectacles put in their sheath, and the text had been given out, an
indignant whispering began.

"Did ye hear that, souls?" Mr. Penny said, in a groaning breath.

"Brazen-faced hussies!" said Bowman.

"True; why, they were every note as loud as we, fiddles and all, if
not louder!"

"Fiddles and all!" echoed Bowman bitterly.

"Shall anything saucier be found than united 'ooman?" Mr. Spinks
murmured.

"What I want to know is," said the tranter (as if he knew already,
but that civilization required the form of words), "what business
people have to tell maidens to sing like that when they don't sit in a
gallery, and never have entered one in their lives? That's the question, my sonnies."

" 'Tis the gallery have got to sing, all the world knows," said Mr.
Penny. "Why, souls, what's the use o' the ancients spending scores of
pounds to build galleries if people down in the lowest depths of the
church sing like that at a moment's notice?"

"Really, I think we useless ones had better march out of the church,
fiddles and all!" said Mr. Spinks, with a laugh which, to a stranger,

would have sounded mild and real. Only the initiated body of men he addressed could understand the horrible bitterness of irony that lurked under the quiet words "useless ones," and the ghastliness of the laughter apparently so natural.

"Never mind! Let 'em sing too—'twill make it all the louder—hee, hee!" said Leaf.

"Thomas Leaf, Thomas Leaf! Where have you lived all your life?" said grandfather William sternly.

The quailing Leaf tried to look as if he had lived nowhere at all. "When all's said and done, my sonnies," Reuben said, "there'd have been no real harm in their singing if they had let nobody hear 'em, and only jined in now and then."

From *Under the Greenwood Tree*

CRISP NEW BILLS FOR MR. TEAGLE

By Frank Sullivan

COMING down in the elevator, Clement Teagle noticed an unwonted cordiality in Steve, the elevator boy, and Harry, the doorman, but thought nothing of it until he stopped at the bank on the corner to cash a cheque and noticed the date.

December the twenty-fourth.

"Good gosh," Mr. Teagle thought, "I haven't bought a present for Essie yet."

Then he remembered Steve and Harry.

His eye caught a legend on a Christmas placard on the wall. "It is more blessed to give than to receive," said the placard.

"Oh, yeah?" remarked Mr. Teagle, who, alas, was somewhat of a cynic.

Grumbling, he tore up the cheque he had started to write, and made out another, for a larger amount.

"Will you please give me new bills?" he asked.

"Indeed I shall," said Mr. Freyer, the teller, cordially.

He counted out one hundred dollars in new bills—*crisp* new bills—and passed them over to Mr. Teagle.

Then he tore up the cheque and handed the fragments to Mr. Teagle.

"Don't be alarmed, Mr. Teagle," said Mr. Freyer. "The bank of the Manhattan Company wants you to accept that one hundred dollars as a slight token of its esteem, with its best wishes for a Merry Christmas. You have been a loyal depositor here these many years. You have overdrawn fewer times than most of your fellow-depositors. You never argue about your monthly statements. You never feel insulted when a new teller identifies your signature before cashing your cheque. You are the kind of depositor who makes banking a joy, and I want to take this opportunity to tell you that we fellows around here, although we are not very demonstrative about that sort of thing, love you very much. A merry Christmas to you."

"You mean the bank is *giving* me this money?" said Mr. Teagle.

"That is the impression I was trying to convey," said Mr. Freyer, with a chuckle.

"Why—uh, thanks, Mr. Freyer. And—and thank the bank. This is—um—quite a surprise."

"Say no more about it, Mr. Teagle. And every Christmas joy to you, sir."

When Mr. Teagle left the bank he was somewhat perturbed, and a little stunned. He went back to the apartment to place the crisp new bills in envelopes for the boys, and as he left the elevator at his floor, Steve handed him an envelope.

"Merry Christmas, Mr. Teagle," said Steve.

"Thanks, Steve," said Mr. Teagle. "I'll—I'll be wishing you one a little later," he added significantly.

"You don't need to, Mr. Teagle," said Steve. "A man like you wishes the whole world a merry Christmas every day, just by living."

"Oh, Steve, damn nice of you to say that, but I'm sure it's not deserved," said Mr. Teagle, modestly struggling with a feeling that Steve spoke no more than the simple truth.

"Well, I guess we won't argue about *that*," said Steve, gazing affectionately at Mr. Teagle.

"I really believe that lad meant it," thought Mr. Teagle, as he let himself into the apartment. "I really believe he did."

Mr. Teagle opened the envelope Steve had handed him. A crisp new five-dollar bill fell out.

Downstairs in the lobby, a few minutes later, Steve was protesting.

"I tell you it wasn't a mistake, Mr. Teagle. I put the bill in there on purpose. For you."

"Steve, I couldn't take—"

"But you *can* take it, and you *will*, Mr. Teagle. And a very merry Christmas to you."

"Then you accept this, Steve, and a merry Christmas to *you*."

"Oh, no, Mr. Teagle. Not this year. You have been pretty swell to we fellows all the years you've lived here. Now it's our turn."

"You bet it is," said Harry the doorman, joining them and pressing a crisp new ten-dollar bill into Mr. Teagle's hand. "Merry Christmas, Mr. Teagle. Buy yourself something foolish with this. I only wish it could be more, but I've had rather a bad year in the market."

"I think the boys on the night-shift have a little surprise for Mr. Teagle, too," said Steve, with a twinkle in his eye.

Just then the superintendent came up.

"Well, well, well," he said jovially. "Who have we got here? Mr. Teagle, it may interest you to hear that I've been having a little chat about you with a certain old gentleman with a long, snowy beard and twinkling little eyes. Know who I mean?"

"Santa Claus?" Mr. Teagle asked.

"None other. And guess what! He asked me if you had been a good boy this year, and I was delighted to be able to tell him you had been, that you hadn't complained about the heat, hadn't run your radio after eleven at night, and hadn't had any late parties. Well, sir, you should have seen old Santa's face. He was tickled to hear it. Said he always knew you were a good boy. And what do you suppose he did?"

"What?" asked Mr. Teagle.

"He asked me to give you this and to tell you to buy yourself something for Christmas with it. Something foolish."

The super pressed a crisp new twenty-dollar bill upon Mr. Teagle.

"Merry Christmas, Mr. Teagle," said the super.

"Merry Christmas, Mr. Teagle," said Steve the elevator boy.

"Merry Christmas, Mr. Teagle," said Harry the doorman.

"Merry Christmas," said Mr. Teagle, in a voice you could scarcely hear. Remembering that he had to buy a present for Essie, he walked out, with the air of a bewildered gazelle. He was in a very, very puzzled state of mind as he walked down East Fifty-first Street, an agitation which did not subside when the proprietor of a cigar-store on Third Avenue rushed out, pressed a box of cigars on him, cried, "Merry Christmas, stranger!" and rushed back into his shop without another word.

To rush out of your store and give a box of cigars to a perfect stranger! And those boys at the apartment house! *And* the super!

Mr. Teagle thought of the many times he had grumbled at being kept waiting a few minutes for the elevator or for a taxi. He felt ashamed. "By George," Mr. Teagle thought, "maybe Dickens was right."

Mr. Teagle approached the business of choosing a present for his wife in a far less carping spirit than was his Christmas wont.

"I'll get Essie something that'll knock her eye out," he thought. "She's a good old girl and she deserves a lot of credit for living with a grouch like me all these years. The best is none too good for her."

Suiting the action to the word, Mr. Teagle turned in at Cartier's and asked to see some square-cut emeralds. He selected one that could have done duty on a traffic light.

"I'm afraid I haven't the cash on me," he told the clerk. "I'll give you a cheque, and you can call the bank and verify—"

"That will not be necessary, sir," said the clerk, with a radiant smile. "You are Mr. Clement Teagle, I believe. In that case, Cartier wishes you to accept this trinket with the Christmas greetings of the firm. We are only sorry that you did not see fit to choose a diamond stomacher. Cartier will feel honoured that one of its emeralds is adorning the finger of the wife of a man like Clement Teagle, a man four-square, a man who is a credit— All right, all right, all *right*, Mr. Teagle! Not another word, please. Cartier is adamant. You take this emerald or we may grow ugly about it. And don't lose it, sir, or I venture to say your good wife will give you Hail Columbia. Good day, sir, and God rest ye."

Mr. Teagle found himself on the street. He accosted the first passer-by.

"Excuse me, stranger, but would you mind pinching me?"

"Certainly not, certainly not," said the stranger, cheerily. "There. Feel better?"

"Yes. Thank you very much," said Mr. Teagle.

"Here, buy yourself something for Christmas," said the stranger, pressing Mr. Teagle's hand. Mr. Teagle looked in the hand and found himself the possessor of a crisp new fifty-dollar bill.

At Fifth Avenue and Fifty-seventh Street, a Park & Tilford attendant rushed out and draped a huge basket, bedecked with ribbons and holly, on Mr. Teagle's arm.

"Everything drinkable for the Yuletide dinner, with love and kisses from Park & Tilford," whispered the clerk jovially. "Tell your wife to be sure and put the champagne in ice early, so it will be nice and cold."

"Oh, come on, come on," protested the butcher at Madison Avenue and Sixty-first Street. "Don't tell me you're too loaded down to carry a simple little turkey home, with the affectionate Christmas wishes of Shaffer's Market."

Mr. Shaffer laughed the rich laugh of the contented butcher.

"Don't take me too seriously when I say 'simple little turkey,'" he said. "That bird you got would make Roosevelt's Christmas turkey look like a humming-bird. An undernourished humming-bird. Pay for it? Certainly you won't pay for it! What do you take me for? It's Christmas. And you are Clement Teagle."

"Am I?" said Mr. Teagle, humbly.

Long before he reached home, Mr. Teagle had had such a plethora of gifts pressed upon him by friendly strangers that there was nothing to do but load them into a taxi-cab. And Mr. Teagle was not quite as surprised as he might have been earlier in the day when the driver refused to accept any money, but grinned and said: "Let's just charge this trip to good old St. Nick."

"Why, Clem!" said Mrs. Teagle, when, with the aid of the entire house staff, Mr. Teagle had deposited his gifts in the dining-room. "Why, Clem, I already *bought* a turkey! Clem, you've been drinking."

"I have *not!*" Mr. Teagle shouted.

"Well, don't get on your high horse," said Mrs. Teagle. "It's Christmas Eve. I don't mind. Only—you know your stomach. And you do look funny."

"I may look funny, but I have not been drinking," Mr. Teagle insisted. "Look! H-h-h-h-h-h."

His breath was as the new-mown hay.

"See what I got you for Christmas, Essie." Mrs. Teagle opened the jewel-case and the emerald gleamed up at her. It was a moment before she could speak.

"No, Clem," she said. "You work too hard for your money. I don't deserve this. I won't take it from you. You've been too good to me as it is. I don't want any Christmas present from you, dear. I want to *give* you one—and oh, by the way, Clem, before I forget it, the funniest thing happened this afternoon. The income-tax man was here, the federal income-tax man. Said he just dropped in to wish you a merry Christmas. He left this cheque for your entire last year's income-tax. He said the Government wants to give it back to you as a token of affection and in recognition of your many superb qualities as a citizen and—oh, I can't remember everything he said, but he made quite a flowery speech about you, dear— Why, Clem, what's the matter?"

Mr. Teagle had burst into tears.

"A merry Christmas, Essie," he said, through his sobs, "and, in the language of Tiny Tim, 'God bless us every one.'"

A CHRISTMAS PRESENT FOR A LADY

By Myra Kelly

IT was the week before Christmas, and the First-Reader Class had, almost to a man, decided on the gifts to be lavished on "Teacher." She was quite unprepared for any such observance on the part of her small adherents, for her first study of the roll-book had shown her that its numerous Jacobs, Isidores, and Rachels belonged to a class to which Christmas Day was much as other days. And so she went serenely on her way, all unconscious of the swift and strict relation between her manner and her chances. She was, for instance, the only person in the room who did not know that her criticism of Isidore Belchatosky's hands and face cost her a tall "three for ten cents" candlestick and a plump box of candy.

But Morris Mogilewsky, whose love for Teacher was far greater than the combined loves of all the other children, had as yet no present to bestow. That his "kind feeling" should be without proof when the lesser loves of Isidore Wishnewsky, Sadie Gonorowsky, and Bertha Binderwitz were taking the tangible but surprising forms which were daily exhibited to his confidential gaze, was more than he could bear. The knowledge saddened all his hours and was the more maddening because it could in no wise be shared by Teacher, who noticed his altered bearing and tried with all sorts of artful beguilements to make him happy and at ease. But her efforts served only to increase his unhappiness and his love. And he loved her! Oh, how he loved her! Since first his dreading eyes had clung for a breath's space to her "like man's shoes" and had then crept timidly upward past a black skirt, a "from silk" apron, a red "jumper," and "from gold" chain to her "light face," she had been mistress of his heart of hearts. That was more than three months ago. And well he remembered the day!

His mother had washed him horribly, and had taken him into the big, red school-house, so familiar from the outside, but so full of unknown terrors within. After his dusty little shoes had stumbled over the threshold he had passed from ordeal to ordeal until at last he was torn in mute and white-faced despair from his mother's skirts.

He was then dragged through long halls and up tall stairs by a large boy, who spoke to him disdainfully as "greenie," and cautioned him as to the laying down softly and taking up gently of those poor dusty shoes, so that his spirit was quite broken and his nerves were all unstrung when he was pushed into a room full of bright sunshine and of children who laughed at his frightened little face. The sunshine smote his timid eyes, the laughter smote his timid heart, and he turned to flee. But the door was shut, the large boy gone, and despair took him for its own.

Down upon the floor he dropped, and wailed, and wept, and kicked. It was then that he heard, for the first time the voice which now he loved. A hand was forced between his aching body and the floor, and the voice said:

"Why, my dear little chap, you mustn't cry like that. What's the matter?"

The hand was gentle and the question kind, and these, combined with a faint perfume suggestive of drug stores and barber shops—but nicer than either—made him uncover his hot little face. Kneeling beside him was a lady, and he forced his eyes to that perilous ascent; from shoes to skirt, from skirt to jumper, from jumper to face, they trailed in dread uncertainty, but at the face they stopped. They had found—rest.

Morris allowed himself to be gathered into the lady's arms and held upon her knee, and when his sobs no longer rent the very foundations of his pink and wide-spread tie, he answered her question in a voice as soft as his eyes, and as gently sad.

"I ain't so big, und I don't know where is my mamma."

So, having cast his troubles on the shoulders of the lady, he had added his throbbing head to the burden, and from that safe retreat had enjoyed his first day at school immensely.

Thereafter he had been the first to arrive every morning, and the last to leave every afternoon; and under the care of Teacher, his liege lady, he had grown in wisdom and love and happiness. But the greatest of these was love. And now, when the other boys and girls were planning surprises and gifts of price for Teacher, his hands were as empty as his heart was full. Appeal to his mother met with denial prompt and energetic.

"For what you go und make, over Christmas, presents? You ain't no Krisht; you should better have no kind feelings over Krishts, neither; your papa could to have a mad."

"Teacher ain't no Krisht," said Morris stoutly; "all the other fellows buys her presents, und I'm loving mit her too; it's polite I gives her presents the while I'm got such a kind feeling over her."

"Well, we ain't got no money for buy nothings," said Mrs. Mogilewsky. "No money, und your papa, he has all times a scare he shouldn't to get no more, the while the boss"—and here followed incomprehensible, but depressing, financial details, until the end of the interview found Morris and his mother sobbing and rocking in one another's arms. So Morris was helpless, his mother poor, and Teacher all unknowing.

And the great day, the Friday before Christmas came, and the school was, for the first half hour, quite mad. Doors opened suddenly and softly to admit small persons, clad in wondrous ways and bearing wondrous parcels. Room 18, generally so placid and so peaceful, was a howling wilderness full of brightly coloured, quickly changing groups of children, all whispering, all gurgling and all hiding queer bundles. A newcomer invariably caused a diversion; the assembled multitude, athirst for novelty, fell upon him and clamoured for a glimpse of his bundle and a statement of its price.

Teacher watched in dumb amaze. What could be the matter with the children, she wondered. They could not have guessed the shrouded something in the corner to be a Christmas-tree. What made them behave so queerly, and why did they look so strange? They seemed to have grown stout in a single night, and Teacher, as she noted this, marvelled greatly. The explanation was simple, though it came in alarming form. The sounds of revelry were pierced by a

long, shrill yell, and a pair of agitated legs sprang suddenly into view
between two desks. Teacher, rushing to the rescue, noted that the
legs formed the unsteady stem of an upturned mushroom of brown
flannel and green braid, which she recognized as the outward seeming of her cherished Bertha Binderwitz; and yet, when the desks were
forced to disgorge their prey, the legs restored to their normal position were found to support a fat child—and Bertha was best described as "skinny"—in a dress of the Stuart tartan tastefully
trimmed with purple. Investigation proved that Bertha's accumula-
tive taste in dress was an established custom. In nearly all cases the
glory of holiday attire was hung upon the solid foundation of everyday clothes as bunting is hung upon a building. The habit was economical of time, and produced a charming embonpoint.

Teacher, too, was more beautiful than ever. Her dress was blue,
and "very long down, like a lady," with bands of silk and scraps of
lace distributed with the eye of art. In her hair she wore a bow of
what Sadie Gonorowsky, whose father "worked by fancy goods," described as black "from plush ribbon—costs ten cents."

Isidore Belchatosky, relenting, was the first to lay tribute before
Teacher. He came forward with a sweet smile and a tall candlestick
—the candy had gone to its long home—and Teacher, for a moment,
could not be made to understand that all that length of bluish-white
china was really hers "for keeps."

"It's to-morrow holiday," Isidore assured her; "and we gives you
presents, the while we have a kind feeling. Candlesticks could to cost
twenty-five cents."

"It's a lie. Three for ten," said a voice in the background, but
Teacher hastened to respond to Isidore's test of her credulity:

"Indeed, they could. This candlestick could have cost fifty cents,
and it's just what I want. It is very good of you to bring me a present."

"You're welcome," said Isidore, retiring; and then, the ice being
broken, the First-Reader Class in a body rose to cast its gifts on
Teacher's desk, and its arms around Teacher's neck.

Nathan Horowitz presented a small cup and saucer; Isidore Applebaum bestowed a large calendar for the year before last; Sadie Gonorowsky brought a basket containing a bottle of perfume, a thimble, and a bright silk handkerchief; Sarah Schrodsky offered a pen-wiper and a yellow celluloid collar-button; and Eva Kidansky gave an elaborate nasal douche, under the pleasing delusion that it was an atomizer.

Once more sounds of grief reached Teacher's ears. Rushing again to the rescue, she threw open the door and came upon Woe personified. Eva Gonorowsky, her hair in wildest disarray, her stocking fouled, ungartered, and down-gyved to her ankle, appeared before her teacher. She bore all the marks of Hamlet's excitement, and many more including a tear-stained little face and a gilt saucer clasped to a panting breast.

"Eva, my dearest Eva, what's happened to you *now?*" asked Teacher, for the list of ill-chances which had befallen this one of her charges was very long. And Eva's wail was that a boy, a very big boy, had stolen her golden cup "what I had for you by present," and had left her only the saucer and her undying love to bestow.

Before Eva's sobs had quite yielded to Teacher's arts, Jacob Spitsky pressed forward with a tortoise-shell comb of terrifying aspect and hungry teeth, and an air showing forth a determination to adjust it in its destined place. Teacher meekly bowed her head; Jacob forced his offering into her long-suffering hair, and then retired with the information, "Costs fifteen cents, Teacher," and the courteous phrase—by etiquette prescribed—"Wish you health to wear it." He was plainly a hero, and was heard remarking to less favoured admirers that "Teacher's hair is awful softy, and smells off of perfumery."

Here a big boy, a very big boy, entered hastily. He did not belong to Room 18, but he had long known Teacher. He had brought her a present; he wished her a Merry Christmas. The present, when produced, proved to be a pretty gold cup, and Eva Gonorowsky, with renewed emotion, recognized the boy as her assailant and the cup as her property. Teacher was dreadfully embarrassed; the boy not at all so. His policy was simple and entire denial, and in this he persevered, even after Eva's saucer had unmistakably proclaimed its relationship to the cup.

Meanwhile the rush of presentation went steadily on. Other cups and saucers came in wild profusion. The desk was covered with them, and their wrappings of purple tissue paper required a monitor's whole attention. The soap, too, became urgently perceptible. It was of all sizes, shapes and colours, but of uniform and dreadful power of perfume. Teacher's eyes filled with tears—of gratitude—as each new piece or box was pressed against her nose, and Teacher's mind was full of wonder as to what she could ever do with all of it. Bottles of perfume vied with one another and with the all-pervading soap until the air was heavy and breathing grew laborious. But pride swelled the hearts of the assembled multitude. No other Teacher had so many helps to the toilet. None other was so beloved.

Teacher's aspect was quite changed, and the "blue long down like a lady dress" was almost hidden by the offerings she had received. Jacob's comb had two massive and bejewelled rivals in the "softy hair." The front of the dress, where aching or despondent heads were wont to rest, glittered with campaign buttons of American celebrities, beginning with James G. Blaine and extending into modern history as far as Patrick Divver, Admiral Dewey, and Captain Dreyfus. Outside the blue belt was a white one, nearly clean, and bearing in "sure 'nough golden words" the curt, but stirring, invitation, "Remember the Maine." Around the neck were three chaplets of beads, wrought by chubby fingers and embodying much love, while the waist-line was further adorned by tiny and beribboned aprons. Truly, it was a day of triumph.

When the waste-paper basket had been twice filled with wrappings and twice emptied; when order was emerging out of chaos; when the Christmas-tree had been disclosed and its treasures distributed, a timid hand was laid on Teacher's knee and a plaintive voice whispered, "Say, Teacher, I got something for you;" and Teacher turned quickly to see Morris, her dearest boy charge, with his poor little body showing quite plainly between his shirt-waist buttons and through the gashes he called pockets. This was his ordinary costume, and the funds of the house of Mogilewsky were evidently unequal to an outer layer of finery.

"Now, Morris dear," said Teacher, "you shouldn't have troubled to get me a present; you know you and I are such good friends that—"

"Teacher, yiss ma'an," Morris interrupted, in a bewitching and rising inflection of his soft and plaintive voice. "I know you got a kind feeling by me, and I couldn't to tell even how I got a kind feeling by you. Only it's about that kind feeling I should give you a present. I didn't"—with a glance at the crowded desk—"I didn't to have no soap nor no perfumery, and my mamma she couldn't to buy none by the store; but, Teacher, I'm got something awful nice for you by present."

"And what is it, deary?" asked the already rich and gifted young person. "What is my new present?"

"Teacher, it's like this: I don't know; I ain't so big like I could to know"—and, truly, God pity him! he was passing small—"it ain't for boys—it's for ladies. Over yesterday on the night comes my papa to my house, und he gives my mamma the present. Sooner she looks on it, sooner she has a awful glad; in her eyes stands tears, und she says, like that—out of Jewish—'Thanks,' un' she kisses my papa a kiss. Und my papa, *how* he is polite! he says—out of Jewish too— 'You're welcome, all right,' un' he kisses my mamma a kiss. So my mamma, she sets und looks on the present, und all the time she looks she has a glad over it. Und I didn't to have no soap, so you could to have the present."

"But did your mother say I might?"

"Teacher, no ma'an; she didn't say like that, und she didn't to say *not* like that. She didn't to know. But it's for ladies, un' I didn't to have no soap. You could to look on it. It ain't for boys."

And here Morris opened a hot little hand and disclosed a tightly folded pinkish paper. As Teacher read it he watched her with eager, furtive eyes, dry and bright, until hers grew suddenly moist, when he promptly followed suit. As she looked down at him, he made his moan once more:

"It's for ladies, und I didn't to have no soap."

"But, Morris, dear," cried Teacher unsteadily, laughing a little, and yet not far from tears, "this is ever so much nicer than soap—a thousand times better than perfume; and you're quite right, it is for ladies, and I never had one in all my life before. I am so very thankful."

"You're welcome, all right. That's how my papa says; it's polite," said Morris proudly. And proudly he took his place among the very little boys, and loudly he joined in the ensuing song. For the rest of that exciting day he was a shining point of virtue in the rest of that confused class. And at three o'clock he was at Teacher's desk again, carrying on the conversation as if there had been no inter ruption.

"Und my mamma," he said insinuatingly—"she kisses my papa a kiss."

"Well?" said Teacher.

"Well," said Morris, "you ain't never kissed me a kiss, und I seen how you kissed Eva Gonorowsky. I'm loving mit you too. Why don't you never kiss me a kiss?"

"Perhaps," suggested Teacher mischievously, "perhaps it ain't for boys."

But a glance at her "light face," with its crown of surprising combs, reassured him.

"Teacher, yiss ma'an; it's for boys," he cried as he felt her arms about him, and saw that in her eyes, too, "stands tears."

"It's polite you kisses me a kiss over that for ladies' present."

Late that night Teacher sat in her pretty room—for she was, un officially, a greatly pampered young person—and reviewed her treas ures. She saw that they were very numerous, very touching, very whimsical, and very precious. But above all the rest she cherished a frayed and pinkish paper, rather crumpled and a little soiled. For it held the love of a man and a woman and a little child, and the magic of a home, for Morris Mogilewsky's Christmas present for ladies was the receipt for a month's rent for a room on the top floor of a Monroe Street tenement.

CHRISTMAS CALORIES

By Merrill Denison

O N some one significant day in the late autumn, the old couple began to think of Christmas with its annual ritualistic orgy of fine food. Of victuals compounded of startlingly perfect materials, founded on recipes long since faded to yellow, and hallowed by the devotional praises of three generations. Of the worshipful family gathering that year after year crowded into the tiny cottage kitchen to gasp its wondering gratitude that such food could really be.

The day of contemplation came along about Thanksgiving. Not that Thanksgiving had anything to do with it. The choice fell more subtler than by days legislated red on calendars. Just how or why, none of the family ever quite knew. Some years Aunt Jane brought up the subject, some years Uncle Henry. Each knew secret signs to wait for, infinitely delicate signals that nature gave at the proper moment. For Jane, it may have been the big elm outside that dropped its shrivelled leaves so deliberately in the fall. For Henry, a queer tang in the morning air when he opened the low front door to bring in the pint bottle of milk.

When the day came, the old couple grew restless. The ivory tranquility of the cottage was disturbed. There were interludes when Jane's knitting lay forgotten while she watched her old comrade, and wondered if his zeal for mighty cooking might not at last burn dimly. When, unsatisfied, she picked up again the soft wool in her lap, Henry's newspaper slid to rest on the rocker's arm, while he in turn watched Jane, and thought perhaps these Christmas festivals were growing too much for her.

As each watched, memories welled to flood the interludes. Memories of classic dinners when the small cottage was rich with the odor of steamed turkey and the heady breath of burning brandy sauce. Dinners at which they had been hosts at a lavish board dispensing great joy to those they loved. Dinners that were the crown of that one day when they emerged from the year's slough of mean economies to give bounteously. To them, forced through necessity to receive so much, Christmas was a truly Christian festival. For them it was much better to give than to receive.

Neither ever thought seriously that the other was not eager to undertake the herculean work involved in compounding the plum-pudding, although each year both proclaimed that it would be the last. But in the period of indecision there came a certain exquisite fear that age might have at last conquered the gay ritual of fifty years.

It was Jane this year who found the day. It was not the sight of the canning factory through the elm's branches that gave it to her, nor the sight of Mrs. Dancy walking out to the post-office with her hands tucked thinly in her seal skin muff, nor the small flurry of snow that swirled pompously for a few minutes across the window panes. It came to her when the grocer's boy from the corner laconically delivered an exciting message.

"That niece of your'n, Aunt Jane," he said as casually as he would deliver a pound of butter. "That Miss Nan. She rung up long distance to say she was motoring through and 'd try and get in to see you. Asked if we'd give you the message."

The old lady's hands fluttered to her neck in anxious disbelief. "Not my Nan? It wasn't Nan Hogarth? Why, she's away down in New York."

"That's what she claimed, Aunt Jane. 'Course we never seen her. The message came over the long distance from Belleville. She oughta be in here in a couple of hours."

The grocer's boy tried to escape, but in a town poked away from the main highways, news of an impending visit is too rare not to be wrung dry of its last drop of detail. When he was at last able to sever her bonds of interest, and break away, Aunt Jane stood for some moments happily surveying the small kitchen.

"Well, now," she marveled, "Nan's coming. Well, now. It's certainly time we began to think about Christmas."

Henry's mid-day meal on the stove, Aunt Jane busied herself putting the house to rights. Fluffing out the parlor curtains; sternly shaking a sofa cushion into perk uprightness; stuffing Henry's pile of newspapers behind the woodbox in the kitchen. . . . As she jovially blustered over her poor furnishings, she beamed at the thought of Nan's coming. And not only coming but having the kindness to think of coming, which seemed to the old lady even more important.

Of all the scattered tribe of sons and daughters, nieces and nephews, cousins and friends, none was so adored as Nan. Nan had always been adored. Adored as a fat lump of a baby for the trills and ripples in her laugh. Adored as a child for the gay mirth with which she jostled life. Adored as a young girl for the fun she always found in the quaint cottage under the big elm on a side street, or in the shavings that softened the floor of Uncle Henry's turning shop. And when she had grown up, and gone away, and made a name for herself drawing pictures of very fat children with very thin lines, she had sent them clippings of her work, and funny jokes cut from newspapers.

But greater than all else in the esteem of Aunt Jane and Uncle Henry, Nan had worshipped food more than any other member of the family. Nan knew good food, she loved eating and she had the tongue and disposition to lavish with unbounded praise the skill and generosity of those who gave it to her.

Aunt Jane paused by the parlor window, and counted back on her fingers to place the date of Nan's last visit. Remembered events took her haltingly from thumb to little finger. Five years! Nan was eighteen then, a strong, fair dumpling of a girl who had almost swooned in ecstasy when Uncle Henry ladled the flaming brandy over the bursting sides of the brown plum pudding. Five years . . .

Uncle Henry came down the other side of the street. He walked strongly enough, but with legs wide spread as if his body needed a broader base than in its younger days. He studied with great care the ground in front of him. Watching him, Aunt Jane forgot Nan's coming for an instant, and when it flashed back to mind again, decided quite suddenly that it should be kept a secret; a surprise for dear old Hunk.

She opened the door for him and blocked his way with mock ferocity. "You can just take that apron off, now, Henry," she said.

"I'm not going to have this house tracked up with shavings." Obediently Henry took off his coat and slipped his arms out of the apron straps. "And you can't leave it out here either," she cried, emitting a feminine cluck that conveyed her never ending wonder at the stupidity of all males.

With practiced docility, Henry watched his old shop apron carried to the kitchen as if it were a chalice of spun glass, meekly took his place at the table, and waited while Jane tweaked a spent leaf from the red geranium on the window sill, bustled his food on the table, put the tea to steep, and at last sat down herself.

"Henry, it just came over me we ought to be getting our heads on Christmas. Here it's along toward the middle of November."

"It's getting on," said Henry. "We ought to be thinking about it, getting things together. Spinks was telling me he had some fine turkeys."

"And you'll want one with the right looks and disposition and family connections before you'll buy it."

"There's no sense buying anything but the best."

"I suppose we'll make plum puddings?"

"I don't know who'll eat 'em. Everybody's so sort of scattered. There mightn't be a soul come. Last year, there wasn't but four, counting us. 'Tain't like the old days when we had a 32 pound bird and it didn't last through to New Year's. The time Nan ate so much turkey she had to have a sleep before she could get around to the plum puno. She always called it plum poono."

"Nan might be here."

"Nan's in New York."

"Well, she's not in New York for life, is she?"

"It's quite aways away."

"Nan will be here."

"How do you know?"

"I don't know. I just feel she will."

And so the planning grew. Faintly at first, like a radio before the tubes are warm, and then with increased strength and volume. Querulous objections dwindled as incidents of other Christmas dinners were recalled and dwelt upon. Henry's fear that none would come to share the festival was stilled by Jane. She did not tell him Nan was at that moment on her way from Belleville, but she convinced him that she would be there at Christmas. It was not very hard. He was so anxious to be convinced.

"Nan loved oyster sauce," he said.

"Then you'll have to arrange to have the oysters sent over fresh from Belleville on the truck."

Other things were planned. The old recipe with its firm black characters on paper charred with age was brought out from its secure hiding place in the clock. "English Plum Pudding, The Genuine" it was headed in the bold, slanting script of Henry's great grandmother. It might have been his great great grandmother. No one was ever very sure. But the recipe was very old, and very perfect.

"I didn't like those raisins we had from Walmsley's last year. Nor their citron, nor their allspice," Jane primly agreed. "They fell off right after they joined the chain."

"It didn't do their quality any good."

"We might try the Red Front—old Dunlops."

"They had some fine currants yesterday."

One by one the ingredients were checked, the place of purchase decided upon and the quantities noted. Flour, currants, allspice, mace, cinnamon, nutmeg, flour, candied peel, orange peel, lemon peel. There was the annual bitterness about the suet. Henry fought yearly for the best, whatever the cost in time or money. The suet must come from western baby beef, fattened in the neighborhood. Henry always chose his suet on the hoof, was present at the killing, and superintended the hanging of the beef.

Eggs were another difficult problem. Despite Jane's protests Henry never bought his eggs in a store however many seals of rubber stamped approval government and merchant might emblazon on them. Henry had to know the hen. At Spinks' there was a hen of which he approved. A hen that laid eggs of calcined whiteness, faultless as to shape and of a size that made an egg an egg.

As they talked it became more and more Nan's dinner. Enough food was planned to feed a starving multitude. Steamed turkey, with oyster sauce, potatoes creamed, cranberries and other vegetables. Nuts, malaga grapes, and oranges. The brandy, a most important thing, was conspiratorially arranged for. The old copper wash boiler was hauled down from the wood-shed, examined with affectionate thoroughness and pronounced sound.

Ahead of them lay six tremendous weeks, weeks crammed with buying, smelling, tasting, complaining, dredging, steaming, wrapping. Ten plum puddings to be made. A big one, seven pounds for Nan, and littler ones for those who could not come. Jane's plum puddings wore like iron. During the war one had followed her favorite nephew all over France for two years before it finally reached him and it was still perfect then.

In the rich satisfaction of planning, Aunt Jane had almost forgotten about Nan's coming. Even when the mellow rootee-too-toot of an expensive motor horn sounded in the street, she continued to peer critically over her glasses at the folds of cotton that would guard her puddings. The sound spread through the house a second time.

"What's that?" exclaimed Uncle Henry.

Questioned, Jane recalled the sound and knew at once. Its silvery insolence, its lazy warning challenge could mean but one person— Nan. There was a commotion at the door. A pounding and it seemed to burst inwards with exuberance.

"It's Nan," gasped Aunt Jane. "It's our own little Nan."

Both saw her framed against the gloom of the small hall. Her gay blue eyes shone at them through a blurr of watery radiance. From the tight blue hat her golden hair repeated the curves of laughter in her wind touched cheeks. A babble of words broke out and she ran to kiss them. It seemed that five years hadn't changed her in the slightest. The affectionate turmoil of welcome over, Uncle Henry reverted to the last topic in his mind—the Christmas dinner. Aunt Jane, to whom hospitality meant succoring the starving, poked around her cupboard. While she looked, Uncle Henry discovered that Nan might possibly spend Christmas with them.

"Jennie, Jennie!" he shouted. "Do you hear that? Little Nan might be here for Christmas."

"Only might, Aunt Jane," cautioned the radiant visitor. "A teeny, weeny little might. It depends . . ." she grew mysterious, "Upon a MAN."

"We're going to have plum poono and oyster sauce," Uncle Henry said coquettishly, leaning forward to pat his niece's fur clad knee. A slight frown crossed Nan's face. Henry did not notice it. The promise of her being at the Christmas board wiped out any insight his old eyes still had.

"Stop talking about Christmas," ordered Jane. "The poor child's almost starving." She turned to the starving young woman in the coon skin coat. "There's some pork sausages—the kind you always liked, the plump kind—some hashed brown potatoes with brown gravy and I have some real strawberry preserves and bread and butter."

A strange expression clouded Nan's face. When her Aunt Jane mentioned potatoes a faint shudder rippled down the coon skin coat.

"Or perhaps some cottage cheese," Aunt Jane added, oblivious to the pained look that greeted each tempting new article of food.

"You poor dears," said Nan enigmatically. "It must be this coon skin coat." She stood up and opened the great fur coat, holding the lapels at arm's length. "Look at me!" she commanded.

"You're thinner," said Uncle Henry after much deliberation.

"Yes," agreed Aunt Jane accusingly. "You are thinner."

"And there, God help me, is my luncheon," said Nan, wrenching a grape fruit out of her pocket and placing it on the table. "I ought to be thinner. I'm on an eighteen day diet." She slipped her coat off then, and tore her small turban from her head, and shook her shining crown of gold. "Give me a knife till I fix this damn thing," she said.

Nothing Nan could have said would have shocked the old couple so deeply. Liberal, tolerant and wise for all that they had lived out their lives in a small town, Nan might have returned to them with confessions of unhappy escapades, of foolish actions, of a stupid life. She might even have turned up with an unnamed child and found nothing but sympathy and understanding for her misfortunes. But to say with undoubted pride that she was on a diet and produce a large yellow globular mass of sour pulp and water for her dinner was a profanation of the household altars.

The old people talked to her as backsliders should be talked to, but neither cajolery, pleading, abuse nor realistic drawings of a hereafter void of nourishment had any effect on Nan. "I simply had to do something," she explained. "I couldn't go around looking like a tub any longer. You remember what a baby elephant I was, Uncle Hank?"

"There was nothing wrong with you that I ever saw," he indignantly retorted. "And I don't suppose this fool dieting will last long. You wouldn't keep it up till Christmas, surely?"

Nan caught the note of wistful anxiety in the old man's voice. She was aware too that Aunt Jane was standing quite still, waiting.

"You mustn't count on me too much for Christmas," she said evasively. "You see, it depends upon a certain MAN." Her eyes and voice put "man" in capitals. "He's gone up north, somewhere with some other men looking over mines. It will depend on when he gets back."

"Couldn't you bring him too?" asked Jane.

"But Aunt Jane, he doesn't eat anything either!"

"Surely steamed turkey and oyster sauce and a little plum pudding couldn't do either of you any harm."

"You don't understand this dieting," explained Nan. "It isn't the effect a decent meal might have on my weight, but the effect it would be sure to have on my soul. It's so long since I've had anything really fit to eat, that I'm terrified of what would happen if I allowed myself to eat anything I really loved. I'd probably go on gorging like a starved python until I could hold no more. It would take me weeks to recover, if I ever did."

By this and other statements of principle, philosophy, strategy and tactics, and by a spirited reference to the similarity of food and liquor reduction, Nan finally convinced her aunt and uncle of her earnestness. The argument hurt her more than it did them, if that was possible, and consumed most of her short visit. As a compromise, she did definitely promise that she would be with them on Christmas day. Before she left much of the old happiness was recaptured despite the cloud of heresy that hovered over her.

They saw her to the front door, and watched her light blue roadster disappear around the corner into Main Street. One instant she was waving madly to them; the next there was nothing to look at but the mildewed brick corner of the furnishing shop. They went back into the cottage together.

"She's coming back. That's something," said Aunt Jane.

"Yes, she'll be back," said Uncle Henry, "but there don't seem much sense going to a lot of trouble and expense making plum puddings and the rest of it if there's no one will eat 'em."

"There's us, isn't there?" said Jane.

"Aw, shucks. What do we care about it, for ourselves."

Aunt Jane understood exactly what he meant. There was little sense in going to all that trouble for themselves alone.

"Won't hardly seem natural without turkey and oyster sauce."

"Or plum puddings."

"We might better get a few lamb chops and a bale of hay. That's what they eat on diets."

"Oysters. We could have some raw oysters."

"Not worth the trouble. All the way from Belleville."

"No, I guess not. We'll just use the money we put by for something else. You've needed a new overcoat for years, Henry."

"No more than you've needed a new dress."

"You need an overcoat more."

"I'll get no overcoat without you get a dress."

"We can't get both."

"No, we can't get both."

"I'd ruther have spent the money on a turkey."

"Yes, but there is no sense to it now is there?"

"No."

"It isn't like the old days when we had to have a thirty-two pound turkey?"

"We'd better just forget about Christmas this year, and not making ourselves miserable either remembering or planning."

So it was agreed. Christmas dinner was to be no different from any other dinner. If Nan wanted starvation she was to have it with little compromise.

But while each was content whatever the pain to sacrifice their one great event of the year, neither felt strong enough to ask that the other share the sacrifice. And so, as November swung grayly by, the little cottage was a place of small secrecies and elaborate, transparent evasions. Neither had any definite plan of action. Neither could have, for to prepare plum pudding alone and undiscovered in the three room cottage would have taxed Aladdin's wit. But each accumulated things.

By small discoveries and little carelessnesses the seeds of mutual suspicion were sown. Uncle Henry discovered one day that a bag supposed to contain soap chips actually harbored the best sultana raisins. He also noted a new package of allspice. Aunt Jane, quite inadvertently, also found out, from Mrs. Dancy, that old Henry had been trapesing around the country with her boy Dick in his old car, when he was supposed to be down at the shop. She faced him with it.

"Henry, where were you last Tuesday?" she said.

"Oh, I don't know," he replied evasively. "Down to the shop most of the day."

"Henry, you were out with young Dancy. You were out to Spinks'."

"Well, I might've gone out for a few minutes."

"Did you order a turkey?"

"What would I order a turkey for? when we aren't going to have none?"

"Did you order a turkey?"

"No, I didn't order no turkey."

Both knew he was lying, splendidly lying. That night Uncle Henry, prowling out in the woodshed, discovered hidden in the copper wash boiler a number of small packages containing condiments. Two days later Mrs. Dancy reported that Uncle Henry had been seen down at the stock pen during the arrival of a carload of fat steers from the lake townships.

"Henry," demanded Jane. "What were you doing down to the stock pen?"

This time Henry attempted no evasion. He marched instead to the woodshed and returned with the wash boiler.

"And what are these here packages doing here?" he demanded. "Raisins, Zante currants, orange peel, Granberry's flour? Why, there ain't a store in town sells Granberry's."

"I got it from Belleville," said Jane.

"You couldn't stick to the bargain, eh?" said Henry.

"No more'n you could," said Jane.

The tremendous undertaking was launched again. Henry rediscovered his favorite hen. Jane scoured the great wooden mixing bowls. The raisins were dredged, the suet chopped with a jeweler's care, the loaves of flawless bread staled and crumbed. All one afternoon they spent mixing the rich, rich food, with the care of ancient alchemists seeking magic that might turn lead to gold. But if they lost themselves as great artists are prone to do, in the joys of technical mastery, the spirit of the work seemed flat and empty. It seemed harder than it used to, and at times purposeless. They heard from Nan along in November. A deft, sharp letter that said she had lost six pounds and would be with them Christmas day. There was no news yet of her man.

Two days before Christmas Uncle Henry drove again to Spinks' place. True to their ancient friendship old Peter Spinks had fed Henry's turkey as no turkey was ever fed before. Henry was horrified when he saw it—a thirty-one pound bird, and not a soul to eat it but themselves. He was ashamed to take it home to show to Jane.

He did not summon courage to take it home to her until the afternoon of Christmas eve. He struggled in with it and dropped it on a kitchen chair.

"For land's sakes, Henry, what have you got there," exclaimed Jane, curiously fingering the brown wrapping.

"Our turkey," Henry said gloomily. "Spinks fed it like it was a balloon."

The wrappings taken off, together they placed it on the table and studied, with frank distaste, its monstrous nudity. Throughout supper it remained there a fleshy tombstone to the glories of the past.

"I never seen a better turkey," Henry morosely observed.

"It could've fed the whole family, counting Maggie's tribe," said Jane. "And there's no one but Nan and she's dieting." She peered admiringly at the turkey, testing first one spot and then another with her fingers.

"Henry," she said at last, and her gaze still lingered on its plump and perfect curves, "it's nothing but a selfish crime for us to keep that bird. There's many a poor family in town would welcome such a meal. There's the Salvation Army for one. And it'll mean nothing but wastage and hard work for us."

"We might as well give 'em the oysters too," said Henry. "They're little use without the turkey. I wisht we hadn't made them plum puddings."

"Don't worry about what's done, dear. We're just a pair of sentimental old fools, that's all we are. It's time we admitted what we are. The days of real eating are past, Henry. You just wrap that bird up and take it over to the army captain."

But Henry seemed reluctant. Now that they had made up their minds to part with such a prize, each wished wistfully that they didn't have to. It was Aunt Jane, realizing something of the agony of Henry's soul, through the acute pain in her own, who rose and found some paper in the cupboard.

"Henry, you might as well get it over with."

Dispiritedly Henry rose to do her bidding. There was a knock at the front door. "I'll go," said Jane. "It might be the army now. They come usually on Christmas eve." She hustled back again a moment later. It was not the army but the boy from the grocery store to say she was wanted on the phone.

"You better go, Henry, you hear better on the phone. It must be Nan."

"You wrap up this bird then," said Henry, "I'll see what she wants. She most likely isn't coming."

"Yes, I'm afraid that's what it will be."

Henry walked up to the corner and turned into Main street feeling that nothing mattered very much anyway. What if Nan wasn't coming? She wouldn't eat anyway.

"Hurry up there, Uncle Henry," the boy called from the doorway.

"I'm coming. There ain't no rush anyways."

Crowded in between the cash desk and the glass cheese case in the far corner of the store, Henry picked up the receiver and fitted it laboriously to his ear. He piped disapprovingly at the mouthpiece: "Well, well. What is it?" Nan's words came rushing back to him. "Uncle Henry, the most terrible thing has happened. It's simply awful. I'm afraid to tell you."

"Well, well. What is it, girl? Speak up. Can't you come?"

"Of course, I can come, but there are six others that want to come with me."

"Eh, what's that."

"The MAN, the man I told you about, Uncle Hank. My man. He just came back today with five friends. They haven't had anything fit to eat for six weeks. I told them about you and Aunt Jane. They insist on coming down with me for Christmas dinner."

"Well, well. I'm sure they'll be welcome."

"But, Uncle Henry, I know you have nothing in the house. I know you haven't anything ready, or prepared or anything because of my diet!" Her voice rose to an anxious wail. "Do you think you can get anything tonight. Roast beef, or a few chickens or anything? They insist on coming. . . ."

"I guess we might find something in the town. Scare up some kind of food."

"Anything will do, Uncle Hank. Anything. As long as there's lots of it."

Uncle Henry could hold the triumph from his voice no longer. "Oh, there'll be lots of it all right. 'n good bye, I got to get to work."

Down Main Street and around the corner he flew like the Hound of Heaven. In his own gateway, and through the front door. In the yellow lamplight beyond, he saw Aunt Jane laboriously knotting string on the clumsy bulk of their turkey.

"Get away from that bird, old woman," he cried. "Leave it be and get my knives. Little Nan's coming and bringing two dozen starving mining engineers with her."

"Well for land's sakes, Henry. You might've got a bigger bird."

ONE THOUSAND AVES

By Louis Hémon

SINCE the coming of winter they had often talked at the Chapdelaines about the holidays, and now these were drawing near.

"I am wondering whether we shall have any callers on New Year's Day," said Madame Chapdelaine one evening. She went over the list of all relatives and friends able to make the venture. "Azalma Larouche does not live so far away, but she—she is not very energetic. The people at St. Prime would not care to take the journey. Possibly Wilfrid or Ferdinand might drive from St. Gedeon if the ice on the lake were in good condition." A sigh disclosed that she still was dreaming of the coming and going in the old parishes at the time of the New Year, the family dinners, the unlooked-for visits of kindred arriving by sleigh from the next village, buried under rugs and furs, behind a horse whose coat was white with frost.

Maria's thoughts were turning in another direction. "If the roads are as bad as they were last year," said she, "we shall not be able to attend the midnight mass. And yet I should so much have liked it this time, and father promised . . ."

Through the little window they looked on the grey sky, and found little to cheer them. To go to midnight mass is the natural and strong desire of every French-Canadian peasant, even of those living farthest from the settlements. What do they not face to accomplish it! Arctic cold, the woods at night, obliterated roads, great distances do but add to the impressiveness and the mystery. This anniversary of the birth of Jesus is more to them than a mere fixture in the calendar with rites appropriate; it signifies the renewed promise of salvation, an occasion of deep rejoicing, and those gathered in the wooden church are imbued with sincerest fervour, are pervaded with a deep sense of the supernatural. This year, more than ever, Maria yearned to attend the mass after many weeks of remoteness from houses and from churches; the favours she would fain demand seemed more likely to be granted were she able to prefer them before the altar, aided in heavenward flight by the wings of music.

But toward the middle of December much snow fell, dry and fine as dust, and three days before Christmas the north-west wind arose and made an end of the roads. On the morrow of the storm Chapdelaine harnessed Charles Eugene to the heavy sleigh and departed with Tit'Bé; they took shovels to clear the way or lay out another route. The two men returned by noon, worn out, white with snow, asserting that there would be no breaking through for several days. The disappointment must be borne; Maria sighed, but the idea came to her that there might be other means of attaining the divine goodwill.

"Is it true, mother," she asked as evening was falling, "that if you repeat a thousand Aves on the day before Christmas you are always granted the thing you seek?"

"Quite true," her mother reverently answered. "One desiring a favour who says her thousand Aves properly before midnight on Christmas Eve, very seldom fails to receive what she asks."

On Christmas Eve the weather was cold but windless. The two men went out betimes in another effort to beat down the road, with no great hope of success; but long before they left, and indeed long before daylight, Maria began to recite her Aves. Awakening very early, she took her rosary from beneath the pillow and swiftly repeated the prayer, passing from the last word to the first without stopping, and counting, bead by bead.

The others were still asleep; but Chien left his place at the stove when he saw that she moved, and came to sit beside the bed, gravely reposing his head upon the coverings. Maria's glance wandered over the long white muzzle resting upon the brown wool, the liquid eyes filled with the dumb creature's pathetic trustfulness, the drooping glossy ears; while she ceased not to murmur the sacred words:—"Hail Mary, full of grace . . ."

Soon Tit'Bé jumped from bed to put wood upon the fire; an impulse of shyness caused Maria to turn away and hide her rosary under the coverlet as she continued to pray. The stove roared; Chien went back to his usual spot, and for another half-hour nothing was stirring in the house save the fingers of Maria numbering the boxwood beads, and her lips as they moved rapidly in the task she had laid upon herself.

Then must she arise, for the day was dawning; make the porridge and the pancakes while the men went to the stable to care for the animals, wait upon them when they returned, wash the dishes, sweep the house. What time she attended to these things, Maria was ever raising a little higher toward heaven the monument of her Aves; but the rosary had to be laid aside and it was hard to keep a true reckoning. As the morning advanced however, no urgent duty calling, she was able to sit by the window and steadily pursue her undertaking.

Noon; and already three hundred Aves. Her anxiety lessens, for now she feels almost sure of finishing in time. It comes to her mind that fasting would give a further title to heavenly consideration, and might, with reason, turn hopes into certainties; wherefore she ate but little, foregoing all those things she liked the best.

Throughout the afternoon she must knit the woollen garment designed for her father as a New Year's gift, and though the faithful repetition ceased not, the work of her fingers was something of a distraction and a delay; then came the long preparations for supper, and finally Tit'Bé brought his mittens to be mended, so all this time the Aves made slow and impeded progress, like some devout procession brought to halt by secular interruption.

But when it was evening and the tasks of the day were done, she could resume her seat by the window where the feeble light of the lamp did not invade the darkness, look forth upon the fields hidden beneath their icy cloak, take the rosary once more in her hands and throw her heart into the prayer. She was happy that so many Aves were left to be recited, since labour and difficulty could only add merit to her endeavour; even did she wish to humble herself further and give force to her prayer by some posture that would bring uneasiness and pain, by some chastening of the flesh.

Her father and Tit'Bé smoked, their feet against the stove; her mother sewed new ties to old moose-hide moccasins. Outside, the moon had risen, flooding the chill whiteness with colder light, and the heavens were of a marvellous purity and depth, sown with stars that shone like that wondrous star of old.

"Blessed art Thou amongst women . . ."

Through repeating the short prayer oftentimes and quickly she grew confused and sometimes stopped, her dazed mind lost among the well-known words. It is only for a moment; sighing she closes her eyes, and the phrase which rises at once to her memory and her lips ceases to be mechanical, detaches itself, again stands forth in all its hallowed meaning.

"Blessed art Thou amongst women . . ."

At length a heaviness weighs upon her, and the holy words are spoken with greater effort and slowly; yet the beads pass through her fingers in endless succession, and each one launches the offering of an Ave to that sky where Mary the compassionate is surely seated on her throne, hearkening to the music of prayers that ever rise, and brooding over the memory of that blest night.

"The Lord is with Thee . . ."

The fence-rails were very black upon the white expanse palely lighted by the moon; trunks of birch trees standing against the dark background of forest were like the skeletons of living creatures smitten with the cold and stricken by death; but the glacial night was awesome rather than affrighting.

"With the roads as they are we will not be the only ones who have to stay at home this evening," said Madame Chapdelaine. "But is there anything more lovely than the midnight mass at Saint Coeur de Marie, with Yvonne Boilly playing the harmonium, and Pacifique Simard who sings the Latin so beautifully!" She was very careful to say nothing that might seem reproachful or complaining on such a night as this, but in spite of herself the words and tone had a sad ring of loneliness and remoteness. Her husband noticed it, and, himself under the influence of the day, was quick to take the blame.

"It is true enough, Laura, that you would have had a happier life with some other man than me, who lived on a comfortable farm, near the settlements."

"No, Samuel; what the good God does is always right. I grumble . . . Of course I grumble. Is there anyone who hasn't something to grumble about? But we have never been unhappy, we two; we have managed to live without faring over-badly; the boys are fine boys, hard-working, who bring us nearly all they earn; Maria too is a good girl . . ."

Affected by these memories of the past, they also were thinking of the candles already lit, of the hymns soon to be raised in honour of the Saviour's birth. Life had always been a simple and a straight-forward thing for them; severe but inevitable toil, a good under-standing between man and wife, obedience alike to the laws of nature and of the Church. Everything was drawn into the same woof; the rites of their religion and the daily routine of existence so woven to-gether that they could not distinguish the devout emotion possessing them from the mute love of each for each.

Little Alma Rose heard praises in the air and hastened to demand her portion. "I have been a good girl too, haven't I, father?"

"Certainly . . . Certainly. A black sin indeed if one were naughty on the day when the little Jesus was born."

To the children, Jesus of Nazareth was ever "the little Jesus," the curly-headed babe of the sacred picture; and in truth, for the parents as well, such was the image oftenest brought to mind by the Name. Not the sad enigmatic Christ of the Protestant, but a being more familiar and less august, a new-born infant in his mother's arms, or at least a tiny child who might be loved without great effort of the mind or any thought of the coming sacrifice.

"Would you like me to rock you?"

"Yes."

He took the little girl on his knees and began to swing her back and forth.

"And are we going to sing too?"

"Yes."

"Very well; now sing with me":

> Dans son étable,
> Que Jésus est charmant!
> Qu'il est aimable
> Dans son abaissement . . .

He began in quiet tones that he might not drown the other slender voice; but soon emotion carried him away and he sang with all his might, his gaze dreamy and remote. Telesphore drew near and looked at him with worshipping eyes. To these children brought up in a lonely house, with only their parents for companions, Samuel Chapdelaine embodied all there was in the world of wisdom and might. As he was ever gentle and patient, always ready to take the children on his knee and sing them hymns, or those endless old songs he taught them one by one, they loved him with a rare affection.

> . . . Tous les palais des rois
> N'ont rien de comparable
> Aux beautés que je vois
> Dans cette étable.

"Once more? Very well."

This time the mother and Tit'Bé joined in. Maria could not resist staying her prayers for a few moments that she might look and hearken; but the words of the hymn renewed her ardour, and she soon took up the task again with a livelier faith . . ."Hail Mary, full of grace . . ."

> Trois gros navires sont arrivés,
> Chargés d'avoine, chargés de blé.
> Nous irons sur l'eau nous y prom-promener,
> Nous irons jouer dans l'île . . .

"And now? Another song: which?" Without waiting for a reply he struck in . . .

"No? not that one . . . *Claire Fontaine?* Ah! That's a beautiful one, that is! We shall all sing it together."

He glanced at Maria, but seeing the beads ever slipping through her fingers he would not intrude.

> A la claire fontaine
> M'en allant promener,
> J'ai trouvé l'eau si belle
> Que je m'y suis baigné . . .
> Il y a longtemps que je t'aime,
> Jamais je ne t'oublierai. . .

Words and tune alike haunting; the unaffected sadness of the refrain lingering in the ear, a song that well may find its way to any heart.

> . . . Sur la plus haute branche,
> Le rossignol chantait.
> Chante, rossignol, chante,
> Toi qui a le cœur gai . . .
> Il y a longtemps que je t'aime
> Jamais je ne t'oublierai . . .

The rosary lay still in the long fingers. Maria did not sing with the others; but she was listening, and this lament of a love that was unhappy fell very sweetly and movingly on her spirit a little weary with prayer.

> . . . Tu as le cœur à rire,
> Moi je l'ai à pleurer,
> J'ai perdu ma maîtresse
> Sans pouvoir la r'trouver,
> Pour un bouquet de roses
> Que je lui refusai
> Il y a longtemps que je t'aime,
> Jamais je ne t'oublierai.

Maria looked through the window at the white fields circled by mysterious forest; the passion of religious feeling, the tide of young love rising within her, the sound of the familiar voices, fused in her heart to a single emotion. Truly the world was filled with love that evening, with love human and divine, simple in nature and mighty in strength, one and the other most natural and right; so intermingled that the beseeching of heavenly favour upon dear ones was scarcely more than the expression of an earthly affection, while the artless love songs were chanted with solemnity of voice and exaltation of spirit fit for addresses to another world.

> . . . Je voudrais que la rose
> Fût encore au rosier,
> Et que le rosier même
> A la mer fût jeté.
> Il y a longtemps que je t'aime,
> Jamais je ne t'oublierai . . .

"Hail Mary, full of grace . . ."

The song ended, Maria forthwith resumed her prayers with zeal refreshed, and once again the tale of the Aves mounted.

Little Alma Rose, asleep on her father's knee, was undressed and put to bed; Telesphore followed; Tit'Bé arose in turn, stretched himself, and filled the stove with green birch logs; the father made a last trip to the stable and came back running, saying that the cold was increasing. Soon all had retired, save Maria.

"You won't forget to put out the lamp?"

"No, father."

Forthwith she quenched the light, preferring it so, and seated herself again by the window to repeat the last Aves. When she had finished, a scruple assailed her, and a fear lest she had erred in the reckoning, because it had not always been possible to count the beads of her rosary. Out of prudence she recited yet another fifty and then was silent—jaded, weary, but full of happy confidence, as though the moment had brought her a promise inviolable.

The world outside was lit; wrapped in that frore splendour which the night unrolls over lands of snow when the sky is clear and the moon is shining. Within the house was darkness, and it seemed that wood and field had illumined themselves to signal the coming of the holy hour.

"The thousand Aves have been said," murmured Maria to herself, "but I have not yet asked for anything . . . not in words." She had thought that perhaps it were not needful; that the Divinity might

understand without hearing wishes shaped by lips—Mary above all
. . . Who had been a woman upon earth. But at the last her simple
mind was taken with a doubt, and she tried to find speech for the
favour she was seeking.

François Paradis . . . Most surely it concerns François Paradis.
Hast Thou already guessed it, O Mary, full of grace? How might she
frame this her desire without impiety? That he should be spared
hardship in the woods . . . That he should be true to his word and
give up drinking and swearing . . . That he return in the spring . . .

That he return in the spring . . . She goes no farther, for it seems
to her that when he is with her again, his promise kept, all the happiness in the world must be within their reach, unaided . . . almost
unaided . . . If it be not presumptuous so to think . . .

That he return in the spring . . . Dreaming of his return, of
François, the handsome sunburnt face turned to hers, Maria forgets
all else, and looks long with unseeing eyes at the snow-covered ground
which the moonlight has turned into a glittering fabric of ivory and
mother-of-pearl—at the black pattern of the fences outlined upon it,
and the menacing ranks of the dark forest.

.   .   .   .

New Year's Day, and not a single caller! Toward evening the mother
of the family, a trifle cast down, hid her depression behind a mask of
extra cheeriness. "Even if no one comes," said she, "that is no reason
for allowing ourselves to be unhappy. We are going to make *la tire*."

The children exclaimed with delight, and followed the preparations with impatient eyes. Molasses and brown sugar were set on
the stove to boil, and when this had proceeded far enough Telesphore
brought in a large dish of lovely white snow. They all gathered about
the table as a few drops of the boiling syrup were allowed to fall upon
the snow where they instantly became crackly bubbles, deliciously
cold.

Each was helped in turn, the big people making a merry pretence
of the children's unfeigned greed; but soon, and very wisely, the tasting was checked, that appetite might not be in peril for the real *la tire*,

the confection of which had only begun. After further cooking, and just at the proper moment, the cooling toffee must be pulled for a long time. The mother's strong hands plied unceasingly for five minutes, folding and drawing out the sugary skein; the movement became slower and slower, until, stretched for the last time to the thickness of a finger, it was cut into lengths with scissors—not too easily, for it was already hard. The *la tire* was made.

The children were busy with their first portions, when a knocking was heard on the door. "Eutrope Gagnon," at once declared Chapdelaine. "I was just saying to myself that it would be an odd thing if he did not come and spend the evening with us."

Eutrope Gagnon it was in truth. Entering, he bade them all good evening, and laid his woollen cap upon the table. Maria looked at him, a blush upon her cheek. Custom ordains that on the first day of the year the young men shall kiss the women-folk, and Maria knew well enough that Eutrope, shy as he was, would exercise his privilege; she stood motionless by the table, unprotesting, yet thinking of another kiss she would have dearly welcomed. But the young man took the chair offered him and sat down, his eyes upon the floor.

"You are the only visitor who has come our way today," said Chapdelaine, "and I suppose you have seen no one either. I felt pretty certain you would be here this evening."

"Naturally . . . . I would not let New Year's Day go by without paying you a visit. But, besides that, I have news to tell."

"News?"

Under the questioning eyes of the household he did not raise his eyes.

"By your face I am afraid you have bad news."

"Yes."

With a start of fear the mother half rose. "Not about the boys?"

"No, Madame Chapdelaine. Esdras and Da'Bé are well, if that be God's pleasure. The word I bring is not of them—not of your own kin. It concerns a young man you know." Pausing a moment he spoke a name under his breath:—"François Paradis."

His glance was lifted to Maria and as quickly fell, but she did not so much as see his look of honest distress. Deep stillness weighed upon the house—upon the whole universe. Everything alive and dead was breathlessly awaiting news of such dreadful moment—touching him that was for her the one man in all the world . . .

"This is what happened. You knew perhaps that he was foreman in a shanty above La Tuque, on the Vermilion River. About the middle of December he suddenly told the boss that he was going off to spend Christmas and New Year at Lake St. John—up here. The boss objected, naturally enough; for if the men take ten or fifteen days' leave right in the middle of the winter you might as well stop the work altogether. The boss did not wish him to go and said so plainly; but you know François—a man not to be thwarted when a notion entered his head. He answered that he was set on going to the lake for the holidays, and that go he would. Then the boss let him have his way, afraid to lose a man useful beyond the common, and of such experience in the bush."

Eutrope Gagnon was speaking with unusual ease, slowly, but without seeking words, as though his story had been shaped beforehand. Amid her overwhelming grief the thought flitted through Maria's heart:—"François wished to come here . . . to me," and a fugitive joy touched it as a swallow in flight ruffles the water with his wing.

"The shanty was not very far in the woods, only two days' journey from the Transcontinental which passes La Tuque. But as the luck was, something had happened to the line and the trains were not running. I heard all this through Johnny Niquette of St. Henri, who arrived from La Tuque two days ago."

"Yes."

"When François found that he could not take the train he burst into a laugh, and in that sort of a humour said that as it was a case of walking he would walk all the way—reaching the lake by following the rivers, first the Croche and then the Ouatchouan which falls in near Roberval."

"That is so," said Chapdelaine. "It can be done. I have gone that way."

"Not at this time of year, Mr. Chapdelaine, certainly not just at this time. Everyone there told François that it would be foolhardy to attempt such a trip in midwinter, about Christmas, with the cold as great as it was, some four feet of snow lying in the woods, and alone. But he only laughed and told them that he was used to the woods and that a little difficulty was not going to frighten him, because he was bound to get to the upper side of the lake for the holidays, and that where the Indians were able to cross he could make the crossing too. Only—you know it very well, Mr. Chapdelaine—when the Indians take that journey it is in company, and with their dogs. François set off alone, on snow-shoes, pulling his blankets and provisions on a toboggan."

No one had uttered a word to hasten or check the speaker. They listened as to him whose story's end stalks into view, before the eyes but darkly veiled, like a figure drawing near who hides his face.

"You will remember the weather a week before Christmas—the heavy snow that fell, and after it the nor'west gale. It happened that François was then in the great burnt lands, where the fine snow drives and drifts so terribly. In such a place the best of men have little chance when it is very cold and the storm lasts. And, if you recall it, the nor'- wester was blowing for three days on end, stiff enough to flay you."

"Yes, and then?"

The narrative he had framed did not carry him further, or perhaps he could not bring himself to speak the final words, for it was some time before the low-voiced answer came:—"He went astray . . ."

Those who have passed their lives within the shadow of the Canadian forests know the meaning but too well. The daring youths to whom this evil fortune happens in the woods, who go astray—are lost —but seldom return. Sometimes a search-party finds their bodies in the spring, after the melting of the snows. In Quebec, and above all in the far regions of the north, the very word, *écarté,* has taken on a new and sinister import, from the peril overhanging him who loses his way, for a short day only, in that limitless forest.

"He went astray . . . The storm caught him in the burnt country and he halted for a day. So much we know, for the Indians found a shelter of fir branches he had made for himself, and they saw his tracks.

He set out again because his provisions were low and he was in haste to reach the end of his journey, as I suppose; but the weather did not mend, snow was falling, the nor'west wind never eased, and it is likely he caught no glimpse of the sun to guide him, for the Indians said that his tracks turned off from the river Croche which he had been following and wandered away, straight to the north."

There was no further speech; neither from the two men who had listened with assenting motions of their heads while they followed every turn of Eutrope's grim story; nor from the mother whose hands were clasped upon her knees, as in a belated supplication; nor from Maria . . .

"When they heard this, men from Ouatchouan set forth after the weather was a little better. But all his footsteps were covered, and they returned saying that they had found no trace; that was three days ago. . . . He is lost . . ."

The listeners stirred, and broke the stillness with a sigh; the tale was told, nor was there a word that anyone might speak. The fate of François Paradis was as mournfully sure as though he were buried in the cemetery at St. Michel de Mistassini to the sound of chants, with the blessing of a priest.

Silence fell upon the house and all within it. Chapdelaine was leaning forward, elbows on his knees, his face working, mechanically striking one fist upon the other. At length he spoke:—"It shows we are but little children in the hand of the good God. François was one of the best men of these parts in the woods, and at finding his way; people who came here used to take him as guide, and always did he bring them back without mishap. And now he himself is lost. We are but little children. Some there be who think themselves pretty strong—able to get on without God's help in their houses and on their lands . . . but in the bush . . ." With solemn voice and slowly-moving head he repeated: "We are but little children."

"A good man he was," said Eutrope Gagnon, "in very truth a good man, strong and brave, with ill-will to none."

"Indeed that is true. I am not saying that the good God had cause to send him to his death—him more than another. He was a fine fellow, hard-working, and I loved him well. But it shows you . . ."

"No one ever had a thing against him." Eutrope's generous insistence carried him on. "A man hard to match for work, afraid of nothing and obliging withal. Everyone who knew him was fond of him —you will not find his like."

Raising his eyes to Maria he repeated with emphasis:—"He was a good man, you will not find his like."

"When we were at Mistassini," began Madame Chapdelaine, "seven years ago, he was only a lad, but very strong and quick and as tall as he is now—I mean as he was when he came here last summer. Always good-natured too. No one could help liking him."

They all looked straight before them in speaking, and yet what they said seemed to be for Maria alone, as if the dear secret of her heart were open to them. But she spoke not, nor moved, her eyes fixed upon the frosted panes of the little window, impenetrable as the wall.

Eutrope Gagnon did not linger. The Chapdelaines, left to themselves, were long without speech. At last the father said in a halting voice: "François Paradis was almost alone in the world; now, as we all had an affection for him, we perhaps might have a mass or two said. What do you think, Laura?"

"Yes indeed. Three high masses with music, and when the boys return from the woods—in health, if such be the will of the good God—three more for the repose of his soul, poor lad! And every Sunday we shall say a prayer for him."

"He was like the rest of us," Chapdelaine continued, "not without fault, of course, but kindly and well-living. God and the Holy Virgin will have pity on him."

Again silence. Maria well knew it was for her they said these things —aware of her grief and seeking to assuage it; but she was not able to speak, either to praise the dead or utter her sorrow. A hand had fastened upon her throat, stifling her, as the narrative unfolded and the end loomed inevitable; and now this hand found its way into her breast and was crushing her heart. Presently she would know a yet more intolerable pain, but now she only felt the deadly grasp of those five fingers closed about her heart.

Other words were said, but they scarce reached her ear; then came the familiar evening stir of preparation for the night, the father's departure on a last visit to the stable and his swift return, face red with the cold, slamming the door hastily in a swirl of frosty vapour.

"Come, Maria." The mother called her very gently, and laid a hand upon her shoulder. She rose and went to kneel and pray with the others. Voice answered to voice for ten minutes, murmuring the sacred words in low monotone.

The usual prayer at an end, the mother whispered:—"Yet five Paters and five Aves for the souls of those who have suffered misfortune in the forest." And the voices again rose, this time more subdued, breaking sometimes to a sob.

When they were silent, and all had risen after the last sign of the cross, Maria went back to the window. The frost upon the panes made of them so many fretted squares through which the eye could not penetrate, shutting away the outside world; but Maria saw them not, for the tears welled to her eyes and blinded her. She stood there motionless, with arms hanging piteously by her side, a stricken figure of grief; then a sudden anguish yet keener and more unbearable seized upon her; blindly she opened the door and went out upon the step.

The world that lay beyond the threshold, sunk in moveless white repose, was of an immense serenity; but when Maria passed from the sheltering walls the cold smote her like the hungry blade of a sword and the forest leaped toward her in menace, its inscrutable face concealing a hundred dreadful secrets which called aloud to her in lamentable voices. With a little moan she drew back, and closing the door sat shivering beside the stove. Numbness was yielding, sorrow taking on an edge, and the hand that clutched her heart set itself to devising new agonies, each one subtler and more cruel than the last.

How he must have suffered, far off there amid the snows! So thought she, as still her own face remembered the sting of the bitter air. Men threatened by this fate had told her that death coming in such a guise smote with gentle and painless hand—a hand that merely lulled to sleep; but she could not make herself believe it, and all the sufferings that François might have endured before giving up and falling to the white ground passed before her eyes.

No need for her to see the spot; too well she knew the winter terrors of the great forest, the snow heaped to the firs' lower branches, alders almost buried beneath it, birches and aspens naked as skeletons and shuddering in the icy wind, a sunless sky above the massed and gloomy spires of green. She sees François making his way through the close-set trees, limbs stiffened with the cold, his skin raw with that pitiless nor'wester, gnawed by hunger, stumbling with fatigue, his feet so weary that with no longer strength to lift them his snow-shoes often catch the snow and throw him to his knees.

Doubtless when the storm abated he saw his error, knew that he was walking toward the barren northland, turned at once and took the right course—he so experienced, the woods his home from boyhood. But his food is nearly gone, the cold tortures him; with lowered head and clenched teeth he fights the implacable winter, calling to aid his every reserve of strength and high courage. He thinks of the road he must follow, the miles to be overcome, measures his chances of life; and fitful memories arise of a house, so warm and snug, where all will greet him gladly; of Maria who, knowing what he has dared for her sake, will at length raise to him her truthful eyes shining with love.

Perhaps he fell for the last time when succour was near, a few yards only from house or shanty. Often so it happens. Cold and his ministers of death flung themselves upon him as their prey; they have stilled the strong limbs forever, covered his open handsome face with snow, closed the fearless eyes without gentleness or pity, changed his living body into a thing of ice. . . . Maria has no more tears that she may shed, but she shivers and trembles as he must have trembled and shivered before he sank into merciful unconsciousness; horror and pity in her face, Maria draws nearer the stove as though she might thus bring him warmth and shield his dear life against the assassin.

"O Christ Jesus, who didst stretch forth Thine arm to those in need, why didst Thou not disperse the snows with those pale hands of Thine? Holy Virgin, why didst Thou not sustain him by Thy power when, for the last time, his feet were stumbling? In all the legions of heaven why was there found no angel to show him the way?"

But it is her grief that utters these reproaches, and the steadfast heart of Maria is fearful of having sinned in yielding to it. Another dread is soon to assail her. Perhaps François Paradis was not able quite faithfully to keep the promises he made to her. In the shanty, among rough and careless men, may he not have had moments of weakness; blasphemed or taken the names of the saints in vain, and thus have gone to his death with sin upon his conscience, under the weight of divine wrath.

Her parents had promised but a little ago that masses should be said. How good they were! Having guessed her secret how kindly had they been silent! But she herself might help with prayers the poor soul in torment. Her beads still lay upon the table; she takes them in her hands, and forthwith the words of the Ave mount to her lips:— "Hail, Mary, full of grace . . ."

Did you doubt of her, O mother of the Galilean? Since that only eight days before she strove to reach your ear with her thousand prayers, and you but clothed yourself in divine impassivity while fate accomplished its purpose, think you that she questions your goodness or your power? It would indeed have been to misjudge her. As once she sought your aid for a man, so now she asks your pardon for a soul, in the same words, with the same humility and boundless faith.

"Blessed art Thou amongst women, and blessed is the fruit of Thy womb, Jesus."

But still she cowers by the great stove, and though the fire's heat strikes through her, she ceases not to shudder as she thinks of the frozen world about her, of François Paradis, who cannot be insentient, who must be so bitter cold in his bed of snow. . . .

IN THE STORM COUNTRY

By Marian Hurd McNeely

THERE are three ways of starting a Christmas story:

It was very early Christmas morning, and the soft snow, falling about the housetops, left peace and purity in its wake . . .

The fragrance of Christmas greens—of pine and hemlock and holly—greeted Molly as she opened the chapel door . . .

It was the day before Christmas, and great preparations were going on in the Maxfield kitchen . . .

The last beginning is the one that belongs to this. Now go on with the story:

There was a delicious odor in the air—a smell compounded of roasting coffee, of almond extract, of cloves and cinnamon and onions and sage. Alice, who was seeding raisins at the window, sniffed hungrily.

"Smells like Arabia," she said.

Ben laughed. It was a nicely graded laugh, intended to convey incredulity, scorn, and derision, rather than amusement, and it achieved its end perfectly.

"How do *you* know what Arabia smells like?" he questioned.

"If you ever looked at your geography you'd know too," retorted his young sister. "Course, any one who gets sixty-one for a month's mark wouldn't be likely to know that spices come from Arabia."

"Sixty-one in geography is no worse than seventy in arithmetic. Even Teacher's Pet, who takes her books home every night, can't get her problems."

"There's the place to stop," said Mrs. Maxfield, crumbling dry sage into a bowl of bread crumbs. "You children act like five and six instead of twelve and thirteen. If you're going to quarrel all vacation, as you've started in, I'll be glad to see school open again. Keep your hands out of those raisins, Ben."

"He eats faster'n I can seed," complained his sister.

"Please let the raisins alone, and put some corn-cobs into the fire," said Mrs. Maxfield. "I want a quick oven for my cookies. And then thread that long needle for me, so I can sew up the goose when this stuffing's ready."

"Gee, that looks swell," said her son, emptying the corncobs out of the hod. "I'm glad we're going to have goose tomorrow."

"Wish we could have a turkey, the way we used to have in Iowa," sighed Alice.

"Why don't you wish for broiled peacock?" taunted her brother. "You're lucky to see goose on the prairie."

"That's all I do see—except Mother."

Ben caught it.

"You ought never feel lonesome, then!"

"Stop it," commanded Mrs. Maxfield. "That kind of bickering always leads to something worse. I do wish you children would agree, occasionally. Look how gray it is outside; we'll probably have more snow for Christmas."

Alice looked.

"We've had enough, now, I should say. There's some one coming down the trail, Mother. Must be one of the Pinchams. Yes, it's Lyd. Maybe she can stay awhile."

Visitors were warmly welcomed in the thinly settled homesteading country, and in spite of the fact that Lydia was only ten, and a "primary," both children were waiting at the door when she arrived.

"Come in," they urged.

"I can't stay," said Lydia, stamping the snow off her overshoes. "I got to go right back; Ma's took awful bad this morning, an' she wants Mis' Maxfield to come over. She's all alone, except us kids."

"What's the matter with her?"

"Oh, chills like, an' fever. An' she's got a terrible pain in her side. Pa's gone fer the doctor."

Mrs. Maxfield had laid down the wooden spoon, and was unbuttoning her apron.

"How did you get over?"

"Walked. Pa had the horses."

"We'd better drive back; it will save time. Sit by the fire and get warm, while Ben hitches up Joanna. Alice, please finish that cup of raisins, and set it away in the pantry. And put the goose in there too, till I get back."

"Shall I bake the cookies?"

Her mother was putting hot-water bag, flannel cloth, and fever thermometer into a basket.

"No, I'd better do it after I come home; I don't want to take any risks with the Christmas cooking. You'll have to get your own lunch, and Ben's, and if I don't get back until late afternoon you can start supper. Keep up the fires, and I'll tell Ben to bring in plenty of coal, in case of snow. And *do* see if you can keep out of a fight while I'm gone. Was your mother suffering when you came away?"

"She was crying when I come," said the little girl, the tears running down her own cheeks at the thought. "I hated to leave her. She couldn't sleep all last night."

"We'll hurry," comforted Mrs. Maxfield. "It won't take us half so long to drive back as it took you to walk over here. How's the lane down to your house? Is the snow deep there?"

"They's two deep drifts. Pa had to shovel his way out this morning."

"Seems as though it couldn't stop snowing," remarked Alice, getting out her mother's galoshes. "It's begun again. I hate to see any more of it. We may get snowed in during vacation."

Mrs. Maxfield was putting on overshoes and getting out her mittens. "There comes Joanna," she said. "Thank you, Ben. You'd better carry in enough coal to last us all day tomorrow, for it looks threatening. You'll be glad enough not to have to do it on Christmas Day. I'll be back for supper at the very latest. Fix up the cottage cheese with cream, and you can cut the fresh spice cake. And start the potatoes at five if I'm not home. *Don't* quarrel, now!"

"No'm," said the two, as Joanna drove away. They watched soberly from the window until the trail melted into a sea of snow, and the buggy became a black speck on the prairie. It was no unusual thing for Mrs. Maxfield to be summoned in cases of illness, but this was the twenty-fourth of December. And when you said to yourself. "All alone the day before Christmas!" that made you at once a martyr. Alice began to feel very sorry for herself, but she found relief in the thought that Ben had some prescribed work ahead of him.

"Don't you think you'd better start at the coal, now?" she suggested.

"That's none of your beeswax," said her brother. "I'll tend to the ole coal."

"Mother said to get it in before it snowed, and it's snowing now." As she spoke the few flakes that had begun to flutter down became more numerous and decided.

"Now don't begin that bossing business," said Ben. "It'll take all your time and attention to cook decent food for us. You needn't try any more of that fairy gingerbread on me."

His sister flushed angrily. The fairy gingerbread, an experiment of her own, warranted to be wafted lightly through the esophagus, had been wingless when the baking powder was forgotten. The subject was not a tactful one. But she set her lips tightly, and gave her brother a taste of the silence that was her most devastating weapon when she had strength to use it. He tried several avenues of approach, but finding none successful, he got out the old coal hod and his heavy mittens. "Might as well start in while I have my things on," he explained, lest his sister might feel that any word of hers had influenced him. Then he called Bounce and slowly ambled out to the coal shed.

The snow was falling in earnest now. No more feathers in the air, but white slants that meant business. A wind had sprung up too—a biting north wind that stung the boy's face and whirled the snow dizzily ahead of his path. Ben fell to briskly, and carried hod after hod from the shed to the big piano box that stood under the kitchen stoop.

"Hope that young lady doesn't think I'm doing this for *her!*" he remarked darkly to himself.

For half an hour he worked on. The snow was falling so thickly now that he could not see far ahead of him, and it was not until Bounce gave a bark that the boy looked up to see a rider on a bay pony come around the side of the house, and stop at the shed.

"How?" said the visitor.

"How."

"S'pose I could drop in on you till this storm lets up? I'm on my way to Calome, and I don't like the looks of this sky. Your dad home?"

"I haven't a father; he's dead."

"What's your name? I'm Red Deneen."

"Maxfield. Ben Maxfield."

"Your pa Doc Maxfield?"

"Yes, sir. Did you know my father?"

"I sure did. He lanced my throat when I had quinsy. And if you've ever had quinsy, Boy, you know that that proceeding makes intimate friends. I almost fell on his neck with thankfulness. How about your mother? Will she let a stray sheep in?"

"She's over at Pincham's. There's some one sick over there."

"Yes, I've heard that the woman over there was down. Who is the boss of your ranch if your mother's gone? I'd like to send in a petition for parking space."

"I am, when mother's gone. But Alice does the cooking. She's my sister."

"The cook is always the boss; I'd better ask her. I might stay to a meal if I was invited."

"Oh, Alice'll like that, and so will I. We don't have company any too often. Come on in."

"Wait until I put up the mare, and I'll help you with that coal."

"No, I'm just through carrying. Put the horse in the barn. Here, this way."

The boy, helping to unsaddle the pony, jumped as she took a nip at his shoulder.

"Don't let that make you nervous. That's one of her tricks. Unbutton him, Lady." At this command, the horse gently nuzzled along Ben's breast. His canvas coat was pulled open.

"How on earth did you teach her to do that?" cried Ben.

"Easy enough. She's like all women—she'll do anything for sugar. Take off his mittens, Lady."

Lady swung Ben's gloves into the air from her mouth.

"I do wish Alice had seen that. She'd never believe it if I told her."

"Lady can give an exhibition before she leaves. She knows dozens of stunts, and loves to show off. May I give her some hay?"

"Sure, and oats, too," said Ben. With the pitchfork he pulled down some fresh hay for Lady's stall. He threw another forkful into her bin, and poured a measure of oats on top. The barn was cold; hoarfrost hung thick upon the rafters and in the crack of the door; but Ben stopped to pat the soft bay nose and to rub Lady's sleek neck.

"Like horses, don't you?" said Red.

"You bet I do. Dad always promised us a pony—me and Alice. We would have had it this fall if he hadn't—hadn't died." He gave the horse another pat. "C'mon, let's go in the house."

Alice looked up in surprise as they entered, and Ben introduced his sister clumsily.

"This is my sister," he said.

"I'm Red Deneen, from down near Dog Ear Buttes," amended the stranger. "I knew your dad. I'm on my way to Calome, and I don't like the looks of this snow for so long a trip."

"No," said Ben. "The drifts are bad enough now without any more on top of them."

"If the storm quits I'll go on; if it keeps up tonight I might ask your mother for a chair by the fire."

Alice gave a quick look at the curly red hair, the decided chin, the bluest eyes she ever saw, and liked him at once. He was past thirty, she thought, and thirty was old, but there were smile wrinkles about his eyes, and a merry cock of the head that appealed to both children.

"I know Mother'd let you stay," said Ben.

The visitor took off his sheep-lined coat, and the heavy sweater he wore underneath. He took the coal scuttle out of Alice's hands, and replenished the big base-burner. He washed at the kitchen sink, and ran his damp hands through his curls. He glanced around the clean living room, at the glowing fire, the old piano, the bookshelves, and the bowl of red berries in the south window.

"Gee!" he said. "This looks like a real home."

"Haven't you a home?" inquired Alice.

"I got half a shack, or did have until this morning. I had a bust-up with my pard a while ago, and he lit out."

"What was the matter?"

"Oh, weather, mostly, I guess; though it's been nip and tuck about as long as we could make it go, together. He held the claim next to mine, so we built our shack together for convenience's sake, and tackled the farming on the shares. This was his idea, and it seemed good, because we could pool our stock. But it didn't work long. All people are divided into lemons and squeezers, and I soon found that he wasn't a lemon."

"What do you mean?" asked the literal Ben.

Red Deneen settled back in the rocker with a sigh of satisfaction.

"I haven't set in a rocking-chair for six years, I'll bet. Why, I mean that he laid back on his oars, and let me do all the pulling. Last up in the morning, and first to bed at night. Had a crick in his back at ploughing time, and a lame finger when there were dishes to wash. Said he'd be perfectly willing to do his share of the meals, only he knew I'd never like his cooking as well as my own. You know the kind —strong on alibis and weak on exercise."

Alice stared at Ben.

"I know," she said.

"At first I didn't mind carrying the main part of the work, because he wasn't overly strong, and he never did anything right, anyway. We didn't have time to scrap, because when night came I was too tired to do anything but cook our meal and fall into bed. But after the crops was all in it was a different story."

"What happened then?" inquired Ben, with interest. A chatty visitor like this was manna to the lonely children.

"Nerves," said Red. "Shut in the house all day we got on each other something terrible. You know how touchy two people get when they see nobody but each other. One turns the lamp wick up and the other goes and turns it down. One saws wood in the room when the other fellow wants to sleep. And fresh air! Some folks think that a draft is as sacred as the Bible—when it's blowing on some one else. More marriages has been broken up by fresh air than by drunkenness.

I got so I couldn't stand that bird around; couldn't stand the way he stretched hisself when he yawned, or the way he bit his nails, or the way he et oysters out of a can."

"I know," said Alice, feelingly.

"I guess *your* daily habits, Allie, aren't anything to brag about," retorted Ben. "And I can't imagine you ever keeping still about mine. Always shooting off your mouth—"

"Well, I got to the place where I couldn't keep still either," went on the guest hastily. "And he didn't like it when I told him how he got on my nerves. He was too hasty, that fellow. I got a quick temper, I'll admit, but it's all over in a week or two; only he wasn't willing to wait that long. So when I told him to get out of doors till I could make up my mind to stand him around, he did, and he didn't come back. I washed up his blankets, and cleaned out the dirt he left behind, and I been batching it ever since. I ain't crazy about batching, either."

"Why don't you get married?"

"Well, sister, I ain't any crazier about matrimony. I never seen but one girl that I wanted."

"Why didn't you marry her?"

"Oh, I heard something about her that made it impossible."

"What?" Ben's curiosity was aroused.

"That she was John D. Rockefeller's granddaughter."

"Are you going back to your home for Christmas?" asked Alice. "I mean the home where you lived when you were little."

Red shook his head.

"No, nothing for me to go home to. I got a brother and a sister down in Missouri, but it's been twenty years since I set eyes on 'em. I run away when I was twelve. And they never meant much to me when I *was* there. We used to fight like cats and dogs."

"Just like Ben and me," said Alice.

"You got that habit, too? It's a bad one."

"I wouldn't fight if it wasn't for Ben. He's the most aggravating—"

"It's your tongue that makes all the trouble," snapped Ben. "You're always—"

"My tongue! I like that."

"Whoa, whoa, there," said their guest. "Too much weather is what's the matter with you kids. Look at that snow come down! It's drifting, too. Your ma had better start back soon."

"She'll probably start home as soon as the doctor gets there with Mr. Pincham. She's got to be back in time to fix for Christmas dinner. She was just in the middle of her baking when they sent for her."

"What was she cooking?"

"Oh, she had the cookies all ready to roll out, and was making mince pies. And the goose was about ready to stuff."

"What say if we finish things up for her? She'll be dead tired if she faces this snowstorm."

"She said to leave them until she came back," said Alice, a little doubtfully. "She didn't want any accidents about the Christmas dinner."

"There won't be no accidents," said Red, confidently. "I know a lot about cooking. I been a regular chef in a hotel more than once, since the war. Let's see how your ma left things."

Alice brought out the half finished Christmas dinner, and Red surveyed it with a professional eye.

"Most everything's done already," he said. "Goose all cleaned and everything started. Let's go ahead and have 'em all ready when she gets in. Gimme an apron an' a clean dust cloth."

He rolled up the sleeves of his gray flannel shirt, washed his hands again, donned the apron, and tied the white cloth about his head.

"These cookies were all ready to roll, weren't they? Is that oven good and hot? Where do you keep the rolling-pin?"

The dubious look left Alice's face as she saw him sprinkle flour on the molding board, scrape out a third of the cookie dough, and begin to roll it out with a practiced hand.

"Where did you learn to cook?"

Red laughed.

"In the war. When we enlisted each soldier had to write down his former employment on his enlistment sheet. I was sparing of my handwriting, which was none too good, anyway, and wrote chauf. instead of chauffeur. They read it 'chef,' and nothing I could say would make any difference. I had to cook, instead of fight, for three solid years. When I got out I was a graduate baker, but the boys had to put up with a great deal while I was learning on them. Oh, I learned a real trade. I've been head cook at the Planter's Hotel in New Orleans, and I was chef at the Edgewater Beach in Chicago for nearly a year."

"Why didn't you stick?"

Red was cutting out cookies with a deft hand.

"I get tired staying in one place. I got spring heels on me, and as soon as the snow melts I want to be moving. I'm about through with farming. If it wasn't for Lady I don't believe I'd come back next summer."

"And throw up your claim when you're so near to proving up?"

Red blushed through his freckles.

"That's the trouble with me—I ain't no sticker. That's why I'm thirty-two with no property but a mare and a mouth organ."

"Can you play the mouth organ? Let's hear you."

"Wait till our cooking's done." He turned over the big pan, arranging the cookies on the bottom, and "tried" the oven with his bare hand. "That's right, Ben; put 'em in, two pans at a time."

From the cookies the "chauf" turned to the pies. He set the two children at finishing the mince-meat, mixed the crust, and turned out the finished product. Three golden-brown pies, with flaky ruching around the edge and a floral design atop, soon stood side by side on the pantry shelf. He finished stuffing the goose, sewed it up and put it into the roaster. He made cranberry sauce, and mayonnaise for cabbage, and a pan of molasses candy. He even pared the potatoes and peeled the onions for the Christmas meal next day.

"Gee!" said Ben. "You sure are some cook! Did you make lots of mince pies in the army? The soldiers must have liked them."

"Mince pies!" said Red. "We was lucky to get crackers and canned salmon most of the time. We moved so fast that I didn't have time to bake for days, sometimes. But whenever we stopped to take breath I did the best I could with what I had. The boys were crazy for pie. Sometimes I'd get dried apples or apricots, and sometimes a Frog would bring a mess of berries into camp. Feeding 'em was all I *could* do. It made me crazy to be stirring a spoon all time instead of firing a gun."

"I s'pose though, you *saw* a lot of fighting?"

"I saw plenty."

"Were you close enough to see men shot?"

"I was in the trenches for five months, just back of the firing-line," said Red. His face looked old. "I don't like to talk about it," he added.

"You said you'd play the mouth organ for us," suggested Alice.

"I will, a little later," promised the guest. "But it's about noon-time. Aren't you kids about ready to eat? How about getting dinner?"

"That's Allie's work," remarked Ben.

"But Mother expected you to *help*."

"No, I did the coal; the meals are up to you."

"I never saw such a lazy boy!"

"How many boys have you seen in all your travels?"

"At it, again, ain't you?" said Red. "You kids just seem to take naturally to scrapping. I should think it would be easier to cook the meal than to think up new comebacks. What say if we all fall to? We can get done quicker."

Stirred by their visitor's example, the children went to work. They cooked the meal together, ate together, and amiably united in clearing away the remains. Then Red went to the gunny sack which had swung over the horn of his saddle when he arrived, and produced a large and ornamental harmonica. With lip and hand he turned that crude instrument into a concert piano. He played jigs and hymns, negro melodies and old-time songs, jazz and classical music, while the children listened spellbound. Then he laid down the mouth organ, and became an entertainer himself. He gave imitations of a band, of a crying baby, of a dog, a sheep, a calliope. He performed sleight-of-hand tricks, and made voices come from wall and ceiling. He danced as Javanese girls dance, as the Sioux Indians dance. He told them how the East Indian fakirs walked on nails, how Eskimo dogs were trained, and how lions were hunted. For hours the children sat entranced, only occasionally bickering about which one must do the necessary chores that took them away, momentarily, from the scene of entertainment. There had never been such a day on the claim—no, never *anywhere,* before.

"Where did you ever learn all these things?" asked Alice, as he stopped for breath.

"Oh, I've been a lot of places. I was a sailor for eight years, and I never shipped for the same port twice. This last twelve months have been the longest time I ever stuck in one place. My feet are beginning to itch again; that's why I'm moving on."

"Where are you going now?"

"Well, I dunno, exactly. Thought I'd try Florida, first. I might ship to Cuba while the cold weather lasts. I never know just where I *am* bound for till I get on the train."

The children gazed at each other. This was the life! No day after day existence in one place, covered by the same roof, cupped by the same sky, hemmed in by prairie grass or drifts of snow. A life of change, of freedom; of moving trains and shifting climates, and new people . . . "I never know just where I *am* bound for till I get on the train!" . . .

"Gee!" said Ben.

The afternoon's entertainment had so engrossed the children that they had lost all interest in what was going on out-of-doors. When their exclamations over the vaudeville stopped they were surprised to find that snow was beginning to bank against the windowpane. It was falling, not in a shower of flakes, but in slanting lines that shut away trail and barn and shed. And with it had come a wind that whirled the downfall in dizzying spirals in the air.

"Oh, heck!" exclaimed Ben. "Look at that snow, will you!"

"We must get a move on us," said the guest. "We got to feed the animals before dark."

"Ain't time, yet."

"Can't go by a clock in weather like this. We must get out there before the drifts get any deeper. That cow of yours will have to be milked and the chickens fed."

Ben groaned.

"You'd better get the pail. I can bed the horses and feed the chickens while you milk."

"I hope Mother isn't out in this storm," said Alice.

"She'd never start out with the weather this way. You won't see your mother till morning."

"But this is Christmas Eve. She'll be sure to come home for that."

"Judging from her children I take it that your ma has got some brain cell-arage," remarked Red. "Any one that's lived a winter on this prairie wouldn't take no chances with a blizzard, Christmas or no Christmas. Come along with that bucket, Ben."

"Good thing you're here, or Ben wouldn't be so ready to milk," commented Alice.

Ben put the empty pail over his sister's head and held it there until the guest came to her rescue.

"That's a fine way to treat a girl," said Red.

"She deserved it."

"I'll admit she did, but you don't have to give women all that's coming to them. The Lord attends to that. Come on, now; we've got to get a hustle on us."

Alice had the lamps lighted and the supper started when the two came back with the pail of milk, a thin coating of ice already over the top of it. They reported an increasing fall of snow, and a wind that almost took them off their feet. Their canvas coats were covered with sleet.

"There are a whole lot of horses down in the draw," said Alice. "I saw them coming in there when I was looking out of the window. If I could have made you hear I would have called you to throw some hay down to them. I'll bet they're hungry and cold."

"Probably hungry," said Red. "But those range horses grow pretty thick coats, and those high banks will keep off the wind. Their owners ought to round 'em up. It's no kind of weather to have animals out."

"No weather for anybody to be out," said Alice. "I wish Mother were home."

"Look here," remarked Red. "You two have got to give up your ma for tonight. She won't be home. There's no horse in the world, except Lady, that could bring her through such a storm like this."

"How could Lady do it?"

"I don't know; nose, most likely. She can smell—or feel—her way through any blizzard I ever saw in Dakota. But your ma *ain't* got her, and no horse could make it. She'll be home as soon as this storm stops, and not before."

"But we've never had a Christmas without her," quavered Alice.

"Well, you got to have a first time for everything. The blizzard may let up in the morning, so she can get back. If I was you I'd clean up my dishes and get to bed early. Then the waiting won't seem so long."

"Will you stay till she comes?"

Red looked pleased.

"I'm not longing to hit the trail in this storm," he said.

The children obediently went at the dishwashing. Red presided over the pan, and succeeded in keeping both wipers busy. On the kitchen side of the house they could get the full violence of the storm. It sounded as though the prairie were a vast carpet which the wind was beating. The house creaked and shook; a border of frost outlined the outer door; an icy draft blew in under it, and in the warm room their feet were cold. Alice got a rug to cover the crack.

"I can't help thinking of those horses out in the draw," she said, as she hung up the dishpan.

For once Ben did not jeer. He was silent.

"They must be almost frozen," she went on.

"No," said Red, "I don't think it is quite cold enough to freeze them. They know how to get behind a windbreak and huddle together. It's the wind that cuts."

"But they're hungry."

There was another long silence. Then Ben got up and began to pull on his galoshes.

"Where you going?" asked Red.

"Going to throw some hay down to those horses."

"Oh, those beasts won't freeze. We'll feed 'em in the morning."

Ben went on buckling his arctics.

"You'd better keep out of that snow. Night's no time to be fooling around in drifts."

"Yes," said Alice. "You might get lost in the dark."

Ben turned on her fiercely.

"I s'pose you think I *want* to go—that I'm going out to make a snowman, or something! That's just like you—always stirring up trouble, in the beginning, and then getting scared. If you'd kept your mouth shut about those horses, I wouldn't have to go. But now that I know they're there I can't let 'em go hungry."

"We'll both go," said Red. He put on his overshoes and his still sleety canvas coat. "It'll take two; one to carry the hay and one to hold the lantern."

Alice, from the window, watched the glow of the lantern move slowly between barn and draw. It was twenty minutes before the two got back into the house—cold, weather-beaten, and tired from fighting the wind. As Red predicted, they had found the animals huddled into a group behind a thin fringe of poplar trees. The high banks of the draw sheltered them from the bitter wind, but they had gratefully accepted the great armfuls of hay thrown down to them, and had begun to eat ravenously.

"I can sleep better now," said Alice.

The guest suggested pinochle, and the three had a few games. Then, quite willingly, the children turned in for the night.

"I'm not going to hang up my stockings," said Alice, virtuously. "I think Mother'd rather have us wait till she gets home."

"You've *got* to," said Ben. "She's got all the presents hid."

"I guess I could find 'em if I wanted to."

"Been peeking?" taunted Ben.

"Alice is right," put in their guest, hastily. "I'd wait if I were you. You'll have more fun over your Christmas with your ma here."

"You can have her bed tonight," said Alice, hospitably.

"No," said Red, "I guess I better not. A bed is sort of sacred to a housekeeper, and she might not like an unknown soldier kicking around under her best quilts. Besides, I got to keep up the fire. I'll just camp on this here lounge if you can lend me a couple of blankets."

Alice got out pillow and sheets, as well as blankets, and made up a bed on the couch.

"I don't know what we'd do if you weren't here," she confided gratefully to her visitor. "I wish Mother knew we had you; she wouldn't be worrying so."

Before long the house was dark and still. The snow whirled around the eaves, and slammed shutters, and shook window casings, but the two children slept. And Red, watching the cheery glow of the base-burner through isinglass, went back twenty years.

At five in the morning he got up in the freezing room to turn on the dampers. Then he heard, from Alice's room, the sound of suppressed sobs. He was about to speak to her, when he heard Ben say, in a half-whisper, "Say, what's eating you?"

"I'm worried over Mother."

"So'm I, but crying ain't going to do any good."

"But I'm afraid she got caught in this storm."

"Don't be an idiot. Mother wouldn't start home in a blizzard."

"She would for Christmas."

Ben did not reply for a moment. Then he said:

"Well, crying ain't going to help any. Cut it out until morning, when we get out and do something. We'll ride over to Pincham's and see."

Alice sobbed again.

"Quit that!" he snapped.

"You're almost crying yourself!"

Ben did not answer. The stifled sobs went on for a few minutes longer. Then the house was still again.

Red lay for a few minutes till he was sure the children had gone to sleep. Then he went to the window and looked out. The snow had stopped, the wind had gone down, and the storm was over. A full moon made the prairie as white as day. The trail was covered, and a great white sheet stretched from the farmhouse to the hill that led to Pincham's. He hesitated but a moment, and then began to hurry on his clothes. He added coal to the fire with a shovel, that he might not disturb the sleepers, folded his bedding in a neat pile on the couch, and put on his outer clothing. On the pillow he pinned a penciled note:

"Back soon. Don't go out till I come."

Then, with a stealthy glance at the bedroom door, he stole quietly out of the house.

It was past seven o'clock when Alice was awakened by the sound of voices outside, and the closing of the front door. As she opened her eyes she heard a familiar voice and the sound of a horse trotting away.

"Mother," she called.

Mrs. Maxfield, her coat still on, opened the bedroom door.

"Merry Christmas!" she said.

"Oh, Mother, I was so worried! I thought you might have started."

"I did start, last night, but I had to go back. I couldn't make it."

"How'd you get here so early this morning? I was afraid you couldn't get through for Christmas."

"I couldn't have done it if it hadn't been for your Mr. Deneen. He came over for me this morning before sun-up, and told me how worried you were."

"Did he drive you home?"

"No, we never could have made it with a buggy. The trail is terribly drifted in some places. He brought his horse, and a bridle for Joanna. How he got through the first time I don't know, but he broke a trail for us, and it wasn't so bad coming back. He took Joanna, and let me ride his horse, and she's a wonder."

"Did he tell you we were scared?"

"Yes, he said that you cried in the night, and he couldn't have that going on at Christmas time. He said he'd have me back for breakfast with you if I were willing to try, and I knew that if he'd got over we could get back. Lots of folks wouldn't have taken the risk of that first trip before daylight. A lovely thing for a stranger to do."

Alice hugged her mother's skirts.

"Where's he?"

"He wouldn't come in. I tried to get him to spend the day with us, but he said that Christmas was for families, and while he was saddled he guessed he'd go on to Calome. The snow is melting, and he wanted to catch that morning train. He left good-by to you both, and told you not to fight until the next war broke out. Must have got pretty well acquainted with your habits in one day."

Alice looked disappointed.

"I should a' thought he'd come in to say good-by before he left."

"He said you'd hear from him again." Her mother smiled as she turned to take off her outer garments. "You didn't hang your stockings, did you? Well, go in and wake Ben, and by the time you're both dressed the stockings will be ready."

The Northwestern train was just pulling into Calome when a red-headed man on a bay pony drove up to the station. He dismounted from the horse, gave her a piece of candy, and handed her bridle to a half-grown boy that stood waiting there.

"Here she is. See that she gets a good rub-down when she gets to the stable, and don't take her out of the barn today. Tell your father that I've changed my mind about keeping her in Calome this winter. There's a family named Maxfield—the doc's folks—down near White Water, that's going to board her for me till I get back. If the road's clear you can drive her there tomorrow."

The boy mounted the saddle. Deneen patted the bay neck, and watched the two ride away. Then he made his way to the train, and mounted the steps of the single coach.

"How are you, Red?" called the engineer.

Red waved a hand in greeting.

"Back to the road again?" asked the engineer.

"Yep, back again."

"We been expecting you. Where you bound for, this time? Africa or Australia?"

"Neither," said Red. "I'm going back to see my sister in Missouri."

"I didn't know you had any folks."

Red planted his feet firmly on the platform.

"Well, I haven't given 'em much attention for twenty years," he admitted. "But I spent Christmas Eve at a claim-house where there were a coupla kids, and it made me lonesome."

"Got the Christmas spirit, did you?"

"Christmas spirit nothing," said Red Deneen. "I was with two kids that fought all day long, and it got the best of me. I haven't been homesick before since I was twelve. But that fighting carried me back twenty years, and I made up my mind I'd go home and see that sister of mine!"

THE BLOSSOMING ROD

By Mary Stewart Cutting

MR. LANGSHAW had vaguely felt unusual preparations for a Christmas gift to him this year; he was always being asked for "change" to pay the children for services rendered.

It might have seemed a pity that calculation as to dollars and cents entered so much into the Christmas festivities of the family, if it were not that it entered so largely into the scheme of living that it was naturally interwoven with every dearest hope and fancy; the overcoming of its limitations gave a zest to life. Langshaw himself, stopping now, as was his daily habit, to look at the display made by the sporting-goods shop on his way home the Friday afternoon before Christmas Monday, wondered, as his hand touched the ten-dollar bill in his pocket—a debt unexpectedly paid him that day—if the time had actually arrived at last when he might become the possessor of the trout-rod that stood in the corner of the window; reduced, as the ticket proclaimed, from fifteen dollars to ten.

The inspiration was the more welcome because the moment before his mind had been idly yet disquietingly filled with the shortcomings of George, his eldest child and only son, aged ten, who didn't seem to show that sense of responsibility which his position and advanced years called for—even evading his duties to his fond mother when he should be constituting himself her protector. He was worried as to the way George would turn out when he grew up.

This particular trout-rod, however, had an attraction for Langshaw of long standing. He had examined it carefully more than once when in the shop with his neighbour, Wickersham; it wasn't a fifty-dollar rod, of course, but it seemed in some ways as good as if it were—it was expensive enough for him! He had spoken of it once to his wife, with a craving for her usual sympathy, only to meet with a surprise that seemed carelessly disapproving.

"Why, you have that old one of your father's and the bass-rod already; I can't see why you should want another. You always say you can't get off to go fishing as it is."

He couldn't explain that to have this particular split bamboo would be almost as good as going on a fishing trip; with it in his hand he could feel himself between green meadows, the line swirling down the rushing brook. But later Clytie had gone back to the subject with pondering consideration:

"Ten dollars seems an awful price for a rod! I'm sure I could buy the same thing for much less uptown; wouldn't you like me to see about it some day?"

"Great Scott! Never think of such a thing!" he had replied in horror. "I could get much cheaper ones myself! If I ever have the money I'll do the buying—you hear?"

"—Hello, Langshaw! Looking at that rod again? Why don't you blow yourself to a Christmas present? Haven't you got the nerve?"

"That's what I don't know!" called Langshaw with a wave of the hand as Wickersham passed by. Yet, even as he spoke he felt he did know—his mind was joyously, adventurously made up to have "the nerve"; he had a right, for once in the twelve years of his married life, to buy himself a Christmas present that he really wanted, in distinction to the gift that family affection prompted, and held dear as such, but which had no relation to his needs or desires. Children and friends were provided for; his wife's winter suit—a present by her transforming imagination—already in the house; the Christmas turkey for the janitor of the children's school subscribed to—sometimes he had wished himself the janitor! and all the small demands that drain the purse at the festal season carefully counted up and allowed for. There was no lien on this unexpected sum just received. The reel and the line, and the flies and such, would have to wait until another time, to be sure; but no one could realize what it would be to him to come home and find that blessed rod there. He had a wild impulse to go in and buy it that moment, but such haste seemed too slighting to the dignity of that occasion, which should allow the sweets of anticipation—though no one knew better than he the danger of delay where money was concerned: it melted like snow in the pocket. Extra funds always seemed to bring an extra demand.

The last time there was ten dollars to spare there had been a letter from Langshaw's mother, saying that his sister Ella, whose husband was unfortunately out of a position, had developed flat-foot; and a pair of suitable shoes, costing nine-fifty, had been prescribed by the physician. Was it possible for her dear boy to send the money? Ella was so depressed.

The ten dollars had, of course, gone to Ella. Both Langshaw and his wife had an unsympathetic feeling that if they developed flat-foot now they would have to go without appropriate shoes.

"You look quite gay!" said his wife as she greeted him on his return, her pretty oval face, with its large dark eyes and dark curly locks, held up to be kissed. "Has anything nice happened?"

"You look gay too!" he evaded laughingly, as his arms lingered round her. Clytie was always a satisfactory person for a wife. "What's this pink stuff on your hair—popcorn?"

"Oh, goodness! Baby has been so bad, she has been throwing it around everywhere," she answered, running ahead of him upstairs to a room that presented a scene of brilliant disorder.

On the bed was a large box of tinselled Christmas-tree decorations and another of pink and white popcorn—the flotsam and jetsam of which strewed the counterpane and the floor to its farthest corners, mingled with scraps of glittering paper, an acreage of which surrounded a table in the centre of the room that was adorned with mucilage pot and scissors. A large feathered hat, a blue silk dress, and a flowered skirt were on the rug, near which a very plump child of three, with straggling yellow hair, was trying to get a piece of gilt paper off her shoe. She looked up with roguish blue eyes to say rapidly:

"Fardie doesn't know what baby goin' a give'm for Kissemus!"

"Hello! This looks like the real thing," said Langshaw, stepping over the débris; "but what are all these clothes on the floor for?"

"Oh, Mary was dressing up and just dropped those things when she went to the village with Viney, though I called her twice to come back and pick them up," said the mother, sweeping the garments out of the way. "It's so tiresome of her! Oh, I know you stand up for everything Mary does, Joe Langshaw; but she is the hardest child to manage!"

Her tone insensibly conveyed a pride in the difficulty of dealing with her elder daughter, aged six.

"But did you ever see anything like Baby? She can keep a secret as well as any one! It does look Christmassy, though—doesn't it? Of course all the work of the tree at the mission comes on me as usual. The children, with the two Wickersham girls, were helping me until they got tired. Why don't you come and kiss father, Baby? She is going to sweep up the floor with her little broom so that father will give her five cents."

"I don't want to fweep 'e floor!" said the child, snapping her blue eyes.

"She shall get her little broom and fardie will help her," said Langshaw, catching the child up in his arms and holding the round little form closely to him before putting her down carefully on her stubby feet.

Later, when the game of clearing up was over and the nickel clutched in Baby's fat palm, he turned to his wife with a half-frown:

"Don't you think you are making the children rather mercenary, Clytie? They seem to want to be paid for everything they do. I'm just about drained out of change!"

"Oh, at Christmas!" said the wife expressively.

"Well, I hope nobody is going to spend any money on me; the only presents I want are those you make for me," said Langshaw warningly. He gave the same warning each year, undeterred by the nature of the articles produced. His last year's "Christmas" from Clytie had been a pair of diaphanous blue China-silk pajamas that were abnormally large in chest and sleeves—as for one of giant proportions—and correspondingly contracted in the legs, owing to her cutting out the tops first and having to get the other necessary adjuncts out of the scant remainder of the material. "You hear me, Clytie?"

"Yes, I hear," returned Clytie in a bored tone.

"Do you know—" Langshaw hesitated, a boyish smile overspreading his countenance. "I was looking at that trout-rod in Burchell's window to-day. I don't suppose you remember my speaking of it, but I've had my eye on it for a long time." He paused, expectant of encouraging interest.

"Oh, have you, dear?" said Clytie absently. The room was gradually, under her fingers, resuming its normal appearance. She turned suddenly with a vividly animated expression.

"I must tell you that you're going to get a great surprise to-night— it isn't a Christmas present, but it's something that you'll like even better, I know. It's about something that George has been doing. You'll never guess what it is!"

"Is that so?" said Langshaw absently in his turn. He had a momentary sense of being set back in his impulse to confidences that was not, after all, untinged with pleasure. His delightful secret was still his own, unmarred by unresponsive criticism. "By the way, Clytie, I don't like the way George has been behaving lately. He hasn't shown me his report from school in months; whenever I ask him for it he has some excuse. Hello! Is that little Mary crying?"

"I wonder what on earth has happened now!" exclaimed the mother, rushing from the room to return the next instant, pulling after her a red-cloaked and red-hatted little girl who sought to hide behind her.

"Well, what do you think she's done?" Clytie's tone was withering as she haled forth the shrinking culprit, her small hands over her eyes. "She lost her purse with the dollar she had saved up for your Christmas present—lost the money for dear father's present; and all because she took it with her to buy a five-cent pencil—a green pencil with purple glass in the end of it; to buy something for *herself* before Christmas!" Clytie paused tragically. "Of course, if she hadn't taken her money out to spend it on herself she wouldn't have lost it!"

"I don't care!" burst out the culprit, her big, dark eyes, just like her mother's, flashing from under her brown curls, and her red lips set defiantly. "It was my own money, anyhow, if I did lose it. I earned it all myself. It wasn't yours!"

"Oh! Oh! Oh!" interposed the father in gentle reproof. "Little girls mustn't talk like that to dear mother. Come, get up here on father's knee—so." He took off the red cap, tucked the brown curly head in the bend of his arm, his chin resting on the top of it as he went on, with the child's small hands clutching at his. "Mary must always do what mother says; but, so far as this money is concerned, you can make me something that I would like far better than anything you could buy. Why don't you make me another pincushion, for instance? The one you gave me last year is quite worn out."

"A pink one?" asked Mary faintly.

"Yes. What's the matter now?" The child had suddenly wriggled to a kneeling posture in his hold and had her little strangling arms round his neck in a tempest of sobs.

"I don't want to give you a pi-ink pincushion—I don't want to! I want my dollar! I want my dollar—to spend! I want—— Father, I want my dollar—my do-o-ol-lar! I want my——"

"What did I tell you, Mary Langshaw?" cried Clytie. She appealed to her husband. "It's just the way I knew she'd act. Now I suppose you'll have to give it to her. Mary, be still a moment—her head is so hot!"

"There, there!" said Langshaw soothingly. "She shall have her money this minute."

"Of course she doesn't deserve it," said Clytie, but with a tone of relief in her voice that seemed oddly greater than the occasion warranted. Mary had wound herself round him passionately; her sobs were dying away happily in long, deep breaths at intervals. Baby, being undressed on her mother's lap, was laughing over some pieces of gilt paper. In the heart of this domesticity it was as if the father and mother were embarked with this little company on a full and swelling river of love, of which they felt the exquisite soothing ripples.

Langshaw put his hand into his pocket.

"No, I can't give you the dollar this minute, little girl; father has only a ten-dollar bill. I'll get it changed right after dinner. Isn't dinner 'most ready, Clytie?"

"We'll go down just as soon as I get Baby in bed," said the mother peacefully. "I don't see why George isn't here. Goodness! There he is now," she added as a tremendous slam of the front door announced the fact. The next moment a small boy, roguishly blue-eyed and yellow-haired like Baby, with an extremely dirty face and a gray sweater half covered with mud, hurled himself into the room, surreptitiously tickling one of Baby's bare feet and pulling Mary's curls on his way to greet his father.

"What have you been doing to get so dirty?"

"Playing cops and robbers," said the boy, serenely. His dimples appeared suddenly; his eyes lit up. "Say, mother"—he turned to her irresolutely—"shall I tell father now?"

"Not until after dinner," returned the mother inexorably. "Go and make yourself clean!"

"May I put on my white silk tie?" George's white tie was the banner of festivity.

"Yes."

"You rouse my curiosity. This seems to be a great occasion," said Langshaw.

"Oh, it is!" agreed the mother happily. She murmured in his ear as they went downstairs: "I hope you'll show that you're pleased, dear. You know sometimes when you really are pleased you don't show it at once—and George has been trying so hard. If you'll only show that you're pleased—"

"Yes—all right!" returned the husband a little impatiently. Clytie had a sensitive consideration for her son's feelings which struck him at times as exaggerated. He thought of the delightful secret back in his own mind; there was no reason for talking any more about the rod until he brought it; he would manage to replace the dollar abstracted from the reserve fund.

If he gave absent answers during the meal Clytie seemed to be preoccupied also. Little Mary, who sat by him, tucked her hand into his as she prattled.

"Now, George!" said his mother at last suddenly when the rice pudding had been finished. George rose, clean and red-cheeked, looking more than ever like a large edition of Baby, in spite of his jacket and knickerbockers, as he stepped over to his father with a new dignity and handed him a folded sheet of paper.

"What's this?" asked Langshaw genially opening it. He read aloud the words within, written laboriously in a round, boyish hand:

To George Brander Langshaw, from father.
   You Oh me five dolers.

                           Reseived paiment.

"Hello! Hello! What does this mean?" asked Langshaw slowly with an unpleasant startled sensation that any such sum in connection with George was out of all reason.

"It means a bill for you from me!" announced George. His cheeks grew redder, his blue eyes looked squarely at his father. "It's for this!" He pulled from his pocket a school report card divided into tiny ruled squares, filled with figures for half its length, and flung it down proudly on the table before his parent.

"It's the Deportment—since September. You said when Miss Skinner sent that last note home about me that if I could get a hundred in Deportment for every month up to Christmas you'd be willing to pay me five dollars. You can see there for yourself, father, the three one hundreds—no, not that line—that's only fifty-five for spelling; nobody ever knows their spelling! Here is the place to look—in the Deportment column. I've tried awful hard to be good, father, to surprise you."

"The way that child has tried!" burst forth Clytie, her dark eyes drowned in sparkles. "And they're so unfair at school—giving you a mark if you squeak your chair, or speak, or look at anybody; as if any child could be expected to sit like a stone all the time! I'm sure I love to hear children laughing—and you know yourself how hard it is for George to be quiet! We had a little talk about it together, he and I; and now you see! It's been such work keeping his card from you each month when you asked for it. One day he thought he had a bad mark and he couldn't eat any dinner—you thought he was ill; but he went to Miss Skinner the next day and she took it off because he had been trying so hard to be good. Joe, why don't you speak?"

"George, I'm proud of you!" said Langshaw simply. There was a slight huskiness in his voice; the round face and guileless blue eyes of his little boy, who had tried "awful hard to be good," seemed to have acquired a new dignity. The father saw in him the grown-up son who could be depended upon to look after his mother if need were. Langshaw held out his hand as man to man; the two pairs of eyes met squarely. "Nothing you could have done would have pleased me more than this, George. I value it more than any Christmas present I could have."

"Mother said you'd like it," said the beaming George, ducking his head suddenly and kicking out his legs from behind.

"And you'll pay the five dollars?" supplemented Clytie anxiously.

"Surely!" said Langshaw. The glances of the parents met in one of the highest pleasures that life affords: the approval together of the good action of their dear child. "George can go out and get this ten-dollar bill changed."

"If you can't spare it, father—" suggested the boy with some new sense of manliness, hanging back.

"I'm glad to be able to spare it," said the father soberly. "It's a good deal of money," he added. "I suppose, of course, you'll put it in the bank, George?"

"Now you mustn't ask what he's going to do with it," said Clytie.

"Oh, isn't it much!" cried little Mary.

"Dear me, there's the doorbell," said Clytie. "Who can it be at this hour? Run, George, and see!"

"It's a letter for you, mother," announced George, reappearing. "There's a man in the hall, waiting for an answer."

"It looks like a bill," said Clytie nervously, tearing open the envelope; "but I don't owe any bill. Why, it's two and a quarter, from the tailor, for fixing over my old suit last fall! I'm positive I paid it weeks ago. There's some mistake."

"He says he's been here three times, but you were out."

"Have you any money for it, Clytie?" asked her husband.

Clytie looked as if a thunderbolt had struck her.

"Yes, I have; but—oh, I don't want to take it for that! I need every penny I've got."

"Well, there's no need of feeling so badly about it," said Langshaw resignedly.

"Give the ten-dollar bill to the man, George, and see if he can change it." He couldn't resist a slight masculine touch of severity at her incapacity. "I wish you'd tend to these things at the time, Clytie, or let me know about them." He took the money when George returned. "Here's your dollar now, Mary—don't lose it again!—and your five, George. You might as well take another dollar yourself. Clytie, for extras."

He pocketed the remainder of the change carelessly. After his first pang at the encroachment on the reserve fund the rod had sunk so far out of sight that it was almost as if it had never been. He had, of course, known all along that he would not buy it. Even the sting of the "Amount due" quickly evaporated.

Little Mary gave a jump that bumped her brown curly head against him.

"You don't know what I'm going to give you for Christmas!" she cried joyously.

II

Langshaw was one of those men who have an inherited capacity for enjoying Christmas. He lent it his attention with zest, choosing the turkey himself with critical care as he went through the big market in town, from whence he brought also wreaths and branches of holly that seemed to have larger and redder berries than could be bought in the village. On Christmas Eve he put up the greens that decorated the parlour and dining-room—a ceremony that required large preparations with a step-ladder, a hammer, tacks, and string, the removal of his coat, and a lighted pipe in one corner of his mouth; and which proceeded with such painstaking slowness on account of his coming down from the ladder every other moment to view the artistic effect of the arrangements, that it was only by sticking the last branches up any old way at Clytie's wild appeal that he ever got it finished at all.

Then he helped her fill the stockings, his own fingers carefully giving the crowning effect of orange and cornucopia in each one, and arranging the large packages below, after tiptoeing down the stairs with them so as not to wake the officially sleeping children, who were patently stark awake, thrashing or coughing in their little beds. The sturdy George had never been known to sleep on Christmas Eve, always coming down the next day esthetically pale and with abnormally large eyes, to the feast of rapture.

On this Saturday—Christmas Eve's eve—when Langshaw finally reached home, laden with all the "last things" and the impossible packages of tortuous shapes left by fond relatives at his office for the children—one pocket of his overcoat weighted with the love-box of really good candy for Clytie—it was evident as soon as he opened the hall door that something unusual was going on upstairs. Wild shrieks of "It's father! It's father!" rent the air.

"It's father!"

"Fardie! Fardie, don't come up!"

"Father, don't come up!"

"Father, it's your present!"

There was hasty scurrying of feet, racing to and fro, and further shrieks. Langshaw waited, smiling. It was evidently a "boughten" gift then; the last had been a water pitcher, much needed in the household. He braced himself fondly for immense enthusiasm over this.

An expression of intense excitement was visible on each face when finally he was allowed to enter the upper room. Mary and Baby rushed at him to clasp his leg, while his wife leaned over to kiss him as he whispered:

"I brought out a lot of truck; it's all in the closet in the hall."

George, standing with his hands in his pockets, proclaimed loudly, with sparkling eyes:

"You nearly saw your present! It's from mother and us. Come here, Baby, and pull brother's leg. Say, father, do you like cut glass?"

"O-oh!" came in ecstatic chorus from the other two, as at a delightful joke.

"It's a secret!" announced Baby, her yellow hair falling over one round, blue eye.

"I believe it's a pony," said the father. "I'm sure I heard a pony up here!"

Shouts of renewed joy greeted the jest.

All the next day, Christmas Eve itself, whenever two or three of the family were gathered together there were secret whisperings, more scurryings, and frenzied warnings for the father not to come into the room. In spite of himself, Langshaw began to get a little curious as to the tobaco jar or the fire shovel, or whatever should be his portion. He not only felt resigned to not having the trout-rod, but a sort of wonder also rose in him that he had been bewitched—even momentarily—into thinking he could have it. What did it matter anyway?

"It's worth it, old girl, isn't it?" he said cryptically as he and Clytie met once unexpectedly in the hall, and he put his arm round her.

"Yes!" answered his wife, her dark eyes lustrous. Sometimes she didn't look much older than little Mary. "One thing though I must say: I do hope, dear, that—the children have been thinking so much of our present to you and saving up so for it—I do hope, Joe, that if you are pleased you'll show it. So far as I'm concerned, it doesn't matter; but sometimes—when, of course, I know how pleased you really are—you don't show it at once to others. That's why I hope you'll show it to-morrow if—"

"Great Scott! Clytie, let up on it! What do you want me to do— jump up and down and make a fool of myself?" asked her husband scornfully. "You leave me alone!"

It was Langshaw's firm rule, vainly protested even by his wife, that the household should have breakfast on Christmas Day before tackling the stockings—a hurried mockery of a meal, to be sure, yet to his masculine idea a reënforcement of food for the infant stomach before the long, hurtling joy of the day. The stockings and the piles under them were taken in order, according to age—the youngest first and the others waiting in rapt interest and admiration until their turn arrived—a pretty ceremony.

In the delicious revelry of Baby's joy, as her trembling, fat little fingers pulled forth dolls and their like, all else was forgotten until it was Mary's turn, and then George's and then the mother's. And then, when he had forgotten all about it: "Now father!" There was seemingly a breathless moment while all eyes turned to him.

"It's father's turn now; father's going to have his presents. Father, sit down here on the sofa—it's your turn now."

There were only a blue cornucopia and an orange and a bottle of olives in his stocking, a Christmas card from his sister Ella, a necktie from grandmamma, and nothing, as his quick eye had noted, under it on the floor; but now George importantly stooped down, drew a narrow package from under the sofa and laid it beside his father, pulling off the paper. Inside was a slim, longish, gray linen bag. Langshaw studied it for a moment before opening it.

"Well, I'll be jiggered!" he breathed, with a strange glance round at the waiting group and an odd, crooked smile. "I'll be jiggered!"

There in its neatly grooved sections lay the rod, ready to be put together—not *a* rod, but, as his eye almost unbelievingly reassured him, *the* rod—the ticket of the shop adorning it—in all its beauty of golden shellac and delicate tip. His fingers touched the pieces reverently.

"Well, will you look at that! How did you ever think of getting it?"

"How did I think of it? Because you talked about it all the time," said his wife scornfully, with her arms round his neck from behind, while the children flung themselves upon him. "Oh, I know you thought you didn't; but you did just the same. George heard you too. We got Mr. Wickersham to pick it out. He said it was the one you wanted. And the reel—you haven't noticed that box there—the reel is the right kind, he says; and the line is silk—the best. There's the book of flies too—six. Baby's crazy over them! Mr. Wickersham said it was all just what you ought to have. We've been saving up for the longest time; but we had to wait, you see, for George's deportment before the things could be bought. If it isn't right—"

"Right? Say, this is the finest present I ever had!" said Langshaw with glittering eyes and that little crooked smile. "It just beats everything!"

He rose, scattering his adoring family, and, walking to the window, threw it open to the frosty December air and called across to a neighbour standing on the walk.

"Want to come over here, Hendon? Got something to show you. Will you look at this! Present from my wife and the kids—been saving up for it. It's a peach, I'll tell you that! I'm going to take George off fishing this spring— What? Well, come over later, when you've got time to take a good look at it."

"Do you like it, father?" came from three different voices at once.

"Do I like it? You can just bet I do," said Langshaw emphatically. He bent and kissed the three upturned faces, and leaned toward his wife afterward to press her sweet waiting lips with his; but his eyes, as if drawn by a magnet, were only on the rod—not the mere bundle of sticks he might have bought, but transformed into one blossoming with love.

"And do you know, we hardly saw a thing of him all day!" Clytie proudly recounted afterward to her sister. "My dear, he would hardly take time to eat his dinner or speak to any one; he was out in the back yard with Henry Wickersham and Mr. Hendon until dark, flapping that rod in circles—the silliest thing! He nearly sent a hook into George's eye once. George acted as bewitched as he did. Joe kept telling every single person who came along that it was 'a present from his wife and the kids.' He certainly showed that he was pleased."

"It's been a pretty nice day, hasn't it?" Langshaw said to his wife that Christmas night when the children were at last in bed. "Best Christmas I ever had! To think of you and the kids doing all this for me."

His hand rested lovingly on the rod, now once again swathed in the gray linen bag. He would have been the last to realize that, in his humble way, he typified a diviner Fatherhood to the little family who trusted in his care for them—for all things came of him and of his own had they given him.

OLD FOLKS' CHRISTMAS

By Ring Lardner

TOM and Grace Carter sat in their living-room on Christmas Eve, sometimes talking, sometimes pretending to read and all the time thinking things they didn't want to think. Their two children, Junior, aged nineteen, and Grace, two years younger, had come home that day from their schools for the Christmas vacation. Junior was in his first year at the university and Grace attending a boarding-school that would fit her for college.

I won't call them Grace and Junior any more, though that is the way they had been christened. Junior had changed his name to Ted and Grace was now Caroline, and thus they insisted on being addressed, even by their parents. This was one of the things Tom and Grace the elder were thinking of as they sat in their living-room Christmas Eve.

Other university freshmen who had lived here had returned on the twenty-first, the day when the vaction was supposed to begin. Ted had telegraphed that he would be three days late owing to a special examination which, if he passed it, would lighten the terrific burden of the next term. He had arrived at home looking so pale, heavy-eyed and shaky that his mother doubted the wisdom of the concentrated mental effort, while his father secretly hoped the stuff had been non-poisonous and would not have lasting effects. Caroline, too, had been behind schedule, explaining that her laundry had gone astray and she had not dared trust others to trace it for her.

Grace and Tom had attempted, with fair success, to conceal their disappointment over this delayed home-coming and had continued with their preparations for a Christmas that would thrill their children and consequently themselves. They had bought an imposing lot of presents, costing twice or three times as much as had been Tom's father's annual income when Tom was Ted's age, or Tom's own income a year ago, before General Motors' acceptance of his new weather-proof paint had enabled him to buy this suburban home and luxuries such as his own parents and Grace's had never dreamed of, and to give Ted and Caroline advantages that he and Grace had perforce gone without.

Behind the closed door of the music-room was the elaborately decked tree. The piano and piano bench and the floor around the tree were covered with beribboned packages of all sizes, shapes and weights, one of them addressed to Tom, another to Grace, a few to the servants and the rest to Ted and Caroline. A huge box contained a sealskin coat for Caroline, a coat that had cost as much as the Carters had formerly paid a year for rent. Even more expensive was a "set" of jewelry consisting of an opal brooch, a bracelet of opals and gold filigree, and an opal ring surrounded by diamonds.

Grace always had preferred opals to any other stone, but now that she could afford them, some inhibition prevented her from buying them for herself; she could enjoy them much more adorning her pretty daughter. There were boxes of silk stockings, lingerie, gloves and handkerchiefs. And for Ted, a three-hundred-dollar watch, a de-luxe edition of Balzac, an expensive bag of shiny, new steel-shafted golf-clubs and the last word in portable phonographs.

But the big surprise for the boy was locked in the garage, a black Gorham sedan, a model more up to date and better-looking than Tom's own year-old car that stood beside it. Ted could use it during the vacation if the mild weather continued and could look forward to driving it around home next spring and summer, there being a rule at the university forbidding undergraduates the possession or use of private automobiles.

Every year for sixteen years, since Ted was three and Caroline one, it had been the Christmas Eve custom of the Carters' to hang up their children's stockings and fill them with inexpensive toys. Tom and Grace had thought it would be fun to continue the custom this year; the contents of the stockings—a mechanical negro dancing doll, music-boxes, a kitten that meowed when you pressed a spot on her back, et cetera—would make the "kids" laugh. And one of Grace's first pronouncements to her returned offspring was that they must go to bed early so Santa Claus would not be frightened away.

But it seemed they couldn't promise to make it so terribly early. They both had long-standing dates in town. Caroline was going to dinner and a play with Beatrice Murdock and Beatrice's nineteen-year-old brother Paul. The latter would call for her in his car at half past six. Ted had accepted an invitation to see the hockey match with two classmates, Herb Castle and Bernard King. He wanted to take his father's Gorham, but Tom told him untruthfully that the foot-brake was not working; Ted must be kept out of the garage till tomorrow morning.

Ted and Caroline had taken naps in the afternoon and gone off together in Paul Murdock's stylish roadster, giving their word that they would be back by midnight or a little later and that tomorrow night they would stay home.

And now their mother and father were sitting up for them, because the stockings could not be filled and hung till they were safely in bed, and also because trying to go to sleep is a painful and hopeless business when you are kind of jumpy.

"What time is it?" asked Grace, looking up from the third page of a book that she had begun to "read" soon after dinner.

"Half past two," said her husband. (He had answered the same question every fifteen or twenty minutes since midnight.)

"You don't suppose anything could have happened?" said Grace.

"We'd have heard if there had," said Tom.

"It isn't likely, of course," said Grace, "but they might have had an accident some place where nobody was there to report it or telephone or anything. We don't know what kind of a driver the Murdock boy is."

"He's Ted's age. Boys that age may be inclined to drive too fast, but they drive pretty well."

"How do you know?"

"Well, I've watched some of them drive."

"Yes, but not all of them."

"I doubt whether anybody in the world has seen every nineteen-year-old boy drive."

"Boys these days seem so kind of irresponsible."

"Oh, don't worry! They probably met some of their young friends and stopped for a bite to eat or something." Tom got up and walked to the window with studied carelessness. "It's a pretty night," he said. "You can see every star in the sky."

But he wasn't looking at the stars. He was looking down the road for headlights. There were none in sight and after a few moments he returned to his chair.

"What time is it?" asked Grace.

"Twenty-two of," he said.

"Of what?"

"Of three."

"Your watch must have stopped. Nearly an hour ago you told me it was half past two."

"My watch is all right. You probably dozed off."

"I haven't closed my eyes."

"Well, it's time you did. Why don't you go to bed?"

"Why don't *you?*"

"I'm not sleepy."

"Neither am I. But honestly, Tom, it's silly for you to stay up. I'm just doing it so I can fix the stockings, and because I feel so wakeful. But there's no use of your losing your sleep."

"I couldn't sleep a wink till they're home."

"That's foolishness! There's nothing to worry about. They're just having a good time. You were young once yourself."

"That's just it! When I was young, I was young." He picked up his paper and tried to get interested in the shipping news.

"What time is it?" asked Grace.

"Five minutes of three."

"Maybe they're staying at the Murdocks' all night."

"They'd have let us know."

"They were afraid to wake us up, telephoning."

At three-twenty a car stopped at the front gate.

"There they are!"

"I told you there was nothing to worry about."

Tom went to the window. He could just discern the outlines of the Murdock boy's roadster, whose lighting system seemed to have broken down.

"He hasn't any lights," said Tom. "Maybe I'd better go out and see if I can fix them."

"No, don't!" said Grace sharply. "He can fix them himself. He's just saving them while he stands still."

"Why don't they come in?"

"They're probably making plans."

"They can make them in here. I'll go out and tell them we're still up."

"No, don't!" said Grace as before, and Tom obediently remained at the window.

It was nearly four when the car lights flashed on and the car drove away. Caroline walked into the house and stared dazedly at her parents.

"Heavens! What are you doing up?"

Tom was about to say something, but Grace forestalled him.

"We were talking over old Christmases," she said. "Is it very late?"

"I haven't any idea," said Caroline.

"Where is Ted?"

"Isn't he home? I haven't seen him since we dropped him at the hockey place."

"Well, you go right to bed," said her mother. "You must be worn out."

"I am, kind of. We danced after the play. What time is breakfast?"

"Eight o'clock."

"Oh, Mother, can't you make it nine?"

"I guess so. You used to want to get up early on Christmas."

"I know, but—"

"Who brought you home?" asked Tom.

"Why, Paul Murdock—and Beatrice."

"You look rumpled."

"They made me sit in the 'rumple' seat."

She laughed at her joke, said good night and went upstairs. She had not come even within hand-shaking distance of her father and mother.

"The Murdocks," said Tom, "must have great manners, making their guest ride in that uncomfortable seat."

Grace was silent.

"You go to bed, too," said Tom. "I'll wait for Ted."

"You couldn't fix the stockings."

"I won't try. We'll have time for that in the morning; I mean, later in the morning."

"I'm not going to bed till you do," said Grace.

"All right, we'll both go. Ted ought not to be long now. I suppose his friends will bring him home. We'll hear him when he comes in."

There was no chance not to hear him when, at ten minutes before six, he came in. He had done his Christmas shopping late and brought home a package.

Grace went downstairs again at half past seven, telling the servants breakfast would be postponed till nine. She nailed the stockings beside the fireplace, went into the music-room to see that nothing had been disturbed and removed Ted's hat and overcoat from where he had carefully hung them on the hall floor.

Tom appeared a little before nine and suggested that the children ought to be awakened.

"I'll wake them," said Grace, and went upstairs. She opened Ted's door, looked and softly closed it again. She entered her daughter's room and found Caroline semiconscious.

"Do I have to get up now? Honestly I can't eat anything. If you could just have Molla bring me some coffee. Ted and I are both invited to the Murdock's for breakfast at half past twelve, and I could sleep for another hour or two."

"But dearie, don't you know we have Christmas dinner at one?"

"It's a shame, Mother, but I thought of course our dinner would be at night."

"Don't you want to see your presents?"

"Certainly I do, but can't they wait?"

Grace was about to go to the kitchen to tell the cook that dinner would be at seven instead of one, but she remembered having promised Signe the afternoon and evening off, as a cold, light supper would be all anyone wanted after the heavy midday meal.

Tom and Grace breakfasted alone and once more sat in the living-room, talking, thinking and pretending to read.

"You ought to speak to Caroline," said Tom.

"I will, but not today. It's Christmas."

"And I intend to say a few words to Ted."

"Yes, dear, you must. But not today."

"I suppose they'll be out again tonight."

"No, they promised to stay home. We'll have a nice cozy evening."

"Don't bet too much on that," said Tom.

At noon the "children" made their entrance and responded to their parents' salutations with almost the proper warmth. Ted declined a cup of coffee and he and Caroline apologized for making a "breakfast" date at the Murdocks'.

"Sis and I both thought you'd be having dinner at seven, as usual."

"We've always had it at one o'clock on Christmas," said Tom.

"I'd forgotten it was Christmas," said Ted.

"Well, those stockings ought to remind you."

Ted and Caroline looked at the bulging stockings.

"Isn't there a tree?" asked Caroline.

"Of course," said her mother. "But the stockings come first."

"We've only a little time," said Caroline. "We'll be terribly late as it is. So can't we see the tree now?"

"I guess so," said Grace, and led the way into the music-room.

The servants were summoned and the tree stared at and admired.

"You must open your presents," said Grace to her daughter.

"I can't open them all now," said Caroline. "Tell me which is special."

The cover was removed from the huge box and Grace held up the coat.

"Oh, Mother!" said Caroline. "A sealskin coat!"

"Put it on," said her father.

"Not now. We haven't time."

"Then look at this!" said Grace, and opened the case of jewels.

"Oh, Mother! Opals!" said Caroline.

"They're my favorite stone," said Grace quietly.

"If nobody minds," said Ted, "I'll postpone my personal investigation till we get back. I know I'll like everything you've given me. But if we have no car in working order, I've got to call a taxi and catch a train."

"You can drive in," said his father.

"Did you fix the brake?"

"I think it's all right. Come up to the garage and we'll see."

Ted got his hat and coat and kissed his mother good-by.

"Mother," he said, "I know you'll forgive me for not having any presents for you and Dad. I was so rushed the last three days at school. And I thought I'd have time to shop a little when we got in yesterday, but I was in too much of a hurry to be home. Last night, everything was closed."

"Don't worry," said Grace. "Christmas is for young people. Dad and I have everything we want."

The servants had found their gifts and disappeared, expressing effusive Scandinavian thanks.

Caroline and her mother were left alone.

"Mother, where did the coat come from?"

"Lloyd and Henry's."

"They keep all kinds of furs, don't they?"

"Yes."

"Would you mind horribly if I exchanged this?"

"Certainly not, dear. You pick out anything you like, and if it's a little more expensive, it won't make any difference. We can go in town tomorrow or next day. But don't you want to wear your opals to the Murdocks'?"

"I don't believe so. They might get lost or something. And I'm not —well, I'm not so crazy about—"

"I think they can be exchanged, too," said Grace. "You run along now and get ready to start."

Caroline obeyed with alacrity, and Grace spent a welcome moment by herself.

Tom opened the garage door.

"Why, you've got two cars!" said Ted.

"The new one isn't mine," said Tom.

"Whose is it?"

"Yours. It's the new model."

"Dad, that's wonderful! But it looks just like the old one."

"Well, the old one's pretty good. Just the same, yours is better. You'll find that out when you drive it. Hop in and get started. I had her filled with gas."

"I think I'd rather drive the old one."

"Why?"

"Well, what I really wanted, Dad, was a Barnes sport roadster, something like Paul Murdock's, only a different color scheme. And if I don't drive this Gorham at all, maybe you could get them to take it back or make some kind of a deal with the Barnes people."

Tom didn't speak till he was sure of his voice. Then: "All right, son. Take my car and I'll see what can be done about yours."

Caroline, waiting for Ted, remembered something and called to her mother. "Here's what I got for you and Dad," she said. "It's two tickets to 'Jolly Jane,' the play I saw last night. You'll love it!"

"When are they for?" asked Grace.

"Tonight," said Caroline.

"But dearie," said her mother, "we don't want to go out tonight, when you promised to stay home."

"We'll keep our promise," said Caroline, "but the Murdocks may drop in and bring some friends and we'll dance and there'll be music.

And Ted and I both thought you'd rather be away somewhere so our noise wouldn't disturb you."

"It was sweet of you to do this," said her mother, "but your father and I don't mind noise as long as you're enjoying yourselves."

"It's time anyway that you and Dad had a treat."

"The real treat," said Grace, "would be to spend a quiet evening here with just you two."

"The Murdocks practically invited themselves and I couldn't say no after they'd been so nice to me. And honestly, Mother, you'll love this play!"

"Will you be home for supper?"

"I'm pretty sure we will, but if we're a little late, don't you and Dad wait for us. Take the seven-twenty so you won't miss anything. The first act is really the best. We probably won't be hungry, but have Signe leave something out for us in case we are."

Tom and Grace sat down to the elaborate Christmas dinner and didn't make much impression on it. Even if they had had any appetite, the sixteen-pound turkey would have looked almost like new when they had eaten their fill. Conversation was intermittent and related chiefly to Signe's excellence as a cook and the mildness of the weather. Children and Christmas were barely touched on.

Tom merely suggested that on account of its being a holiday and their having theatre tickets, they ought to take the six-ten and eat supper at the Metropole. His wife said no; Ted and Caroline might come home and be disappointed at not finding them. Tom seemed about to make some remark, but changed his mind.

The afternoon was the longest Grace had ever known. The children were still absent at seven and she and Tom taxied to the train. Neither talked much on the way to town. As for the play, which Grace was sure to love, it turned out to be a rehash of "Cradle Snatchers" and "Sex," retaining the worst features of each.

When it was over, Tom said: "Now I'm inviting you to the Cove Club. You didn't eat any breakfast or dinner or supper and I can't have you starving to death on a feast-day. Besides, I'm thirsty as well as hungry."

They ordered the special *table d'hôte* and struggled hard to get away with it. Tom drank six high-balls, but they failed to produce the usual effect of making him jovial. Grace had one high-ball and some kind of cordial that gave her a warm, contented feeling for a moment. But the warmth and contentment left her before the train was half way home.

The living-room looked as if Von Kluck's army had just passed through. Ted and Caroline had kept their promise up to a certain point. They had spent part of the evening at home, and the Murdocks must have brought all their own friends and everybody else's, judging from the results. The tables and floors were strewn with empty glasses, ashes and cigaret stubs. The stockings had been torn off their nails and the wrecked contents were all over the place. Two sizable holes had been burnt in Grace's favorite rug.

Tom took his wife by the arm and led her into the music-room.

"You never took the trouble to open your own present," he said.

"And I think there's one for you, too," said Grace. "They didn't come in here," she added, "so I guess there wasn't much dancing or music."

Tom found his gift from Grace, a set of diamond studs and cuff buttons for festive wear. Grace's present from him was an opal ring.

"Oh, Tom!" she said.

"We'll have to go out somewhere tomorrow night, so I can break these in," said Tom.

"Well, if we do that, we'd better get a good night's rest."

"I'll beat you upstairs," said Tom.

A CHRISTMAS CAROL

BY CHARLES DICKENS

STAVE ONE

Marley's Ghost

MARLEY was dead, to begin with. There is no doubt whatever about that. The register of his burial was signed by the clergyman, the clerk, the undertaker, and the chief mourner. Scrooge signed it. And Scrooge's name was good upon 'Change for anything he chose to put his hand to.

Old Marley was as dead as a door-nail.

Mind! I don't mean to say that I know, of my own knowledge, what there is particularly dead about a door-nail. I might have been inclined, myself, to regard a coffin-nail as the deadest piece of ironmongery in the trade. But the wisdom of our ancestors is in the simile; and my unhallowed hands shall not disturb it, or the Country's done for. You will therefore permit me to repeat, emphatically, that Marley was as dead as a door-nail.

Scrooge knew he was dead? Of course he did. How could it be otherwise? Scrooge and he were partners for I don't know how many years. Scrooge was his sole executor, his sole administrator, his sole assign, his sole residuary legatee, his sole friend, and sole mourner. And even Scrooge was not so dreadfully cut up by the sad event, but that he was an excellent man of business on the very day of the funeral, and solemnized it with an undoubted bargain.

The mention of Marley's funeral brings me back to the point I started from. There is no doubt that Marley was dead. This must be distinctly understood, or nothing wonderful can come of the story I am going to relate. If we were not perfectly convinced that Hamlet's father died before the play began, there would be nothing more remarkable in his taking a stroll at night, in an easterly wind, upon his own ramparts, than there would be in any other middle-aged gentleman rashly turning out after dark in a breezy spot—say Saint Paul's Churchyard for instance—literally to astonish his son's weak mind.

Scrooge never painted out old Marley's name. There it stood, years afterward, above the warehouse door: Scrooge and Marley. The firm was known as Scrooge and Marley. Sometimes people new to the business called Scrooge Scrooge, and sometimes Marley, but he answered to both names. It was all the same to him.

Oh! but he was a tight-fisted hand at the grindstone, Scrooge! a squeezing, wrenching, grasping, scraping, clutching, covetous old sinner! Hard and sharp as flint, from which no steel had ever struck out generous fire, secret, and self-contained, and solitary as an oyster. The cold within him froze his old features, nipped his pointed nose, shriveled his cheek, stiffened his gait, made his eyes red, his thin lips blue, and spoke out shrewdly in his grating voice. A frosty rime was on his head, and on his eyebrows, and his wiry chin. He carried his own low temperature always about with him; he iced his office in the dog-days; and didn't thaw it one degree at Christmas.

External heat and cold had little influence on Scrooge. No warmth could warm, no wintry weather chill him. No wind that blew was bitterer than he, no falling snow was more intent upon its purpose, no pelting rain less open to entreaty. Foul weather didn't know where to have him. The heaviest rain, and snow, and hail, and sleet, could boast of the advantage over him in only one respect. They often "came down" handsomely, and Scrooge never did.

Nobody ever stopped him in the street to say, with gladsome looks, "My dear Scrooge, how are you? When will you come to see me?" No beggars implored him to bestow a trifle, no children asked him what it was o'clock, no man or woman ever once in all his life inquired the way to such and such a place, of Scrooge. Even the blind men's dogs appeared to know him; and, when they saw him coming on, would tug their owners into doorways and up courts; and then would wag their tails as though they said, "No eye at all is better than an evil eye, dark master!"

But what did Scrooge care? It was the very thing he liked. To edge his way along the crowded paths of life, warning all human sympathy to keep its distance, was what the knowing ones call "nuts" to Scrooge.

Once upon a time—of all the good days in the year, on Christmas Eve—old Scrooge sat busy in his counting-house. It was cold, bleak, biting weather, foggy withal, and he could hear the people in the court outside go wheezing up and down, beating their hands upon their breasts, and stamping their feet upon the pavement stones to warm them. The city clocks had only just gone three, but it was quite dark already—it had not been light all day—and candles were flaring in the windows of the neighboring offices, like ruddy smears upon the palpable brown air. The fog came pouring in at every chink and key-hole, and was so dense without, that, although the court was of the narrowest, the houses opposite were mere phantoms. To see the dingy cloud come drooping down, obscuring everything, one might have thought that Nature lived hard by, and was brewing on a large scale.

The door of Scrooge's counting-house was open, that he might keep his eye upon his clerk, who, in a dismal little cell beyond, a sort of tank, was copying letters. Scrooge had a very small fire, but the clerk's fire was so very much smaller that it looked like one coal. But he couldn't replenish it, for Scrooge kept the coal-box in his own room; and so surely as the clerk came in with the shovel, the master predicted that it would be necessary for them to part. Wherefore the clerk put on his white comforter, and tried to warm himself at the candle; in which effort, not being a man of a strong imagination, he failed.

"A merry Christmas, uncle! God save you!" cried a cheerful voice. It was the voice of Scrooge's nephew, who came upon him so quickly that this was the first intimation he had of his approach.

"Bah!" said Scrooge. "Humbug!"

He had so heated himself with rapid walking in the fog and frost, this nephew of Scrooge's, that he was all in a glow; his face was ruddy and handsome; his eyes sparkled, and his breath smoked again.

"Christmas a humbug, uncle!" said Scrooge's nephew. "You don't mean that, I am sure?"

"I do," said Scrooge. "Merry Christmas! What right have you to be merry? What reason have you to be merry? You're poor enough."

"Come, then," returned the nephew gaily. "What right have you to be dismal? What reason have you to be morose? You're rich enough."

Scrooge, having no better answer ready on the spur of the moment, said "Bah!" again; and followed it up with "Humbug!"

"Don't be cross, uncle!" said the nephew.

"What else can I be," returned the uncle, "when I live in such a world of fools as this? Merry Christmas! Out upon merry Christmas! What's Christmas-time to you but a time for paying bills without money; a time for finding yourself a year older, and not an hour richer; a time for balancing your books, and having every item in 'em through a round dozen of months presented dead against you? If I could work my will," said Scrooge indignantly, "every idiot who goes about with 'Merry Christmas' on his lips should be boiled with his own pudding, and buried with a stake of holly through his heart. He should!"

"Uncle!" pleaded the nephew.

"Nephew!" returned the uncle sternly, "keep Christmas in your own way, and let me keep it in mine."

"Keep it!" repeated Scrooge's nephew. "But you don't keep it."

"Let me leave it alone, then," said Scrooge. "Much good may it do you! Much good it has ever done you!"

"There are many things from which I might have derived good by which I have not profited, I dare say," returned the nephew, "Christmas among the rest. But I am sure I have always thought of Christmas-time, when it has come round—apart from the veneration due to its sacred name and origin, if anything belonging to it can be apart from that—as a good time; a kind, forgiving, charitable, pleasant time; the only time I know of, in the long calendar of the year, when men and women seem by one consent to open their shut-up hearts freely, and to think of people below them as if they really were fellow-passengers to the grave, and not another race of creatures bound on other journeys. And therefore, uncle, though it has never put a scrap of gold or silver in my pocket, I believe that it *has* done me good, and *will* do me good; and I say, God bless it!"

The clerk in the tank involuntarily applauded. Becoming immediately sensible of the impropriety, he poked the fire, and extinguished the last frail spark forever.

"Let me hear another sound from *you*," said Scrooge, "and you'll keep your Christmas by losing your situation! You're quite a powerful speaker, sir," he added, turning to his nephew. "I wonder you don't go into Parliament."

"Don't be angry, uncle. Come! Dine with us to-morrow."

Scrooge said that he would see him— Yes, indeed he did. He went the whole length of the expression, and said that he would see him in that extremity first.

"But why?" cried Scrooge's nephew. "Why?"

"Why did you get married?" said Scrooge.

"Because I fell in love."

"Because you fell in love!" growled Scrooge, as if that were the only one thing in the world more ridiculous than a merry Christmas. "Good afternoon!"

"Nay, uncle, but you never came to see me before that happened. Why give it as a reason for not coming now?"

"Good afternoon," said Scrooge.

"I want nothing from you; I ask nothing of you; why cannot we be friends?"

"Good afternoon!" said Scrooge.

"I am sorry, with all my heart, to find you so resolute. We have never had any quarrel, to which I have been a party. But I have made the trial in homage to Christmas, and I'll keep my Christmas humor to the last. So a merry Christmas, uncle!"

"Good afternoon," said Scrooge.

"And a happy New Year!"

"Good afternoon!" said Scrooge.

His nephew left the room without an angry word, notwithstanding. He stopped at the outer door to bestow the greetings of the season on the clerk, who, cold as he was, was warmer than Scrooge, for he returned them cordially.

"There's another fellow," muttered Scrooge, who overheard him; "my clerk, with fifteen shillings a week, and a wife and family, talking about a merry Christmas. I'll retire to Bedlam."

This lunatic, in letting Scrooge's nephew out, had let two other people in. They were portly gentlemen, pleasant to behold, and now stood with their hats off, in Scrooge's office. They had books and papers in their hands, and bowed to him.

"Scrooge and Marley's, I believe," said one of the gentlemen, referring to his list. "Have I the pleasure of addressing Mr. Scrooge, or Mr. Marley?"

"Mr. Marley has been dead these seven years," Scrooge replied. "He died seven years ago, this very night."

"We have no doubt his liberality is well represented by his surviving partner," said the gentleman, presenting his credentials.

It certainly was: for they had been two kindred spirits. At the ominous word "liberality," Scrooge frowned, and shook his head, and handed the credentials back.

"At this festive season of the year, Mr. Scrooge," said the gentleman, taking up a pen, "it is more than usually desirable that we should make some slight provision for the poor and destitute, who suffer greatly at the present time. Many thousands are in want of common necessaries; hundreds of thousands are in want of common comforts, sir."

"Are there no prisons?" asked Scrooge.

"Plenty of prisons," said the gentleman, laying down the pen again.

"And the Union workhouses?" demanded Scrooge. "Are they still in operation?"

"They are. Still," returned the gentleman, "I wish I could say they were not."

"The Treadmill and the Poor Law are in full vigor, then?" said Scrooge.

"Both very busy, sir."

"Oh! I was afraid, from what you said at first, that something had occurred to stop them in their useful course," said Scrooge. "I'm very glad to hear it."

"Under the impression that they scarcely furnish Christian cheer of mind or body to the multitude," returned the gentleman, "a few of us are endeavoring to raise a fund to buy the poor some meat and drink, and means of warmth. We choose this time, because it is a time, of all others, when Want is keenly felt, and Abundance rejoices. What shall I put you down for?"

"Nothing!" Scrooge replied.

"You wish to be anonymous?"

"I wish to be left alone," said Scrooge. "Since you ask me what I wish, gentlemen, that is my answer. I don't make merry myself at Christmas, and I can't afford to make idle people merry. I help to support the establishments I have mentioned—they cost enough; and those who are badly off must go there."

"Many can't go there; and many would rather die."

"If they would rather die," said Scrooge, "they had better do it, and decrease the surplus population. Besides—excuse me—I don't know that."

"But you might know it," observed the gentleman.

"It's not my business," Scrooge returned. "It's enough for a man to understand his own business, and not to interfere with other people's. Mine occupies me constantly. Good afternoon, gentlemen!"

Seeing clearly that it would be useless to pursue their point, the gentlemen withdrew. Scrooge resumed his labors with an improved opinion of himself, and in a more facetious temper than was usual with him.

Meanwhile the fog and darkness thickened so that people ran about with flaring links, proffering their services to go before horses in carriages, and conduct them on their way. The ancient tower of a church, whose gruff old bell was always peeping slyly down at Scrooge out of a Gothic window in the wall, became invisible, and struck the hours and quarters in the clouds, with tremulous vibrations afterward, as if its teeth were chattering in its frozen head up there. The cold became intense. In the main street, at the corner of the court, some laborers were repairing the gas-pipes, and had lighted a great fire in a brazier, round which a party of ragged men and boys were gathered, warming their hands and winking their eyes before the blaze, in rapture. The water-plug being left in solitude, its overflowings suddenly congealed, and turned to misanthropic ice. The brightness of the shops, where holly sprigs and berries crackled in the lamp heat of the windows, made pale faces ruddy as they passed. Poulterers' and grocers' trades became a splendid joke; a glorious pageant, with which it was next to impossible to believe that such dull principles as bargain and sale had anything to do. The Lord Mayor, in the stronghold of the mighty Mansion House, gave orders to his fifty cooks and butlers to keep Christmas as a Lord Mayor's household should; and even the little tailor, whom he had fined five shillings on the previous Monday for being drunk and bloodthirsty in the streets, stirred up tomorrow's pudding in his garret, while his lean wife and baby sallied out to buy the beef.

Foggier yet, and colder! Piercing, searching, biting cold. If the good Saint Dunstan had but nipped the Evil Spirit's nose with a touch of such weather as that, instead of using his familiar weapons, then, indeed, he would have roared to lusty purpose. The owner of one scant young nose, gnawed and mumbled by the hungry cold as bones are gnawed by dogs, stooped down at Scrooge's keyhole to regale him with a Christmas carol; but at the first sound of

"God rest you, merry gentleman,
May nothing you dismay,

Scrooge seized the ruler with such energy of action, that the singer fled in terror, leaving the keyhole to the fog and even more congenial frost.

At length the hour of shutting up the counting-house arrived. With an ill will Scrooge dismounted from his stool, and tacitly admitted the fact to the expectant clerk in the tank, who instantly snuffed his candle out, and put on his hat.

"You'll want all day to-morrow, I suppose?" said Scrooge.

"If quite convenient, sir."

"It's not convenient," said Scrooge, "and it's not fair. If I was to stop half a crown for it, you'd think yourself ill used, I'll be bound?"

The clerk smiled faintly.

"And yet," said Scrooge, "you don't think *me* ill used when I pay a day's wages for no work."

The clerk observed that it was only once a year.

"A poor excuse for picking a man's pocket every twenty-fifth of December!" said Scrooge, buttoning his greatcoat to the chin. "But I suppose you must have the whole day. Be here all the earlier next morning."

The clerk promised that he would; and Scrooge walked out with a growl. The office was closed in a twinkling, and the clerk, with the long ends of his white comforter dangling below his waist (for he boasted no greatcoat), went down a slide on Cornhill, at the end of a lane of boys, twenty times, in honor of its being Christmas Eve, and then ran home to Camden Town, as hard as he could pelt, to play at blind-man's buff.

Scrooge took his melancholy dinner in his usual melancholy tavern; and having read all the newspapers, and beguiled the rest of the evening with his banker's book, went home to bed. He lived in chambers which had once belonged to his deceased partner. They were a gloomy suite of rooms, in a lowering pile of building up a yard, where it had so little business to be, that one could scarcely help fancying it must have run there when it was a young house, playing at hide-and-seek with other houses, and have forgotten the way out again. It was old enough now, and dreary enough, for nobody lived in it but Scrooge, the other rooms being all let out as offices. The yard was so dark that even Scrooge, who knew its every stone, was fain to grope with his hands. The fog and frost so hung about the black old gateway of the house, that it seemed as if the Genius of the Weather sat in mournful meditation on the threshold.

Now it is a fact that there was nothing at all particular about the knocker on the door, except that it was very large. It is also a fact that Scrooge had seen it, night and morning, during his whole residence in that place; also that Scrooge had as little of what is called fancy about him as any man in the City of London, even including—which is a bold word—the corporation, aldermen, and livery. Let it also be borne in mind that Scrooge had not bestowed one thought on Marley, since his last mention of his seven-years-dead partner that afternoon. And then let any man explain to me, if he can, how it happened that Scrooge, having his key in the lock of the door, saw in the knocker, without its undergoing any intermediate process of change—not a knocker, but Marley's face.

Marley's face. It was not in impenetrable shadow, as the other objects in the yard were, but had a dismal light about it, like a bad lobster in a dark cellar. It was not angry or ferocious, but looked at Scrooge as Marley used to look: with ghostly spectacles turned up on its ghostly forehead. The hair was curiously stirred, as if by breath or hot air; and though the eyes were wide open, they were perfectly motionless. That, and its livid color, made it horrible; but its horror seemed to be in spite of the face, and beyond its control, rather than a part of its own expression.

As Scrooge looked fixedly at this phenomenon it was a knocker again.

To say that he was not startled, or that his blood was not conscious of a terrible sensation to which it had been a stranger from infancy, would be untrue. But he put his hand upon the key he had relinquished, turned it sturdily, walked in, and lighted his candle.

He *did* pause, with a moment's irresolution, before he shut the door; and he *did* look cautiously behind it first, as if he half expected to be terrified with the sight of Marley's pigtail sticking out into the hall. But there was nothing on the back of the door, except the screws and nuts that held the knocker on, so he said, "Pooh, pooh!" and closed it with a bang.

The sound resounded through the house like thunder. Every room above, and every cask in the wine-merchant's cellars below, appeared to have a separate peal of echoes of its own. Scrooge was not a man to be frightened by echoes. He fastened the door, and walked across the hall, and up the stairs, slowly, too, trimming his candle as he went.

You may talk vaguely about driving a coach and six up a good old flight of stairs, or through a bad young Act of Parliament; but I mean to say you might have got a hearse up that staircase, and taken it broadwise, with the splinter-bar toward the wall, and the door toward the balustrade, and done it easy. There was plenty of width for that, and room to spare; which is perhaps the reason why Scrooge thought he saw a locomotive hearse going on before him in the gloom. Half a dozen gas-lamps out of the street wouldn't have lighted the entry too well, so you may suppose that it was pretty dark with Scrooge's dip.

Up Scrooge went, not caring a button for that. Darkness is cheap, and Scrooge liked it. But before he shut his heavy door, he walked through his rooms to see that all was right. He had just enough recollection of the face to desire to do that.

Sitting-room, bedroom, lumber-room. All as they should be. Nobody under the table, nobody under the sofa; a small fire in the grate; spoon and basin ready; and the little saucepan of gruel (Scrooge had a cold in his head) upon the hob. Nobody under the bed; nobody in the closet; nobody in his dressing-gown, which was hanging up in a suspicious attitude against the wall. Lumber-room as usual. Old fire-guard, old shoes, two fish-baskets, washing-stand on three legs, and a poker.

Quite satisfied, he closed his door, and locked himself in; double-locked himself in, which was not his custom. Thus secured against surprise, he took off his cravat, put on his dressing-gown and slippers, and his night-cap, and sat down before the fire to take his gruel.

It was a very low fire indeed; nothing on such a bitter night. He was obliged to sit close to it, and brood over it, before he could extract the least sensation of warmth from such a handful of fuel. The fireplace was an old one, built by some Dutch merchant long ago, and paved all round with quaint Dutch tiles, designed to illustrate the Scriptures. There were Cains and Abels, Pharaoh's daughters, Queens of Sheba, angelic messengers descending through the air on clouds like feather-beds, Abrahams, Belshazzars, Apostles putting off to sea in butter-boats, hundreds of figures to attract his thoughts; and yet that face of Marley, seven years dead, came like the ancient Prophet's rod, and swallowed up the whole. If each smooth tile had been a blank at first, with power to shape some picture on its surface from the disjointed fragments of his thoughts, there would have been a copy of old Marley's head on every one.

"Humbug!" said Scrooge; and walked across the room.

After several turns, he sat down again. As he threw his head back in the chair, his glance happened to rest upon a bell, a disused bell, that hung in the room, and communicated, for some purpose now forgotten, with a chamber in the highest story of the building. It was with great astonishment, and with a strange, inexplicable dread, that, as he looked, he saw this bell begin to swing. It swung so softly in the outset that it scarcely made a sound; but soon it rang out loudly, and so did every bell in the house.

This might have lasted half a minute, or a minute, but it seemed an hour. The bells ceased, as they had begun, together. They were succeeded by a clanking noise, deep down below; as if some person were dragging a heavy chain over the casks in the wine-merchant's cellar. Scrooge then remembered to have heard that ghosts in haunted houses were described as dragging chains.

The cellar door flew open with a booming sound, and then he heard the noise, much louder, on the floors below; then coming up the stairs; then coming straight toward his door.

"It's humbug still!" said Scrooge. "I won't believe it!"

His color changed, though, when, without a pause, it came on through the heavy door, and passed into the room before his eyes. Upon its coming in, the dying flame leaped up, as though it cried, "I know him! Marley's Ghost!" and fell again.

The same face, the very same. Marley, in his pigtail, usual waistcoat, tights and boots; the tassels on the latter bristling like his pigtail, and his coat-skirts, and the hair upon his head. The chain he drew was clasped about his middle. It was long, and wound about him like a tail; and it was made (for Scrooge observed it closely) of cash-boxes, keys, padlocks, ledgers, deeds, and heavy purses wrought in steel. His body was transparent; so that Scrooge, observing him, and looking through his waistcoat, could see the two buttons on his coat behind.

Scrooge had often heard it said that Marley had no bowels, but he had never believed it until now.

No, nor did he believe it even now. Though he looked the phantom through and through, and saw it standing before him; though he felt the chilling influence of its death-cold eyes, and marked the very texture of the folded kerchief bound about its head and chin, which wrapper he had not observed before, he was still incredulous, and fought against his senses.

"How now!" said Scrooge, caustic and cold as ever. "What do you want with me?"

"Much!"—Marley's voice, no doubt about it.

"Who are you?"

"Ask me who I *was.*"

"Who *were* you, then?" said Scrooge, raising his voice. "You're particular, for a shade." He was going to say, "*to* a shade," but substituted this, as more appropriate.

"In life I was your partner, Jacob Marley."

"Can you—can you sit down?" asked Scrooge, looking doubtfully at him.

"I can."

"Do it, then."

Scrooge asked the question, because he didn't know whether a ghost so transparent might find himself in a condition to take a chair; and felt in the event of its being impossible, it might involve the necessity of an embarrassing explanation. But the Ghost sat down on the opposite side of the fireplace, as if he were quite used to it.

"You don't believe in me," observed the Ghost.

"I don't," said Scrooge.

"What evidence would you have of my reality beyond that of your own senses?"

"I don't know," said Scrooge.

"Why do you doubt your senses?"

"Because," said Scrooge, "a little thing affects them. A slight disorder of the stomach makes them cheats. You may be an undigested bit of beef, a blot of mustard, a crumb of cheese, a fragment of an underdone potato. There's more of gravy than of grave about you, whatever you are!"

Scrooge was not much in the habit of cracking jokes, nor did he feel, in his heart, by any means waggish then. The truth is, that he tried to be smart, as a means of distracting his own attention, and keeping down his terror, for the specter's voice disturbed the very marrow in his bones.

To sit staring at those fixed glazed eyes in silence, for a moment, would play, Scrooge felt, the very deuce with him. There was something very awful, too, in the specter's being provided with an infernal atmosphere of his own. Scrooge could not feel it himself, but this was clearly the case; for though the Ghost sat perfectly motionless, his hair, and skirts, and tassels were still agitated as by the hot vapor from an oven.

"You see this toothpick?" said Scrooge, returning quickly to the charge, for the reason just assigned; and wishing, though it were only for a second, to divert the vision's stony gaze from himself.

"I do," replied the Ghost.

"You are not looking at it," said Scrooge.

"But I see it," said the Ghost, "notwithstanding."

"Well!" returned Scrooge, "I have but to swallow this, and be for the rest of my days persecuted by a legion of goblins, all my own creation. Humbug, I tell you; humbug!"

At this the spirit raised a frightful cry, and shook his chain with such a dismal and appalling noise, that Scrooge held on tight to his chair, to save himself from falling in a swoon. But how much greater was his horror when, the phantom taking off the bandage round his head, as if it were too warm to wear indoors, his lower jaw dropped down upon his breast!

Scrooge fell upon his knees, and clasped his hands before his face.

"Mercy!" he said. "Dreadful apparition, why do you trouble me?"

"Man of the worldly mind!" replied the Ghost, "do you believe in me or not?"

"I do," said Scrooge. "I must. But why do spirits walk the earth, and why do they come to me?"

"It is required of every man," the Ghost returned, "that the spirit within him should walk abroad among his fellow-men, and travel far and wide; and if that spirit goes not forth in life, it is condemned to do so after death. It is doomed to wander through the world—oh, woe is me!—and witness what it cannot share, but might have shared on earth, and turned to happiness!"

Again the specter raised a cry, and shook his chain and wrung his shadowy hands.

"You are fettered," said Scrooge trembling. "Tell me why?"

"I wear the chain I forged in life," replied the Ghost. "I made it link by link, and yard by yard; I girded it on of my own free will, and of my own free will I wore it. Is its pattern strange to *you?*"

Scrooge trembled more and more.

"Or would you know," pursued the Ghost, "the weight and length of the strong coil you bear yourself? It was full as heavy and as long as this, seven Christmas Eves ago. You have labored on it, since. It is a ponderous chain!"

Scrooge glanced about him on the floor, in the expectation of finding himself surrounded by some fifty or sixty fathoms of iron cable; but he could see nothing.

"Jacob!" he said imploringly. "Old Jacob Marley, tell me more! Speak comfort to me, Jacob!"

"I have none to give," the Ghost replied. "It comes from other regions, Ebenezer Scrooge, and is conveyed by other ministers, to other kinds of men. Nor can I tell you what I would. A very little more is all permitted to me. I cannot rest, I cannot stay, I cannot linger anywhere. My spirit never walked beyond our counting-house—mark me! —in life my spirit never roved beyond the narrow limits of our money-changing hole; and weary journeys lie before me!"

It was a habit with Scrooge, whenever he became thoughtful, to put his hands in his breeches pockets. Pondering on what the Ghost had said, he did so now, but without lifting up his eyes, or getting off his knees.

"You must have been very slow about it, Jacob," Scrooge observed in a business-like manner, though with humility and deference.

"Slow!" the Ghost repeated.

"Seven years dead," mused Scrooge. "And traveling all the time?"

"The whole time," said the Ghost. "No rest, no peace. Incessant torture of remorse."

"You travel fast?" said Scrooge.

"On the wings of the wind," replied the Ghost.

"You might have got over a great quantity of ground in seven years," said Scrooge.

The Ghost, on hearing this, set up another cry, and clanked his chain so hideously in the dead silence of the night, that the Ward would have been justified in indicting it for a nuisance.

"Oh! captive, bound and double-ironed," cried the phantom, "not to know that ages of incessant labor, by immortal creatures, for this earth, must pass into eternity before the good of which it is susceptible is all developed! Not to know that any Christian spirit working kindly in its little sphere, whatever it may be, will find its mortal life too short for its vast means of usefulness! Not to know that no space of regret can make amends for one life's opportunities misused! Yet such was I! Oh! such was I!"

"But you were always a good man of business, Jacob," faltered Scrooge, who now began to apply this to himself.

"Business!" cried the Ghost, wringing his hands again. "Mankind was my business. The common welfare was my business; charity, mercy, forbearance, and benevolence were all my business. The dealings of my trade were but a drop of water in the comprehensive ocean of my business!"

He held up his chain at arm's-length, as if that were the cause of all his unavailing grief, and flung it heavily upon the ground again.

"At this time of the rolling year," the specter said, "I suffer most. Why did I walk through crowds of fellow-beings with my eyes turned down, and never raise them to that blessed Star which led the Wise Men to a poor abode? Were there no poor homes to which its light would have conducted *me?*"

Scrooge was very much dismayed to hear the specter going on at this rate, and began to quake exceedingly.

"Hear me!" cried the Ghost. "My time is nearly gone."

"I will," said Scrooge. "But don't be hard upon me! Don't be flowery, Jacob! Pray!"

"How it is that I appear before you in a shape that you can see, I may not tell. I have sat invisible beside you many and many a day.

It was not an agreeable idea. Scrooge shivered, and wiped the perspiration from his brow.

"That is no light part of my penance," pursued the Ghost. "I am here to-night to warn you, that you have yet a chance and hope of escaping my fate. A chance and hope of my procuring, Ebenezer."

"You were always a good friend to me," said Scrooge. "Thankee!"

"You will be haunted," resumed the Ghost, "by Three Spirits."

Scrooge's countenance fell almost as low as the Ghost's had done.

"Is that the chance and hope you mentioned, Jacob?" he demanded in a faltering voice.

"It is."

"I—I think I'd rather not," said Scrooge.

"Without their visits," said the Ghost, "you cannot hope to shun the path I tread. Expect the first to-morrow when the bell tolls One."

"Couldn't I take 'em all at once, and have it over, Jacob?" hinted Scrooge.

"Expect the second on the next night at the same hour. The third, upon the next night when the last stroke of Twelve has ceased to vibrate. Look to see me no more; and look that, for your own sake, you remember what has passed between us!"

When he had said these words, the specter took his wrapper from the table, and bound it round his head, as before. Scrooge knew this, by the smart sound his teeth made when the jaws were brought together by the bandage. He ventured to raise his eyes again, and found his supernatural visitor confronting him in an erect attitude, with his chain wound over and about his arm.

The apparition walked backward from him; and at every step he took, the window raised itself a little, so that when the specter reached it, it was wide open. He beckoned Scrooge to approach, which he did. When they were within two paces of each other, Marley's Ghost held up his hand, warning him to come no nearer. Scrooge stopped.

Not so much in obedience, as in surprise and fear; for on the raising of the hand he became sensible of confused noises in the air; incoherent sounds of lamentation and regret; wailings inexpressibly sorrowful and self-accusatory. The specter, after listening for a moment, joined in the mournful dirge; and floated out upon the bleak, dark night.

Scrooge followed to the window, desperate in his curiosity. He looked out.

The air was filled with phantoms, wandering hither and thither in restless haste, and moaning as they went. Every one of them wore chains like Marley's Ghost; some few (they might be guilty governments were linked together; none were free. Many had been personally known to Scrooge in their lives. He had been quite familiar with one old ghost, in a white waistcoat, with a monstrous iron safe attached to his ankle, who cried piteously at being unable to assist a wretched woman with an infant, whom he saw below, upon a door-step. The misery with them all was, clearly, that they sought to interfere, for good, in human matters, and had lost the power forever.

Whether these creatures faded into mist, or mist enshrouded them, he could not tell. But they and their spirit voices faded together; and the night became as it had been when he walked home.

Scrooge closed the window, and examined the door by which the Ghost had entered. It was double-locked, as he had locked it with his own hands, and the bolts were undisturbed. He tried to say "Humbug!" but stopped at the first syllable. And being, from the emotion he had undergone, or the fatigues of the day, or his glimpse of the Invisible World, or the dull conversation of the Ghost, or the lateness of the hour, much in need of repose, went straight to bed, without undressing, and fell asleep on the instant.

STAVE TWO

The First of the Three Spirits

When Scrooge awoke it was so dark, that, looking out of bed, he could scarcely distinguish the transparent window from the opaque walls of his chamber. He was endeavoring to pierce the darkness with his ferret eyes, when the chimes of a neighboring church struck the four quarters. So he listened for the hour.

To his great astonishment the heavy bell went on from six to seven, and from seven to eight, and regularly up to twelve; then stopped. Twelve! It was past two when he went to bed. The clock was wrong. An icicle must have got into the works. Twelve!

He touched the spring of his repeater, to correct this most preposterous clock. Its rapid little pulse beat twelve; and stopped.

"Why, it isn't possible," said Scrooge, "that I can have slept through a whole day and far into another night. It isn't possible that anything has happened to the sun, and this is twelve at noon!"

The idea being an alarming one, he scrambled out of bed, and groped his way to the window. He was obliged to rub the frost off with the sleeve of his dressing-gown before he could see anything; and could see very little then. All he could make out was, that it was still very foggy and extremely cold, and that there was no noise of people running to and fro, and making a great stir, as there unquestionably would have been if night had beaten off bright day, and taken possession of the world. This was a great relief, because "Three days after sight of this First of Exchange pay to Mr. Ebenezer Scrooge or his order," and so forth, would have become a mere United States security if there were no days to count by.

Scrooge went to bed again, and thought, and thought, and thought it over and over, and could make nothing of it. The more he thought, the more perplexed he was; and the more he endeavored not to think, the more he thought.

Marley's Ghost bothered him exceedingly. Every time he resolved within himself, after mature inquiry, that it was all a dream, his mind flew back again, like a strong spring released, to its first position, and presented the same problem to be worked all through, "Was it a dream or not?"

Scrooge lay in this state until the chime had gone three quarters more, when he remembered, on a sudden, that the Ghost had warned him of a visitation when the bell tolled One. He resolved to lie awake until the hour was passed; and, considering that he could no more go to sleep than go to Heaven, this was, perhaps, the wisest resolution in his power.

The quarter was so long, that he was more than once convinced he must have sunk into a doze unconsciously, and missed the clock. At length it broke upon his listening ear.

"Ding, dong!"

"A quarter past," said Scrooge, counting.

"Ding, dong!"

"Half past," said Scrooge.

"Ding, dong!"

"A quarter to it," said Scrooge.

"Ding, dong!"

"The hour itself," said Scrooge triumphantly, "and nothing else!"

He spoke before the hour bell sounded, which it now did with a deep, dull, hollow, melancholy ONE. Lights flashed up in the room upon the instant, and the curtains of his bed were drawn.

The curtains of his bed were drawn aside, I tell you, by a hand. Not the curtains at his feet, nor the curtains at his back, but those to which his face was addressed. The curtains of his bed were drawn aside; and Scrooge, starting up into a half-recumbent attitude, found himself face to face with the unearthly visitor who drew them: as close to it as I am now to you, and I am standing in the spirit at your elbow.

It was a strange figure—like a child; yet not so like a child as like an old man, viewed through some supernatural medium, which gave him the appearance of having receded from the view, and being diminished to a child's proportions. Its hair, which hung about its neck and down its back, was white, as if with age; and yet the face had not a wrinkle in it, and the tenderest bloom was on the skin. The arms were very long and muscular; the hands the same, as if its hold were of uncommon strength. Its legs and feet, most delicately formed, were, like those upper members, bare. It wore a tunic of the purest white; and round its waist was bound a lustrous belt, the sheen of which was beautiful. It held a branch of fresh, green holly in its hand; and, in singular contradiction to that wintry emblem, had its dress trimmed with summer flowers. But the strangest thing about it was, that from the crown of its head there sprung a bright, clear jet of light, by which all this was visible; and which was doubtless the occasion of its using, in its duller moments, a great extinguisher for a cap, which it now held under its arm.

Even this, though, when Scrooge looked at it with increasing steadiness, was *not* its strangest quality. For as its belt sparkled and glittered now in one part and now in another, and what was light one instant at another time was dark, so the figure itself fluctuated in its distinctness: being now a thing with one arm, now with one leg, now with twenty legs, now a pair of legs without a head, now a head without a body; of which dissolving parts no outline would be visible in the dense gloom wherein they melted away. And, in the very wonder of this, it would be itself again, distinct and clear as ever.

"Are you the Spirit, sir, whose coming was foretold to me?" asked Scrooge.

"I am!"

The voice was soft and gentle. Singularly low, as if instead of being so close beside him, it were at a distance.

"Who, and what are you?" Scrooge demanded.

"I am the Ghost of Christmas Past."

"Long Past?" inquired Scrooge, observant of its dwarfish stature.

"No. Your past."

Perhaps Scrooge could not have told anybody why, if anybody could have asked him, but he had a special desire to see the Spirit in his cap, and begged him to be covered.

"What!" exclaimed the Ghost, "would you so soon put out, with worldly hands, the light I give? Is it not enough that you are one of those whose passions made this cap, and force me through whole trains of years to wear it low upon my brow?"

Scrooge reverently disclaimed all intention to offend or any knowledge of having wilfully "bonneted" the Spirit at any period of his life. He then made bold to inquire what business brought him there.

"Your welfare!" said the Ghost.

Scrooge expressed himself as much obliged, but could not help thinking that a night of unbroken rest would have been more conducive to that end. The Spirit must have heard him thinking, for it said immediately:

"Your reclamation, then. Take heed!"

It put out its strong hand as it spoke, and clasped him gently by the arm.

"Rise, and walk with me!"

It would have been in vain for Scrooge to plead that the weather and the hour were not adapted to pedestrian purposes; that his bed was warm, and the thermometer a long way below freezing; that he was clad but lightly in his slippers, dressing-gown, and nightcap; and that he had a cold upon him at that time. The grasp, though gentle as a woman's hand, was not to be resisted. He rose; but finding that the Spirit made toward the window, clasped its robe in supplication.

"I am a mortal," Scrooge remonstrated, "and liable to fall."

"Bear but a touch of my hand *there,*" said the Spirit, laying it upon his heart, "and you shall be upheld in more than this!"

As the words were spoken, they passed through the wall, and stood upon an open country road, with fields on either hand. The city had entirely vanished. Not a vestige of it was to be seen. The darkness and the mist had vanished with it, for it was a clear, cold, winter day, with snow upon the ground.

"Good Heaven!" said Scrooge, clasping his hands together, as he looked about him. "I was bred in this place. I was a boy here!"

The Spirit gazed upon him mildly. Its gentle touch, though it had been light and instantaneous, appeared still present to the old man's sense of feeling. He was conscious of a thousand odors floating in the air, each one connected with a thousand thoughts, and hopes, and joys, and cares long, long forgotten!

"Your lip is trembling," said the Ghost. "And what is that upon your cheek?"

Scrooge muttered, with an unusual catching in his voice, that it was a pimple, and begged the Ghost to lead him where he would.

"You recollect the way?" inquired the Spirit.

"Remember it!" cried Scrooge with fervor, "I could walk it blind-fold."

"Strange to have forgotten it for so many years!" observed the Ghost. "Let us go on."

They walked along the road, Scrooge recognizing every gate, and post, and tree; until a little market-town appeared in the distance, with its bridge, its church, and winding river. Some shaggy ponies now were seen trotting toward them, with boys upon their backs, who called to other boys in country gigs and carts, driven by farmers. All these boys were in great spirits, and shouted to each other, until the broad fields were so full of merry music that the crisp air laughed to hear it.

"These are but shadows of the things that have been," said the Ghost. "They have no consciousness of us."

The jocund travelers came on; and as they came, Scrooge knew and named them every one. Why was he rejoiced beyond all bounds to see them? Why did his cold eye glisten, and his heart leap up as they went past? Why was he filled with gladness when he heard them give each other merry Christmas, as they parted at cross-roads and byways, for their several homes? What was merry Christmas to Scrooge? Out upon merry Christmas! What good had it ever done to him?

"The school is not quite deserted," said the Ghost. "A solitary child, neglected by his friends, is left there still."

Scrooge said he knew it. And he sobbed.

They left the highroad, by a well-remembered lane, and soon approached a mansion of dull red brick, with a little weathercock-surmounted cupola, on the roof, and a bell hanging in it. It was a large house, but one of broken fortunes; for the spacious offices were little used, their walls were damp and mossy, their windows broken, and their gates decayed. Fowls clucked and strutted in the stables, and the coach-houses and sheds were overrun with grass. Nor was it more retentive of its ancient state, within; for entering the dreary hall, and glancing through the open doors of many rooms, they found them poorly furnished, cold, and vast. There was an earthy savor in the air, a chilly bareness in the place, which associated itself somehow with too much getting up by candle-light, and not too much to eat.

They went, the Ghost and Scrooge, across the hall, to a door at the back of the house. It opened before them, and disclosed a long, bare, melancholy room, made barer still by lines of plain deal forms and desks. At one of these a lonely boy was reading near a feeble fire; and Scrooge sat down upon a form, and wept to see his poor forgotten self as he had used to be.

Not a latent echo in the house, not a squeak and scuffle from the mice behind the paneling, not a drip from the half-thawed water-spout in the dull yard behind, not a sigh among the leafless boughs of one despondent poplar, not the idle swinging of an empty storehouse door, no, not a clicking in the fire, but fell upon the heart of Scrooge with softening influence, and gave a freer passage to his tears.

The Spirit touched him on the arm, and pointed to his younger self, intent upon his reading. Suddenly a man, in foreign garments, won-derfully real and distinct to look at, stood outside the window, with an ax stuck in his belt, and leading by the bridle an ass laden with wood.

"Why, it's Ali Baba!" Scrooge exclaimed in ecstasy. "It's dear old honest Ali Baba! Yes, yes, I know! One Christmas-time, when yonder solitary child was left here all alone, he *did* come, for the first time, just like that. Poor boy! And Valentine," said Scrooge, "and his wild brother Orson; there they go! And what's his name, who was put down in his drawers, asleep, at the Gate of Damascus; don't you see him? And the Sultan's Groom turned upside down by the Genii; there he is upon his head! Serve him right! I'm glad of it. What business had *he* to be married to the Princess?"

To hear Scrooge expending all the earnestness of his nature on such subjects, in a most extraordinary voice between laughing and crying, and to see his heightened and excited face, would have been a surprise to his business friends in the City, indeed.

"There's the Parrot!" cried Scrooge. "Green body and yellow tail, with a thing like a lettuce growing out of the top of his head; there he is! Poor Robin Crusoe, he called him, when he came home again, after sailing round the island. 'Poor Robin Crusoe, where have you been, Robin Crusoe?' The man thought he was dreaming, but he wasn't. It was the Parrot, you know. There goes Friday, running for his life to the little creek! Halloa! Hoop! Halloa!"

Then, with a rapidity of transition very foreign to his usual character, he said, in pity for his former self, "Poor boy!" and cried again.

"I wish," Scrooge muttered, putting his hand in his pocket, and looking about him, after drying his eyes with his cuff, "but it's too late now."

"What is the matter?" asked the Spirit.

"Nothing," said Scrooge, "nothing. There was a boy singing a Christmas carol at my door last night. I should like to have given him something, that's all."

The Ghost smiled thoughtfully, and waved its hand, saying, as it did so, "Let us see another Christmas!"

Scrooge's former self grew larger at the words, and the room became a little darker and more dirty. The panels shrunk, the windows cracked; fragments of plaster fell out of the ceiling, and the naked laths were shown instead; but how all this was brought about, Scrooge knew no more than you do. He only knew that it was quite correct; that everything had happened so; that there he was, alone again, when all the other boys had gone home for the jolly holidays.

He was not reading now, but walking up and down despairingly. Scrooge looked at the Ghost, and, with a mournful shaking of his head, glanced anxiously toward the door.

It opened, and a little girl, much younger than the boy, came darting in, and, putting her arms about his neck, and often kissing him, addressed him as her "dear, dear brother."

"I have come to bring you home, dear brother!" said the child, clapping her tiny hands, and bending down to laugh. "To bring you home, home, home!"

"Home, little Fan?" returned the boy.

"Yes!" said the child, brimful of glee. "Home, for good and all. Home, for ever and ever. Father is so much kinder than he used to be, that home's like Heaven! He spoke so gently to me one dear night when I was going to bed that I was not afraid to ask him once more if you might come home; and he said Yes, you should; and sent me in a

coach to bring you. And you're to be a man!" said the child, opening
her eyes, "and are never to come back here; but first, we're to be together all the Christmas long, and have the merriest time in all the
world."

"You are quite a woman, little Fan!" exclaimed the boy.

She clapped her hands and laughed, and tried to touch his head; but,
being too little, laughed again, and stood on tiptoe to embrace him.
Then she began to drag him, in her childish eagerness, toward the
door; and he, nothing loath to go, accompanied her.

A terrible voice in the hall cried, "Bring down Master Scrooge's box,
there!" and in the hall appeared the schoolmaster himself, who glared
on Master Scrooge with a ferocious condescension, and threw him
into a dreadful state of mind by shaking hands with him. He then
conveyed him and his sister into the veriest old well of a shivering best
parlor that ever was seen, where the maps upon the wall, and the
celestial and terrestrial globes in the windows, were waxy with cold.
Here he produced a decanter of curiously light wine, and a block of
curiously heavy cake, and administered instalments of those dainties
to the young people; at the same time, sending out a meager servant to
offer a glass of "something" to the postboy, who answered that he
thanked the gentleman, but if it was the same tap as he had tasted before, he had rather not. Master Scrooge's trunk being by this time tied
on to the top of the chaise, the children bade the schoolmaster good-by
right willingly; and, getting into it, drove gaily down the garden sweep,
the quick wheels dashing the hoar-frost and snow from off the dark
leaves of the evergreens like spray.

"Always a delicate creature, whom a breath might have withered,"
said the Ghost. "But she had a large heart!"

"So she had," cried Scrooge. "You're right. I will not gainsay it,
Spirit. God forbid!"

"She died a woman," said the Ghost, "and had, as I think, children."

"One child," Scrooge returned.

"True," said the Ghost. "Your nephew!"

Scrooge seemed uneasy in his mind and answered briefly, "Yes."

Although they had but that moment left the school behind them, they were now in the busy thoroughfares of a city, where shadowy passengers passed and repassed, where shadowy carts and coaches battled for the way, and all the strife and tumult of a real city were. It was made plain enough, by the dressing of the shops, that here, too, it was Christmas-time again, but it was evening, and the streets were lighted up.

The Ghost stopped at a certain warehouse door, and asked Scrooge if he knew it.

"Know it!" said Scrooge. "Was I apprenticed here?"

They went in. At sight of an old gentleman in a Welsh wig, sitting behind such a high desk that if he had been two inches taller he must have knocked his head against the ceiling, Scrooge cried in great excitement:

"Why, it's old Fezziwig! Bless his heart; it's Fezziwig alive again!"

Old Fezziwig laid down his pen, and looked up at the clock, which pointed to the hour of seven. He rubbed his hands, adjusted his capacious waistcoat, laughed all over himself, from his shoes to his organ of benevolence and called out, in a comfortable, oily, rich, fat, jovial voice:

"Yo ho, there! Ebenezer! Dick!"

Scrooge's former self, now grown a young man, came briskly in, accompanied by his fellow-prentice.

"Dick Wilkins, to be sure!" said Scrooge to the Ghost. "Bless me, yes. There he is. He was very much attached to me, was Dick. Poor Dick! Dear, dear!"

"Yo ho, my boys!" said Fezziwig. "No more work to-night. Christmas Eve, Dick. Christmas, Ebenezer! Let's have the shutters up," cried old Fezziwig, with a sharp clap of his hands, "before a man can say Jack Robinson!"

You wouldn't believe how those two fellows went at it! They charged into the street with the shutters—one, two, three—had 'em up in their places—four, five, six—barred 'em and pinned 'em—seven, eight, nine—and came back before you could have got to twelve, panting like racehorses.

"Hilli-ho!" cried old Fezziwig, skipping down from the high desk with wonderful agility. "Clear away, my lads, and let's have lots of room here! Hilli-ho, Dick! Chirrup, Ebenezer!"

Clear away! There was nothing they wouldn't have cleared away, or couldn't have cleared away, with old Fezziwig looking on. It was done in a minute. Every movable was packed off, as if it were dismissed from public life forevermore; the floor was swept and watered, the lamps were trimmed, fuel was heaped upon the fire; and the warehouse was as snug, and warm, and dry, and bright a ball-room as you would desire to see upon a winter's night.

In came a fiddler with a music-book, and went up to the lofty desk, and made an orchestra of it, and tuned like fifty stomach-aches. In came Mrs. Fezziwig, one vast, substantial smile. In came the three Miss Fezziwigs, beaming and lovable. In came the six young followers whose hearts they broke. In came all the young men and women employed in the business. In came the house-maid, with her cousin, the baker. In came the cook, with her brother's particular friend, the milkman. In came the boy from over the way, who was suspected of not having board enough from his master, trying to hide himself behind the girl from next door but one, who was proved to have had her ears pulled by her mistress. In they all came, one after another; some shyly, some boldly, some gracefully, some awkwardly, some pushing, some pulling; in they all came, anyhow and everyhow. Away they all went, twenty couple at once; hands half round and back again the other way; down the middle and up again; round and round in various stages of affectionate grouping; old top couple always turning up in the wrong place; new top couple starting off again, as soon as they got there; all top couples at last, and not a bottom one to help them! When this result was brought about, old Fezziwig, clapping his hands to stop the dance, cried out, "Well done!" and the fiddler plunged his hot face into a pot of porter, especially provided for that purpose. But, scorning rest, upon his reappearance he instantly began again, though there were no dancers yet, as if the other fiddler had been carried home, exhausted, on a shutter, and he were a brand-new man resolved to beat him out of sight, or perish.

There were more dances, and there were forfeits, and more dances, and there was cake, and there was negus, and there was a great piece of cold roast, and there was a great piece of cold boiled, and there were mince-pies, and plenty of beer. But the great effect of the evening came after the roast and boiled, when the fiddler (an artful dog, mind! the sort of man who knew his business better than you or I could have told it him!) struck up "Sir Roger de Coverley." Then old Fezziwig stood out to dance with Mrs. Fezziwig. Top couple, too, with a good stiff piece of work cut out for them; three or four and twenty pair of partners; people who were not to be trifled with; people who *would* dance, and had no notion of walking.

But if they had been twice as many—ah, four times—old Fezziwig would have been a match for them, and so would Mrs. Fezziwig. As to *her,* she was worthy to be his partner in every sense of the term. If that's not high praise, tell me higher, and I'll use it. A positive light appeared to issue from Fezziwig's calves. They shone in every part of the dance like moons. You couldn't have predicted, at any given time, what would become of them next. And when old Fezziwig and Mrs. Fezziwig had gone all through the dance: advance and retire, both hands to your partner, bow and curtsey, corkscrew, thread-the-needle, and back again to your place, Fezziwig "cut"—cut so deftly, that he appeared to wink with his legs, and came upon his feet again without a stagger.

When the clock struck eleven, this domestic ball broke up. Mr. and Mrs. Fezziwig took their stations, one on either side of the door, and shaking hands with every person individually as he or she went out, wished him or her a merry Christmas. When everybody had retired but the two prentices, they did the same to them; and thus the cheerful voices died away, and the lads were left to their beds, which were under a counter in the back shop.

During the whole of this time, Scrooge had acted like a man out of his wits. His heart and soul were in the scene, and with his former self. He corroborated everything, remembered everything, enjoyed everything, and underwent the strangest agitation. It was not until now, when the bright faces of his former self and Dick were turned from them, that he remembered the Ghost, and became conscious that it was looking full upon him, while the light upon its head burned very clear.

"A small matter," said the Ghost, "to make these silly folks so full of gratitude."

"Small!" echoed Scrooge.

The Spirit signed to him to listen to the two apprentices, who were pouring out their hearts in praise of Fezziwig, and, when he had done so, said:

"Why! Is it not? He has spent but a few pounds of your mortal money: three or four, perhaps. Is that so much that he deserves this praise?"

"It isn't that," said Scrooge, heated by the remark, and speaking unconsciously like his former, not his latter self—"it isn't that, Spirit. He has the power to render us happy or unhappy, to make our service light or burdensome, a pleasure or a toil. Say that his power lies in words and looks, in things so slight and insignificant that it is impossible to add and count 'em up; what then? The happiness he gives is quite as great as if it cost a fortune."

He felt the Spirit's glance, and stopped.

"What is the matter?" asked the Ghost.

"Nothing particular," said Scrooge.

"Something, I think?" the Ghost insisted.

"No," said Scrooge—"no. I should like to be able to say a word or two to my clerk just now. That's all."

His former self turned down the lamps as he gave utterance to the wish; and Scrooge and the Ghost again stood side by side in the open air.

"My time grows short," observed the Spirit. "Quick!"

Scrooge turned upon the Ghost and wrestled with it.

In the struggle, if that can be called a struggle in which the Ghost with no visible resistance on his part was undisturbed by any effort of its adversary, Scrooge observed that its light was burning high and bright; and dimly connecting that with its influence over him, he seized the extinguisher-cap, and by a sudden action pressed it down upon its head.

The Spirit dropped beneath it, so that the extinguisher covered its whole form, but though Scrooge pressed it down with all his force, he could not hide the light, which streamed from under it in an unbroken flood upon the ground.

He was conscious of being exhausted, and overcome by an irresistible drowsiness, and, further, of being in his own bedroom. He gave the cap a parting squeeze, in which his hand relaxed, and had barely time to reel to bed before he sank into a heavy sleep.

STAVE THREE

The Second of the Three Spirits

Awaking in the middle of a prodigiously tough snore, and sitting up in bed to get his thoughts together, Scrooge had no occasion to be told that the bell was again upon the stroke of One. He felt that he was restored to consciousness in the right nick of time, for the especial purpose of holding a conference with the second messenger despatched to him through Jacob Marley's intervention. But, finding that he turned uncomfortably cold when he began to wonder which of his curtains this new specter would draw back, he put them every one aside with his own hands, and, lying down again, established a sharp lookout all round the bed. For he wished to challenge the Spirit on the moment of its appearance, and did not wish to be taken by surprise, and made nervous.

Now, being prepared for almost anything, he was not by any means prepared for nothing; and, consequently, when the bell struck One, and no shape appeared, he was taken with a violent fit of trembling. Five minutes, ten minutes, a quarter of an hour went by, yet nothing came. All this time he lay upon his bed, the very core and center of a blaze of ruddy light, which streamed upon it when the clock proclaimed the hour; and which, being only light, was more alarming than a dozen ghosts, as he was powerless to make out what it meant, or would be at and was sometimes apprehensive that he might be at that very moment an interesting case of spontaneous combustion, without having the consolation of knowing it. At last, however, he began to think—as you or I would have thought at first; for it is always the person not in the predicament who knows what ought to have been done in it, and would unquestionably have done it too—at last, I say, he began to think that the source and secret of this ghostly light might be in the adjoining room, from whence, on further tracing it, it seemed to shine. This idea taking full possession of his mind, he got up softly, and shuffled in his slippers to the door.

The moment Scrooge's hand was on the lock, a strange voice called him by his name, and bade him enter. He obeyed.

It was his own room. There was no doubt about that. But it had undergone a surprising transformation. The walls and ceiling were so hung with living green that it looked a perfect grove; from every part of which bright, gleaming berries glistened. The crisp leaves of holly, mistletoe, and ivy reflected back the light, as if so many little mirrors had been scattered there, and such a mighty blaze went roaring up the chimney, as that dull petrifaction of a hearth had never known in Scrooge's time, or Marley's, or for many a winter season gone. Heaped up on the floor, to form a kind of throne, were turkeys, geese, game, poultry, brawn, great joints of meat, sucking-pigs, long wreaths of sausages, mince-pies, plum-puddings, barrels of oysters, red-hot chestnuts, cherry-cheeked apples, juicy oranges, luscious pears, immense twelfth-cakes, and seething bowls of punch, that made the chamber dim with their delicious steam. In easy state upon this couch, there sat a jolly Giant, glorious to see who bore a glowing torch, in shape not unlike Plenty's horn, and held it up, high up, to shed its light on Scrooge, as he came peeping round the door.

"Come in!" exclaimed the Ghost—"come in! and know me better, man!"

Scrooge entered timidly, and hung his head before this Spirit. He was not the dogged Scrooge he had been and though the Spirit's eyes were clear and kind, he did not like to meet them.

"I am the Ghost of Christmas Present," said the Spirit. "Look upon me!"

Scrooge reverently did so. It was clothed in one simple, deep-green robe, or mantle, bordered with white fur. This garment hung so loosely on the figure that its capacious breast was bare, as if disdaining to be warded or concealed by any artifice. Its feet, observable beneath the ample folds of the garment, were also bare, and on its head it wore no other covering than a holly wreath, set here and there with shining icicles. Its dark-brown curls were long and free, free as its genial face, its sparkling eye, its open hand, its cheery voice, its unconstrained demeanor, and its joyful air. Girded round its middle was an antique scabbard, but no sword was in it, and the ancient sheath was eaten up with rust.

"You have never seen the like of me before!" exclaimed the Spirit.

"Never," Scrooge made answer to it.

"Have never walked forth with the younger members of my family, meaning (for I am very young) my elder brothers born in these later years?" pursued the Phantom.

"I don't think I have," said Scrooge. "I am afraid I have not. Have you had many brothers, Spirit?"

"More than eighteen hundred," said the Ghost.

"A tremendous family to provide for," muttered Scrooge.

The Ghost of Christmas Present rose.

"Spirit," said Scrooge submissively, "conduct me where you will. I went forth last night on compulsion, and I learned a lesson which is working now. To-night, if you have aught to teach me, let me profit by it."

"Touch my robe!"

Scrooge did as he was told, and held it fast.

Holly, mistletoe, red berries, ivy, turkeys, geese, game, poultry, brawn, meat, pigs, sausages, oysters, pies, puddings, fruit, and punch, all vanished instantly. So did the room, the fire, the ruddy glow, the hour of the night, and they stood in the city streets on Christmas morning, where (for the weather was severe) the people made a rough, but brisk and not unpleasant kind of music, in scraping the snow from the pavement in front of their dwellings, and from the tops of their houses, whence it was mad delight to the boys to see it come plumping down into the road below, and splitting into artificial little snow-storms.

The house-fronts looked black enough, and the windows blacker, contrasting with the smooth white sheet of snow upon the roofs, and with the dirtier snow upon the ground which last deposit had been plowed up in deep furrows by the heavy wheels of carts and wagons, furrows that crossed and recrossed each other hundreds of times where the great streets branched off, and made intricate channels, hard to trace, in the thick yellow mud and icy water. The sky was gloomy, and the shortest streets were choked up with a dingy mist, half thawed, half frozen, whose heavier particles descended in a shower of sooty atoms, as if all the chimneys in Great Britain had, by one consent, caught fire, and were blazing away to their dear hearts' content. There was nothing very cheerful in the climate or the town, and yet there was an air of cheerfulness abroad that the clearest summer air and brightest summer sun might have endeavored to diffuse in vain.

For the people who were shoveling away on the housetops were jovial and full of glee, calling out to one another from the parapets, and now and then exchanging a facetious snowball—better-natured missile far than many a wordy jest—laughing heartily if it went right, and not less heartily if it went wrong. The poulterers' shops were still half open, and the fruiterers' were radiant in their glory. There were great, round, pot-bellied baskets of chestnuts, shaped like the waistcoats of jolly old gentlemen, lolling at the doors, and tumbling out into the street in their apoplectic opulence. There were ruddy, brown-faced, broad-girthed Spanish onions, shining in the fatness of their growth like Spanish friars, and winking from their shelves in wanton slyness at the girls as they went by, and glanced demurely at the hung-up mistletoe. There were pears and apples, clustered high in blooming pyramids; there were bunches of grapes, made, in the shop-keepers' benevolence, to dangle from conspicuous hooks, that people's mouths might water gratis as they passed; there were piles of filberts, mossy and brown, recalling, in their fragrance, ancient walks among the woods, and pleasant shufflings ankle-deep through withered leaves; there were Norfolk biffins, squab and swarthy, setting off the yellow of the oranges and lemons, and, in the great compactness of their juicy persons, urgently entreating and beseeching to be carried home in paper bags and eaten after dinner. The very gold- and silverfish, set forth among these choice fruits in a bowl, though members of a dull and stagnant-blooded race, appeared to know that there was something going on and, to a fish, went gasping round and round their little world in slow and passionless excitement.

The grocers! oh, the grocers! nearly closed, with perhaps two shutters down, or one, but through those gaps such glimpses! It was not alone that the scales descending on the counter made a merry sound, or that the twine and roller parted company so briskly, or that the canisters were rattled up and down like juggling tricks, or even that the blended scents of tea and coffee were so grateful to the nose, or even that the raisins were so plentiful and rare, the almonds so extremely white, the sticks of cinnamon so long and straight, the other spices so delicious, the candied fruits so caked and spotted with molten sugar as to make the coldest lookers-on feel faint, and subsequently bilious. Nor was it that the figs were moist and pulpy, or that the French plums blushed in modest tartness from their highly decorated boxes, or that everything was good to eat and in its Christmas dress, but the customers were all so hurried and so eager in the hopeful promise of the day, that they tumbled up against each other at the door, crashing their wicker baskets wildly, and left their purchases upon the counter, and came running back to fetch them, and committed hundreds of the like mistakes, in the best humor possible; while the grocer and his people were so frank and fresh that the polished hearts with which they fastened their aprons behind might have been their own, worn outside for general inspection, and for Christmas daws to peck at, if they chose.

But soon the steeples called good people all to church and chapel, and away they came, flocking through the streets in their best clothes, and with their gayest faces. And at the same time there emerged from scores of by-streets, lanes, and nameless turnings, innumerable people, carrying their dinners to the bakers' shops. The sight of these poor revelers appeared to interest the Spirit very much, for he stood, with Scrooge beside him, in a baker's doorway, and, taking off the covers as their bearers passed, sprinkled incense on their dinners from his torch. And it was a very uncommon kind of torch, for once or twice when there were angry words between some dinner-carriers who had jostled each other, he shed a few drops of water on them from it, and their good humor was restored directly. For they said, it was a shame to quarrel upon Christmas Day. And so it was! God love it, so it was!

In time the bells ceased, and the bakers were shut up, and yet there was a genial shadowing forth of all these dinners, and the progress of their cooking, in the thawed blotch of wet above each baker's oven, where the pavement smoked as if its stones were cooking too.

"Is there a peculiar flavor in what you sprinkle from your torch?" asked Scrooge.

"There is. My own."

"Would it apply to any kind of dinner on this day?" asked Scrooge.

"To any kindly given. To a poor one most."

"Why to a poor one most?" asked Scrooge.

"Because it needs it most."

And perhaps it was the pleasure the good Spirit had in showing off this power of his, or else it was his own kind, generous, hearty nature, and his sympathy with all poor men, that led him straight to Scrooge's clerk's; for there he went, and took Scrooge with him, holding to his robe and on the threshold of the door the Spirit smiled, and stopped to bless Bob Cratchit's dwelling with the sprinklings of his torch. Think of that! Bob had but fifteen "Bob" a week himself; he pocketed on Saturdays but fifteen copies of his Christian name and yet the Ghost of Christmas Present blessed his four-roomed house!

Then up rose Mrs. Cratchit, Cratchit's wife, dressed out but poorly in a twice-turned gown, but brave in ribbons, which are cheap and make a goodly show for sixpence, and she laid the cloth, assisted by Belinda Cratchit, second of her daughters, also brave in ribbons, while Master Peter Cratchit plunged a fork into the saucepan of potatoes, and getting the corners of his monstrous shirt-collar (Bob's private property, conferred upon his son and heir in honor of the day) into his mouth, rejoiced to find himself so gallantly attired, and yearned to show his linen in the fashionable Parks. And now two smaller Cratchits, boy and girl, came tearing in, screaming that outside the baker's they had smelled the goose, and known it for their own and, basking in luxurious thoughts of sage and onion, these young Cratchits danced about the table, and exalted Master Peter Cratchit to the skies, while he (not proud, although his collars nearly choked him) blew the fire, until the slow potatoes, bubbling up, knocked loudly at the saucepan lid to be let out and peeled.

"What has ever got your precious father, then?" said Mrs. Cratchit. "And your brother, Tiny Tim? And Martha warn't as late last Christmas Day by half an hour!"

"Here's Martha, mother," said a girl, appearing as she spoke.

"Here's Martha, mother!" cried the two young Cratchits. "Hurrah! There's *such* a goose, Martha!"

"Why, bless your heart alive, my dear, how late you are!" said Mrs. Cratchit, kissing her a dozen times, and taking off her shawl and bonnet for her with officious zeal.

"We'd a deal of work to finish up last night," replied the girl, "and had to clear away this morning, mother!"

"Well! Never mind so long as you are come," said Mrs. Cratchit. "Sit ye down before the fire, my dear, and have a warm, Lord bless ye!"

"No, no! There's father coming," cried the two young Cratchits, who were everywhere at once. "Hide, Martha, hide!"

So Martha hid herself, and in came little Bob, the father, with at least three feet of comforter, exclusive of the fringe, hanging down before him, and his threadbare clothes darned up and brushed, to look seasonable, and Tiny Tim upon his shoulder. Alas for Tiny Tim, he bore a little crutch, and had his limbs supported by an iron frame!

"Why, where's our Martha?" cried Bob Cratchit, looking round.

"Not coming," said Mrs. Cratchit.

"Not coming!" said Bob, with a sudden declension in his high spirits for he had been Tim's blood-horse all the way from church, and had come home rampant. "Not coming upon Christmas Day!"

Martha didn't like to see him disappointed, if it were only a joke so she came out prematurely from behind the closet door, and ran into his arms, while the two young Cratchits hustled Tiny Tim, and bore him off into the wash-house, that he might hear the pudding singing in the copper.

"And how did little Tim behave?" asked Mrs. Cratchit, when she had rallied Bob on his credulity, and Bob had hugged his daughter to his heart's content.

"As good as gold," said Bob, "and better. Somehow he gets thoughtful, sitting by himself so much, and thinks the strangest things you ever heard. He told me, coming home, that he hoped the people saw him in the church, because he was a cripple, and it might be pleasant to them to remember, upon Christmas Day, who made lame beggars walk and blind men see."

Bob's voice was tremulous when he told them this, and trembled more when he said that Tiny Tim was growing strong and hearty.

His active little crutch was heard upon the floor, and back came Tiny Tim before another word was spoken, escorted by his brother and sister to his stool beside the fire, and while Bob, turning up his cuffs—as if, poor fellow, they were capable of being made more shabby —compounded some hot mixture in a jug with gin and lemons, and stirred it round and round, and put it on the hob to simmer, Master Peter and the two ubiquitous young Cratchits went to fetch the goose, with which they soon returned in high procession.

Such a bustle ensued that you might have thought a goose the rarest of all birds, a feathered phenomenon, to which a black swan was a matter of course—and in truth it was something very like it in that house. Mrs. Cratchit made the gravy (ready beforehand in a little saucepan) hissing hot, Master Peter mashed the potatoes with incredible vigor, Miss Belinda sweetened up the apple sauce, Martha dusted the hot plates, Bob took Tiny Tim beside him in a tiny corner at the table, the two young Cratchits set chairs for everybody, not forgetting themselves, and, mounting guard upon their posts, crammed spoons into their mouths, lest they should shriek for goose before their turn came to be helped. At last the dishes were set on, and grace was said. It was succeeded by a breathless pause, as Mrs. Cratchit, looking slowly all along the carving-knife, prepared to plunge it in the breast, but when she did, and when the long-expected gush of stuffing issued forth, one murmur of delight arose all round the board, and even Tiny Tim, excited by the two young Cratchits, beat on the table with the handle of his knife, and feebly cried Hurrah!

There never was such a goose. Bob said he didn't believe there ever was such a goose cooked. Its tenderness and flavor, size and cheapness, were the themes of universal admiration. Eked out by apple sauce and mashed potatoes, it was a sufficient dinner for the whole family; indeed, as Mrs. Cratchit said with great delight (surveying one small atom of a bone upon the dish), they hadn't ate it all at last! Yet every one had enough, and the youngest Cratchits in particular were steeped in sage and onion to the eyebrows! But now, the plates being changed by Miss Belinda, Mrs. Cratchit left the room alone—too nervous to bear witness—to take the pudding up, and bring it in.

Suppose it should not be done enough! Suppose it should break in turning out! Suppose somebody should have got over the wall of the back yard, and stolen it, while they were merry with the goose—a supposition at which the two young Cratchits became livid! All sorts of horrors were supposed.

Hallo! A great deal of steam! The pudding was out of the copper. A smell like a washing-day! That was the cloth. A smell like an eating-house and a pastry-cook's next door to each other, with a laundress's next door to that! That was the pudding! In half a minute Mrs. Cratchit entered—flushed, but smiling proudly—with the pudding, like a speckled cannon-ball, so hard and firm, blazing in half of half a quartern of ignited brandy, and bedight with Christmas holly stuck into the top.

Oh, a wonderful pudding! Bob Cratchit said, and calmly, too, that he regarded it as the greatest success achieved by Mrs. Cratchit since their marriage. Mrs. Cratchit said that, now the weight was off her mind, she would confess she had her doubts about the quantity of flour. Everybody had something to say about it, but nobody said or thought it was at all a small pudding for a large family. It would have been flat heresy to do so. Any Cratchit would have blushed to hint at such a thing.

At last the dinner was all done, the cloth was cleared, the hearth swept, and the fire made up. The compound in the jug being tasted, and considered perfect, apples and oranges were put upon the table, and a shovelful of chestnuts on the fire. Then all the Cratchit family drew round the hearth in what Bob Cratchit called a circle, meaning half a one, and at Bob Cratchit's elbow stood the family display of glass—two tumblers and a custard-cup without a handle.

These held the hot stuff from the jug, however, as well as golden goblets would have done and Bob served it out with beaming looks, while the chestnuts on the fire sputtered and crackled noisily. Then Bob proposed:

"A merry Christmas to us all, my dears. God bless us!"

Which all the family re-echoed.

"God bless us, every one!" said Tiny Tim, the last of all.

He sat very close to his father's side, upon his little stool. Bob held his withered little hand in his, as if he loved the child, and wished to keep him by his side, and dreaded that he might be taken from him.

"Spirit," said Scrooge, with an interest he had never felt before, "tell me if Tiny Tim will live."

"I see a vacant seat," replied the Ghost, "in the poor chimney-corner, and a crutch without an owner, carefully preserved. If these shadows remain unaltered by the Future, the child will die."

"No, no," said Scrooge. "Oh, no, kind Spirit! say he will be spared."

"If these shadows remained unaltered by the Future, none other of my race," returned the Ghost, "will find him here. What then? If he be like to die, he had better do it, and decrease the population."

Scrooge hung his head to hear his own words quoted by the Spirit, and was overcome with penitence and grief.

"Man," said the Ghost, "if man you be in heart, not adamant, forbear that wicked cant until you have discovered what the surplus is, and where it is. Will you decide what men shall live, what men shall die? It may be that in the sight of Heaven you are more worthless and less fit to live than millions like this poor man's child. O God! to hear the insect on the leaf pronouncing on the too much life among his hungry brothers in the dust!"

Scrooge bent before the Ghost's rebuke, and, trembling, cast his eyes upon the ground. But he raised them speedily, on hearing his own name.

"Mr. Scrooge!" said Bob; "I'll give you Mr. Scrooge, the Founder of the Feast!"

"The Founder of the Feast, indeed!" cried Mrs. Cratchit, reddening. "I wish I had him here. I'd give him a piece of my mind to feast upon, and I hope he'd have a good appetite for it."

"My dear," said Bob, "the children! Christmas Day."

"It should be Christmas Day, I am sure," said she, "on which one drinks the health of such an odious, stingy, hard, unfeeling man as Mr. Scrooge. You know he is, Robert! Nobody knows it better than you do, poor fellow!"

"My dear," was Bob's mild answer, "Christmas Day."

"I'll drink his health for your sake, and the Day's," said Mrs. Cratchit, "not for his. Long life to him! A merry Christmas and a happy New Year! He'll be very merry and very happy, I have no doubt!"

The children drank the toast after her. It was the first of their proceedings which had no heartiness in it. Tiny Tim drank it last of all, but he didn't care twopence for it. Scrooge was the Ogre of the family. The mention of his name cast a dark shadow on the party, which was not dispelled for full five minutes.

After it had passed away, they were ten times merrier than before, from the mere relief of Scrooge the Baleful being done with. Bob Cratchit told them how he had a situation in his eye for Master Peter, which would bring in, if obtained, full five and sixpence weekly. The two young Cratchits laughed tremendously at the idea of Peter's being a man of business, and Peter himself looked thoughtfully at the fire from between his collars, as if he were deliberating what particular investments he should favor when he came into the receipt of that bewildering income. Martha, who was a poor apprentice at a milliner's, then told them what kind of work she had to do, and how many hours she worked at a stretch, and how she meant to lie abed to-morrow morning for a good long rest, to-morrow being a holiday she passed at home. Also how she had seen a countess and a lord some days before, and how the lord "was much about as tall as Peter"; at which Peter pulled up his collars so high that you couldn't have seen his head if you had been there. All this time the chestnuts and the Jug went round and round, and by and by they had a song, about a lost child traveling in the snow, from Tiny Tim, who had a plaintive little voice, and sang it very well indeed.

There was nothing of high mark in this. They were not a handsome family, they were not well dressed, their shoes were far from being waterproof, their clothes were scanty, and Peter might have known, and very likely did, the inside of a pawnbroker's. But they were happy, grateful, pleased with one another, and contented with the time; and when they faded, and looked happier yet in the bright sprinklings of the Spirit's torch at parting, Scrooge had his eye upon them, and especially on Tiny Tim, until the last.

By this time it was getting dark, and snowing pretty heavily and as Scrooge and the Spirit went along the streets, the brightness of the roaring fires in kitchens, parlors, and all sorts of rooms was wonderful. Here, the flickering of the blaze showed preparations for a cozy dinner, with hot plates baking through and through before the fire, and deep-red curtains, ready to be drawn to shut out cold and darkness. There, all the children of the house were running out into the snow to meet their married sisters, brothers, cousins, uncles, aunts, and be the first to greet them. Here, again, were shadows on the window-blinds of guests assembling, and there a group of handsome girls, all hooded and fur-booted, and all chattering at once, tripped lightly off to some near neighbor's house, where, woe upon the single man who saw them enter —artful witches! well they knew it—in a glow.

But, if you had judged from the numbers of people on their way to friendly gatherings, you might have thought that no one was at home to give them welcome when they got there, instead of every house expecting company, and piling up its fires half-chimney high. Blessings on it, how the Ghost exulted! How it bared its breadth of breast, and opened its capacious palm, and floated on, outpouring, with a generous hand, its bright and harmless mirth on everything within its reach! The very lamplighter, who ran on before, dotting the dusky street with specks of light, and who was dressed to spend the evening somewhere, laughed out loudly as the Spirit passed, though little kenned the lamplighter that he had any company but Christmas!

And now, without a word of warning from the Ghost, they stood upon a bleak and desert moor, where monstrous masses of rude stone were cast about, as though it were the burial-place of giants, and water spread itself wheresoever it listed, or would have done so, but for the frost that held it prisoner, and nothing grew but moss and furze, and coarse, rank grass. Down in the west the setting sun had left a streak of fiery red, which glared upon the desolation for an instant, like a sullen eye, and, frowning lower, lower, lower yet, was lost in the thick gloom of darkest night.

"What place is this?" asked Scrooge.

"A place where miners live, who labor in the bowels of the earth," returned the Spirit. "But they know me. See!"

A light shone from the window of a hut, and swiftly they advanced toward it. Passing through the wall of mud and stone, they found a cheerful company assembled round a glowing fire. An old, old man and woman, with their children and their children's children, and another generation beyond that, all decked out gaily in their holiday attire. The old man, in a voice that seldom rose above the howling of the wind upon the barren waste, was singing them a Christmas song— it had been a very old song when he was a boy—and from time to time they all joined in the chorus. So surely as they raised their voices, the old man got quite blithe and loud, and so surely as they stopped, his vigor sank again.

The Spirit did not tarry here, but bade Scrooge hold his robe, and, passing on above the moor, sped—whither? Not to sea? To sea. To Scrooge's horror, looking back, he saw the last of the land, a frightful range of rocks, behind them and his ears were deafened by the thundering of water, as it rolled, and roared, and raged among the dreadful caverns it had worn, and fiercely tried to undermine the earth.

Built upon a dismal reef of sunken rocks, some leagues or so from shore, on which the waters chafed and dashed, the wild year through, there stood a solitary lighthouse. Great heaps of seaweed clung to its base, and storm-birds—born of the wind, one might suppose, as seaweed of the water—rose and fell about it, like the waves they skimmed.

But even here, two men who watched the light had made a fire, that through the loophole in the thick stone wall shed out a ray of brightness on the awful sea. Joining their horny hands over the rough table at which they sat, they wished each other Merry Christmas in their can of grog, and one of them, the elder, too, with his face all damaged and scarred with hard weather, as the figurehead of an old ship might be, struck up a sturdy song that was like a gale in itself.

Again the Ghost sped on, above the black and heaving sea—on, on —until, being far away, as he told Scrooge, from any shore, they lighted on a ship. They stood beside the helmsman at the wheel, the lookout in the bow, the officers who had the watch, dark, ghostly figures in their several stations, but every man among them hummed a Christmas tune, or had a Christmas thought, or spoke below his breath to his companion of some bygone Christmas Day, with homeward hopes belonging to it. And every man on board, waking or sleeping, good or bad, had had a kinder word for one another on that day in the year, and had shared to some extent in its festivities, and had remembered those he cared for at a distance, and had known that they delighted to remember him.

It was a great surprise to Scrooge, while listening to the moaning of the wind, and thinking what a solemn thing it was to move on through the lonely darkness over an unknown abyss, whose depths were secrets as profound as death—it was a great surprise to Scrooge, while thus engaged, to hear a hearty laugh. It was a much greater surprise to Scrooge to recognize it as his own nephew's and to find himself in a bright, dry, gleaming room, with the Spirit standing smiling by his side, and looking at that same nephew with approving affability!

"Ha, ha!" laughed Scrooge's nephew. "Ha, ha, ha!"

When Scrooge's nephew laughed in this way, holding his sides, rolling his head, and twisting his face into the most extravagant contortions, Scrooge's niece, by marriage, laughed as heartily as he. And their assembled friends, being not a bit behindhand, roared out lustily.

"Ha, ha! Ha, ha, ha, ha!"

"He said that Christmas was a humbug, as I live!" cried Scrooge's nephew. "He believed it, too!"

"More shame for him, Fred!" said Scrooge's niece indignantly. Bless those women! they never do any thing by halves. They are always in earnest.

She was very pretty; exceedingly pretty. With a dimpled, surprised-looking capital face, a ripe little mouth that seemed made to be kissed —as no doubt it was, all kinds of good little dots about her chin, that melted into one another when she laughed, and the sunniest pair of eyes you ever saw in any little creature's head. Altogether she was what you would have called provoking, you know, but satisfactory, too. Oh, perfectly satisfactory!

"He's a comical old fellow," said Scrooge's nephew, "that's the truth; and not so pleasant as he might be. However, his offenses carry their own punishment, and I have nothing to say against him."

"I'm sure he is very rich, Fred," hinted Scrooge's niece. "At least you always tell *me* so."

"What of that, my dear?" said Scrooge's nephew. "His wealth is of no use to him. He doesn't do any good with it. He doesn't make himself comfortable with it. He hasn't the satisfaction of thinking—ha, ha, ha!—that he is ever going to benefit us with it."

"I have no patience with him," observed Scrooge's niece. Scrooge's niece's sisters, and all the other ladies, expressed the same opinion.

"Oh, I have!" said Scrooge's nephew. "I am sorry for him: I couldn't be angry with him if I tried. Who suffers by his ill whims? Himself, always. Here, he takes it into his head to dislike us, and he won't come and dine with us. What's the consequence? He doesn't lose much of a dinner."

"Indeed, I think he loses a very good dinner," interrupted Scrooge's niece. Everybody else said the same, and they must be allowed to have been competent judges, because they had just had dinner and, with the dessert upon the table, were clustered round the fire, by lamplight.

"Well! I am very glad to hear it," said Scrooge's nephew, "because I haven't any great faith in these young housekeepers. What do *you* say, Topper?"

Topper had clearly got his eye upon one of Scrooge's niece's sisters, for he answered that a bachelor was a wretched outcast, who had no right to express an opinion on the subject. Whereat Scrooge's niece's sister—the plump one with the lace tucker, not the one with the roses —blushed.

"Do go on, Fred," said Scrooge's niece, clapping her hands. "He never finishes what he begins to say! He is such a ridiculous fellow!"

"I was only going to say," said Scrooge's nephew, "that the consequence of his taking a dislike to us, and not making merry with us, is, as I think, that he loses some pleasant moments, which could do him no harm. I am sure he loses pleasanter companions than he can find in his own thoughts, either in his moldy old office or his dusty chambers. I mean to give him the same chance every year, whether he likes it or not, for I pity him. He may rail at Christmas till he dies, but he can't help thinking better of it—I defy him—if he finds me going there, in good temper, year after year, and saying, 'Uncle Scrooge, how are you?' If it only puts him in the vein to leave his poor clerk fifty pounds, *that's* something, and I think I shook him, yesterday."

It was their turn to laugh now, at the notion of his shaking Scrooge. But being thoroughly good-natured, and not much caring what they laughed at, so that they laughed at any rate, he encouraged them in their merriment, and passed the bottle, joyously.

After tea, they had some music. For they were a musical family, and knew what they were about, when they sung a glee or catch, I can assure you: especially Topper, who could growl away in the bass like a good one, and never swell the large veins in his forehead, or get red in the face over it. Scrooge's niece played well upon the harp and played, among other tunes, a simple little air (a mere nothing: you might learn to whistle it in two minutes) which had been familiar to the child who fetched Scrooge from the boarding-school, as he had been reminded by the Ghost of Christmas Past. When this strain of music sounded, all the things that Ghost had shown him came upon his mind; he softened more and more and thought that if he could have listened to it often, years ago, he might have cultivated the kindness of life for his own happiness with his own hands, without resorting to the sexton's spade that buried Jacob Marley.

But they didn't devote the whole evening to music. After a while they played at forfeits, for it is good to be children sometimes, and never better than at Christmas, when its mighty Founder was a child himself. Stop! There was first a game at blindman's-buff. Of course there was. And I no more believe Topper was really blind than I believe he had eyes in his boots. My opinion is, that it was a done thing between him and Scrooge's nephew, and that the Ghost of Christmas Present knew it. The way he went after that plump sister in the lace tucker was an outrage on the credulity of human nature. Knocking down the fire-irons, tumbling over the chairs, bumping up against the piano, smothering himself among the curtains, wherever she went, there went he! He always knew where the plump sister was. He wouldn't catch anybody else. . . .

Scrooge's niece was not one of the blindman's-buff party, but was made comfortable with a large chair and a footstool, in a snug corner, where the Ghost and Scrooge were close behind her. But she joined in the forfeits, and loved her love to admiration with all the letters of the alphabet. Likewise at the game of How, When, and Where, she was very great, and, to the secret joy of Scrooge's nephew, beat her sisters hollow, though they were sharp girls, too, as Topper could have told you. There might have been twenty people there, young and old, but they all played, and so did Scrooge for, wholly forgetting, in the interest he had in what was going on, that his voice made no sound in their ears, he sometimes came out with his guess quite loud, and very often guessed right, too; for the sharpest needle, best Whitechapel, warranted not to cut in the eye, was not sharper than Scrooge, blunt as he took it in his head to be.

The Ghost was greatly pleased to find him in this mood, and looked upon him with such favor, that he begged like a boy to be allowed to stay until the guests departed. But this the Spirit said could not be done.

"Here is a new game," said Scrooge. "One half-hour, Spirit, only one!"

It was a game called Yes and No, where Scrooge's nephew had to think of something, and the rest must find out what, he only answering to their questions yes or no, as the case was. The brisk fire of questioning to which he was exposed, elicited from him that he was thinking of an animal, a live animal, rather a disagreeable animal, a savage animal, an animal that growled and grunted sometimes, and talked sometimes, and lived in London, and walked about the streets, and wasn't made a show of, and wasn't led by anybody, and didn't live in a menagerie, and was never killed in a market, and was not a horse, or an ass, or a cow, or a bull, or a tiger, or a dog, or a pig, or a cat, or a bear. At every fresh question that was put to him, this nephew burst into a fresh roar of laughter and was so inexpressibly tickled, that he was obliged to get up off the sofa and stamp. At last the plump sister, falling into a similar state, cried out:

"I have found it out! I know what it is, Fred! I know what it is!"

"What is it?" cried Fred.

"It's your uncle Scro-o-o-o-oge!"

Which it certainly was. Admiration was the universal sentiment, though some objected that the reply to "Is it a bear?" ought to have been "Yes," inasmuch as an answer in the negative was sufficient to have diverted their thoughts from Mr. Scrooge, supposing they had ever had any tendency that way.

"He has given us plenty of merriment, I am sure," said Fred, "and it would be ungrateful not to drink his health. Here is a glass of mulled wine ready to our hand at the moment and I say, 'Uncle Scrooge!' "

"Well! Uncle Scrooge!" they cried.

"A merry Christmas and a happy New Year to the old man, whatever he is!" said Scrooge's nephew. "He wouldn't take it from me, but may he have it, nevertheless. Uncle Scrooge!"

Uncle Scrooge had imperceptibly become so gay and light of heart, that he would have pledged the unconscious company in return, and thanked them in an inaudible speech, if the Ghost had given him time. But the whole scene passed off in the breath of the last word spoken by his nephew, and he and the Spirit were again upon their travels.

Much they saw, and far they went, and many homes they visited, but always with a happy end. The Spirit stood beside sick-beds, and they were cheerful; on foreign lands, and they were close at home; by struggling men, and they were patient in their greater hope; by poverty, and it was rich. In almshouse, hospital, and jail, in misery's every refuge, where vain man in his little brief authority had not made fast the door, and barred the Spirit out, he left his blessing, and taught Scrooge his precepts.

It was a long night, if it were only a night, but Scrooge had his doubts of this, because the Christmas holidays appeared to be condensed into the space of time they passed together. It was strange, too, that while Scrooge remained unaltered in his outward form, the Ghost grew older, clearly older. Scrooge had observed this change, but never spoke of it, until they left a children's Twelfth Night party, when, looking at the Spirit as they stood together in an open place, he noticed that its hair was gray.

"Are spirits' lives so short?" asked Scrooge.

"My life upon this globe is very brief," replied the Ghost. "It ends to-night."

"To-night!" cried Scrooge.

"To-night at midnight. Hark. The time is drawing near."

The chimes were ringing the three quarters past eleven at that moment.

"Forgive me if I am not justified in what I ask," said Scrooge, looking intently at the Spirit's robe, "but I see something strange, and not belonging to yourself, protruding from your skirts. Is it a foot or a claw?"

"It might be a claw, for the flesh there is upon it," was the Spirit's sorrowful reply. "Look here."

From the foldings of its robe, it brought two children, wretched, abject, frightful, hideous, miserable. They knelt down at its feet, and clung upon the outside of its garment.

"O Man! look here! Look, look, down here!" exclaimed the Ghost.

They were a boy and girl. Yellow, meager, ragged, scowling, wolfish;

but prostrate, too, in their humility. Where graceful youth should have filled their features out, and touched them with its freshest tints, a stale and shriveled hand, like that of age, had pinched and twisted them, and pulled them into shreds. Where angels might have sat enthroned, devils lurked, and glared out menacing. No change, no degradation, no perversion of humanity, in any grade, through all the mysteries of wonderful creation, has monsters half so horrible and dread.

Scrooge started back, appalled. Having them shown to him in this way, he tried to say they were fine children, but the words choked themselves, rather than be parties to a lie of such enormous magnitude.

"Spirit! are they yours?" Scrooge could say no more.

"They are Man's," said the Spirit, looking down upon them. "And they cling to me, appealing from their fathers. This boy is Ignorance. This girl is Want. Beware of them both, and all of their degree, but most of all beware this boy, for on his brow I see that written which is Doom, unless the writing be erased. Deny it!" cried the Spirit, stretching out its hand toward the city. "Slander those who tell it ye! Admit it for your factious purposes, and make it worse! And bide the end!"

"Have they no refuge or resource?" cried Scrooge.

"Are there no prisons?" said the Spirit, turning on him for the last time with his own words. "Are there no workhouses?"

The bell struck Twelve.

Scrooge looked about him for the Ghost, and saw it not. As the last strike ceased to vibrate, he remembered the prediction of old Jacob Marley, and, lifting up his eyes, beheld a solemn Phantom, draped and hooded, coming, like a mist along the ground, toward him.

STAVE FOUR

The Last of the Spirits

The phantom slowly, gravely, silently, approached. When it came near him, Scrooge bent down upon his knee, for in the very air through which this Spirit moved it seemed to scatter gloom and mystery.

It was shrouded in a deep black garment, which concealed its head, its face, its form, and left nothing of it visible save one outstretched hand. But for this it would have been difficult to detach its figure from the night, and separate it from the darkness by which it was surrounded.

He felt that it was tall and stately when it came beside him, and that its mysterious presence filled him with a solemn dread. He knew no more, for the Spirit neither spoke nor moved.

"I am in the presence of the Ghost of Christmas Yet to Come?" said Scrooge.

The Spirit answered not, but pointed onward with its hand.

"You are about to show me shadows of the things that have not happened, but will happen in the time before us," Scrooge pursued. "Is that so, Spirit?"

The upper portion of the garment was contracted for an instant in its folds, as if the Spirit had inclined its head. That was the only answer he received.

Although well used to ghostly company by this time, Scrooge feared the silent shape so much that his legs trembled beneath him, and he found that he could hardly stand when he prepared to follow it. The Spirit paused a moment, as if observing his condition, and giving him time to recover.

But Scrooge was all the worse for this. It thrilled him with a vague uncertain horror, to know that, behind the dusky shroud, there were ghostly eyes intently fixed upon him, while he, though he stretched his own to the utmost, could see nothing but a spectral hand and one great heap of black.

"Ghost of the Future!" he exclaimed, "I fear you more than any specter I have seen. But as I know your purpose is to do me good, and as I hope to live to be another man from what I was, I am prepared to bear you company, and do it with a thankful heart. Will you not speak to me?"

It gave him no reply. The hand was pointed straight before them.

"Lead on!" said Scrooge—"lead on! The night is waning fast, and it is precious time to me, I know. Lead on, Spirit!"

The Phantom moved away as it had come toward him. Scrooge followed in the shadow of its dress, which bore him up, he thought, and carried him along.

They scarcely seemed to enter the City, for the City rather seemed to spring up about them, and encompass them of its own act. But there they were, in the heart of it, on 'Change, among the merchants, who hurried up and down, and chinked the money in their pockets, and conversed in groups, and looked at their watches, and trifled thoughtfully with their great gold seals, and so forth, as Scrooge had seen them often.

The Spirit stopped beside one little knot of business men. Observing that the hand was pointed to them, Scrooge advanced to listen to their talk.

"No," said a great fat man with a monstrous chin, "I don't know much about it either way. I only know he's dead."

"When did he die?" inquired another.

"Last night, I believe."

"Why, what was the matter with him?" asked a third, taking a vast quantity of snuff out of a very large snuff-box. "I thought he'd never die."

"God knows," said the first, with a yawn.

"What has he done with his money?" asked a red-faced gentleman with a pendulous excrescence on the end of his nose, that shook like the gills of a turkey-cock.

"I haven't heard," said the man with the large chin, yawning again. "Left it to his company, perhaps. He hasn't left it to *me*. That's all I know."

This pleasantry was received with a general laugh.

"It's likely to be a very cheap funeral," said the same speaker, "for, upon my life, I don't know of anybody to go to it. Suppose we make up a party, and volunteer?"

"I don't mind going if a lunch is provided," observed the gentleman with the excrescence on his nose. "But I must be fed, if I make one."

Another laugh.

"Well, I am the most disinterested among you, after all," said the first speaker, "for I never wear black gloves, and I never eat lunch. But I'll offer to go, if anybody else will. When I come to think of it, I'm not at all sure that I wasn't his most particular friend, for we used to stop and speak whenever we met. By-by!"

Speakers and listeners strolled away, and mixed with other groups. Scrooge knew the men, and looked toward the Spirit for an explanation.

The Phantom glided on into a street. Its finger pointed to two persons meeting. Scrooge listened again, thinking that the explantaion might lie here.

He knew these men, also, perfectly. They were men of business, very wealthy, and of great importance. He had made a point always of standing well in their esteem—in a business point of view, that is, strictly in a business point of view.

"How are you?" said one.

"How are you?" returned the other.

"Well!" said the first. "Old Scratch has got his own at last, hey?"

"So I am told," returned the second. "Cold, isn't it?"

"Seasonable for Christmas-time. You are not a skater, I suppose?"

"No. No. Something else to think of. Good morning!"

Not another word. That was their meeting, their conversation, and their parting.

Scrooge was at first inclined to be surprised that the Spirit should attach importance to conversations apparently so trivial, but feeling assured that they must have some hidden purpose, he set himself to consider what it was likely to be. They could scarcely be supposed to have any bearing on the death of Jacob, his old partner, for that was Past, and this Ghost's province was the Future. Nor could he think of any one immediately connected with himself, to whom he could apply them. But nothing doubting that, to whomsoever they applied, they had some latent moral for his own improvement, he resolved to treasure up every word he heard, and everything he saw, and especially to observe the shadow of himself when it appeared. For he had an expectation that the conduct of his future self would give him the clue he missed, and would render the solution of these riddles easy.

He looked about in that very place for his own image, but another man stood in his accustomed corner, and though the clock pointed to his usual time of day for being there, he saw no likeness of himself among the multitudes that poured in through the Porch. It gave him little surprise, however, for he had been revolving in his mind a change of life, and thought and hoped he saw his newborn resolutions carried out in this.

Quiet and dark, beside him stood the Phantom, with its outstretched hand. When he roused himself from his thoughtful quest, he fancied, from the turn of the hand and its situation in reference to himself, that the Unseen Eyes were looking at him keenly. It made him shudder, and feel very cold.

They left the busy scene, and went into an obscure part of the town, where Scrooge had never penetrated before, although he recognized its situation, and its bad repute.

Far in this den of infamous resort, there was a low-browed, beetling shop, below a pent-house roof, where iron, old rags, bottles, bones, and greasy offal were bought. Sitting in among the wares he dealt in, by a charcoal stove, made of old bricks, was a gray-haired rascal, nearly seventy years of age, who had screened himself from the cold air without by a frowzy curtaining of miscellaneous tatters, hung upon a line, and smoked his pipe in all the luxury of calm retirement.

Scrooge and the Phantom came into the presence of this man, just as a woman with a heavy bundle slunk into the shop. But she had scarcely entered, when another woman, similarly laden, came in too, and she was closely followed by a man in faded black, who was no less startled by the sight of them than they had been upon the recognition of each other. After a short period of blank astonishment, in which the old man with the pipe had joined them, they all three burst into a laugh.

"Let the charwoman alone to be the first!" cried she who had entered first. "Let the laundress alone to be the second, and let the undertaker's man alone to be the third. Look here, old Joe, here's a chance! If we haven't all three met here without meaning it!"

"You couldn't have met in a better place," said old Joe, removing his pipe from his mouth. "Come into the parlor. You were made free of it long ago, you know, and the other two ain't strangers. Stop till I shut the door of the shop. Ah! How it skreeks! There ain't such a rusty bit of metal in the place as its own hinges, I believe, and I'm sure there's no such old bones here as mine. Ha, ha! We're all suitable to our calling, we're well matched. Come into the parlor. Come into the parlor."

The parlor was the space behind the screen of rags. The old man raked the fire together with an old stair-rod, and having trimmed his smoky lamp (for it was night) with the stem of his pipe, put it in his mouth again.

While he did this, the woman who had already spoken threw her bundle on the floor, and sat down in a flaunting manner on a stool, crossing her elbows on her knees, and looking with a bold defiance at the other two.

"What odds, then? What odds, Mrs. Dilber?" said the woman. "Every person has a right to take care of themselves. *He* always did!"

"That's true, indeed!" said the laundress. "No man more so."

"Why, then, don't stand staring as if you was afraid, woman! Who's the wiser? We're not going to pick holes in each other's coats, I suppose?"

"No, indeed!" said Mrs. Dilber and the man together. "We should hope not."

"Very well, then!" cried the woman. "That's enough. Who's the worse for the loss of a few things like these? Not a dead man, I suppose?"

"No, indeed," said Mrs. Dilber, laughing.

"If he wanted to keep 'em after he was dead, a wicked old screw," pursued the woman, "why wasn't he natural in his lifetime? If he had been, he'd have had somebody to look after him when he was struck with Death, instead of lying gasping out his last there, alone by himself."

"It's the truest word that ever was spoke," said Mrs. Dilber. "It's a judgment on him."

"I wish it was a little heavier judgment," replied the woman, "and it should have been, you may depend upon it, if I could have laid my hands on anything else. Open that bundle, old Joe, and let me know the value of it. Speak out plain."

But the gallantry of her friends would not allow of this, and the man in faded black, mounting the breach first, produced *his* plunder. It was not extensive. A seal or two, a pencil-case, a pair of sleeve-buttons, and a brooch of no great value, were all. They were severally examined and appraised by old Joe, who chalked the sums he was disposed to give for each upon the wall, and added them up into a total when he found that there was nothing more to come.

"That's your account," said Joe, "and I wouldn't give another six-pence, if I was to be boiled for not doing it. Who's next?"

Mrs. Dilber was next. Sheets and towels, a little wearing-apparel, two old-fashioned silver teaspoons, a pair of sugar-tongs, and a few boots. Her account was stated on the wall in the same manner.

"I always give too much to ladies. It's a weakness of mine, and that's the way I ruin myself," said old Joe. "That's your account. If you asked me for another penny, and made it an open question, I'd repent of be-ing so liberal, and knock off half a crown."

"And now undo *my* bundle, Joe," said the first woman.

Joe went down on his knees for the greater convenience of opening it, and, having unfastened a great many knots, dragged out a large, heavy roll of some dark stuff.

"What do you call this?" said Joe. "Bed-curtains?"

"Ah!" returned the woman, laughing and leaning forward on her crossed arms. "Bed-curtains!"

"You don't mean to say you took 'em down, rings and all, with him lying there?" said Joe.

"Yes, I do," replied the woman. "Why not?"

"You were born to make your fortune," said Joe, "and you'll cer-tainly do it."

"I certainly sha'n't hold my hand, when I can get anything in it by reaching it out, for the sake of such a man as He was, I promise you, Joe," returned the woman coolly. "Don't drop that oil upon the blankets now."

"His blankets?" asked Joe.

"Whose else's do you think?" replied the woman. "He isn't likely to take cold without 'em, I dare say."

Scrooge listened to this dialogue in horror. As they sat grouped about their spoil, in the scanty light afforded by the old man's lamp, he viewed them with a detestation and disgust which could hardly have been greater though they had been obscene demons, marketing the corpse itself.

"Ha, ha!" laughed the same woman, when old Joe, producing a flannel bag with money in it, told out their several gains upon the ground. "This is the end of it, you see! He frightened every one away from him when he was alive, to profit us when he was dead! Ha, ha, ha!"

"Spirit!" said Scrooge, shuddering from head to foot. "I see, I see. The case of this unhappy man might be my own. My life tends that way now. Merciful Heaven, what is this?"

He recoiled in terror, for the scene had changed, and now he almost touched a bed—a bare, uncurtained bed, on which, beneath a ragged sheet, there lay a something covered up, which, though it was dumb, announced itself in awful language.

The room was very dark, too dark to be observed with any accuracy, though Scrooge glanced round it in obedience to a secret impulse, anxious to know what kind of room it was. A pale light, rising in the outer air, fell straight upon the bed, and on it, plundered and bereft, unwatched, unwept, uncared for, was the body of this man.

Scrooge glanced toward the Phantom. Its steady hand was pointed to the head. The cover was so carelessly adjusted that the slightest raising of it, the motion of a finger upon Scrooge's part, would have disclosed the face. He thought of it, felt how easy it would be to do, and longed to do it, but had no more power to withdraw the veil than to dismiss the specter at his side.

Oh cold, cold, rigid, dreadful Death, set up thine altar here, and dress it with such terrors as thou hast at thy command, for this is thy dominion! But of the loved, revered, and honored head, thou canst

not turn one hair to thy dread purposes, or make one feature odious.
It is not that the hand is heavy, and will fall down when released; it
is not that the heart and pulse are still: but that the hand was open,
generous, and true, the heart brave, warm, and tender, and the pulse
a man's. Strike, Shadow, strike! And see his good deeds springing
from the wound, to sow the world with life immortal!

No voice pronounced these words in Scrooge's ears, and yet he heard
them when he looked upon the bed. He thought, if this man could
be raised up now, what would be his foremost thoughts? Avarice, hard
dealing, griping cares? They have brought him to a rich end, truly!

He lay, in the dark, empty house, with not a man, a woman, or a
child to say he was kind to me in this or that, and for the memory of
one kind word I will be kind to him. A cat was tearing at the door,
and there was a sound of gnawing rats beneath the hearthstone. What
they wanted in the room of death, and why they were so restless and
disturbed, Scrooge did not dare to think.

"Spirit!" he said, "this is a fearful place. In leaving it, I shall not
leave its lesson, trust me. Let us go!"

Still the Ghost pointed with an unmoved finger to the head.

"I understand you," Scrooge returned, "and I would do it, if I
could. But I have not the power, Spirit. I have not the power."

Again it seemed to look upon him.

"If there is any person in the town who feels emotion caused by
this man's death," said Scrooge, quite agonized, "show that person to
me, Spirit, I beseech you!"

"Let me see some tenderness connected with a death," said Scrooge,
"or that dark chamber, Spirit, which we left just now will be forever
present to me."

The Ghost conducted him through several streets familiar to his
feet and, as they went along, Scrooge looked here and there to find
himself, but nowhere was he to be seen. They entered poor Bob
Cratchit's house—the dwelling he had visited before—and found the
mother and the children seated round the fire.

Quiet. Very quiet. The noisy little Cratchits were as still as statues
in one corner, and sat looking up at Peter, who had a book before him.

The mother and her daughters were engaged in sewing. But surely they were very quiet!

"'And he took a child, and set him in the midst of them.'"

Where had Scrooge heard those words? He had not dreamed them. The boy must have read them out, as he and the Spirit crossed the threshold. Why did he not go on?

The mother laid her work upon the table, and put her hand up to her face.

"The color hurts my eyes," she said.

The color? Ah, poor Tiny Tim!

"They're better now again," said Cratchit's wife. "It makes them weak by candle-light; and I wouldn't show weak eyes to your father when he comes home, for the world. It must be near his time."

"Past it, rather," Peter answered, shutting up his book. "But I think he has walked a little slower than he used, these few last evenings, mother."

They were very quiet again. At last she said, and in a steady, cheerful voice, that only faltered once:

"I have known him walk with—I have known him walk with Tiny Tim upon his shoulder very fast indeed."

"And so have I," cried Peter. "Often."

"And so have I," exclaimed another. So had all.

"But he was very light to carry," she resumed, intent upon her work, "and his father loved him so, that it was no trouble—no trouble. And there is your father at the door!"

She hurried out to meet him, and little Bob in his comforter—he had need of it, poor fellow—came in. His tea was ready for him on the hob, and they all tried who should help him to it most. Then the two young Cratchits got upon his knees, and laid, each child, a little cheek against his face, as if they said, "Don't mind it, father. Don't be grieved!"

Bob was very cheerful with them, and spoke pleasantly to all the family. He looked at the work upon the table, and praised the industry and speed of Mrs. Cratchit and the girls. They would be done long before Sunday, he said.

"Sunday! You went to-day, then, Robert?" said his wife.

"Yes, my dear," returned Bob. "I wish you could have gone. It would have done you good to see how green a place it is. But you'll see it often. I promised him that I would walk there on a Sunday. My little, little child!" cried Bob. "My little child!"

He broke down all at once. He couldn't help it. If he could have helped it, he and his child would have been farther apart, perhaps, than they were.

He left the room, and went up-stairs into the room above, which was lighted cheerfully, and hung with Christmas. There was a chair set close beside the child, and there were signs of some one having been there lately. Poor Bob sat down in it, and when he had thought a little and composed himself, he kissed the little face. He was reconciled to what had happened, and went down again quite happy.

They drew about the fire and talked, the girls and mother working still. Bob told them of the extraordinary kindness of Mr. Scrooge's nephew, whom he had scarcely seen but once, and who, meeting him in the street that day, and seeing that he looked a little—"just a little down, you know," said Bob, inquired what had happened to distress him. "On which," said Bob, "for he is the pleasantest-spoken gentleman you ever heard, I told him. 'I am heartily sorry for it, Mr. Cratchit,' he said, 'and heartily sorry for your good wife.' By the by, how he ever knew *that*, I don't know."

"Knew what, my dear?"

"Why, that you were a good wife," replied Bob.

"Everybody knows that," said Peter.

"Very well observed, my boy!" cried Bob. "I hope they do. 'Heartily sorry,' he said, 'for your good wife. If I can be of service to you in any way,' he said, giving me his card, 'that's where I live. Pray come to me.' Now it wasn't," cried Bob, "for the sake of anything he might be able to do for us, so much as for his kind way, that this was quite delightful. It really seemed as if he had known our Tiny Tim, and felt with us."

"I'm sure he's a good soul!" said Mrs. Cratchit.

"You would be sure of it, my dear," returned Bob, "if you saw and spoke to him. I shouldn't be at all surprised—mark what I say!—if he got Peter a better situation.

"Only hear that, Peter," said Mrs. Cratchit.

"And then," cried one of the girls, "Peter will be keeping company with some one, and setting up for himself."

"Get along with you!" retorted Peter, grinning.

"It's just as likely as not," said Bob, "one of these days, though there's plenty of time for that, my dear. But, however and whenever we part from one another, I am sure we shall none of us forget poor Tiny Tim—shall we?—or this first parting that there was among us?"

"Never, father!" cried they all.

"And I know," said Bob—"I know, my dears, that when we recollect how patient and how mild he was, although he was a little, little child, we shall not quarrel easily among ourselves, and forget poor Tiny Tim in doing it."

"No, never, father!" they all cried again.

"I am very happy," said little Bob—"I am very happy!"

Mrs. Cratchit kissed him, his daughters kissed him, the two young Cratchits kissed him, and Peter and himself shook hands. Spirit of Tiny Tim, thy childish essence was from God!

"Specter," said Scrooge, "something informs me that our parting moment is at hand. I know it, but I know not how. Tell me what man that was whom we saw lying dead."

The Ghost of Christmas Yet to Come conveyed him, as before—though at a different time, he thought; indeed, there seemed no order in these latter visions, save that they were in the Future—into the resorts of business men, but showed him not himself. Indeed, the Spirit did not stay for anything, but went straight on, as to the end just now desired, until besought by Scrooge to tarry for a moment.

"This court," said Scrooge, "through which we hurry now is where my place of occupation is, and has been for a length of time. I see the house. Let me behold what I shall be, in days to come!"

The Spirit stopped; the hand was pointed elsewhere.

"The house is yonder," Scrooge exclaimed. "Why do you point away?"

The inexorable finger underwent no change.

Scrooge hastened to the window of his office, and looked in. It was an office still, but not his. The furniture was not the same, and the figure in the chair was not himself. The Phantom pointed as before.

He joined it once again, and, wondering why and whither he had gone, accompanied it until they reached an iron gate. He paused to look round before entering.

A churchyard. Here, then, the wretched man whose name he had now to learn lay underneath the ground.

The Spirit stood among the graves, and pointed down to One. He advanced toward it, trembling. The Phantom was exactly as it had been, but he dreaded that he saw new meaning in its solemn shape.

"Before I draw nearer to that stone to which you point," said Scrooge, "answer me one question. Are these the shadows of the things that Will be or are they shadows of the things that May be, only?"

Still the Ghost pointed downward to the grave by which it stood.

"Men's courses will foreshadow certain ends, to which, if persevered in, they must lead," said Scrooge. "But if the courses be departed from, the ends will change. Say it is thus with what you show me!"

The Spirit was immovable as ever.

Scrooge crept toward it, trembling as he went; and following the finger, read upon the stone of the neglected grave his own name, EBENEZER SCROOGE.

"Am *I* that man who lay upon the bed," he cried, upon his knees.

The finger pointed from the grave to him, and back again.

"No, Spirit! Oh, no, no!"

The finger still was there.

"Spirit!" he cried, tight clutching at its robe, "hear me! I am not the man I was. I will not be the man I must have been but for this intercourse. Why show me this, if I am past all hope?"

For the first time the hand appeared to shake.

"Good Spirit," he pursued, as down upon the ground he fell before it, "your nature intercedes for me, and pities me. Assure me that I yet may change these shadows you have shown me, by an altered life!"

The kind hand trembled.

"I will honor Christmas in my heart, and try to keep it all the year. I will live in the Past, Present, and the Future. The Spirits of all Three shall strive within me. I will not shut out the lessons that they teach. Oh, tell me I may sponge away the writing on this stone!"

In his agony he caught the spectral hand. It sought to free itself, but he was strong in his entreaty, and detained it. The Spirit, stronger yet, repulsed him.

Holding up his hands in a last prayer to have his fate reversed, he saw an alteration in the Phantom's hood and dress. It shrunk, collapsed, and dwindled down into a bedpost.

STAVE FIVE

The End of It

Yes! and the bedpost was his own. The bed was his own, the room was his own. Best and happiest of all, the Time before him was his own, to make amends in!

"I will live in the Past, the Present, and the Future!" Scrooge repeated, as he scrambled out of bed. "The Spirits of all Three shall strive within me. O Jacob Marley! Heaven and the Christmas-time be praised for this! I say it on my knees, old Jacob, on my knees!"

He was so fluttered and so glowing with his good intentions, that his broken voice would scarcely answer to his call. He had been sobbing violently in his conflict with the Spirit, and his face was wet with tears.

"They are not torn down," cried Scrooge, folding one of his bedcurtains in his arms—"they are not torn down, rings and all. They are here—I am here—the shadows of the things that would have been may be dispelled. They will be. I know they will!"

His hands were busy with his garments all this time; turning them inside out, putting them on upside down, tearing them, mislaying them, making them parties to every kind of extravagance.

"I don't know what to do!" cried Scrooge, laughing and crying in the same breath, and making a perfect Laocoön of himself with his stockings. "I am as light as a feather, I am as happy as an angel, I am as merry as a schoolboy. I am as giddy as a drunken man. A merry Christmas to everybody! A happy New Year to all the world! Hallo here! Whoop! Hallo!"

He had frisked into the sitting-room, and was now standing there, perfectly winded.

"There's the saucepan that the gruel was in" cried Scrooge, starting off again, and going round the fireplace. "There's the door by which the Ghost of Jacob Marley entered! There's the corner where the Ghost of Christmas Present sat! There's the window where I saw the wandering Spirits! It's all right, it's all true, it all happened. Ha, ha, ha!"

Really, for a man who had been out of practice for so many years, it was a splendid laugh, a most illustrious laugh. The father of a long, long line of brilliant laughs!

"I don't know what day of the month it is," said Scrooge. "I don't know how long I have been among the Spirits. I don't know anything. I'm quite a baby. Never mind. I don't care. I'd rather be a baby. Hallo! Whoop! Hallo here!"

He was checked in his transports by the churches ringing out the lustiest peals he had ever heard. Clash, clash, hammer; ding, dong, bell! Bell, dong, ding; hammer, clang, clash! Oh, glorious, glorious!

Running to the window, he opened it, and put out his head. No fog, no mist; clear, bright, jovial, stirring, cold; cold, piping for the blood to dance to; golden sunlight; heavenly sky; sweet fresh air; merry bells. Oh, glorious! Glorious!

"What's to-day?" cried Scrooge, calling downward to a boy in Sunday clothes, who perhaps had loitered in to look about him.

"Eh?" returned the boy, with all his might of wonder.

"What's to-day, my fine fellow?" said Scrooge.

"To-day!" replied the boy. "Why, *Christmas Day.*"

"It's Christmas Day!" said Scrooge to himself. "I haven't missed it. The Spirits have done it all in one night. They can do anything they like. Of course they can. Of course they can. Hallo, my fine fellow!"

"Hallo!" returned the boy.

"Do you know the poulterer's, in the next street but one, at the corner?" Scrooge inquired.

"I should hope I did," replied the lad.

"An intelligent boy!" said Scrooge. "A remarkable boy! Do you know whether they've sold the prize Turkey that was hanging up there?—Not the little prize Turkey, the big one?"

"What, the one as big as me?" returned the boy.

"What a delightful boy!" said Scrooge. "It's a pleasure to talk to him. Yes, my buck!"

"It's hanging there now," replied the boy.

"Is it?" said Scrooge. "Go and buy it."

"Walk-ER!" exclaimed the boy.

"No, no," said Scrooge. "I am in earnest. Go and buy it, and tell 'em to bring it here, that I may give them the directions where to take it. Come back with the man, and I'll give you a shilling. Come back with him in less than five minutes, and I'll give you half a crown!"

The boy was off like a shot. He must have had a steady hand at a trigger who could have got a shot off half so fast.

"I'll send it to Bob Cratchit's," whispered Scrooge, rubbing his hands, and splitting with a laugh. "He sha'n't know who sends it. It's twice the size of Tiny Tim. Joe Miller never made such a joke as sending it to Bob's will be!"

The hand in which he wrote the address was not a steady one, but write it he did, somehow, and went down-stairs to open the street door, ready for the coming of the poulterer's man. As he stood there, waiting his arrival, the knocker caught his eye.

"I shall love it as long as I live!" cried Scrooge, patting it with his hand. "I scarcely ever looked at it before. What an honest expression it has in its face! It's a wonderful knocker!—Here's the Turkey. Hallo! Whoop! How are you? Merry Christmas!"

It *was* a Turkey! He never could have stood upon his legs, that bird. He would have snapped 'em short off in a minute, like sticks of sealing-wax.

"Why, it's impossible to carry that to Camden Town," said Scrooge.

"You must have a cab."

The chuckle with which he said this, and the chuckle with which he paid for the Turkey, and the chuckle with which he paid for the cab, and the chuckle with which he recompensed the boy, were only to be exceeded by the chuckle with which he sat down breathless in his chair again, and chuckled till he cried.

Shaving was not an easy task, for his hand continued to shake very much and shaving requires attention, even when you don't dance while you are at it. But if he had cut the end of his nose off, he would have put a piece of sticking-plaster over it, and been quite satisfied.

He dressed himself "all in his best," and at last got out into the streets. The people were by this time pouring forth, as he had seen them with the Ghost of Christmas Present; and walking with his hands behind him, Scrooge regarded every one with a delighted smile. He looked so irresistibly pleasant, in a word, that three or four good-humored fellows said, "Good morning, sir! A merry Christmas to you!" And Scrooge said often afterward, that of all the blithe sounds he had ever heard, those were the blithest in his ears.

He had not gone far, when, coming on toward him he beheld the portly gentleman who had walked into his counting-house the day before, and said, "Scrooge and Marley's, I believe?" It sent a pang across his heart to think how this old gentleman would look upon him when they met, but he knew what path lay straight before him, and he took it.

"My dear sir," said Scrooge, quickening his pace, and taking the old gentleman by both his hands, "how do you do? I hope you succeeded yesterday. It was very kind of you. A Merry Christmas to you, sir!"

"Mr. Scrooge?"

"Yes," said Scrooge. "That is my name, and I fear it may not be pleasant to you. Allow me to ask your pardon. And will you have the goodness—" Here Scrooge whispered in his ear.

"Lord bless me!" cried the gentleman, as if his breath were taken away. "My dear Mr. Scrooge, are you serious?"

"If you please," said Scrooge. "Not a farthing less. A great many back payments are included in it, I assure you. Will you do me that favor?"

"My dear sir," said the other, shaking hands with him, "I don't know what to say to such munifi—"

"Don't say anything, please," retorted Scrooge. "Come and see me. Will you come and see me?"

"I will!" cried the old gentleman. And it was clear he meant to do it.

"Thankee," said Scrooge. "I am much obliged to you. I thank you fifty times. Bless you!"

He went to church, and walked about the streets, and watched the people hurrying to and fro, and patted the children on the head, and questioned beggars, and looked down into the kitchens of houses, and up to the windows, and found that everything could yield him pleasure. He had never dreamed that any walk—that anything—could give him so much happiness. In the afternoon, he turned his steps toward his nephew's house.

He passed the door a dozen times before he had the courage to go up and knock. But he made a dash, and did it.

"Is your master at home, my dear?" said Scrooge to the girl. Nice girl! Very.

"Yes, sir."

"Where is he, my love?" said Scrooge.

"He's in the dining-room, sir, along with mistress. I'll show you up-stairs, if you please."

"Thankee. He knows me," said Scrooge, with his hand already on the dining-room lock. "I'll go in here, my dear."

He turned it gently, and sidled his face in, round the door. They were looking at the table (which was spread out in great array); for these young housekeepers are always nervous on such points, and like to see that everything is right.

"Fred!" said Scrooge.

Dear heart alive, how his niece by marriage started! Scrooge had forgotten, for the moment, about her sitting in the corner with the footstool, or he wouldn't have done it, on any account.

"Why, bless my soul!" cried Fred, "who's that?"

"It's I. Your uncle Scrooge. I have come to dinner. Will you let me in, Fred?"

Let him in! It is a mercy he didn't shake his arm off. He was at home in five minutes. Nothing could be heartier. His niece looked just the same. So did Topper, when *he* came. So did the plump sister, when *she* came. So did every one, when *they* came. Wonderful party, wonderful games, wonderful unanimity, won-der-ful happiness!

But he was early at the office next morning. Oh, he was early there! If he could only be there first, and catch Bob Cratchit coming late! That was the thing he had set his heart upon.

And he did it, yes, he did! The clock struck nine. No Bob. A quarter past. No Bob. He was full eighteen minutes and a half behind his time. Scrooge sat with his door wide open, that he might see him come into the tank.

His hat was off before he opened the door, his comforter, too. He was on his stool in a jiffy, driving away with his pen, as if he were trying to overtake nine o'clock.

"Hallo!" growled Scrooge, in his accustomed voice as near as he could feign it. "What do you mean by coming here at this time of day?"

"I am very sorry, sir," said Bob. "I *am* behind my time."

"You are?" repeated Scrooge. "Yes. I think you are. Step this way, sir, if you please."

"It's only once a year, sir," pleaded Bob, appearing from the tank. "It shall not be repeated. I was making rather merry yesterday, sir."

"Now, I'll tell you what, my friend," said Scrooge, "I am not going to stand this sort of thing any longer. And therefore," he continued, leaping from his stool, and giving Bob such a dig in the waistcoat that he staggered back into the tank again—"and therefore, I am about to raise your salary!"

Bob trembled, and got a little nearer to the ruler. He had a momentary idea of knocking Scrooge down with it, holding him, and calling to the people in the court for help and a strait-waistcoat.

"A merry Christmas, Bob!" said Scrooge, with an earnestness that could not be mistaken, as he clapped him on the back. "A merrier Christmas, Bob, my good fellow, than I have given you for many a year! I'll raise your salary, and endeavor to assist your struggling family, and we will discuss your affairs this very afternoon, over a Christmas bowl of smoking bishop, Bob! Make up the fires, and buy another coal-scuttle before you dot another *i*, Bob Cratchit!"

SCROOGE was better than his word. He did it all, and infinitely more; and to Tiny Tim, who did NOT die, he was a second father. He became as good a friend, as good a master, and as good a man as the good old City knew, or any other good old city, town, or borough in the good old world. Some people laughed to see the alteration in him, but he let them laugh, and little heeded them, for he was wise enough to know that nothing ever happened on this globe, for good, at which some people did not have their fill of laughter in the outset; and knowing that such as these would be blind anyway, he thought it quite as well that they should wrinkle up their eyes in grins, as have the malady in less attractive forms. His own heart laughed, and that was quite enough for him.

He had no further intercourse with Spirits, but lived upon the Total Abstinence Principle ever afterward; and it was always said of him, that he knew how to keep Christmas well, if any man alive possessed the knowledge. May that be truly said of us, and all of us! And so, as Tiny Tim observed, God Bless Us, Every One!

CHRISTMAS BELLS

I heard the bells on Christmas Day
Their old, familiar carols play,
   And wild and sweet
   The words repeat
Of peace on earth, good-will to men!

And thought how, as the day had come,
The belfries of all Christendom
    Had rolled along
    The unbroken song
Of peace on earth, good-will to men!

Till, ringing, swinging on its way,
The world revolved from night to day
    A voice, a chime,
    A chant sublime
Of peace on earth, good-will to men!

Then from each black, accursèd mouth
The cannon thundered in the South
    And with the sound
    The carols drowned
Of peace on earth, good-will to men!

It was as if an earthquake rent
The hearth-stones of a continent,
    And made forlorn
    The households born
Of peace on earth, good-will to men!

And in despair I bowed my head;
"There is no peace on earth," I said;
    "For hate is strong
    And mocks the song
Of peace on earth, good-will to men!"

Then pealed the bells more loud and deep.
"God is not dead; nor doth He sleep!
    The Wrong shall·fail,
    The Right prevail,
With peace on earth, good-will to men!"
                    HENRY WADSWORTH LONGFELLOW

IT IS THE BIRTHDAY OF THY KING

Awake, glad heart! get up and sing!
It is the Birthday of thy King.
    Awake! awake!
    The sun doth shake
Light from his locks, and, all the way
Breathing perfumes, doth spice the day.

Awake! awake! hark how th' wood rings,
Winds whisper, and the busy springs
    A concert make!
    Awake! awake!
Man is their high-priest, and should rise
To offer up the sacrifice.

I would I were some bird, or star,
Fluttering in woods, or lifted far
    Above this inn,
    And road of sin!
Then either star or bird should be
Shining or singing still to thee.

I would I had in my best part
Fit rooms for thee! or that my heart
    Where so clean as
    Thy manger was!
But I am all filth, and obscene;
Yet, if thou wilt, thou canst make clean.

Sweet Jesu! will then. Let no more
This leper haunt and soil thy door!
    Cure him, ease him,
    O release him!
And let once more, by mystic birth,
The Lord of life be born in earth.

                HENRY VAUGHAN

CHRISTMAS IN THE OLDEN TIME

On Christmas-eve the bells were rung;
The damsel donned her kirtle sheen;
The hall was dressed with holly green;
Forth to the wood did merry men go,
To gather in the mistletoe.
Thus opened wide the baron's hall
To vassal, tenant, serf and all;
Power laid his rod of rule aside
And ceremony doffed his pride.
The heir, with roses in his shoes,
That night might village partner choose;
The lord, underogating, share
The vulgar game of "Post and Pair."
All hailed, with uncontrolled delight,
And general voice, the happy night
That to the cottage, as the crown,
Brought tidings of salvation down.

The fire, with well-dried logs supplied,
Went roaring up the chimney wide;
The huge hall-table's oaken face,
Scrubbed till it shone, the day to grace,
Bore then upon its massive board
No mark to part the squire and lord.
Then was brought in the lusty brawn
By old blue-coated serving man;
Then the grim boar's head frowned on high,
Crested with bays and rosemary.
Well can the green-garbed ranger tell
How, when and where the monster fell;
What dogs before his death he tore,

And all the baitings of the boar.
The wassal round, in good brown bowls,
Garnished with ribbons, blithely trowls.
There the huge sirloin reeked: hard by
Plum-porridge stood, and Christmas pye;
Nor failed old Scotland to produce,
At such high-tide, her savory goose.

Then came the merry maskers in,
And carols roared with blithesome din.
If unmelodious was the song,
It was a hearty note, and strong;
Who lists may in their murmuring see
Traces of ancient mystery;
White shirts supplied the masquerade,
And smutted cheeks the visors made;
But O, what maskers richly dight,
Can boast of bosoms half so light!
England was "merry England" when
Old Christmas brought his sports again;
'Twas Christmas broached the mightiest ale,
'Twas Christmas told the merriest tale;
A Christmas gambol oft would cheer
The poor man's heart through half the year.

SIR WALTER SCOTT

THE STOCKINGS

THREE STOCKINGS

By Jan Struther

HOWEVER much one groaned about it beforehand, however much one hated making arrangements and doing up parcels and ordering several days' meals in advance—when it actually happened Christmas Day was always fun.

It began in the same way every year: the handle of her bedroom door being turned just loudly enough to wake her up, but softly enough not to count as waking her up on purpose; Toby glimmering like a moth in the dark doorway, clutching a nobbly Christmas stocking in one hand and holding up his pyjama trousers with the other. (He insisted upon pyjamas, but he had not yet outgrown his sleeping-suit figure.)

"Toby! It's only just after six. I did say not till seven."

"But, Mummy, I can't tell the time." He was barefoot and shivering, and his eyes were like stars.

"Come here and get warm, you little *goat*." He was into her bed in a flash, stocking and all. The tail of a clockwork dog scratched her shoulder. A few moments later another head appeared round the door, a little higher up.

"Judy, darling, it's *too* early, honestly."

"I know, but I heard Toby come in, so I knew you must be awake."

"All right, you can come into bed, but you've got to keep quiet for a bit. Daddy's still asleep."

And then a third head, higher up still, and Vin's voice, even deeper than it had been at Long Leave.

"I say, are the others in here? I thought I heard them."

He curled himself up on the foot of his father's bed. And by that time, of course, Clem was awake too. The old transparent stratagem had worked to perfection once more: there was nothing for it but to switch on the lights, shut the windows, and admit that Christmas Day had insidiously but definitely begun.

The three right hands—Vin's strong and broad, Judy's thin and flexible, Toby's still a star-fish—plunged in and out of the three distorted stockings, until there was nothing left but the time-hallowed tangerine in the toe. (It was curious how that tradition lingered, even nowadays when children had a good supply of fruit all the year round.) Their methods were as different as their hands. Vin, with little grunts of approval, examined each object carefully as he drew it out, exploring all its possibilities before he went on to the next. Judy, talking the whole time, pulled all her treasures out in a heap, took a quick glance at them and went straight for the one she liked best—a minikin black baby in a wicker cradle. Toby pulled all his out, too, but he arranged them in a neat pattern on the eiderdown and looked at them for a long time in complete silence. Then he picked up one of them—a big glass marble with coloured squirls inside—and put it by itself a little way off. After that he played with the other toys, appreciatively enough; but from time to time his eyes would stray towards the glass marble, as though to make sure it was still waiting for him.

Mrs. Miniver watched him with a mixture of delight and misgiving. It was her own favourite approach to life: but the trouble was that sometimes the marble rolled away. Judy's was safer; Vin's, on the whole, the wisest of the three.

To the banquet of real presents which was waiting downstairs, covered with a red and white dust-sheet, the stocking-toys, of course, were only an *apéritif;* but they had a special and exciting quality of their own. Perhaps it was the atmosphere in which they were opened—the chill, the black window-panes, the unfamiliar hour; perhaps it was the powerful charm of the miniature, of toy toys, of smallness squared; perhaps it was the sense of limitation within a strict form, which gives to both the filler and the emptier of a Christmas stocking something of the same enjoyment which is experienced by the writer and the reader of a sonnet; or perhaps it was merely that the spell of the old legend still persisted, even though for everybody in the room except Toby the legend itself was outworn.

There were cross-currents of pleasure, too: smiling glances exchanged by her and Vin about the two younger children (she remembered suddenly, having been an eldest child, the unsurpassable sense of grandeur that such glances gave one); and by her and Clem, because they were both grown-ups; and by her and Judy, because they were both women; and by her and Toby, because they were both the kind that leaves the glass marble till the end. The room was laced with an invisible network of affectionate understanding.

This was one of the moments, thought Mrs. Miniver, which paid off at a single stroke all the accumulations on the debit side of parenthood: the morning sickness and the quite astonishing pain; the pram in the passage, the cold mulish glint in the cook's eye; the holiday nurse who had been in the best families; the pungent white mice, the shrivelled caterpillars; the plasticine on the door-handles, the face-flannels in the bathroom, the nameless horrors down the crevices of armchairs; the alarms and emergencies, the swallowed button, the inexplicable earache, the ominous rash appearing on the eve of a journey; the school bills and the dentists' bills; the shortened step, the tempered pace, the emotional compromises, the divided loyalties, the adventures continually forsworn.

And now Vin was eating his tangerine, pig by pig; Judy had undressed the nigger baby and was putting on its frock again back to front; Toby was turning the glass marble round and round against the light, trying to count the squirls. There were sounds of movement in the house; they were within measurable distance of the blessed chink of early morning tea. Mrs. Miniver looked towards the window. The dark sky had already paled a little in its frame of cherry-pink chintz. Eternity framed in domesticity. Never mind. One had to frame it in something, to see it at all.

EARLY IN THE MORNING

By Susan Warner

CHRISTMAS morning was dawning gray, but it was still far from broad daylight, when Ellen was awakened. She found little Ellen Chauncey pulling and pushing at her shoulders, and whispering "Ellen! Ellen!"—in a tone that showed a great fear of waking somebody up. There she was, in nightgown and nightcap, and barefooted too, with a face brim-full of excitement and as wide awake as possible. Ellen roused herself in no little surprise and asked what the matter was.

"I am going to look at my stocking," whispered her visitor,—"don't you want to get up and come with me? it's just here in the other room, —come!—don't make any noise."

"But what if you should find nothing in it?" said Ellen laughingly, as she bounded out of bed.

"Ah but I shall, I know;—I always do;—never fear. Hush! step ever so softly—I don't want to wake anybody."

"It's hardly light enough for you to see," whispered Ellen, as the two little barefooted white figures glided out of the room.

"O yes it is—that's all the fun. Hush!—don't make a bit of noise— I know where it hangs—mamma always puts it at the back of her big easy chair—come this way—here it is! O Ellen! there's two of 'em! There's one for you! There's one for you!"

In a tumult of delight one Ellen capered about the floor on the tips of her little bare toes, while the other, not less happy, stood still for pleasure. The dancer finished by hugging and kissing her with all her heart, declaring she was so glad she didn't know what to do.

"But how shall we know which is which?"

"Perhaps they are both alike," said Ellen.

"No—at any rate one's for me, and t'other's for you. Stop! here are pieces of paper, with our names on I guess—let's turn the chair a little bit to the light—there—yes!—Ellen—M-o-n,—there, that's yours; my name doesn't begin with an M; and this is mine!"

Another caper round the room, and then she brought up in front of the chair where Ellen was still standing.

"I wonder what's in 'em," she said; "I want to look and I *don't* want to. Come, you begin."

"But that's no stocking of mine," said Ellen, a smile gradually breaking upon her sober little face; "my leg never was as big as that."

"Stuffed, isn't it?" said Ellen Chauncey. "O do make haste, and see what is in yours. I want to know so I don't know what to do."

"Well, will you take out of yours as fast as I take out of mine?"

"Well!"—

O mysterious delight, and delightful mystery, of the stuffed stocking! Ellen's trembling fingers sought the top, and then very suddenly left it.

"I can't think what it is," said she laughing,—"it feels so funny."

"O never mind! make haste," said Ellen Chauncey; "it won't hurt you, I guess."

"No, it won't hurt me," said Ellen,—"but"—

She drew forth a great bunch of white grapes.

"Splendid! isn't it?" said Ellen Chauncey. "Now for mine."

It was the counterpart of Ellen's bunch.

"So far, so good," said she. "Now for the next."

The next thing in each stocking was a large horn of sugar-plums.

"Well that's fine, isn't it?" said Ellen Chancey;—"your's is tied with white ribbon and mine with blue; that's all the difference. O, and your paper's red and mine is purple."

"Yes, and the pictures are different," said Ellen.

"Well, I had rather they would be different, wouldn't you? I think it's just as pleasant. One's as big as the other, at any rate. Come—what's next?"

Ellen drew out a little bundle, which being opened proved to be a nice little pair of dark kid gloves.

"O I wonder who gave me this!" she said,—"it's just what I wanted. How pretty! O I'm so glad. I guess who it is."

"O look here," said the other Ellen, who had been diving into *her* stocking,—"I've got a ball—this is just what I wanted too; George told me if I'd get one he'd show me how to play. Isn't it pretty? Isn't it funny we should each get just what we wanted? O this is a very nice ball. I'm glad I've got it. Why here is another great round thing in my stocking!—what can it be? they wouldn't give me *two* balls," said she, chuckling.

"So there is in mine!" said Ellen. "Maybe they're apples?"

"They aren't! they wouldn't give us apples; besides, it is soft. Pull it out and see."

"Then they are oranges," said Ellen laughing.

"*I* never felt such a soft orange," said little Ellen Chauncey. "Come Ellen! stop laughing, and let's see."

They were two great scarlet satin pincushions, with E. C. and E. M. very neatly stuck in pins.

"Well, we sha'n't want pins for a good while, shall we?" said Ellen. "Who gave us these?"

"I know," said little Ellen Chauncey,—"Mrs. Bland."

"She was very kind to make one for me," said Ellen. "Now for the next!"

Her next thing was a little bottle of Cologne water.

"I can tell who put that in," said her friend,—"aunt Sophia. I know her little bottles of Cologne water. Do you love Cologne water? Aunt Sophia's is delicious."

Ellen did like it very much, and was extremely pleased. Ellen Chauncey had also a new pair of scissors which gave entire satisfaction.

"Now I wonder what all this toe is stuffed with," said she,—"raisins and almonds, I declare! and yours the same, isn't it? Well, don't you think we have got enough sweet things? Isn't this a pretty good Christmas?"

"What are you about, you monkeys?" cried the voice of aunt Sophia from the dressing-room door. "Alice, Alice! do look at them. Come, right back to bed both of you. Crazy pates! It is lucky it is Christmas day—if it was any other in the year we should have you both sick in bed; as it is I suppose you will go scot free."

Laughing, and rosy with pleasure, they came back and got into bed together; and for an hour afterwards the two kept up a most animated conversation, intermixed with long chuckles and bursts of merriment, and whispered communications of immense importance. The arrangement of the painted needlebook was entirely decided upon in this consultation; also two or three other matters; and the two children seemed to have already lived a day since daybreak by the time they came down to breakfast.

After breakfast Ellen applied secretly to Alice to know if she could write *very* beautifully; she exceedingly wanted something done.

"I should not like to venture, Ellie, if it must be so superfine; but John can do it for you."

"Can he? Do you think he would?"

"I am sure he will if you ask him."

"But I don't like to ask him," said Ellen, casting a doubtful glance at the window.

"Nonsense! he's only reading the newspaper. You won't disturb him."

"Well you won't say anything about it?"

"Certainly not."

Ellen accordingly went near and said gently, "Mr. Humphreys,"— but he did not seem to hear her. "Mr. Humphreys!"—a little louder.

"He has not arrived yet," said John, looking round gravely.

He spoke so gravely that Ellen could not tell whether he were joking or serious. Her face of extreme perplexity was too much for his command of countenance. "Whom do you want to speak to?" said he, smiling.

"I wanted to speak to you, sir," said Ellen, "if you are not too busy."

"*Mr. Humphreys* is always busy," said he, shaking his head; "but *Mr. John* can attend to you at any time, and *John* will do for you whatever you please to ask him."

"Then, Mr. John," said Ellen laughing, "if you please I wanted to ask you to do something for me very much indeed, if you are not too busy; Alice said I shouldn't disturb you."

"Not at all; I've been long enough over this stupid newspaper.

What is it?"

"I want you, if you will be so good," said Ellen, "to write a little bit for me on something, very beautifully."

" 'Very beautifully!' Well—come to the library; we will see."

"But it is a great secret," said Ellen; "you won't tell anybody?"

"Tortures sha'n't draw it from me—when I know what it is," said he, with one of his comical looks.

In high glee Ellen ran for the pieces of Bristol board which were to form the backs of the needlebook, and brought them to the library; and explained how room was to be left in the middle of each for a painting, a rose on one, a butterfly on the other; the writing to be as elegant as possible, above, beneath, and roundabout, as the fancy of the writer should choose.

"Well, what is to be inscribed on this most original of needlebooks?" John said, as he carefully mended his pen.

"Stop!"—said Ellen,—"I'll tell you in a minute—on this one, the front you know, is to go, 'To my dear mother, many happy New Years;'—and on this side, 'From her dear little daughter, Ellen Chauncey.' You know," she added, "Mrs. Chauncey isn't to know anything about it till New Year's Day; nor anybody else."

Gilbert was next applied to, to paint the rose and the butterfly, which, finding so elegant a beginning made in the work, he was very ready to do. The girls were then free to set about the embroidery of the leaves, which was by no means the business of an hour.

A very happy Christmas day was that. With their needles and thimbles, and rose-colored silk, they kept by themselves in a corner, or in the library, out of the way; and sweetening their talk with a sugar-plum now and then, neither tongues nor needles knew any flagging. It was wonderful what they found so much to say, but there was no lack. Ellen Chauncey especially was inexhaustible. Several times too that day the Cologne bottle was handled, the gloves looked at and fondled, the ball tried, and the new scissors extolled as "just the thing for their work."

Then came the great merry Christmas dinner, when the girls had, not talked themselves out, but tired themselves with working. Young and old dined together to-day, and the children not set by themselves but scattered among the grown-up people; and as Ellen was nicely placed between Alice and little Ellen Chauncey, she enjoyed it all very much. The large long table surrounded with happy faces; tones of cheerfulness and looks of kindness, and lively talk; the superb display of plate and glass and china; the stately dinner; and last but not least, the plum pudding. There was sparkling wine too, and a great deal of drinking of healths; but Ellen noticed that Alice and her brother smilingly drank all theirs in water; so when old Mr. Marshman called to her to "hold out her glass," she held it out to be sure and let him fill it, but she lifted her tumbler of water to her lips instead, after making him a very low bow. Mr. Marshman laughed at her a great deal, and asked her if she was "a proselyte to the new notions;" and Ellen laughed with him, without having the least idea what he meant, and was extremely happy. It was very pleasant too when they went into the drawing-room to take coffee. The young ones were permitted to have coffee to-night as a great favor.

After tea there was a great call for games, and young and old joined in them. They played the Old Curiosity Shop; and Ellen thought Mr. John's curiosities could not be matched. They played the Old Family Coach, Mr. Howard Marshman being the manager, and Ellen laughed till she was tired; she was the coach door, and he kept her opening and shutting and swinging and breaking, it seemed all the while, though most of the rest were worked just as hard. When they were well tired they sat down to rest and hear music, and Ellen enjoyed that exceedingly. Alice sang, and Mrs. Gillespie, and Miss Sophia, and another lady, and Mr. Howard; sometimes alone, sometimes three or four or all together.

At last came ten o'clock and the young ones were sent off; and from beginning to end that had been a Christmas day of unbroken and unclouded pleasure. Ellen's last act was to take another look at her Cologne bottle, gloves, pincushions, grapes, and paper of sugar-plums, which were laid side by side carefully in a drawer.

CHRISTMAS AT CONCORD

By Louisa May Alcott

I

"CHRISTMAS won't be Christmas without any presents," grumbled Jo, lying on the rug.

"It's so dreadful to be poor!" sighed Meg, looking down at her old dress.

"I don't think it's fair for some girls to have lots of pretty things, and other girls nothing at all," added little Amy, with an injured sniff.

"We've got father and mother, and each other, anyhow," said Beth, contentedly, from her corner.

The four young faces on which the firelight shone brightened at the cheerful words, but darkened again as Jo said sadly,—

"We haven't got father, and shall not have him for a long time." She didn't say "perhaps never," but each silently added it, thinking of father far away, where the fighting was.

Nobody spoke for a minute; then Meg said in an altered tone,—

"You know the reason mother proposed not having any presents this Christmas, was because it's going to be a hard winter for every one; and she thinks we ought not to spend money for pleasure, when our men are suffering so in the army. We can't do much, but we can make our little sacrifices, and ought to do it gladly. But I am afraid I don't"; and Meg shook her head, as she thought regretfully of all the pretty things she wanted.

"But I don't think the little we should spend would do any good. We've each got a dollar, and the army wouldn't be much helped by our giving that. I agree not to expect anything from mother or you, but I do want to buy *Undine and Sintram* for myself; I've wanted it *so* long," said Jo, who was a bookworm.

"I planned to spend mine in new music," said Beth, with a little sigh, which no one heard but the hearth brush and kettle-holder.

"I shall get a nice box of Faber's drawing pencils; I really need them," said Amy, decidedly.

"Mother didn't say anything about our money, and she won't wish us to give up everything. Let's each buy what we want, and have a little fun; I'm sure we grub hard enough to earn it," cried Jo, examining the heels of her boots in a gentlemanly manner.

"I know *I* do,—teaching those dreadful children nearly all day, when I'm longing to enjoy myself at home," began Meg, in the complaining tone again.

"You don't have half such a hard time as I do," said Jo. "How would you like to be shut up for hours with a nervous, fussy old lady, who keeps you trotting, is never satisfied, and worries you till you're ready to fly out of the window or box her ears?"

"It's naughty to fret,—but I do think washing dishes and keeping things tidy is the worst work in the world. It makes me cross; and my hands get so stiff, I can't practise good a bit." And Beth looked at her rough hands with a sigh that any one could hear that time.

"I don't believe any of you suffer as I do," cried Amy; "for you don't have to go to school with impertinent girls, who plague you if you don't know your lessons, and laugh at your dresses, and label your father if he isn't rich, and insult you when your nose isn't nice."

"If you mean *libel* I'd say so, and not talk about *labels,* as if Pa was a pickle-bottle," advised Jo, laughing.

"I know what I mean, and you needn't be 'statirical' about it. It's proper to use good words, and improve your *vocabilary,*" returned Amy, with dignity.

"Don't peck at one another, children. Don't you wish we had the money Papa lost when we were little, Jo? Dear me, how happy and good we'd be, if we had no worries," said Meg, who could remember better times.

"You said the other day you thought we were a deal happier than the King children, for they were fighting and fretting all the time, in spite of their money."

"So I did, Beth. Well, I guess we are; for though we do have to work, we make fun for ourselves, and are a pretty jolly set, as Jo would say."

"Jo does use such slang words," observed Amy, with a reproving look at the long figure stretched on the rug. Jo immediately sat up, put her hands in her apron pockets, and began to whistle.

"Don't, Jo; it's so boyish."

"That's why I do it."

"I detest rude, unladylike girls."

"I hate affected, niminy piminy chits."

"Birds in their little nests agree," sang Beth, the peacemaker, with such a funny face that both sharp voices softened to a laugh, and the "pecking" ended for that time.

"Really, girls, you are both to be blamed," said Meg, beginning to lecture in her elder sisterly fashion. "You are old enough to leave off boyish tricks, and behave better, Josephine. It didn't matter so much when you were a little girl; but now you are so tall, and turn up your hair, you should remember that you are a young lady."

"I ain't! and if turning up my hair makes me one, I'll wear it in two tails till I'm twenty," cried Jo, pulling off her net, and shaking down a chestnut mane. "I hate to think I've got to grow up and be Miss March, and wear long gowns, and look as prim as a China-aster. It's bad enough to be a girl, any way, when I like boys' games, and work, and manners. I can't get over my disappointment in not being a boy, and it's worse than ever now, for I'm dying to go and fight with Papa, and I can only stay at home and knit like a poky old woman"; and Jo shook the blue army-sock till the needles rattled like castanets, and her ball bounded across the room.

"Poor Jo; it's too bad! But it can't be helped, so you must try to be contented with making your name boyish, and playing brother to us girls," said Beth, stroking the rough head at her knee with a hand that all the dish washing and dusting in the world could not make ungentle in its touch.

"As for you, Amy," continued Meg, "you are altogether too particular and prim. Your airs are funny now, but you'll grow up an affected little goose if you don't take care. I like your nice manners, and refined ways of speaking, when you don't try to be elegant; but your absurd words are as bad as Jo's slang."

"If Jo is a tom-boy, and Amy a goose what am I, please?" asked Beth, ready to share the lecture.

"You're a dear, and nothing else," answered Meg, warmly; and no one contradicted her, for the "Mouse" was the pet of the family.

It was a comfortable old room, though the carpet was faded and the furniture very plain, for a good picture or two hung on the walls, books filled the recesses, chrysanthemums and Christmas roses bloomed in the windows, and a pleasant atmosphere of home peace pervaded it.

Margaret, the eldest of the four, was sixteen, and very pretty, being plump and fair, with large eyes, plenty of soft brown hair, a sweet mouth, and white hands, of which she was rather vain. Fifteen-year-old Jo was very tall, thin and brown, and reminded one of a colt; for she never seemed to know what to do with her long limbs, which were very much in her way. She had a decided mouth, a comical nose, and sharp gray eyes, which appeared to see everything, and were by turns fierce, funny, or thoughtful. Her long, thick hair was her one beauty; but it was usually bundled into a net, to be out of her way. Round shoulders had Jo, big hands and feet, a fly-away look to her clothes, and the uncomfortable appearance of a girl who was rapidly shooting up into a woman, and didn't like it. Elizabeth—or Beth, as every one called her—was a rosy, smooth-haired, bright-eyed girl of thirteen, with a shy manner, a timid voice, and a peaceful expression, which was seldom disturbed. Her father called her "Little Tranquillity," and the name suited her excellently; for she seemed to live in a happy world of her own, only venturing out to meet the few whom she trusted and loved. Amy, though the youngest, was a most important person, in her own opinion at least. A regular snow maiden, with blue eyes, and yellow hair curling on her shoulders; pale and slender, and always carrying herself like a young lady mindful of her manners. What the characters of the four sisters were, we will leave to be found out.

The clock struck six; and, having swept up the hearth, Beth put a pair of slippers down to warm. Somehow the sight of the old shoes had a good effect upon the girls, for Mother was coming, and every one brightened to welcome her. Meg stopped lecturing, and lit the lamp, Amy got out of the easy chair without being asked, and Jo forgot how tired she was as she sat up to hold the slippers nearer to the blaze.

"They are quite worn out; Marmee must have a new pair."

"I thought I'd get her some with my dollar," said Beth.

"No, I shall!" cried Amy.

"I'm the oldest," began Meg, but Jo cut in with a decided—

"I'm the man of the family, now Papa is away, and *I* shall provide the slippers, for he told me to take special care of Mother while he was gone."

"I'll tell you what we'll do," said Beth; "let's each get her something for Christmas, and not get anything for ourselves."

"That's like you, dear! What will we get?" exclaimed Jo.

Every one thought soberly for a minute; then Meg announced, as if the idea was suggested by the sight of her own pretty hands, "I shall give her a nice pair of gloves."

"Army shoes, best to be had," cried Jo.

"Some handkerchiefs, all hemmed," said Beth.

"I'll get a little bottle of Cologne; she likes it, and it won't cost much, so I'll have some left to buy something for me," added Amy.

"How will we give the things?" asked Meg.

"Put 'em on the table, and bring her in and see her open the bundles. Don't you remember how we used to do on our birthdays?" answered Jo.

"I used to be *so* frightened when it was my turn to sit in the big chair with a crown on, and see you all come marching round to give the presents, with a kiss. I liked the things and the kisses, but it was dreadful to have you sit looking at me while I opened the bundles," said Beth, who was toasting her face and the bread for tea, at the same time.

"Let Marmee think we are getting things for ourselves, and then surprise her. We must go shopping tomorrow afternoon, Meg; there is lots to do about the play for Christmas night," said Jo, marching up and down with her hands behind her back, and her nose in the air.

"I don't mean to act any more after this time; I'm getting too old for such things," observed Meg, who was as much a child as ever about "dressing up" frolics.

"You won't stop, I know, as long as you can trail round in a white gown with your hair down, and wear gold-paper jewelry. You are the best actress we've got, and there'll be an end of everything if you quit the boards," said Jo. "We ought to rehearse tonight; come here, Amy, and do the fainting scene, for you are as stiff as a poker in that."

"I can't help it; I never saw any one faint, and I don't choose to make myself all black and blue, tumbling flat as you do. If I can go down easily, I'll drop; if I can't, I shall fall into a chair and be graceful; I don't care if Hugo does come at me with a pistol," returned Amy, who was not gifted with dramatic power, but was chosen because she was small enough to be borne out shrieking by the hero of the piece.

"Do it this way; clasp your hands so, and stagger across the room, crying frantically, 'Roderigo! save me! save me!'" and away went Jo, with a melodramatic scream which was truly thrilling.

Amy followed, but she poked her hands out stiffly before her, and jerked herself along as if she went by machinery; and her "Ow!" was more suggestive of pins being run into her than of fear and anguish. Jo gave a despairing groan, and Meg laughed outright, while Beth let her bread burn as she watched the fun, with interest.

"It's no use! do the best you can when the time comes, and if the audience shout, don't blame me. Come on, Meg."

Then things went smoothly, for Don Pedro defied the world in a speech of two pages without a single break; Hagar, the witch, chanted an awful incantation over her kettleful of simmering toads, with weird effect; Roderigo rent his chains asunder manfully, and Hugo died in agonies of remorse and arsenic, with a wild "Ha! ha!"

"It's the best we've had yet," said Meg, as the dead villain sat up and rubbed his elbows.

"I don't see how you can write and act such splendid things, Jo. You're a regular Shakespeare!" exclaimed Beth, who firmly believed that her sisters were gifted with wonderful genius in all things.

"Not quite," replied Jo, modestly. "I do think 'The Witch's Curse, an Operatic Tragedy,' is rather a nice thing; but I'd like to try Macbeth, if we only had a trap-door for Banquo. I always wanted to do the killing part. 'Is that a dagger that I see before me?' " muttered Jo, rolling her eyes and clutching at the air, as she had seen a famous tragedian do.

"No, it's the toasting fork, with Ma's shoe on it instead of the bread. Beth's stage-struck!" cried Meg, and the rehearsal ended in a general burst of laughter.

"Glad to find you so merry, my girls," said a cheery voice at the door, and actors and audience turned to welcome a stout, motherly lady, with a "can-I-help-you" look about her which was truly delightful. She wasn't a particularly handsome person, but mothers are always lovely to their children, and the girls thought the gray cloak and unfashionable bonnet covered the most splendid woman in the world.

"Well, dearies, how have you got on today? There was so much to do, getting the boxes ready to go tomorrow, that I didn't come home to dinner. Has any one called, Beth? How is your cold, Meg? Jo, you look tired to death. Come and kiss me, baby."

While making these maternal inquiries Mrs. March got her wet things off, her hot slippers on, and sitting down in the easy chair, drew Amy to her lap, preparing to enjoy the happiest hour of her busy day. The girls flew about, trying to make things comfortable, each in her own way. Meg arranged the tea table; Jo brought wood and set chairs, dropping, overturning, and clattering everything she touched; Beth trotted to and fro between parlor and kitchen, quiet and busy; while Amy gave directions to every one, as she sat with her hands folded.

As they gathered about the table, Mrs. March said, with a particularly happy face, "I've got a treat for you after supper."

A quick, bright smile went round like a streak of sunshine. Beth clapped her hands, regardless of the hot biscuit she held, and Jo tossed up her napkin, crying, "A letter! a letter! Three cheers for Father!"

"Yes, a nice long letter. He is well, and thinks he shall get through the cold season better than we feared. He sends all sorts of loving wishes for Christmas, and an especial message to you girls," said Mrs. March, patting her pocket as if she had got a treasure there.

"Hurry up, and get done. Don't stop to quirk your little finger, and prink over your plate, Amy," cried Jo, choking in her tea, and dropping her bread, butter side down, on the carpet, in her haste to get at the treat.

Beth ate no more, but crept away, to sit in her shadowy corner and brood over the delight to come, till the others were ready.

"I think it was so splendid in Father to go as a chaplain when he was too old to be drafted, and not strong enough for a soldier," said Meg, warmly.

"Don't I wish I could go as a drummer, a *vivan*—what's its name? or a nurse, so I could be near him and help him," exclaimed Jo, with a groan.

"It must be very disagreeable to sleep in a tent, and eat all sorts of bad-tasting things, and drink out of a tin mug," sighed Amy.

"When will he come home, Marmee?" asked Beth, with a little quiver in her voice.

"Not for many months, dear, unless he is sick. He will stay and do his work faithfully as long as he can, and we won't ask for him back a minute sooner than he can be spared. Now come and hear the letter."

They all drew to the fire, Mother in the big chair with Beth at her feet, Meg and Amy perched on either arm of the chair, and Jo leaning on the back, where no one would see any sign of emotion if the letter should happen to be touching.

Very few letters were written in those hard times that were not touching, especially those which fathers sent home. In this one little was said of the hardships endured, the dangers faced, or the home-sickness conquered; it was a cheerful, hopeful letter, full of lively descriptions of camp life, marches, and military news; and only at the end did the writer's heart overflow with fatherly love and longing for the little girls at home.

"Give them all my dear love and a kiss. Tell them I think of them by day, pray for them by night, and find my best comfort in their affection at all times. A year seems very long to wait before I see them, but remind them that while we wait we may all work, so that these hard days need not be wasted. I know they will remember all I said to them, that they will be loving children to you, will do their duty faithfully, fight their bosom enemies bravely, and conquer themselves so beautifully, that when I come back to them I may be fonder and prouder than ever of my little women."

Everybody sniffed when they came to that part; Jo wasn't ashamed of the great tear that dropped off the end of her nose, and Amy never minded the rumpling of her curls as she hid her face on her mother's shoulder and sobbed out, "I *am* a selfish pig! but I'll truly try to be better, so he mayn't be disappointed in me by and by."

"We all will!" cried Meg. "I think too much of my looks, and hate to work, but won't any more, if I can help it."

"I'll try and be what he loves to call me, 'a little woman,' and not be rough and wild; but do my duty here instead of wanting to be somewhere else," said Jo, thinking that keeping her temper at home was a much harder task than facing a rebel or two down South.

Beth said nothing, but wiped away her tears with the blue army-sock, and began to knit with all her might, losing no time in doing the duty that lay nearest her, while she resolved in her quiet little soul to be all that Father hoped to find her when the year brought round the happy coming home.

Mrs. March broke the silence that followed Jo's words, by saying in her cheery voice, "Do you remember how you used to play Pilgrim's Progress when you were little things? Nothing delighted you more than to have me tie my piece-bags on your backs for burdens, give you hats and sticks, and rolls of paper, and let you travel through the house from the cellar, which was the City of Destruction, up, up, to the house-top, where you had all the lovely things you could collect to make a Celestial City."

"What fun it was, especially going by the lions, fighting Apollyon, and passing through the Valley where the hobgoblins were," said Jo.

"I liked the place where the bundles fell off and tumbled down stairs," said Meg.

"My favorite part was when we came out on the flat roof where our flowers and arbors, and pretty things were, and all stood and sung for joy up there in the sunshine," said Beth, smiling, as if that pleasant moment had come back to her.

"I don't remember much about it, except that I was afraid of the cellar and the dark entry, and always liked the cake and milk we had up at the top. If I wasn't too old for such things, I'd rather like to play it over again," said Amy, who began to talk of renouncing child- ish things at the mature age of twelve.

"We never are too old for this, my dear, because it is a play we are playing all the time in one way or another. Our burdens are here, our road is before us, and the longing for goodness and happiness is the guide that leads us through many troubles and mistakes to the peace which is a true Celestial City. Now, my little pilgrims, suppose you begin again, not in play, but in earnest, and see how far on you can get before Father comes home."

"Really, Mother? where are our bundles?" asked Amy, who was a very literal young lady.

"Each of you told what your burden was just now, except Beth; I rather think she hasn't got any," said her mother.

"Yes, I have; mine is dishes and dusters, and envying girls with nice pianos, and being afraid of people."

Beth's bundle was such a funny one that everybody wanted to laugh; but nobody did, for it would have hurt her feelings very much.

"Let us do it," said Meg, thoughtfully. "It is only another name for trying to be good, and the story may help us; for though we do want to be good, it's hard work, and we forget, and don't do our best."

"We were in the Slough of Despond tonight, and Mother came and pulled us out as Help did in the book. We ought to have our roll of directions, like Christian. What shall we do about that?" asked Jo, delighted with the fancy which lent a little romance to the very dull task of doing her duty.

"Look under your pillows, Christmas morning, and you will find your guide-book," replied Mrs. March.

II

Jo was the first to wake in the gray dawn of Christmas morning. No stockings hung at the fireplace, and for a moment she felt as much disappointed as she did long ago, when her little sock fell down because it was so crammed with goodies. Then she remembered her mother's promise, and slipping her hand under her pillow, drew out a little crimson-covered book. She knew it very well, for it was that beautiful old story of the best life ever lived, and Jo felt that it was a true guide-book for any pilgrim going the long journey. She woke Meg with a "Merry Christmas," and bade her see what was under her pillow. A green-covered book appeared, with the same picture inside, and a few words written by their mother, which made their one present very precious in their eyes. Presently Beth and Amy woke, to rummage and find their little books also,—one dove-colored, the other blue; and all sat looking at and talking about them, while the East grew rosy with the coming day.

In spite of her small vanities, Margaret had a sweet and pious nature, which unconsciously influenced her sisters, especially Jo, who loved her very tenderly, and obeyed her because her advice was so gently given.

"Girls," said Meg, seriously, looking from the tumbled head beside her to the two little night-capped ones in the room beyond, "mother wants us to read and love and mind these books, and we must begin at once. We used to be faithful about it; but since Father went away, and all this war trouble unsettled us, we have neglected many things. You can do as you please; but I shall keep my book on the table here, and read a little every morning as soon as I wake, for I know it will do me good, and help me through the day."

Then she opened her new book and began to read. Jo put her

arm around her, and, leaning cheek to cheek, read also, with the quiet expression so seldom seen on her restless face.

"How good Meg is! Come, Amy, let's do as they do. I'll help you with the hard words, and they'll explain things if we don't understand," whispered Beth, very much impressed by the pretty books and her sister's example.

"I'm glad mine is blue," said Amy; and then the rooms were very still while the pages were softly turned, and the winter sunshine crept in to touch the bright heads and serious faces with a Christmas greeting.

"Where is Mother?" asked Meg, as she and Jo ran down to thank her for their gifts, half an hour later.

"Goodness only knows. Some poor creeter come a-beggin', and your ma went straight off to see what was needed. There never *was* such a woman for givin' away vittles and drink, clothes, and firin'," replied Hannah, who had lived with the family since Meg was born, and was considered by them all more as a friend than a servant.

"She will be back soon, I guess; so do your cakes, and have everything ready," said Meg, looking over the presents which were collected in a basket and kept under the sofa, ready to be produced at the proper time. "Why, where is Amy's bottle of Cologne?" she added, as the little flask did not appear.

"She took it out a minute ago, and went off with it to put a ribbon on it, or some such notion," replied Jo, dancing about the room to take the first stiffness off the new army-slippers.

"How nice my handkerchiefs look, don't they? Hannah washed and ironed them for me, and I marked them all myself," said Beth, looking proudly at the somewhat uneven letters which had cost her such labor.

"Bless the child, she's gone and put 'Mother' on them instead of 'M. March'; how funny!" cried Jo, taking up one.

"Isn't it right? I thought it was better to do it so, because Meg's initials are 'M. M.,' and I don't want any one to use these but Marmee," said Beth, looking troubled.

"It's all right, dear, and a very pretty idea; quite sensible, too, for no one can ever mistake now. It will please her very much, I know," said Meg, with a frown for Jo, and a smile for Beth.

"There's Mother; hide the basket, quick!" cried Jo, as a door slammed, and steps sounded in the hall.

Amy came in hastily, and looked rather abashed when she saw her sisters all waiting for her.

"Where have you been, and what are you hiding behind you?" asked Meg, surprised to see, by her hood and cloak, that lazy Amy had been out so early.

"Don't laugh at me, Jo, I didn't mean any one should know till the time came. I only meant to change the little bottle for a big one, and I gave *all* my money to get it, and I'm truly trying not to be selfish any more."

As she spoke, Amy showed the handsome flask which replaced the cheap one; and looked so earnest and humble in her little effort to forget herself, that Meg hugged her on the spot, and Jo pronounced her "a trump," while Beth ran to the window, and picked her finest rose to ornament the stately bottle.

"You see, I felt ashamed of my present, after reading and talking about being good this morning, so I ran round the corner and changed it the minute I was up; and I'm glad, for mine is the handsomest now."

Another bang of the street-door sent the basket under the sofa, and the girls to the table eager for breakfast.

"Merry Christmas, Marmee! Lots of them! Thank you for our books; we read some, and mean to every day," they cried, in chorus.

"Merry Christmas, little daughters! I'm glad you began at once, and hope you will keep on. But I want to say one word before we sit down. Not far away from here lies a poor woman with a little new-born baby. Six children are huddled into one bed to keep from freezing, for they have no fire. There is nothing to eat over there; and the oldest boy came to tell me they were suffering hunger and cold. My girls, will you give them your breakfast as a Christmas present?"

They were all unusually hungry, having waited nearly an hour, and for a minute no one spoke; only a minute, for Jo exclaimed impetuously,—

"I'm so glad you came before we began!"

"May I go and help carry the things to the poor little children?" asked Beth, eagerly.

"*I* shall take the cream and the muffins," added Amy, heroically giving up the articles she most liked.

Meg was already covering the buckwheats, and piling the bread into one big plate.

"I thought you'd do it," said Mrs. March, smiling as if satisfied. "You shall all go and help me, and when we come back we will have bread and milk for breakfast, and make it up at dinner-time."

They were soon ready, and the procession set out. Fortunately it was early, and they went through back streets, so few people saw them, and no one laughed at the funny party.

A poor, bare, miserable room it was, with broken windows, no fire, ragged bed-clothes, a sick mother, wailing baby, and a group of pale, hungry children cuddled under one old quilt, trying to keep warm. How the big eyes stared, and the blue lips smiled, as the girls went in!

"Ach, mein Gott! it is good angels come to us!" cried the poor woman, crying for joy.

"Funny angels in hoods and mittens," said Jo, and set them laughing.

In a few minutes it really did seem as if kind spirits had been at work there. Hannah, who had carried wood, made a fire, and stopped up the broken panes with old hats, and her own shawl. Mrs. March gave the mother tea and gruel, and comforted her with promises of help, while she dressed the little baby as tenderly as if it had been her own. The girls, meantime, spread the table, set the children round the fire, and fed them like so many hungry birds; laughing, talking, and trying to understand the funny broken English.

"Das ist gute!" "Der angel-kinder!" cried the poor things, as they ate, and warmed their purple hands at the comfortable blaze. The girls had never been called angel children before, and thought it very agreeable, especially Jo, who had been considered "a Sancho" ever since she was born. That was a very happy breakfast, though they didn't get any of it; and when they went away, leaving comfort behind, I think there were not in all the city four merrier people than the hungry little girls who gave away their breakfasts, and contented themselves with bread and milk on Christmas morning.

"That's loving our neighbor better than ourselves, and I like it," said Meg, as they set out their presents, while their mother was upstairs collecting clothes for the poor Hummels.

Not a very splendid show, but there was a great deal of love done up in the few little bundles; and the tall vase of red roses, white chrysanthemums, and trailing vines, which stood in the middle, gave quite an elegant air to the table.

"She's coming! strike up, Beth, open the door, Amy. Three cheers for Marmee!" cried Jo, prancing about, while Meg went to conduct Mother to the seat of honor.

Beth played her gayest march, Amy threw open the door, and Meg enacted escort with great dignity. Mrs. March was both surprised and touched; and smiled with her eyes full as she examined her presents, and read the little notes which accompanied them. The slippers went on at once, a new handkerchief was slipped into her pocket, well scented with Amy's Cologne, the rose was fastened in her bosom, and the nice gloves were pronounced "a perfect fit."

There was a good deal of laughing, and kissing, and explaining, in the simple, loving fashion which makes these home-festivals so pleasant at the time, so sweet to remember long afterward, and then all fell to work.

The morning charities and ceremonies took so much time, that the rest of the day was devoted to preparations for the evening festivities. Being still too young to go often to the theatre, and not rich enough to afford any great outlay for private performances, the girls put their wits to work, and, necessity being the mother of invention, made whatever they needed. Very clever were some of their productions; pasteboard guitars, antique lamps made of old-fashioned butter-boats, covered with silver paper, gorgeous robes of old cotton, glittering with tin spangles from the pickle factory, and armor covered with the same useful diamond-shaped bits, left in sheets when the lids of tin preserve-pots were cut out. The furniture was used to being turned topsy-turvy, and the big chamber was the scene of many innocent revels.

No gentlemen were admitted; so Jo played male parts to her heart's content, and took immense satisfaction in a pair of russet-leather boots given her by a friend, who knew a lady who knew an actor. These boots, an old foil, and a slashed doublet once used by an artist for some picture, were Jo's chief treasures, and appeared on all occasions. The smallness of the company made it necessary for the two principal actors to take several parts apiece; and they certainly deserved some credit for the hard work they did in learning three or four different parts, whisking in and out of various costumes, and managing the stage besides. It was excellent drill for their memories, a harmless amusement, and employed many hours which otherwise would have been idle, lonely, or spent in less profitable society.

On Christmas night, a dozen girls piled on to the bed, which was the dress circle, and sat before the blue and yellow chintz curtains, in a most flattering state of expectancy. There was a good deal of rustling and whispering behind the curtain, a trifle of lamp-smoke, and an occasional giggle from Amy, who was apt to get hysterical in the excitement of the moment. Presently a bell sounded, the curtains flew apart, and the Operatic Tragedy began.

"A gloomy wood," according to the one play-bill, was represented by a few shrubs in pots, a green baize on the floor, and a cave in the distance. This cave was made with a clothes-horse for a roof, bureaus for walls; and in it was a small furnace in full blast, with a black pot on it, and an old witch bending over it. The stage was dark, and the glow of the furnace had a fine effect, especially as real steam issued from the kettle when the witch took off the cover. A moment was allowed for the first thrill to subside; then Hugo, the villain, stalked in with a clanking sword at his side, a slouched hat, black beard, mysterious cloak, and the boots. After pacing to and fro in much agitation, he struck his forehead and burst out in a wild strain, sing-

ing of his hatred to Roderigo, his love for Zara, and his pleasing
resolution to kill the one and win the other. The gruff tones of Hugo's
voice, with an occasional shout when his feelings overcame him, were
very impressive, and the audience applauded the moment he paused
for breath. Bowing with the air of one accustomed to public praise,
he stole to the cavern and ordered Hagar to come forth with a commanding "What ho! minion! I need thee!"

Out came Meg, with gray horse-hair hanging about her face, a red
and black robe, a staff, and cabalistic signs upon her cloak. Hugo demanded a potion to make Zara adore him, and one to destroy Roderigo. Hagar, in a fine dramatic melody, promised both, and proceeded
to call up the spirit who would bring the love philter:—

> Hither, hither, from thy home,
> Airy sprite, I bid thee come.
> Born of roses, fed on dew,
> Charms and potions canst thou brew?
> Bring me here, with elfin speed,
> The fragrant philter which I need;
> Make it sweet, and swift and strong;
> Spirit, answer now my song!

A soft strain of music sounded, and then at the back of the cave appeared a little figure in cloudy white, with glittering wings, golden
hair, and a garland of roses on its head. Waving a wand, it sung:—

> Hither I come,
> From my airy home,
> Afar in the silver moon;
> Take the magic spell,
> Oh, use it well!
> Or its power will vanish soon!

and dropping a small gilded bottle at the witch's feet, the spirit vanished. Another chant from Hagar produced another apparition,—not
a lovely one, for, with a bang, an ugly, black imp appeared, and having
croaked a reply, tossed a dark bottle at Hugo, and disappeared with

a mocking laugh. Having warbled his thanks, and put the potions in his boots, Hugo departed; and Hagar informed the audience that, as he had killed a few of her friends in times past, she has cursed him, and intends to thwart his plans, and be revenged on him. Then the curtain fell, and the audience reposed and ate candy while discussing the merits of the play.

A good deal of hammering went on before the curtain rose again; but when it became evident what a masterpiece of stage carpentering had been got up, no one murmured at the delay. It was truly superb! A tower rose to the ceiling; half-way up appeared a window with a lamp burning at it, and behind the white curtain appeared Zara in a lovely blue and silver dress, waiting for Roderigo. He came, in gorgeous array, with plumed cap, red cloak, chestnut love-locks, a guitar, and the boots, of course. Kneeling at the foot of the tower, he sung a serenade in melting tones. Zara replied, and after a musical dialogue, consented to fly. Then came the grand effect of the play. Roderigo produced a rope-ladder with five steps to it, threw up one end, and invited Zara to descend. Timidly she crept from her lattice, put her hand on Roderigo's shoulder, and was about to leap gracefully down, when, "alas, alas for Zara!" she forgot her train,—it caught in the window; the tower tottered, leaned forward, fell with a crash and buried the unhappy lovers in the ruins!

A universal shriek arose as the russet boots waved wildly from the wreck, and a golden head emerged, exclaiming, "I told you so! I told you so!" With wonderful presence of mind Don Pedro, the cruel sire, rushed in, dragged out his daughter with a hasty aside,—

"Don't laugh, act as if it was all right!" and ordering Roderigo up, banished him from the kingdom with wrath and scorn. Though decidedly shaken by the fall of the tower upon him, Roderigo defied the old gentleman, and refused to stir. This dauntless example fired Zara; she also defied her sire, and he ordered them both to the deepest dungeons of the castle. A stout little retainer came in with chains, and led them away, looking very much frightened, and evidently forgetting the speech he ought to have made.

Act third was the castle hall; and here Hagar appeared, having come to free the lovers and finish Hugo. She hears him coming, and hides; sees him put the potions into two cups of wine, and bid the timid little servant "Bear them to the captives in their cells, and tell them I shall come anon." The servant takes Hugo aside to tell him something, and Hagar changes the cups for two others which are harmless. Ferdinando, the "minion," carries them away, and Hagar puts back the cup which holds the poison meant for Roderigo. Hugo, getting thirsty after a long warble, drinks it, loses his wits, and after a good deal of clutching and stamping, falls flat and dies; while Hagar informs him what she has done in a song of exquisite power and melody.

This was a truly thrilling scene; though some persons might have thought that the sudden tumbling down of a quantity of long hair rather marred the effect of the villain's death. He was called before the curtain, and with great propriety appeared leading Hagar, whose singing was considered more wonderful than all the rest of the performance put together.

Act fourth displayed the despairing Roderigo on the point of stabbing himself, because he has been told that Zara has deserted him. Just as the dagger is at his heart, a lovely song is sung under his window, informing him that Zara is true, but in danger, and he can save her if he will. A key is thrown in, which unlocks the door, and in a spasm of rapture he tears off his chains, and rushes away to find and rescue his lady-love.

Act fifth opened with a stormy scene between Zara and Don Pedro. He wishes her to go into a convent, but she won't hear of it; and, after a touching appeal, is about to faint, when Roderigo dashes in and demands her hand. Don Pedro refuses, because he is not rich. They shout and gesticulate tremendously, but cannot agree, and Roderigo is about to bear away the exhausted Zara, when the timid servant enters with a letter and a bag from Hagar, who has mysteriously disappeared. The letter informs the party that she bequeaths untold wealth to the young pair, and an awful doom to Don Pedro if he doesn't make them happy. The bag is opened, and several quarts of tin money shower down upon the stage, till it is quite glorified with the glitter. This entirely softens the "stern sire"; he consents without a murmur, all join in a joyful chorus, and the curtain falls upon the lovers kneeling to receive Don Pedro's blessing, in attitudes of the most romantic grace.

Tumultuous applause followed, but received an unexpected check; for the cot-bed on which the "dress circle" was built, suddenly shut up, and extinguished the enthusiastic audience. Roderigo and Don Pedro flew to the rescue, and all were taken out unhurt, though many were speechless with laughter. The excitement had hardly subsided when Hannah appeared, with "Mrs. March's compliments, and would the ladies walk down to supper."

This was a surprise, even to the actors; and when they saw the table they looked at one another in rapturous amazement. It was like "Marmee" to get up a little treat for them, but anything so fine as this was unheard of since the departed days of plenty. There was ice cream, actually two dishes of it,—pink and white,—and cake, and fruit, and distracting French bonbons, and in the middle of the table four great bouquets of hot-house flowers!

It quite took their breath away; and they stared first at the table and then at their mother, who looked as if she enjoyed it immensely.

"Is it fairies?" asked Amy.

"It's Santa Claus," said Beth.

"Mother did it"; and Meg smiled her sweetest, in spite of her gray beard and white eyebrows.

"Aunt March had a good fit, and sent the supper," cried Jo, with a sudden inspiration.

"All wrong; old Mr. Laurence sent it," replied Mrs. March.

"The Laurence boy's grandfather! What in the world put such a thing into his head? We don't know him," exclaimed Meg.

"Hannah told one of his servants about your breakfast party; he is an odd old gentleman, but that pleased him. He knew my father, years ago, and he sent me a polite note this afternoon, saying he hoped I would allow him to express his friendly feeling toward my children by sending them a few trifles in honor of the day. I could not refuse, and so you have a little feast at night to make up for the bread and milk breakfast."

"That boy put it into his head, I know he did! He's a capital fellow, and I wish we could get acquainted. He looks as if he'd like to know us; but he's bashful, and Meg is so prim she won't let me speak to him when we pass," said Jo, as the plates went round, and the ice began to melt out of sight, with ohs! and ahs! of satisfaction.

"You mean the people who live in the big house next door, don't you?" asked one of the girls. "My mother knows old Mr. Laurence, but says he's very proud, and don't like to mix with his neighbors. He keeps his grandson shut up when he isn't riding or walking with his tutor, and makes him study dreadful hard. We invited him to our party, but he didn't come. Mother says he's very nice, though he never speaks to us girls."

"Our cat ran away once, and he brought her back, and we talked over the fence, and were getting on capitally, all about cricket, and so on, when he saw Meg coming, and walked off. I mean to know him some day, for he needs fun, I'm sure he does," said Jo, decidedly.

"I like his manners, and he looks like a little gentleman, so I've no objection to your knowing him if a proper opportunity comes. He brought the flowers himself, and I should have asked him in if I had been sure what was going on upstairs. He looked so wistful as he went away, hearing the frolic, and evidently having none of his own."

"It's a mercy you didn't, Mother," laughed Jo, looking at her boots. "But we'll have another play some time, that he *can* see. Maybe he'll help act; wouldn't that be jolly?"

"I never had a bouquet before; how pretty it is," and Meg examined her flowers with great interest.

"They *are* lovely, but Beth's roses are sweeter to me," said Mrs. March, sniffing at the half-dead posy in her belt.

Beth nestled up to her, and whispered, softly, "I wish I could send my bunch to Father. I'm afraid he isn't having such a merry Christmas as we are."

CHRISTMAS PRESENTS IN THE EIGHTIES

CAIRO, ILLINOIS

I have not told you about my Christmas presents.

Mamma. Lemon colored dress and nearly six yards satin to go with it.

Papa. Morocco music-case and embroidered handkerchief.

Elmer. Daintily exquisite book of paintings and poems entitled "Heart's Ease and Happy Days." Also a pretty table with a drawer in it on which was a costly and sweet-toned telegraph instrument— a beauty. (P.S. I'd made him promise to get something simple.)

Aunt Amarala. Wine-colored plush hand-bag.

I gave Mamma a banjo covered with pale pink satin, hand-painted roses and lilacs, morning-glories under silver strings in handle pale blue velvet round the bowl.

[She also received] about a peck of Christmas cards, the handsomest among them being one of Prang's, an immense thing, the back of which was imitation alligator-skin, and inside on one side a satin hand-painted sachet, on the other a dark rich painting with holly-berries all round it.

From the journal of Isabella Maud Rittenhouse,
December, 1883, as recorded in *Maud*

MARY PAXON'S DIARY

BUCKS COUNTY, PENNSYLVANIA, 1882

(TEN YEARS OLD)

Christmas Day. Maggie and I have a very beautiful Christmas tree. I got 2 bottles of colone and so did Maggie and I got little cups and saucers. Mamma gave me 1 and the Quimby girls gave me 1 too, and Hanna gave my doll Winifred a beautiful coat and cap and they are pink and Win gave her new stuff to make a pink dress out of and pink buttons because she is named for him, his name is Winfield but she has to be named Winifred because she is a girl that's why, Mamma and Papa gave us each a book and I have a new game too and each of us a new collar and hair ribbons and gloves for best and mittens for school and oranges and nuts and candies and things.

THE TREE

THE CHRISTMAS TREE

I know you're in the house;
I know you are in there;
I feel the green and breathing
All around the air.
I know you're safe and warm;
I know you're very near—
        Oh, darling Tree,
                Do you hear?

I promised not to look
(The way I did before)
But I can hear you purring,
Purring through the door:
A green, soft, purring
Just as if you knew
        Everybody here
                Loves you.

Don't feel lonely
Now you are indoors;
Wait for all the shining things
To-morrow—all yours!
Then you won't know what to think,
All over Candle-light—
        Oh, darling Tree,
                Good-night!

And I love you, I love you,
And everybody, to;
And so does the marketman

That brought us you!
And if you haven't Anything·
For Me, this year,
I love you. Good-night!
Do you hear?
JOSEPHINE PRESTON PEABODY

THE FIR TREE

BY HANS CHRISTIAN ANDERSEN

OUT in the forest stood a pretty little Fir Tree. It had a good place; it could have sunlight, air there was in plenty, and all around grew many larger comrades—pines as well as firs. But the little Fir Tree wished ardently to become greater. It did not care for the warm sun and the fresh air; it took no notice of the peasant children, who went about talking together, when they had come out to look for strawberries and raspberries. Often they came with a whole potful, or had strung berries on a straw; then they would sit down by the little Fir Tree and say, "How pretty and small that one is!" and the Fir Tree did not like to hear that at all.

Next year he had grown a great joint, and the following year he was longer still, for in fir trees one can always tell by the number of rings they have how many years they have been growing.

"Oh, if I were only as great a tree as the others!" sighed the little Fir, "then I would spread my branches far around, and look out from my crown into the wide world. The birds would then build nests in my boughs, and when the wind blew I could nod just as grandly as the others yonder."

He took no pleasure in the sunshine, in the birds, and in the red clouds that went sailing over him morning and evening.

When it was winter, the snow lay all around, white and sparkling, a hare would often come jumping along, and spring right over the little Fir Tree. Oh! this made him so angry. But two winters went by, and when the third came the little Tree had grown so tall that the hare was obliged to run around it.

"Oh! to grow, to grow, and become old; that's the only fine thing in the world," thought the Tree.

In the autumn woodcutters always came and felled a few of the largest trees; that was done this year too, and the little Fir Tree, that was now quite well grown, shuddered with fear, for the great stately trees fell to the ground with a crash, and their branches were cut off, so that the trees looked quite naked, long, and slender—they could hardly be recognized. But then they were laid upon wagons, and horses dragged them away out of the wood. Where were they going? What destiny awaited them?

In the spring when the Swallows and the Stork came, the tree asked them, "Do you know where they were taken? Did you not meet them?"

The Swallows knew nothing about it, but the Stork looked thoughtful, nodded his head, and said:

"Yes, I think so. I met many new ships when I flew out of Egypt; on the ships were stately masts; I fancy these were the trees. They smelled like fir. I can assure you they're stately—very stately."

"Oh that I were only big enough to go over the sea! What kind of thing is this sea, and how does it look?"

"It would take too long to explain all that," said the Stork, and he went away.

"Rejoice in thy youth," said the Sunbeams; "rejoice in thy fresh growth, and in the young life that is within thee."

And the wind kissed the Tree, and the dew wept tears upon it; but the Fir Tree did not understand about that.

When Christmas time approached, quite young trees were felled, sometimes trees which were neither so old nor so large as this Fir Tree, that never rested, but always wanted to go away. These young trees, which were always the most beautiful, kept all their branches; they were put upon wagons, and horses dragged them away out of the wood.

"Where are they all going?" asked the Fir Tree. "They are not greater than I—indeed, one of them was much smaller. Why do they keep all their branches? Whither are they taken?"

"We know that! We know that!" chirped the Sparrows. "Yonder in the town we looked in at the windows. We know where they go. Oh! they are dressed up in the greatest pomp and splendor that can be imagined. We have looked in at the windows, and have perceived that they are planted in the middle of a warm room, and adorned with the most beautiful things—gilt apples, honey cakes, playthings, and many hundreds of candles."

"And then?" asked the Fir Tree, and trembled through all its branches. "And then? What happens then?"

"Why, we have not seen anything more. But it is incomparable."

"Perhaps I may be destined to tread this glorious path one day!" cried the Fir Tree, rejoicingly. "That is even better than traveling across the sea. How painfully I long for it! If it were only Christmas now! Now I am great and grown up, like the rest who were led away last year. Oh, if I were only on the carriage! If I were only in the warm room, among all the pomp and splendor! And then? Yes, then something even better will come, something far more charming, or else why should they adorn me so? There must be something grander, something greater still to come; but what? Oh! I'm suffering, I'm longing! I don't know myself what is the matter with me!"

"Rejoice in us," said the Air and Sunshine. "Rejoice in thy fresh youth here in the woodland."

But the Fir Tree did not rejoice at all, but it grew and grew; winter and summer it stood there, green, dark green. The people who saw it said, "That's a handsome tree!" and at Christmas time it was felled before any of the others. The ax cut deep into its marrow, and the tree fell to the ground with a sigh; it felt a pain, a sensation of faintness, and could not think at all of happiness, for it was sad at parting from its home, from the place where it had grown up; it knew that it should never again see the dear old companions, the little bushes and flowers all around—perhaps not even the birds. The parting was not at all agreeable.

The Tree only came to itself when it was unloaded in a yard, with other trees, and heard a man say:

"This one is famous; we want only this one!"

Now two servants came in gay liveries, and carried the Fir Tree into a large, beautiful salon. All around the walls hung pictures, and by the great stove stood large Chinese vases with lions on the covers; there were rocking-chairs, silken sofas, great tables covered with picture-books, and toys worth a hundred times a hundred dollars, at least the children said so. And the Fir Tree was put into a great tub filled with sand; but no one could see that it was a tub, for it was hung round with green cloth, and stood on a large, many-colored carpet. Oh, how the Tree trembled! What was to happen now? The servants, and the young ladies also, decked it out. On one branch they hung little nets, cut out of colored paper; every net was filled with sweetmeats; golden apples and walnuts hung down, as if they grew there, and more than a hundred little candles, red, white, and blue, were fastened to the different boughs. Dolls that looked exactly like real people—the tree had never seen such before—swung among the foliage, and high on the summit of the Tree was fixed a tinsel star. It was splendid, particularly splendid.

"This evening," said all, "this evening it will shine."

"Oh," thought the Tree, "that it were evening already! Oh, that the lights may soon be lit up! When may that be done? Will the sparrows fly against the panes? Shall I grow fast here, and stand adorned in summer and winter?"

Yes, he did not guess badly. But he had a complete backache from mere longing, and backache is just as bad for a tree as a headache for a person.

At last the candles were lighted. What a brilliance, what a splendor! The Tree trembled so in all its branches that one of the candles set fire to a green twig, and it was scorched.

"Heaven preserve us!" cried the young ladies; and they hastily put the fire out.

Now the Tree might not even tremble. Oh, that was terrible! It was so afraid of setting fire to some of its ornaments, and it was quite bewildered with all the brilliance. And now the folding doors were thrown wide open, and a number of children rushed in as if they would have overturned the whole Tree; the older people followed more deliberately. The little ones stood quite silent, but only for a minute; then they shouted till the room rang: they danced gleefully round the Tree, and one present after another was plucked from it.

"What are they about?" thought the Tree. "What's going to be done?"

And the candles burned down to the twigs, and as they burned down they were extinguished, and then the children received permission to plunder the Tree. Oh! they rushed in upon it, so that every branch cracked again: if it had not been fastened by the top and by the golden star to the ceiling, it would have fallen down.

The children danced about with their pretty toys. No one looked at the Tree except one old man, who came up and peeped among the branches, but only to see if a fig or an apple had not been forgotten.

"A story! A story!" shouted the children; and they drew a little fat man toward the tree; and he sat down just beneath it—"for then we shall be in the green wood," said he, "and the tree may have the advantage of listening to my tale. But I can only tell one. Will you hear the story of Ivede-Avede, or of Klumpey-Dumpey, who fell downstairs, and still was raised up to honor and married the Princess?"

"Ivede-Avede!" cried some, "Klumpey-Dumpey!" cried others, and there was a great crying and shouting. Only the Fir Tree was quite silent, and thought, "Shall I not be in it? Shall I have nothing to do in it?" But he had been in the evening's amusement, and had done what was required of him.

And the fat man told about Klumpey-Dumpey who fell downstairs, and yet was raised to honor and married a Princess. And the children clapped their hands and cried, "Tell another! tell another!" and they wanted to hear about Ivede-Avede; but they only got the story of Klumpey-Dumpey. The Fir Tree stood quite silent and thoughtful; never had the birds in the wood told such a story as that. Klumpey-Dumpey fell downstairs, and yet came to honor and married a Princess!

"Yes, so it happens in the world!" thought the Fir Tree, and believed it must be true, because that was such a nice man who told it.

"Well, who can know? Perhaps I shall fall downstairs, too, and marry a Princess!" And it looked forward with pleasure to being adorned again, the next evening, with candles and toys, gold and fruit. "To-morrow I shall not tremble," it thought.

"I shall rejoice in all my splendor. Tomorrow I shall hear the story of Klumpey-Dumpey again, and perhaps that of Ivede-Avede, too."

And the Tree stood all night quiet and thoughtful.

In the morning the servants and the chambermaid came in.

"Now my splendor will begin afresh," thought the Tree. But they dragged him out of the room, and upstairs to the garret, and here they put him in a dark corner where no daylight shone.

"What's the meaning of this?" thought the Tree. "What am I to do here? What is to happen?"

And he leaned against the wall, and thought, and thought. And he had time enough, for days and nights went by, and nobody came up; and when at length some one came, it was only to put some great boxes in a corner. Now the Tree stood quite hidden away, and the supposition is that it was quite forgotten.

"Now it's winter outside," thought the Tree. "The earth is hard and covered with snow, and people cannot plant me; therefore I suppose I'm to be sheltered here until spring comes. How considerate that is! How good people are! If it were only not so dark here, and so terribly solitary!—not even a little hare? That was pretty out there in the wood, when the snow lay thick and the hare sprang past; yes, even when he jumped over me; but then I did not like it. It is terribly lonely up here!"

"Piep! piep!" said a little Mouse, and crept forward, and then came another little one. They smelled at the Fir Tree, and then slipped among the branches.

"It's horribly cold," said the two little Mice, "or else it would be comfortable here. Don't you think so, old Fir Tree?"

"I'm not old at all," said the Fir Tree. "There are many much older than I."

"Where do you come from?" asked the Mice. "And what do you know?" They were dreadfully inquisitive. "Tell us about the most beautiful spot on earth. Have you been there? Have you been in the storeroom, where cheeses lie on the shelves, and hams hang from the ceiling, where one dances on tallow candles, and goes in thin and comes out fat?"

"I don't know that," replied the Tree; "but I know the wood, where the sun shines and the birds sing."

And then it told all about its youth.

And the little Mice had never heard anything of the kind; and they listened and said:

"What a number of things you have seen! How happy you must have been!"

"I?" replied the Fir Tree; and it thought about what it had told. "Yes, those were really quite happy times." But then he told of the Christmas Eve, when he had been hung with sweetmeats and candles.

"Oh!" said the little Mice, "how happy you have been, you old Fir Tree!"

"I'm not old at all," said the Tree. "I only came out of the wood this winter. I'm only rather backward in my growth."

"What splendid stories you can tell!" said the little Mice.

And the next night they came with four other little Mice, to hear what the Tree had to relate; and the more it said, the more clearly did it remember everything, and thought, "Those were quite merry days! But they may come again. Klumpey-Dumpey fell downstairs, and yet he married a Princess. Perhaps I shall marry a Princess, too!" And the Fir Tree thought of a pretty little Birch Tree that grew out in the forest; for the Fir Tree, that Birch was a real Princess.

"Who's Klumpey-Dumpey?" asked the little Mice.

And then the Fir Tree told the whole story. It could remember every single word; and the little Mice were ready to leap to the very top of the Tree with pleasure. Next night a great many more Mice came, and on Sunday two Rats even appeared; but these thought the story was not pretty, and the little Mice were sorry for that, for now they also did not like it so much as before.

"Do you know only one story?" asked the Rats.

"Only that one," replied the Tree. "I heard that on the happiest evening of my life; I did not think then how happy I was."

"That's a very miserable story. Don't you know any about bacon and tallow candles—a storeroom story?"

"No," said the Tree.

"Then we'd rather not hear you," said the Rats.

And they went back to their own people. The little Mice at last stayed away also; and then the Tree sighed and said:

"It was very nice when they sat round me, the merry little Mice, and listened when I spoke to them. Now that's past too. But I shall remember to be pleased when they take me out."

But when did that happen? Why, it was one morning that people came and rummaged in the garret; the boxes were put away, and the Tree brought out; they certainly threw him rather roughly on the floor, but a servant dragged him away at once to the stairs, where the daylight shone.

"Now life is beginning again!" thought the Tree.

It felt the fresh air and the first sunbeam, and now it was out in the courtyard. Everything passed so quickly that the Tree quite forgot to look at itself, there was so much to look at all round. The courtyard was close to a garden, and here everything was blooming; the roses hung fresh over the paling, the linden trees were in blossom, and the swallows cried, "Quinze-wit! quinze-wit! my husband's come!" But it was not the Fir Tree that they meant.

"Now I shall live!" said the Tree, rejoicingly, and spread its branches far out; but, alas! they were all withered and yellow; and it lay in the corner among nettles and weeds. The tinsel star was still upon it, and shone in the bright sunshine.

In the courtyard a couple of the merry children were playing who had danced round the tree at Christmas time, and had rejoiced over it. One of the youngest ran up and tore off the golden star.

"Look what is sticking to the ugly old fir tree!" said the child, and he trod upon the branches till they cracked again under his boots.

And the Tree looked at all the blooming flowers and the splendor of the garden, and then looked at itself, and wished it had remained in the dark corner of the garret; it thought of its fresh youth in the wood, of the merry Christmas Eve, and of the little Mice which had listened so pleasantly to the story of Klumpey-Dumpey.

"Past! past!" said the old Tree. "Had I but rejoiced when I could have done so! Past! past!"

And the servant came and chopped the Tree into little pieces; a whole bundle lay there; it blazed brightly under the great brewing copper, and it sighed deeply, and each sigh was like a little shot; and the children who were at play there ran up and seated themselves at the fire, looked into it, and cried "Puff! puff!" But at each explosion, which was a deep sigh, the Tree thought of a summer day in the woods, or of a winter night there, when the stars beamed; he thought of Christmas Eve and of Klumpey-Dumpey, the only story he had ever heard or knew how to tell; and then the Tree was burned.

The boys played in the garden, and the youngest had on his breast a golden star, which the Tree had worn on its happiest evening. Now that was past, and the Tree's life was past, and the story is past too: past! past!—and that's the way with all stories.

THE CHRISTMAS TREE

AN OLD STORY RETOLD

BY GERALDINE GORDON

ONCE upon a time long, long ago before that magical night when the star-led shepherds found their way to the stable in Bethlehem, there dwelt in the deep forests of central Europe and along the bleak shores of the North Sea men to whom the endless winters meant not only cold and hunger and darkness, but ravening beasts and attacks from savage foemen. Small wonder they watched the signs of the changing seasons and welcomed with a fierce joy the first indication of lengthening days! How better celebrate the passing of the longest night than by dragging from the forest a great tree and setting it ablaze in the open clearing before the circle of crowded huts? It was an appropriate rite, for the tree, Yggdrasil, was to them the symbol of their universe. In its topmost evergreen branches near the stars and sun and moon the gods reigned, and there plain to be seen perched the dark eagle of Thor. In the great mid-branches men lived with their flocks and herds. At the foot of the tree lay coiled the old dragon, ancient enemy of men and gods, forever gnawing at the roots of the tree, forever working destruction. One day he would have finished his work and the great tree would topple over. The awful end of the world would come in that mighty crash.

Such a tree, widespreading, ever green, symbolizing their life, was used by these dwellers in darkness to send its flaming message into the angry skies as a signal of welcome to Freya, the goddess of the spring, whose advent they awaited with such impatient longing. Then as they watched the slow procession of the days and nights bring the inevitable change—the sun lingering longer and longer, the dark nights growing shorter and shorter—they knew that the goddess had answered their signal and returned to bless them.

Into that northern world came at length the first Christian missionaries from the south. To them it seemed a happy omen that the joyous celebration of the winter solstice by these northern heathen should come at the season when all good Christians were remembering the Holy Night of Christ's Nativity. The lighted tree took on new meaning. Was not their Master's sign a star? Had He not come to a people who sat in great darkness? The flames of the World Tree leaping high into the winter sky proclaimed for them the end of gods who ruled men's hearts by terror, and heralded a new Saviour who bade them be of good cheer. In the deep forests a new word was spoken— *God is Love. . . . Underneath are the everlasting arms. . . . Fear not.*

Out of that remote past comes our Christmas tree with its balls of gold and silver, its long streamers of tinsel, its flowers and fruits, blooming anew each year beside our hearths, making us glad with its fragrance and beauty. The lights that sparkle in its branches, once a signal to Freya, today remind us only of the Light that lighteth every man that cometh into the world. In the topmost branch where Thor's eagle once flapped his dark wings, an angel shines—the angel of the Annunciation, the angel of the shepherds, the angel whose message is "Fear not." There in the heaven at the top of our tree we hang the golden ball of the sun, the silver ball of the moon, and the myriad starry host. On the widespreading branches we place little figures of animals, all the friendly beasts that serve man; and the flowers and fruits that reward his labors and make his heart rejoice.

According to ancient custom there are four great reindeer on our tree, and as they feed on the branches the four seasons pass. Twelve lesser reindeer nibble away at the little green twigs, and as they eat the twelve months pass. The chattering squirrel who ran up and down the old World Tree, creating discord in the home of the gods and in the lair of the dragon, is on our tree, a reformed, delightful Christian squirrel. Certain other creatures find an honored place because they belong especially to the Christmas story. The camels that brought the Magi to the new-born King; the ox and the ass; the shepherd boy's dog; the cock and the raven and the lamb; and the fish, first symbol of Christ's name. No Christmas tree is really complete without these, and no child quite satisfied until he has heard again each year the old tale of what the animals said when on the first Christmas night they were permitted to speak in the language of men.

The cock began it. Speaking boldly in the Latin tongue, as a good Roman bird should, he cried aloud for all the world to hear:

> *"Christus natus est!*
> *Christus natus est!"*

The raven, circling above the Inn in Bethlehem, queried, *"Quando? Quando?"* To which the ass, close beside the manger, replied, *"Hac nocte! Hac nocte!"* Then the lowing ox asked softly, (though well he knew the answer) *"Ubi? Ubi?"* The little lamb, white and fleecy, snuggling close to Mary, gave the word all men waited to hear, *"Beth-le-hem! Beth-le-hem!"*

It is said by wise old folk who remember many things that on that wonderful first Christmas the trees bore fruit and the flowers burst into bloom. It is in memory of that lovely miracle that we hang glowing fruits on our evergreen tree and fasten roses and lilies to the tips of its branches. Was He not called Rose of Sharon and Lily of the Valley? All the gleaming strands of tinsel shining in the dark branches —are they the rays of the sun, the golden hair of the goddess Freya who brings again the spring to warm and cheer us? Are they not rather faint reflections of those rays of glory that stream down upon us from the star of Bethlehem?

The beauty and pungent fragrance of the Christmas tree gladden our homes but its power over our hearts lies in the loveliest of all its symbols. From the foot of the tree the old dragon has been forever banished. No longer does he fill men's hearts with terror working his evil spell. There where he once lay coiled and venomous we find today the crêche—the Holy Child in the strawfilled manger, His blessed mother, faithful St. Joseph, adoring shepherds, worshiping kings with their royal gifts of gold and frankincense and myrrh. There at the foot of the tree is the whole meaning of Christmas. Perfect love has cast out fear.

O come let us adore Him!

THE TREE THAT DIDN'T GET TRIMMED

By Christopher Morley

IF YOU walk through a grove of balsam trees you will notice that the young trees are silent; they are listening. But the old tall ones —especially the firs—are whispering. They are telling the story of The Tree That Didn't Get Trimmed. It sounds like a painful story, and the murmur of the old trees as they tell it is rather solemn; but it is an encouraging story for young saplings to hear. On warm autumn days when your trunk is tickled by ants and insects climbing, and the resin is hot and gummy in your knots, and the whole glade smells sweet, drowsy, and sad, and the hardwood trees are boasting of the gay colours they are beginning to show, many a young evergreen has been cheered by it.

All young fir trees, as you know by that story of Hans Andersen's—if you've forgotten it, why not read it again?—dream of being a Christmas Tree some day. They dream about it as young girls dream of being a bride, or young poets of having a volume of verse published. With the vision of that brightness and gayety before them they patiently endure the sharp sting of the ax, the long hours pressed together on a freight car. But every December there are more trees cut down than are needed for Christmas. And that is the story that no one—not even Hans Andersen—has thought to put down.

The tree in this story should never have been cut. He wouldn't have been, but it was getting dark in the Vermont woods, and the man with the ax said to himself, "Just one more." Cutting young trees with a sharp, beautifully balanced ax is fascinating; you go on and on; there's a sort of cruel pleasure in it. The blade goes through the soft wood with one whistling stroke and the boughs sink down with a soft swish.

He was a fine, well-grown youngster, but too tall for his age; his branches were rather scraggly. If he'd been left there he would have been an unusually big tree some day; but now he was in the awkward age and didn't have the tapering shape and the thick, even foliage that people like on Christmas trees. Worse still, instead of running up to a straight, clean spire, his top was a bit lop-sided, with a fork in it.

But he didn't know this as he stood with many others, leaning against the side wall of the green-grocer's shop. In those cold December days he was very happy, thinking of the pleasures to come. He had heard of the delights of Christmas Eve: the stealthy setting-up of the tree, the tinsel balls and coloured toys and stars, the peppermint canes and birds with spun-glass tails. Even that old anxiety of Christmas trees—burning candles—did not worry him, for he had been told that nowadays people use strings of tiny electric bulbs which cannot set one on fire. So he looked forward to the festival with a confident heart.

"I shall be very grand," he said. "I hope there will be children to admire me. It must be a great moment when the children hang their stockings on you!" He even felt sorry for the first trees that were chosen and taken away. It would be best, he considered, not to be bought until Christmas Eve. Then, in the shining darkness someone would pick him out, put him carefully along the running board of a car, and away they would go. The tire-chains would clack and jingle merrily on the snowy road. He imagined a big house with fire glowing on a hearth; the hushed rustle of wrapping paper and parcels being unpacked. Someone would say, "Oh, what a beautiful tree!" How erect and stiff he would brace himself in his iron tripod stand.

But day after day went by, one by one the other trees were taken, and he began to grow troubled. For everyone who looked at him seemed to have an unkind word. "Too tall," said one lady. "No, this one wouldn't do, the branches are too skimpy," said another. "If I chop off the top," said the greengrocer, "it wouldn't be so bad?" The tree shuddered, but the customer had already passed on to look at others. Some of his branches ached where the grocer had bent them upward to make his shape more attractive.

Across the street was a Ten Cent Store. Its bright windows were full of scarlet odds and ends; when the doors opened he could see people crowded along the aisles, cheerfully jostling one another with bumpy packages. A buzz of talk, a shuffle of feet, a constant ringing of cash drawers came noisily out of that doorway. He could see flashes of marvellous colour, ornaments for luckier trees. Every evening, as the time drew nearer, the pavements were more thronged. The handsomer trees, not so tall as he but more bushy and shapely, were ranked in front of him; as they were taken away he could see the gayety only too well. Then he was shown to a lady who wanted a tree very cheap. "You can have this one for a dollar," said the grocer. This was only one third of what the grocer had asked for him at first, but even so the lady refused him and went across the street to buy a little artificial tree at the toy store. The man pushed him back carelessly, and he toppled over and fell alongside the wall. No one bothered to pick him up. He was almost glad, for now his pride would be spared.

Now it was Christmas Eve. It was a foggy evening with a drizzling rain; the alley alongside the store was thick with trampled slush. As he lay there among broken boxes and fallen scraps of holly strange thoughts came to him. In the still northern forest already his wounded stump was buried in forgetful snow. He remembered the wintry sparkle of the woods, the big trees with crusts and clumps of silver on their broad boughs, the keen singing of the lonely wind. He remembered the strong, warm feeling of his roots reaching down into the safe earth. That is a good feeling; it means to a tree just what it means to you to stretch your toes down toward the bottom of a well-tucked bed. And he had given up all this to lie here, disdained and forgotten, in a littered alley. The splash of feet, the chime of bells, the cry of cars went past him. He trembled a little with self-pity and vexation. "No toys and stockings for me," he thought sadly, and shed some of his needles.

Late that night, after all the shopping was over, the grocer came out to clear away what was left. The boxes, the broken wreaths, the empty barrels, and our tree with one or two others that hadn't been sold, all were thrown through the side door into the cellar. The door was locked and he lay there in the dark. One of his branches, doubled under him in the fall, ached so he thought it must be broken. "So this is Christmas," he said to himself.

All that day it was very still in the cellar. There was an occasional creak as one of the bruised trees tried to stretch itself. Feet went along the pavement overhead, and there was a booming of church bells, but everything had a slow, disappointed sound. Christmas is always a little sad, after such busy preparations. The unwanted trees lay on the stone floor, watching the furnace light flicker on a hatchet that had been left there.

The day after Christmas a man came in who wanted some green boughs to decorate a cemetery. The grocer took the hatchet, and seized the trees without ceremony. They were too disheartened to care. Chop, chop, chop, went the blade, and the sweet-smelling branches were carried away. The naked trunks were thrown into a corner.

And now our tree, what was left of him, had plenty of time to think. He no longer could feel anything, for trees feel with their branches, but they think with their trunks. What did he think about as he grew dry and stiff? He thought that it had been silly of him to imagine such a fine, gay career for himself, and he was sorry for other young trees, still growing in the fresh hilly country, who were enjoying the same fantastic dreams.

Now perhaps you don't know what happens to the trunks of left-over Christmas trees. You could never guess. Farmers come in from the suburbs and buy them at five cents each for bean-poles and grape arbours. So perhaps (here begins the encouraging part of this story) they are really happier, in the end, than the trees that get trimmed for Santa Claus. They go back into the fresh, moist earth of spring, and when the sun grows hot the quick tendrils of the vines climb up them and presently they are decorated with the red blossoms of the bean or the little blue globes of the grape, just as pretty as any Christmas trinkets.

So one day the naked, dusty fir-poles were taken out of the cellar, and thrown into a truck with many others, and made a rattling journey out into the land. The farmer unloaded them in his yard and was stacking them up by the barn when his wife came out to watch him. "There!" she said. "That's just what I want, a nice long pole with a fork in it. Jim, put that one over there to hold up the clothesline." It was the first time that anyone had praised our tree, and his dried-up heart swelled with a tingle of forgotten sap. They put him near one end of the clothesline, with his stump close to a flower bed. The fork that had been despised for a Christmas star was just the thing to hold up a clothesline. It was washday, and soon the farmer's wife began bringing out wet garments to swing and freshen in the clean, bright air. And the very first thing that hung near the top of the Christmas pole was a cluster of children's stockings.

That isn't quite the end of the story, as the old fir trees whisper it in the breeze. The Tree That Didn't Get Trimmed was so cheerful watching the stockings, and other gay little clothes that plumped out in the wind just as though waiting to be spanked, that he didn't notice what was going on—or going up—below him. A vine had caught hold of his trunk and was steadily twisting upward. And one morning, when the farmer's wife came out intending to shift him, she stopped and exclaimed. "Why, I mustn't move this pole," she said. "The morning glory has run right up it." So it had, and our bare pole was blue and crimson with colour.

Something nice, the old firs believe, always happens to the trees that don't get trimmed. They even believe that some day one of the Christmas-tree bean-poles will be the starting point for another Magic Beanstalk, as in the fairy tale of the boy who climbed up the bean-tree and killed the giant. When that happens, fairy tales will begin all over again.

BALSAM AND MISTLETOE

By Donald Culross Peattie

WHEN I set out to buy a Christmas tree, I have my choice of long-needled pines, red cedars, and fragrant spruces with narrow spire-like tops, the branches beautifully up-curved at the dark tips. But I am looking for a balsam, which has this inestimable advantage over all the spruces, that even in the warmth of the house its needles do not drop.

You many know a balsam from a spruce in this way, that the leaves of the balsam are flattish, and the cones are borne erect; on many of the branches the leaves are two-ranked, so that they appear to form a flat spray, while in the spruces the needles are scattered, bristling out in every direction from the stem, to the touch seeming four-sided; and the cones of a fir always droop.

Time was, not long ago, when a man bought a Christmas tree in all innocence, feeling that it was no really material expenditure but a symbol, almost intangible, which gave beauty and good cheer to all who beheld it. Now come the tree conservationists, to reproach us with the forests that we slay to make a brief holiday, to let them die then ingloriously upon the rubbish heap. But balsam is only used in a small way in the crafts and sciences, while the spruces, by far the commonest holiday trees, have, otherwise, only the pulp mill for their destiny.

And the Christmas trees cut for the city across the river would not suffice to put out the combined Sunday editions of its newspapers in one week, bearing into every home their freight of unchallenged intellectual poison—the brutal humor, the wordly inanity, the crime and pseudo-science.

The old Saxon name of *mistl-tan,* from which we have the name of mistletoe, has debated meanings. One of them is "different branch," because, though it sprouts from a tree like one of the tree's own branches, it is in reality a parasite, a very different branch indeed. I find no mistletoe about my house, but it grows thickly nearer to the sea, on gum and maple. In Europe it is the missel thrush that carries the berries from tree to tree, wiping the seed from its beak off upon the bark. Here the waxwings perform the same involuntary office. Once upon the tree the viscid pulp soon hardens fast like a sucker, and instead of an honest root this green parasite thrusts a claw down into its victim.

The druids considered that the mistletoe represented pure spirit, since it never touches earth—quite a different view of it than we take either of its aspect as a parasite or as an opportunity. Druids cut it with a golden sickle, and caught it in a clean white cloth; Keltic women wore it in the hope that they would soon go freighted with child. Pseudo-Aristotle's *Golden Cabinet of Secrets* mentions it as a love powder. But wicked Loki put it as an arrow in blind Hoder's hand that he might kill Balder the young god of light. And here, if you like, you may read an allegory of the winter solstice—the sun god slain upon the twenty-second, revived upon the third day, after the mistletoe had promised never again to slay but only to bring life.

All this is legend, one may say. But legend concerning events of earth and heaven is part of the natural history of humanity, and you may pity the man who has so blunted his perceptions that he can feel no old racial associations with the things that grow and the things that creep.

From *An Almanac for Moderns*

THE PETERKINS' CHRISTMAS TREE

By Lucretia P. Hale

EARLY in the autumn the Peterkins began to prepare for their Christmas tree. Everything was done in great privacy, as it was to be a surprise to the neighbors, as well as to the rest of the family. Mr. Peterkin had been up to Mr. Bromwick's wood-lot, and, with his consent, selected the tree. Agamemnon went to look at it occasionally after dark, and Solomon John made frequent visits to it mornings, just after sunrise. Mr. Peterkin drove Elizabeth Eliza and her mother that way, and pointed furtively to it with his whip; but none of them ever spoke of it aloud to each other. It was suspected that the little boys had been to see it Wednesday and Saturday afternoons. But they came home with their pockets full of chestnuts, and said nothing about it.

At length Mr. Peterkin had it cut down and brought secretly into the Larkins' barn. A week or two before Christmas a measurement was made of it with Elizabeth Eliza's yard-measure. To Mr. Peterkin's great dismay it was discovered that it was too high to stand in the back parlor.

This fact was brought out at a secret council of Mr. and Mrs. Peterkin, Elizabeth Eliza, and Agamemnon.

Agamemnon suggested that it might be set up slanting; but Mrs. Peterkin was very sure it would make her dizzy, and the candles would drip.

But a brilliant idea came to Mr. Peterkin. He proposed that the ceiling of the parlor should be raised to make room for the top of the tree.

Elizabeth Eliza thought the space would need to be quite large. It must not be like a small box, or you could not see the tree.

"Yes," said Mr. Peterkin, "I should have the ceiling lifted all across the room; the effect would be finer."

Elizabeth Eliza objected to having the whole ceiling raised, because her room was over the back parlor, and she would have no floor while the alteration was going on, which would be very awkward. Besides, her room was not very high now, and, if the floor were raised, perhaps she could not walk in it upright.

Mr. Peterkin explained that he didn't propose altering the whole ceiling, but to lift up a ridge across the room at the back part where the tree was to stand. This would make a hump, to be sure, in Elizabeth Eliza's room; but it would go across the whole room.

Elizabeth Eliza said she would not mind that. It would be like the cuddy thing that comes up on the deck of a ship, that you sit against, only here you would not have the seasickness. She thought she should like it, for a rarity. She might use it for a divan.

Mr. Peterkin thought it would come in the worn place of the carpet, and might be a convenience in making the carpet over.

Agamemnon was afraid there would be trouble in keeping the matter secret, for it would be a long piece of work for a carpenter; but Mr. Peterkin proposed having the carpenter for a day or two, for a number of other jobs.

One of them was to make all the chairs in the house of the same height, for Mrs. Peterkin had nearly broken her spine by sitting down in a chair that she had supposed was her own rocking-chair, and it had proved to be two inches lower. The little boys were now large enough to sit in any chair; so a medium was fixed upon to satisfy all the family, and the chairs were made uniformly of the same height.

On consulting the carpenter, however, he insisted that the tree could be cut off at the lower end to suit the height of the parlor, and demurred at so great change as altering the ceiling. But Mr. Peterkin had set his mind upon the improvement, and Elizabeth Eliza had cut her carpet in preparation for it.

So the folding-doors into the back parlor were closed, and for nearly a fortnight before Christmas there was great litter of fallen plastering, and laths, and chips, and shavings; and Elizabeth Eliza's carpet was taken up, and the furniture had to be changed, and one night she had to sleep at the Bromwicks', for there was a long hole in her floor that might be dangerous.

All this delighted the little boys. They could not understand what was going on. Perhaps they suspected a Christmas tree, but they did not know why a Christmas tree should have so many chips, and were still more astonished at the hump that appeared in Elizabeth Eliza's room. It must be a Christmas present, or else the tree in a box.

Some aunts and uncles, too, arrived a day or two before Christmas, with some small cousins. These cousins occupied the attention of the little boys, and there was a great deal of whispering and mystery, behind doors, and under the stairs, and in the corners of the entry.

Solomon John was busy, privately making some candles for the tree. He had been collecting some bayberries, as he understood they made very nice candles, so that it would not be necessary to buy any.

The elders of the family never all went into the back parlor together, and all tried not to see what was going on. Mr. Peterkin would go in with Solomon John, or Mr. Peterkin with Elizabeth Eliza, or Elizabeth Eliza and Agamemnon and Solomon John. The little boys and the small cousins were never allowed even to look inside the room.

Elizabeth Eliza meanwhile went into town a number of times. She wanted to consult Amanda as to how much ice-cream they should need, and whether they could make it at home, as they had cream and ice. She was pretty busy in her own room; the furniture had to be changed, and the carpet altered. The "hump" was higher than she expected. There was danger of bumping her own head whenever she crossed it. She had to nail some padding on the ceiling for fear of accidents.

The afternoon before Christmas, Elizabeth Eliza, Solomon John, and their father collected in the back parlor for a council. The carpenters had done their work, and the tree stood at its full height at the back of the room, the top stretching up into the space arranged for it. All the chips and shavings were cleared away, and it stood on a neat box.

But what were they to put upon the tree?

Solomon John had brought in his supply of candles; but they proved to be very "stringy" and very few of them. It was strange how many bayberries it took to make a few candles! The little boys had helped him, and he had gathered as much as a bushel of bayberries. He had put them in water, and skimmed off the wax, according to the directions; but there was so little wax!

Solomon John had given the little boys some of the bits sawed off from the legs of the chairs. He had suggested that they should cover them with gilt paper, to answer for gilt apples, without telling them what they were for.

These apples, a little blunt at the end, and the candles, were all they had for the tree!

After all her trips into town Elizabeth Eliza had forgotten to bring anything for it.

"I thought of candies and sugar-plums," she said; "but I concluded if we made caramels ourselves we should not need them. But, then, we have not made caramels. The fact is, that day my head was full of my carpet. I had bumped it pretty badly, too."

Mr. Peterkin wished he had taken, instead of a fire-tree, an apple-tree he had seen in October, full of red fruit.

"But the leaves would have fallen off by this time," said Elizabeth Eliza.

"And the apples, too," said Solomon John.

"It is odd I should have forgotten, that day I went in on purpose to get the things," said Elizabeth Eliza, musingly. "But I went from shop to shop, and didn't know exactly what to get. I saw a great many gilt things for Christmas-trees; but I knew the little boys were making the gilt apples; there were plenty of candles in the shops, but I knew Solomon John was making the candles."

Mr. Peterkin thought it was quite natural.

Solomon John wondered if it were too late for them to go into town now.

Elizabeth Eliza could not go in the next morning, for there was to be a grand Christmas dinner, and Mr. Peterkin could not be spared, and Solomon John was sure he and Agamemnon would not know what to buy. Besides, they would want to try the candles tonight.

Mr. Peterkin asked if the presents everybody had been preparing would not answer. But Elizabeth Eliza knew they would be too heavy.

A gloom came over the room. There was only a flickering gleam from one of Solomon John's candles that he had lighted by way of trial.

Solomon John again proposed going into town. He lighted a match to examine the newspaper about the trains. There were plenty of trains coming out at that hour, but none going in except a very late one. That would not leave time to do anything and come back.

"We could go in, Elizabeth Eliza and I," said Solomon John, "but we should not have time to buy anything."

Agamemnon was summoned in. Mrs. Peterkin was entertaining the uncles and aunts in the front parlor. Agamemnon wished there was time to study up something about electric lights. If they could only have a calcium light! Solomon John's candles sputtered and went out.

At this moment there was a loud knocking at the front door. The little boys, and the small cousins, and the uncles and aunts, and Mrs. Peterkin, hastened to see what was the matter.

The uncles and aunts thought somebody's house must be on fire. The door was opened, and there was a man, white with flakes, for it was beginning to snow, and he was pulling in a large box.

Mrs. Peterkin supposed it contained some of Elizabeth Eliza's purchases, so she ordered it to be pushed into the back parlor, and hastily called back her guests and the little boys into the other room. The little boys and the small cousins were sure they had seen Santa Claus himself.

Mr. Peterkin lighted the gas. The box was addressed to Elizabeth Eliza. It was from the lady from Philadelphia! She had gathered a hint from Elizabeth Eliza's letters that there was to be a Christmas tree, and had filled this box with all that would be needed.

It was opened directly. There was every kind of gilt hanging- thing, from gilt pea-pods to butterflies on springs. There were shining flags and lanterns, and bird-cages, and nests with birds sitting on them, baskets of fruit, gilt apples and bunches of grapes, and, at the bottom of the whole, a large box of candles and a box of Philadelphia bon-bons!

Elizabeth Eliza and Solomon John could scarcely keep from screaming. The little boys and the small cousins knocked on the folding-doors to ask what was the matter.

Hastily Mr. Peterkin and the rest took out the things and hung them on the tree, and put on the candles.

When all was done, it looked so well that Mr. Peterkin exclaimed:

"Let us light the candles now, and send to invite all the neighbors tonight, and have the tree on Christmas Eve!"

And so it was that the Peterkins had their Christmas tree the day before, and on Christmas night could go and visit their neighbors.

THE FIRST CHRISTMAS TREE

By Eugene Field

ONCE upon a time the forest was in a great commotion. Early in the evening the wise old cedars had shaken their heads ominously and predicted strange things. They had lived in the forest many, many years; but never had they seen such marvellous sights as were to be seen now in the sky, and upon the hills, and in the distant village.

"Pray tell us what you see," pleaded a little vine; "we who are not as tall as you can behold none of these wonderful things. Describe them to us, that we may enjoy them with you."

"I am filled with such amazement," said one of the cedars, "that I can hardly speak. The whole sky seems to be aflame, and the stars appear to be dancing among the clouds; angels walk down from heaven to the earth, and enter the village or talk with the shepherds upon the hills."

The vine listened in mute astonishment. Such things never before had happened. The vine trembled with excitement. Its nearest neighbor was a tiny tree, so small it scarcely ever was noticed; yet it was a very beautiful little tree, and the vines and ferns and mosses and other humble residents of the forest loved it dearly.

"How I should like to see the angels!" sighed the little tree, "and how I should like to see the stars dancing among the clouds! It must be very beautiful."

As the vine and the little tree talked of these things, the cedars watched with increasing interest the wonderful scenes over and beyond the confines of the forest. Presently they thought they heard music, and they were not mistaken, for soon the whole air was full of the sweetest harmonies ever heard upon earth.

"What beautiful music!" cried the little tree. "I wonder whence it comes."

"The angels are singing," said a cedar; "for none but angels could make such sweet music."

"But the stars are singing, too," said another cedar; "yes, and the shepherds on the hills join in the song, and what a strangely glorious song it is!"

The trees listened to the singing, but they did not understand its meaning: it seemed to be an anthem, and it was of a Child that had been born; but further than this they did not understand. The strange and glorious song continued all the night; and all that night the angels walked to and fro, and the shepherd-folk talked with the angels, and the stars danced and carolled in high heaven. And it was nearly morning when the cedars cried out, "They are coming to the forest! the angels are coming to the forest!" And, surely enough, this was true. The vine and the little tree were very terrified, and they begged their older and stronger neighbors to protect them from harm. But the cedars were too busy with their own fears to pay any heed to the faint pleadings of the humble vine and the little tree. The angels came into the forest, singing the same glorious anthem about the Child, and the stars sang in chorus with them, until every part of the woods rang with echoes of that wondrous song. There was nothing in the appearance of this angel host to inspire fear; they were clad all in white, and there were crowns upon their fair heads, and golden harps in their hands; love, hope, charity, compassion, and joy beamed from their beautiful faces, and their presence seemed to fill the forest with a divine peace. The angels came through the forest to where the little tree stood, and gathering around it, they touched it with their hands, and kissed its little branches, and sang even more sweetly than before. And their song was about the Child, the Child, the Child that had been born. Then the stars came down from the skies and danced and hung upon the branches of the tree, and they, too, sang that song,—the song of the Child. And all the other trees and the vines and the ferns and the mosses beheld in wonder; nor could they understand why all these things were being done, and why this exceeding honor should be shown the little tree.

When the morning came the angels left the forest,—all but one angel, who remained behind and lingered near the little tree. Then a cedar asked: "Why do you tarry with us, holy angel?" And the angel answered: "I stay to guard this little tree, for it is sacred, and no harm shall come to it."

The little tree felt quite relieved by this assurance, and it held up its head more confidently than ever before. And how it thrived and grew, and waxed in strength and beauty! The cedars said they never had seen the like. The sun seemed to lavish its choicest rays upon the little tree, heaven dropped its sweetest dew upon it, and the winds never came to the forest that they did not forget their rude manners and linger to kiss the little tree and sing it their prettiest songs. No danger ever menaced it, no harm threatened; for the angel never slept, —through the day and through the night the angel watched the little tree and protected it from all evil. Oftentimes the trees talked with the angel; but of course they understood little of what he said, for he spoke always of the Child who was to become the Master; and always when thus he talked, he caressed the little tree, and stroked its branches and leaves, and moistened them with his tears. It all was so very strange that none in the forest could understand.

So the years passed, the angel watching his blooming charge. Sometimes the beasts strayed toward the little tree and threatened to devour its tender foliage; sometimes the woodman came with his axe, intent upon hewing down the straight and comely thing; sometimes the hot, consuming breath of drought swept from the south, and sought to blight the forest and all its verdure: the angel kept them from the little tree. Serene and beautiful it grew, until now it was no longer a little trees, but the pride and glory of the forest.

One day the tree heard some one coming through the forest. Hitherto the angel had hastened to its side when men approached; but now the angel strode away and stood under the cedars yonder.

"Dear angel," cried the tree, "can you not hear the footsteps of some one approaching? Why do you leave me?"

"Have no fear," said the angel; "for He who comes is the Master."

The Master came to the tree and beheld it. He placed His hands upon its smooth trunk and branches, and the tree was thrilled with a strange and glorious delight. Then He stooped and kissed the tree, and then He turned and went away.

Many times after that the Master came to the forest, and when He came it always was to where the tree stood. Many times He rested beneath the tree and enjoyed the shade of its foliage, and listened to the music of the wind as it swept through the rustling leaves. Many times He slept there, and the tree watched over Him, and the forest was still, and all its voices were hushed. And the angel hovered near like a faithful sentinel.

Ever and anon men came with the Master to the forest and sat with Him in the shade of the tree, and talked with Him of matters which the tree never could understand; only it heard that the talk was of love and charity and gentleness, and it saw that the Master was beloved and venerated by the others. It heard them tell of the Master's goodness and humility,—how He had healed the sick and raised the dead and bestowed inestimable blessings wherever He walked. And the tree loved the Master for His beauty and His goodness; and when He came to the forest it was full of joy, but when He came not it was sad. And the other trees of the forest joined in its happiness and its sorrow, for they, too, loved the Master. And the angel always hovered near.

The Master came one night alone into the forest, and His face was pale with anguish and wet with tears, and He fell upon His knees and prayed. The tree heard Him, and all the forest was still, as if it were standing in the presence of death. And when the morning came, lo! the angel had gone.

Then there was a great confusion in the forest. There was a sound of rude voices, and a clashing of swords and staves. Strange men appeared, uttering loud oaths and cruel threats, and the tree was filled with terror. It called aloud for the angel, but the angel came not.

"Alas," cried the vine, "they have come to destroy the tree, the pride and glory of the forest!"

The forest was sorely agitated, but it was in vain. The strange men plied their axes with cruel vigor, and the tree was hewn to the ground. Its beautiful branches were cut away and cast aside, and its soft, thick foliage was strewn to the tenderer mercies of the winds.

"They are killing me!" cried the tree; "why is not the angel here to protect me?"

But no one heard the piteous cry,—none but the other trees of the forest; and they wept, and the little vine wept too.

Then the cruel men dragged the despoiled and hewn tree from the forest, and the forest saw that beauteous thing no more.

But the night wind that swept down from the City of the Great King that night to ruffle the bosom of distant Galilee, tarried in the forest awhile to say that it had seen that day a cross upraised on Calvary,—the tree on which was stretched the body of the dying Master.

THE LITTLE MATCH GIRL

By Hans Christian Andersen

IT was late on a bitterly cold, snowy, New Year's Eve. A poor little girl was wandering in the dark cold streets; she was bareheaded and barefooted. She certainly had had shoes on when she left home, but they were not much good, for they were so huge. They had last been worn by her mother, and they fell off the poor little girl's feet when she was running across the street to avoid two carriages that were rolling rapidly by. One of the shoes could not be found at all; and the other was picked up by a boy, who ran off with it, saying that it would do for a cradle when he had children of his own. So the poor little girl had to go on with her little bare feet, which were blue with the cold. She carried a quantity of matches in her old apron, and held a packet of them in her hand. Nobody had bought any from her during all the long day; nobody had even given her a copper.

The poor little creature was hungry and perishing with cold, and she looked the picture of misery. The snowflakes fell upon her long yellow hair, which curled so prettily round her face, but she paid no attention to that. Lights were shining from every window, and there was a most delicious odour of roast goose in the streets, for it was New Year's Eve—she could not forget that. She found a protected place where one house projected a little beyond the next one, and here she crouched, drawing up her feet under her, but she was colder than ever. She did not dare to go home, for she had not sold any matches and had not earned a single penny. Her father would beat her; besides, it was almost as cold at home as it was here. They lived in a house where the wind whistled through every crack, although they tried to stuff up the biggest ones with rags and straw. Her tiny hands were almost paralyzed with cold. Oh, if she could only find some way to warm them! Dared she pull one match out of the bundle and strike it on the wall to warm her fingers? She pulled one out. "Ritsch!" How it spluttered, how it blazed! It burnt with a bright clear flame, just like a little candle when she held her hand round it. It was a very curious candle, too. The little girl fancied that she was sitting in front of a big stove with polished brass feet and handles. There was a splendid fire blazing in it and warming her so beautifully, but— what happened? Just as she was stretching out her feet to warm them, the blaze went out, the stove vanished, and she was left sitting with the end of the burnt-out match in her hand. She struck a new one, it burnt, it blazed up, and where the light fell upon the wall against which she lay, it became transparent like gauze, and she could see right through it into the room inside. There was a table spread with a snowy cloth and pretty china; a roast goose stuffed with apples and prunes was steaming on it. And what was even better, the goose hopped from the dish with the carving knife and fork sticking in his back, and it waddled across the floor. It came right up to the poor child, and then—the match went out and there was nothing to be seen but the thick black wall.

She lit another match. This time she was sitting under a lovely Christmas tree. It was much bigger and more beautifully decorated than the one she had seen when she had peeped through the glass doors at the rich merchant's house this Christmas day. Thousands of lighted candles gleamed upon its branches, and coloured pictures such as she had seen in the shop windows looked down upon her. The little girl stretched out both her hands towards them—then out went the match. All the Christmas candles rose higher and higher, till she saw that they were only the twinkling stars. One of them fell and made a bright streak of light across the sky. "Some one is dying," thought the little girl; for her old grandmother, the only person who had ever been kind to her, used to say, "When a star falls a soul is going up to God."

Now she struck another match against the wall, and this time it was her grandmother who appeared in the circle of flame. She saw her quite clearly and distinctly, looking so gentle and happy.

"Grandmother!" cried the little creature. "Oh, do take me with you! I know you will vanish when the match goes out; you will vanish like the warm stove, the delicious goose, and the beautiful Christmas tree!"

She hastily struck a whole bundle of matches, because she did so want to keep her grandmother with her. The light of the matches made it as bright as day. Grandmother had never before looked so big or so beautiful. She lifted the little girl up in her arms, and they soared in a halo of light and joy, far, far above the earth, where there was no more cold, no hunger, no pain, for they were with God.

LORD, KEEP MY MEMORY GREEN

By Charles Dickens

"WHAT is that the old man has in his arms?" asked Mr. Redlaw, as he sat down to his solitary meal.

"Holly, Sir," replied the quiet voice of Milly.

"That's what I say myself, Sir," interposed Mr. William, striking in with the butter-boat. "Berries is so seasonable to the time of year!"

"Another Christmas come, another year gone!" murmured the Chemist, with a gloomy sigh. "More figures in the lengthening sum of recollection that we work and work at to our torment, till Death idly jumbles all together, and rubs all out. So, Philip!" breaking off, and raising his voice as he addressed the old man, standing apart, with his glistening burden in his arms, from which the quiet Mrs. William took small branches, which she noiselessly trimmed with her scissors, and decorated the room with, while her aged father-in-law looked on much interested in the ceremony.

"My duty to you, Sir," returned the old man. "Should have spoke before, Sir, but know your ways, Mr. Redlaw—proud to say—and wait till spoke to! Merry Christmas, Sir, and Happy New Year, and many of 'em. Have had a pretty many of 'em myself—ha, ha!—and may take the liberty of wishing 'em. I'm eighty-seven!"

"Have you had so many that were happy and merry?" asked the other.

"Ay, Sir, ever so many," returned the old man.

"Is his memory impaired with age? It is to be expected now," said Mr. Redlaw, turning to the son, and speaking lower.

"Not a morsel of it, Sir," replied Mr. William. "That's exactly what I say myself. There was never such a memory as my father's. He's the most wonderful man in the world. He don't know what forgetting means. It's the very observation I'm always making to Mrs. William, Sir, if you'll believe me!"

Mr. Swidger, in his polite desire to seem to acquiesce at all events, delivered this as if there were no iota of contradiction in it, and it were all said in unbounded and unqualified assent.

The Chemist pushed his plate away, and, rising from the table, walked across the room to where the old man stood looking at a little sprig of holly in his hand.

"It recalls the time when many of these years were old and new, then?" he said, observing him attentively, and touching him on the shoulder. "Does it?"

"Oh, many, many!" said Philip, half-awakening from his reverie. "I'm eighty-seven!"

"Merry and happy, was it?" asked the Chemist, in a low voice. "Merry and happy, old man?"

"Maybe as high as that, no higher," said the old man, holding out his hand a little way above the level of his knee, and looking retrospectively at his questioner, "when I first remember 'em! Cold, sunshiny day it was, out a-walking, when some one—it was my mother as sure as you stand here, though I don't know what her blessed face was like, for she took ill and died that Christmas-time—told me they were food for birds. The pretty little fellow thought—that's me, you understand—that birds' eyes were so bright, perhaps, because the berries that they lived on in the winter were so bright. I recollect that. And I'm eighty-seven!"

"Merry and happy!" mused the other, bending his dark eyes upon the stooping figure, with a smile of compassion. "Merry and happy—and remember well?"

"Ay, ay, ay," resumed the old man, catching the last words. "I remember 'em well in my school time, year after year, and all the merrymaking that used to along with them. I was a strong chap then, Mr. Redlaw: and, if you'll believe me, hadn't my match at football within ten miles. Where's my son William? Hadn't my match at football, William, within ten mile!"

"That's what I always say, father!" returned the son promptly, and with great respect. "You ARE a Swidger, if ever there was one of the family! "

"Dear!" said the old man, shaking his head as he again looked at the holly. "His mother—my son William's my youngest son—and I, have sat among 'em all, boys and girls, little children and babies, many a year, when the berries like these were not shining half so bright all round us, as their bright faces. Many of 'em are gone; she's gone; and my son George (our eldest, who was our pride more than all the rest) is fallen very low; but I can see them, when I look here, alive and healthy, as they used to be in those days; and I can see him, thank God, in his innocence. It's a blessed thing to me, at eighty-seven."

The keen look that had been fixed upon him with so much earnestness, had gradually sought the ground.

"When my circumstances got to be not so good as formerly, through not being honestly dealt by, and I first come here to be custodian," said the old man, "which was upwards of fifty years ago—where's my son William? More than half a century ago, William!"

"That's what I say, father," replied the son, as promptly and dutifully as before; "that's exactly where it is. Two times ought's an ought, and twice five ten, and there's a hundred of 'em."

"It was quite a pleasure to know that one of our founders—or more correctly speaking," said the old man, with a great glory in his subject and his knowledge of it, "one of the learned gentlemen that helped endow us in Queen Elizabeth's time, for we were founded afore her day—left in his will, among the other bequests he made us, so much to buy holly, for garnishing the walls and windows, come Christmas. There was something homely and friendly in it. Being but strange here, then, and coming at Christmas time, we took a liking for his very picter that hangs in what used to be, anciently, afore our ten poor gentlemen commuted for an annual stipend in money, our great Dinner Hall. A sedate gentleman in a peaked beard, with a ruff round his neck, and a scroll below him, in old English letters, 'Lord! keep my memory green.' You know all about him, Mr. Redlaw?"

"I know the portrait hangs there, Philip."

"Yes, sure, it's the second on the right, above the panelling. I was going to say—he has helped to keep *my* memory green, I thank him;

for going round the building every year, as I'm doing now, and freshening up the bare rooms with these branches and berries, freshens up my bare old brain. One year brings back another, and that year another, and those others numbers! At last, it seems to me as if the birth-time of our Lord was the birth-time of all I have ever had affection for, or mourned for, or delighted in—and they're pretty many, for I'm eighty-seven!"

TO THE FIR-TREE

O Fir-tree green! O Fir-tree green!
  Your leaves are constant ever,
Not only in the summer time,
But through the winter's snow and rime
O Fir-tree green! O Fir-tree green!
  You're fresh and green forever.

O Fir-tree green! O Fir-tree green!
  I still shall love you dearly!
How oft to me on Christmas night
Your laden boughs have brought delight.
O Fir-tree green! O Fir-tree green!
  I still shall love you dearly.

FROM THE GERMAN

THE CHRISTMAS TREE IN THE NURSERY

With wild surprise
Four great eyes
In two small heads,
From neighboring beds
Looked out—and winked—
And glittered and blinked
At a very queer sight
In the dim starlight.
As plain as can be

A fairy tree
Flashes and glimmers
And shakes and shimmers.
Red, green and blue
Meet their view;
Silver and gold
Their sharp eyes behold;
Small moon, big stars;
And jams in jars,
And cakes, and honey
And thimbles, and money,
Pink dogs, blue cats,
Little squeaking rats,
And candles, and dolls,
And crackers, and polls,
A real bird that sings,
And tokens and favors,
And·all sorts of things
For the little shavers.

Four black eyes
Grow big with surprise;
And then grow bigger
When a tiny figure,
Jaunty and airy,
(Is it a fairy?)
From the tree-top cries,
"Open wide! Black Eyes!
Come, children, wake now!
Your joys you may take now!"

Quick as you can think
  Twenty small toes
  In four pretty rows,
Like little piggies pink,
  All kick in the air—
And before you can wink
  The tree stands bare!

RICHARD WATSON GILDER

SANTA CLAUS

IS THERE A SANTA CLAUS?

An Editorial reprinted from the New York Sun, *September 21, 1897*

By Francis P. Church

WE take pleasure in answering at once and thus prominently the communication below, expressing at the same time our great gratification that its faithful author is numbered among the friends of *The Sun:*

> *Dear Editor:*
> *I am 8 years old.*
> *Some of my little friends say there is no Santa Claus.*
> *Papa says "If you see it in 'The Sun' it's so."*
> *Please tell me the truth, is there a Santa Claus?*
> > *Virginia O'Hanlon,*
> > *115 West 95th Street,*
> > *New York City.*

Virginia, your little friends are wrong. They have been affected by the skepticism of a skeptical age. They do not believe except they see. They think that nothing can be which is not comprehensible by their little minds. All minds, Virginia, whether they be men's or children's, are little. In this great universe of ours man is a mere insect, an ant, in his intellect, as compared with the boundless world about him, as measured by the intelligence capable of grasping the whole of truth and knowledge.

Yes, Virginia, there is a Santa Claus. He exists as certainly as love and generosity and devotion exist, and you know that they abound and give to your life its highest beauty and joy. Alas! how dreary would be the world if there were no Santa Claus! It would be as dreary as if there were no Virginias. There would be no childlike faith, then, no poetry, no romance to make tolerable this existence.

451

We should have no enjoyment, except in sense and sight. The eternal light with which childhood fills the world would be extinguished.

Not believe in Santa Claus! You might as well not believe in fairies! You might get your papa to hire men to watch in all the chimneys on Christmas Eve to catch Santa Claus, but even if they did not see Santa Claus coming down, what would that prove? Nobody sees Santa Claus, but that is no sign that there is no Santa Claus. The most real things in the world are those that neither children nor men can see. Did you ever see fairies dancing on the lawn? Of course not, but that's no proof that they are not there. Nobody can conceive or imagine all the wonders there are unseen and unseeable in the world.

You tear apart the baby's rattle and see what makes the noise inside, but there is a veil covering the unseen world which not the strongest man, nor even the united strength of all the strongest men that ever lived, could tear apart. Only faith, fancy, poetry, love, romance, can push aside that curtain and view and picture the supernal beauty and glory beyond. Is it all real? Ah, Virginia, in all this world there is nothing else real and abiding.

No Santa Claus! Thank God he lives, and he lives forever. A thousand years from now, Virginia, nay, ten times ten thousand years from now, he will continue to make glad the heart of childhood.

THE MOUSE THAT DIDN'T BELIEVE IN SANTA CLAUS

Adapted from "The Mouse and the Moonbeam"

By EUGENE FIELD

THE clock stood, of course, in the corner; a moonbeam floated idly on the floor, and a little mauve mouse came from the hole in the chimney corner and frisked and scampered in the light of the moonbeam upon the floor. The little mauve mouse was particularly merry; sometimes she danced upon two legs and sometimes upon four legs, but always very daintily and always very merrily.

"Ah, me!" sighed the old clock, "how different mice are nowadays from the mice we used to have in the old times! Now there was your grandma, Mistress Velvetpaw, and there was your grandpa, Master Sniffwhisker—how grave and dignified they were! Many a night have I seen them dancing up on the carpet below me, but always that stately minuet and never that crazy frisking which you are executing now, to my surprise—yes, and to my horror, too."

"But why shouldn't I be merry?" asked the little mauve mouse. "Tomorrow is Christmas, and this is Christmas Eve."

"So it is," said the old clock. "I had really forgotten all about it. But, tell me, what is Christmas to you, little Miss Mauve Mouse?"

"A great deal to me!" cried the little mauve mouse. "I have been very good for a very long time; I have not used any bad words, nor have I gnawed any holes, nor have I stolen any canary seed, nor have I worried my mother by running behind the flour barrel where that horrid trap is set. In fact, I have been so good that I'm very sure Santa Claus will bring me something very pretty."

This seemed to amuse the old clock mightily; in fact, the old clock fell to laughing so heartily that in an unguarded moment she struck twelve instead of ten, which was exceedingly careless.

"Why, you silly little mauve mouse," said the old clock, "you don't believe in Santa Claus, do you?"

"Of course I do," answered the mauve mouse. "Believe in Santa Claus? Why shouldn't I? Didn't Santa Claus bring me a beautiful butter cracker last Christmas, and a lovely gingersnap, and a delicious rind of cheese, and—lots of things? I should be very ungrateful if I did *not* believe in Santa Claus, and I certainly shall not disbelieve in him at the very moment when I am expecting him to arrive with a bundle of goodies for me.

"I once had a little sister," continued the little mauve mouse, "who did not believe in Santa Claus, and the very thought of the fate that befell her makes my blood run cold and my whiskers stand on end. She died before I was born, but my mother has told me all about her. Her name was Squeaknibble, and she was in stature one of those long, low, rangy mice that are seldom found in well-stocked pantries. Mother says that Squeaknibble took after our ancestors who came from New England, and seemed to inherit many ancestral traits, the most conspicuous of which was a disposition to sneer at some of the most respected dogmas in mousedom. From her very infancy she doubted, for example, the widely accepted theory that the moon was composed of green cheese; and this heresy was the first intimation her parents had of her sceptical turn of mind. Of course, her parents were vastly annoyed, for they saw that this youthful scepticism would lead to serious, if not fatal consequences. Yet all in vain did they reason and plead with their headstrong and heretical child.

"For a long time Squeaknibble would not believe that there was any such archfiend as a cat; but she came to be convinced one memorable night, on which occasion she lost two inches of her beautiful tail, and received so terrible a fright that for fully an hour afterward her little heart beat so violently as to lift her off her feet and bump her head against the top of our domestic hole. The cat that deprived my sister of so large a percentage of her tail was the same ogress that nowadays steals into this room, crouches treacherously behind the sofa, and feigns to be asleep, hoping, forsooth, that some of us, heedless of her hated presence, will venture within reach of her claws. So enraged was this ferocious monster at the escape of my sister that she ground her fangs viciously together, and vowed to take no pleasure in life until she held in her devouring jaws the innocent little mouse which belonged to the mangled bit of tail she even then clutched in her remorseless claws."

"Yes," said the old clock, "now that you recall the incident, I recollect it well. I was here then, and I remember that I laughed at the cat and chided her for her awkwardness. My reproaches irritated her; she told me that a clock's duty was to run itself down, *not* to be depreciating the merits of others! Yes, I recall the time; that cat's tongue is fully as sharp as her claws."

"Be that as it may," said the little mauve mouse, "it is a matter of history, and therefore beyond dispute, that from that very moment the cat pined for Squeaknibble's life; it seemed as if that one little two-inch taste of Squeaknibble's tail had filled the cat with a consuming appetite for the rest of Squeaknibble. So the cat waited and watched and hunted and schemed and devised and did everything possible for a cat—a cruel cat—to do in order to gain her murderous ends.

"One night—one fatal Christmas Eve—our mother had undressed the children for bed, and was urging upon them to go to sleep earlier than usual, since she fully expected that Santa Claus would bring each of them something very nice before morning. Thereupon the little dears whisked their cunning tails, pricked up their beautiful ears, and began telling one another what they hoped Santa Claus would bring. One asked for a slice of Roquefort, another for Swiss, another for Brick, and a fourth for Edam; one expressed a preference for Cream cheese, while another hoped for Camembert. There were fourteen little ones then, and consequently there were diverse opinions as to the kind of gift which Santa Claus should best bring; still there was, as you can readily understand, an enthusiastic agreement upon this point, namely, that the gift should be cheese of some brand or other.

" 'My dears,' said our mother, 'we should be content with whatsoever Santa Claus bestows, so long as it is cheese, disjoined from all traps whatsoever, unmixed with Paris green, and free from glass, strychnine, and other harmful ingredients. As for myself, I shall be satisfied with a cut of nice, fresh American cheese. So run away to your dreams now, that Santa Claus may find you sleeping.'

"The children obeyed—all but Squeaknibble. 'Let the others think what they please,' said she, 'but *I* don't believe in Santa Claus. I'm not going to bed, either. I'm going to creep out of this dark hole and have a quiet romp, all by myself, in the moonlight.' Oh, what a vain, foolish, wicked little mouse was Squeaknibble! But I will not reproach the dead; her punishment came all too swiftly. Now listen: who do you suppose overheard her talking so disrespectfully of Santa Claus?"

"Why, Santa Claus himself," said the old clock.

"Oh, no," answered the little mauve mouse. "It was that wicked, murderous cat! Just as Satan lurks and lies in wait for bad children, so does the cruel cat lurk and lie in wait for naughty little mice. And you can depend upon it that, when that awful cat heard Squeaknibble speak so disrespectfully of Santa Claus, her wicked eyes glowed with joy, her sharp teeth watered, and her bristling fur emitted electric sparks as big as peas. Then what did that bloody monster do but scuttle as fast as she could into Dear-my-Soul's room, leap up into Dear-my-Soul's crib, and walk off with the pretty little white muff which Dear-my-Soul used to wear when she went for a visit to the little girl in the next block! What upon earth did the horrid old cat want with Dear-my-Soul's pretty little white muff? Ah, the ingenuity of that cat! Listen.

"In the first place," resumed the little mauve mouse, after a pause that showed the depth of her emotion, "in the first place, that wretched cat dressed herself up in that pretty little white muff, by which you are to understand that she crawled through the muff just so far as to leave her four cruel legs at liberty."

"Yes, I understand," said the old clock.

"Then she put on the boy doll's cap," said the little mauve mouse, "and when she was arrayed in the boy doll's fur cap and Dear-my-Soul's pretty little white muff, of course she didn't look like a cruel cat at all. But whom did she look like?"

"Like the boy doll," suggested the old clock.

"No, no!" cried the little mauve mouse.

"Like Dear-my-Soul?" asked the old clock.

"How stupid you are!" exclaimed the little mauve mouse. "Why she looked like Santa Claus, of course!"

"Oh, yes; I see," said the old clock. "Now I begin to be interested; go on."

"Alas!" sighed the little mauve mouse, "not much remains to be told; but there is more of my story left than there was of Squeaknibble when that horrid cat crawled out of that miserable disguise. You are to understand that, contrary to her mother's warning, Squeaknibble issued from the friendly hole in the chimney corner, and gamboled about over this very carpet, and, I dare say, in this very moonlight.

"Right merrily was Squeaknibble gamboling," continued the little mauve mouse, "and she had just turned a double somersault without the use of what remained of her tail, when, all of a sudden, she beheld, looming up like a monster ghost, a figure all in white fur? Oh, how frightened she was, and how her little heart did beat! 'Purr, purr-r-r,' said the ghost in white fur. 'Oh, please don't hurt me!' pleaded Squeaknibble. 'No; I'll not hurt you,' said the ghost in white fur; 'I'm Santa Claus, and I've brought you a beautiful piece of savory old cheese, you dear little mousie, you.' Poor Squeaknibble was deceived; a sceptic all her life, she was at last befooled by the most fatal of frauds. 'How good of you!' said Squeaknibble. 'I didn't believe there was a Santa Claus, and—' but before she could say more she was seized by two sharp, cruel claws that conveyed her crushed body to the murderous mouth of the cat. I can dwell no longer upon this harrowing scene. Before the morrow's sun rose upon the spot where that tragedy had been enacted, poor Squeaknibble passed to that bourne to which two inches of her beautiful tail had preceded her by the space of three weeks to a day. As for Santa Claus, when he came that Christmas Eve, bringing cheese and goodies for the other little mice, he heard with sorrow of Squeaknibble's fate; and ere he departed he said that in all his experience he had never known of a mouse or a child that had prospered after once saying he didn't believe in Santa Claus."

THE REVENGE OF SAINT NICHOLAS

A TALE FOR THE HOLIDAYS

By James K. Paulding

EVERYBODY knows that, in the famous city of New York, whose proper name is Nieuw Amsterdam, the excellent St. Nicholas— who is worth a dozen St. Georges, with dragons to boot, and who, if every tub stood on its right bottom, would be at the head of the Seven

Champions of Christendom—I say, everybody knows that the excellent St. Nicholas, in holiday times, goes about among the people in the middle of the night, distributing all sorts of toothsome and becoming gifts to the good boys and girls in this his favorite city. Some say that he comes down the chimneys in a little Jersey wagon; others, that he wears a pair of Holland skates, with which he travels like the wind; and others, who pretend to have seen him, maintain that he has lately adopted a locomotive, and was once actually detected on the *Albany* railroad. But this last assertion is looked upon to be entirely fabulous, because St. Nicholas has too much discretion to trust himself in such a new-fangled jarvie; and so I leave this matter to be settled by whomsoever will take the trouble. My own opinion is, that his favorite mode of travelling is on the canal, the motion and speed of which aptly comport with the philosophic dignity of his character.

It was in the year one thousand seven hundred and sixty, or sixty-one, for the most orthodox chronicles differ in this respect; but it was a very remarkable year, and it was called *annus mirabilis* on that account. . . . What contributed to render this year still more remarkable was the building of six new three-story brick houses in the city, and the fact of three persons' setting up equipages, who, I cannot find, ever failed in business afterwards, or compounded with their creditors at a pistareen in the pound. . . .

But the most extraordinary thing of all was the confident assertion that there was but one *gray mare* within the bills of mortality, and, incredible as it may appear, she was the wife of a responsible citizen, who, it was affirmed, had grown rich by weaving velvet purses out of sows' ears. But this we look upon as being somewhat of the character of the predictions of almanac-makers. Certain it is, however, that Amos Shuttle possessed the treasure of a wife who was shrewdly suspected of having established within doors a system of government not laid down in Aristotle or the Abbé Sièyes, who made a constitution for every day in the year, and two for the first of April.

Amos Shuttle, though a mighty pompous little man out of doors, was the humblest of human creatures within. He belonged to that class of people who pass for great among the little, and little among the

great; and he would certainly have been master in his own house, had
it not been for a woman. . . . Amos had grown rich, Heaven knows
how—he did not know himself; but, what was somewhat extraordinary, he considered his wealth a signal proof of his talents and sagac-
ity, and valued himself according to the infallible standard of pounds,
shillings, and pence. But, though he lorded it without, he was, as we
have just said, the most gentle of men within doors. The moment he
stepped inside of his own house, his spirit cowered down, like that of
a pious man entering a church; he felt as if he was in the presence of
a superior being—to wit, Mrs. Amos Shuttle. . . .

Such as he was, Mr. Amos Shuttle waxed richer and richer every day,
insomuch that those who envied his prosperity were wont to say "that
he had certainly been born with a dozen silver spoons in his mouth, or
such a great blockhead would never have got together such a heap
of money." When he had become worth ten thousand pounds, he
launched his shuttle magnanimously out of the window, ordered his
weaver's beam to be split up for oven-wood, and Mrs. Amos turned his
weaver's shop into a boudoir. Fortune followed him faster than he ran
away from her. In a few years the ten thousand doubled, and in a few
more trebled, quadrupled—in short, Amos could hardly count his
money.

"What shall we do now, my dear?" asked Mrs. Shuttle, who never
sought his opinion, that I can learn, except for the pleasure of con-
tradicting him.

"Let us go and live in the country, and enjoy ourselves," quoth
Amos.

"Go into the country? go to—" I could never satisfy myself what
Mrs. Shuttle meant; but she stopped short, and concluded the sentence with a withering look of scorn, that would have cowed the
spirits of nineteen weavers.

Amos named all sorts of places, enumerated all sorts of modes of
life he could think of, and every pleasure that might enter into the
imagination of a man without a soul. His wife despised them all; she
would not hear of them.

"Well, my dear, suppose you suggest something; do now, Abby," at length said Amos, in a coaxing whisper; "will you, my oneydoney?"

"Ony fiddlestick! I wonder you repeat such vulgarisms. But if I must say what I should like, I should like to travel."

"Well let us go and make a tour as far as Jamaica, or Hackensack, or Spiking-devil. There is excellent fishing for striped-bass there."

"Spiking-devil!" screamed Mrs. Shuttle; "a'n't you ashamed to swear so, you wicked mortal? I won't go to Jamaica, nor to Hackensack among the Dutch Hottentots, nor to Spiking-devil to catch striped-bass. I'll go to Europe!"

. . . When Mrs. Shuttle said a thing, it was settled. They went to Europe, taking their only son with them. The lady ransacked all the milliners' shops in Paris, and the gentleman visited all the restaurants. He became such a desperate connoisseur and gourmand, that he could almost tell an *omelette au jambon* from a gammon of bacon. After consummating the polish, they came home, the lady with the newest old fashions, and the weaver with a confirmed preference of *potage à la Turque* over pepperpot. It is said the city trembled, as with an earthquake, when they landed; but the notion was probably superstitious.

They arrived near the close of the year, the memorable year, the *annus mirabilis,* one thousand seven hundred and sixty. Everybody that had ever known the Shuttles flocked to see them, or rather to see what they had brought with them; and such was the magic of a voyage to Europe, that Mr. and Mrs. Shuttle, who had been nobodies when they departed, became somebodies when they returned, and mounted at once to the summit of *ton.*

"You have come in good time to enjoy the festivities of the holidays," said Mrs. Hubblebubble, an old friend of Amos the weaver and his wife.

"We shall have a merry Christmas and a happy New-year," exclaimed Mrs. Doubletrouble, another old acquaintance of old times.

"The holidays?" drawled Mrs. Shuttle; "the holidays? Christmas and New-year? Pray, what are they?"

It is astonishing to see how people lose their memories abroad, sometimes. They often forget their old friends and old customs; and, occasionally, themselves.

"Why, la! now, who'd have thought it?" cried Mrs. Doubletrouble; "why, sure you haven't forgot the oly koeks and the mince-pies, the merry meetings of friends, the sleigh-rides, the Kissing-Bridge, and the family parties?"

"Family parties!" shrieked Mrs. Shuttle, and held her salts to her nose; "family parties! I never heard of anything so Gothic in Paris or Rome; and oly koeks—oh shocking! and mince-pies—detestable! and throwing open one's doors to all one's old friends, whom one wishes to forget as soon as possible—Oh! the idea is insupportable!" And again she held the salts to her nose.

Mrs. Hubblebubble and Mrs. Doubletrouble found they had exposed themselves sadly and were quite ashamed. A real genteel, well-bred, enlightened lady of fashion ought to have no rule of conduct, no conscience but Paris—whatever is fashionable there is genteel—whatever is not fashionable is vulgar. At least so thought Mrs. Hubblebubble and Mrs. Doubletrouble.

"But is it possible that all these things are out of fashion, abroad?" asked the latter, beseechingly.

"They never were in," said Mrs. Amos Shuttle. "For my part, I mean to close my doors and windows on New-year's day—I'm determined."

"And so am I," said Mrs. Hubblebubble.

"And so am I," said Mrs. Doubletrouble.

And it was settled that they should make a combination among themselves and their friends to put down the ancient and good customs of the city, and abolish the sports and enjoyments of the jolly New-year.

[*St. Nicholas is much displeased by such unfeeling conduct. He resolves that they shall never have another comfortable sleep.*]

Mrs. Amos Shuttle could not sleep, because something had whispered in her apprehensive ear, that her son, her only son, whom she had engaged to the daughter of Count Grenouille in Paris, then about three years old, was actually at that moment crossing Kissing-Bridge, in company with little Susan Varian, and some others. Now Susan was the fairest little lady of all the land. . . . She was, moreover, a good little girl, and an accomplished little girl—but alas! she had not mounted to that step in the Jacob's ladder of fashion which qualifies a person for the heaven of high *ton,* and Mrs. Shuttle had not been to Europe for nothing. . . . It kept her awake all the livelong night; and the only consolation she had was scolding poor Amos, because the sleigh-bells made such a noise.

As for Mrs. Hubblebubble and Mrs. Doubletrouble, neither of the wretches got a wink of sleep during a whole week, for thinking of the beautiful French chairs and damask curtains Mrs. Shuttle had brought from Europe. They forthwith besieged their good men, leaving them no rest until they sent out orders to Paris for just such rich chairs and curtains as those of the thrice-happy Mrs. Shuttle, from whom they kept the affair a profound secret, each meaning to treat her to an agreeable surprise. In the mean while they could not rest, for fear the vessel which was to bring these treasures might be lost on her passage. Such was the dreadful judgment inflicted on them by the good St. Nicholas.

The perplexities of Mrs. Shuttle increased daily. In the first place, do all she could, she could not make Amos a fine gentleman. . . . He would be telling the price of everything in his house, his furniture, his wines and his dinners, insomuch that those who envied his prosperity, or, perhaps, only despised his pretensions, were wont to say, after eating his venison and drinking his old Madeira, "that he ought to have been a tavernkeeper, he knew so well how to make out a bill." Mrs. Shuttle once overheard a speech of this kind, and the good St. Nicholas himself, who had brought it about, almost felt sorry for the mortification she endured on the occasion.

Scarcely had she got over this, when she was invited to a ball by Mrs. Hubblebubble, and the first thing she saw on entering the drawing-room was a suit of damask curtains and chairs, as much like her own as two peas, only the curtains had far handsomer fringe. Mrs. Shuttle came very near fainting away, but escaped for that time, determining to mortify this impudent creature, by taking not the least notice of her finery. But St. Nicholas ordered it otherwise, so that she was at last obliged to acknowledge they were very elegant indeed. Nay, this was not the worst, for she overheard one lady whisper to another, that Mrs. Hubblebubble's curtains were much richer than Mrs. Shuttle's.

"Oh, I dare say," replied the other—"I dare say Mrs. Shuttle bought them second-hand, for her husband is as mean as pursley."

This was too much. The unfortunate woman was taken suddenly ill—called her carriage, and went home, where it is supposed she would have died that evening, had she not wrought upon Amos to promise her an entire new suit of French furniture for her drawing-room and parlour to boot, besides a new carriage. But for all this she could not close her eyes that night, for thinking of the "second-hand curtains."

Nor was the wicked Mrs. Doubletrouble a whit better off, when her friend Mrs. Hubblebubble treated her to the agreeable surprise of the French window-curtains and chairs. "It is too bad—too bad, I declare," said she to herself: "but I'll pay her off soon." Accordingly she issued invitations for a grand ball and supper, at which both Mrs. Shuttle and Mrs. Hubblebubble were struck dumb at beholding a suit of curtains and a set of chairs exactly of the same pattern with theirs. The shock was terrible, and it is impossible to say what might have been the consequences, had not the two ladies all at once thought of uniting in abusing Mrs. Doubletrouble for her extravagance.

"I pity poor Mr. Doubletrouble," said Mrs. Shuttle, shrugging her shoulders significantly, and glancing at the room.

"And so do I," said Mrs. Hubblebubble, doing the same.

Mrs. Doubletrouble had her eye upon them, and enjoyed their mortification, until her pride was brought to the ground by a dead shot from Mrs. Shuttle, who was heard to exclaim, in reply to a lady who observed that the chairs and curtains were very handsome:

"Why, yes; but they have been out of fashion in Paris a long time; and, besides, really they are getting so common, that I intend to have mine removed to the nursery."

Heavens! what a blow! Poor Mrs. Doubletrouble hardly survived it. . . .

Thus were these wicked and miserable women spurred on by witchcraft from one piece of prodigality to another, and a deadly rivalship grew up between them, which destroyed their own happiness and that of their husbands. . . . But they still shut their doors on the jolly anniversary of St. Nicholas, though the old respectable burghers and their wives, who had held up their heads time out of mind, continued the good custom, and laughed at the presumption of these upstart interlopers, who were followed only by a few people of silly pretensions, who had no more soul than Amos Shuttle himself.

[*Young Johnny Shuttle wishes to marry Susan Varian. His mother refuses her consent and says that his father will disinherit him.*]

"If my father goes on as he has done lately," sighed the youth, "he won't have anything left to disinherit me of but his affection, I fear. But if he had millions, I would not abandon Susan."

"Are you not ashamed of such a plebeian attachment? You, that have been to Europe! But, once for all, remember this, renounce this low-born upstart, or quit your father's home for ever."

"Upstart!" thought young Shuttle:—"one of the oldest families in the city!" He made his mother a respectful bow, bade Heaven bless her, and left the house. He was, however, met at the door by his father, who said to him,

"Johnny, I give my consent; but mind, don't tell your mother a word of the matter. I'll let her know I've a soul, as well as other people"; and he tossed his head like a war-horse.

.   .   .   .

No fortune, be it ever so great, can stand the eternal sapping of wasteful extravagance, engendered and stimulated by the baleful passion of envy. In less than ten years from the hatching of the diabolical conspiracy of these three wicked women against the supremacy of the excellent St. Nicholas, their spendthrift rivalship had ruined the fortunes of their husbands, and entailed upon themselves misery and remorse. Rich Amos Shuttle became at last as poor as a church-mouse.

and would have been obliged to take to the loom again in his old age, had not Johnny, now rich, and a worshipful magistrate of the city, afforded him and his better half a generous shelter under his own happy roof. Mrs. Hubblebubble and Mrs. Doubletrouble had scarcely time to condole with Mrs. Shuttle, and congratulate each other, when their husbands went the way of all flesh; that is to say, failed for a few tens of thousands, and called their creditors together to hear the good news. The two wicked women lived long enough after this to repent of their offense against St. Nicholas; but they never imported any more French curtains, and at last perished miserably in an attempt to set the fashions in Pennypot Alley. . . .

Such was the terrible revenge of St. Nicholas, which ought to be a warning to all who attempt to set themselves up against the venerable customs of their ancestors, and backslide from the hallowed institutions of the blessed Saint, to whose good offices, without doubt, it is owing, that this his favorite city has transcended all others of the universe in beautiful damsels, valorous young men, mince-pies, and New-year cookies. . . .

HOW SANTA CLAUS CAME TO SIMPSON'S BAR

By Bret Harte

IT had been raining in the valley of the Sacramento. The North Fork had overflowed its banks, and Rattlesnake Creek was impassable. The few boulders that had marked the summer ford at Simpson's Crossing were obliterated by a vast sheet of water stretching to the foothills. The up stage was stopped at Grangers; the last mail had been abandoned in the *tules,* the rider swimming for his life.

Nor was the weather any better in the foothills. The mud lay deep on the mountain road; the way to Simpson's Bar was indicated by broken-down teams and hard swearing. And farther on, cut off and inaccessible, rained upon and bedraggled, smitten by high winds and threatened by high water, Simpson's Bar, on the eve of Christmas day, 1862, clung like a swallow's nest to the rocky entablature and splintered capitals of Table Mountain, and shook in the blast.

As night shut down on the settlement, a few lights gleamed through the mist from the windows of cabins on either side of the highway. Happily most of the population were gathered at Thompson's store, clustered around a red-hot stove, at which they silently spat in some accepted sense of social communion that perhaps rendered conversation unnecessary.

Even the sudden splashing of hoofs before the door did not arouse them. Dick Bullen alone paused in the act of scraping out his pipe, and lifted his head, but no other one of the group indicated any interest in, or recognition of, the man who entered.

It was a figure familiar enough to the company, and known in Simpson's Bar as "The Old Man." A man of perhaps fifty years; grizzled and scant of hair, but still fresh and youthful of complexion. A face full of ready, but not very powerful sympathy, with a chameleon-like aptitude for taking on the shade and color of contiguous moods and feelings. He had evidently just left some hilarious companions, and did not at first notice the gravity of the group, but clapped the shoulder of the nearest man jocularly, and threw himself into a vacant chair.

"Jest heard the best thing out, boys! Ye know Smiley, over yar— Jim Smiley—funniest man in the Bar? Well, Jim was jest telling the richest yarn about ——"

"Smiley's a —— fool," interrupted a gloomy voice.

"A particular —— skunk," added another in sepulchral accents.

A silence followed these positive statements. The Old Man glanced quickly around the group. Then his face slowly changed. "That's so," he said, reflectively, after a pause, "certingly a sort of a skunk and suthin' of a fool. In course." He was silent for a moment as in painful contemplation of the unsavoriness and folly of the unpopular Smiley. "Dismal weather, ain't it?" he added, now fully embarked on the current of prevailing sentiment. "Mighty rough papers on the boys, and no show for money this season. And tomorrow's Christmas."

There was a movement among the men at this announcement, but whether of satisfaction or disgust was not plain. "Yes," continued the Old Man in the lugubrious tone he had, within the last few moments, unconsciously adopted—"yes, Christmas, and tonight's Christmas Eve. Ye see, boys, I kinder thought—that is, I sorter had an idee, jest passin' like, you know—that maybe ye'd all like to come over to my house tonight and have a sort of tear 'round. But I suppose, now, you wouldn't? Don't feel like it, maybe?" he added with anxious sympathy, peering into the faces of his companions.

"Well, I don't know," responded Tom Flynn with some cheerfulness. "P'r'aps we may. But how about your wife, Old Man? What does *she* say to it?"

The Old Man hesitated. His conjugal experience had not been a happy one, and the fact was known to Simpson's Bar. His first wife, a delicate, pretty little woman, had suffered keenly and secretly from the jealous suspicions of her husband, until one day he invited the whole Bar to his house to expose her infidelity. On arriving, the party found the shy, petite creature quietly engaged in her household duties, and retired abashed and discomfited. But the sensitive woman did not easily recover from the shock of this extraordinary outrage. It was with difficulty she regained her equanimity sufficiently to release her lover from the closet in which he was concealed and escape with him. She left a boy of three years to comfort her bereaved husband. The Old Man's present wife had been his cook. She was large, loyal, and aggressive.

Before he could reply, Joe Dimmick suggested with great directness that it was the "Old Man's house," and that, invoking the Divine Power, if the case were his own, he would invite whom he pleased, even if in so doing he imperiled his salvation. The Powers of Evil, he further remarked, should contend against him vainly. All this delivered with a terseness and vigor lost in this necessary translation.

"In course. Certainly. Thet's it," said the Old Man with a sympathetic frown. "Thar's no trouble about *thet*. It's my own house, built every stick on it myself. Don't you be afeard o' her, boys. She *may* cut up a trifle rough—ez wimmin do—but she'll come 'round."

Secretly the Old Man trusted to the exaltation of liquor and power of courageous example to sustain him in such an emergency.

As yet, Dick Bullen, the oracle and leader of Simpson's Bar, had not spoken. He now took his pipe from his lips. "Old Man, how's that yer Johnny gettin' on? Seems to me he didn't look so peart last time I seed him on the bluff heavin' rocks at Chinamen. Didn't seem to take much interest in it. Thar was a gang of 'em by yar yesterday—drownded out up the river—and I kinder thought o' Johnny, and how he'd miss 'em! Maybe, now, we'd be in the way ef he wus sick?"

The father, evidently touched not only by this pathetic picture of Johnny's deprivation, but by the considerate delicacy of the speaker, hastened to assure him that Johnny was better and that a "little fun might 'liven him up." Whereupon Dick arose, shook himself, and saying, "I'm ready. Lead the way, Old Man: here goes," himself led the way with a leap, a characteristic howl, and darted out into the night. As he passed through the outer room he caught up a blazing brand from the hearth. The action was repeated by the rest of the party, closely following and elbowing each other, and before the astonished proprietor of Thompson's grocery was aware of the intention of his guests, the room was deserted.

The night was pitchy dark. In the first gust of wind their temporary torches were extinguished, and only the red brands dancing and flitting in the gloom like drunken will-o'-the-wisps indicated their whereabouts. Their way led up Pine-Tree Cañon, at the head of which a broad, low, bark-thatched cabin burrowed in the mountainside. It was the home of the Old Man, and the entrance to the tunnel in which he worked when he worked at all. Here the crowd paused for a moment, out of delicate deference to their host, who came up panting in the rear.

"P'r'aps ye'd better hold on a second out yer, whilst I go in and see thet things is all right," said the Old Man, with an indifference he was far from feeling. The suggestion was graciously accepted, the door opened and closed on the host, and the crowd, leaning their backs against the wall and cowering under the eaves, waited and listened.

For a few moments there was no sound but the dripping of water from the eaves, and the stir and rustle of wrestling boughs above them. Then the men became uneasy, and whispered suggestion and suspicion passed from the one to the other. "Reckon she's caved in his head the first lick!" "Decoyed him inter the tunnel and barred him up, likely." "Got him down and sittin' on him." "Prob'ly b'ilin' suthin' to heave on us: stand clear the door, boys!" For just then the latch clicked, the door slowly opened, and a voice said, "Come in out o' the wet."

The voice was neither that of the Old Man nor of his wife. It was the voice of a small boy, its weak treble broken by that preternatural hoarseness which only vagabondage and the habit of premature self-assertion can give. It was the face of a small boy that looked up at theirs—a face that might have been pretty and even refined but that it was darkened by evil knowledge from within, and dirt and hard experience from without. He had a blanket around his shoulders and had evidently just risen from his bed. "Come in," he repeated, "and don't make no noise. The Old Man's in there talking to mar," he continued, pointing to an adjacent room which seemed to be a kitchen, from which the Old Man's voice came in deprecating accents. "Let me be," he added, querulously, to Dick Bullen, who had caught him up, blanket and all, and was affecting to toss him into the fire, "let go o' me, you d——d old fool, d'ye hear?"

Thus adjured, Dick Bullen lowered Johnny to the ground with a smothered laugh, while the men, entering quietly, ranged themselves around a long table of rough boards which occupied the center of the room. Johnny then gravely proceeded to a cupboard and brought out several articles which he deposited on the table. "Thar's whisky. And crackers. And red herons. And cheese." He took a bite of the latter on his way to the table. "And sugar." He scooped up a mouthful en route with a small and very dirty hand. "And terbacker. Thar's dried appils too on the shelf, but I don't admire 'em. Appils is swellin'. Thar," he concluded, "now wade in, and don't be afeard. *I* don't mind the old woman. She don't b'long to *me*. S'long."

He had stepped to the threshold of a small room, scarcely larger than a closet, partitioned off from the main apartment, and holding in its dim recess a small bed. He stood there a moment looking at the company, his bare feet peeping from the blanket, and nodded.

"Hello, Johnny! You ain't goin' to turn in ag'in, are ye?" said Dick.

"Yes, I are," responded Johnny, decidedly.

"Why, wot's up, old fellow?"

"I'm sick."

"How sick?"

"I've got a fevier. And childblains. And roomatiz," returned Johnny, and vanished within. After a moment's pause, he added in the dark, apparently from under the bedclothes, "And biles!"

There was an embarrassing silence. The men looked at each other, and at the fire. Even with the appetizing banquet before them, it seemed as if they might again fall into the despondency of Thompson's grocery, when the voice of the Old Man, incautiously lifted, came deprecatingly from the kitchen.

"Certainly! Thet's so. In course they is. A gang o' lazy drunken loafers, and that ar Dick Bullen's the orneriest of all. Didn't hev no more *sabe* than to come round yar with sickness in the house and no provision. Thet's what I said: 'Bullen, sez I, 'it's crazy drunk you are, or a fool,' sez I, 'to think o' such a thing.' 'Staples, I sez, be you a man, Staples, and 'spect to raise h-ll under my roof and invalids lyin' round?' But they would come—they would. Thet's wot you must 'spect o' such trash as lays round the Bar."

A burst of laughter from the men followed this unfortunate exposure. Whether it was overheard in the kitchen, or whether the Old Man's irate companion had just then exhausted all other modes of expressing her contemptuous indignation, I cannot say, but a back door was suddenly slammed with great violence. A moment later and the Old Man reappeared, haply unconscious of the cause of the late hilarious outburst, and smiled blandly.

"The old woman thought she'd jest run over to Mrs. McFadden's for a sociable call," he explained, with jaunty indifference, as he took a seat at the board.

Oddly enough, it needed this untoward incident to relieve the embarrassment that was beginning to be felt by the party, and their natural audacity returned with their host. I do not propose to record the convivialities of that evening. The inquisitive reader will accept the statement that the conversation was characterized by the same intellectual exaltation, the same cautious reverence, the same fastidious delicacy, the same rhetorical precision, and the same logical and coherent discourse somewhat later in the evening, which distinguish similar gatherings of the masculine sex in more civilized localities and under more favorable auspices. No glasses were broken in the absence of any; no liquor was uselessly spilled on floor or table in the scarcity of that article.

It was nearly midnight when the festivities were interrupted. "Hush," said Dick Bullen, holding up his hand. It was the querulous voice of Johnny from his adjacent closet: "Oh, dad!"

The Old Man arose hurriedly and disappeared in the closet. Presently he reappeared. "His rheumatiz is coming on ag'in bad," he explained, "and he wants rubbin'." He lifted the demijohn of whisky from the table and shook it. It was empty. Dick Bullen put down his tin cup with an embarrassed laugh. So did the others. The Old Man examined their contents and said, hopefully, "I reckon that's enough; he don't need much. You hold on, all o' you, for a spell, and I'll be back"; and vanished in the closet with an old flannel shirt and the whisky. The door closed but imperfectly, and the following dialogue was distinctly audible:

"Now, sonny, whar does she ache worst?"

"Sometimes over yar and sometimes under yer; but it's most powerful from yer to yer. Rub yer, dad."

A silence seemed to indicate a brisk rubbing. Then Johnny:

"Hevin' a good time out yer, dad?"

"Yes, sonny."

"Tomorrer's Chrismiss; ain't it?"

"Yes, sonny. How does she feel now?"

"Better. Rub a little furder down. Wot's Chrismiss, anyway? Wot's it all about?"

"Oh, it's a day."

This exhaustive definition was apparently satisfactory, for there was a silent interval of rubbing. Presently Johnny again:

"Mar sez that everywhere else but yer everybody gives things to everybody Chrismiss, and then she jist waded inter you. She sez thar's a man they call Sandy Claws, not a white man, you know, but a kind o' Chinemin, comes down the chimbley night afore Chrismiss and gives things to chillern—boys like me. Puts 'em in their butes. Thet's what she tried to play upon me. Easy now, pop, whar are you rubbin' to; thet's a mile from the place. She jest made that up, didn't she, jest to aggrewate me and you? Don't rub thar. . . . Why, dad!"

In the great quiet that seemed to have fallen upon the house the sigh of the near pines and the drip of leaves without were very distinct. Johnny's voice, too, was lowered as he went on: "Don't you take on now, fur I'm gettin' all right fast. Wot's the boys doin' out thar?"

The Old Man partly opened the door and peered through. His guests were sitting there sociably enough, and there were a few silver coins and a lean buckskin purse on the table. "Bettin' on suthin— some little game or 'nother. They're all right," he replied to Johnny, and recommenced his rubbing.

"I'd like to take a hand and win some money," said Johnny, reflectively, after a pause.

The Old Man glibly repeated what was evidently a familiar formula, that if Johnny would wait until he struck it rich in the tunnel he'd have lots of money, etc., etc.

"Yes," said Johnny, "but you don't. And whether you strike it or I win it, it's about the same. It's all luck. But it's mighty cur'o's about Chrismiss, ain't it? Why do they call it Chrismiss?"

Perhaps from some instinctive deference to the overhearing of his guests, or from some vague sense of incongruity, the Old Man's reply was so low as to be inaudible beyond the room.

"Yes," said Johnny, with some slight abatement of interest, "I've heard o' *him* before. Thar, that 'll do, dad. I don't ache near so bad as I did. Now wrap me tight in this yer blanket. So. Now," he added in a muffled whisper, "sit down yer by me till I go asleep." To assure himself of obedience, he disengaged one hand from the blanket and, grasping his father's sleeve, again composed himself to rest.

For some moments the Old Man waited patiently. Then the unwonted stillness of the house excited his curiosity, and without moving from the bed, he cautiously opened the door with his disengaged hand, and looked into the main room. To his infinite surprise it was dark and deserted. But even then a smoldering log on the hearth broke, and by the upspringing blaze he saw the figure of Dick Bullen sitting by the dying embers.

"Hello!"

Dick started, rose, and came somewhat unsteadily toward him.

"Whar's the boys?" said the Old Man.

"Gone up the cañon on a little *pasear*. They're coming back for me in a minit. I'm waitin' round for 'em. What are you you starin' at, Old Man?" he added, with a forced laugh. "Do you think I'm drunk?"

The Old Man might have been pardoned the supposition, for Dick's eyes were humid and his face flushed. He loitered and lounged back to the chimney, yawned, shook himself, buttoned up his coat, and laughed. "Liquor ain't so plenty as that, Old Man. Now don't you git up," he continued, as the Old Man made a movement to release his sleeve from Johnny's hand. "Don't you mind manners. Sit jest whar you be; I'm goin' in a jiffy. Thar, that's them now."

There was a low tap at the door. Dick Bullen opened it quickly, nodded "good night" to his host, and disappeared. The Old Man would have followed him but for the hand that still unconsciously grasped his sleeve. He could have easily disengaged it: it was small, weak, and emaciated. But perhaps because it *was* small, weak, and emaciated, he changed his mind, and, drawing his chair closer to the bed, rested his head upon it. The room flickered and faded before his eyes, reappeared, faded again, went out, and left him—asleep.

Meantime Dick Bullen, closing the door, confronted his companions.

"Are you ready?" said Staples.

"Ready," said Dick. "What's the time?"

"Past twelve," was the reply.

"Can you make it?—it's nigh on fifty miles, the round trip hither and yon."

"I reckon," returned Dick, shortly. "Whar's the mare?"

"Bill and Jack's holdin' her at the crossin'."

"Let 'em hold on a minit longer," said Dick.

He turned and re-entered the house softly. By the light of the guttering candle and dying fire he saw that the door of the little room was open. He stepped toward it on tiptoe and looked in. The Old Man had fallen back in his chair, snoring, his helpless feet thrust out in a line with his collapsed shoulders, and his hat pulled over his eyes. Beside him, on a narrow wooden bedstead, lay Johnny, muffled tightly in a blanket that hid all save a strip of forehead and a few curls damp with perspiration. Dick Bullen made a step forward, hesitated, and glanced over his shoulder into the deserted room. Everything was quiet. With a sudden resolution he parted his huge mustaches with both hands and stooped over the sleeping boy. But even as he did so a mischievous blast, lying in wait, swooped down the chimney, rekindled the hearth, and lit up the room with a shameless glow from which Dick fled in bashful terror.

His companions were already waiting for him at the crossing. Two of them were struggling in the darkness with some strange misshapen bulk, which, as Dick came nearer, took the semblance of a great yellow horse.

It was the mare. She was not a pretty picture. From her Roman nose to her rising haunches, from her arched spine hidden by the stiff *machillas* of a Mexican saddle, to her thick, straight, bony legs, there was not a line of equine grace. In her half-blind but wholly vicious white eyes, in her protruding under lip, in her monstrous color, there was nothing but ugliness and vice.

"Now then," said Staples, "stand cl'ar of her heels, boys, and up with you. Don't miss your first holt of her mane, and mind ye get your off stirrup *quick*. Ready!"

There was a leap, a scrambling struggle, a bound, a wild retreat of the crowd, a circle of flying hoofs, two springless leaps that jarred the

earth, a rapid play and jingle of spurs, a plunge and then the voice of
Dick somewhere in the darkness, "All right!"

A splash, a spark struck from the ledge in the road, a clatter in
the rocky cut beyond, and Dick was gone.

Sing, O Muse, the ride of Richard Bullen! Sing, O Muse, of chivalrous men! the sacred quest, the doughty deeds, the battery of low
churls, the fearsome ride and grewsome perils of the Flower of Simpson's Bar! Alack! she is dainty, this Muse! She will have none of this
bucking brute and swaggering, ragged rider, and I must fain follow
him in prose, afoot!

It was one o'clock, and yet he had only gained Rattlesnake Hill.
For in that time Jovita had rehearsed to him all her imperfections and
practiced all her vices. Thrice had she thrown up her Roman nose in
a straight line with the reins, and, resisting bit and spur, struck out
madly across country. Twice had she reared, and, rearing, fallen backward; and twice had the agile Dick, unharmed, regained his seat before she found her vicious legs again. And a mile beyond them, at
the foot of a long hill, was Rattlesnake Creek. Dick knew that here was
the crucial test of his ability to perform his enterprise, set his teeth
grimly, put his knees well into her flanks, and changed his defensive
tactics to brisk aggression. Bullied and maddened, Jovita began the
descent of the hill. Here the artful Richard pretended to hold her in
with ostentatious objurgation and well-feigned cries of alarm. It is
unnecessary to add that Jovita instantly ran away. Nor need I state
the time made in the descent; it is written in the chronicles of Simpson's Bar. Enough that in another moment, as it seemed to Dick, she
was splashing on the overflowed banks of Rattlesnake Creek. As Dick
expected, the momentum she had acquired carried her beyond the
point of balking, and, holding her well together for a mighty leap,
they dashed into the middle of the swiftly flowing current. A few moments of kicking, wading, and swimming, and Dick drew a long breath
on the opposite bank.

The road from Rattlesnake Creek to Red Mountain was tolerably
level. Either the plunge in Rattlesnake Creek had dampened her bale-

ful fire, or the art which led to it had shown her the superior wickedness of her rider, for Jovita no longer wasted her surplus energy in wanton conceits. Hollows, ditches, gravelly deposits, patches of freshly springing grasses, flew from beneath her rattling hoofs. She began to smell unpleasantly, once or twice she coughed slightly, but there was no abatement of her strength or speed. By two o'clock he had passed Red Mountain and begun the descent to the plain. At half past two Dick rose in his stirrups with a great shout. Stars were glittering through the rifted clouds, and beyond him, out of the plain, rose two spires, a flagstaff, and a straggling line of black objects. Dick jingled his spurs and swung his *riata,* Jovita bounded forward, and in another moment they swept into Tuttleville and drew up before the wooden piazza of "The Hotel of All Nations."

What transpired that night at Tuttleville is not strictly a part of this record. Briefly I may state, however, that after Jovita had been handed over to a sleepy ostler, whom she at once kicked into unpleasant consciousness, Dick sallied out with the barkeeper for a tour of the sleeping town. Lights still gleamed from a few saloons and gambling houses; but, avoiding these, they stopped before several closed shops, and by persistent tapping and judicious outcry roused the proprietors from their beds, and made them unbar the doors of their magazines and expose their wares. Sometimes they were met by curses, but oftener by interest and some concern in their needs, and the interview was invariably concluded by a drink. It was three o'clock before this pleasantry was given over, and with a small waterproof bag of India-rubber strapped on his shoulders Dick returned to the hotel. But here he was waylaid by Beauty—Beauty opulent in charms, affluent in dress, persuasive in speech, and Spanish in accent! In vain she repeated the invitation in "Excelsior," happily scorned by all Alpine-climbing youth, and rejected by this child of the Sierras—a rejection softened in this instance by a laugh and his last gold coin. And then he sprang to the saddle and dashed down the lonely street and out into the lonelier plain, where presently the lights, the black line of houses, the spires, and the flagstaff sank into the earth behind him again and were lost in the distance.

The storm had cleared away, the air was brisk and cold, the outlines of adjacent landmarks were distinct, but it was half past four before Dick reached the meeting-house and the crossing of the county road. To avoid the rising grade he had taken a longer and more circuitous road, in whose viscid mud Jovita sank fetlock deep at every bound. It was a poor preparation for a steady ascent of five miles more; but Jovita, gathering her legs under her, took it with her usual blind, unreasoning fury, and a half-hour later reached the long level that led to Rattlesnake Creek. Another half-hour would bring him to the creek. He threw the reins lightly upon the neck of the mare, chirruped to her, and began to sing.

Suddenly Jovita shied with a bound that would have unseated a less practiced rider. Hanging to her rein was a figure that had leaped from the bank, and at the same time from the road before her arose a shadowy horse and rider. "Throw up your hands," commanded this second apparition, with an oath.

Dick felt the mare tremble, quiver, and apparently sink under him. He knew what it meant and was prepared.

"Stand aside, Jack Simpson. I know you, you d——d thief. Let me pass or ——"

He did not finish the sentence. Jovita rose straight in the air with a terrific bound, throwing the figure from her bit with a single shake of her vicious head, and charged with deadly malevolence down on the impediment before her. An oath, a pistol-shot, horse and highwayman rolled over in the road, and the next moment Jovita was a hundred yards away. But the good right arm of her rider, shattered by a bullet, dropped helplessly at his side.

Without slacking his speed he shifted the reins to his left hand. But a few moments later he was obliged to halt and tighten the saddle-girths that had slipped in the onset. This in his crippled condition took some time. He had no fear of pursuit, but looking up he saw that the eastern stars were already paling, and that the distant peaks had lost their ghostly whiteness, and now stood out blackly against a lighter sky. Day was upon him. Then completely absorbed in a single idea, he forgot the pain of his wound, and mounting again dashed on toward Rattlesnake Creek. But now Jovita's breath came broken by gasps, Dick reeled in his saddle, and brighter and brighter grew the sky.

Ride, Richard; run, Jovita; linger, O day!

For the last few rods there was a roaring in his ears. Was it exhaustion from loss of blood, or what? He was dazed and giddy as he swept down the hill, and did not recognize his surroundings. Had he taken the wrong road, or was this Rattlesnake Creek?

It was. But the brawling creek he had swam a few hours before had risen, more than doubled its volume, and now rolled a swift and resistless river between him and Rattlesnake Hill. For the first time that night Richard's heart sank within him. The river, the mountain, the quickening east, swam before his eyes. He shut them to recover his self-control. In that brief interval, by some fantastic mental process, the little room at Simpson's Bar and the figures of the sleeping father and son rose upon him. He opened his eyes wildly, cast off his coat, pistol, boots, and saddle, bound his precious pack tightly to his shoulders, grasped the bare flanks of Jovita with his bared knees, and with a shout dashed into the yellow water. A cry rose from the opposite bank as the head of a man and horse struggled for a few moments against the battling current, and then were swept away amidst uprooted trees and whirling driftwood.

The Old Man started and woke. The fire on the hearth was dead, the candle in the outer room flickering in its socket, and somebody was rapping at the door. He opened it, but fell back with a cry before the dripping, half-naked figure that reeled against the doorpost.

"Dick?"

"Hush! Is he awake yet?"

"No,—but, Dick? ——"

"Dry up, you old fool! Get me some whisky *quick!*" The Old Man flew and returned with—an empty bottle! Dick would have sworn, but his strength was not equal to the occasion. He staggered, caught at the handle of the door, and motioned to the Old Man.

"Thar's suthin' in my pack yer for Johnny. Take it off. I can't."

The Old Man unstrapped the pack and laid it before the exhausted man.

"Open it, quick!"

He did so with trembling fingers. It contained only a few poor toys —cheap and barbaric enough, goodness knows, but bright with paint and tinsel. One of them was broken; another, I fear, was irretrievably ruined by water; and on the third—ah me! there was a cruel spot.

"It don't look like much, that's a fact," said Dick, ruefully, "but it's the best we could do. . . . Take 'em, Old Man, and put 'em in his stocking, and tell him—tell him, you know. . . . Hold me, Old Man—" The Old Man caught at his sinking figure. "Tell him"— said Dick, with a weak little laugh, "tell him Sandy Claus has come."

And even so, bedraggled, ragged, unshaven, and unshorn, with one arm hanging helplessly at his side, Santa Claus came to Simpson's Bar and fell fainting on the first threshold. The Christmas dawn came slowly after, touching the remoter peaks with the rosy warmth of ineffable love. And it looked so tenderly on Simpson's Bar that the whole mountain, as if caught in a generous action, blushed to the skies.

THE ERRORS OF SANTA CLAUS

By Stephen Leacock

IT was Christmas Eve.

The Browns, who lived in the adjoining house, had been dining with the Joneses.

Brown and Jones were sitting over wine and walnuts at the table. The others had gone upstairs.

"What are you giving to your boy for Christmas?" asked Brown.

"A train," said Jones, "new kind of thing—automatic."

"Let's have a look at it," said Brown.

Jones fetched a parcel from the sideboard and began unwrapping it.

"Ingenious thing, isn't it?" he said, "goes on its own rails. Queer how kids love to play with trains, isn't it?"

"Yes," assented Brown, "how are the rails fixed?"

"Wait, I'll show you," said Jones, "just help me to shove these dinner things aside and roll back the cloth. There! See! You lay the rails like that and fasten them at the ends, so—"

"Oh, yes, I catch on, makes a grade, doesn't it? Just the thing to amuse a child, isn't it? I got Willie a toy aeroplane."

"I know, they're great. I got Edwin one on his birthday. But I thought I'd get him a train this time. I told him Santa Claus was going to bring him something altogether new this time. Edwin, of course, believes in Santa Claus absolutely. Say, look at this locomotive, would you? It has a spring coiled up inside the fire box."

"Wind her up," said Brown with great interest, "let's see her go."

"All right," said Jones, "just pile up two or three plates or something to lean the end of the rails on. There, notice the way it buzzes before it starts. Isn't that a great thing for a kid, eh?"

"Yes," said Brown, "and say! see this little string to pull the whistle. By Gad, it toots, eh? Just like real?"

"Now then, Brown," Jones went on, "you hitch on those cars and I'll start her. I'll be engineer, eh!"

Half an hour later Brown and Jones were still playing trains on the dining-room table.

But their wives upstairs in the drawing room hardly noticed their absence. They were too much interested.

"Oh, I think it's perfectly sweet," said Mrs. Brown, "just the loveliest doll I've seen in years. I must get one like it for Ulvina. Won't Clarisse be perfectly enchanted?"

"Yes," answered Mrs. Jones, "and then she'll have all the fun of arranging the dresses. Children love that so much. Look! there are three little dresses with the doll, aren't they cute? All cut out and ready to stitch together."

"Oh, how perfectly lovely," exclaimed Mrs. Brown, "I think the mauve one would suit the doll best—don't you?—with such golden hair—only don't you think it would make it much nicer to turn back the collar, so, and to put a little band—so?"

"*What* a good idea!" said Mrs. Jones, "do let's try it. Just wait, I'll get a needle in a minute. I'll tell Clarisse that Santa Claus sewed it himself. The child believes in Santa Claus absolutely."

And half an hour later Mrs. Jones and Mrs. Brown were so busy stitching dolls' clothes that they could not hear the roaring of the little train up and down the dining table, and had no idea what the four children were doing.

Nor did the children miss their mothers.

"Dandy, aren't they?" Edwin Jones was saying to little Willie Brown, as they sat in Edwin's bedroom. "A hundred in a box, with cork tips, and see, an amber mouthpiece that fits into a little case at the side. Good present for dad, eh?"

"Fine!" said Willie, appreciatively, "I'm giving father cigars."

"I know, I thought of cigars too. Men always like cigars and cigarettes. You can't go wrong on them. Say, would you like to try one or two of these cigarettes? We can take them from the bottom. You'll like them, they're Russian,—away ahead of Egyptian."

"Thanks," answered Willie. "I'd like one immensely. I only started smoking last spring—on my twelfth birthday. I think a feller's a fool to begin smoking cigarettes too soon, don't you? It stunts him. I waited till I was twelve."

"Me too," said Edwin, as they lighted their cigarettes. "In fact, I wouldn't buy them now if it weren't for dad. I simply *had* to give him something from Santa Claus. He believes in Santa Claus absolutely, you know."

And while this was going on, Clarisse was showing little Ulvina the absolutely lovely little bridge set that she got for her mother. "Aren't these markers perfectly charming?" said Ulvina, "and don't you love this little Dutch design—or is it Flemish, darling?"

"Dutch," said Clarisse, "isn't it quaint? And aren't these the dearest little things—for putting the money in when you play. I needn't have got them with it—they'd have sold the rest separately—but I think it's too utterly slow playing without money, don't you?"

"Oh, abominable," shuddered Ulvina, "but your mamma never plays for money, does she?"

"Mamma! Oh, gracious, no. Mamma's far too slow for that. But I shall tell her that Santa Claus insisted on putting in the little money boxes."

"I suppose she believes in Santa Claus, just as my Mamma does."

"Oh, absolutely," said Clarisse, and added, "What if we play a little game! With a double dummy, the French way, or Norwegian Skat, if you like. That only needs two."

"All right," agreed Ulvina, and in a few minutes they were deep in a game of cards with a little pile of pocket money beside them.

About half an hour later, all the members of the two families were down again in the drawing room. But of course nobody said anything about the presents. In any case they were all too busy looking at the beautiful big Bible, with maps in it, that the Joneses had bought to give to Grandfather. They all agreed that with the help of it, Grandfather could hunt up any place in Palestine in a moment, day or night.

But up stairs, away upstairs in a sitting room of his own, Grandfather Jones was looking with an affectionate eye at the presents that stood beside him. There was a beautiful whiskey decanter, with silver filigree outside (and whiskey inside) for Jones, and for the little boy a big nickel-plated Jew's harp.

Later on, far in the night, the person, or the influence, or whatever it is called Santa Claus, took all the presents and placed them in the people's stockings.

And, being blind as he always has been, he gave the wrong things to the wrong people—in fact, he gave them just as indicated above.

But the next day, in the course of Christmas morning, the situation straightened itself out, just as it always does.

Indeed, by ten o'clock, Brown and Jones were playing with the train, and Mrs. Brown and Mrs. Jones were making dolls' clothes, and the boys were smoking cigarettes, and Clarisse and Ulvina were playing cards for their pocket money.

And upstairs—away up—Grandfather was drinking whiskey and playing the Jew's harp.

And so Christmas, just as it always does, turned out all right after all.

JOLLY OLD SAINT NICHOLAS

Jolly old Saint Nicholas,
   Lean your ear this way!
Don't you tell a single soul
   What I'm going to say;
Christmas Eve is coming soon;
   Now you dear old man,
Whisper what you'll bring to me;
   Tell me if you can.

When the clock is striking twelve,
   When I'm fast asleep,
Down the chimney broad and black,
   With your pack you'll creep;
All the stockings you will find
   Hanging in a row;
Mine will be the shortest one,
   You'll be sure to know.

Johnny wants a pair of skates;
   Susy wants a sled;
Nellie wants a picture book;
   Yellow, blue and red;
Now I think I'll leave to you
   What to give the rest;
Choose for me, dear Santa Claus,
   You will know the best.

OLD SONG

SLY SANTA CLAUS

All the house was asleep,
　And the fire burning low,
When, from far up the chimney,
　Came down a "Ho! ho!"
And a little, round man,
　With a terrible scratching,
Dropped into the room
　With a wink that was catching.
Yes, down he came, bumping,
And thumping, and jumping,
　And picking himself up without sign of a bruise!

"Ho! ho!" he kept on,
　As if bursting with cheer.
"Good children, gay children,
　Glad children, see here!
I have brought you fine dolls,
　And gay trumpets, and rings,
Noah's arks, and bright skates,
　And a host of good things!
I have brought a whole sackful,
A packful, a hackful!
　Come hither, come hither, come hither and choose!

"Ho! ho! What is this?
　Why, they all are asleep!
But their stockings are up,
　And my presents will keep!
So, in with the candies,
　The books, and the toys;

All the goodies I have
   For the good girls and boys.
I'll ram them, and jam them,
And slam them, and cram them;
   All the stockings will hold while the tired youngsters snooze."

All the while his round shoulders
   Kept ducking and ducking;
And his little, fat fingers
   Kept tucking and tucking;
Until every stocking
   Bulged out, on the wall,
As if it were bursting,
   And ready to fall.
And then, all at once,
   With a whisk and a whistle,
And twisting himself
   Like a tough bit of gristle,
He bounced up again,
   Like the down of a thistle,
     And nothing was left but the prints of his shoes.

                  MRS. C. S. STONE

A VISIT FROM ST. NICHOLAS

'Twas the night before Christmas, when all through the house
Not a creature was stirring, not even a mouse;
The stockings were hung by the chimney with care,
In hopes that St. Nicholas soon would be there;
The children were nestled all snug in their beds,
While visions of sugar-plums danced through their heads;
And mamma in her kerchief, and I in my cap,
Had just settled our brains for a long winter's nap,—

When out on the lawn there arose such a clatter,
I sprang from my bed to see what was the matter.
Away to the window I flew like a flash,
Tore open the shutters and threw up the sash.
The moon, on the breast of the new-fallen snow,
Gave a lustre of midday to objects below;
When what to my wondering eyes should appear,
But a miniature sleigh and eight tiny reindeer,
With a little old driver, so lively and quick
I knew in a moment it must be St. Nick.
More rapid than eagles his coursers they came,
And he whistled and shouted and called them by name:
"Now, Dasher! now, Dancer! now, Prancer and Vixen!
On, Comet! on, Cupid! on, Donder and Blitzen!
To the top of the porch, to the top of the wall!
Now, dash away, dash away, dash away all!"
As dry leaves that before the wild hurricane fly,
When they meet with an obstacle, mount to the sky,
So, up to the house-top the coursers they flew,
With a sleigh full of toys,—and St. Nicholas too.
And then in a twinkling I heard on the roof
The prancing and pawing of each little hoof,
As I drew in my head and was turning around,
Down the chimney St. Nicholas came with a bound.
He was dressed all in fur from his head to his foot,
And his clothes were all tarnished with ashes and soot;
A bundle of toys he had flung on his back,
And he looked like a pedler just opening his pack.
His eyes how they twinkled! his dimples how merry!
His cheeks were like roses, his nose like a cherry;
His droll little mouth was drawn up like a bow,
And the beard on his chin was as white as the snow.
The stump of a pipe he held tight in his teeth,
And the smoke it encircled his head like a wreath.
He had a broad face, and a little round belly

That shook, when he laughed, like a bowl full of jelly.
He was chubby and plump,—a right jolly old elf—
And I laughed when I saw him, in spite of myself.
A wink of his eye and a twist of his head
Soon gave me to know I had nothing to dread.
He spoke not a word, but went straight to his work,
And filled all the stockings; then turned with a jerk,
And laying his finger aside of his nose,
And giving a nod, up the chimney he rose.
He sprang to his sleigh, to his team gave a whistle,
And away they all flew like the down of a thistle;
But I heard him exclaim, ere he drove out of sight:
"Happy Christmas to all, and to all a goodnight!"

CLEMENT C. MOORE

READING ALOUD TO YOUNG PEOPLE

CHRISTMAS AND THE BIBLE STORY

By May Lamberton Becker

THE New Testament, it seems to me, should come first to a little child by word of mouth—preferably his mother's mouth, or his grandmother's. The natural time to begin it would be Christmas, and a natural beginning would be made in the course of preparations for the first Christmas on which the child is old enough to listen to stories and take part, if ever so small a part, in the family's Christmas ritual.

For every family that keeps Christmas at all seems to evolve, in the course of time, a sort of secular ritual that belongs to this family and no other, through which it goes every year, obscurely resenting changes. When Jo made her famous statement that "Christmas won't be Christmas without any presents," she was not regretting the trinkets and trifles she might have received—gifts never cost much in Orchard House—but protesting against this break in the March family ritual. It stays in the mind and under the mind years after it has ceased to be celebrated—for as the children grow up and marry and have families of their own they evolve a ritual of that family with only a basic resemblance to the one on which they were brought up. Somehow the memory of those family rites and observances never comes back, even to a solitary grown-up, bringing a sense of loneliness with it, but with a sense of being, as long as one is remembering, part of a company. It has so chanced that I have spent but one Christmas of all my life quite alone, and that was some years ago. As I came back to my apartment after an early dinner, there in the hall outside the door of a family that had just moved in, stood a man with a curly-headed three-year old. "Listen!" said he, *"schon klingt der Weinachtsmann!"* and sure enough just as I came level with the door I heard a little bell tinkling inside, and Mamma, who had been putting the last touches to the tree, opened wide the door. Down the hall I could see the glow of candles;

491

they shone into a rapt, upturned little face. I went on without stopping, but a long time after, when we had been for years good neighbors, I told them that all this night I had been one of their Christmas party, because I too had heard so many times the ringing of that little bell and the singing of "O Tannenbaum" before the glowing tree.

I know a family whose Christmas ritual involved reading Dickens' "Christmas Carol" aloud, all the way through by various members of the family, between Christmas and New Year's Day. My own custom, which I suggest to those who take Christmas too hard and reach it all played out, is to re-read this book every year, closing ten days before Christmas. It sets a good tone for the holidays. There should be always story-telling or reading-aloud before and during these holidays, as part of everybody's home ritual, and the Christmas story is naturally told then.

Of course an ideal way to hear it would be as I did in 1926, in Bethlehem, Pennsylvania, after dusk on any day between Christmas and New Year's. If you rang the bell of any house whose front door was wreathed with green, studded with colored lights, and surmounted by a many-pointed, star-shaped lantern, and asked to "see the Putz," you would at once be led to the place—it might be a corner of the parlor or a whole room upstairs—where under a grove of Christmas trees stood the tableau of the Nativity in little figures arranged as naïvely as in a fourteenth-century crêche. Certain features must be there: the lighted stable, the Holy Family, the shepherds, the angels, the star: but as everything is kept from generation to generation and new figures are added from time to time, the nicest Putz I saw had not only angels seventy-five years old floating from the blue-calico sky, but no less than nine Wise Men of various sizes. You may have a working waterfall in your Putz, or an electric train, so long as it is to the glory of God, but the heart of it must be at the manger and Grandmother must be ready to tell the story to any child who comes. She tells it sitting with the child under the tree. Then the visitor is given a dozen kinds of Christmas cookies that began to be baked the day after Thanksgiving—the same day that people bring out the rock-paper from the attic and look about for conveniently shaped boxes out of which to construct the terrain—and off you go after another lighted door. They told me that I could "go putzing" every evening for two weeks, if I should go even unto Bethlehem.

But if you stay in New York and on the streets and in the shops, it may be hard to keep your mind on Christmas as a religious festival, even if you theoretically hold it to be one. So far as many a city child is concerned, red-wrapped Santa Clauses, wagging their beards in every shop-window, have captured Christmas just as in New York at Easter the rabbit has routed the Resurrection. If you prefer that your child shall not be thus confused, you will have to do something about it yourself.

So if you wish to come as near as a picture-book can bring you to this friendly respect for the Christmas story, have "The Christ Child," illustrated in color by the Petershams, in the house for little children from four to eight, or for children even younger to look at and listen. You can read words familiar to you from Matthew and from Luke, telling the story as far as the visit to the Temple, while the littlest in your lap looks on at the Nativity in many colors, with quite the most ingratiating animals around the manger that ever I saw in anything but a very primitive picture. There is a glow and a tenderness about every picture in the big book: I do not know one more likely to be loved a long time.

Another picture-book seems to go along with it, though it is not especially a Christmas book: "The Lord's Prayer," pictured in lithographs drawn on stone by Ingri and Edgar Parin D'Aulaire. The Lord's Prayer has been many times "embellished with woodcuts." But no one, so far as I know, has put its petitions, without a word of explanation or homily, into pictures that translate them directly in terms of a little child's experience. The result is a book a child can love and its parents find touching, pathetic, or satisfying, according as they have kept or departed from the spirit and the faith of childhood.

The only text is the words of the prayer—there is a Protestant edition and a Catholic edition—each petition separately, in large clear lettering upon a fairly large page. Turn the leaf and there is a double-page picture in the colors of spring, illustrating these words within the limits of a child's view of life. For example, *Thy Will be Done*. Every one who has come to grips with life interprets these words in terms of his own experience, sadly or joyfully according as he has understood their meaning. No words carry a greater weight of human woe or cover a wider field of human experience. Out of all these possible experiences the artists chose one a little child takes in at the first glance—a little convalescent, tucked up in bed and in the society of a sympathetic Sealyham and kitten, but hearing through the open window, where the curtain blows, the voices of children dancing in a ring. Something in the child's face goes to the heart, for it has gone to the heart of *Fiat Voluntas Tua*—not submission to, but coöperation with, the will of God.

The one I like best is *Thy Kingdom Come*. In a sunny suburban garden in whose trees birds in their little nests agree and on whose lawn a dog is curled up comfortably with a cat, children are happily at play. The gate is open and others in darker garments are being welcomed in to share the toys. A little girl nurses her baby brother; a woman opens a cottage window to look out on sunflowers turning intently toward the sun. It is so simple, so possible—so like that Land of the Righteous that Gorky talked about. There was a man in Siberia, he said, who believed that somewhere on this earth there was a Land of the Righteous, where people were kind to one another and wished each other well. He could put up with his hard life because when things got too bad he could always pack up and start for that Land. So when some one proved to him on the map that in all the world there was no such place, he destroyed the map—and then himself. There is something so humanly possible about the D'Aulaires' little kingdom of God that it may have, to some of us, the intolerable sweetness of a lost Paradise.

An older person who distrusts his ability as a story-teller for very little children can read aloud from "A Baby's Life of Jesus Christ," by Mary Rolt, one of the simplest possible re-tellings for a quite tiny child, and get the effect of story-telling. Sir Arthur Quiller-Couch and others arranged selections from the Authorized Version, with occasional slight changes, in the book for five to seven, "The Little Children's Bible." In all these there are pictures, and there always should be in a Bible or a book of Bibles stories to which children have access, if you want them to read it for themselves. Literary autobiography is full of references to illustrated Bibles—such as the one that so enthralled Anatole France—and their effect on children who have read, so to speak, around the pictures, to find out what they were about, until if these were many they had of their own free will absorbed a good part of the narrative.

One of the most richly beautiful of recent books is "The Ageless Story," with pictures in color by the celebrated American artist Lauren Ford. The ageless story is that of the child Jesus as told in the Gospel of Luke, up to the verse, "He went down with them and came to Nazareth and was subject to them. And His mother kept all these words in her heart." The pictures are twelve in number, in four colors with gold bordering. They glow with more than the hues of ancient illuminated manuscripts, for they have the same sort of personal conviction and lively faith that make those pictures glow. Here is a Holy Family against the hilly country of Connecticut; the Magi coming in sleighs to see the baby, wrapped in a fur robe in Mary's arms while Joseph, bundled in such a sheepskin coat as farmers wear, looks lovingly upon child and mother. The Visitation shows an aged Elizabeth in a lace collar and Paisley shawl, meeting Mary on a white porch beside a patchwork-cushioned chair. The Annunciation angel appears to a girl in blue gingham shelling peas. Painters thus presented the Holy Family in ages of faith: that is, in the costume of their own time and country, not in fancy dress. Miss Ford paints in her own time, in the same spirit. She says to her god-daughter: "The Baby Jesus is born in the barn down the hill. It is because He belongs to you and me. He is living inside our hearts, just as the barn is." Above the little town of Bethlehem, Connecticut, the silent stars go by.

Opposite each picture is the music of an antiphon, handdrawn with a border in color. If these borders are combined of ancient patchwork patterns and New England daisies, I do not think those who made old designs out of flowers and patterns of their day would find anything to criticize in her choice of material.

The loveliest of the illustrated introductions to the Bible now offered directly to a child is "A First Bible," illustrated with some of the most appropriate, reverent and sympathetic full-page woodcuts—by Helen Sewell—that have been made for the Bible in our time. Flowing through its gracious pages—whose typography is so good that you notice it no more than you do a good digestion—is a running series of selections from Old and New Testaments, from Noah through Paul's speech at Mars Hill, arranged by Jean West Maury to give the effect of continuous narrative. There is no attempt to condense the Bible or even to present its essential doctrines; the scenes are those a young reader might be expected to know about in later life, scenes that by their inherent interest and beauty will lead him to go on reading for himself. The skill of the artist is used in the service of a spirit in the deepest sense religious.

I like the Old Testament stories as re-told by Sholem Asch in "In the Beginning," because he has performed the not inconsiderable feat of combining reverence with an occasional dancing humor. That is, when the story itself is funny, he makes the child laugh in glee, but he never once makes a child laugh at the story. For children old enough to read easily Frances J. Olcott has selected one hundred and fifty Bibles stories from the King James Version to form an outline of Old Testament history, omitting some words and passages not clear to a modern child.

"The Life of Our Lord," Charles Dickens' effort to express to his children what the story of Jesus meant to him, makes a determined try at reducing the New Testament to what this father thought were its essential points and concentrating on these, and conveys a sense that these points are essentially important in the life of man. It will be welcomed or otherwise by parents in proportion to their agreement with him on these essentials.

There are two illustrated versions of the whole Bible made expressly for the use of children, that have been used by them so long one can scarcely wonder that in many homes they would be, so to speak, fought for against any newcomer in the field, however good that newcomer might be—just as there is no use in trying to prove the merits of the Moffatt or the Goodchild version to a family thoroughly committed to the Authorized. These are the long-standing "Bible for Young People" and "The Children's Bible" edited by Sherman and Kent; in the first, stories are told in Bible language but grouped into subjects to give complete narratives, and in the second—which has color-pictures—"the text is that of the King James Version but in the language of the child." But Dr. Bowie, rector of Grace Church, New York, has produced a modern narrative rendering of the Old and New Testaments for young people in "The Story of the Bible" which combines so many good features in what amounts to an entirely new manner of treatment, that it should be generally brought to the attention of parents looking for an introduction that will take their children a long way. It gives the scriptural story in whatever version best gives the meaning of a particular passage, whether this is the Authorized, the Revised, the sturdy contemporary rendering of Moffatt, or Dr. Bowie's own translation, together with explanations deftly interwoven wherever needed, drawn from rich scholarship and warm love of the subject and the task. To old or young, but to the inquiring mind of youth especially, he presents the Bible as literature and as history and as something to be treasured for itself. The teens can make the most of it, but it might well be in the house ahead of the teens.

A good first book of saints is the bedtime story-book of Joan Windham, "Six O'Clock Saints" and its continuing volume. Its stories have a contemporary touch, and an affectionate understanding of a child's way of saying things or of translating to himself what is said by his elders. Thus when the Archangel Raphael visits St. Gregory disguised as a sailor and tries in vain to make the saint lose his patience, after the identity of the heavenly visitor is revealed St. Gregory says, "Wasn't it lucky that I was Forebearing and everything just when you happened to come?" "Yes," replies the archangel, "it was, rather."

Children a trifle older find the sympathetic "Ten Saints," of Eleanor Farjeon, a happy introduction. They range from the third to the fourteenth century and are accompanied by large pictures after the manner of old colored woodcuts, by Helen Sewell.

THE MONKEY'S REVENGE

By E. V. Lucas

O NCE upon a time there was a little girl named Clara Anabell Platts. She lived in Kensington, near the Gardens, and every day when it was fine she walked with Miss Hobbs round the Round Pond. Miss Hobbs was her governess. When it was wet she read a book, or as much of a book as she could, being still rather weak in the matter of long words. When she did not read she made wool-work articles for her aunts, and now and then something for her mother's birthday present, which was supposed to be a secret, but which her mother, however hard she tried not to look, always knew all about. But this did not prevent her mother, who was a very nice lady, from being extraordinarily surprised when the present was given to her. (That word "extraordinarily," by the way, is one of the words which Clara would have had to pass over if she were reading this story to herself; but you, of course, are cleverer.)

It was generally admitted by Mrs. Platts, and also by Miss Hobbs and Kate Woodley, the nurse, that Clara was a very good girl; but she had one fault which troubled them all, and that was too much readiness in saying what came into her mind. Mrs. Platts tried to check her by making her count five before she made any comment on what was happening, so that she could be sure that she really ought to say it; and Kate Woodley used often to click her tongue when Clara was rattling on; but Miss Hobbs had another and more serious remedy. She used to tell Clara to ask herself three questions before she made any of her quick little remarks. These were the questions: (1) "Is it kind?" (2) "Is it true?" (3) "Is it necessary?" If the answer to all three was "Yes," then Clara might say what she wanted to; otherwise not. The result was that when Clara and Miss Hobbs walked round the Round Pond Clara had very little to say; because, you know, if it comes to that, hardly anything is necessary.

Well, on December 20, 1907, the postman brought Mrs. Platts a letter from Clara's aunt, Miss Anabell Patterson of Chistlehurst, and it was that letter which makes this story. It began by saying that Miss Patterson would very much like Clara to have a nice Christmas present, and it went on to say that if she had been very good up to the time of buying the present, it was to cost seven-and-six, but if she had not been very good it was only to cost a shilling. This shows you the kind of aunt Miss Patterson was. For myself, I don't think that at Christmastime a matter of good or bad behavior ought to be remembered at all. And I think that everything then ought to cost seven-and-six. But Miss Patterson had her own way of doing things; and it did not really matter about the shilling at all, because, as it was agreed that Clara had been very good for a long time, Mrs. Platts (who did not admire Miss Patterson's methods any more than we do) naturally decided that unless anything still were to happen (which is very unlikely with seven-and-sixpence at stake) the present should cost seven-and-six, just as if nothing about a shilling had ever been said.

Unless anything were to happen. Ah! Everything in this story depends on that.

Clara was as good as gold all the morning, and she and Miss Hobbs marched round the Round Pond like soldiers, Miss Hobbs talking all the time and Clara as dumb as a fish. At dinner also she behaved beautifully, although the pudding was not at all what she liked; and then it was time for her mother to take her out to buy the present. So, still good, Clara ran upstairs to be dressed.

As I dare say you know, there are in Kensington High Street a great many large shops, and the largest of these, which is called Biter's, has a very nice way every December of filling one of its windows (which for the rest of the year is full of dull things, such as tables, and rolls of carpets, and coal scuttles) with such seasonable and desirable articles as boats for the Round Pond, and dolls of all sorts and sizes, and steam engines with quite a lot of rails and signals, and clockwork animals, and guns. And when you go inside you can't help hearing the gramophone.

It was into this shop that Mrs. Platts and Clara went, wondering whether they would buy just one thing that cost seven-and-six all at once or a lot of smaller things that came to seven-and-six altogether; which is one of the pleasantest problems to ponder over that this life holds. Well, everything was going splendidly, and Clara, after many changings of her minds, had just decided on a beautiful wax doll with cheeks like tulips and real black hair, when she chanced to look up and saw a funny little old gentleman come in at the door; and all in a flash she forgot her good resolutions and everything that was depending upon them, and seizing her mother's arm, and giving no thought at all to Miss Hobb's three questions, or to Kate Woodley's clicking tongue, or to counting five, she cried in a loud quick whisper, "Oh, mother, do look at that queer little man! Isn't he just like a monkey?"

Now there were two dreadful things about this speech. One, that it was made before Aunt Anabell's present had been bought, and therefore Mrs. Platts was only entitled to spend a shilling, and the other was that the little old gentleman quite clearly heard it, for his face flushed and he looked exceedingly uncomfortable. Indeed, it was an uncomfortable time for everyone, for Mrs. Platts was very unhappy to think that her little girl not only should have lost the nice doll, but also have been so rude; the little old gentleman was confused and nervous; the girl who was waiting on them was distressed when she knew what Clara's unlucky speech had cost her; and Clara herself was in a passion of tears. After some time, in which Mrs. Platts and the girl did their best to soothe her, Clara consented to receive a shilling box of chalks as her present, and was led back still sobbing. Never was there such a sad ending to an exciting expedition.

Miss Hobbs luckily had gone home; but Kate Woodley made things worse by being very sorry and clicking away like a Bee clock, and Clara hardly knew how to get through the rest of the day.

Clara's bedtime came always at a quarter to eight, and between her supper, which was at half-past six, and that hour she used to come downstairs and play with her father and mother. On this evening she was very quiet and miserable, although Mrs. Platts and Mr. Platts did all they could to cheer her; and she even committed the most extraordinary action of her life, for she said, when it was still only half-past seven, that she should like to go to bed.

And she would have gone had not at that very moment a tremendous knock sounded at the front door—so tremendous that, in spite of her unhappiness, Clara had, of course to wait and see what it was.

And what do you think it was? It was a box addressed to Mrs. Platts, and it came from Biter's, the very shop where the tragedy had occurred.

"But I haven't ordered anything," said Mrs. Platts.

"Never mind," said Mr. Platts, who had a practical mind. "Open it."

So the box was opened, and inside was a note and this is what it said:

"Dear Madam:
I am so distressed to think that I am the cause of your little girl losing her present, that I feel that there is nothing I can do but give her one myself. For if I had not been so foolish—at my age too!— as to go to Biter's this afternoon, without any real purpose but to look around, she would never have got into trouble. Biter's is for children, not for old men with queer faces. And so I beg leave to send her this doll, which I hope is the right one, and with it a few clothes and necessaries, and I am sure she will not forget how it was that she very nearly lost it altogether.
                Believe me, yours penitently,
        The-little-old-gentleman-who-really-is (as-his
        looking-glass-has-too-often-told-him) -like-a
        monkey."

To Clara this letter, when Mrs. Platts read it to her, seemed like something in a dream, but when the box was unpacked it was found to contain, truly enough, not only the identical doll which she had wanted, with cheeks like tulips and real black hair, but also frocks for it, and nightdresses and petticoats, and a card of tortoise shell toilet requisites, and three hats, and a diabolo set, and a tiny doll's parasol for Kensington Gardens on sunny days.

Poor Clara didn't know what to do, and so she simply sat down with the doll in her arms and cried again; but this was a totally different kind of crying from that which had gone before. And when Kate Woodley came to take her to bed she cried, too.

And the funny thing is that, though the little old gentleman's present looks much more like a reward for being naughty than a punishment, Clara has hardly ever since said a quick, unkind thing that she could be sorry for, and Miss Hobb's three questions are never wanted at all, and Kate Woodley has entirely given up clicking.

HOW THE GOOD GIFTS WERE USED BY TWO

By Howard Pyle

THIS is the way that this story begins: Once upon a time there was a rich brother and a poor brother, and the one lived across the street from the other.

The rich brother had all the world's gear that was good for him and more besides; as for the poor brother, why, he had hardly enough to keep soul and body together, yet he was contented with his lot, and Contentment did not sit back of the stove in the rich brother's house; wherefore in this the rich brother had less than the poor brother.

Now these things happened in the good old days when the saints used to be going hither and thither in the world upon this business and that. So one day, who should come traveling through the town where the rich brother and the poor brother lived, but Saint Nicholas himself.

Just beside the town gate stood the great house of the rich brother; thither went the saint and knocked at the door, and it was the rich brother himself who came and opened it.

Now, Saint Nicholas had had a long walk of it that day, so that he was quite covered with dust, and looked no better than he should. Therefore he seemed to be only a common beggar; and when the rich brother heard him ask for a night's lodging at his fine, great house, he gaped like a toad in a rain-storm. What! Did the traveler think that he kept a free lodging house for beggars? If he did he was bringing his grist to the wrong mill; there was no place for the likes of him in the house, and that was the truth. But yonder was a poor man's house across the street, if he went over there perhaps he could get a night's lodging and a crust of bread. That was what the rich brother said, and after he had said it he banged to the door, and left Saint Nicholas standing on the outside under the blessed sky.

So now there was nothing for good Saint Nicholas to do but to go across the street to the poor brother's house, as the other had told him to do. Rap! tap! tap! he knocked at the door, and it was the poor brother who came and opened it for him.

"Come in, come in!" says he, "come in and welcome!"

So in came Saint Nicholas, and sat himself down behind the stove where it was good and warm, while the poor man's wife spread before him all that they had in the house—a loaf of brown bread and a crock of cold water from the town fountain.

"And is that all that you have to eat?" said Saint Nicholas. Yes; that was all that they had.

"Then, maybe, I can help you to better," said Saint Nicholas. "So bring me hither a bowl and a crock."

You may guess that the poor man's wife was not long in fetching what he wanted. When they were brought the saint blessed the one and passed his hand over the other.

Then he said, "Bowl be filled!" and straightway the bowl began to boil up with a good rich meat pottage until it was full to the brim. Then the saint said, "Bowl be stilled!" and it stopped making the broth, and there stood as good as feast as man could wish for.

Then Saint Nicholas said, "Crock be filled!" and the crock began to bubble up with the best of beer. Then he said, "Crock be stilled!" and there stood as good drink as man ever poured down his throat.

Down they all sat, the saint and the poor man and the poor man's wife, and ate and drank till they could eat and drink no more, and whenever the bowl and crock grew empty, the one and the other became filled at the bidding.

The next morning the saint trudged off the way he was going, but he left behind him the bowl and the crock, so that there was no danger of hunger and thirst to that house.

Well, the world jogged along for a while, maybe a month or two, and life was as easy for the poor man and his wife as an old shoe. One day the rich brother said to his wife, "See now, luck seems to be striking our brother over there the right way; I'll just go and see what it all means."

So over the street he went, and found the poor man at home. Down he sat back of the stove and began to chatter and talk and talk and chatter, and the upshot of the matter was that bit by bit, he dragged out the whole story from the poor man. Then nothing would do but he must see the bowl and the crock at work. So the bowl and the crock were brought and set to work and—Hui! how the rich brother opened his eyes when he saw them making good broth and beer by themselves.

And now he must and would have that bowl and crock. At first the poor brother said, "No" but the other bargained and bargained until, at last, the poor man consented to let him have the two for a hundred dollars. So the rich brother paid down the hundred dollars, and off he marched with what he wanted.

When the next day had come, the rich brother said to his wife, "Never you mind about the dinner today. Go you into the harvest field and I will see to the dinner." So off went the wife with the harvesters, and the husband stayed at home and smoked his pipe all the morning, for he knew that the dinner would be ready at his bidding. So when noontime had come he took out the bowl and the crock, and, placing them on the table, said, "Bowl be filled! Crock be filled!" and straightway they began making broth and beer as fast as they could.

In a little while the bowl and the crock were filled, and then they could hold no more, so that the broth and the beer ran down all over the table and the floor. Then the rich brother was in a pretty pickle, for he did not know how to bid the bowl and the crock to stop from making what they were making. Out he ran and across the street to the poor man's house, and meanwhile the broth and beer filled the whole room until it could hold no more, and then ran out into the gutters so that all the pigs and dogs in town had a feast that day.

"Oh, dear brother!" cried the rich man to the poor man, "do tell me what to do or the whole town will soon be smothered in broth and beer."

But, no; the poor brother was not to be stirred in such haste; they would have to strike a bit of bargain first. So the upshot of the matter was that the rich brother had to pay the poor brother another hundred dollars to take the crock and the bowl back again.

See, now, what comes of being coveteous!

As for the poor man, he was well off in the world, for he had all that he could eat and drink, and a stockingful of money back of the stove besides.

Well, time went along as time does, and now it was Saint Christopher who was thinking about taking a little journey below.

"See, Brother," says Saint Nicholas to him, "if you chance to be jogging by yonder town, stop at the poor man's house, for there you will have a warm welcome and plenty to eat."

But when Saint Christopher came to town, the rich man's house was so much larger and finer than the poor man's house, that he thought that he would ask for lodging there.

But it fared the same with him that it did with Saint Nicholas. Prut! Did he think that the rich man kept free lodgings for beggars? And—bang!—the door was slammed in his face, and off packed the saint with a flea in his ear.

Over he went to the poor man's house, and there was a warm welcome for him, and good broth and beer from the bowl and the crock that Saint Nicholas had blessed. After he had supped he went to bed, where he slept as snug and warm as a mouse in the nest.

Then the good wife said to the husband, "See, now, the poor fellow's shirt is none too good for him to be wearing. I'll just make him another while he is sleeping, so that he'll have a decent bit of linen to wear in the morning."

So she brought her best roll of linen out of her closet and set to work stitching and sewing, and never stopped till she had made the new shirt to the last button. The next morning, when the saint awoke, there lay the nice, new, clean shirt, and he put it on and gave thanks to it.

Before he left the house the poor man took him aside, and emptied the stockingful of silver money on the table, and bade the saint take what he wanted, "for," he says, "a penny or two is never amiss in the great world."

After that it was time for the traveler to be jogging; but before he went he said, "See, now, because you have both been so kind and good to a poor wayfarer, I will give you a blessing; whatever you begin doing this morning, you shall continue doing till sunset." So saying he took up his staff and went his way.

After Saint Christopher had gone the poor man and his wife began talking together as to what would be best for them to be doing all the day, and one said one thing and the other said another, but every plug was too small for the hole, as we say in our town, for nothing seemed to fit the case.

"Come, come," said the good woman, "here we are losing time that can never be handled again. While we are talking the matter over I will be folding the linen that is left from making the shirt."

"And I," said the good man, "will be putting the money away that the holy man left behind him."

So the wife began folding the linen into a bundle again, and the man began putting away the money he had offered in charity. Thus they began doing, and thus they kept on doing; so that by the time the evening had come the whole house was full of fine linen, and every tub and bucket and mug and jug about the place was brimming with silver money. As for the good couple, their fortune was made, and that is the heart of the whole matter in four words.

That night who should come over from across the street but the rich brother, with his pipe in his mouth and his hands in his pockets. But when he saw how very rich the poor man had become all of a sudden, and what a store of fine linen and silver money he had, he was so wonder-struck that he did not know whither to look and what to think.

Dear heart's sake alive! Where did all those fine things come from? That was what he should like to know.

Oh! there was nothing to hide in the matter and the poor man told all about what had happened.

As for the rich brother, when he had found how he had shut his door in the face of good-fortune, he rapped his head with his knuckles because he was so angry at his own foolishness. However, crying never mended a jacket, so he made the poor brother promise that if either of the saints came that way again, they should be sent over to his house for a night's lodging, for it was only fair and just that he should have a share of the same cake his brother had eaten.

So the poor brother promised to do what the other wanted, and after that the rich brother went back home again.

Well, a year and a day passed, and then, sure enough, who should come along that way but both the saints together, arm in arm. Rap! tap! tap! they knocked at the poor man's door, for they thought that where they had had good lodgings before they could get again. And so they could and welcome, only the poor brother told them that his rich brother across the street had asked that they should come and lodge at the fine house when they came that way again.

The saints were willing enough to go to the rich brother's house, though they would rather have stayed with the other. So over they went, and when the rich brother saw them coming he ran out to meet them, and shook each of them by the hand, and bade them to come in and sit down back of the stove where it was warm.

But you should have seen the feast that was set for the two saints at the rich brother's house! I can only say that I have never seen the like, and I only wish that I had been there with my legs under the table. After supper they were shown to a grand room, where each saint had a bed all to his own self, and before they were fairly asleep the rich man's wife came and took away their old shirts, and laid a shirt of fine fabric linen in place of each. When the next morning came and the saints were about to take their leave, the rich brother brought out a great bag of golden money, and bade them to stuff what they could of it into their pockets.

Well, all this was as it should be, and before the two went on their way they said they would give the same blessing to him and his wife that they had given to the other couple—that whatsoever they should begin doing that morning, that they should continue doing until sunset.

After that they put on their hats and took up their staffs and off they plodded.

Now the rich brother was a very envious man, and was not content to do only as well as his brother had done, no indeed! He would do something that would make him even richer than counting out money for himself all day. So down he sat back of the stove and began turning the matter over in his mind, and rubbing up his wits to make them brighter.

In the meantime the wife said to herself, "See, now, I shall be folding fine cambric linen all day, and the pigs will have to go with nothing to eat. I have no time to waste in feeding them, but I'll just run out and fill their troughs with water at any rate."

So out she went with a bucket full of water which she began pouring into the troughs for the pigs. That was the first thing that she did, and after that there was no leaving off, but pour water she must until sunset.

All this while the man sat back of the stove, warming his wits and saying to himself, "Shall I do this? Shall I do that?" and answering "no" to himself every time. At last he began wondering what his wife was doing so he went out to find her. Find her he did, for there she was pouring out water to the pigs. Then if anybody was angry it was the rich man.

"What!" cried he, "and is this the way that you waste the gifts of the blessed saints?"

So saying he looked around, and there lay a bit of switch on the ground near by. He picked up the bit of switch and struck the woman across the shoulders with it, and that was the first thing he began doing. After that he had to keep on doing the same.

So the woman poured water, and the man stood by and beat her with the little switch until there was nothing left of it, and that was what they did all day.

And what is more, they made such a hubbub that the neighbors came to see what was going forward. They loked aud laughed and went away again, and others came, and there stood the two—the woman pouring water and the man beating her with the bit of a switch.

When the evening came, and they left off their work, they were so weary that they could hardly stand; and nothing was to show for it but a broken switch and a wet sty, for even the blessed saints cannot give wisdom to those who will have none of it, and that is the truth.

And such is the end of the story, with only this to tell: Tommy Pfounce tells me that there are folks, even in these wise times, who, if they did all day what they began in the morning, would find themselves at sunset doing no better than pouring pure water to pigs.

That is the kernel to this great nut.

From The Wonder Clock

WHY SANTA CLAUS CHOSE
THE REINDEER

By E. H. Lane

THIS is a story about the very first Christmas eve that Santa Claus ever made his trip around the world. He was quite a young man then, and he had found it rather dreary at the North Pole, with nothing to do but slide down icebergs and play with the Polar Bears. One day, some of the Snow Birds that come north for the summer told him about many children living in the rest of the world, who were sad because they had no toys. That gave Santa Claus an idea. He built a great big work shop and called together the Elves and Brownies and Fairies, who were his good friends. All the year long, they worked together, making dolls and sleds and games and books.

The animals wanted to help. They, too, were Santa Claus' friends. He let them into the shop, but it just didn't work very well. The Polar Bears, who insisted on playing with the dolls, were so clumsy they were always dropping and breaking them. The seals *would* stand up on their tails and dance to the tunes of the music boxes, and were in everybody's way. The Arctic Dogs just couldn't resist shaking up all the stuffed cats and bunnies. The Reindeer suddenly became quite frivolous when they saw all the gay balloons. They tossed them into the air with their noses, but the balloons caught on their antlers and broke with a bang.

Santa Claus finally just had to put out the animals and lock the door. They stood in the snow, looked longingly into the windows, and felt hurt because Santa Claus didn't come out to play with them any more. In fact, they grumbled a good deal.

Finally, the toys were all completed. The shop was overflowing. Santa Claus drew a long breath and sat down to rest, while all the Elves and Brownies and Fairies curled up and went to sleep, they were so tired.

"Now," said Santa Claus, "the next question is how to get all these things to the children! Here are the toys and there is my sleigh waiting to take them, but who will pull it?"

"We will," cried the Polar Bears, delighted at a chance to have a share in things again.

"We will!" cried the Reindeer.

"Oh, please let us!" exclaimed the Seals, flopping up to Santa and crowding around him.

"The idea!" cried the Dogs. "The very idea of Seals drawing a sleigh! They're so slow they wouldn't get there for a year. We are the ones to do it, of course."

This hurt the Seals' feelings. They were very sensitive about being so slow on land. When Santa Claus saw big tears rolling down from their eyes and dropping onto their flippers, he just couldn't stand it, for he was very tender hearted.

"Of course, the Seals shall do it," he said. "What if they are a little slow? If they keep at it, they'll get there all right."

He hitched the Seals up to the sleigh, and away they went, flopping along over the ice. It was a little slow, but Santa Claus was very patient. When however, they were about 15 degrees from the North

Pole and Santa Claus told them to head first for Alaska, one Seal said:

"Oh no! Let's go to Greenland first. I have a third cousin who lives in Greenland, and I've always wanted to see that country. This is a great chance!" And he set out for Greenland.

"I should say not!" said the second Seal. "I've always heard that the fish in the waters of Australia are the most delicious in the world. We'll go to Australia first," and he set out for Australia.

Each Seal wanted to go in a different direction. Santa Claus tried to reason with them.

"But the main thing is to get these gifts to the children. We can see everyone of these countries in the end, if only you will all pull together and follow my directions."

But the Seals were very stubborn; and Santa Claus had to give up and go back to the North Pole.

"I'll let the Dogs do it," he said to himself. "After all, they are the ones best fitted to draw the sleigh."

He hitched up the Dogs and set out again. But before they had reached Alaska the Dogs began to quarrel with each other.

"You've got to pull your share of the load or I won't pull mine," said the first Dog.

"I *am* pulling my share. You're the one that's holding back," snarled the second Dog.

"I think you're all leaving most of it to me!" whined another Dog.

"Come! Come!" said Santa, "this is no way to do. Let's stop trying to see who's *not* doing his share. Let's all try to pull as hard as we can ourselves and never mind what the other Dog does. After all, the main thing is to get these gifts to the children, isn't it?"

The Dogs agreed that it was. They all wanted to get the gifts to the children, but each one was so afraid he was doing more than his share.

Finally, the first Dog stopped short. That stopped the rest of them. It stopped Santa Claus and the sleigh, too.

"I'm not going any further unless the rest will do their share," said the first Dog.

Then Santa Claus almost lost his patience.

"If you can't all forget yourselves and work together, we'll never get there," he said, and he took them back to the North Pole.

Both the Reindeer and the Polar Bears wanted very much to help, but the Reindeer, being always unselfish, gave in to the Polar Bears, and off they went.

"Now we'll surely get there," said Santa Claus to himself, for the Polar Bears were always very good natured and obliging. They trotted along merrily, Santa Claus singing lustily as they went, until they came down to the timber line.

"Oh, just wait a minute while I go and climb that tree!" said the first Polar Bear, and before Santa Claus could stop him, he was off, taking most of the team with him.

"No! No!" shouted the second Bear, "I want to explore that cave," and he set out in the other direction.

"Oh dear!" exclaimed Santa Claus, very much discouraged, "I had forgotten how curious these Bears always are. We'll never get this job done, if they have to investigate everything they see."

He got out of the sleigh and made them all sit down in the snow, while he talked to them very seriously.

"Don't you see," he said, "that the main thing is to get these gifts to the children? We must do that whether or not we do all these other things."

The Polar Bears agreed, and promised to be good, and they went on again. But every time they came to something new, they forgot all about the children and the toys and started to investigate.

Santa Claus was pretty discouraged, when he had to turn back for the third time. As he finally set out with the Reindeer harnessed to the sleigh, he wondered if he'd have to give up the whole thing.

Before they went far, the first Reindeer said to the others, "Remember, we all want one thing more than anything else—to get these gifts to the children. So let's forget everything else we might like to do and all pull together until the job is done." And away they went like the wind.

The other animals were very cross. The Seals went and banged their heads against an iceberg. The Dogs crowded into a corner of the work shop and sulked. The Polar Bears spent their time teasing the Brownies. They tickled the Fairies and woke them up.

But because they forgot themselves and all pulled together, the Reindeer carried Santa's sleigh safely and swiftly around the world. And that's why they have been doing it ever since.

JIMMY SCARECROW'S CHRISTMAS

By Mary E. Wilkins Freeman

JIMMY SCARECROW led a sad life in the winter. Jimmy's greatest grief was his lack of occupation. He liked to be useful, and in winter he was absolutely of no use at all.

He wondered how many such miserable winters he would have to endure. He was a young scarecrow, and this was his first one. He was strongly made, and, although his wooden joints creaked a little when the wind blew, he did not grow in the least rickety. Every morning, when the wintry sun peered like a hard, yellow eye across the corn stubble, Jimmy felt sad, but at Christmas time his heart nearly broke.

On Christmas Eve Santa Claus came in his sledge, heaped high with presents, urging his team of reindeer across the field. He was on his way to the farmhouse where Betsey lived with her Aunt Hannah.

Betsey was a very good little girl with very smooth yellow curls, and she had a great many presents. Santa Claus had a large wax doll-baby for her on his arm, tucked up against the fur collar of his coat. He was afraid to trust it in the pack, lest it get broken.

When poor Jimmy Scarecrow saw Santa Claus his heart gave a great leap.

"Santa Claus! Here I am!" he cried out, but Santa Claus did not hear him.

"Santa Claus, please give me a little present. I was good all summer and kept the crows out of the corn," pleaded the poor scarecrow, but Santa Claus passed by with a merry halloo and a great clamor of bells.

Then Jimmy Scarecrow stood in the corn stubble and shook with sobs until his joints creaked.

"I am of no use in the world, and everybody has forgotten me," he moaned. But he was mistaken.

The next morning Betsey sat at the window holding her Christmas doll-baby, and looked out at Jimmy Scarecrow standing alone in the field amidst the corn stubble.

"Aunt Hannah?" she said. Aunt Hannah was making a crazy patch-work quilt, and she frowned hard at a triangular piece of red silk and circular piece of pink, wondering how to fit them together.

"Well?" she said.

"Did Santa Claus bring the scarecrow any Christmas present?"

"No, of course he didn't."

"Why not?"

"Because he's a scarecrow. Don't ask silly questions."

"I wouldn't like to be treated so, if I were a scarecrow," said Betsey, but her Aunt Hannah did not hear her. She was busy cutting a tri-angular snip out of the round piece of pink silk so the red silk could be feather-stitched into it.

It was snowing hard out of doors, and the north wind blew. The scarecrow's poor old coat got whiter and whiter with snow. Sometimes he almost vanished in the thick white storm. Aunt Hannah worked until the middle of the afternoon on her crazy quilt. Then she got up and spread it out over the sofa with an air of pride.

"There," she said, "that's done, and that makes the eighth. I've got one for every bed in the house, and I've given four away. I'd give this away if I knew of anybody that wanted it."

Aunt Hannah put on her hood and shawl, and drew some blue yarn stockings on over her shoes, and set out through the snow to carry a slice of plum pudding to her sister Susan, who lived down the road. Half an hour after Aunt Hannah had gone, Betsey put her little red plaid shawl over her head, and ran across the field to Jimmy Scarecrow. She carried her new doll-baby snuggled up under her shawl.

"Wish you a Merry Christmas!" she said to Jimmy Scarecrow.

"Wish you the same," said Jimmy, but his voice was choked with sobs, and was also muffled, for his old hat had slipped down over his chin. Betsey looked pitifully at the old hat fringed with icicles, like frozen tears, and the old snow-laden coat.

"I've brought you a Christmas present," she said, and with that she tucked her doll-baby inside Jimmy Scarecrow's coat, sticking its tiny feet into a pocket.

"Thank you," said Jimmy Scarecrow faintly.

"You're welcome," she said. "Keep her under your overcoat, so the snow won't wet her, and she won't catch cold. She's delicate."

"Yes, I will," said Jimmy Scarecrow, and he tried hard to bring one of his stiff, outstretched arms around to clasp the doll-baby.

"Don't you feel cold in that old summer coat?" asked Betsey.

"If I had a little exercise, I should be warm," he replied. But he shivered, and the wind whistled through his rags.

"You wait a minute," said Betsey, and she was off across the field.

Jimmy Scarecrow stood in the corn-stubble, with the doll-baby under his coat, and waited, and soon Betsey was back again with Aunt Hannah's crazy quilt trailing in the snow behind her.

"Here," she said, "here is something to keep you warm," and she folded the crazy quilt around the scarecrow and pinned it.

"Aunt Hannah wants to give it away if anybody wants it," she explained. "She's got too many crazy quilts in the house now that she doesn't know what to do with. Good-bye—be sure you keep the doll-baby covered up." And with that she ran across the field, and left Jimmy Scarecrow alone with the crazy quilt and the doll-baby.

The bright flash of colors under Jimmy's hat brim dazzled his eyes, and he felt a little alarmed. "I hope this quilt is harmless if it *is* crazy," he said. But the quilt was warm, and he dismissed his fears. Soon the doll-baby whimpered, but he creaked his joints a little, and that amused it, and he heard it cooing inside his coat.

Jimmy Scarecrow had never felt so happy in his life as he did for an hour or so. But after that the snow began to turn to rain, and the crazy quilt was soaked through and through, and not only that, but his coat and the poor doll-baby. It cried pitifully for a while, and then it was still, and he was afraid it was dead.

It grew very dark, and the rain fell in sheets, the snow melted, and Jimmy Scarecrow stood half-way up his old boots in water. He was saying to himself that the saddest hour of his life had come, when suddenly he again heard Santa Claus' sleigh bells and his merry voice talking to his reindeer. It was after midnight; Christmas was over, and Santa was hastening home to the North Pole.

"Santa Claus! dear Santa Claus!" cried Jimmy Scarecrow with a great sob, and that time Santa Claus heard him and drew rein.

"Who's there?" he shouted out of the darkness.

"It's only me," replied the Scarecrow.

"Who's me?" shouted Santa Claus.

"Jimmy Scarecrow!"

Santa got out of his sledge and waded up.

"Have you been standing here ever since corn was ripe?" he asked pityingly, and Jimmy replied that he had.

"What's that over your shoulders?" Santa Claus continued, holding up his lantern.

"It's a crazy quilt."

"And what are you holding under your coat?"

"The doll-baby that Betsey gave me, and I'm afraid it's dead," poor Jimmy Scarecrow sobbed.

"Nonsense!" cried Santa Claus. "Let me see it!" And with that he pulled the doll-baby out from under the Scarecrow's coat, and patted its back, and shook it a little, and it began to cry, and then to crow. "It's all right," said Santa Claus. "This is the doll-baby that I gave Betsey, and it is not at all delicate. It went through the measles, and the chicken pox, and the mumps, and the whooping cough, before it left the North Pole. Now get into the sledge, Jimmy Scarecrow, and bring the doll-baby and the crazy quilt. I have never had any quilts that weren't in their right minds at the North Pole, but maybe I can cure this one. Get in!" Santa chirruped to his reindeer, and they drew the sledge up close in a beautiful curve.

"Get in, Jimmy Scarecrow, and come with me to the North Pole!" he cried.

"Please, how long shall I stay?" asked Jimmy Scarecrow.

"Why you are going to live with me," replied Santa Claus. "I've been looking for a person like you for a long time."

"Are there any crows to scare at the North Pole? I want to be useful," Jimmy Scarecrow said, anxiously.

"No," answered Santa Claus, "but I don't want you to scare away crows. I want you to scare away Arctic Explorers. I can keep you in work for a thousand years, and scaring away Arctic Explorers from the North Pole is much more important than scaring away crows from corn. Why, if they found the pole, there wouldn't be a piece an inch long left in a week's time, and the earth would cave in like an apple without a core! They would whittle it all to pieces, and carry it away in their pockets for souvenirs. Come along; I am in a hurry."

"I will go on two conditions," said Jimmy. "First, I want to make a present for Aunt Hannah and Betsey, next Christmas."

"You shall make any present you choose. What else?"

"I want some way provided to scare the crows out of the corn next summer, while I am away," said Jimmy.

"That is easily managed," said Santa Claus. "Just wait a minute."

Santa took his stylographic pen out of his pocket, went with his lantern close to one of the fence posts, and wrote these words upon it:

NOTICE TO CROWS

Whichever crow shall hereafter hop, fly, or flop into this field during the absence of Jimmy Scarecrow, and therefrom purloin, steal, or abstract corn, shall be instantly, in a twinkling and a thrice, turned snow-white, and be ever after a disgrace, a byword and a reproach to his whole race.

Per order of Santa Claus

"The corn will be safe now," said Santa Claus; "get in." Jimmy got into the sledge and they flew away over the fields, out of sight, with merry halloos and a great clamor of bells.

The next morning there was much surprise at the farmhouse, when Aunt Hannah and Betsey looked out of the window and the scarecrow was not in the field holding out his stiff arms over the corn stubble. Betsey had told Aunt Hannah she had given away the crazy quilt and the doll-baby, but had been scolded very little.

"You must not give away anything of yours again without asking permission," said Aunt Hannah. "And you have no right to give away anything of mine, even if you know I don't want it. Now both my pretty quilt and your beautiful doll-baby are spoiled."

That was all that Aunt Hannah had said. She thought she would send John after the quilt and the doll-baby the next morning as soon as it was light.

But Jimmy Scarecrow was gone, and the crazy quilt and the doll-baby with him. John, the servant-man, searched everywhere, but not a trace of them could he find.

"They must have all blown away, mum," he said to Aunt Hannah.

"We shall have to have another scarecrow next summer," said she.

But the next summer there was no need of a scarecrow, for not a crow came past the fence post on which Santa Claus had written his notice to the crows. The cornfield was never so beautiful, and not a single grain was stolen by a crow, and everyone wondered at it, for they could not read the crow-language in which Santa Claus had written.

"It is a great mystery to me why the crows don't come into our cornfield, when there is no scarecrow," said Aunt Hannah.

But she had a still greater mystery to solve when Christmas came round again. Then she and Betsey each had a strange present. They found them in the sitting room on Christmas morning. Aunt Hannah's present was her old crazy quilt, remodeled, with every piece cut square and true, and matched exactly to its neighbor.

"Why it's my old crazy quilt, but it isn't crazy now!" cried Aunt Hannah, and her very spectacles seemed to glisten with amazement.

Betsey's present was her doll-baby of the Christmas before; but the doll was a year older. She had grown an inch, and could walk and say, "mamma," and "how do?" She was changed a good deal, but Betsey knew her at once.

"It's my doll-baby!" she cried, and snatched her up and kissed her.

But neither Aunt Hannah nor Betsey ever knew that the quilt and doll were Jimmy Scarecrow's Christmas presents to them.

ABOUT THREE KINGS, UNCLE HERMAN'S UNIFORM, AND CHRISTMAS NIGHT IN THE TYROL

By Ludwig Bemelmans

"CHRISTMAS EVE," thought Hansi, "should start with the evening. There should be no day on that day at all."

Certainly it was the biggest day in the year and the longest to wait around in.

He was sent from the house on errands as soon as he came in. Packages wandered around. One room was locked and even the keyhole stuffed so one could see nothing.

The children weren't hungry though there were the most wonderful things on the table.

"Hansi, nothing is going to happen until this plate is empty. Lieserl, stop wiggling on that chair." Uncle Herman finally looked at his watch and got up. Soon a little silver bell rang, and sparkling across the hall stood the Christmas tree. It turned slowly to music, as glass angels, cookies and burning candles rode around.

The best skis in the whole world are made of Norwegian spruce with long tapered ends. Such a pair stood beside the tree—new and with a binding like that the champion jumpers use. Next to them a skiing cap with a long tassel. Aunt Amalie had knitted it for Hansi. The skis, of course, were from his mother. Uncle Herman had given Hansi a skiing jacket, bright red and warm so that one could get lost and yet stay warm and easily be found in the white snow.

Lieserl had a doll carriage with a big doll dressed like a peasant girl on Sunday. This doll could go to sleep and even said "Mamma," when she was pinched.

"Yes, Lieserl, I see," said Hansi, and looked at his skis again.

Hansi had barely slipped into the skis to try them on and put the stocking cap on his head, when singing was heard outside the house.

"Here they are," said Uncle Herman. Everybody tiptoed to the door, and quietly it swung open.

Three Kings stood majestically in the starry night and sang in verses. They told how they had come from the sands of the desert and were passing this house on the way to visit the Christ Kinderl, to offer Him their precious gifts. Long heavy robes of scarlet flowed off them into the snow. Over their serious devout faces shone tall crowns of pure gold. Their hands were hidden in the deep folds of scarlet sleeves and one of them held a silver lance on which shone the star that had guided the Kings from the East past this house.

After they had finished their song, Uncle Herman invited them to enter his home. He did so singing a verse to which they answered with singing and came in.

Aunt Amalie had brought three cups of hot chocolate and a big plate of Lebkuchen. The Kings seemed to be very hungry indeed after the hard trip from the hot desert and over the cold mountains. Each took three Lebkuchen as they sat down, falling over the plate in their hurry to reach it. One Lebkuchen was left and, as one of the Kings tried to reach for it, the biggest one hit him on the fingers with the silver lance to which was attached the morning star, which broke off and fell into the chocolate. Uncle Herman seemed to know these Kings very well. He took the lances away from them so they would not hurt each other any more.

Lieserl sat down next to the smallest King, who was black, and looked at him very closely. Then she wet her finger and rubbed his nose. The King started to cry and his nose turned white.

"I knew it all the time," said Lieserl. "It's Frau Kofler's little boy Peterl."

Now Hansi came to the table, and he could see that the King, outside of a black face, had only black fingernails. His hands were white —almost white. They were boys from the village. The beautiful stars and crowns were made of cardboard with gold and silver paper pasted over it and the little King was blackened with burnt cork.

They had to sing at three more houses, they said. Aunt Amalie brought two more Lebkuchen, so each could eat another, and Uncle

Herman repaired the little King's pale nose with stove blacking. They gave thanks with a little verse for the shelter and food and bowed and walked back into the night. The cold light of the moon gave them back their lost majesty. As they left everyone was serious and quiet. Their stars and crowns had turned again to purest beaten gold.

The evening passed as quickly as the day had been slow in going. Soon it was time to go to midnight services.

This was one of three days in the year when Uncle Herman stood in front of a mirror. He buttoned his tunic and pinned his medals on according to regulation, "six fingers down from the seam of the collar, three fingers over from the second button—right over the heart." Belt and saber were adjusted carefully. Uncle Herman breathed on the buckle and polished it with his sleeve.

Aunt Amalie said, "Why don't you ask for a piece of cloth? It's a shame—the nice new uniform."

The feathers on the green huntsman's hat were straightened out, the white gloves put on.

The children looked up in awe at their new uncle who looked like a picture of his old emperor.

Aunt Amalie had her best dress on with a wide silk shawl around her shoulders and silver lacing from which jingled heavy thalers as she walked.

Hansi and Lieserl sat around like pictures painted on the wall. They had been ready for an hour, and held the little lanterns that were used to light the way down the path.

Aunt Amalie put some things on the table for a small supper when they came back.

The night helped to make Christmas. All the stars were out. The windows of the mountain church shone out into the blue night from the valley and from high up little rows of lights came towards the church. People carried them. They shone up into happy, quiet faces. Silent, holy night—only the bells of the churches rang from near and from the far white fields.

They scraped the snow from their shoes and entered the church. It smelled like a cool forest at noontime when the sun shines through the tall pines. Pines stood in rows along the walls reaching almost to the tower. Candles flickered everywhere.

Hansi walked up the creaky stairway that led through the tower and opened into the choir. A big oil lamp hung over the organ that was built a century ago. In front of it sat the village schoolmaster. He gave Hansi notes and nodded to the place where he was to stand with other boys. Behind him a man was tuning two large copper kettle-drums. He bent his ear close to them and struck them with a softly padded hammer. It was a lovely warm sound that made Hansi feel hollow inside.

Post Seppl was up here with a trumpet, and there were the players of two more instruments—a flute and a fiddle.

In front of the organ above the schoolmaster's head was a little mirror. In this the teacher watched the services. He could tell when to play, and he kept the time by nodding with his head.

The church below was filled to the doors with kindly people who thanked God for their beautiful mountains and asked no more of Him than that He keep them as He had all the years of their plain good lives.

The old teacher lifted his eyes and asked in addition for His help in repairing this poor tired organ. Not only were many important sounds missing—there were others that did not make melodies, and of the two wooden angels that flew to left and right of it, one needed his robe painted and the other had lost a wing.

After services Uncle Herman waited below with Aunt Amalie and Lieserl for Hansi. They went home together as they had come, with other little lights that wandered from the church to the houses on the mountain.

From *Hansi*

MASTER JACK'S SONG

WRITTEN AFTER SPENDING THE CHRISTMAS HOLIDAYS AT
GRANDMAMMA'S

You may talk about your groves,
Where you wander with your loves;
You may talk about your moonlit waves that fall and flow.
Something fairer far than these
I can show you, if you please.
'Tis the charming little cupboard where the jam-pots grow.

Chorus

There the golden peaches shine
In their syrup clear and fine,
And the raspberries are blushing with a dusky glow;
And the cherry and the plum
Seem to beckon you to come
To the charming little cupboard where the jam-pots grow.

Chorus

There the sprightly pickles stand,
With the catsup close at hand,
And the marmalades and jellies in a goodly row;
While the quinces' ruddy fire
Would an anchorite inspire
To seek the little cupboard where the jam-pots grow.

Chorus

Never tell me of your bowers
That are full of bugs and flowers!
Never tell me of your meadows where the breezes blow!
But sing me, if you will,
Of the house beneath the hill,
And the darling little cupboard where the jam-pots grow.

Chorus

Where the jam-pots grow!
Where the jam-pots grow!
Where the jelly jolly, jelly jolly jam-pots grow.
The fairest spot to me,
On the land or on the sea,
Is the charming little cupboard where the jam-pots grow.

LAURA E. RICHARDS

FOOD AND FUN

CHRISTMAS AT DINGLEY DELL

By Charles Dickens

THE best sitting room at Manor Farm was a good, long, dark-pannelled room with a high chimney piece, and a capacious chimney, up which you could have driven one of the new patent cabs, wheels and all. At the upper end of the room, seated in a shady bower of holly and evergreens, were the two best fiddlers, and the only harp, in all Muggleton. In all sorts of recesses, and on all kinds of brackets, stood massive old silver candlesticks with four branches each. The carpet was up, the candles burnt bright, the fire blazed and crackled on the hearth; and merry voices and light-hearted laughter rang through the room. If any of the old English yeomen had turned into fairies when they died, it was just the place in which they would have held their revels.

If any thing could have added to the interest of this agreeable scene, it would have been the remarkable fact of Mr. Pickwick's appearing without his gaiters, for the first time within the memory of his oldest friends.

"You mean to dance?" said Wardle.

"Of course I do," replied Mr. Pickwick, "Don't you see I am dressed for the purpose?" and Mr. Pickwick called attention to his speckled silk stockings, and smartly tied pumps.

"*You* in silk stockings!" exclaimed Mr. Tupman jocosely.

"And why not Sir—why not?" said Mr. Pickwick, turning warmly upon him.

"Oh, of course there is no reason why you shouldn't wear them," responded Mr. Tupman.

"I imagine not Sir—I imagine not," said Mr. Pickwick in a very peremptory tone.

Mr. Tupman had contemplated a laugh, but he found it was a

527

serious matter; so he looked grave, and said they were a very pretty pattern.

"I hope they are," said Mr. Pickwick fixing his eyes upon his friend. "You see nothing extraordinary in these stockings, *as* stockings, I trust Sir?"

"Certainly not—oh certainly not," replied Mr. Tupman. He walked away; and Mr. Pickwick's countenance resumed its customary benign expression.

"We are all ready, I believe," said Mr. Pickwick, who was stationed with the old lady at the top of the dance, and had already made four false starts, in his excessive anxiety to commence.

"Then begin at once," said Wardle. "Now."

Up struck the two fiddles and the one harp, and off went Mr. Pickwick into hands across, when there was a general clapping of hands, and a cry of "Stop, stop."

"What's the matter?" said Mr. Pickwick, who was only brought to, by the fiddles and harp desisting, and could have been stopped by no other earthly power, if the house had been on fire.

"Where's Arabella Allen?" said a dozen voices.

"And Winkle?" added Mr. Tupman.

"Here we are!" exclaimed that gentleman, emerging with his pretty companion from the corner; and, as he did so, it would have been hard to tell which was the redder in the face, he or the young lady with the black eyes.

"What an extraordinary thing it is, Winkle," said Mr. Pickwick, rather pettishly, "that you wouldn't have taken your place before."

"Not at all extraordinary," said Mr. Winkle.

"Well," said Mr. Pickwick, with a very expressive smile, as his eyes rested on Arabella, "well, I don't know that it *was* extraordinary, either, after all."

However, there was no time to think more about the matter, for the fiddles and harp began in real earnest. Away went Mr. Pickwick—hands across, down the middle to the very end of the room, and half way up the chimney, back again to the door—poussette everywhere—loud stamp on the ground—ready for the next couple—off again—all the figure over once more—another stamp to beat out the time—next couple, and the next, and the next again—never was such going; and at last, after they had reached the bottom of the dance, and full fourteen couple after the old lady had retired in an exhausted state, and the clergyman's wife had been substituted in her stead, did that gentleman, when there was no demand whatever on his exertions, keep perpetually dancing in his place, to keep time to the music, smiling on his partner all the while with a blandness of demeanour which baffles all description. . . .

"And so your family has games in the kitchen to-night, my dear, has they?" inquired Sam of Emma.

"Yes, Mr. Weller," replied Emma; "we always have on Christmas eve. Master wouldn't neglect to keep it up on any acount."

"Your master's a wery pretty notion of keepin' anythin' up, my dear," said Mr. Weller; "I never see such a sensible sort of man as he is, or such a reg'lar gen'l'm'n." . . .

From the centre of the ceiling of this kitchen, old Wardle had just suspended with his own hands a huge branch of mistletoe, and this same branch of mistletoe instantaneously gave rise to a scene of general and most delightful struggling and confusion; in the midst of which Mr. Pickwick with a gallantry which would have done honour to a descendant of Lady Tollimglower herself, took the old lady by the hand, led her beneath the mystic branch, and saluted her in all courtesy and decorum. The old lady submitted to this piece of practical politeness with all the dignity which befitted so important and serious a solemnity, but the younger ladies not being so thoroughly imbued with a superstitious veneration of the custom, or imagining that the value of a salute is very much enhanced if it cost a little trouble to obtain it, screamed and struggled, and ran into corners, and threatened and remonstrated, and did every thing but leave the room, until some of the less adventurous gentlemen were on the point of desisting, when they all at once found it useless to resist any longer, and submitted to be kissed with a good grace. Mr. Winkle kissed the young lady with the black eyes, and Mr. Snodgrass kissed Emily; and Mr. Weller, not being particular about the form of being under the mistletoe, kissed Emma and the other female servants, just as he caught them. As to the poor relations, they kissed everybody, not even excepting the plainer portion of the young-lady visitors, who, in their excessive confusion, ran right under the mistletoe, directly it was hung up, without knowing it! Wardle stood with his back to the fire, surveying the whole scene, with the utmost satisfaction; and the fat boy took the opportunity of appropriating to his own use, and summarily devouring, a particularly fine mince-pie, that had been carefully put by, for somebody else.

Now the screaming had subsided, and faces were in a glow and curls in a tangle, and Mr. Pickwick, after kissing the old lady as before-mentioned, was standing under the mistletoe, looking with a very pleased countenance on all that was passing around him, when the young lady with the black eyes, after a little whispering with the other young ladies, made a sudden dart forward, and, putting her arm round Mr. Pickwick's neck, saluted him affectionately on the left cheek; and before Mr. Pickwick distinctly knew what was the matter, he was surrounded by the whole body, and kissed by every one of them.

It was a pleasant thing to see Mr. Pickwick in the centre of the group, now pulled this way, and then that, and first kissed on the chin and then on the nose, and then on the spectacles, and to hear the peals of laughter which were raised on every side; but it was a still more pleasant thing to see Mr. Pickwick, blinded shortly afterwards with a silk-handkerchief, falling up against the wall, and scrambling into corners, and going through all the mysteries of blind-man's buff, with the utmost relish for the game, until at last he caught one of the poor relations; and then had to evade the blind-man himself, which he did with a nimbleness and agility that elicited the admiration and applause of all beholders. The poor relations caught just the people whom they thought would like it; and when the game flagged, got caught themselves. When they were all tired of blind-man's buff, there was a great game at snap-dragon, and when fingers enough were burned with that, and all the raisins gone, they sat down by the huge fire of blazing logs to a substantial supper, and a mighty bowl of wassail, something smaller than an ordinary wash-house copper, in which the hot apples were hissing and bubbling with a rich look, and a jolly sound, that were perfectly irresistible.

"This," said Mr. Pickwick, looking round him, "this is, indeed, comfort."

"Our invariable custom," replied Mr. Wardle. "Every body sits down with us on Christmas eve, as you see them now—servants and all; and here we wait till the clock strikes twelve, to usher Christmas in, and wile away the time with forfeits and old stories. Trundle, my boy, rake up the fire."

Up flew the bright sparks in myriads as the logs were stirred, and the deep red blaze sent forth a rich glow, that penetrated into the furthest corner of the room, and cast its cheerful tint on every face.

"Come," said Wardle, "a song—a Christmas song. I'll give you one, in default of a better."

"Bravo," said Mr. Pickwick.

"Fill up," cried Wardle. "It will be two hours good, before you see the bottom of the bowl through the deep rich colour of the was-sail; fill up all round, and now for the song."

Thus saying, the merry old gentleman, in a good, round, sturdy voice, commenced without more ado—

A CHRISTMAS CAROL

I care not for Spring; on his fickle wing
Let the blossoms and buds be borne:
He woos them amain with his treacherous rain,
And he scatters them ere the more.
An inconstant elf, he knows not himself,
Of his own changing mind an hour,
He'll smile in your face, and, with wry grimace,
He'll wither your youngest flower.

But my song I troll out, for Christmas stout,
The hearty, the true, and the bold;
A bumper I drain, and with might and main

Give three cheers for this Christmas old.
We'll usher him in with a merry din
That shall gladden his joyous heart
And we'll keep him up while there's bite or sup,
And in fellowship good, we'll part.

This song was tumultuously applauded, for friends and dependents make a capital audience; and the poor relations especially were in perfect ecstasies of rapture.

From *Pickwick Papers*

CHRISTMAS AT BRACEBRIDGE HALL

By Washington Irving

THE dinner was served up in the great hall, where the Squire always held his Christmas banquet. A blazing crackling fire of logs had been heaped on to warm the spacious apartment, and the flame went sparkling and wreathing up the wide-mouthed chimney. The great picture of the crusader and his white horse had been profusely decorated with greens for the occasion; and holly and ivy had likewise been wreathed round the helmet and weapons on the opposite wall, which I understood were the arms of the same warrior. I must own, by the bye, I had strong doubts about the authenticity of the painting and armour as having belonged to the crusader, they certainly having the stamp of more recent days; but I was told that the painting had been so considered time out of mind; and that as to the armour, it had been found in a lumber room, and elevated to its present situation by the Squire, who at once determined it to be the armour of the family hero; and as he was absolute authority on all such subjects in his own household, the matter had passed into current acceptation. A sideboard was set out just under this chivalric trophy, on which was a display of plate that might have vied (at least in variety) with Belshazzar's parade of the vessels of the temple;

"flagons, cans, cups, beakers, goblets, basins, and ewers"; the gorgeous utensils of good companionship, that had gradually accumulated through many generations of jovial housekeepers. Before these stood the two Yule candles beaming like two stars of the first magnitude; other lights were distributed in branches, and the whole array glittered like a firmament of silver.

We were ushered into this banqueting scene with the sound of minstrelsy, the old harper being seated on a stool beside the fireplace, and twanging his instrument with a vast deal more power than melody. Never did Christmas board display a more goodly and gracious assemblage of countenances: those who were not handsome were, at least, happy; and happiness is a rare improver of your hard-favoured visage. I always consider an old English family as well worth studying as a collection of Holbein's portraits or Albert Durer's prints. There is much antiquarian lore to be acquired; much knowledge of the physiognomies of former times. Perhaps it may be from having continually before their eyes those rows of old family portraits, with which the mansions of this country are stocked; certain it is, that the quaint features of antiquity are often most faithfully perpetuated in these ancient lines; and I have traced an old family nose through a whole picture gallery, legitimately handed down from generation to generation, almost from the time of the Conquest. Something of the kind was to be observed in the worthy company around me. Many of their faces had evidently originated in a Gothic age, and been merely copied by succeeding generations; and there was one little girl, in particular, of staid demeanour, with a high Roman nose, and an antique vinegar aspect, who was a great favourite of the Squire's, being, as he said, a Bracebridge all over, and the very counterpart of one of his ancestors who figured in the court of Henry VIII.

The parson said grace, which was not a short familiar one, such as is commonly addressed to the Deity, in these unceremonious days; but a long, courtly, well-worded one of the ancient school. There was now a pause, as if something was expected; when suddenly the butler entered the hall with some degree of bustle; he was attended by a servant on each side with a large wax-light, and bore a silver dish, on which

was an enormous pig's head decorated with rosemary, with a lemon
in its mouth, which was placed with great formality at the head of
the table. The moment this pageant made its appearance, the harper
struck up a flourish; at the conclusion of which the young Oxonian,
on receiving a hint from the Squire, gave, with an air of the most
comic gravity, an old carol, the first verse of which was as follows:

> Caput apri defero
> Reddens laudes Domino.
> The boar's head in hand bring I,
> With garlands gay and rosemary.
> I pray you all sing merrily
> Qui estis in convivio.

Though prepared to witness many of these little eccentricities,
from being apprised of the peculiar hobby of mine host; yet, I confess,
the parade with which so odd a dish was introduced somewhat perplexed me, until I gathered from the conversation of the Squire and
the parson that it was meant to represent the bringing in of the boar's
head: a dish formerly served up with much ceremony, and the sound
of minstrelsy and song, at great tables on Christmas day. "I like the
old custom," said the Squire, "not merely because it is stately and
pleasing in itself, but because it was observed at the College of Oxford, at which I was educated. When I hear the old song chanted, it
brings to mind the time when I was young and gamesome—and the
noble old college-hall—and my fellow students loitering about in
their black gowns; many of whom, poor lads, are now in their graves!"

The parson, however, whose mind was not haunted by such associations, and who was always more taken up with the text than the
sentiment, objected to the Oxonian's version of the carol: which he
affirmed was different from that sung at college. He went on, with the
dry perseverance of a commentator, to give the college reading, accompanied by sundry annotations: addressing himself at first to the
company at large; but finding their attention gradually diverted to
other talk, and other objects, he lowered his tone as his number of
auditors diminished, until he concluded his remarks, in an under

voice, to a fat-headed old gentleman next him, who was silently engaged in the discussion of a huge plateful of turkey.

The table was literally loaded with good cheer, and presented an epitome of country abundance, in this season of overflowing larders. A distinguished post was allotted to "ancient sirloin," as mine host termed it; being, as he added, "the standard of old English hospitality, and a joint of goodly presence, and full of expectation." There were several dishes quaintly decorated, and which had evidently something traditionary in their embellishments; but about which, as I did not like to appear over-curious, I asked no questions.

I could not, however, but notice a pie, magnificently decorated with peacocks' feathers, in imitation of the tail of that bird, which overshadowed a considerable tract of the table. This the Squire confessed, with some little hesitation, was a pheasant-pie, though a peacock-pie was certainly the most authentical; but there had been such a mortality among the peacocks this season, that he could not prevail upon himself to have one killed.

When the cloth was removed, the butler brought in a huge silver vessel of rare and curious workmanship, which he placed before the Squire. Its appearance was hailed with acclamation; being the Wassail Bowl, so renowned in Christmas festivity. The contents had been prepared by the Squire himself; for it was a beverage in the skilful mixture of which he particularly prided himself; alleging that it was too abstruse and complex for the comprehension of an ordinary servant. It was a potation, indeed, that might well make the heart of a toper leap within him; being composed of the richest and raciest wines, highly spiced and sweetened, with roasted apples bobbing about the surface.

The old gentleman's whole countenance beamed with a serene look of indwelling delight, as he stirred this mighty bowl. Having raised it to his lips, with a hearty wish of a merry Christmas to all present, he sent it brimming round the board, for every one to follow his example, according to the primitive style; pronouncing it "the ancient fountain of good feeling, where all hearts met together."

There was much laughing and rallying as the honest emblem of

Christmas joviality circulated, and was kissed rather coyly by the ladies. When it reached Master Simon he raised it in both hands, and with the air of a boon companion struck up an old Wassail chanson. . . .

Much of the conversation during dinner turned upon family topics, to which I was a stranger. There was, however, a great deal of rallying of Master Simon about some gay widow, with whom he was accused of having a flirtation. This attack was commenced by the ladies; but it was continued throughout the dinner by the fat-headed old gentleman next the parson, with the persevering assiduity of a slow-hound; being one of those long-winded jokers, who, though rather dull at starting game, are unrivalled for their talents in hunting it down. At every pause in the general conversation, he renewed his bantering in pretty much the same terms; winking hard at me with both eyes whenever he gave Master Simon what he considered a home thrust. The latter, indeed, seemed fond of being teased on the subject, as old bachelors are apt to be; and he took occasion to inform me, in an under-tone, that the lady in question was a prodigiously fine woman, and drove her own curricle.

The dinner-time passed away in this flow of innocent hilarity; and, though the old hall may have resounded in its time with many a scene of broader rout and revel, yet I doubt whether it ever witnessed more honest and genuine enjoyment. How easy it is for one benevolent being to diffuse pleasure around him; and how truly is a kind heart a fountain of gladness, making everything in its vicinity to freshen into smiles! The joyous disposition of the worthy Squire was perfectly contagious; he was happy himself, and disposed to make all the world happy; and the little eccentricities of his humour did but season, in a manner, the sweetness of his philanthropy.

When the ladies had retired, the conversation, as usual, became still more animated; many good things were broached which had been thought of during dinner, but which would not exactly do for a lady's ear; and though I cannot positively affirm that there was much wit uttered, yet I have certainly heard many contests of rare wit produce much less laughter.

I found the tide of wine and wassail fast gaining on the dry land of sober judgment. The company grew merrier and louder as their jokes grew duller. Master Simon was in as chirping a humour as a grasshopper filled with dew; his old songs grew of a warmer complexion, and he began to talk maudlin about the widow. He even gave a long song about the wooing of a widow, which he informed me he had gathered from an excellent black-letter work, entitled *Cupid's Solicitor for Love,* containing store of good advice for bachelors, and which he promised to lend me. The first verse was to this effect:

> He that will woo a widow must not dally,
> He must make hay while the sun doth shine;
> He must not stand with her, Shall I, Shall I?
> But boldly say, Widow, thou must be mine.

This song inspired the fat-headed old gentleman, who made several attempts to tell a rather broad story out of Joe Miller, that was pat to the purpose; but he always stuck in the middle, everybody recollecting the latter part excepting himself. The parson, too, began to show the effects of good cheer, having gradually settled down into a doze, and his wig sitting most suspiciously on one side. Just at this juncture we were summoned to the drawing-room, and, I suspect, at the private instigation of mine host, whose joviality seemed always tempered with a proper love of decorum.

After the dinner-table was removed, the hall was given up to the younger members of the family, who, prompted to all kind of noisy mirth by the Oxonian and Master Simon, made its old walls ring with their merriment, as they played at romping games. I delight in witnessing the gambols of children, and particularly at this happy holiday season, and could not help stealing out of the drawing-room on hearing one of their peals of laughter. I found them at the game of blind-man's buff. Master Simon, who was the leader of their revels, and seemed on all occasions to fulfil the office that of ancient potentate, the Lord of Misrule, was blinded in the midst of the hall. The little beings were as busy about him as the mock fairies about Falstaff, pinching him, plucking at the skirts of his coat, and tickling him with straws. One fine blue-eyed girl of about thirteen, with her flaxen hair all in beautiful confusion, her frolic face in a glow, her frock half torn off her shoulders, a complete picture of a romp, was the chief tormentor; and from the slyness with which Master Simon avoided the smaller game, and hemmed this wild little nymph in corners, and obliged her to jump shrieking over chairs, I suspected the rogue of being not a whit more blinded than was convenient. . . .

Whilst we were all attention to the parson's stories, our ears were suddenly assailed by a burst of heterogeneous sounds from the hall, in which was mingled something like the clang of rude minstrelsy, with the uproar of many small voices and girlish laughter. The door suddenly flew open, and a train came trooping into the room, that might almost have been mistaken for the breaking up of the court of Fairy. That indefatigable spirit, Master Simon, in the faithful discharge of his duties as Lord of Misrule, had conceived the idea of a Christmas mummery, or masking; and having called in to his assistance the Oxonian and the young officer, who were equally ripe for anything that should occasion romping and merriment, they had carried it into instant effect. The old house-keeper had been consulted; the antique clothes-presses and wardrobes rummaged and made to yield up the relics of finery that had not seen the light for several generations; the younger part of the company had been privately convened from the parlour and hall, and the whole had been bedizened out, into a burlesque imitation of an antique masque.

Master Simon led the van, as "Ancient Christmas," quaintly apparelled in a ruff, a short cloak, which had very much the aspect of one of the old housekeeper's petticoats, and a hat that might have served for a village steeple, and must indubitably have figured in the days of the Covenanters. From under this his nose curved boldly forth, flushed with a frost-bitten bloom, that seemed the very trophy of a December blast. He was accompanied by the blue-eyed romp, dished up as "Dame Mince-Pie," in the venerable magnificence of faded brocade, long stomacher, peaked hat, and high-heeled shoes. The young officer appeared as Robin Hood, in a sporting dress of

Kendal green, and a foraging cap with a gold tassel. The costume, to be sure, did not bear testimony to deep research, and there was an evident eye to the picturesque, natural to a young gallant in the presence of his mistress. The fair Julia hung on his arm in a pretty rustic dress, as "Maid Marian." The rest of the train had been metamorphosed in various ways; the girls trussed up in the finery of the ancient belles of the Bracebridge line, and the striplings bewhiskered with burnt cork, and gravely clad in broad skirts, hanging sleeves, and full-bottomed wigs, to represent the characters of Roast Beef, Plum Pudding, and other worthies celebrated in ancient maskings. The whole was under the control of the Oxonian, in the appropriate character of Misrule; and I observed that he exercised rather a mischievous sway with his wand over the smaller personages of the pageant.

The irruption of this motley crew, with beat of drum, according to ancient custom, was the consummation of uproar and merriment. Master Simon covered himself with glory by the stateliness with which, as Ancient Christmas, he walked a minuet with the peerless, though giggling, Dame Mince-Pie. It was followed by a dance of all the characters, which, from its medley of costumes, seemed as though the old family portraits had skipped down from their frames to join in the sport. Different centuries were figuring at cross hands and right and left; the dark ages were cutting pirouettes and rigadoons; and the days of Queen Bess jigging merrily down the middle, through a line of succeeding generations.

The worthy Squire contemplated these fantastic sports, and this resurrection of his old wardrobe, with the simple relish of childish delight. He stood chuckling and rubbing his hands, and scarcely hearing a word the parson said, notwithstanding that the latter was discoursing most authentically on the ancient and stately dance of the Paon, or Peacock, from which he conceived the minuet to be derived. For my part, I was in a continual excitement, from the varied scenes of whim and innocent gaiety passing before me. It was inspiring to see wild-eyed frolic and warm-hearted hospitality breaking out from among the chills and glooms of winter, and old age throwing off his apathy, and catching once more the freshness of youthful enjoyment.

I felt also an interest in the scene, from the consideration that these fleeting customs were posting fast into oblivion, and that this was, perhaps, the only family in England in which the whole of them were still punctiliously observed. There was a quaintness, too, mingled with all this revelry that gave it a peculiar zest; it was suited to the time and place; and as the old Manor House almost reeled with mirth and wassail, it seemed echoing back the joviality of long-departed years.

THE CHRISTMAS PLAY OF ST. GEORGE AND THE DRAGON

From a Lost Mediaeval Miracle Play

CHARACTERS.

SAINT GEORGE. KING OF EGYPT.

THE DRAGON. TURKISH KNIGHT.

FATHER CHRISTMAS. THE GIANT TURPIN.

THE DOCTOR.

Enter the Turkish Knight.

Open your doors, and let me in,
I hope your favors I shall win;
Whether I rise or whether I fall,
I'll do my best to please you all.
St. George is here, and swears he will come in,
And, if he does, I know he'll pierce my skin.
If you will not believe what I do say,
Let Father Christmas come in—clear the way.

[*Retires.*]

Enter Father Christmas.

Here come I, old Father Christmas,
    Welcome, or welcome not,
I hope old Father Christmas
    Will never be forgot.
I am not come here to laugh or to jeer,
But for a pocketfull of money, and a skinfull of beer,
If you will not believe what I do say,
Come in the King of Egypt—clear the way.

Enter the King of Egypt.

Here I, the King of Egypt, boldly do appear,
St. George, St. George, walk in, my only son and heir.
Walk in, my son St. George, and boldly act thy part,
That all the people here may see thy wond'rous art.

Enter Saint George.

Here come I, St. George, from Britain did I spring,
I'll fight the Dragon bold, my wonders to begin.
I'll clip his wings, he shall not fly;
I'll cut him down, or else I die.

Enter the Dragon.

Who's he that seeks the Dragon's blood,
And calls so angry, and so loud?
That English dog, will he before me stand?
I'll cut him down with my courageous hand.
With my long teeth, and scurvy jaw,
Of such I'd break up half a score,
And stay my stomach, till I'd more.

      [*St. George and the Dragon fight, the latter is killed.*]

Father Christmas.

Is there a doctor to be found
　　All ready, near at hand,
To cure a deep and deadly wound,
　　And make the champion stand.

Enter Doctor.

Oh! yes, there is a doctor to be found
　　All ready, near at hand,
To cure a deep and deadly wound,
　　And make the champion stand.

Father Christmas.

What can you cure?

Doctor.

All sorts of diseases,
Whatever you pleases,
The phthisic, the palsy, and the gout;
If the devil's in, I'll blow him out.

Father Christmas.

What is your fee?

Doctor.

Fifteen pound, it is my fee,
　　The money to lay down.
But, as 'tis such a rogue as thee,
　　I cure for ten pound.

I carry a little bottle of alicumpane;
 Here Jack, take a little of my flip flop,
 Pour it down thy tip top;
Rise up and fight again.

 [*The Doctor performs his cure, the fight is renewed,
 and the Dragon again killed.*]

Saint George.

Here am I, St. George,
 That worthy champion bold,
And with my sword and spear
 I won three crowns of gold.
I fought the fiery dragon,
 And brought him to the slaughter;
By that I won fair Sabra,
 The King of Egypt's daughter.
Where is the man, that now will me defy?
I'll cut his giblets full of holes, and make his buttons fly.

The Turkish Knight advances.

Here come I, the Turkish Knight,
Come from the Turkish land to fight.
I'll fight St. George, who is my foe,
I'll make him yield before I go;
He brags to such a high degree,
He thinks there's none can do the like of he.

Saint George.

Where is the Turk, that will before me stand?
I'll cut him down with my courageous hand.

 [*They fight, the Knight is overcome, and falls on one knee.*]

Turkish Knight.

Oh! pardon me, St. George, pardon of thee I crave,
Oh! pardon me this night, and I will be thy slave.

Saint George.

No pardon shalt thou have, while I have foot to stand,
So rise thee up again, and fight out sword in hand.

    [*They fight again, and the Knight is killed. Father Christmas
        calls for the Doctor, with whom the same dialogue occurs as
        before, and the cure is performed.*]

Enter the Giant Turpin.

Here come I, the Giant, bold Turpin is my name,
And all the nations round do tremble at my fame.
Wher'ere I go, they tremble at my sight,
No lord or champion long with me would fight.

Saint George.

Here's one that dares to look thee in the face,
And soon will send thee to another place.

    [*They fight and the Giant is killed; medical aid is called in as
        before, and the cure performed by the Doctor, to whom then
        is given a basin of girdy grout and a kick and driven out.*]

Father Christmas.

Now ladies and gentlemen, your sport is most ended,
So prepare for the hat, which is highly commended.
The hat it would speak, if it had but a tongue;
Come throw in your money and think it no wrong.

THE CHRISTMAS MUMMERS OF EGDON

By Thomas Hardy

A TRADITIONAL pastime is to be distinguished from a mere revival in no more striking feature than in this, that while in the revival all is excitement and fervor, the survival is carried on with a stolidity and absence of stir which sets one wondering why a thing that is done so perfunctorily should be kept up at all. Like Balaam and other unwilling prophets, the agents seem moved by an inner compulsion to say and do their allotted parts whether they will or no. This unweeting manner of performance is the true ring by which, in the refurbishing age, a fossilized survival may be known from a spurious reproduction.

The piece was the well-known play of "Saint George," and all who were behind the scenes assisted in the preparations, including the women of each household. Without the cooperation of sisters and sweethearts the dresses were likely to be a failure; but on the other hand, this class of assistance was not without its drawbacks. The girls could never be brought to respect tradition in designing and decorating the armour; they insisted on attaching loops and bows of silk and velvet in any situation pleasing to their taste. Gorget, gusset, basinet, cuirass, gauntlet, sleeve, all alike in the view of these feminine eyes were practicable spaces whereon to sew scraps of fluttering color.

It might be that Joe, who fought on the side of Christendom, had a sweetheart, and that Jim, who fought on the side of the Moslem, had one likewise. During the making of the costumes it would come to the knowledge of Joe's sweetheart that Jim's was putting brilliant silk scallops at the bottom of her lover's surcoat, in addition to the ribbons of the visor, the bars of which, being invariably formed of colored strips about half an inch wide hanging before the face, were mostly of that material. Joe's sweetheart straightway placed brilliant silk on the scallops of the hem in question, and, going a little further, added ribbon tufts to the shoulder pieces. Jim's, not to be outdone, would affix bows and rosettes everywhere.

The result was that in the end the Valiant Soldier, of the Christian army, was distinguished by no peculiarity of accoutrement from the Turkish Knight; and what was worse, on a casual view Saint George himself might be mistaken for his deadly enemy, the Saracen. The guisers themselves, though inwardly regretting this confusion of persons, could not afford to offend those by whose assistance they so largely profited, and the innovations were allowed to stand.

There was, it is true, a limit to this tendency to uniformity. The Leech or Doctor preserved his character intact: his darker habiliments, peculiar hat, and the bottle of physic slung under his arm, could never be mistaken. And the same might be said for the conventional figure of Father Christmas, with his gigantic club, an older man, who accompanied the band as general protector in long night journeys from parish to parish, and was bearer of the purse. . . .

As they drew nearer to the front of the house the mummers became aware that music and dancing were briskly flourishing within. Every now and then a long low note from the serpent, which was the chief wind instrument played at these times, advanced further into the heath than the thin treble part, and reached their ears alone; and next a more than usually loud tread from a dancer would come the same way. With nearer approach these fragmentary sounds became pieced together, and were found to be the salient points of the tune called "Nancy's Fancy."

. . . "They won't be much longer," said Father Christmas. . .

At this moment the fiddles finished off with a screech, and the serpent emitted a last note that nearly lifted the roof. When, from the comparative quiet within, the mummers judged that the dancers had taken their seats, Father Christmas advanced, lifted the latch, and put his head inside the door.

"Ah, the mummers, the mummers!" cried several guests at once. "Clear a space for the mummers!"

Hump-backed Father Christmas then made a complete entry, swinging his huge club, and in a general way clearing the stage for the actors proper, while he informed the company in smart verse that he was come, welcome or welcome not; concluding his speech with

"Make room, make room, my gallant boys,
And give us space to rhyme;
We've come to show Saint George's play,
Upon this Christmas time."

The guests were now arranging themselves at one end of the room, the fiddler was mending a string, the serpent player was emptying his mouthpiece, and the play began. First of those outside the Valiant Soldier entered, in the interest of Saint George—

"Here come I, the Valiant Soldier;
Slasher is my name;"

and so on. This speech concluded with a challenge to the infidel, at the end of which it was Eustacia's duty to enter as the Turkish Knight. She, with the rest who were not yet on, had till now remained in the moonlight which streamed under the porch. With no apparent effort or backwardness she came in, beginning—

"Here come I, a Turkish Knight,
Who learnt in Turkish land to fight;
I'll fight this man with courage bold:
If his blood's hot I'll make it cold!"

During her declamation Eustacia held her head erect, and spoke as roughly as she could, feeling pretty secure from observation. But the concentration upon her part necessary to prevent discovery, the newness of the scene, the shine of the candles, and the confusing effect upon her vision of the ribboned visor which hid her features, left her absolutely unable to perceive who were present as spectators. On the further side of a table bearing candles she could faintly discern faces, and that was all.

Meanwhile Jim Starks as the Valiant Soldier had come forward, and, with a glare upon the Turk, replied—

> "If, then, thou art that Turkish Knight,
> Draw out thy sword, and let us fight!"

And fight they did; the issue of the combat being that the Valiant
Soldier was slain by a preternaturally inadequate thrust from Eustacia, Jim, in his ardor for genuine histrionic art, coming down like
a log upon the stone floor with force enough to dislocate his shoulder.
Then, after more words from the Turkish Knight, rather too faintly
delivered, and statements that he'd fight Saint George and all his crew.
Saint George himself magnificently entered with the well-known
flourish—

> "Here come I, Saint George, the valiant man,
> With naked sword and spear in hand,
> Who fought the dragon and brought him to the slaughter,
> And by this won fair Sabra, the King of Egypt's daughter;
> What mortal man would dare to stand
> Before me with my sword in hand?"

This was the lad who had first recognized Eustacia; and when she
now, as the Turk, replied with suitable defiance, and at once began
the combat, the young fellow took especial care to use his sword as
gently as possible. Being wounded, the Knight fell upon one knee,
according to the direction. The Doctor now entered, restored the
Knight by giving him a draught from the bottle which he carried,
and the fight was again resumed, the Turk sinking by degrees until
quite overcome—dying as hard in this venerable drama as he is said
to do at the present day.

The remainder of the play ended: the Saracen's head was cut off,
and Saint George stood as victor. Nobody commented, any more than
they would have commented on the fact of mushrooms coming in
autumn or snowdrops in spring. They took the piece as phlegmati-
cally as did the actors themselves. It was a piece of cheerfulness which
was, as a matter of course, to be passed through every Christmas; and
there was no more to be said.

From *The Return of the Native*

CHRISTMAS WITH OUR BILL

By Frederick H. Grisewood

IT really was a ridiculous day; when you consider that Christmas was so near. The sun was quite hot, the air warm and balmy—spring might well have been round the corner instead of several months away.

Bill, whom I met on my way to the village shop which served as post office, was evidently of the same opinion. "Nothing, don't seem right somehow these 'ere days," he said. "I just picked a rose in my garden. That tree 'ad ought to 'a' known better—'er 'ad ought to 'a' bin asleep a long while since, instead o' gallivantin' about like that. But it ain't only the weather as be different—things ain't what they was."

Bill was evidently in one of his reminiscent moods, so I encouraged him to go on.

"Well, sir," he said, "fer one thing, us don't get what us 'ad used to get at Christmas time. In the old days it were coal an' beef fer all on us as worked on the estate. 'Ad used to come round in a waggin, an' us 'ad it reg'lar. Still, I will say as us used to work fer it. There weren't no talk o' overtime in those days. If your carter 'ad a sick mare 'e'd sit up all night along of 'er, an' such a thing as extra payment fer it never crossed 'is mind. You see, sir," he went on, "us took a proper pride in our jobs those days—an' the carter 'e didn't want 'is team spoilt by a sick 'un, so o' course 'e done what 'e could to keep all 'is beasts fit. But these young lads as works nowadays—the only thing as they thinks on be their 'alf 'oliday o' Saturdays. If you take five minutes out o' a man's dinner hour now 'e'll charge you overtime fer it. Well, that's the way things goes, and if that's what they wants they can 'ave it, but it don't suit me, I can tell 'ee. All comes o' tryin' to run farmin' like a factory—that's what it is.

"Th' old Christmases were fine. Us used to go a' carol singin',' and then there was the Mummers an' such like."

But here I lost Bill and his grievances. That magic word "Mummers" had opened the floodgates of memory. I was back in those far-off days—long before the Great War was even dreamed of—when, indeed, the Boer War was only a cloud on the horizon. I was a little boy again in a navy suit. For days there had been rumours of these strange things, Mummers. What could they be? But even Jane, the parlourmaid, who was my informant on all the important events in life, refused to tell me.

"You wait and see," she would say. So for the time being Mummers remained a mystery.

Christmas Day came and passed, and still no sign of these queer things. And then—two nights after—just as we had finished tea—we were allowed down into the drawing-room as it was Christmas time—Jane appeared at the door and said with a knowing look in my direction: "Please, ma'am, the Mummers are here, and we've cleared the servants' hall."

My father was fetched from his study, and we all made our way downstairs. The cook and the other servants were there with an air of expectancy on their faces, but who could these dreadful strangers be with black faces, gleaming eyes, and outlandish dresses, who were stamping the snow from their boots in the stone passage outside? Could these frightful objects really be the Mummers? Tremblingly, I hid my face in my mother's dress. "What's the matter?" she asked; "you're not afraid of the Mummers, are you?" And then one of them spoke, and I withdrew my face from its hiding-place and gazed in amazement. Could it be possible that concealed behind that blackened face and nightmare clothes lurked the familiar person of Bert, the boot boy? It certainly was his voice—a trifle self-conscious, but unmistakably it was Bert's voice.

This put quite a different complexion on the whole affair. With renewed courage I looked about me. That familiar shuffle could only belong to one person. I should have known it in a million in spite of its owner's disguise. It was fat George, the landlord of "The Spotted Dog." And over there, brandishing a wooden sword, in all the finery of Bold Slasher was—yes, it was none other than dear old Joe Allen, our postman.

This was fine—this was the real thing. And so the play began. The players were introduced—each one walking round and round the room reciting his lines in his homely Oxfordshire: "In comes I, King George, fine fellar be I. To fight for the good o' England will I try." Bold Slasher with his challenge. The mortal combat and defeat of the challenger. The frenzied appeal for a doctor. "Be there a doctor outside?" "There be." "I'll give thee ten pun' if thou'll come." "Won't come for that." "I'll give thee five pun' if thou'll come." "Won't come for that." "I'll give thee three brass fardens if thou'll come." "Come for that and glad o' the money. In comes I, the Doctor," etc.

The examination of the wounded man: "What's the matter with this 'ere man? Pain in the leg?" "No, pain in the 'ead." "What's best for a pain in the 'ead?" "Draw a tooth." "What, draw an arm?" "No, draw a tooth." The operation. Those frightful pincers. Were they really going to pull out one of Joe's teeth?

This was too much. I started up from my chair, but Ernest, the pseudo-doctor, grinned all over his black face and gave me a portentous wink. The pincers were inserted; every one pulled—once, twice, three times—and there, gripped firmly in the jaws of the murderous instrument, was an enormous tooth, which Ernest displayed in triumph. So Bold Slasher was made whole again and lived to fight another day.

What a splendid climax, and how we applauded—nor did the fearsome apparition of Beelzebub—"On my shoulder I carries my club"—evoke any feeling from me beyond that of wonder that our usually mild gardener could transform himself into such a demon.

Then there were songs from the company, congratulations, much shaking of hands and drinking of beer—and—

Here I came back to earth again to hear Bill saying: "An' one o' they young rapscallions clumb up into the branches o' Hassams' oak and very nigh startled old Polly Chivers out o' 'er senses. You knows as they says as that there oak be 'aunted. A lot o' nonsense, I sez."

"You don't believe in ghosts then, Bill?" I asked, pulling myself together. "Ghosts," said Bill, and I wish I could portray the scorn in his voice. "I don't set no store by they—why, ol' Ted as lived next door to me 'e 'ad used to see 'em every Saturday night. 'It at 'em wi' a stick, that he did—reg'lar."

And with that he turned and trudged slowly towards "The Spotted Dog."

THE CHRISTMAS FAMILY-PARTY

By Charles Dickens

THE Christmas family-party that we mean, is not a mere assemblage of relations, got up at a week or two's notice, originating this year, having no family precedent in the last, and not likely to be repeated in the next. It is an annual gathering of all the accessible members of the family, young or old, rich or poor; and all the children look forward to it, for two months beforehand, in a fever of anticipation. Formerly it was held at grandpapa's; but grandpapa getting old, and grandmamma getting old too, and rather infirm, they have given up housekeeping, and domesticated themselves with uncle George, so the party always takes place at uncle George's house, but grandmamma sends in most of the good things, and grandpapa always *will* toddle down, all the way to Newgate-market, to buy the turkey, which he engages a porter to bring home behind him in triumph, always insisting on the man's being rewarded with a glass of spirits, over and above his hire, to drink "a merry Christmas and a happy New Year" to aunt George. As to grandmamma, she is very secret and mysterious for two or three days beforehand, but not sufficiently so to prevent rumours getting afloat that she has purchased a beautiful new cap with pink ribbons for each of the servants, together with sundry books, and penknives, and pencil-cases, for the younger branches; to say nothing of divers secret additions to the order originally given by aunt George at the pastrycook's, such as another dozen of mince-pies for the dinner, and a large plum-cake for the children.

On Christmas-eve, grandmamma is always in excellent spirits, and after employing all the children, during the day, in stoning the plums and all that, insists regularly every year on uncle George coming down into the kitchen, taking off his coat, and stirring the pudding for half an hour or so, which uncle George good-humouredly does, to the vociferous delight of the children and servants, and the evening concludes with a glorious game of blind-man's-buff, in an early stage of which grandpapa takes great care to be caught, in order that he may have an opportunity of displaying his dexterity.

On the following morning, the old couple, with as many of the children as the pew will hold, go to church in great state, leaving aunt George at home dusting decanters and filling castors, and uncle George carrying bottles into the dining-parlour, and calling for corkscrews, and getting into everybody's way.

When the church-party return to lunch, grandpapa produces a small sprig of mistletoe from his pocket, and tempts the boys to kiss their little cousins under it—a proceeding which affords both the boys and the old gentleman unlimited satisfaction, but which rather outrages grandmamma's ideas of decorum, until grandpapa says, that when he was just thirteen years and three months old, *he* kissed grandmamma under a mistletoe too, on which the children clap their hands, and laugh very heartily, as do aunt George and uncle George; and grandmamma looks pleased, and says, with a benevolent smile, that grandpapa always was an impudent dog, on which the children laugh very heartily again, and grandpapa more heartily than any of them.

But all these diversions are nothing to the subsequent excitement when grandmamma in a high cap, and slate-coloured silk gown, and grandpapa with a beautifully plaited shirt-frill, and white neckerchief, seat themselves on one side of the drawing-room fire, with uncle George's children and little cousins innumerable, seated in the front, waiting the arrival of the anxiously expected visitors. Suddenly a hackney-coach is heard to stop, and uncle George, who has been looking out of the window, exclaims "Here's Jane!" on which the children rush to the door, and helter-skelter down stairs; and uncle Robert and aunt Jane, and the dear little baby, and the nurse, and the whole party, are ushered up stairs amidst tumultuous shouts of "Oh, my!" from the children, and frequently repeated warnings not to hurt baby from the nurse: and grandpapa takes the child, and grandmamma kisses her daughter, and the confusion of this first entry has scarcely subsided, when some other aunts and uncles with more cousins arrive, and the grown-up cousins flirt with each other, and so do the little cousins too, for that matter, and nothing is to be heard but a confused din of talking, laughing, and merriment.

A hesitating double knock at the street-door, heard during a momentary pause in the conversation, excites a general inquiry of "Who's that?" and two or three children, who have been standing at the window, announce in a low voice, that it's "poor aunt Margaret." Upon which aunt George leaves the room to welcome the new comer, and grandmamma draws herself up rather stiff and stately, for Margaret married a poor man without her consent, and poverty not being a sufficiently weighty punishment for her offence, has been discarded by her friends, and debarred the society of her dearest relatives. But Christmas has come round, and the unkind feelings that have struggled against better dispositions during the year, have melted away before its genial influence, like half-formed ice beneath the morning sun. It is not difficult in a moment of angry feeling for a parent to denounce a disobedient child; but to banish her at a period of general good-will and hilarity, from the hearth round which she has sat on so many anniversaries of the same day, expanding by slow degrees from infancy to girlhood, and then bursting, almost imperceptibly, into the high-spirited and beautiful woman, is widely different. The air of conscious rectitude and cold forgiveness, which the old lady has assumed, sits ill upon her; and when the poor girl is led in by her sister, pale in looks and broken in spirit—not from poverty, for that she could bear, but from the consciousness of undeserved neglect, and unmerited unkindness—it is easy to see how much of it is assumed. A momentary pause succeeds; the girl breaks suddenly from her sister and throws herself, sobbing, on her mother's neck. The father steps hastily forward, and grasps her husband's hand. Friends crowd round to offer their hearty congratulations, and happiness and harmony again prevail.

As to the dinner, it's perfectly delightful—nothing goes wrong, and everybody is in the very best of spirits, and disposed to please and be pleased. Grandpapa relates a circumstantial account of the purchase of the turkey, with a slight digression relative to the purchase of previous turkeys, on former Christmas-days, which grandmamma corroborates in the minutest particular. Uncle George tells stories, and carves poultry, and takes wine, and jokes with the children at the side-table, and winks at the cousins that are making love, or being made love to, and exhilarates everybody with his good humour and hospitality; and when at last a stout servant staggers in with a gigantic pudding, with a sprig of holly in the top, there is such a laughing and shouting, and clapping of little chubby hands, and kicking up of fat dumpy legs, as can only be equalled by the applause with which the astonishing feat of pouring lighted brandy into mince-pies, is received by the younger visitors. Then the dessert!—and the wine!— and the fun! Such beautiful speeches, and *such* songs, from aunt Margaret's husband, who turns out to be such a nice man, and *so* attentive to grandmamma! Even grandpapa not only sings his annual song with unprecedented vigour, but on being honoured with an unanimous *encore*, according to annual custom, actually comes out with a new one which nobody but grandmamma ever heard before: and a young scape-grace of a cousin, who has been in some disgrace with the old people, for certain heinous sins of omission and commission—neglecting to call, and persisting in drinking Burton Ale— astonishes everybody into convulsions of laughter by volunteering the most extraordinary comic songs that were ever heard. And thus the evening passes, in a strain of rational good-will and cheerfulness, doing more to awaken the sympathies of every member of the party in behalf of his neighbour, and to perpetuate their good feeling during the ensuing year, than all the homilies that have ever been written, by all the divines that have ever lived.

From *Sketches by Boz*

RECIPES FOR FOOD AND DRINK

ROAST GOOSE À LA CRATCHIT

First, estimate the roasting time from the weight of the dressed goose; allow 25 to 30 minutes per pound. The temperature is moderate, 350 degrees F. (or use 450 degrees F. for 20 minutes, then reduce to moderate, 350 degrees, for remainder of time.)

Place goose, breast up, on a rack or trivet in a shallow, uncovered pan. Do not stuff—yet. The first part of the roasting will be a fat-trying-out process. Roast at the above temperature for one hour. Then remove from the oven, allow to stand until rather cool; pour off all the fat in the pan. Then, if you are going to stuff, do it just before completing the roasting. That may be now or next day. If the goose seems to have an unusually heavy fat layer, pour off fat again at the end of the second hour. And remember; no water; no basting. The fattiness of the bird makes basting unnecessary when roasted at this low temperature. If you prefer not to stuff the goose, the roasting may be continuous except for pouring off the fat. If you do want to make a stuffing, a tart one will be best. Use plain sauerkraut for this, or a mixture of chopped tart apples and dried fruit.

ROAST TURKEY: AMERICAN STYLE

1 (15 to 16 pound) turkey	Sage and onion dressing
1 tablespoon salt	¾ cup melted butter
⅛ teaspoon pepper	1 cup hot water

Wash and dry ready-dressed turkey. Singe. Sprinkle inside and out with combined salt and pepper. Stuff with sage and onion dressing, packing in firmly. Truss bird and place in shallow roasting pan. Brush all over with some of the melted butter and place in a moderate oven (350 degrees) and allow about 25 minutes per pound. Slices of bread arranged over the places which seem to brown faster than others will ensure an even brown color all over the bird. Remove string or skewers to serve. Approximate yield: 16 portions.

ROAST PIG

[From Martha Washington's Cook Book]

1 small pig	¾ cup butter
Bread crumbs	sprigs of thyme
Salt and pepper	½ teasp. sugar

Thoroughly clean a young suckling pig. Dust over with salt. Put in hot oven. After about an hour, when half roasted, pull off the skin and stick the pig full of sprigs of thyme. Return to oven and baste frequently with ¾ cup butter, melted and mixed with a few coarse breadcrumbs. It requires about 2 hrs. to roast the pig. Serve with Bread Sauce.

CHICKEN PIE

[Martha Washington's Recipe]

1 Chicken	mace
1 ½ lb. forequarter of Lamb	butter
1 small onion	1 tablespoonful flour
stalk of celery	grated nutmeg
bay leaf	salt
whole cloves	peppercorns
6 hard boiled eggs	¾ cup white wine
	lemon juice

Pastry

Disjoint the chicken and place in a stewing pan, together with the onion, bay leaf, celery, cloves, salt and peppercorns. Cover with boiling water and cook gently until tender. Cut lamb into small pieces, remove any skin or fat, roll in flour seasoned with pepper and salt, brown in a little butter, add boiling water ½ to cover, stew till tender. Remove chicken from stock, remove bones and skin and cut in pieces. Line deep, round dish with pastry. Lay in the chicken, lamb, and quartered hard boiled eggs. Sprinkle in salt, pepper, grated nutmeg and a little mace; dot thickly with butter. Then to 1¼ cups chicken stock add ¾ cups white wine, and if desired, some lemon juice.

Thicken with flour mixed with 1 tablespoonful butter and pour into the pie. Put on top crust, slash, and bake in a moderate oven 1 hour.

(For those who like sweets, shredded dates, sugar, citron, raisins, currants and candied lettuce may be added.)

KING GEORGE I'S CHRISTMAS PUDDING

(*This recipe is said to have been in the possession of the Royal Family from the days of George I.*)

Ingredients: Suet 1 ½ lb. finely shredded; Demerara sugar 1 lb.; small raisins 1 lb.; plums 1 lb. (stoned and cut in half); candied citron peel 4 oz.; mixed spice 1 teaspoonful; nutmeg ½; salt 2 teaspoonfuls; breadcrumbs 1 lb.; sifted flour 1 lb.; eggs 1 lb. (weighed in their shells); new milk ½ pt.; brandy 1 wineglassful.

Time: Stand after mixing for 12 hours in a cool place; and boil 8 hours.

Method:
1. Mix all the dry ingredients together.
2. Beat the eggs to a froth.
3. Add ½ pt. new milk, and the brandy.
4. Use this mixture to moisten the dry ingredients.
5. Stand 12 hours in a cool place.
6. Then put in buttered moulds which should be filled.
7. Cover with buttered paper.
8. Tie down with a cloth and boil 8 hours.
9. When required boil up for another 2 hours. Sufficient for 3 medium sized puddings each weighing about 3 lb.

WARTIME PLUM PUDDING

Ingredients: Potatoes ½ lb.; carrots ½ lb.; sugar 3 oz.; currants and raisins mixed ¼ lb.; flour ¼ lb.; suet 3 oz.; candied peel ½ oz.; eggs 1.

Time: steam 3 hours

Method:
1. Butter pudding basin.
2. Peel and grate the potatoes (you want ¼ lb. weighed after they have been grated).
3. Peel and grate the carrots (must weigh ¼ lb. when grated).

4. Mix the potatoes and carrots, sugar, currants, raisins and all the dry ingredients well together; and
5. Blend them with the egg and milk.
6. Mix well.

[NOTE: A spoonful in England means as much above the bowl as in it. An English teaspoonful = 1 third dram, or 30 drops. 3 English teasp. = 1 American tablespoon]

MINCEMEAT FOR CHRISTMAS

[*The Priory. Melton Mowbray.*]

Ingredients: Apples 4 lb.; fine chopped suet, stoned raisins, 2 lb. of each; granulated sugar 2 lb.; lemons, the grated rinds of 3 and juice of 1; mixed spice to taste; salt ½ oz.; brandy or wine, or both, to moisten.

N.B.—Do not let any flour of any kind touch the suet, or the mince-meat will ferment.

(These mince pies are what in America we call tarts: no larger than the palm of the hand. For a long time I thought English families must have Gargantuan appetites, because Grandma so casually—in "Sketches by Boz"—added to the baker's order an "extra dozen of mince-pies.")

COLONIAL PUMPKIN PIE

Pastry for 2 9-inch shells
6 eggs
1 cup granulated sugar
½ teaspoon ginger
½ teaspoon cinnamon
½ teaspoon nutmeg
½ teaspoon salt
2 cups cooked pumpkin
2 cups cream or rich milk

Line 2 9-inch pie plates with pastry. Beat eggs until light; combine with sugar, spices, salt and pumpkin. Gradually add cream or milk; stir until well combined. Pour into pastry-lined plates and bake in hot oven (450 degrees F.) 10 minutes; then reduce temperature to moderate (350 degrees F.) and continue baking about 30 minutes longer or until knife comes out clean when inserted in custard. Yield: 2 (9-inch) pies.

DARK FRUITCAKE

2 lb. seeded and quartered raisins
½ lb. figs cut fine
½ lb. finely shaved citron
½ lb. mixed candied peel
½ lb. blanched almonds cut in slivers
½ lb. walnut meats chopped
1 lb. dried currants
1½ cup sherry

4 to 5 cups flour
1 lb. butter
1 lb. brown sugar
1 cup molasses
10 eggs
1 tablespoon cinnamon
2 grated nutmegs
½ teaspoon allspice
1 scant teaspoon soda
½ cup orange juice

Bake in two large tube pans. When taken from pan, sprinkle with French wine or brandy, wrap in linen and store till Christmas in crock.

OLYKOEK: AN ANCESTRAL NEW AMSTERDAM CHRISTMAS CAKE

1 cup milk, scalded
1 teaspoon salt
¼ cup sugar
2⅔ tablespoons shortening

1 cake compressed yeast
1 egg, well beaten
3½ cups sifted flour (about)
Brandied raisins
Powdered sugar

Place milk, salt, sugar and 1 tablespoon shortening in large mixing bowl, and cool. When lukewarm, add crumbled yeast cake and well beaten egg. Add 1½ cups flour and beat thoroughly. Gradually stir in remaining flour, adding just enough to make a dough slightly softer than that of bread. Turn out on floured board and knead until smooth and elastic, adding flour as necessary. Place dough in greased bowl and brush with melted shortening; cover and let rise in warm place until doubled in bulk (for 2 to 4 hours). Knead, cut off small pieces of dough and enclose brandied raisins or citron in center of each when shaping into small balls. Let stand until light. Fry in hot deep fat (360–370 degrees F.) about 3 minutes. Roll in powdered sugar while warm. This is an early American favorite; the epicures of New Amsterdam soaked the olykoeks in Santa Cruz rum and served them with whipped cream.

CHRISTMAS APPLE PIE: ENGLAND, 1770

At Polton, Bedfordshire, and places adjacent, it was the custom at Christmas festivities, to place on the table a large apple pie called an "Apple Florentine." This was made in a huge dish of pewter or Sheffield plate, or silver (or perhaps gold), filled with "good baking apples, sugar and lemon to the very brim, with a covering of rich pastry." When baked and before serving up, the crust was taken off and cut into triangular portions ready to be replaced on the apples, but before this was done a full quart of well-spiced ale was poured in hissing hot. I do not know whether apple pies are still called Florentines in Bedfordshire, but I do know that an apple pie is considered as much an indispensable part of the Christmas feast in some places as orange jelly is in others.

Florence White, *Good Things in England*

YULE CAKE, WHITBY

An ancestral cake with which old ladies regale their friends who call between Christmas and New Year's, together with a glass of cherry brandy, in Whitby, Yorkshire.

Ingredients: Plain flour, 1½ lb.; butter ¾ lb.; moist sugar ½ lb.; cinnamon ½ oz.; ½ nutmeg grated; raisins ½ lb.; currants ½ lb.; unlimited candied lemon peel and almonds; eggs 3; 1 glass of brandy and a little cream sufficient to make the whole into a paste.

Method:
1. Rub the butter into the flour.
2. Mix in the dry ingredients.
3. Mix well.
4. Beat up the eggs very well with the brandy.
5. Mix with the dry ingredients.
6. Work into a dough with a little cream.
7. Press into a flat tin—it will half fill.
8. Cut it half through each way into small squares.
9. Bake in a moderate oven for 3 hours.

10. Turn out of the tin on to a wire pastry tray when you take it from the oven, and
11. When cold break into rough pieces where the knife indicated before cooking.

NEW YEAR'S EGGNOG

6 eggs

¾ cup sugar

1½ cups cognac brandy

½ cup rum

4 cups heavy cream

4 cups milk

½ cup powdered sugar

Nutmeg

Separate egg whites from yolks. Beat yolks until very light, add sugar and continue beating until well blended; slowly add brandy and rum, then 3 cups of cream and milk. Beat egg whites until stiff but not dry and fold into above mixture. Whip the remaining cup of cream and add powdered sugar. Top each glass with the sweetened whipped cream and sprinkle lightly with nutmeg before serving. Approximate yield: 26 portions.

SOLLAGHAN

[*This dish is served at breakfast on Christmas Day in the Isle of Man.*]

1. Put some oat meal in a pan on the fire, and
2. Keep stirring till it is dry and crisp.
3. Then skim the top of the broth pot on to it and stir well.
4. Eat with pepper and salt.

GLOUCESTER'S CHRISTMAS PIE

A Lamprey Pie embellished with golden ornaments was sent annually as a Christmas present from the Corporation of Gloucester to the Sovereign of the realm down to the time of Corporation reform in 1830. The custom was revived in 1893. The pie was sent to Queen Victoria in her Diamond Jubilee Year; it weighed 20 lb., was oval in shape, the crust garnished with truffles and crayfish on gold skewers, and aspic jelly; on the top was a gold crown and sceptre and at the base four gold lions. The gold skewer heads were in the form of crowns and on either side of the pie was a white silk banner with the Gloucester coat of arms and two lampreys entwined with the inscription "Royal Lamprey Pie, Gloucester's Ancient Custom from the Norman Period to the Victorian Era."

WASSAIL BOWL

1 quart ale	½ bottle sherry
¼ ounce grated nutmeg	2 slices toasted bread ½ inch thick
¼ ounce grated ginger	1 lemon, juice and peel
¼ ounce grated cinnamon	Sugar to taste
	2 well-baked apples

Put ale in sauce pan and cook gently until it foams, then stir in the spices, add the sherry, lemon peel and juice with the sugar. When sugar is dissolved, set the pan aside on the stove for 20 minutes to infuse. Then warm up, pour into the punch bowl, let the toast and apples float in this and serve in cups.

The Wassail, prepared by Charles Dickens for the entertainment, on Christmas Eve, at the Charity of Richard Watts, Rochester, Kent, of seven poor travellers not being rogues or proctors; as reported in the Christmas Number of "Household Words" for 1854:

It was high time to make the Wassail now; therefore I had up the materials (which, together with their proportions and combinations, I must decline to impart, as the only secret of my own I was ever known to keep) and made a glorious jorum. Not in a bowl; for a bowl anywhere but on a shelf is a low superstition, fraught with cooling and slopping; but in a brown earthenware pitcher, tenderly suffocated, when full, with a coarse cloth.

PUNCH À LA MICAWBER

I informed Mr. Micawber that I relied upon him for a bowl of punch, and led him to the lemons. His recent despondency, not to say despair, was gone in a moment. I never saw a man so thoroughly enjoy himself amid the fragrance of lemon-peel and sugar, the odour of burning rum, and the steam of boiling water, as Mr. Micawber did that afternoon. It was wonderful to see his face shining at us out of a thin cloud of these delicious fumes, as he stirred, and mixed, and tasted, and looked as if he were making, instead of punch, a fortune for his family down to the latest posterity.

Charles Dickens, *David Copperfield*

BURNT SHERRY AT A THAMESIDE INN

"They burn sherry very well here," said the Inspector, as a piece of local intelligence. "Perhaps you gentlemen might like a bottle?" . . .

Bob's reappearance with a steaming jug broke off the conversation. But although the jug steamed forth a delicious perfume, its contents had not received that last happy touch which the Six Jolly Fellowship Porters imparted on such momentous occasions. Bob carried in his left hand one of those iron models of sugar-loaf hats—made in that shape that they might, with their pointed ends, seek out for themselves glowing nooks in the depths of the red coals—into which he emptied the jug and the pointed end of which he thrust deep down into the fire, so leaving it for a few moments while he disappeared and reappeared with three bright drinking glasses. Placing these on the table and bending over the fire, meritoriously sensible of the trying nature of his duty, he watched the wreaths of steam, until at the special instant of projection he caught up the iron vessel and gave it one delicate twirl, causing it to send forth one gentle hiss. Then he restored the contents to the jug; held over the steam of the jug, each of the 3 bright glasses in succession; finally filled them all, and with a clear conscience awaited the applause of his fellow creatures.

Charles Dickens, *Our Mutual Friend*

MULLED CIDER PUNCH

3 large tart apples	½ teaspoon nutmeg
¼ cup water	½ teaspoon allspice
1 teaspoon cinnamon	6 cups cider

Peel and core apples, place in baking dish, add water, cover and bake in moderate oven (350 degrees F.) 30 minutes or until very soft.

Put pulp through a sieve and combine with spices. When ready to serve, heat cider to boiling and pour over the spiced apple pulp. Mix well and serve at once. Approximate yield: 6 portions.

MULLED PORT

½ nutmeg	sugar
2 cups port	4 eggs, separated

Grate the nutmeg into the wine, add sugar if desired, cover and heat just to the boiling point. Remove from fire and let cool slightly. Beat egg yolks until thick and lemon colored. Blend with a little cold wine and then gradually with the hot wine. Pour it back and forth in two containers several times until it is light and thoroughly mixed. Place it over low heat and stir it constantly until mixture coats a metal spoon. Do not let it boil. Pour into chocolate cups and top with beaten egg white if desired. Serve with slightly sweetened wafers. Yield 4 portions.

BEEFSTEAK PUDDING

[Christmas with a travelling Cheap Jack]

I am a neat hand at cookery, and I'll tell you what I knocked up for my Christmas eve dinner in the Library Cart. I knocked up a beefsteak pudding for one, with two-kidneys, a dozen oysters, and a couple of mushrooms thrown in. It's a pudding to put a man in good humour with everything, except the two bottom buttons of his waistcoat.

Charles Dickens, *Dr. Marigold's Prescriptions*

But for most of us, the beefsteak pudding that lives in literature was made by Ruth Pinch in "Martin Chuzzlewit." She used, according to Florence White of the English Folk Cookery Association, "6 oz. butter for the crust of her pudding instead of 6 oz. suet, and moistened the flour, etc. into a paste with the well-beaten yolks of four eggs, mixed with a little water (an extravagant young woman that!) Otherwise the ingredients and directions for making are the same as in Miss Acton's recipe (1845)." For a basin that holds 1 ½ pints, the following quantities will be required:

Ingredients: Flour 1 lb.; beef suet finely minced 6 oz. (or if you are a Ruth Pinch, 6 oz. butter); beefsteak 1 lb. (the skirt makes an excellent pudding and is economical); salt ½ oz.; pepper ½ teaspoonful; water ½ pint; mutton may be substituted for beef and half a dozen or a dozen oysters interspersed with it. Time: to boil 3½ hours.

Method: 1. Grease a basin, put a large pot of water on to boil.
2. Make the pastry with the flour, suet, salt and water.
3. Roll it out and line the basin leaving a piece for a lid.
4. Cut the steak into convenient pieces; flour them, season with pepper and salt; put them in the pudding.
5. Pour in the ½ pint of water and put on the lid.
6. Tie over with a floured cloth and boil as above.

"IT'S A STEW OF TRIPE"

There was a deep red ruddy blush upon the room, and when the landlord stirred the fire, sending the flames skipping and leaping up—when he took off the lid of the iron pot and there rushed out a savoury smell, while the bubbling sound grew deeper and more rich, and an unctuous steam came floating out, hanging in a delicious mist above their heads—when he did this. . . . Mr. Codlin drew his sleeve across his lips, and said in a murmuring voice, "What is it?"

"It's a stew of tripe," said the landlord smacking his lips, "and cow-heel," smacking them again, "and bacon," smacking them once more, "and steak," smacking them for the fourth time, "and peas, cauliflowers, new potatoes and sparrow-grass, all working up together in one delicious gravy."

"Then," said Mr. Codlin, "fetch me a pint of warm ale, and don't let anybody bring into the room even so much as a biscuit until the time arrives."

Charles Dickens, *Old Curiosity Shop*

[*Though this is a summer concoction—as its ingredients imply—the famous old restaurant of Simpson's on the Strand, London, prepares it in the Christmas holidays as a special feature of this time of good cheer—and will concoct it at other times if given due notice.*]

SONGS AND VERSES

JINGLE BELLS

Dashing thro' the snow,
In a one-horse open sleigh;
O'er the fields we go,
Laughing all the way;
Bells on bob-tail ring
Making spirits bright;
What fun it is to ride and sing
A sleighing song to-night!

Chorus: Accompanied by jingling glasses.

Jingle, bells! Jingle, bells!
Jingle all the way!
Oh! what fun it is to ride
In a one-horse open sleigh!
Jingle, bells! Jingle, bells!
Jingle all the way!
Oh! what fun it is to ride
In a one-horse open sleigh!

A day or two ago
I thought I'd take a ride,
And soon Miss Fannie Bright
Was seated by my side.
The horse was lean and lank;
Misfortune seem'd his lot;
He got into a drifted bank,
And we, we got up-sot.

Now the ground is white;
Go it while you're young;
Take the girls to-night,
And sing this sleighing song.
Just get a bob-tail'd bay,
Two-forty for his speed;
Then hitch him to an open sleigh,
And crack! you'll take the lead.

J. PIERPONT

CHRISTMAS TIME IS COMING ROUND

Christmas time is coming round.
Geese are getting fat,
Please to put a penny
In an old man's hat!
If you haven't got a penny,
A ha'penny will do,
If you haven't got a ha'penny,
God
      bless
         you!

NURSERY RHYME

AULD LANG SYNE

Should auld acquaintance be forgot,
  And never brought to min'?
Should auld acquaintance be forgot,
  And days o' auld lang syne?

For auld lang syne, my dear,
   For auld lang syne,
We'll tak a cup o' kindness yet
   For auld lang syne.

We twa hae run about the braes,
   And pu'd the gowans fine;
But we've wandered monie a weary fit
   Sin' auld lang syne.

We twa hae paidl't i' the burn,
   Frae mornin' sun till dine;
But seas between us braid hae roared
   Sin auld lang syne.

And here's a hand, my trusty fiere,
   And gie's a hand o' thine;
And we'll tak a right guid willie-waught
   For auld lang syne.

And surely ye'll be your pint-stowp,
   And surely I'll be mine,
And we'll tak a cup o' kindness yet
   For auld lang syne!

ROBERT BURNS

WE WILL SING A NEW SONG

We will sing a new song
That sounds like the old:
     Noël.

We will tell an old tale
That has often been told:
     Noël.

We will build a tall town:
We will watch for the Star:
Noël.

We will build a new world,
Without War.

Ernest Rhys

HEIGH HO, THE HOLLY!

Blow, blow, thou winter wind—
Thou art not so unkind
    As man's ingratitude!
Thy tooth is not so keen,
Because thou are not seen,
    Although thy breath be rude.
Heigh ho! sing heigh ho! unto the green holly:
Most friendship is feigning, most loving mere folly.
    Then heigh ho! the holly!
    This life is most jolly!

Freeze, freeze, thou bitter sky—
Thou dost not bite so nigh
    As benefits forgot!
Though thou the waters warp,
Thy sting is not so sharp
    As friend remembered not.
Heigh ho! sing heigh ho! unto the green holly,
Most friendship is feigning, most loving mere folly.
    Then heigh ho, the holly!
    This life is most jolly!

William Shakespeare

THE MAHOGANY-TREE

Christmas is here;
Winds whistle shrill,
Icy and chill,
Little care we;
Little we fear
Weather without,
Sheltered about
The Mahogany-Tree.

Once on the boughs
Birds of rare plume
Sang in its bloom;
Night-birds are we;
Here we carouse,
Singing, like them,
Perched round the stem
Of the jolly old tree.

Here let us sport,
Boys, as we sit—
Laughter and wit
Flashing so free.
Life is but short—
When we are gone,
Let them sing on,
Round the old tree.

Evenings we knew,
Happy as this;
Faces we miss,
Pleasant to see.

Kind hearts and true,
Gentle and just,
Peace to your dust!
We sing round the tree.

Care like a dun,
Lurks at the gate;
Let the dog wait;
Happy we'll be!
Drink, every one;
Pile up the coals;
Fill the red bowls,
Round the old tree!

Drain we the cup.—
Friend, art afraid?
Spirits are laid
In the Red Sea.
Mantle it up;
Empty it yet;
Let us forget,
Round the old tree!

Sorrows begone!
Life and its ills,
Duns and their bills,
Bid we to flee.
Come with the dawn,
Blue-devil sprite!
Leave us tonight,
Round the old tree!

WILLIAM MAKEPEACE THACKERAY

CEREMONIES FOR CHRISTMAS

Come, bring with a noise,
My merry, merry boys,
The Christmas log to the firing,
While my good dame, she
Bids ye all be free,
And drink to your heart's desiring.

With the last year's brand
Light the new block, and
For good success in his spending,
On your psalteries play,
That sweet luck may
Come while the log is a-tending.

Drink now the strong beer,
Cut the white loaf here,
The while the meat is a-shredding;
For the rare mince-pie,
And the plums stand by,
To fill the paste that's a-kneading.

            ROBERT HERRICK

BUT A SINGLE THOUGHT

Bring us in good ale, and bring us in good ale:
For our blessèd Lady's sake, bring us in good ale!

Bring us in no beef, for there is many bones,
Bring us in good ale, for *that* goth down at ones.

Bring us in no bacon, for that is passing fat,
But bring us in good ale, and give us enough of that.

Bring us in no mutton, for that is often lene,
Nor bring us in no trypes, for they be seldom clene.

Bring us in no egges, for there are many shelles,
But bring us in good ale, and give us nothing elles.

Bring us in no butter, for therein are many heres,
Nor bring us in no pigges flesh, for that will make us boars.

Bring us in good ale, and bring us in good ale:
For our blessèd Lady's sake, bring us in good ale!

FROM THE FIFTEENTH CENTURY

OLD CHRISTMAS RETURNED

All you that to feasting and mirth are inclined,
Come here is good news for to pleasure your mind,
Old Christmas is come for to keep open house,
He scorns to be guilty of starving a mouse:
Then come, boys, and welcome for diet the chief,
Plum-pudding, goose, capon, minced pies, and roast beef.

The holly and ivy about the walls wind
And show that we ought to our neighbors be kind,
Inviting each other for pastime and sport,
And where we best fare, there we most do resort;
We fail not of victuals, and that of the chief,
Plum-pudding, goose, capon, minced pies, and roast beef.

All travellers, as they do pass on their way,
At gentlemen's halls are invited to stay,
Themselves to refresh, and their horses to rest,
Since that he must be Old Christmas's guest;
Nay, the poor shall not want, but have for relief,
Plum-pudding, goose, capon, minced pies, and roast beef.

TRADITIONAL

CHRISTMAS POEM FOR MOTORISTS

The light that's red like a holly berry
I find irritating, very;
But the light that's green and bids me go
Pleases me like mistletoe.
I pay no heed to the light that's yellow,
But leave that for the other fellow.

P. E. G. Quercus

BELLS ACROSS THE SNOW

O Christmas, merry Christmas!
  Is it really come again,
With its memories and greetings,
  With its joy and with its pain?
There's a minor in the carol,
  And a shadow in the light,
And a spray of cypress twining
  With the holly wreath to-night.
And the hush is never broken
  By laughter light and low,
As we listen in the starlight
  To the "bells across the snow."

O Christmas, merry Christmas!
  'Tis not so very long
Since other voices blended
  With the carol and the song!
If we could but hear them singing
  As they are singing now,

If we could but see the radiance
    Of the crown on each dear brow;
There would be no sigh to smother,
    No hidden tear to flow,
As we listen in the starlight
    To the "bells across the snow."

O Christmas, merry Christmas!
    This never more can be;
We cannot bring again the days
    Of our unshadowed glee.
But Christmas, happy Christmas,
    Sweet herald of good-will,
With holy songs of glory
    Brings holy gladness still.
For peace and hope may brighten,
    And patient love may glow,
As we listen in the starlight
    To the "bells across the snow."
                    FRANCES RIDLEY HAVERGAL

SO, NOW IS COME OUR JOYFULST FEAST

So, now is come our joyfulst feast,
    Let every man be jolly;
Each room with ivy leaves is drest,
    And every post with holly.
Though some churls at our mirth repine,
Round your foreheads garlands twine;
Drown sorrow in a cup of wine,
    And let us all be merry.

Now all our neighbours' chimnies smoke,
   And Christmas logs are burning;
Their ovens they with baked meats choke,
   And all their spits are turning.
Without the door let sorrow lie;
And if for cold it hap to die,
We'll bury't in a Christmas pie,
   And evermore be merry.

Now every lad is wondrous trim,
   And no man minds his labour;
Our lasses have provided them
   A bag-pipe and a tabor;
Young men and maids, and girls and boys,
Give life to one another's joys;
And you anon shall by their noise
   Perceive that they are merry.

Rank misers now do sparing shun;
   Their hall of music soundeth;
And dogs thence with whole shoulders run,
   So all things there aboundeth.
The country folks themselves advance
For crowdy-mutton's * come out of France;
And Jack shall pipe, and Jill shall dance,
   And all the town be merry.

                            GEORGE WITHER

* Fiddlers.

IT WAS THE CALM AND SILENT NIGHT!

It was the calm and silent night!
   Seven hundred years and fifty-three
Had Rome been growing up to might,
   And now was Queen of land and sea.
No sound was heard of clashing wars;
   Peace brooded o'er the hush'd domain;
Apollo, Pallas, Jove and Mars,
   Held undisturb'd their ancient reign,
      In the solemn midnight
        Centuries ago.

'T was in the calm and silent night!
   The senator of haughty Rome
Impatient urged his chariot's flight,
   From lordly revel rolling home.
Triumphal arches gleaming swell
   His breast with thoughts of boundless sway;
What reck'd the Roman what befell
   A paltry province far away,
      In the solemn midnight
        Centuries ago!

Within that province far away
   Went plodding home a weary boor:
A streak of light before him lay,
   Fall'n through a half-shut stable door
Across his path. He pass'd—for nought
   Told what was going on within;
How keen the stars! his only thought;
   The air how calm and cold and thin,
      In the solemn midnight
        Centuries ago!

O strange indifference!—low and high
  Drows'd over common joys and cares:
The earth was still—but knew not why;
  The world was listening—unawares.
How calm a moment may precede
  One that shall thrill the world for ever!
To that still moment none would heed,
  Man's doom was link'd, no more to sever,
     In the solemn midnight
      Centuries ago.

It *is* the calm and solemn night!
  A thousand bells ring out, and throw
Their joyous peals abroad, and smite
  The darkness, charm'd and holy now.
The night that erst no name had worn,
  To it a happy name is given;
For in that stable lay new-born
  The peaceful Prince of Earth and Heaven,
     In the solemn midnight
      Centuries ago.
              ALFRED DOMETT

BRIGHTEST AND BEST

Brightest and best of the Sons of the morning!
  Dawn on our darkness and lend us thine aid!
Star of the East, the horizon adorning,
  Guide where our Infant Redeemer is laid!

Cold on His cradle the dewdrops are shining,
  Low lies His head with the beasts of the stall;
Angels adore Him in slumber reclining,
  Maker and Monarch and Saviour of all!

Say, shall we yield Him, in costly devotion,
   Odors of Edom and offerings divine?
Gems of the mountain and pearls of the ocean,
   Myrrh from the forest, or gold from the mine?

Vainly we offer each ample oblation;
   Vainly with gifts would His favor secure:
Richer by far is the heart's adoration;
   Dearer to God are the prayers of the poor.

Brightest and best of the Sons of the morning!
   Dawn on our darkness and lend us thine aid!
Star of the East, the horizon adorning,
   Guide where our Infant Redeemer is laid!

REGINALD HEBER

HARK, HARK, MY SOUL

Hark, hark, my soul! angelic songs are swelling
   O'er earth's green fields and ocean's wave-beat shore;
How sweet the truth those blessèd strains are telling
   Of that new life when sin shall be no more!

     Angels of Jesus, angels of light,
     Singing to welcome the pilgrims of the night!

Onward we go, for still we hear them singing,
   "Come, weary souls, for Jesus bids you come;"
And through the dark, its echoes sweetly ringing,
   The music of the gospel leads us home.

Far, far away, like bells at evening pealing,
   The voice of Jesus sounds o'er land and sea,
And laden souls by thousands, meekly stealing,
   Kind Shepherd, turn their weary steps to thee.

Rest comes at length, though life be long and dreary;
   The day must dawn, and darksome night be past;
All journeys end in welcome to the weary,
   And heaven, the heart's true home, will come at last.

Angels, sing on! your faithful watches keeping;
   Sing us sweet fragments of the songs above;
Till morning's joy shall end the night of weeping,
   And life's long shadows break in cloudless love.

FREDERICK W. FABER

ODE

In numbers, and but these few,
I sing Thy birth, O Jesu!
Thou pretty Baby, born here
With sup'rabundant scorn here.
Who for Thy princely port here,
   Hadst for Thy place
   Of birth a base
Out-stable for Thy court here.

Instead of neat enclosures
Of interwoven osiers,
Instead of fragrant posies
Of daffodils and roses,
Thy cradle, Kingly Stranger,
   As Gospel tells,
   Was nothing else
But here a homely manger.

But we with silks, not crewels,
With sundry precious jewels,
And lily-work, will dress Thee;

And as we dispossess Thee
Of clouts, we'll make a chamber,
    Sweet Babe, for Thee
    Of ivory,
And plastered round with amber.

The Jews they did disdain Thee,
But we will entertain Thee
With glories to await here
Upon Thy princely state here,
And more for love than pity,
    From year to year
    We'll make Thee, here,
A freeborn of our city.
                ROBERT HERRICK

CHRISTMAS-GREETINGS

FROM A FAIRY TO A CHILD

Lady, dear, if Fairies may
    For a moment lay aside
Cunning tricks and elfish play,
    'Tis at happy Christmas-tide.

We have heard the children say—
    Gentle children, whom we love—
Long ago, on Christmas Day,
    Came a message from above.

Still, as Christmas-tide comes round,
    They remember it again—
Echo still the joyful sound
    "Peace on earth, good-will to men!"

Yet the hearts must childlike be
   Where such heavenly guests abide;
Unto children, in their glee,
   All the year is Christmas-tide!

Thus, forgetting tricks and play
   For a moment, Lady dear,
We would wish you, if we may
   Merry Christmas, glad New Year!

                  LEWIS CARROLL

Christmas, 1867.

EX ORE INFANTIUM

Little Jesus, wast Thou shy
Once, and just so small as I?
And what did it feel like to be
Out of Heaven, and just like me?
Didst Thou sometimes think of *there*,
And ask where all the angels were?
I should think that I would cry
For my house all made of sky;
I would look about the air,
And wonder where my angels were;
And at waking 'twould distress me—
Not an angel there to dress me!

Hadst Thou ever any toys,
Like us little girls and boys?
And didst Thou play in Heaven with all
The angels, that were not too tall,
With stars for marbles? Did the things
Play *Can you see me?* through their wings?

Didst Thou kneel at night to pray,
And didst Thou join Thy hands, this way?
And did they tire sometimes, being young,
And make the prayer seem very long?
And dost Thou like it best, that we
Should join our hands to pray to Thee?
I used to think, before I knew,
The prayer not said unless we do.
And did Thy Mother at the night
Kiss Thee, and fold the clothes in right?
And didst Thou feel quite good in bed,
Kissed, and sweet, and Thy prayers said?

Thou canst not have forgotten all
That it feels like to be small:
And Thou know'st I cannot pray
To Thee in my father's way—
When Thou wast so little, say,
Couldst Thou talk Thy Father's way?—
So, a little Child, come down
And hear a child's tongue like Thy own;
Take me by the hand and walk,
And listen to my baby-talk.
To Thy Father show my prayer
(He will look, Thou art so fair),
And say: "O Father, I, Thy Son,
Bring the prayer of a little one."

And He will smile, that children's tongue
Has not changed since Thou wast young!

FRANCIS THOMPSON

THE STORKE

A CHRISTMAS BALLAD

From the Fly-leaf of King Edward VI's Prayer-book, 1549

The Storke shee rose on Christmas Eve
And sayed unto her broode,
I nowe muste fare to Bethleem
To viewe the Sonne of God.

Shee gave to eche his dole of mete,
Shee stowed them fayrlie in,
And faire shee flew and faste shee flew
And came to Bethleem.

Now where is He of David's lynne?
Shee asked at house and halle.
He is not here, they spake hardlye,
But in the maungier stalle.

Shee found hym in the maungier stalle
With that most Holye Mayde;
The gentyle Storke shee wept to see
The Lord so rudelye layde.

Then from her panntynge brest shee plucked
The fethers whyte and warm;
Shee strawed them in the maungier bed
To kepe the Lorde from harm.

Now blessed bee the gentyle Storke
Forever more quothe Hee
For that shee saw my sadde estate
And showed Pytye.

Full welkum shall shee ever bee
In hamlet and in halle,
And hight henceforth the Blessed Byrd
And friend of babyes all.

CAROLS

GOD REST YOU MERRY, GENTLEMEN

God rest you merry, gentlemen,
  Let nothing you dismay,
For Jesus Christ, our Saviour,
  Was born upon this day.
To save us all from Satan's pow'r
  When we were gone astray.
    O tidings of comfort and joy!
    For Jesus Christ, our Saviour,
    Was born on Christmas Day.

In Bethlehem, in Jewry,
  This blessed Babe was born,
And laid within a manger,
  Upon this blessed morn;
The which His mother, Mary,
  Nothing did take in scorn.

From God our Heavenly Father,
  A blessed angel came;
And unto certain shepherds
  Brought tidings of the same:
How that in Bethlehem was born
  The Son of God by name.

"Fear not," then said the angel,
  "Let nothing you affright,
This day is born a Saviour
  Of virtue, power, and might,
So frequently to vanquish all
  The friends of Satan quite."

591

The shepherds at those tidings
   Rejoicèd much in mind,
And left their flocks a-feeding
   In tempest, storm, and wind,
And went to Bethlehem straightway,
   This blessed Babe to find.

But when to Bethlehem they came,
   Whereat this infant lay,
They found Him in a manger,
   Where oxen feed on hay,
His mother Mary kneeling,
   Unto the Lord did pray.

Now to the Lord sing praises,
   All you within this place,
And with true love and brotherhood
   Each other now embrace;
This holy tide of Christmas
   All others doth deface.
     O tidings of comfort and joy!
For Jesus Christ, our Saviour,
   Was born on Christmas Day.

TRADITIONAL

CHRISTIANS, AWAKE, SALUTE THE HAPPY MORN

Christians, awake, salute the happy morn,
Where on the Saviour of mankind was born;
Rise to adore the mystery of love,
Which host of angels chanted from above;
With them the joyful tidings first begun
Of God incarnate and the Virgin's Son.

Then to the watchful shepherds it was told,
Who heard th' angelic herald's voice Behold,
I bring good tidings of a Saviour's birth
To you and all the nations upon earth;
This day hath God fulfill'd His promised word
This day is born a Saviour, Christ the Lord.

He spake; and straight-way the celestial choir
In hymns of joy, unknown before, conspire:
The praises of redeeming love they sang,
And heav'n's whole arch with alleluias rang:
God's highest glory was their anthem still,
Peace upon earth, and unto men good-will.

TRADITIONAL

WE THREE KINGS OF ORIENT ARE

All: We three kings of Orient are,
                Bearing gifts we traverse afar,
                Field and fountain, moor and mountain,
                Following yonder star.

                    O star of wonder, star of night,
                    Star with royal beauty bright,
                    Westward leading, still proceeding,
                    Guide us to thy perfect light.

Melchior: Born a king on Bethlehem's plain,
                Gold I bring, to crown Him again,
                King for ever, ceasing never,
                Over us all to reign.

Caspar: Frankincense to offer have I,
                Incense owns a Deity nigh,
                Prayer and praising, all men raising,
                Worship Him, God most high.

Balthazar: Myrrh is mine, its bitter perfume
           Breathes a life of gathering gloom;
           Sorrowing, sighing, bleeding, dying,
           Sealed in the stone-cold tomb.

All: Glorious now behold Him arise,
           King and God and sacrifice,
           Alleluia, alleluia;
           Earth to the heavens replies.

                   JOHN HENRY HOPKINS

THE FIRST NOWELL

The first nowell the angel did say
Was to certain poor shepherds in fields as they lay;
In fields where they lay, keeping their sheep,
In a cold winter's night that was so deep.
   Nowell, nowell, nowell, nowell!
   Born is the King of Israel.

They lookèd up and saw a star,
Shining in the east, beyond them far,
And to the earth it gave great light,
And so it continued both day and night.

And by the light of that same star,
Three wise man came from country far;
To seek for a king was their intent,
And to follow the star wheresoever it went.

This star drew nigh to the north-west,
O'er Bethlehem it took its rest,
And there it did both stop and stay,
Right over the place where Jesus lay.

Then did they know assuredly
Within that house the King did lie:
One entered in then for to see,
And found the Babe in poverty.

Then entered in those wise men three,
Full reverently upon their knee,
And offered there, in His presence,
Their gold, and myrrh, and frankincense.

Between an ox-stall and an ass
This Child truly there born He was;
For want of clothing they did Him lay
All in the manger, among the hay.

Then let us all with one accord,
Sing praises to our Heavenly Lord,
That hath made Heaven and earth of naught,
And with His blood mankind hath brought.

If we in our time shall do well,
We shall be free from death and hell;
For God hath preparèd for us all
A resting-place in general.

FROM THE SEVENTEENTH CENTURY

GOOD KING WENCESLAS

Good King Wenceslas look'd out
   On the feast of Stephen,
When the snow lay round about,
   Deep and crisp and even.
Brightly shone the moon that night,
   Though the frost was cruel,
When a poor man came in sight,
   Gathering winter fuel.

"Hither, page, and stand by me,
　If thou know'st it, telling,
Yonder peasant, who is he?
　Where and what his dwelling?"
"Sire, he lives a good league hence,
　Underneath the mountain;
Right against the forest fence,
　By Saint Agnes' fountain."

"Bring me flesh and bring me wine,
　Bring me pine-logs hither;
Thou and I will see him dine,
　When we bear them thither."
Page and monarch, forth they went,
　Forth they went together;
Through the rude wind's wild lament,
　And the bitter weather.

"Sire, the night is darker now,
　And the wind blows stronger;
Fails my heart, I know not how,
　I can go no longer."
"Mark my footsteps, good my page,
　Tread thou in them boldly;
Thou shalt find the winter's rage
　Freeze thy blood less coldly."

In his master's steps he trod,
　Where the snow lay dinted;
Heat was in the very sod
　Which the saint had printed.
Therefore, Christian men, be sure,
　Wealth or rank possessing,
Ye who now will bless the poor,
　Shall yourselves find blessing.

J. M. NEALE

THE WASSAIL SONG

Here we come a-wassailing
  Among the leaves so green;
Here we come a-wandering,
  So fair to be seen:

> *Love and joy come to you*
> *And to you your wassail too,*
> *And God bless you, and send you*
> *A happy new year;*
> *And God send you a happy new year.*

Our wassail-cup is made
  Of the rosemary tree,
And so is your beer
  Of the best barley:

We are not daily beggars
  That beg from door to door,
But we are neighbours' children
  Whom you have seen before:

Good master and good mistress,
  As you sit by the fire,
Pray think of us poor children
  Who are wandering in the mire:

We have a little purse
  Made of ratching leather skin;
We want some of your small change
  To line it well within:

Call up the butler of this house,
    Put on his golden ring;
Let him bring us a glass of beer,
    And better we shall sing:

Bring us out a table,
    And spread it with a cloth;
Bring us out a mouldy cheese,
    And some of your Christmas loaf:

God bless the master of this house,
    Likewise the mistress too;
And all the little children
    That round the table go:

Yorkshire

THE BOAR'S HEAD CAROL *

The boar's head in hand bear I,
Bedeck'd with bays and rosemary;
And I pray you, my masters, be merry;
Quot estis in convivio.

Caput apri defero,
Reddens laudes Domino.

The boar's head, as I understand,
Is the rarest dish in all this land;
Which thus bedeck'd with a gay garland,
Let us *servire cantico.*

* This carol is still sung annually on Christmas Day at Queen's College, Oxford.

Our steward hath provided this
In honour of the King of Bliss;
Which on this day to be servèd is,
In Reginensi atrio.

OLD ENGLISH

O SHEPHERDS, SAY?

(QUELLE EST CETTE ODEUR AGRÉABLE?)

What perfume this, O Shepherds, say,
That sweetens all the cold night air?
Faint breath of ev'ry sweet spring flower
Making the winter snowfields fair?
    What perfume this, O shepherds, say,
    That sweetens all the cold night air?

O whence this star that sudden shines
Across the dark upon our sight?
Never the sun in all his glory
Shed such a wondrous tender light.
    O whence this star that sudden shines
    Across the dark upon our sight?

In Bethlehem a cradle rocks
A babe—our Savior and our King.
Come let us kneel in adoration,
While angels hosts His praises sing.
    In Bethlehem a cradle rocks
    A babe—our Savior and our King.

FAITH LIDDELL

A BABE IS BORN

A Babe is born all of a may,
　To bring salvation unto us.
To Him we sing both night and day
　Veni Creator Spiritus.

At Bethlehem, that blessed place,
　The Child of bliss then born He was;
And Him to serve God give us grace,
　O Lux beata Trinitas.

There came three kings out of the East,
　To worship there that King so free;
With gold and myrrh and frankincense,
　A solis ortus cardine.

The shepherds heard an angel's cry,
　A merry song that night sang he,
"Why are ye so sore aghast?"
　Jam lucis orto sidere?

The angel came down with a cry,
　A fair and joyful song sang he,
All in the worship of that Child,
　Gloria tibi Domine.

FROM THE FIFTEENTH CENTURY

I SAW THREE SHIPS

I saw three ships come sailing in
  On Christmas day, on Christmas day;
I saw three ships some sailing in
  On Christmas day in the morning.

And what was in those ships all three
  On Christmas day, on Christmas day . . .

Our Saviour Christ and His lady,
  On Christmas day, on Christmas day . . .

Pray whither sailed those ships all three
  On Christmas day, on Christmas day . . .

O they sailed into Bethlehem
  On Christmas day, on Christmas day . . .

And all the bells on earth shall ring
  On Christmas day, on Christmas day . . .

And all the angels in heaven shall sing
  On Christmas day, on Christmas day . . .

And all the souls on earth shall sing
  On Christmas day, on Christmas day . . .

Then let us all rejoice amain!
  On Christmas day, on Christmas day . . .
                     FROM THE FIFTEENTH CENTURY

THE HOLLY AND THE IVY

The Holly and the Ivy,
  When they are both full grown
Of all the trees are in the wood,
  The Holly bears the crown.

O the rising of the sun,
  And the running of the deer,
The playing of the merry organ,
  Sweet singing in the choir.

The Holly bears a blossom
  As white as any flower;
And Mary bore sweet Jesus Christ
  To be our sweet Saviour.

The Holly bears a berry
  As red as any blood;
And Mary bore sweet Jesus Christ
  To do poor sinners good.

The Holly bears a prickle
  As sharp as any thorn;
And Mary bore sweet Jesus Christ
  On Christmas in the morn.

The Holly bears a bark
  As bitter as any gall;
And Mary bore sweet Jesus Christ
  For to redeem us all.

The Holly and the Ivy
  Now both are full well grown:
Of all the trees are in the wood
  The Holly bears the crown.

FROM THE FIFTEENTH CENTURY

BELLMAN'S SONG

The moon shines bright, and the stars give a light
    A little before the day,
Our mighty Lord He looked on us,
    And bade us awake and pray.

Awake, awake, good people all,
    Awake, and you shall hear,
Our Lord, our God, died on the Cross,
    For us He loved so dear.

O fair, O fair Jerusalem,
    When shall I come to thee?
When shall my sorrows have an end
    The joy that I may see?

The fields were green as green could be,
    When from His glorious seat
Our Lord, our God, He watered us
    With His heavenly dew so sweet.

And for the saving of our souls
    Christ died upon the cross.
We ne'er shall do for Jesus Christ,
    As He hath done for us.

The life of man is but a span,
    And cut down in its flower,
We're here to-day, to-morrow gone,
    The creatures of an hour.

Instruct and teach your children well,
  The while that you are here;
It will be better for your soul,
  When your corpse lies on the bier.

To-day you may be alive and well,
  Worth many a thousand pound;
To-morrow dead and cold as clay,
  Your corpse laid underground.

With one turf at thine head, O man,
  And another at thy feet:
Thy good deeds and thy bad, O man.
  Will all together meet.

My song is done, I must be gone,
  I can stay no longer here;
God bless you all, both great and small,
  And send you a joyful new year.

THE OLD "WAITS" CAROL

IN BETHLEHEM CITY

In Bethlehem city, in Judea it was,
That Joseph and Mary together did pass,
All for to be taxèd when thither they came,
For Caesar Augustus commanded the same.
  Chorus Then let us be merry, cast sorrow away,
        Our Saviour Christ Jesus was born on this day.

But Mary's full time being come as we find,
She brought forth her first-born to save all mankind;
The inn being full of the heavenly Guest,
No place could she find to lay Him to rest.
  Chorus Then let us, &c.

Blest Mary, blest Mary, so meek and so mild,
All wrapped up in swathing this heavenly Child,
Contented she laid where oxen do feed,
The great God of nature approved of the deed.
  Chorus Then let us, &c.

To teach us humility all this was done,
To learn us from hence haughty pride for to shun,
The manger His cradle Who came from above,
The great God of mercy, of peace and of love.
  Chorus Then let us, &c.

Then presently after the shepherds did spy,
Vast numbers of angels did stand in the sky;
So merry were talking, so sweetly did sing,
"All glory and praise to the heavenly King!"
  Chorus Then let us sing, &c.

NORTHAMPTONSHIRE

THE CHERRY TREE CAROL

Joseph was an old man,
  An old man was he,
When he married Mary,
  In the land of Galilee.

Joseph and Mary walked
  Through an orchard green,
Where was cherries and berries
  As thick as might be seen.

O then bespoke Mary,
  Her sweet lips so mild,
"Pluck me a cherry, Joseph,
  For I am with child."

O then bespoke Joseph
  With answer unkind,
"Let him pluck thee a cherry
  That brought thee with child."

O then bespoke the Baby
  Within His mother's womb,
"Bow down then the tallest tree,
  For My mother to have some."

The uppermost sprig then
  Bowed down to her knee,
"Thus you may see, Joseph,
  These cherries are for me."

"O eat your cherries, Mary,
  O eat your cherries now,
O eat your cherries, Mary,
  That grow upon the bough."

OLD ENGLISH

THE MISTLETOE BOUGH

The mistletoe hung in the castle hall,
The holly branch shone on the old oak wall,
And the Baron's retainers were blithe and gay,
And keeping their Christmas holiday.
The Baron beheld with a father's pride
His beautiful child, young Lovel's bride,
While she with her bright eyes, seem'd to be
  The star of the goodly company.
    Oh, the mistletoe bough!
    Oh, the mistletoe bough!

"I'm weary of dancing, now," she cried,
"Here tarry a moment; I'll hide, I'll hide.
And Lovel, be sure thou 'rt the first to trace
The clue to my secret lurking place."
Away she ran, and her friends began
Each tower to search and each nook to scan,
And young Lovel cried: "Oh, where dost thou hide?
I'm lonesome without thee, my own dear bride."

They sought her that night and they sought her next day,
And they sought her in vain till a week pass'd away.
In the highest, the lowest, the loneliest spot,
Young Lovel sought wildly but found her not.
And years flew by, and their grief at last
Was told as a sorrowful tale long past,
And when Lovel appear'd the children cried,
"See, the old man weeps for his fairy bride!"

At length an oak chest that had long lain hid
Was found in the castle; they rais'd the lid;
And a skeleton form lay mould'ring there
In the bridal wreath of the lady fair.
Oh, sad was her fate! In sportive jest
She hid from her lord in the old oak chest.
It closed with a spring, and her bridal bloom
Lay withering there in a living tomb.

THOMAS HAYNES BAYLY

THE TWELVE DAYS OF CHRISTMAS

A PARTRIDGE IN A PEAR TREE

On the first day of Christmas my true love sent to me
A partridge in a pear tree.
On the second day of Christmas my true love sent to me
Two turtle doves and a partridge in a pear tree.
On the third day of Christmas my true love sent to me
Three French hens, two turtle doves, and a partridge in a pear tree.
On the fourth day of Christmas my true love sent to me
Four colly birds, three French hens, two turtle doves, and a partridge
    in a pear tree.
On the fifth day of Christmas my true love sent to me
Five gold rings, four colly birds, three French hens, two turtle doves,
    and a partridge in a pear tree.
On the sixth day of Christmas my true love sent to me
Six geese a-laying, five gold rings, four colly birds, three French hens,
    two turtle doves, and a partridge in a pear tree.
On the seventh day of Christmas my true love sent to me
Seven swans a-swimming, six geese a-laying, five gold rings, four colly
    birds, three French hens, two turtle doves, and a partridge in a
    pear tree.
On the eighth day of Christmas my true love sent to me
Eight maids a-milking, seven swans a-swimming, six geese a-laying,
    five gold rings, four colly birds, three French hens, two turtle
    doves, and a partridge in a pear tree.
On the ninth day of Christmas my true love sent to me
Nine ladies dancing, eight maids a-milking, seven swans a-swimming,
    six geese a-laying, five gold rings, four colly birds, three French
    hens, two turtle doves, and a partridge in a pear tree.
On the tenth day of Christmas my true love sent to me

Ten lords a-leaping, nine ladies dancing, eight maids a-milking, seven
  swans a-swimming, six geese a-laying, five gold rings, four colly
  birds, three French hens, two turtle doves, and a partridge in a
  pear tree.
On the eleventh day of Christmas my true love sent to me
Eleven drummers drumming, ten lords a-leaping, nine ladies dancing,
  eight maids a-milking, seven swans a-swimming, six geese a-laying,
  five gold rings, four colly birds, three French hens, two turtle
  doves, and a partridge in a pear tree.
On the twelfth day of Christmas my true love sent to me
Twelve pipers piping, eleven drummers drumming, ten lords a-leaping, nine ladies dancing, eight maids a-milking, seven swans
  a-swimming, six geese a-laying, five gold rings, four colly birds,
  three French hens, two turtle doves, and a partridge in a pear tree.

TRADITIONAL

WHAT CHILD IS THIS?

What Child is this, Who, laid to rest,
On Mary's lap is sleeping?
Whom angels greet with anthems sweet,
While shepherds watch are keeping?

Why lies He in such mean estate,
Where ox and ass are feeding?
Good Christian, fear; for sinners here
The silent Word is pleading:

So bring Him incense, gold, and myrrh,
Come peasant, king, to own Him;
The King of kings, salvation brings:
Let loving hearts enthrone Him.

WILLIAM C. DIX

SHEPHERDS! SHAKE OFF YOUR DROWSY SLEEP

Shepherds, shake off your drowsy sleep,
Rise and leave your silly sheep.
Angels from heav'n around loud singing,
Tidings of great joy are bringing.

Hark! even now the bells ring round,
Listen to their merry sound;
Hark! how the birds new songs are making,
As if winter's chains were breaking.

Chorus

Shepherds! the chorus come and swell!
Sing noel, O sing Noel!

FROM THE FRENCH

BRING A TORCH, JEANNETTE, ISABELLA

Bring a torch, Jeannette, Isabella!
Bring a torch, to the cradle run!
It is Jesus, good folk of the village;
Christ is born and Mary's calling:
Ah! ah! beautiful is the Mother;
Ah! ah! beautiful is her son!

It is wrong when the Child is sleeping,
It is wrong to talk so loud;
Silence, all, as you gather around,

Lest your noise should waken Jesus:
Hush! hush! see how fast He slumbers:
Hush! hush! see how fast He sleeps!

Softly to the little stable,
Softly for a moment come;
Look and see how charming is Jesus,
How He is white, His cheeks are rosy!
Hush! hush! see how the Child is sleeping;
Hush! hush! see how He smiles in dreams.

FROM THE OLD FRENCH

THE COVENTRY CAROL

Lullay, Thou little tiny Child,
By, by, lully, lullay;
Lullay, Thou little tiny Child,
By, by, lully, lullay.

O sisters too, how may we do,
For to preserve this day,
This poor Youngling for whom we sing,
By, by, lully, lullay?

Herod the king in his raging,
Charged he hath this day
His men of might, in his own sight,
All children young to slay.

Then woe is me, poor Child for Thee,
And ever mourn and say,
For Thy parting nor say nor sing,
By, by, lully, lullay.

FROM THE PAGEANT OF THE SHEARMEN AND TAILORS

HOW THEY SPENT CHRISTMAS

CHRISTMAS EVE IN OLD NEW ENGLAND

By Harriet Beecher Stowe

[Parson Cushing's little daughter Dolly has heard that there is to be an "illumination" that night at the Episcopal Church. It will not be proper for her to go: the Parson thinks "this Christmas dressing" all nonsense. But Dolly longs to see it. . . .]

SLEEP she could not. The wide, bright, wistful blue eyes lay shining like two stars toward the fading light in the window, and the little ears were strained to catch every sound. She heard the shouts of Tom and Bill and the loud barking of Spring as they swept out of the door; and the sound went to her heart. Spring—her faithful attendant, the most loving and sympathetic of dogs, her friend and confidential counselor in many a solitary ramble—Spring had gone with the boys to see the sight, and left her alone. She began to pity herself and cry softly on her pillow. For a while she could hear Nabby's energetic movements below, washing up dishes, putting back chairs, and giving energetic thumps and bangs here and there, as her way was of producing order. But by and by that was all over, and she heard the loud shutting of the kitchen door and Nabby's voice chatting with her attendant as she went off to the scene of gaiety.

In those simple, innocent days in New England villages nobody thought of locking house doors at night. There was in those times no idea either of tramps or burglars, and many a night in summer had Dolly lain awake and heard the voices of tree-toads and whippoorwills mingling with the whisper of leaves and the swaying of elm boughs, while the great outside door of the house lay broad open in the moonlight. But then this was when everybody was in the house and asleep, when the door of her parents' room stood open on the front hall, and she knew she could run to the paternal bed in a minute for protection. Now, however, she knew the house was empty. Everybody had gone out of it; and there is something fearful to a little lonely body in the possibilities of a great, empty house. She got up and opened her door, and the "tick-tock" of the old kitchen clock for a moment seemed like company; but pretty soon its ticking began to strike louder and louder with a nervous insistency on her ear, till the nerves quivered and vibrated, and she couldn't go to sleep. She lay and listened to all the noises outside. It was a still, clear, freezing night, when the least sound clinked with a metallic resonance. She heard the runners of sleighs squeaking and crunching over the frozen road, and the lively jingle of bells. They would come nearer, nearer, pass by the house, and go off in the distance. Those were the happy folks going to see the gold star and the Christmas greens in the church. The gold star, the Christmas greens, had all the more attraction from their vagueness. Dolly was a fanciful little creature, and the clear air and romantic scenery of a mountain town had fed her imagination. Stories she had never read, except in the Bible and the Pilgrim's Progress, but her very soul had vibrated with the descriptions of the celestial city—something vague, bright, glorious, lying beyond some dark river; and Nabby's rude account of what was going on in the church suggested those images.

Finally a bright thought popped into her little head. She could see the church from the front windows of the house; she would go there and look. In haste she sprang out of bed and dressed herself. It was sharp and freezing in the fireless chamber, but Dolly's blood had a racing, healthy tingle to it; she didn't mind cold. She wrapped her cloak around her and tied on her hood and ran to the front windows. There it was, to be sure—the little church with its sharp-pointed windows, every pane of which was sending streams of light across the glittering snow. There was a crowd around the door, and men and boys looking in at the windows. Dolly's soul was fired. But the elm boughs a little obstructed her vision; she thought she would go down and look at it from the yard. So down-stairs she ran, but as she opened the door the sound of the chant rolled out into the darkness with sweet and solemn cadence:

"Glory be to God on high; and on earth peace, good will toward men."

Dolly's soul was all aglow—her nerves tingled and vibrated; she thought of the bells ringing in the celestial city; she could no longer contain herself, but faster and faster the little hooded form scudded across the snowy plain and pushed in among the dark cluster of spectators at the door. All made way for the child, and in a moment, whether in the body or out she could not tell, Dolly was sitting in a little nook under a bower of spruce, gazing at the star and listening to the voices:

"We praise Thee, we bless Thee, we worship Thee, we glorify Thee, we give thanks to Thee for Thy great glory, O Lord God, Heavenly King, God, the Father Almighty."

Her heart throbbed and beat; she trembled with a strange happiness and sat as one entranced till the music was over. Then came reading, the rustle and murmur of people kneeling, and then they all rose and there was the solemn buzz of voices repeating the Creed with a curious lulling sound to her ear. There was old Mr. Danforth with his spectacles on, reading with a pompous tone, as if to witness a good confession for the church; and there were Squire Lewis and old Ma'am Lewis; and there was one place where they all bowed their heads and all the ladies made courtesies—all of which entertained her mightily.

When the sermon began Dolly got fast asleep, and slept as quietly as a pet lamb in a meadow, lying in a little warm roll back under the shadows of the spruces. She was so tired and so sound asleep that she did not wake when the service ended, lying serenely curled up, and having perhaps pleasant dreams. She might have had the fortunes of little Goody Two-Shoes, whose history was detailed in one of the few children's books then printed, had not two friends united to find her out.

Spring, who had got into the slip with the boys, and been an equally attentive and edified listener, after service began a tour of investigation, dog-fashion, with his nose; for how could a minister's dog form a suitable judgment of any new procedure if he was repressed from the use of his own leading faculty? So, Spring went round the church conscientiously, smelling at pew doors, smelling of the greens, smelling at the heels of gentlemen and ladies, till he came near the door of the church, when he suddenly smelt something which called for immediate attention, and he made a side dart into the thicket where Dolly was sleeping, and began licking her face and hands and pulling her dress, giving short barks occasionally, as if to say, "Come, Dolly, wake up!" At the same instant Hiel, who had seen her from the gallery, came down just as the little one was sitting up with a dazed, bewildered air.

"Why, Dolly, how came you out o' bed this time o' night? Don't ye know the nine o'clock bell's jest rung?"

Dolly knew Hiel well enough—what child in the village did not? She reached up her little hands, saying in an apologetic fashion:

"They were all gone away, and I was so lonesome!"

Hiel took her up in his long arms and carried her home, and was just entering the house door with her as the sleigh drove up with Parson Cushing and his wife.

"Wal, Parson, your folks has all ben to the 'lumination—Nabby and Bill and Tom and Dolly here; found her all rolled up in a heap like a rabbit under the cedars."

"Why, Dolly Cushing!" exclaimed her mother. "What upon earth got you out of bed this time of night? You'll catch your death o' cold."

"I was all alone," said Dolly, with a piteous bleat.

"Oh, there, there, wife; don't say a word," put in the parson. "Get her off to bed. Never mind, Dolly, don't you cry"; for Parson Cushing was a soft-hearted gentleman and couldn't bear the sight of Dolly's quivering under lip. So Dolly told her little story, how she had been promised a sugar dog by Nabby if she'd be a good girl and go to sleep, and how she couldn't go to sleep, and how she just went down to look from the yard, and how the music drew her right over.

"There, there," said Parson Cushing, "go to bed, Dolly; and if Nabby don't give you a sugar dog, I will. This Christmas dressing is all nonsense," he added, "but the child's not to blame—it was natural."

"After all," he said to his wife the last thing after they were settled for the night, "our little Dolly is an unusual child. There were not many little girls that would have dared to do that. I shall preach a sermon right away that will set all this Christmas matter straight," said the Doctor. "There is not a shadow of evidence that the first Christians kept Christmas. It wasn't kept for the first three centuries, nor was Christ born anywhere near the 25th of December."

* * * * * *

The next morning found little Dolly's blue eyes wide open with all the wondering eagerness of a new idea.

Dolly had her wise thoughts about Christmas. She had been terribly frightened at first, when she was brought home from the church; but when her papa kissed her and promised her a sugar dog she was quite sure that, whatever the unexplained mystery might be, he did not think the lovely scene of the night before a wicked one. And when Mrs. Cushing came and covered the little girl up warmly in bed, she only said to her, "Dolly, you must never get out of bed again at night after you are put there; you might have caught a dreadful cold and been sick and died, and then we should have lost our little Dolly." So Dolly promised quite readily to be good and lie still ever after, no matter what attractions might be on foot in the community.

Much was gained, however, and it was all clear gain; and forthwith the little fanciful head proceeded to make the most of it, thinking over every feature of the wonder. The child had a vibrating, musical organization, and the sway and rush of the chanting still sounded in her ears and reminded her of that wonderful story in the "Pilgrim's Progress," where the gate of the celestial city swung open, and there were voices that sung, "Blessing and honor and glory and power be unto Him who sitteth on the throne." And then that wonderful star, that shone just as if it were a real star—how could it be! For Miss Ida Lewis, being a young lady of native artistic genius, had cut a little hole in the centre of her gilt paper star, behind which was placed a candle, so that it gave real light, in a way most astonishing to untaught eyes. In Dolly's simple view it verged on the supernatural—perhaps it was *the* very real star read about in the Gospel story. Why not? Dolly was at the happy age when anything bright and heavenly seemed credible, and had the child-faith to which all things were possible.

"I wish, my dear," said Mrs. Cushing, after they were retired to their room for the night, "that to-morrow morning you would read the account of the birth of Christ in St. Matthew, and give the children some advice upon the proper way of keeping Christmas."

"Well, but you know we don't *keep* Christmas; nobody knows anything about Christmas," said the Doctor.

"You know what I mean, my dear," replied his wife. "You know that my mother and her family *do* keep Christmas. I always heard of it when I was a child; and even now, though I have been out of the way of it so long, I cannot help a sort of kindly feeling toward these ways. I am not surprised at all that the children got drawn over last night to the service. I think it's the most natural thing in the world, and I know by experience just how attractive such things are. I shouldn't wonder if this other church should draw very seriously on your congregation; but I don't want it to begin by taking away our own children. Dolly is an inquisitive child; a child that thinks a good deal, and she'll be asking all sorts of questions about the why and wherefore of what she saw last night."

"Oh, yes, Dolly is a bright one. Dolly's an uncommon child," said the Doctor, who had a pardonable pride in his children—they being, in fact, the only worldly treasure that he was at all rich in.

He rose up early on the following Sabbath and proceeded to buy a sugar dog at the store of Lucius Jenks, and when Dolly came down to breakfast he called her to him and presented it, saying as he kissed her:

"Papa gives you this, not because it is Christmas, but because he loves his little Dolly."

"But *isn't* it Christmas?" asked Dolly with a puzzled air.

"No, child; nobody knows when Christ was born, and there is nothing in the Bible to tell us *when* to keep Christmas."

And then in family worship the Doctor read the account of the birth of Christ and of the shepherds abiding in the fields who came at the call of the angels, and they sung the old hymn, "While shepherds watched their flocks by night."

"Now, children," he said when all was over, "you must be good children and go to school. If we are going to keep any day on account of the birth of Christ, the best way to keep it is by doing all our duties on that day better than any other. Your duty is to be good children, go to school and mind your lessons."

Tom and Bill were quite ready to fall in with their father's view of the matter. As for Dolly, she put her little tongue advisedly to the back of her sugar dog and found that he was very sweet indeed—a most tempting little animal. She even went so far as to nibble off a bit of the green ground he stood on—yet resolved heroically not to eat him at once, but to make him last as long as possible. She wrapped him tenderly in cotton and took him to the school with her, and when her confidential friend, Bessie Lewis, displayed her Christmas gifts, Dolly had something on her side to show, though she shook her curly head and informed Bessie in strict confidence that there wasn't any such thing as Christmas, her papa had told her so—a heresy which Bessie forthwith reported when she went home at noon.

"Poor little child—and did she say so?" asked gentle old Grandmamma Lewis. "Well, dear, you mustn't blame her—she don't know any better. You bring the little one in here to-night and I'll give her a Christmas cooky. I'm sorry for such children."

From *Poganuc People*

THE LAST CHRISTMAS

BEFORE THE CIVIL WAR

By Eliza Ripley

CHRISTMAS before the war. There never will be another in any land, with any peoples, like the Christmas of 1859—on the old plantation. Days beforehand preparations were in progress for the wedding at the quarters, and the ball at the "big house." Children coming home for the holidays were both amused and delighted to learn that Nancy Brackenridge was to be the quarter bride. "Nancy a bride! Oh, la!" they exclaimed. "Why Nancy must be forty years old." And she was going to marry Aleck, who, if he would wait a year or two, might marry Nancy's daughter. While the young school-girls were busy "letting out" the white satin balldress that had descended from the parlor dance to the quarter bride, and were picking out and freshening up the wreath and corsage bouquet of lilies of the valley that had been the wedding flowers of the mistress of the big house, and while the boys were ransacking the distant woods for holly branches and magnolia boughs, enough for the ballroom as well as the wedding supper table, the family were busy with the multitudinous preparations for the annual dance, for which Arlington, with its ample parlors and halls, and its proverbial hospitality, was noted far and wide.

The children made molasses gingerbread and sweet potato pies, and one big bride's cake, with a real ring in it. They spread the table in the big quarters nursery, and the boys decorated it with greenery and a lot of cut paper fly catchers, laid on the roast mutton and pig, and hot biscuits from the big house kitchen, and the pies and cakes of the girls' own make. The girls proceeded to dress Nancy Brackenridge, pulling together that refractory satin waist which, though it had been "let out" to its fullest extent, still showed a sad gap, to be concealed by a dextrous arrangement of some discarded hair ribbons. Nancy was black as a crow and had rather a startling look in that dazzling white satin dress and the pure white flowers pinned to her kinks. At length the girls gave a finishing pat to the toilet, and their brothers pronounced her "bully," and called Marthy Ann to see how fine her mammy was.

As was the custom, the whole household went to the quarter to witness the wedding. Lewis, the plantation preacher, in a cast-off swallow-tail coat of Marse Jim's that was uncomfortably tight, especially about the waist line, performed the ceremony. Then my husband advanced and made some remarks, to the effect that this marriage was a solemn tie, and there must be no shirking of its duties; they

must behave and be faithful to each other; he would have no foolishness. These remarks, though by no means elegant, fitted the occasion
to a fraction. There were no high flights of eloquence which the darky
mind could not reach, it was plain, unvarnished admonition.

The following morning, Christmas Day, the field negroes were
summoned to the back porch of the big house, where Marse Jim, after
a few preliminary remarks, distributed the presents—a head handkerchief, a pocketknife, a pipe, a dress for the baby, shoes for the
growing boy (his first pair, maybe), etc., etc., down the list. Each gift
was received with a "Thankee, sir," and, perhaps, also a remark anent
its usefulness. Then after Charlotte brought forth the jug of whiskey
and the tin cups, and everyone had a comfortable dram, they filed
off to the quarters, with a week of holiday before them and a trip
to town to do their little buying.

The very last Christmas on the old plantation we had a tree. None
of us had ever seen a Christmas tree; there were no cedars or pines,
so we finally settled upon a tall althea bush, hung presents on it, for
all the house servants, as well as for the family and a few guests. The
tree had to be lighted up, so it was postponed till evening. The idea
of the house servants having such a celebration quite upset the little
negroes. I heard one remark, "All us house niggers is going to be
hung on a tree." Before the dawn of another Christmas the negroes
had become discontented, demoralized and scattered, freer than the
whites, for the blacks recognized no responsibilities whatsoever. The
family had already abandoned the old plantation home. We could not
stand the changed condition of things any longer, and the Federals
had entered into possession and completed the ruin. Very likely some
reminiscent darky told new-found friends, "All de house niggers was
hung on a tree last Christmas." I have heard from Northern lips even
more astonishing stories of maltreated slaves than a wholesale hanging.

Frequently before the holidays some of the negroes were questioned
as to what they would like to have, and the planter would make notes
and have the order filled in the city. That, I think, was the custom at
Whitehall plantation. I was visiting there on one occasion when a
woman told Judge Chinn she wanted a mourning veil. "A mourning

veil!" he replied. "I thought you were going to marry Tom this Christmas?" "Yis, marster, but you know Jim died last grinding, and I ain't never mourned none for 'im. I want to mourn some 'fore I marries agin." I did not remain to see, but I do not doubt she got the mourning veil and had the melancholy satisfaction of wearing it around the quarter lot a few days before she married Tom.

After the departure of our happy negroes, whose voices and laughter could be heard long after the yard gate was closed and they had vanished out of sight, we rushed around like wild to complete the preparations for the coming ball guests. They began to arrive in the afternoon from down the coast and from the opposite side of the river. Miles and miles some of them drove in carriages, with champagne baskets, capital forerunners of the modern suit case, tied on behind, and, like as not, a dusky maid perched on top of it; poor thing, the carriage being full, she had to travel in this precarious way, holding on for dear life. Those old-time turtle-back vehicles had outside a single seat for the coachman only. Parties came also in skiffs, with their champagne baskets and maids. Long before time for the guests from town to appear, mammas and maids were busy in the bedrooms, dressing their young ladies for the occasion. Meanwhile the plantation musicians were assembling, two violins, a flute, a triangle, and a tambourine. A platform had been erected at one end of the room, with kitchen chairs and cuspidors, for their accommodation. Our own negroes furnished the dance music, but we borrowed Col. Hicky's Washington for the tambourine. He was more expert than any "end man" you ever saw. He kicked it and butted it and struck it with elbow and heel, and rattled it in perfect unison with the other instruments, making more noise, and being himself a more inspiring sight, than all the rest of the band put together. Col. Hicky always said it was the only thing Washington was fit for, and he kept the worthless negro simply because he was the image (in bronze) of Gen. Lafayette. Col. Hicky was an octogenarian, and had seen Gen. Lafayette, so he could not have been mistaken. When Washington flagged, a few drops of whiskey was all he needed to refresh his energies.

The whirl of the dance waxed as the night waned. The tired paterfamiliases sat around the rooms, too true to their mission to retire for a little snooze. They were restored to consciousness at intervals by liberal cups of strong coffee. Black William, our first violin, called out the figures, "Ladies to the right!" "Set to your partners?"—and the young people whirled and swung around in the giddy reel as though they would never have such another opportunity to dance—as, indeed, many of them never did. From the porch and lawn windows black faces gazed on the inspiring scene. They never saw the like again, either.

Laughing, wide-awake girls and tired fathers and mothers started homeward at the first blush of dawn, when they could plainly see their way over the roads. I started too early from a party the year before, and the buggy I was in ran over a dirt-colored cow lying asleep in the road. The nodding maid again perilously perched on top the champagne basket, and skiffs with similar freight plied across the broad river as soon as there was sufficient light to enable them to dodge a passing steamboat.

The last ball was a noble success. We danced on and on, never thinking this was to be our last dance in the big house. Clouds were hovering all about us the following Christmas. No one had the heart to dance then. The negroes had already become restless and discontented. After that the Deluge! The big house long ago slid into the voracious Mississippi. The quarters where the wedding feast was spread have fallen into ruins, the negroes scattered or dead. The children, so happy and so busy then, are now old people—the only ones left to look on this imperfectly drawn picture with any personal interest. We lived, indeed, a life never to be lived again.

From *Social Life in Old New Orleans*

A LETTER TO HER FAMILY

By Louisa May Alcott

Saturday evening, Dec. 25, 1875.

DEAR FAMILY,— . . . I had only time for a word this A. M., as the fourth letter was from Mrs. P. to say they could not go; so I trotted off in the fog at ten to the boat and there found Mr. and Mrs. G. and piles of goodies for the poor children. She is a dear little old lady in a close, Quakerish bonnet and plain suit, but wide-awake and full of energy.

I've had a pretty good variety of Christmases in my day, but never one like this before. First we drove in an old ramshackle hack to the chapel, whither a boy had raced before us, crying joyfully to all he met, "She's come! Miss G.—she's come!" And all faces beamed, as well they might, since for thirty years she has gone to make set after set of little forlornities happy on this day.

The chapel was full. On one side, in front, girls in blue gowns and white pinafores; on the other, small chaps in pinafores likewise; and behind them, bigger boys in gray suits with cropped heads, and larger girls with ribbons in their hair and pink calico gowns. They sang alternately; the girls gave "Juanita" very well, the little chaps a pretty song about poor children asking a "little white angel" to leave the gates of heaven ajar, so they could peep in, if no more. Quite pathetic, coming from poor babies who had no home but this.

The big boys spoke pieces, and I was amused when one bright lad in gray, with a red band on his arm, spoke the lines I gave G.,— "Merry Christmas." No one knew me, so I had the joke to myself; and I found afterward that I was taken for the mayoress, who was expected. Then we drove to the hospital, and there the heart-ache began, for me at least, so sad it was to see these poor babies, born of want and sin, suffering every sort of deformity, disease, and pain.

Cripples half blind, scarred with scrofula, burns, and abuse,—it was simply awful and indescribable!

As we went in, I with a great box of dolls and the young reporter with a bigger box of candy, a general cry of delight greeted us. Some children tried to run, half-blind ones stretched out their groping hands, little ones crawled, and big ones grinned, while several poor babies sat up in their bed, beckoning us to "come quick."

One poor mite, so eaten up with sores that its whole face was painted with some white salve,—its head covered with an oilskin cap; one eye gone, and the other half filmed over; hands bandaged, and ears bleeding,—could only moan and move its feet till I put a gay red dolly in one hand and a pink candy in the other; then the dim eye brightened, the hoarse voice said feebly, "Tanky, lady!" and I left it contentedly sucking the sweetie, and *trying* to *see* its dear new toy. It can't see another Christmas, and I like to think I helped make this one happy, even for a minute.

It was pleasant to watch the young reporter trot round with the candy-box, and come up to me all interest to say, "One girl hasn't got a doll, ma'am, and looks *so* disappointed."

After the hospital, we went to the idiot house; and there I had a chance to see faces and figures that will haunt me a long time. A hundred or so of half-grown boys and girls ranged down a long hall, a table of toys in the middle, and an empty one for Mrs. G.'s gifts. A cheer broke out as the little lady hurried in waving her handkerchief and handful of gay bead necklaces, and "Oh! Ohs!" followed the appearance of the doll-lady and the candy man.

A pile of gay pictures was a new idea, and Mrs. G. told me to hold up some bright ones and see if the poor innocents would understand and enjoy them. I held up one of two kittens lapping spilt milk, and the girls began to mew and say "Cat! ah, pretty." Then a fine horse, and the boys bounced on their benches with pleasure; while a ship in full sail produced a cheer of rapture from them all.

Some were given out to the good ones, and the rest are to be pinned round the room; so the pictures were a great success. All wanted dolls, even boys of nineteen; for all were children in mind. But the girls had them, and young women of eighteen cuddled their babies and were happy. The boys chose from the toy-table, and it was pathetic to see great fellows pick out a squeaking dog without even the wit to pinch it when it was theirs. One dwarf of thirty-five chose a little Noah's ark, and brooded over it in silent bliss.

Some with beards sucked their candy, and stared at a toy cow or box of blocks as if their cup was full. One French girl sang the Marseillaise in a feeble voice, and was so overcome by her new doll that she had an epileptic fit on the spot, which made two others go off likewise; and a slight pause took place while they were kindly removed to sleep it off.

A little tot of four, who hadn't sense to put candy in its mouth, was so fond of music that when the girls sang the poor vacant face woke up, and a pair of lovely soft hazel eyes stopped staring dully at nothing, and went wandering to and fro with light in them, as if to find the only sound that can reach its poor mind.

I guess I gave away two hundred dolls, and a soap-box of candy was empty when we left. But rows of sticky faces beamed at us, and an array of gay toys wildly waved after us, as if we were angels who had showered goodies on the poor souls.

Pauper women are nurses, and Mrs. G. says the babies die like sheep, many being deserted so young nothing can be hoped or done for them. One of the teachers in the idiot home was a Miss C., who remembered Nan at Dr. Wilbur's. Very lady-like, and all devotion to me. But such a life! Oh, me! Who *can* lead it, and not go mad?

At four, we left and came home, Mrs. G. giving a box of toys and sweeties on board the boat for the children of the men who run it. So leaving a stream of blessings and pleasures behind her, the dear old lady drove away, simply saying, "There now, I shall feel better for the next year!" Well she may; bless her!

She made a speech to the chapel children after the Commissioner had prosed in the usual way, and she told 'em that *she* should come as long as she could, and when she was gone her children would still keep it up in memory of her; so for thirty years more she hoped this, their one holiday, would be made happy for them. I could have hugged her on the spot, the motherly old dear!

Next Wednesday we go to the Tombs, and some day I am to visit the hospital with her, for I like this better than parties, etc.

I got home at five, and then remembered that I'd had no lunch; so I took an apple till six, when I discovered that all had dined at one so the helpers could go early this evening. Thus my Christmas day was without dinner or presents, for the first time since I can remember. Yet it has been a very memorable day, and I feel as if I'd had a splendid feast seeing the poor babies wallow in turkey soup, and that every gift I put into their hands had come back to me in the dumb delight of their unchild-like faces trying to smile.

From Life and Letters

THROUGH COBHAM WOOD WITH DICKENS ON CHRISTMAS MORNING

By Charles Dickens

AND now the mists began to rise in the most beautiful manner, and the sun to shine; and as I went on through the bracing air, seeing the hoar-frost sparkle everywhere, I felt as if all Nature shared in the joy of the great Birthday.

Going through the woods, the softness of my tread upon the mossy ground and among the brown leaves enhanced the Christmas sacredness by which I felt surrounded. As the whitened stems environed me, I thought how the Founder of the time had never raised his benignant hand, save to bless and heal, except in the case of one unconscious tree. By Cobham Hall, I came to the village, and the churchyard where the dead had been quietly buried, "in the sure and certain hope" which Christmas time inspired. What children could I see at play, and not be loving of, recalling who had loved them! No garden that I passed was out of unison with the day, for I remembered that the tomb was in a garden, and that "she, supposing him to be the gardener," had said, "Sir, if thou have borne him hence, tell me where thou hast laid him, and I will take him away." In time, the distant river with the ships came full in view, and with it pictures of the poor fishermen, mending their nets, who arose and followed him,—of the teaching of the people from a ship pushed off a little way from shore, by reason of the multitude,—of a majestic figure walking on the water, in the loneliness of night. My very shadow on the ground was eloquent of Christmas; for did not the people lay their sick where the mere shadows of the men who had heard and seen him might fall as they passed along?

Thus Christmas begirt me, far and near, until I had come to Black-heath, and had walked down the long vista of gnarled old trees in Greenwich Park, and was being steam-rattled through the mists now closing in once more, towards the lights of London. Brightly they shone, but not so brightly as my own fire, and the brighter faces around it, when we came together to celebrate the day.

From *Seven Poor Travellers*

CHRISTMAS IN OUR TOWN

DURING THE FIRST WORLD WAR, 1917

BY EMMA BUGBEE

IT was Christmas in Our Town, still very early and dark, with the Christmas stars shining overhead, although the first dull yellow of dawn was creeping above the hills across the river. There was snow on the garden and ice on the streets, so that approaching footsteps crunched noisily on the walk, filling the stillness with a cheerful clatter even before the voices of the carollers rang out in the dark:

> "It came upon the midnight clear,
> That glorious song of old."

Yes, it was really Christmas, just as it used to be before the war, with Mother bending over, whispering: "Wake up, darlings, and hear the Christmas song."

Childish memories cling more fondly in Our Town to those mysterious sweet songs coming so suddenly out of the dark than they do even to the visit of Santa Claus. Perhaps it was because we knew that Santa would leave anything nice he might happen to have, and it would keep until morning; but the carollers were a fragment of wonderfulness that could not be preserved, a moment of sheer delight that could never be recaptured, even by the carols around the piano in the dusk of Christmas afternoon. As children we turned over happily and went to sleep again with the silver song ringing in our ears. But with the years our interest grew, until we knew the words and the entire programme, and could follow the carollers on their way past the schoolhouse and down the hill to the parsonage, where they all went in for coffee. We always thought that quite the most gracious act of hospitality Our Town ever witnessed. It was one thing to lie warm in bed, enjoying the visit of the carollers, but quite another to get up and make coffee for a crowd of half-frozen boys and girls.

"I wonder where the bass voices are. It sounds so weak," whispered Our Mother, and as she spoke she remembered where they were. So the war came with the Christmas dawn.

OUR CAROLLERS

Our carollers were not a native product. The traditions of the Puritans lay stern across Our Town, which grew up around the new church when it was found to be too hard for the farmers to travel eight miles across the hill to meeting. We would never have invented carolling, although we might wish we could. It was the English down in the valley, who came when the mills began to boom, bringing their own Established Church and their own cheerful English customs. That was how it came about that the carollers were weak on the bass, for their best voices were singing in the trenches long since.

As Christmas Day dawned and passed through its merry hours, there was every now and again a reminder as sharp as this of the reality we were trying to forget. The Lady Across the Street had shut up her house and gone away. Her boy was in Scotland, on "Andy" Carnegie's estate, chopping down trees with the lumberjacks. The home from which resounded on other Christmases such huge sounds of collegiate mirth that the whole neighborhood alternately chuckled and cursed was still this year, and undecorated, save for the red gleam of a one-starred service flag in an upper window.

Those flags hung in almost every window on Our Hill. In homes where there was no flag we knew it was because there was no son. From the House Around the Corner the youngest son had gone three years ago to drive an ambulance, and never came back. It may be that his brave young spirit, calling to the boys who used to romp with him over our hills, has been partly responsible for the large number of recruits to army and navy from Our Hill.

THE FIRST WAR CHRISTMAS

Thank God that for this first War Christmas they had not gone so far they could not yet return. It was this that made it merry Christmas still, in spite of everything; and mothers who dared not think of next year busied themselves with turkey and red Santa Clauses with a hilarity never before assumed. And now Our Mother rejoiced with every other mother as the homecomers toiled up the hill after the Christmas morning train!

"Here comes Horace! He's been promoted to first lieutenant. Isn't he splendid in that overcoat! And how little his father looks beside him! His mother has been baking for a week."

"Even Roy is coming—all the way from Allentown—to spend the day with the Smiths. They are as proud of him as if they were his own parents, and he is devoted to them, although Mrs. Smith says he has never given up the search for his own mother. He plans to spend his furloughs in Paris looking for her. Some one has told him she had a French name."

Even the visit of the letter carrier, interest in which is usually purely selfish on Christmas Day, was another chapter in the story of Our Boys.

"Run quick, dear, and ask the letter carrier if his brother has found his knitted helmet."

The report was bad, quite overshadowing ordinary Christmas glee over the letter carrier's burden. The Brother in France said in his last letter that the helmet had evidently been stolen by some soldier who needed it more than he, so rather than impose on the generosity of the Red Cross our letter carrier was going to get somebody in the Old Ladies' Home to knit him another.

Our Town is very proud of its Red Cross, which has supplied a complete outfit of knitted garments—sweater, wristers, muffler, helmet and socks—to every boy who has gone to the army. The Daughters of the American Revolution—and Our Town bristles with them—have done the same for the sailors. Intense rivalry exists between the two circles as to whose boys shall be the best equipped. When Joseph Sargent joined the navy he caused strained relations between them for days. His mother belonged to the Red Cross, and was in duty bound to give all her work to the army, while the Daughters naturally were envious of the honor of providing the first lieutenant from Our Town. Our Town harbors a suspicion that Joseph has two sets of knitted wear, but, of course, nobody knows. He is better off than the boy whose mother refused haughtily to accept a Red Cross outfit for him in the summer, saying that if her boy needed a sweater she guessed she could buy him one; and now he needs one, and the Red Cross supply has given out.

The Lady Next Door brought in a bit of holly as her gift, it being almost unattainable in Our Town this year. She apologized for not having made any presents, but she had worn a hole in the forefinger of her left hand from constant knitting and there was danger of blood poisoning.

That didn't matter, though, in view of the eighteen helmets she had made and two dozen sweaters.

GUNS ABOVE HOLLY

We put the holly in the place of honor over the piano. How essential the little things were a year ago! We would have whined that Christmas was not Christmas without holly and cranberry sauce. That year we commented cheerfully on the fact that we couldn't expect to fill up the railroad cars with holly when there was not room for guns, and that we wouldn't care to waste precious sugar (even supposing we could get it) on cranberry sauce. There was plenty of hemlock for decorations in the woods and plenty of currant jelly in the cupboard, made last summer according to Hoover's orders. The Lieutenant found in his stocking one precious cube of sugar and the War Bride had a whole glass jar of it to take back to the boarding house. The rest of us had learned to drink coffee without it.

And so the first War Christmas came to a merry dusk, when the shadow again fell. The War Bride sat at the piano and we sang again the Christmas carols, all of them—the funny ones and the beautiful ones—but with a new one for the end—not a Christmas song at all, but "My Country 'Tis of Thee"—and for the first time that day the War Bride's fingers faltered a bit and Our Mother's hand crept to the service pin over her heart.

HOOFBEATS ON A BRIDGE

By Alexander Woollcott

LAST December my path by chance at Christmastime crossed that of a neighbor of mine who was also far from home. Thus it befell that Katharine Cornell and I, she trouping with a play and I on a lecture tour, observed the day by dining together in a Seattle hotel. I remember that my present to her was a telephone call whereby she could send her love across the continent to a friend we both cherish —a dear friend, endowed with so many more senses than the paltry five allotted to the rest of us that I have no doubt she knew what we were up to before ever the bell rang in that Connecticut cottage of hers and the operator said, "Seattle calling Miss Helen Keller."

The year before that I had spent every waking hour of the sacred day writing (or rehearsing with the orchestra) for a broadcast that would go out on Christmas night across America and for another that would reach the British Isles at 9 P. M. on Boxing Day. And I ask no greater boon than that this Christmas will once again find me, as often in recent years, so neck-deep in work that from dawn to sundown I shall have no time to remember the Christmases that used to be.

I have said that in that Seattle hotel Miss Cornell and I were two travelers far from home. But mine was more than a mere three thousand miles away. It was three thousand miles and a quarter of a century away. And if nowadays I try to fill each Christmas Eve with the hubbub of many manufactured preoccupations, it is probably in the dread of being trapped alone in the twilight by the ghost of Christmas Past. Then sharp but unmistakable and inexpressibly dear to me, there would be borne across the years a music that is for me more full of Christmas than sleigh bells ever were or all the carols flung down from all the belfries in the world. It is the ghost of a sound that must haunt many an old dirt road—the thud of hoofbeats on a wooden bridge. By them when I was young we could tell on the darkest night that we were nearing home.

The house where I was born was a vast, ramshackle, weather-beaten building, which had already seen better days. But not recently. A tangle of vines—trumpet vines and wistaria and white grape and crimson rambler—curtained the twelve ground-floor windows looking out toward the high road, and tactfully concealed the fact that the house had not been painted since before the Civil War. We used to speak grandly of the ballroom; but I cannot remember a time when the musicians' gallery was not taken up with stacks of old *Harper's* and other dusty, unbound magazines. In my time, at least, we could not hold a dance without sweeping the fallen plaster from the floor. But this dear old house, which had belonged to my grandfather, remained the one constant in the problem of a far-flung tribe, and back to it most of us managed to make our way at Christmastime. Often the railroad fare was hard to come by; but somehow, as long as my mother was alive, from school or college or work I made my way home every Christmas for more than twenty years.

What ticking off of the days on the calendar as the time grew near! Then at last the arrival at the railroad station after dark on Christmas Eve, with home only five miles away. I could always find a hack—it would smell of mothballs and manure—and the driver could usually tell me how many of the cousins had got there ahead of me. A dozen or so, maybe. Then the jog trot in the deepening darkness, with one eager passenger inside—hungry for home and no longer counting the days or even the minutes. By this time I was counting the bridges. I knew them by heart. Three more. Two more. At the next, if I sat forward and peered through the window, I would see the house through the leafless trees, every window down the long front agleam with a welcoming lamp, each light a token of all the loving-kindness that dwelt under that old, shingled roof. Then the long, slow pull up the drive. Before I could get out of the hack and pay the driver, the door would be flung open, and my mother would be standing on the threshold.

Small wonder I like to be busy at Christmas. Small wonder I feel a twist at my heart whenever at any time anywhere in the world I hear the sound of a hoofbeat on a wooden bridge.

LETTER FROM FRA GIOVANNI
TO THE CONTESSINA

Pont' Assieve
Christmas Eve.
Anno Domini 1513.

The Most Illustrious
The Contessina Allagia degl'Aldobrandeschi
On the via de' Martelli—Firenzi—

Most Beloved Contessina:—

I salute you. Believe me your most devoted servant. The rascal who carries this letter, if he devour them not on the way, will crave your acceptance of the fruits of our garden. Would that the Peace of Heaven might reach you through such things of earth!

Contessina, forgive an old man's babble, but I am your friend, and my love for you goes deep. There is nothing I can give you, which you have not got; but there is much, very much that, while I cannot give it, you can take. No Heaven can come to us unless our hearts find rest in it to-day. Take Heaven! No Peace lies in the future which is not hidden in this present little instant. Take Peace! The gloom of the world is but a shadow; behind it, yet within our reach, is joy. There is radiance and glory in the darkness, could we but see; and to see, we have only to look. Contessina, I beseech you to look.

Life is so generous a giver; but we, judging its gifts by their coverings, cast them away as ugly, or heavy or hard. Remove the covering and you will find beneath it a living splendour, woven of love, by wisdom, with power. Welcome it, grasp it, and you touch the Angel's hand that brings it to you. Everything we call a trial, a sorrow or a duty; believe me that Angel's hand is there; the gift is there, and the wonder of an overshadowing presence. Our joys, too; be not content with them as joys; they too conceal divine gifts.

Life is so full of meaning and of purpose, so full of beauty beneath its covering, that you will find that earth but cloaks your heaven. Courage then, to claim it, that is all! The courage you have, and the knowledge that we are pilgrims together, wending through unknown countries, home.

And so, at this Christmas time, I greet you; not quite as the world sends greetings, but with profound esteem, and with the prayer that for you, now and forever, the day breaks and the shadows flee away.

I have the honor to be your servant, though the least worthy of them.

FRA GIOVANNI.

FROM THE KING'S BROADCAST, CHRISTMAS, 1939

By Louise Haskins

I SAID to a man who stood at the gate of the year: "Give me a light that I may tread safely into the unknown," and he replied, "Go out into the darkness and put your hand into the hand of God. That shall be to you better than a light and safer than a known way." So I went forth, and finding the Hand of God, trod gladly into the night.

From *The Gate of the Year*

The Observer commented: "It must have been a thrilling experience for Miss Haskins to hear the King quote in his Christmas Day broadcast a verse from a poem of hers written twenty years ago, and for which the libraries of London and New York had been searching in vain. It had, apparently, come to His Majesty's notice through being printed on a private greeting card."

CHRISTMAS IN VERMONT

By Anne Bosworth Greene

ON Christmas night a brilliant full moon rose, shining on the crust. It was twelve below zero. The rolling hills were like a silver sea. Moonlight gleamed on their tops and made shining paths. The belts of woods were black as ink. Riding home from a festive dinner at the Chickadee's, we gazed, though with teeth chattering; the horses galloped along the lighted roads, but even that exhilarating motion could not keep out the bite of the cold, and we turned gladly down the path to the barn. Before I could dismount, Polly quickly steered me to the watering-trough, with her little chivalrous air of "Oh, do let me save you the trouble of doing this later!" . . . But she bumped her nose on it! It was frozen hard; *and* the fence beside it shivered into bits!

Not a pony was to be found. They had had a kicking-bee by the fence, laid it flat, and departed. The crust was hard; they could go anywhere.

"Elizabeth—out at this hour!" I cried.

"And Donny—she'll freeze!" mourned Babs. The moon, though big, was still low above the hills; so we brought a lantern and scurried through the orchards (magically beautiful, with their purples against shadowy silver). There we discovered a stream of tracks on the hard crust.

It was dreadfully slippery on that crust; we slid along, holding the lantern at the tracks, and feeling every sword-sharp breath of air a stab in our hearts. . . . Would Elizabeth's little round furriness withstand this bitter night? So we hurried perilously over the slopes, where birch clumps sketched enchanting shadows, and the moon, soaring aloft, shone brightly down. The dark blue sky was thick with stars, the Milky Way solid with them; even the needless glory of the northern lights flared tongues of greenish fire upward behind the mountains. A night of celebration above, as well as on earth! and in the midst of such beauty our anxious quest seemed a bad dream. . . . It was Elizabeth's first Christmas! and we had brought her home a lump of sugar tied up with red ribbon. . . .

At the lane, tracks went in both directions, one stream into the dark woods. So we darted into a birchy hollow. Tracks were everywhere now, and round dig-places in the snow, where a hoof had scraped for food. We were both escorted by columns of steaming breath; " 'Valleys where the people went about like smoking chimneys'—remember?" I panted, holding on to my nose, which seemed of a strange numbness. . . .

The bushy lane turned here, and in its shadows we perceived clusters of deeper blackness, from which a certain *breathing* quality arose . . . and then somebody very kindly sneezed!

"I'll get over the fence," whispered my child, with strategy learned of old, "and you go back to the turn and shoo 'em in when you hear 'em coming! I'll yell if I need you!"

Before I could even nod assentingly (as an obedient parent should) she was bobbing away. I dashed desperately back. If they got there before I did,—and if the wrong pony was leading,—all was lost! They would go tearing downhill into the woods. . . . If steady little black Fad had been with them, she would swerve into the home field; but, alas! Fad was now far away, dragging a cart in Connecticut, and Ocean Wave, the swift and tireless, was leader of the gang. Mischief is the spice of Ocean's life. I could just *see* her dashing the whole crowd down into those shadowy depths, like the swine that dashed into the sea. Only it needs no especial devil to inspire my darling children; once get them in a mob, and out jump a dozen busy little devils ready for use—devils that a pony ordinarily keeps tucked away in the back side of his clever little head. And that pitch into the woods was a divine dash-place, geographically—and psychologically; being both a lovely downhill *and* the exact opposite of the direction in which they knew—*ad nauseam!*—they ought to go. How often had they galloped along that very lane and shot piously in at the opening! And Shetlands, like people, can't bear being good *too* long.

Awaiting the onrush, I listened intently. All was still. The moon shone down through the trees, and lay in patterns on the frozen snow. Tiny sounds stole into the night stillness: a rustle, a crisping of crust, a frost-snap from a tree, the fritter of a dry beech-leaf; and, behind all these, the slow rise and fall of a murmur, a vast, slow murmur as from forgotten winds. . . . But from up the lane—silence. I grew anxious. Had they eluded my questing child and careered away? Should I stick to my post, or run and help?

Just then a crunching came to my ears; the crunching became a crashing, and round the corner of the birches dashed an agitated black mass, diving into the hollow, surging up over its crest, and roaring straight at me in full flight—a laneful of wildness! The woods for them! and midnight, and freedom, and frozen ears—hooray! Into the slivers of moonlight came a gallant blink of white; two silver knees flashing, an ink-black mane waving—Ocean Wave, simply going it!

"Hi!" I yelled, swinging my lantern in mad circles, and dancing furiously from one side of the lane to the other. Just as I caught the flash of Ocean's eye, and thought she was going straight through me, she swerved past—into the home field. A clot of others followed, galloping their best, swinging on desperate small legs around the sharp turn; then a single pony, shining golden against the shadow—Marigold; after her a string of slower yearlings, breathing loudly; then Queenie, a little black galloping blot on the moon-lit snow; and last—not to be hurried—the mare Thalma, at a laborious trot, with Elizabeth beside her. Finally, out of the darkness grew two attached but wrestling forms, about which expostulations hovered. "Stop, Superb! . . . Superb, don't be an ass!" and my child appeared, mightily restraining an agonized parent whose son had run on without her. Superb was knit into complete curves, her whole self a tense half-circle of suspense. Once safely in the field we let her go—and a chestnut streak shot into the valley, then up among the frisking mob of home-goers. We smiled at each other. Then our faces sobered.

"My! this cold bites!" muttered Babs.

"Got any nose?" I asked anxiously.

"Not much!" said she cheerfully, clasping it in a mittened hand. "You got any?"

In front of us were roofs and cuddling orchards; and to-night a single light shone out—that light I always longed to see. It made the whole picture; . . . even if one knew it was candlesticks on a side-table under my child's portrait! . . . And the softness of the orchard-darks, above clear lines of silver fields—oh, dear! what a thing to draw—at twelve below zero, and ten o'clock at night! Things are always gorgeous just when it's impossible to get at them. . . .

By the door stood a huddle of forms, meekly awaiting us. As we buttoned the door upon them, a sudden shock struck me.

"Where's Kindness?" I gasped.

"And Donlinna!" breathed Babs.

We had forgotten them completely! After a rueful glance at the freezing hills, we looked at each other and burst into shouts of mirth. Seizing the lantern, we set off, and nearly a mile from home came upon them standing disconsolately before a gray wayside barn, its front brilliant silver in the moonlight. Donlinna sprang to meet us.

"Bless you, Missises!" she wickered, running her nose into my coat-front.

"Why didn't you come home then, idiot?" I said, crossly, petting her; and started to put a halter on her. None of that! With a bound and a flourish she and her tributary pony were off, tails up, for home. Toiling in their wake, we had just one glimpse of them flying along the moon-lit lane. . . .

At exactly 11:15 by the kitchen clock we sat down to a Christmas supper. How marvelous the fire-heat felt; how joyfully the kettles steamed! Which was the greater luxury, to bask or to eat, we did not know. The candles gleamed among the holly; Boo-boo purred like a happy cello; and Goliath, on the hearth-rug, stretched out with a groan of content.

From *Lone Winter*

A CHRISTMAS GUEST

By Ruth McEnery Stuart

A BOY, you say, doctor? An' she don't know it yet? Then what're you tellin' *me* for? No, sir—take it away. I don't want to lay my eyes on it till she's saw it—not if I *am* its father. She's its *mother*, I reckon!

Better lay it down somew'eres an' go to *her*—not there on the rockin'-cheer, for somebody to set on—'n' not on the trunk, please. That ain't none o' yo' ord'nary newborn bundles, to be dumped on a box that'll maybe be opened sudden d'rec'ly for somethin' needed, an' be dropped ag'in the wall-paper behin' it.

It's hers, whether she knows it or not. *Don't,* for *gracious* sakes, lay 'im on the *table! Anybody* knows *that's* bad luck.

You think it might bother her on the bed? She's that bad? An' they ain't no fire kindled in the settin'-room, to lay it in there.

S-i-r? Well, yas, I-I reck'n I'll *haf* to hold it, ef you say so—that is— of co'se—

Wait, doctor! *Don't* let go of it *yet!* Lordy! but I'm thess *shore* to drop it! Lemme set down first, doctor, here by the fire an' git het th'ugh. Not yet! My ol' shinbones stan' up thess like a pair o' dog-irons. Lemme bridge 'em over first 'th somethin' soft. That'll do. She patched that quilt herself. Hold on a minute, 'tel I git the aidges of it under my ol' boots, to keep it f'om saggin' down in the middle.

There, now! Merciful goodness, but I never! I'd ruther trus' myself with a whole playin' fountain in blowed glass'n sech ez this.

Stoop down there, doctor, please, sir, an' shove the end o' this quilt a leetle further under my foot, won't you? Ef it was to let up sudden, I wouldn't have no more lap'n what any other fool man's got.

'N' now—you go to *her.*

I'd feel a heap safer ef this quilt was nailed to the flo' on each side o' my legs. They're trimblin' so I dunno what minute my feet'll let go their holt.

An' she don't know it yet! An' he layin' here, dressed up in all the little clo'es she sewed! She mus' be purty bad. I dunno, though: maybe that's gen'ally the way.

They're keepin' mighty still in that room. Blessed ef I don't begin to feel 'is warmth in my ol' knee-bones! An' he's a-breathin' thess ez reg'lar ez that clock, on'y quicker. Lordy! An' she don't know it yet! An' he a boy! He takes that after the Joneses; we've all been boys in our male branch. When that name strikes, seem like it comes to stay. Now for a girl—

Wonder if he ain't covered up mos' too clos't. Seem like he snuffles purty loud—for a beginner.

Doctor! *oh,* doctor! I say, *doctor!*

Strange he don't hear—'n' I don't like to holler no louder. Wonder ef she could be worse? Ef I could thess reach somethin' to knock with! I daresn't lif' my feet, less'n the whole business'd fall through.

Oh, doc! Here he comes now— *Doctor,* I say, don't you think maybe he's covered up too—

How's *she,* doctor? "Thess the same," you say? 'n' she don't know yet—about him? "In a couple o' hours," you say? Well, don't lemme keep you, doctor. But, tell me, don't you think maybe he's covered up a leetle too close-t?

That's better. An' now I've saw him befo' she did! An' I didn't want to, neither.

Poor, leetle, weenchy bit of a thing! Ef he ain't the *very* littlest! Lordy, Lordy, Lordy! But I s'pose all thet's needed in a baby is a startin'-p'int big enough to hol' the fam'ly characteristics. I s'pose maybe he is, but the po' little thing mus' feel sort o' scrouged with 'em, ef he's got 'em all—the Joneses' an' the Simses'. Seems to me he favors her a little thess aroun' the mouth.

An' she don't know it yet!

Lord! But my legs ache like ez if they was bein' wrenched off. I've got 'em on sech a strain, somehow. An' he on'y a half hour ol', an' two hours mo' 'fo' I can budge! Lord, Lord! how *will* I stand it!

God bless 'im! Doc! He's a-sneezin'! Come quick! Shore ez I'm here, he snez twice-t!

Don't you reckon you better pile some mo' wood on the fire an—

What's that you say? "Fetch 'im along"? An' has she ast for 'im? Bless the Lord! I say. But a couple of you'll have to come help me loosen up 'fo' I can stir, doctor.

Here, you stan' on that side the quilt, whiles I stir my foot to the flo' where it won't slip—an' Dicey—, where's that nigger Dicey? Yo, Dicey, come on here, an' tromp on the other side o' this bedquilt till I h'ist yo' young marster up on to my shoulder.

No, you don't take 'im, neither. I'll tote him myself.

Now, go fetch a piller till I lay 'im on it. That's it. And now git me somethin' stiff to lay the piller on. There! That lapbo'd'll do. Why didn't I think about that befo'? It's a heap safeter 'n my ole knee-j'ints. Now, I've got 'im *se*cure. *Wait*, doctor—hold on! I'm afeered you'll haf to ca'y 'im in to her, after all? I'll cry ef I do it. I'm trimblin' like ez ef I had a 'ager, thess a-startin' in with 'im—an' seein' me give way might make her nervous. You take 'im to her, and lemme come in sort o' unconcerned terreckly, after she an' 'im 've kind o' got acquainted. Dast you hold 'im that-a-way, doctor, 'thout no support to 'is spinal colume? I s'pose he *is* too sof' to snap, but I wouldn't resk it. Reckon I can slip in the other do' where she won't see me, an' view the meetin'.

Yas, I'm right here, honey! (The idea o' her a-callin' for me an' *him* in 'er arms!) I'm right here, honey—mother! Don't min' me a-cryin'! I'm all broke up, somehow; but don't you fret. I'm right here by yo' side on my knees, in pure thankfulness.

Bless His name, I say! You know he's a boy, don't yer? I been a holdin' 'im all day—'t least ever sence they dressed 'im, purty nigh a' hour ago. An' he's slep'—an' waked up—an' yawned—an' snez— an' wunk—an' sniffed—'thout me sayin' a word. Opened an' shet his little fist, once-t, like ez ef he craved to shake hands, howdy! He cer- t'n'ly does perform 'is functions wonderful.

Yas, doctor; I'm a-comin', right now.

Go to sleep now, honey, you an' him, an' I'll be right on the spot when needed. Lemme whisper to her thess a minute, doctor?

I thess want to tell you, honey, thet you never, even in yo' young days, looked ez purty to my eyes ez what you do right now. An' that boy is *yo' boy,* an' I ain't a-goin' to lay no mo' claim to 'im 'n to see thet you have yo' way with 'im—you hear? An' now good night, honey, an' go to sleep.

They wasn't nothin' lef' for me to do but to come out here in this ol' woodshed where nobody wouldn't see me ac' like a plumb baby.

An' now, seem like I *can't* git over it! The idea o' me, fifty year ol', actin' like this!

An' she knows it! An' she's *got* 'im—*a boy*—layin' in the bed 'long- side 'er.

"Mother an' child doin' well!" Lord, Lord! How often I've heerd that said! But it never give me the all-overs like it does now, some way.

Guess I'll gether up a' armful o' wood, an' try to act unconcerned —an' laws-a-mercy-me! Ef—to-day—ain't-been-Christmas! My! my! my! An' it come an' gone befo' I remembered!

I'll haf to lay this wood down ag'in an' *think*.

I've had many a welcome Christmas gif' in my life, but the idee o' the good Lord a-timin' *this* like that!

Christmas! An' a boy! An' she doin' well!

No wonder that ol' turkey-gobbler sets up on them rafters blinkin' at me so peaceful! He knows he's done passed a critical time o' life—

You've done crossed another bridge safe-t, ol' gobbly, an' you can *afford* to blink—an' to set out in the clair moonlight, 'stid o' roostin' back in the shadders same ez you been doin'.

You was to've died by accident las' night, but the new visitor thet's dropped in on us ain't cut 'is turkey teeth yet, an' his mother—

Lord, how that name sounds! Mother! I hardly know 'er by it, long ez I been tryin' to fit it to 'er—an' fearin' to, too, less'n somethin' might go wrong with either one.

I even been callin' him "it" to myse'f, all along, so 'feered thet ef I set my min' on either the "he" or the "she" the other one might take a notion to come—an' I didn't want any disappointment mixed in with the arrival.

But now he's come—an' registered, ez they say at the polls,—I know I sort o' counted on the boy, some way.

Lordy! but he's little! Ef he hadn't 'a' showed up so many of his functions spontaneous, I'd be oneasy less'n he mightn't have 'em; but they're there! Bless goodness, they're there!

An' he snez prezac'ly, for all the world, like my po' ol' pap—a reg'lar little cat sneeze, thess like all the Joneses.

Well, Mr. Turkey, befo' I go back into the house, I'm a-goin' to make you a solemn promise.

You go free till about this time next year, *anyhow*. You an' me'l celebrate the birthday between ourselves with that contrac'. You needn't git oneasy Thanksgivin', or picnic-time, or Easter, or no other time 'twixt this an' nex' Christmas—less'n, of co'se, you stray off an' git stole.

An' this here reprieve, I want you to understand, is a present from the junior member of the firm.

Lord! but I'm that tickled! This here wood ain't much needed in the house,—the wood-boxes 're all full,—but I can't *de*vise no other excuse for vacatin'—thess at this time.

S'pose I *might* gether up some eggs out'n the nests, but it'd look sort o' flighty to go egg-huntin' here at midnight—an' he not two hours ol'.

I dunno, either, come to think; she might need a new-laid egg—sof'-b'iled. Reckon I'll take a couple in my hands—an' one or two sticks o' wood—an' I'll draw a bucket o' water too—an' tote *that* in.

Goodness! but this back yard is bright ez day! Goin' to be a clair, cool night—moon out, full an' white. Ef this ain't the *stillest* stillness!

Thess such a night, for all the world, I reckon, ez the first Christmas, when HE come—

> When shepherds watched their flocks by night,
> All seated on the ground,
> The angel o' the Lord come down,
> En' glory shone around—

thess like the hymn says.

The whole o' this back yard is full o' glory this minute. Th' ain't nothin' too low down an' mean for it to shine on, neither—not even the well-pump or the cattle-trough—'r the pig-pen—'r even me.

Thess look at me, covered over with it! An' how it does shine on the roof o' the house where they lay—her an' him!

I suppose that roof has shined that-a-way frosty nights 'fo' tonight; but some way I never seemed to see it.

Don't reckon the creakin' o' this windlass could disturb her—or him.

Reckon I might go turn a little mo' cotton-seed in the troughs for them cows—an' put some extry oats out for the mules an' the doctor's mare—an' onchain Rover, an' let 'im stretch 'is legs a little. I'd like everythin' on the place to know he's come, an' to feel the diff'ence.

Well, now I'll load up—an' I do hope nobody won't notice the *re-dic'lousness* of it.

You say she's asleep, doctor, an' th' ain't nothin' mo' needed to be did—an' yo' goin'?

Don't, fr' gracious sakes! go, doctor, an' leave me! I won't know what on top o' the round earth to do, ef-ef— You know she—she might wake up—or he!

You say Dicey she knows. But she's on'y a nigger, doctor. Yes: I know she's had exper'ence with the common rin o' babies, but—

Lemme go an' set down this bucket, an' lay this stick o' wood on the fire, an' put these eggs down, so's I can talk with you free-handed.

Step here to the do', doctor. I say, doc, ef it's a question o' the size o' yo' bill, you can make it out to suit yo'self—or, I'll tell you what I'll do? You stay right along here a day or so—tell to-morrow or nex' day, anyhow—an' I'll sen' you a whole bale o' cotton—an' you can sen' back any change you see fit—or none—*or none,* I say. Or, ef you'd ruther take it out in perpaters an' corn an' sorghum, thess say so, an' how much of each.

But *what?* "It wouldn't be right? Th' ain't no use," you say? An' you'll *shore* come back to-morrer? Well. But, by-the-way, doctor, did you know to-day was Christmas? Of co'se I might've knew you did— but I never. An' now it seems to me like Christmas, an' fo'th o' July, an' "Hail Columbia, happy lan' " all b'iled down into one big jubilee!

But tell me, doctor, confidential—Sh!—step here a little further back—tell me, don't you think he's to say a leetle bit undersized? Speak out, ef he is.

Wh—how'd you say? "Mejun," eh? Thess mejun! An' they do come even littler yet? An' you say mejun babies 're thess ez liable to turn out likely an' strong ez over-sizes, eh? Mh—hm! Well, I reckon you *know*—an' maybe the less they have to contend with at the start the better.

Oh, thanky, doctor! Don't be afeerd o' wrenchin' my wris'! A thousand thankies! Yo' word for it, he's a fine boy! An' you've inspected a good many, an' of co'se you know—yas, yas! Shake ez hard ez you like —up an' down—up an' down!

An' now I'll go yit yo' horse—an' don't ride 'er too hard to-night, 'cause I've put a double po'tion of oats in her trough ahile ago. The junior member he give instructions that everything on the place was to have a' extry feed to-night—an' of co'se I went and obeyed orders.

Now—'fo' you start, doctor—I ain't got a thing stronger 'n raspberry corjal in the house—but ef you'll drink a glass o' that with me? (Of co'se he will!)

She made this 'erself, doctor—picked the berries an' all—an' I raised the little sugar thet's in it. Well, good-night, doctor! To-morrer, shore!

SH-H!

How that do' latch does click! Thess like thunder!

Sh-h! Dicey, you go draw yo' pallet close-t outside the do', an' lay down—an' I'll set here by the fire an' keep watch.

How my ol' stockin'-feet do tromp! So lemme hurry an' set down! Seem like this room's awful rackety, the fire a-poppin' an' tumblin', an' me breathin' like a porpoise. Even the clock ticks ez excited ez I feel. Wonder how they sleep through it all! But they do. He beats her a-snorin' a'ready, blest ef he don't! Wonder ef he knows he's born into the world, po' little thing! I reckon not; but they's no tellin'. Maybe that's th' one thing the good Lord gives 'em *to* know, so's they'll realize what to begin to study about—theirselves an' the world—how to fight it an' keep friends with it at the same time. Ef I could giggle an' sigh both at once-t, seem like I'd be relieved. Somehow I feel sort o' tight 'round the heart—an' wide awake an'—

How that clock *does* travel—an' how they all keep time, he an' she—an' it—an' me—an' the fire a roa'in' up the chimbley, playin' a tune all round us like a' organ, an' he—an' she—an' he—an' it—an' he—an'.

Blest ef I don't hear singing—an' how white the moonlight is! They's angels all over the house—an' their robes is breshin' the roof whiles they sing—

His head had fallen. He was dreaming.

CHRISTMAS ON BEE TREE

By Lucy Furman

DECEMBER came in with almost a week of bad rainy weather, which compelled Uncle Lot to stay close in the house.

When, having finished his feeding and wood-chopping for the day, he took his seat by the fire, Bible in hand, Aunt Ailsie stopped long enough in her spinning to hand him his spectacles, which she had been wearing, and then made apparently patient efforts to resume it without the glasses. But the yarn began snapping and flying.

" 'Pears like hit hain't much use," she sighed; "a body can't do right spinning without they can foller the yarn, and my pore old eyes seems like has done their do. I allow I might as well take this here wool up Bee Tree for Cyarline to spin, or somebody else that's got either daylight or good seeing. And maybe to weave, too, for my weaving now wouldn't noways be the pretty weaving hit was, and them women allowed they wanted the best. I hate to give hit up, though, having sot my mind on yearning all that money myself. If there was jest some way for me to get good light to see by, my eyes might hold out to make many a kiver yet."

"You hain't got all the light you might have," said Uncle Lot. "Lemme fix hit brighter." He poked the fire vigorously with the long, homemade poker, threw several chunks in front of the backlog, and, selecting a longer and fatter pine stick from the basket, stuck it into the jamb.

"Now try if you hain't got sufficience of light," he commanded.

She started in again at the spinning; but the yarn continued to snap and fly viciously, and at last she sighed; " Pears like hit hain't no great of help—fire-light and fat-pine both being so flickery. Stiddy light is what is called for when eyes goes to dimming. Don't you mind, paw; I'll go back to the cyarpet rags. I never did set store by wealth, no-how—a body can't sarve both God and Mammon."

She picked up her wheel and set it back in its corner, and taking up the basket of wool, started toward the loft steps.

"How much was it them women agreed to give you?"

"Ten dollars a kiver, and after I oncet had the yarn spun and dyed I could easy weave two kivers a week."

"And how much more spinning you got to do?"

"I could finish maybe in two weeks if I had sight and light."

Uncle Lot, to whose elect soul ten dollars loomed as large as to that of any foredoomed sinner, slowly removed his square silver spectacles and held them toward her.

"Here's my specs," he said. "I allow I can make out to scrouge along without 'em whilst you do the spinning."

She shook her head vehemently. "No, paw, I wouldn't see ary grain of peace if I was to part you from Job and tother ole fellers you set sech store by; hit would be wicked and godless in me; any money I yearnt that way wouldn't never do me no good."

She climbed the lower treads of the ladder-like steps.

Uncle Lot rose this time and came toward her rather hastily, the spectacles outstretched in his hand. "Take 'em," he said, "hit's my will. I got corn to shell, and more odd jobs."

"Well, paw," reluctantly, "the man being the head of the woman, hit's my bounden duty to obey you; but ricollect, hit's again' my jedgment."

Meekly she put on the spectacles, drew out the wheel again, and set it whirring.

Uncle Lot went out in the rain to the barn, shucked his corn and shelled it, and returned to the house with the question, "Hain't it nigh about time to put dinner on?"

"Gee-oh, paw, hit's two good hours yet!"

He sat down by the fire and watched the small hand of the clock, which apparently consumed an age in passing from minute mark to minute mark. After eons of time had passed in this way, he rose desperately, and went out again to the barn. But not a thing could he see there to do. Tom mule and Darb, Old Pied and Blossom, all regarded him with surprise, as if he were an alien and an intruder.

Returning to the house, he sat and fidgeted painfully for another endless period of time, with Job, Solomon, and Jeremiah in full sight on the fireboard, but as unattainable as if in another world.

When Aunt Ailsie at last arose to put dinner on, he plunged instantly into the delights of Lamentations; and while she washed the dishes after dinner he snatched a greedy bit of Job. Then the long afternoon, the sea without a sail, stretched before him. It was too wet for him to ride into the village; the clock ticked more slowly than ever. After nearly three hours of agony, he went up the branch to Link's, only a half mile distant.

"Pore creetur," said Aunt Ailsie, after he was gone, "he's pyorely punishing. I feel for him, too, but hit's his own will; he would make me wear these here specs! Well, I'm proud he's gone to Link's; he'll see how good that-air glass window of Rutheny's lets in the light."

Day after day of rain followed. For almost a week Uncle Lot was a prisoner, without a prisoner's solace. Every morning Aunt Ailsie insisted on giving him the specs; every morning he stubbornly refused to take them. His sufferings were evidently intense, as frequent sighs and groans testified. He began to look so peaked and forlorn that Aunt Ailsie now and then took pity on his desperate condition and threw a sop to Cerberus.

"That air reel of mine," she would say, when things appeared to have reached a breaking-point, "has wanted a new piece for allus. Do you feel to make one for hit, paw? I got to use it soon as I'm through this spinning." Or: "I hain't got nigh enough quills to spool all this yarn on; would hit be axing too much of you to make me some new ones?" or again: "This here old sley is all snaggle-toothed—how about putting some new reeds in hit, paw? The weaving hain't fur off now." These soporific labors and the snatches of reading he got at noon and night took some of the edge off his desperation.

"I'd have you know," he said, on handing over the specs the last afternoon of the rain, "that these-here specs is a burnt offering on the brazen altar of sacrifice."

"I know hit, paw; hit's terrible hard on you, and I feel for you, I do, setting there the livelong day denying yourself this way. Hit's too hard; you oughtn't to treat yourself that way."

"Hit's hard, too," he agreed crossly; "but dollars don't grow up in the sticks; and that-air spinning can't last everly."

"No indeed, paw. And one marciful thing—you got such a lavish of Scripter shet up in your mind, you can allus call hit up and meditate on hit even if you can't read. I'm proud I got me a man with so much larning. I never seed nobody, not even a preacher, knowed Scripter like you."

"Hit's a fact," admitted Uncle Lot, modestly; "but sometimes, even if a body knows a thing, they hain't able to call hit up."

"Not when they get older," sighed Aunt Ailsie. "Law, law, old age is a-creeping up fast on me and you both. God send your mind hain't à-getting failable like my eyes!"

"I may not be as young as I oncet was," he replied, tartly, "but I'll have you know my headpiece is able as ever!"

A week of fair weather followed, during which Uncle Lot was hard at work in the timber, and Aunt Ailsie made good progress with the spinning. At last the yarn was all spun and spooled and she rode in to the Forks on a Saturday to buy the indigo and madder for the dying. While she was trading for these in Madison Lee's store, a wagon, followed by a noisy train of children, passed along the street.

"What air the young uns follering Adam's wagon that way for?" she asked Madison.

"He's fetching in the women's Christmas things—candy and such. They aim to have a Christmas tree at the school."

Quickly as she could get there, Aunt Ailsie was at the women's cottage. Almost every child in town was already hanging over the palings, while Uncle Adam unloaded the wagon, handing out bucket after bucket labeled CANDY, and various mysterious boxes.

"What is a Christmas tree, women?" she asked Amy and Virginia, after they had all come into the house again. "I heared talk of hit downtown."

They told her it was a tree hung with pretties and presents for the children at Christmas time.

"Never heared tell of one in life, or present for Christmas either, till you women sont in that-air box last year, with things for the young uns, and the fine lace collar and necktie for me and Lot. When do you aim to have your tree—New Christmas or Old Christmas?"

It was the women's turn to look puzzled.

"New Christmas," explained Aunt Ailsie, "comes first, along in December, and is the time when young folks frolics, and everybody drinks and cheers themselves. Old Christmas comes the sixth of January, and is *rael* Christmas, and a solemn season; and payrents don't put up with no antic ways from the young then."

"We never heard of any but New Christmas," replied the women.

"That hain't right Christmas, and never was; and the way I know it, the night afore Old Christmas, at midnight, all the cattle gets down on their knees and lows and prays, and the elders puts out a head of blossom. Creeters they know better than humans when Jesus was bornded; and I have heared 'em at their lowing and praying, and have scratched the snow off'n the elders and seed the green shoots next morning. All the old folks will tell you the same."

The women then remembered their English history—how, when the calendar was changed eleven days in the middle of the eighteenth century, the country people of England, and many of the colonists also, refused to accept the new, earlier date for Christmas, but kept their festival on the sixth of January.

Aunt Ailsie was invited to come in on New Christmas Eve and help trim the tree, as well as to be present Christmas morning.

"Women," she replied, "I'll be here if there's any getting here, though I see trouble ahead, my man being again' everything gay and lively."

As she started out the gate, she met Susanna and Christine coming in.

"Hain't it grand about the Christmas tree?" she asked. " 'Pears like I can't hardly wait to see one. I'll come holp you gals trim it if I have good luck."

"Maybe you'll come and help me with the one up Bee Tree for Lowizy and her scholars, just after the one here," said Christine.

"I'll come, too," declared Aunt Ailsie, joyfully.

.   .   .   .

The fine weather continued the third week in December, Aunt Ailsie busily made her dye-pots—indigo, madder, walnut. Then, having run her yarn in the reel into hanks, she dyed and dipped with zest, rejoicing with an artist's delight in the rich colors that resulted. Very beautiful the hanks looked after the dyeing, their deep blues, soft reds and rich browns hanging from the joists of "old house" in every place not already occupied by strings of shucky beans, cushaw, red peppers, and onions. Gazing with pride upon her handiwork,

Aunt Ailsie softly repeated to herself those verses from the last chapter of Proverbs, better known to her, perhaps, than any in the Bible, from ceaseless repetition by Uncle Lot. "She seeketh wool and flax, and worketh willingly with her hands. . . . She layeth her hands to the spindle and her hands hold the distaff. . . . She maketh fine linen . . . she maketh . . . coverings of tapestry . . . feareth not the snow for her household . . . eateth not the bread of idleness—"

"Hit's the pine-blank picter of me," she said to herself. Then another verse smote somewhat sharply upon her conscience. "The heart of her husband doth safely trust in her . . . she will do him good and not evil all the days of her life," and remembering guiltily the plan at that moment enlarging in her mind, she lapsed into an instant of pensiveness. "Well, hain't I trying to do him good? Hain't it as much for his good as mine to have a glass window? Won't hit save his sight as much as mine, and likewise his rheumatiz, from going out in the cold to hunt fat pine?" With which sophistries she quieted the still, small voice.

And now came the most tedious part of her labors, the warping of the big loom. First the thread or chain must be wound on the warping-bars and made into the desired lengths; then it must be beamed—that is, each separate thread of the hundreds composing the bundle must be drawn with a wire hook through the reeds of the sley and tied to the main beam of the loom. No human being can accomplish this alone, and Rutheny was called in for a couple of days, the spectacles also being required every minute. Fortunately Uncle Lot was out snaking logs down the slopes.

When she asked him one night about going to see the women's Christmas tree, he promised that if she would get through everything else and be ready to settle down to weaving by that time, he might take her in. "For I aim to have the last of my logs down by then, and to sarch the Scripters stiddy all winter from then on," he said; "and I want you to get to a job where you won't need my specs no more, which a body knows weaving don't take no eyesight at all, hardly; and atter you once get started on hit, I'll have peace and satisfaction."

He firmly held out against her going in to help trim the tree, however. "Hit hain't nothing but a frolic and a vanity noway—I don't hold with no sech," he said.

So the Christmas tree, a beautiful "spruce-pine," hemlock, had to be trimmed in the school chapel without her aid.

.   .   .   .

Hours before dawn on Christmas morning Aunt Ailsie was up and had Uncle Lot up, and by five-thirty they were ready to start for the tree, which was not to be until eight. Both were dressed in their best, Uncle Lot in a fine linen shirt of her weaving, and a suit of black sheep's-wool likewise spun, woven, and tailored by her. She wore her newest linsey, black with blue stripes, and a new print apron with blue sprig, and her black-silk sunbonnet and home-spun shawl lay on the bed. The two sat stiffly in "old house" until time to start. Then, when Uncle Lot went to saddle the nags, she hurried to the chest of drawers in "tother house," took out the small box containing the women's gifts of a year before, and laying the lace collar about her neck, ran to the small, wavery mirror on the back porch and took a breathless look at herself. How lovely it was! How she longed to wear it! But hearing Uncle Lot's step on the front porch, she quickly tore it off, and stuffed it back, with the black tie, into the box and drawer just as he entered the door.

After bonnet, shawl and mitts were all on, she remembered that she had not gathered the eggs, which would be frozen if left. She was snooping around in the barn loft, amid bundles of fodder and piles of hay, when through a wide crack betwen the logs she saw Uncle Lot emerge from "tother house" on to the back porch, look about in a strange, furtive way, and approach the mirror, where he fumbled with something at his neck. Not until he stood back to observe the effect did she see that it was the "vanity" he had so sternly condemned a year before—the black necktie! Only for an instant, however, did he dally with temptation; in the next he had snatched off the tie and hurried back into the house. When she arrived, his shirt-front was as innocent of a tie as it had always been.

As the two rode up Troublesome through the ice and snow a little later, Uncle Lot, severe and grizzled, in the lead, Aunt Ailsie a picture of wifely meekness, following, one would never have guessed that her bosom was a seething caldron of emotions—joy at the discovery of her lord's weakness, hope that the breach once made would widen, prevision that in the end she would certainly enjoy not only the lace collar and lesser pretties but the glass window too. She saw it plainly, set in the south wall; and the vision nerved her to continued persistence in her plan.

. . . .

. . . The Rideout house was bursting and running over with life. Not only the forty-odd "scholars" were there, but all their younger brothers and sisters, their fathers, mothers, and in some cases their grandmothers. Christine thanked her stars she had brought a hundred candy-stockings.

Everybody had run out of the kitchen, a number of barefoot boys overflowing into the snow of the yard with no apparent discomfort, and Giles then set up the tree David had already cut, and Christine and Phebe trimmed it and tied on dolls and toys. Aunt Ailsie and Uncle Lot arrived just as they were lighting the candles. The door into the other room was thrown open, and the crowd surged in, Lowizy, wrapped in blankets, in her father's arms.

There was silence for a moment as everybody gazed spellbound. Not a child spoke. They scarcely breathed, their eyes glued to the tree.

A few "gee-oh's!" and "eh, laws!" rose softly from the older people, however, and one old lady exclaimed in a rapt voice, "Glory to God, was sech a wonderly sight ever seed afore! Them pretty leetle creeters a-flying in them limbs—air they angels from heaven?"

Aunt Ailsie laid a hand on the speaker's arm. "Them's store poppets, Cyarline," she corrected, in a stage whisper.

Giles, in his impressive way, read the story of the first Christmas from St. Luke, and told why gifts are made to children on this day. Then Christine sang "O Little Town of Bethlehem." Then the gifts were detached from the tree and handed to Lowizy, who read the names and passed them on.

Christine had never in her life seen such decorum. Not a child grabbed or snatched or begged for anything, each taking what came its way in "gladness and singleness of heart." When a "store-poppet" was passed to a grand-daughter of Aunt Cyarline, the old lady promptly seized it from the child's arms, to clasp it to her own hard bosom.

"I jest got a bound to hold it, Cindy," she cried; "seems like I never pined for nothing so bad in all my days! Now hain't hit a picter, people? Look-a-there at them-air blue eyes and rosy jaws and yaller curls! Hit's too pretty to live!"

Aunt Ailsie thereupon possessed herself of little Dovey's doll and, backing into a corner, the two old souls compared eyes, hair, clothes, and size as if they were little girls again, or young mothers with their first babies.

"Yourn's the biggest, but mine's the most prettiest," was Aunt Cyarline's conclusion, which Aunt Ailsie indignantly repudiated.

Their dispute ended at last by an agreement to disagree, Aunt Cyarline said, "The onliest poppets I ever seed afore was them my paw follered cyarving out of a chunk of wood, and rosing their jaws with pokeberry, and burning eyes on 'em with a poker, and tying on black sheep's wool for hair. I allus follered making the same for my young uns and my grands."

"Me, too," said Aunt Ailsie. "And all the time, Cyarline, you and me never drempt there was sech lovelie creeters in this world as these!"

"I don't feel to part with this'n," said Aunt Cyarline. "Seems like I jest got to keep hit. I never seed nothing I liked so well. I could set up all night a-loving on hit!"

"I got me a fine lacy handkerchief off'n the women's tree at The Forks, and Lot a fine silk one; but I'd a sight ruther hit'd been a poppet!" declared Aunt Ailsie fervently.

Christine, overhearing, felt a real pang that there were not enough dolls for the two old ladies to have some of their own.

"I'm dreadfully sorry there are'n't enough for you to have some now," she said to them, "but I'll tell you what I'll do; I'll promise to have one here for each of you by Old Christmas! Will that be all right?"

"Ef hit's got blue eyes and rosy jaws and yaller curls same as this'n," qualified Aunt Cyarline. Then, with an exhaustive look at Christine, "That gal she looks like a poppet herself," she said to Aunt Ailsie.

Aunt Ailsie shook her head somewhat sadly. "She's a red-head," she said, as if that precluded the idea.

"Hit's pretty if hit is red," contended Aunt Cyarline with pleased eyes roaming over the red-gold hair.

Turning away from this naïve inventory of her charms and blemishes, and looking into the hungry eyes of the mothers and grannies as they feasted upon the brightness and beauty and color of the tree, Christine could almost have wept that there was nothing on it for them.

"I'm terribly sorry there's nothing for older folks," she said; "I didn't understand."

"If hit hain't oncivil to ax, 'pears like hit would pleasure me a sight to have one of them pretty chains to hang around my neck," said a tall, weary-looking woman, with one baby tugging vigorously at a bare breast and two or three others at her skirts. She spoke with evident hesitation, and pointed to one of the bright paper kindergarten chains.

"And a string of them berries would set well on me," said another. "I allus did love pretties so good!"

Christine was delighted. Paper chains and strings of holly berries were passed out to all the women-folk, and the festoons of popcorn were distributed among the least-ones, who ate them, strings and all, along with their candy. At last even the tiny candle-holders were given away, and the tree was left absolutely stripped.

After the guests, singing the praises and wonders of the tree, had all departed, little Lowizy lay in her bed again, exhausted and hacking, but blissful. Giles sat in a chair beside her; Christine and Uncle Lot were nearby; her new book and poppet lay in her arms.

Aunt Ailsie, who had gone out to help Phebe with the dinner, poked her head into the room to say to Uncle Lot, "Paw, have you tuck note of Lowizy's glass window there—how hit lets in the light so good for her to read her books?"

Uncle Lot rose and went to the window, which he examined carefully with both hand and eye. "Hit does let in a sight of light," he admitted; "for shet-ins like her I allow hit hain't a bad notion."

From *The Glass Window*

CHRISTMAS AT THE MILL ON THE FLOSS

By George Eliot

FINE old Christmas, with the snowy hair and ruddy face, had done his duty that year in the noblest fashion, and had set off his rich gifts of warmth and colour with all the heightening contrast of frost and snow.

Snow lay on the croft and river-bank in undulations softer than the limbs of infancy; it lay with the neatliest finished border on every sloping roof, making the dark-red gables stand out with a new depth of colour; it weighed heavily on the laurels and fir-trees till it fell from them with a shuddering sound; it clothed the rough turnip-field with whiteness, and made the sheep look like dark blotches; the gates were all blocked up with the sloping drifts, and here and there a disregarded four-footed beast stood as if petrified "in unrecumbent sadness"; there was no gleam, no shadow, for the heavens, too, were one still, pale cloud—no sound or motion in anything but the dark river, that flowed and moaned like an unresting sorrow. But old Christmas smiled as he laid this cruel-seeming spell on the out-door world, for he meant to light up home with new brightness, to deepen all the richness of indoor colour, and give a keener edge of delight to the warm fragrance of food: he meant to prepare a sweet imprisonment that would strengthen the primitive fellowship of kindred, and make the sunshine of familiar human faces as welcome as the hidden daystar. His kindness fell but hardly on the homeless—fell but hardly on the homes where the hearth was not very warm, and where the food had little fragrance; where the human faces had no sunshine in them, but rather the leaden, blank-eyed gaze of unexpectant want. But the fine old season meant well; and if he has not learnt the secret how to bless men impartially, it is because his father Time, with ever-unrelenting purpose, still hides that secret in his own mighty, slow-beating heart.

And yet this Christmas day, in spite of Tom's fresh delight in home, was not, he thought, somehow or other, quite so happy as it 'had always been before. The red berries were just as abundant on the holly, and he and Maggie had dressed all the windows and mantelpieces and picture-frames on Christmas eve with as much taste as ever, wedding the thick-set scarlet clusters with branches of the black-berried ivy. There had been singing under the windows after midnight— supernatural singing, Maggie always felt, in spite of Tom's contemptuous insistence that the singers were old Patch, the parish clerk, and the rest of the church choir: she trembled with awe when their caroling broke in upon her dreams, and the image of men in fustian clothes was always thrust away by the vision of angels resting on the parted cloud. But the midnight chant had helped as usual to lift the morning above the level of common days; and then there was the smell of hot toast and ale from the kitchen, at the breakfast hour; the favourite anthem, the green boughs, and the short sermon, gave the appropriate festal character to the church-going; and aunt and uncle Moss, with all their seven children, were looking like so many reflectors of the bright parlour fire, when the church-goers came back, stamping the snow from their feet. The plum-pudding was of the same handsome roundness as ever, and came in with the symbolic blue flames around it, as if it had been heroically snatched from the nether fires into which it had been thrown by dyspeptic Puritans; the dessert was as splendid as ever, with its golden oranges, brown nuts, and the crystalline light and dark of apple jelly and damson cheese: in all these things Christmas was as it had always been since Tom could remember; it was only distinguished, if by anything, by superior sliding and snowballs.

TWILIGHT OF THE WISE

By James Hilton

WE were talking, on Christmas night, about other Christmas nights. I had said that twenty years ago I was in the trenches somewhere in France. "And I," Middleton countered, "was somewhere in the Bavarian Alps."

It seemed a queer place for an Englishman to have been during the war years, until he explained, with a smile: "I was escaping. We managed it, you know—thanks to luck and Manny Stewart's German."

I guessed then that this fellow Middleton had deliberately stayed up to talk after the others had gone to bed; he knew I had known Manny from the conversation at dinner. I had quoted one of Manny's last poems, and we had all argued about what it probably meant—all of us, that is, except Middleton, who didn't seem the kind of person to argue much about a poem, anyway.

"You must have known him well?" I suggested.

"Not exactly. But it came as a personal loss when I read of his death last year, and again to-night when you quoted that poem. I suppose an experience of the kind he and I had, even if it only lasts a few days, counts for more than years of just 'knowing' somebody."

"Maybe."

"Ordinarily, of course, Manny and I wouldn't have had much in common—even at the prison-camp he'd been with us at least a month before I exchanged more than a few words with him. He had his own friends—chaps interested in art and books and all that. Then one day he came up to me when I was alone and said: 'Is it true you nearly got away once?' It *was* true, and I told him all about it, how I'd been within a mile of the Dutch frontier when things went wrong, all because I didn't know that *Eisenstange* means a sort of iron rod. I was hiding in a railway wagon full of them . . . but that's another story. Manny laughed when I told it him. 'My German's pretty good,' he said. 'How would you like to have another try with me?' I looked at him and I knew damn well I'd like it, and he knew I knew, too—it was a sort of sudden contact between us that didn't have to be argued about."

"Yes," I said. "He made a good many of those contacts."

"So we fixed it right away, and began to make plans. Manny thought we ought to try an escape in midwinter, because of the long nights; and he had an idea that the third week of December might be lucky for us, because even in war-time Germany the Christmas spirit had its manifestations—feasting and jollification and a general slackening of vigilance. The food shortage wasn't too bad in our part of Bavaria, and the people were a comfortable lot compared with the Prussians —as I knew myself from experience. And then, too, he thought we might try to get across the mountains instead of keeping to lowland routes—the idea, you see, being to do just what nobody would expect. Actually, we could be among the mountains within a couple of hours of leaving camp—if we dared to risk it. Do you know the Bavarian Alps? I didn't, and neither did Manny, but we had a map, and we both found we'd had plenty of pre-war climbing experience in Switzerland. It was just a matter of nerve, endurance, food-supply, and luck with the weather. Well, we thought we had the first two, and we prayed for the others. We began to hide food till we had a store; then we collected warm clothing and white coats made of bed-linen, so that we shouldn't be spotted against a snow background. Then we had to make plans for the actual escape, but I needn't tell you about these, partly because they weren't very different from those of other escapes I've read of, and also because the get-away was pretty easy. We were six thousand feet above the camp when dawn broke. We had to put on dark glasses because of the snow dazzle, and we ate chocolate and chaffed each other and stared down at the camp below—just a few littered roofs amongst the pine forests.

"Of course, by that time the hue and cry must surely have been raised, but it didn't worry us much. You can't chase two men over high alps in midwinter, and in practice you don't consider it—because you don't believe the two men would ever be such fools. *We* were, though, and we were quite happy about it. I don't believe I've ever had a feeling of such almighty ecstasy as that morning as we climbed farther and higher up the snow-slopes till we reached the steep rocks.

"The day was glorious, and we lay out in the sun during the afternoon and slept, knowing that it would be bitterly cold at night, and that we should have to keep moving all the time. We didn't talk very much, except that Manny tried to brush up my German. We climbed an icy ridge, and descended the other side. There was no trace after that of any inhabited world—the mountains enclosed us on every hand. Manny led the way, and at nightfall the moon rose, so that we went on without a halt.

"Of course we might have known that it wouldn't be all as easy as that. The next day there was no sunshine at all, and a freezing wind blew; we were utterly exhausted and slept for odd minutes in any sheltered place we could find, until our stiffening limbs awakened us. We began to walk and climb in a daze; Manny recited poetry, and I told him, I remember, about my horses and dogs at home. We were really talking to ourselves—not to each other. That night we began to realize, though neither of us put it into words, the pretty awful chance we were taking. We ate our food, primed ourselves with brandy, smoked our pipes, and drew what consolation we could from the map. It was a good map, and Manny knew exactly the place he was making for. Nevertheless, our spirits sank lower, and lowest of all during the early hours of the morning. But afterwards, when the sun came out, we grew cheerful again.

"I won't try to detail each day as it passed—partly because I can't be sure how many days did pass. During the sunshine we lived; during the cold, dark hours we slipped into a kind of coma. I think there was an exact moment when we both felt that our number was up—though whether this came on the third or the fifth or the seventh day I can't be sure. We had come to the end of our food, we were chilled and utterly wearied, and—to make things worse—the comparatively fine weather broke down and snowstorms began. I think Manny saw the future as I did, for he said once, in that wry way of his: 'I'm afraid we've been guarding against the wrong sort of danger with these white coats of ours. The trouble's going to be that we *shan't* be found, not that we *shall*. All the same, we kept going, though I believe I was the first to collapse, and had to be given what was left of the brandy. The next thing I recollect is a clearing sky and a valley vista opening at our feet, and far down, almost as if we could have jumped on skis to it, a cluster of lights. Rather like Lauterbrunnen seen from Wengenalp, if you happen to know that."

I said I did, and he went on: "There was no discussion about what we should do—we had planned it so many times in our heads. We'd comforted ourselves by thinking that as soon as we came to a house we'd wait till the occupants had gone to bed, break in, and take some food. So with this new and exciting hope we staggered down the slope, running when we came to the level of the pinewoods, and checking our pace by wild grabs from tree to tree. I can remember how dark it was in those woods, and rather terrifying; we kept stumbling and scratching our hands and faces. Then, just ahead of us—almost as if it hadn't been there before, if you know the feeling—we saw the lighted window of a house, shining out exactly like a Christmas card. Yes, and smoke curling up from the chimney. *Exactly* like a Christmas card. Warm and comforting and sentimental.

"But, of course, the light at the window meant that there were still people out of bed, so there was nothing for us to do but wait—and as it was Christmas night, we guessed we might have to wait a long time. Still, there would be some heavy sleeping afterwards, and that would help us. So we crouched down on a sort of grassy ledge, rather like a golf green, where the snow was half melted, and the moonlight lay over it like a sort of trembling sea. I suppose it was *we* who were trembling, really—you know how it feels when you've been hurrying downhill and you come to a level stretch again—your legs seem to sink under you. We were so exhausted we threw ourselves on the grass and rested a minute or two, and as I looked back at the pinewoods reaching up the side of the mountain, I noticed a star touching the dark edge of the tree-tops—just one little star. I'm not much of a person for noticing things like that, but it's a queer thing—I can almost see those woods and that star now, if I shut my eyes.

"I dare say we waited a couple of hours—it seemed twice as long. What began to puzzle us was that there was no sound from the house. We were quite close, and the night was still—surely there ought to have been voices or a dog barking or something? But there wasn't. At last Manny whispered: 'I can't stand this hanging about any longer— I'm going to scout round.'

"We crept to the outside wall, and saw that the place was a mountain chalet, timbered and heavily gabled. We listened awhile but there still wasn't a sound—but I'll tell you what there was. There was a most luscious, and to us an infuriating smell of cooking. In the end that settled it. We groped round to the doorway, and Manny tried the handle. It turned—the door was unlocked. A gust of warm air reached us and—more overpowering than ever—a definite smell of sizzling meat and roasting poultry. I looked at Manny and my look meant: Let's take a chance. . . .

"We entered the house and tiptoed along a corridor. There was a room that had a strip of light under the door, but still no sound. Manny was trying to deduce where the larder was—we daren't strike matches. And then suddenly we heard footsteps on the inside of the lighted room, the door opened, and a young girl came walking straight into us—actually she'd have collided if we hadn't stepped away. I don't think my heart has ever jumped as much as it did at that moment. Manny had the presence of mind to say 'Guten Abend.'

"The light from the doorway shone full on us then, and it suddenly occurred to me what a grim and frightening sight we must look—torn, scratched, dirty, eyes bloodshot, unshaven for days. But she didn't seem alarmed—she just said, in a tranquil voice: 'You are strangers?'

"Manny answered her, and they exchanged a few sentences in such rapid German that I couldn't properly follow it. Then I realized that we were being invited into the room. . . . That room . . . I shall never forget it. . . . It dazzled me, its firelight and lamplight, for the moment; then, as I gathered my wits, I saw a table set for two and food for a banquet warming in front of the log fire. Roast chicken, slices of veal, beans, potatoes. Cheese and a bottle of wine. A little Christmas tree. . . . I just stared and stared and left Manny to do the talking. It seemed to me we'd probably have to surrender and make the best of it—we certainly weren't prepared to terrorize a girl; and for myself, the thought of immediate things that surrender would bring —food, sleep, warmth—nearly outweighed the disappointment I knew I should feel afterwards. I wondered whether Manny felt the same, especially as the girl and he went on talking. At last she smiled and went out of the room. Then Manny turned to me and said: 'It's all right. You can sit down and make yourself at home.'

"I must have looked rather stupid about it, for he added: 'Draw your chair to the table and don't guzzle too much all at once.'

" 'But—have you—told her—who—who we are?' I whispered.

" 'Sssh,' he answered. 'I don't have to. Can't you see . . . she's blind.'

" 'Blind?'

" 'Simply the most incredible piece of luck,' he went on. 'She's alone here—her father's one of the frontier guards—he's out on the mountains with a search-party. The frontier's quite close, too—that's another piece of luck. There's a whole platoon of them looking for the two escaped Englishmen—apparently we've been well advertised.'

"I asked him who she thought we really were. He answered: 'Why, part of the search-party, of course—I've explained to her that we got lost, and are dead tired and hungry. And what's more to the point, my lad, she's going to give us our Christmas dinner!'

" 'But if her father returns?'

" 'Then we shall just be a little less in luck, that's all.' "

"The girl came back then, and laid extra places at the table. She had a very serene face and beautiful hands. Now that the idea was put in my head, it seemed obvious that she was blind. Yet her movements were scarcely less quick and accurate than if she had had sight. She helped us to food and Manny carved the chicken. They talked and laughed a lot together, and though I could follow what they were saying more or less, sometimes they talked too quickly or used words I didn't understand. But the food—and the wine—and the fire! I've never had a dinner that was as good as that. I know now I never shall. . . . The girl showed us photographs of her father and her two brothers who were at the Front. We drank their health and the healths of the German Army and—in our hearts—of the British Army, and of all brave men. Then she and Manny began an argument about the whole war business, and how damsilly it was that men should spend Christmas hunting other men over mountains instead of feasting at home. She agreed, and then added something that made my heart miss another beat. She said: 'I thought at first you were the two English prisoners.'

" 'That would have been awkward for you,' said Manny.

" 'Oh, no, I expect they would have wanted food, just the same.'

" 'They certainly would.'

" 'Because, after all, there's not as much difference between English and German as between tired and hungry people and those who aren't.'

" 'Other people mightn't see that,' said Manny, laughing.

" 'They see other things instead.' "

Middleton glanced round the room as if to reassure himself of privacy before he continued: "I remember this rather strange conversation, because at the time it scared me—I thought it was just the sort of too-clever-by-half stuff that a fellow like Manny would give himself away by, instead of sticking to the proper part of the simple German soldier. Because, you see, I was getting more and more panicky over an idea that had just struck me—that the girl was leading us on with all that sort of talk, that she already suspected who we were, and was deliberately trying to keep us till her father and probably some of the other searchers came back. As soon as she next went out of the room, ostensibly to fetch another bottle of wine, I whispered to Manny just what I felt about it. He seemed surprised, and told me then that the girl had offered to show us a short cut over the mountain that would lead us exactly where he wanted to go.

"I was scared again by that. 'I wouldn't trust a yard of that short cut,' I told Manny. 'She's obviously going to lead us straight into a trap.' He answered, in that dreamy way of his: 'Well, you may be right. Wisdom or cleverness—which are we up against?—that's the question, always.'

" 'That just irritated me—it didn't seem to be the right moment to be so damned philosophical. But he only kept on saying: 'You may be right, and I may be wrong—time will show.'

"But time never did—nor anything else. Because while we were still arguing we heard a commotion outside in the corridor, then the girl's sudden cry amidst men's voices. Both Manny and I took it that our number was up and that the girl was telling them all about us. But she wasn't. We could see what was happening through the gap in the hinge of the door. She was crying because they had brought her father home—on an improvised stretcher.

"Apparently he'd fallen pretty badly somewhere—had a nasty head-wound and an arm was limp. He was in a lot of pain, and we heard the girl imploring the men who had brought him in—there were two of them—to hurry down to the village and bring a doctor. And that would take them a couple of hours at least.

"Well, there isn't much more to tell you. Manny, as you may or may not know, was born to be a surgeon if he hadn't been a poet with a private income, and those soldiers hadn't done a good job with the broken arm. Manny refixed it, and we made the old boy as comfortable as we could before we left. He was semi-conscious and obviously didn't care a damn who we were—you don't you know, if things are hurting and somebody's helping. . . . So we said 'Guten Abend' again, and made off into the woods. We didn't find the short cut, but we did, after sundry other adventures, manage to wriggle across the frontier. And that's the end of the story. I've no doubt Manny would have told it better."

"The odd thing is," I said, "that he never told it at all."

Middleton answered after a pause: "I wonder if he felt about it as I did afterwards—that it all happened in another sort of world? Mind you, it *did* happen—we escaped all right. That much is on record. And the roast chicken was real enough, I'll swear. And yet . . . oh, well, we were dazed with exhaustion, and sick with anxiety, and wild with hunger. And the girl was blind and her father half-crazy with pain. Things don't happen *to* you when you're like that—as Manny said, they happen *in* you."

I agreed, and we smoked awhile, and then he went on: "That's the worst and the best of war—you feel a brotherhood with the other side that you can't get away from, and equally that you can't give way to. I often wonder what became of the old boy—whether he got better; I hope he did. He was really quite a veteran—far too old and fat to be chasing youngsters like us over mountains. A few years after the Armistice, Manny was in Munich and tried to trace both the man and the girl, but he had no luck—couldn't even find the chalet on the hillside. Anyway, it's twenty years ago now—too late to hold an inquiry over it. But you can perhaps understand how . . . I felt . . . when you quoted that poem at dinner."

"Oh, the poem we were all arguing about?"

"Yes. As a matter of fact, I never knew Manny had written it—poetry, I must admit, isn't much in my line. But that poem . . . well, it reminded me."

I nodded. The volume of Manny Stewart's last poems, issued after his death, lay on the shelf at my elbow, and I reached for it, found the page, and leaned forward to catch the firelight as I read, in a sense for the first time:

> You do not know our ways are strange
> 　　In war-perverted brotherhood;
> How white the snow upon the range,
> 　　How warm the window in the wood.
> You do not know, you have not seen
> The moonlight trembling on the green;
> Nor have you watched a single star
> Rise over shades where terrors are.
> Yet in that world whose beauty lies
> 　　Beyond the eye and in the mind,
> Yours is the twilight of the wise,
> 　　And ours the noonday of the blind.

BROADCAST FROM THE TRENCHES

FINLAND, 1939

BY WILLIAM L. WHITE

WILLIAM L. WHITE, speaking to you on this Christmas night from Finland, the country where our legend of Santa Claus and his reindeers first began. Reindeer still pull sleighs in the north of Finland tonight, carrying supplies to the little nation's army which is fighting to press back the great army which would come in. But if part of our Christmas story began in Finland, it, Finland, is also the country where Christmas ends, for beyond the line of its armies lies that great land where there is no Christmas any more, and where the memory of its stories is dimming fast.

And this is why, since I have come from a front-line post of command of this Finnish army, I can tell you tonight about the last Christmas tree. And although you have many finer ones in America tonight, tall trees gay with tinsel, proud with sparkling colored balls, and rich with presents underneath wrapped in pretty papers and tied with silver cords, I think you would like these even better when you know about that brave and sad last little Christmas tree at the very edge of the land where Christmas ends.

Even without our guide we might have found the last Christmas tree by following the sound of big guns from far off. Presently, when they were close, we left our cars and followed a trail in the deep snow which wound toward the guns through a tall spruce forest, the snow on their branches glistening in the moonlight. The trail led past the second-line dugouts on through the woods toward the guns, and sometimes we stepped aside to let pass a horse-drawn sleigh, fitted to carry warm boilers of steaming hot soup up to the men ahead.

We were told to walk quietly now. Talking in whispers, we passed places where the white snow had been gashed deep by shell craters, and at last we came to the front-line post-of-command. The officer here greeted us in a tired voice, saying we should go no further, as this forest had only yesterday been retaken from the Russians, whose lines were a few hundred yards ahead, and his men had not had time to dig safe trenches. Beyond us was no real front line, but only machine-gun nests, dugouts and a few shallow trenches, a place where it was not safe for any man to crawl who had not first seen the country by clear light of day. But perhaps we would like to go down into his front-line command post dugout, talk to his men and see their Christmas tree.

The dugout was deep beneath snow and earth and warmed from the zero weather by a tiny stove. Tired men were lying on the straw-strewn floor and when they rose to greet us we could see by the light of the shaded lantern that their faces were weary and unshaven. The officer explained this, saying fighting had been very hard, the enemy had greatly outnumbered them, so when there was no fighting there was time for little but sleep.

We asked him what the men would have for Christmas dinner and he told us their mess kits would be filled with thick warm pea soup, rich with pieces of mutton and pork, with plenty of bread spread thick with butter and for dessert porridge with sugar. And then, because it was Christmas, the army had sent up four Christmas hams, which would be sliced and eaten with bread.

He said we should remember that several sledges had come laden with Christmas presents for the men—warm sweaters and socks knitted by their wives or Christmas cookies and tarts baked by them and there would be something for each man.

We asked when the men up ahead in the last machine-gun posts and dugouts would get their presents and he said not until tomorrow, but they would not mind, because each man knew why he must be there and what must be done and not one would wish himself in any other place, and because the people of this country love Christmas so much, each one could carry it with him in his heart.

Then we asked if, at our own risk, we might not crawl up and give them some of the cigarettes and sweets and tobacco we had brought.

He shook his head, saying that if we made a noise and attracted Russian artillery there might be losses among his men, and this was not good to happen on Christmas night in any land.

But tomorrow those men would get their presents in this dugout, and also the Christmas tree would be saved for them to see. The tiny tree was standing near the stove. Little red and white wax candles had been tied by men's clumsy fingers to its branches. The officers said the candles could not be lit, because this might be seen by bombers through the dugout's canvas roof. Also tied to the green spruce twigs were a few gumdrops—the kind you buy twisted in colored wax papers. At the very top was tied, not a sparkling glass star, but a cheap cardboard image of Santa Claus—and this was all. No strips of tinsel, no shining balls, no winking electric lights. . . . You can be very glad that the Christmas tree in your home tonight is so much finer. We asked the officer who sent these ornaments, and he smiled kindly and said that they came from a very small girl whose father was out on the last line tonight, and with them a note from her mother explaining that the child was very young, and could not understand why he could not come back to them even on Christmas, and had cried bitterly until they let her send him these little things so that at least he could have his own Christmas tree. So the tree would be kept as it was in the dugout until he came back from his outpost tomorrow.

So when you take your last look at your own fine tree tonight before turning out its lights, I think you will like it even better since you know about the last sad little Christmas tree of all, which could not even have its poor candles lit because it faces the land where there is no Christmas.

Courtesy Columbia Broadcasting System

STILL IS THE NIGHT

By Faith Baldwin

THIS is what happened. It is hard to believe. It is true, as sunrise is true, as death is true. It is true and tragic and very wonderful. Shortly after three on the morning of November 27 of last year the ship Rangitane was attacked by German raiders in the Southern Pacific . . . some four hundred miles east of the New Zealand coast. Among her passengers were a number of the British escorts who had brought evacuated children safely to Australia and New Zealand and were now returning home.

There were three raiders, two sailing under Japanese names and colors and one under Norwegian. When the raid began the Nazi symbols were flown.

Shells screamed, guns spoke, and people died . . . six perished, four women and two men, out of twenty passengers. Many were wounded—men, women, and small children.

Two of the British escort nurses were not wounded. The dead, the maimed, the dying were brought up on deck and transferred to the lifeboats. The British nurses labored over them until at last, leaving the burning ship, they saw the dawn . . . cold, gray . . . over a cold gray swelling sea . . . and the bright flames leaping. . . .

In full uniform, the captain of the Rangitane remained at salute upon the bridge until a boat from one of the raiders came and took him.

The lifeboats were towed to the raiders and sunk. The prisoners were distributed among the raiders . . . which sailed away. . . .

On board one of the raiders a German surgeon, young and capable, worked over the wounded. One of the British nurses had her right arm shot away; part of a thumb and the forefinger of her left hand; and her face was shattered by shrapnel. Once he asked, bending to look in the live, invincible eyes which alone shone from the bandages, "Do you British women never cry?" And she answered, her mouth muffled by the bandages, "Only when we have something to cry about. . . ."

It is on record that he gave her his fruit ration every morning. Fruit was not issued to prisoners.

The men were kept below decks, but the raiders' officers gave up their cabins to the women and set special quarters aside for the wounded. There was food—of a kind. Below decks, very little air. But the children were given their freedom, and those who could run and walk played about the decks, and the crew members were indulgent.

Clothing was scarce. The crew contributed sheets; the women fashioned shorts and shirts. . . . And when one of them woke one morning to realize—how strange, how fantastic!—that it was her birthday, presents were found among the passengers—not alone her fellow passengers on the Rangitane but those already aboard the raider. And such presents . . . a hair clip, and a safety pin, and from the crew a deck of cards.

There were two dogs on the raider, patiently trained by the crew. . . . One of them had had her leg broken three times and each time it had been set by the surgeon. Incredible. . . .

On the twenty-first day of December the raiders landed their prisoners on a tropical island. There were by now nearly five hundred of them, and no more could be accommodated, even in raider fashion. Only the passengers and crew of the ship Tunakina were not released. This ship with one gun had put up a terrific battle in the Tasman Sea in August. Her survivors were not permitted to mingle with the passengers of the other ships when—as they did every day—the raiders met.

It is also on record that when this daily meeting and conference took place between the raiders, the prisoners were ordered below decks . . . all save the children, who were told that their parents had been sent to bed! Such a reversal of the normal procedure greatly charmed the youngsters . . . free to run the decks at liberty while their parents "napped" below."

But very soon the prisoners who had been taken from no less than ten ships would be free—and together . . . on the island of Emirau, ten miles square, two degrees south of the equator, five hundred miles north of the southeast portion of New Guinea.

A little island. Four whites and two hundred and fifty natives . . . all engaged in the copra industry. No radio . . . no means of communication save by cutter to Kavieng, eighty-four miles away.

The prisoners were landed nine miles from the homestead of the white men. . . . But before they were landed the raiders ascertained that water would be available, and they also left stores. Not enough . . . not as much as they had pledged. But stores, at any event.

The day the prisoners were all transferred to one ship for landing, there was rejoicing. . . . Men and women had not been allowed to be together during the long strange voyage. . . . Now they saw one another, were perhaps, in some instances, reunited, father with child, husband with wife, brother with sister. . . .

But some would never return to those who loved them.

There were three pregnant women landed on that little island . . . women who bore hope and life under their hearts, women who must have surrendered to a personal, intimate panic which they had not shown under shellfire in the long terrifying nights aboard the raiders. They had been shown consideration by their captors, and when they were landed on Emirau they were sent by lorry to the home of the copra dealers. The others walked.

There would be ample time, the raiders reasoned, for them to land their prisoners on this island without radio and be far away before a rescue could be attempted.

The whites gave their house to the women, and then, with natives helping, constructed palm shelters for the others. The natives were greatly excited at this innocent invasion. One of the British nurses reported that, as the ship approached the island, she could see them dancing on the beach—that is, she saw the bright red pants which were their only clothing, as the brown bodies were merged into the landscape. . . .

The stores left by the raiders were inadequate, and the islanders and copra dealers could not cope with the situation. But there were coconuts and pawpaws, pineapples, roots, and yams to eke out the meager rations.

More important than food was the fact that the Germans had overlooked a cutter, hidden up one of the creeks, which shortly thereafter put off for Kavieng with a group of sailors, to ask for rescue.

But before resue came it was Christmas Eve.

A group of Polish women among the refugees procured from the island store white calico and the bright red twill—the fabrics worn by the islanders—and from them fashioned, with love, with gratitude, a complete set of vestments for the priest, Father Kelly, who had survived the sinking of the Rangitane and who had been one of the British escorts with the evacuated children.

And so, on Christmas Eve, Father Kelly celebrated Mass on the little island, under a starry sky, for all the people, Catholic and Protestant alike, whose hearts were lifted in thanksgiving.

Carrying lanterns, they marched to the tumbledown boat jetty. There, on the jetty, an altar had been improvised. A cross of bamboo, on a plinth of coconut shell . . . and a Union Jack flying.

Carrying lanterns, they marched . . . through the groves lush with growth and sweet with alien fragrance. The frangipani trees were in bloom, heavy with perfume, those starry white blossoms. The crotons grew tall and thick, bronze and red and green. The wind spoke in the coconut palms with that unforgettable dry rattle, that insistent sighing.

The lanterns shone bravely, and overhead the great stars were clustered like silver grapes, and there was a path of starlight on the water. . . .

As they marched they sang, these indomitable people . . . those who limped, who carried scars; those who carried knowledge of irrevocable loss—and all had known fear and the hot breath of death blowing—and many mourned a wife, a child, a husband, a friend. But they sang. . . .

They sang O Come, All Ye Faithful, and they sang Hark the Herald

Angels Sing, and they sang The First Noel. . . .

And so, marching and singing and carrying the lanterns of their courage, they came to the altar and to Father Kelly in his red and white vestments, and the celebration of the Mass.

Communion was there for the communicants, with a bread especially baked by one of the young Englishwomen.

Surely no stranger Christmas Eve has ever been spent . . . and none which could draw hearts more closely together—the hearts of these rescued people, rescued from sea and flame and shell.

Surely the three women who wore approaching motherhood as a shield heard the understanding voice of that other Mother in their hearts; and those who had lost their sons in a horror too deep for tears drew comfort from one who, too, had lost her Son.

The Polish women stood together and sang Still Is the Night. . . .

That rescue came, the world knows. Yet our world here does not, perhaps, know of this Christmas Eve on a boat jetty on a little island . . . a speck upon the map—a tiny tropical shrine of heroism and generosity, faith renewed and courage justified. . . .

So now you know.

CHRISTMAS EVE AT TOPMAST TICKLE

By Norman Duncan

RETURNING afoot from the bedside of Long John Wise at Run-by-Guess—and from many a bedside and wretched hearth by the way—the doctor and I strapped our packs aback and heartily set out from the Hudson's Bay Company's post at Bread-and-Water Bay in the dawn of the day before Christmas: being then three weeks gone from our harbour, and thinking to reach it next day. We were to chance hospitality for the night; and this must be (they told us) at the cottage of a man of the name of Jonas Jutt, which is at Topmast Tickle.

There was a lusty old wind scampering down the coast, with many a sportive whirl and whoop, flinging the snow about in vast delight— a big, rollicking winter's wind, blowing straight out of the north, at the pitch of half a gale. With this abeam we made brave progress; but yet 'twas late at night when we floundered down the gully called Long-an'-Deep, where the drifts were overhead and each must rescue the other from sudden misfortune: a warm glimmer of light in Jonas Jutt's kitchen window to guide and hearten us.

The doctor beat the door with his fist. "Open, open!" cried he, still furiously knocking. "Good Lord! will you never open?"

So gruff was the voice, so big and commanding—and so sudden was the outcry—and so late was the night and wild the wind and far away the little cottage—that the three little Jutts, who then (as it turned out) sat expectant at the kitchen fire, must all at once have huddled close; and I fancy that Sammy blinked no longer at the crack in the stove, but slipped from his chair and limped to his sister, whose hand he clutched.

"We'll freeze, I tell you!" shouted the doctor. "Open the— Ha! Thank you," in a mollified way, as Skipper Jonas opened the door; and then, most engagingly: "May we come in?"

"An' welcome, zur," said the hearty Jonas, "whoever you be! 'Tis gettin' t' be a wild night."

"Thank you. Yes—a wild night. Glad to catch sight of your light from the top of the hill. We'll leave the racquets here. Straight ahead? Thank you. I see the glow of a fire."

We entered.

"Hello!" cried the doctor, stopping short. "What's this? Kids? Good! Three of them. Ha! How are you?"

The manner of asking the question was most indignant, not to say threatening; and a gasp and heavy frown accompanied it. By this I knew that the doctor was about to make sport for Martha and Jimmie and Sammy Jutt (as their names turned out to be): which often he did for children by pretending to be in a great rage; and invariably they found it delicious entertainment, for however fiercely he blustered, his eyes twinkled most merrily all the time, so that one was irresistibly moved to chuckle with delight at the sight of them, no matter how suddenly or how terribly he drew down his brows.

"I like kids," said he, with a smack of the lips. "I eat 'em!"

Gurgles of delight escaped from the little Jutts—and each turned to the other: the eyes of all dancing.

"And how are *you?*" the doctor demanded.

His fierce little glance was indubitably directed at little Sammy, as though, God save us! the lad had no right to be anything *but* well, and ought to be, and should be, birched on the instant if he had the temerity to admit the smallest ache or pain from the crown of his head to the soles of his feet. But Sammy looked frankly into the flashing eyes, grinned, chuckled audibly, and lisped that he was better.

"Better?" growled the doctor, searching Sammy's white face and skinny body as though for evidence to the contrary. "I'll attend to *you!*"

Thereupon Skipper Jonas took us to the shed, where we laid off our packs and were brushed clean of snow; and by that time Matilda Jutt, the mother of Martha and Jimmie and Sammy, had spread the table with the best she had—little enough, God knows! being but bread and tea—and was smiling beyond. Presently there was nothing left of the bread and tea; and then we drew up to the fire, where the little Jutts still sat, regarding us with great interest. And I observed that Martha Jutt held a letter in her hand: whereupon I divined precisely what our arrival had interrupted, for I was Labrador born, and knew well enough what went on in the kitchens of our land of a Christmas Eve.

"And now, my girl," said the doctor, "what's what?"

By this extraordinary question—delivered, as it was, in a manner that called imperatively for an answer—Martha Jutt was quite nonplussed: as the doctor had intended she should be.

"What's what?" repeated the doctor.

Quite startled, Martha lifted the letter from her lap. "He's not comin', zur," she gasped, for lack of something better.

"You're disappointed, I see," said the doctor. "So he's not coming?"

"No, zur—not this year."

"That's too bad. But you mustn't mind it, you know—not for an instant. What's the matter with him?"

"He've broke his leg, zur."

"What!" cried the doctor, restored of a sudden to his natural manner. "Poor fellow! How did he come to do that?"

"Catchin' one o' they wild deer, zur."

"Catching a deer!" the doctor exclaimed. "A most extraordinary thing. He was a fool to try it. How long ago?"

"Sure, it can't be more than half an hour; for he've—"

The doctor jumped up. "Where is he?" he demanded, with professional eagerness. "It can't be far. Davy, I must get to him at once. I must attend to that leg. Where is he?"

"Narth Pole, zur," whispered Sammy.

"Oh-h-h!" cried the doctor; and he sat down again, and pursed his lips, and winked at Sammy in a way most peculiar. "I *see!*"

"Ay, zur," Jimmy rattled, eagerly. "We're fair disappointed that he's not—"

"Ha!" the doctor interrupted. "I see. Hum! Well, now!" And having thus incoherently exclaimed for a little, the light in his eyes growing merrier all the time, he most unaccountably worked himself into a great rage: whereby I knew that the little Jutts were in some way to be mightily amused. "The lazy rascal!" he shouted, jumping out of his chair, and beginning to stamp the room, frowning terribly. "The fat, idle, blundering dunderhead! Did they send you that message? Did they, now? Tell me, did they? Give me that letter!" He snatched the letter from Martha's lap. "Sammy," he demanded, "where did this letter come from?"

"Narth Pole, zur!"

Jonas Jutt blushed—and Matilda threw her apron over her head to hide her confusion.

"And *how* did it come?"

"Out o' the stove, zur."

The doctor opened the letter, and paused to slap it angrily, from time to time, as he read it.

North poll

DEER MARTHA

few lines is to let you know on accounts of havin broke me leg cotchin the deer Im sory im in a stat of helth not bein able so as to be out in hevy wether. hopin you is all wel as it leves me

yrs respectful

SANDY CLAWS

Fish was poor and it would not be much this yere anyways. tel little Sammy.

"Ha!" shouted the doctor, as he crushed the letter to a little ball and flung it under the table. "Ha! That's the kind of thing that happens when one's away from home. There you have it! Discipline gone to the dogs. System gone to the dogs. Everything gone to the dogs. Now, what do you think of that?"

He scowled, and gritted his teeth, and puffed, and said "Ha!" in a fashion so threatening that one must needs have fled the room had there not been a curiously reassuring twinkle in his eyes.

"What do you think of that?" he repeated, fiercely, at last. "A countermanded order! I'll attend to *him!*" he burst out. "I'll fix that fellow! The lazy dunderhead, I'll soon fix him! Give me pen and ink. Where's the paper? Never mind. I've some in my pack. One moment, and I'll—"

He rushed to the shed, to the great surprise and alarm of the little Jutts, and loudly called back for a candle, which Skipper Jonas carried to him; and when he had been gone a long time, he returned with a letter in his hand, still ejaculating in a great rage.

"See that?" said he to the three little Jutts. "Well, *that's* for Santa Claus's clerk. That'll fix *him.* That'll blister the stupid fellow."

"Please, zur!" whispered Martha Jutt.

"Well?" snapped the doctor, stopping short in a rush to the stove.

"Please, zur," said Martha, taking courage, and laying a timid hand on his arm. "Sure, I don't know what 'tis all about. I don't know what blunder he've made. But I'm thinkin', zur, you'll be sorry if you acts in haste. 'Tis wise t' count a hundred. Don't be too hard on un, zur.

Tis like the blunder may be mended. 'Tis like he'll do better next time. Don't be hard—"

"*Hard* on him?" the doctor interrupted. "Hard on *him!* Hard on that—"

"Ay, zur," she pleaded, looking fearlessly up. "Won't you count a hundred?"

"Count it," said he, grimly.

Martha counted. I observed that the numbers fell slower—and yet more slowly—from her lips, until (and she was keenly on the watch) a gentler look overspread the doctor's face; and then she rattled them off, as though she feared he might change his mind once more.

"—an' a hundred!" she concluded, breathless.

"Well," the doctor drawled, rubbing his nose, "I'll modify it," whereupon Martha smiled, "just to 'blige *you*," whereupon she blushed.

So he scratched a deal of the letter out; then he sealed it, strode to the stove, opened the door, flung the letter into the flames, slammed the door, and turned with a wondrously sweet smile to the amazed little Jutts.

"There!" he sighed. "I think that will do the trick. We'll soon know, at any rate."

We waited, all very still, all with eyes wide open, all gazing fixedly at the door of the stove. Then, all at once—and in the very deepest of the silence—the doctor uttered a startling "Ha!" leaped from his chair with such violence that he overturned it, awkwardly upset Jimmie Jutt's stool and sent the lad tumbling head over heels (for which he did not stop to apologize); and there was great confusion: in the midst of which the doctor jerked the stove door open, thrust in his arm, and snatched a blazing letter straight from the flames—all before Jimmie and Martha and Sammy Jutt had time to recover from the daze into which the sudden uproar had thrown them.

"There!" cried the doctor, when he had managed to extinguish the blaze. "We'll just see what's in this. Better news, I'll warrant."

You may be sure that the little Jutts were blinking amazement.

There could be no doubt about the authenticity of *that* communication. And the doctor seemed to know it: for he calmly tore the envelope open, glanced the contents over, and turned to Martha, the broadest of grins wrinkling his face.

"Martha Jutt," said he, "will you *please* be good enough to read *that*."

And Martha read:

North Pole, Dec. 24, 10:18 P. M.

To Captain Blizzard,
  Jonas Jutt's Cottage, Topmast Tickle,

Labrador Coast

RESPECTED SIR:

Regret erroneous report. Mistake of a clerk in the Bureau of Information. Santa Claus got away at 9:36. Wind blowing due south, strong and fresh.

SNOW, Chief Clerk.

Then there was a great outburst of glee. It was the doctor who raised the first cheer. Three times three and a tiger! And what a tiger it was! What with the treble of Sammy, which was of the thinnest description, and the treble of Martha, which was full and sure, and the treble of Jimmie, which dangerously bordered on a cracked bass, and what with Matilda's cackle and Skipper Jonas's croak and my own hoorays and the doctor's guttural uproar (which might have been mistaken for a very double bass)—what with all this, as you may be sure, the shout of the wind was nowhere. Then we joined hands— it was the doctor who began it by catching Martha and Matilda—and danced the table round, shaking our feet and tossing our arms, the glee ever more uproarious—danced until we were breathless, every one, save little Sammy, who was not asked to join the gambol, but sat still in his chair, and seemed to expect no invitation.

"Wind blowing due south, strong and fresh," gasped Jimmie, when, at last, we sat down. "He'll be down in a hurry, with they swift deer. My! but he'll just *whizz* in this gale!"

"But 'tis sad 'tis too late t' get word to un," said Martha, the smile gone from her face.

"Sad, is it?" cried the doctor. "Sad! What's the word you want to send?"

" 'Tis something for Sammy, zur."

Sammy gave Martha a quick dig in the ribs. " 'N' mama," he lisped reproachfully.

"Ay, zur; we're wantin' it bad. An' does you think us could get word to un? For Sammy, zur?"

" 'N' mama," Sammy insisted.

"We can try, at any rate," the doctor answered, doubtfully. "Maybe we can catch him on the way down. Where's that pen? Here we are. Now!"

He scribbled rapidly, folded the letter in great haste, and dispatched it to Santa Claus's clerk by the simple process of throwing it in the fire. As before, he went to his pack in the shed, taking the candle with him—the errand appeared to be really most trivial—and stayed so long that the little Jutts, who now loved him very much (as I could see), wished that the need would not arise again. But, all in good time, he returned, and sat to watch for the reply, intent as any of them; and, presently, he snatched the stove door open, creating great confusion in the act, as before; and before the little Jutts could recover from the sudden surprise, he held up a smoking letter. Then he read aloud:

"Try Hamilton Inlet. Touches there 10:48. Time of arrival at Topmast Tickle uncertain. No use waiting up.

SNOW, Clerk."

"By Jove!" exclaimed the doctor. "That's jolly! Touches Hamilton Inlet at 10:48." He consulted his watch. "It's now 10:43 and a half. We've just four and a half minutes. I'll get a message off at once. Where's that confounded pen? Ha! Here we are. Now—what is it you want for Sammy and mamma?"

The three little Jutts were suddenly thrown into a fearful state of excitement. They tried to talk all at once; but not one of them could frame a coherent sentence. It was most distressful to see.

"The Exterminator!" Martha managed to jerk out, at last.

"Oh, ay!" cried Jimmie Jutt. "Quick, zur! Write un down. Pine's Prompt Pain Exterminator. Warranted to cure. Please, zur, make haste!"

The doctor stared at Jimmie.

"Oh, zur," groaned Martha, "don't be starin' like that! Write, zur! 'Twas all in the paper the prospector left last summer. Pine's Prompt Pain Exterminator. Cures boils, rheumatism, pains in the back an' chest, sore throat, an' all they things, an' warts on the hands by a simple application with brown paper. We wants it for the rheumatiz, zur. Oh, zur—"

"None genuine without the label," Jimmie put in, in an excited rattle. "Money refunded if no cure. Get a bottle with the label."

The doctor laughed—laughed aloud, and laughed again. "By Jove!" he roared, "you'll get it. It's odd, but—ha, ha!—by Jove, he has it in stock!"

The laughter and repeated assurance seemed vastly to encourage Jimmie and Martha—the doctor wrote like mad while he talked—but not little Sammy. All that he lisped, all that he shouted, all that he screamed, had gone unheeded. As though unable to put up with the neglect any longer, he limped over the floor to Martha, and tugged her sleeve, and pulled at Jimmie's coat-tail, and jogged the doctor's arm, until, at last, he attracted a measure of attention. Notwithstanding his mother's protests—notwithstanding her giggles and waving hands—notwithstanding that she blushed as red as ink (until, as I perceived, her freckles were all lost to sight)—notwithstanding that she threw her apron over her head and rushed headlong from the room, to the imminent danger of the door-posts—little Sammy insisted that his mother's gift should be named in the letter of request.

"Quick!" cried the doctor. "What is it? We've but half a minute left."

Sammy began to stutter.

"Make haste, b'y!" cried Jimmie.

"One—bottle—of—the—Magic—Egyptian—Beautifier," said Sammy, quite distinctly for the first time in his life.

The doctor looked blank; but he doggedly nodded his head, nevertheless, and wrote it down and off went the letter at precisely 10:47.45, as the doctor said.

Later—when the excitement had all subsided and we sat dreaming in the warmth and glow—the doctor took little Sammy in his lap, and told him he was a very good boy, and looked deep in his eyes, and stroked his hair, and, at last, very tenderly bared his knee. Sammy flinched at that; and he said "Ouch!" once, and screwed up his face, when the doctor—his gruffness all gone, his eyes gentle and sad, his hand as light as a mother's—worked the joint, and felt the knee-cap and socket with the tips of his fingers.

"And is this the rheumatiz the Prompt Exterminator is to cure, Sammy?" he asked.

"Ith, zur."

"Ah, is *that* where it hurts you? Right on the point of the bone, there?"

"Ith, zur."

"And was there no fall on the rock, at all? Oh, there *was* a fall? And the bruise was just there—where it hurts so much? And it's very hard to bear, isn't it?"

Sammy shook his head.

"No? But it hurts a good deal, sometimes, does it not? That's too bad. That's very sad, indeed. But, perhaps—perhaps, Sammy—I can cure it for you, if you are brave. And are you brave? No? Oh, I think you are. And you'll try to be, at any rate, won't you? Of course! That's a good boy."

And so, with his sharp little knives, the doctor cured Sammy Jutt's knee, while the lad lay white and still on the kitchen table. And 'twas not hard to do; but had not the doctor chanced that way, Sammy Jutt would have been a cripple all his life.

"Doctor, zur," said Matilda Jutt, when the children were put to bed, with Martha to watch by Sammy, who was still very sick, "is you really got a bottle o' Pine's Prompt?"

The doctor laughed. "An empty bottle," said he. "I picked it up at Poverty Cove. Thought it might come useful. I'll put Sammy's medicine in that. They'll not know the difference. And you'll treat the knee with it as I've told you. That's all. We must turn in at once; for we must be gone before the children wake in the morning."

"Oh, ay, zur; an'—" she began: but hesitated, much embarrassed.

"Well?" the doctor asked, with a smile.

"Would you mind puttin' some queer lookin' stuff in one o' they bottles o' yours?"

"Not in the least," in surprise.

"An' writin' something on a bit o' paper," she went on, pulling at her apron, and looking down, "an' gluin' it t' the bottle?"

"Not at all. But what shall I write?"

She flushed. "'Magic Egyptian Beautifier,' zur," she answered; "for I'm thinkin' 'twould please little Sammy t' think that Sandy Claws left something—for me—too."

If you think that the three little Jutts found nothing but bottles of medicine in their stockings, when they got down-stairs on Christmas morning, you are very much mistaken. Indeed, there was much more than that—a great deal more than that. I will not tell you what it was; for you might sniff, and say, "Huh! That's little enough!" But there *was* more than medicine. No man—rich man, poor man, beggar-man nor thief, doctor, lawyer nor merchant chief—ever yet left a Hudson's Bay Company's post, stared in the face by the chance of having to seek hospitality of a Christmas Eve—no right-feeling man, I say, ever yet left a Hudson's Bay Company's post, under such circumstances, without putting something more than medicine in his pack. I chance to know, at any rate, that upon this occasion Doctor Luke did not. And I know, too—you may be interested to learn it—that as we floundered through the deep snow, homeward bound, soon after dawn, the next day, he was glad enough that he hadn't. No merry shouts came over the white miles from the cottage of Jonas Jutt, though I am sure that they rang there most heartily; but the doctor did not care: he shouted merrily enough for himself, for he was very happy. And that's the way *you'd* feel, too, if you spent *your* days hunting good deeds to do.

From *Doctor Luke of the Labrador*

WHEN SHALL THESE THREE MEET AGAIN? OR THE MOST MYSTERIOUS CHRISTMAS EVE IN LITERATURE

By Charles Dickens

CHRISTMAS EVE in Cloisterham. A few strange faces in the streets; a few other faces, half strange and half familiar, once the faces of Cloisterham children, now the faces of men and women who come back from the outer world at long intervals to find the city wonderfully shrunken in size, as if it had not washed by any means well in the meanwhile. To these, the striking of the Cathedral clock, and the cawing of the rooks from the Cathedral tower, are like voices of their nursery time. To such as these, it has happened in their dying hours afar off, that they have imagined their chamber-floor to be strewn with the autumnal leaves fallen from the elm-trees in the Close: so have the rustling sounds and fresh scents of their earliest impressions revived when the circle of their lives was very nearly traced, and the beginning and the end were drawing close together.

Seasonable tokens are about. Red berries shine here and there in the lattices of Minor Canon Corner; Mr. and Mrs. Tope are daintily sticking sprigs of holly into the carvings and sconces of the Cathedral stalls, as if they were sticking them into the coat-buttonholes of the Dean and Chapter. Lavish profusion is in the shops: particularly in the articles of currants, raisins, spices, candied peel, and moist sugar. An unusual air of gallantry and dissipation is abroad; evinced in an immense bunch of mistletoe hanging in the green-grocer's shop door-way, and a poor little Twelfth Cake, culminating in the figure of a Harlequin—such a very poor little Twelfth Cake, that one would rather call it a Twenty-fourth Cake or a Forty-eighth Cake—to be raffled for at the pastry-cook's, terms one shilling per member. Public amusements are not wanting. The Wax-Work which made so deep an impression on the reflective mind of the Emperor of China is to be seen by particular desire during Christmas Week only, on the premises of the bankrupt livery-stablekeeper up the lane; and a new grand comic Christmas pantomime is to be produced at the Theatre: the latter heralded by the portrait of Signor Jacksonini the clown, saying "How do you do to-morrow?" quite as large as life, and almost as miserably. In short, Cloisterham is up and doing: though from this description the High School and Miss Twinkleton's are to be excluded. From the former establishment the scholars have gone home, every one of them in love with one of Miss Twinkleton's young ladies (who knows nothing about it); and only the handmaidens flutter occasionally in the windows of the latter. It is noticed, by the bye, that these damsels become, within the limits of decorum, more skittish when thus intrusted with the concrete representation of their sex, than when dividing the representation with Miss Twinkleton's young ladies.

Three are to meet at the gatehouse to-night. How does each one of the three get through the day?

Neville Landless, though absolved from his books for the time by Mr. Crisparkle—whose fresh nature is by no means insensible to the charms of a holiday—reads and writes in his quiet room, with a concentrated air, until it is two hours past noon. He then sets himself to clearing his table, to arranging his books, and to tearing up and burning his stray papers. He makes a clean sweep of all untidy accumulations, puts all his drawers in order, and leaves no note or scrap of paper undestroyed, save such memoranda as bear directly on his studies. This done, he turns to his wardrobe, selects a few articles of ordinary wear—among them, change of stout shoes and socks for walking—and packs these in a knapsack. This knapsack is new, and he bought it in the High Street yesterday. He also purchased, at the same time and at the same place, a heavy walking-stick; strong in the handle for the grip of the hand, and iron-shod. He tries this, swings it, poises it, and lays it by, with the knapsack, on a windowseat. By this time his arrangements are complete.

He dresses for going out, and is in the act of going—indeed has left his room, and has met the Minor Canon on the staircase, coming out of his bedroom upon the same story—when he turns back again for his walking-stick, thinking he will carry it now. Mr. Crisparkle, who has paused on the staircase, sees it in his hand on his immediately reappearing, takes it from him, and asks him with a smile how he chooses a stick?

"Really I don't know that I understand the subject," he answers. "I choose it for its weight."

"Much too heavy, Neville; *much* too heavy."

"To rest upon in a long walk, sir?"

"Rest upon?" repeats Mr. Crisparkle, throwing himself into pedestrian form. "You don't rest upon it; you merely balance with it."

"I shall know better, with practice, sir. I have not lived in a walking country, you know."

"True," says Mr. Crisparkle. "Get into a little training, and we will have a few score miles together. I should leave you nowhere now. Do you come back before dinner?"

"I think not, as we dine early."

Mr. Crisparkle gives him a bright nod and a cheerful good-bye; expressing (not without intention) absolute confidence and ease.

Neville repairs to the Nuns' House, and requests that Miss Landless may be informed that her brother is there, by appointment. He waits at the gate, not even crossing the threshold; for he is on his parole not to put himself in Rosa's way.

His sister is at least as mindful of the obligation they have taken on themselves as he can be, and loses not a moment in joining him. They meet affectionately, avoid lingering there, and walk towards the upper inland country.

"I am not going to tread upon forbidden ground, Helena," says Neville, when they have walked some distance and are turning; "you will understand in another moment that I cannot help referring to —what shall I say?—my infatuation."

"Had you not better avoid it, Neville? You know that I can hear nothing."

"You can hear, my dear, what Mr. Crisparkle has heard, and heard with approval."

"Yes; I can hear so much."

"Well, it is this. I am not only unsettled and unhappy myself, but I am conscious of unsettling and interfering with other people. How do I know that, but for my unfortunate presence, you, and—and—the rest of that former party, our engaging guardian excepted, might be dining cheerfully in Minor Canon Corner to-morrow? Indeed it probably would be so. I can see too well that I am not high in the old lady's opinion, and it is easy to understand what an irksome clog I must be upon the hospitalities of her orderly house—especially at this time of year—when I must be kept asunder from this person, and there is such a reason for my not being brought into contact with that person, and an unfavourable reputation has preceded me with such another person; and so on. I have put this very gently to Mr. Crisparkle, for you know his self-denying ways; but still I have put it. What I have laid much greater stress upon at the same time is, that I am engaged in a miserable struggle with myself, and that a little change and absence may enable me to come through it the better. So, the weather being bright and hard, I am going on a walking expedition, and intend taking myself out of everybody's way (my own included, I hope) to-morrow morning."

"When to come back?"

"In a fortnight."

"And going quite alone?"

"I am much better without company, even if there were any one but you to bear me company, my dear Helena."

Up to this point he has been extremely cheerful. Perhaps, the having to carry his case with her, and therefore to present it in its brightest aspect, has roused his spirits. Perhaps, the having done so with success, is followed by a revulsion. As the day closes in, and the city-lights begin to spring up before them, he grows depressed.

"I wish I were not going to this dinner, Helena."

"Dear Neville, is it worth while to care much about it? Think how soon it will be over."

"How soon it will be over!" he repeats gloomily. "Yes. But I don't like it."

There may be a moment's awkwardness, she cheeringly represents to him, but it can only last a moment. He is quite sure of himself.

"I wish I felt as sure of everything else, as I feel of myself," he answers her.

"How strangely you speak, dear! What do you mean?"

"Helena, I don't know. I only know that I don't like it. What a strange dead weight there is in the air!"

She calls his attention to those copperous clouds beyond the river, and says that the wind is rising. He scarcely speaks again, until he takes leave of her, at the gate of the Nun's House. She does not immediately enter, when they have parted, but remains looking after him along the street. Twice he passes the gatehouse, reluctant to enter. At length, the Cathedral clock chiming one quarter, with a rapid turn he hurries in.

And so *he* goes up the postern stair.

Edwin Drood passes a solitary day. Something of deeper moment than he had thought has gone out of his life; and in the silence of his own chamber he wept for it last night. Though the image of Miss Landless still hovers in the background of his mind, the pretty little affectionate creature, so much firmer and wiser than he had supposed, occupies its stronghold. It is with some misgiving of his own unworthiness that he thinks of her, and of what they might have been to one another, if he had been more in earnest some time ago; if he had set a higher value on her; if, instead of accepting his lot in life as an inheritance of course, he had studied the right way to its appreciation and enhancement. And still, for all this, and though there is a sharp heartache in all this, the vanity and caprice of youth sustain that handsome figure of Miss Landless in the background of his mind.

That was a curious look of Rosa's when they parted at the gate. Did it mean that she saw below the surface of his thoughts, and down into their twilight depths? Scarcely that, for it was a look of astonished and keen inquiry. He decides that he cannot understand it, though it was remarkably expressive.

As he only waits for Mr. Grewgious now, and will depart immediately after having seen him, he takes a sauntering leave of the ancient city and its neighbourhood. He recalls the time when Rosa and he walked here or there, mere children, full of the dignity of being engaged. Poor children! he thinks, with pitying sadness.

Finding that his watch has stopped, he turns into the jeweller's shop, to have it wound and set. The jeweller is knowing on the subject of a bracelet, which he begs leave to submit, in a general and quite aimless way. It would suit (he considers) a young bride to perfection; especially if of a rather diminutive style of beauty. Finding the bracelet but coldly looked at, the jeweller invited attention to a tray of rings for gentlemen; here is a style of ring, now, he remarks—a very chaste signet—which gentlemen are much given to purchasing, when changing their condition. A ring of a very responsible appearance. With the date of their wedding-day engraved inside, several gentlemen have preferred it to any other kind of memento.

The rings are as coldly viewed as the bracelet. Edwin tells the tempter that he wears no jewellery but his watch and chain, which were his father's; and his shirt-pin.

"That I was aware of," is the jeweller's reply, "for Mr. Jasper dropped in for a watch-glass the other day, and, in fact, I showed these articles to him, remarking that if he *should* wish to make a present to a gentleman relative, on any particular occasion— But he said with a smile that he had an inventory in his mind of all the jewellery his gentleman relative ever wore; namely, his watch and chain, and his shirt-pin." Still (the jeweller considers) that might not apply to all times, though applying to the present time. "Twenty minutes past two, Mr. Drood, I set your watch at. Let me recommend you not to let it run down, sir."

Edwin takes his watch, puts it on, and goes out, thinking: "Dear old Jack! If I were to make an extra crease in my neckcloth, he would think it worth noticing!"

He strolls about and about, to pass the time until the dinner-hour.

It somehow happens that Cloisterham seems reproachful to him to-day; has fault to find with him, as if he had not used it well; but is far more pensive with him than angry. His wonted carelessness is replaced by a wistful looking at, and dwelling upon, all the old landmarks. He will soon be far away, and may never see them again, he thinks. Poor youth! Poor youth!

As dusk draws on, he paces the Monks' Vineyard. He has walked to and fro half an hour by the Cathedral chimes, and it was closed in dark, before he becomes quite aware of a woman crouching on the ground near a wicket gate in a corner. The gate commands a cross bye-path, little used in the gloaming; and the figure must have been there all the time, though he has but gradually and lately made it out.

He strikes into that path, and walks up to the wicket. By the light of a lamp near it, he sees that the woman is of a haggard appearance, and that her weazen chin is resting on her hands, and that her eyes are staring—with an unwinking, blind sort of steadfastness—before her.

Always kindly, but moved to be unusually kind this evening, and having bestowed kind words on most of the children and aged people he has met, he at once bends down, and speaks to the woman.

"Are you ill?"

"No, deary," she answers, without looking at him, and with no departure from her strange blind stare.

"Are you blind?"

"No, deary."

"Are you lost, homeless, faint? What is the matter, that you stay here in the cold so long, without moving?"

By slow and stiff efforts, she appears to contract her vision until it can rest upon him; and then a curious film passes over her, and she begins to shake.

He straightens himself, recoils a step, and looks down at her in a dread amazement; for he seems to know her.

"Good Heaven!" he thinks, next moment. "Like Jack that night!"

As he looks down at her, she looks up at him, and whimpers: "My lungs is weakly; my lungs is dreffle bad. Poor me, poor me, my cough is rattling dry!" and coughs in confirmation horribly.

"Where do you come from?"

"Come from London, deary." (Her cough still rending her.)

"Where are you going to?"

"Back to London, deary. I came here, looking for a needle in a haystack, and I ain't found it. Look'ee, deary: give me three-and-sixpence, and don't you be afeared for me. I'll get back to London then, and trouble no one. I'm in a business.—Ah, me! It's slack, it's slack, and times is very bad!—but I can make a shift to live by it."

"Do you eat opium?"

"Smokes it," she replies with difficulty, still racked by her cough. "Give me three-and-sixpence, and I'll lay it out well, and get back. If you don't give me three-and-sixpence, don't give me a brass farden. And if you do give me three-and-sixpence, deary, I'll tell you something."

He counts the money from his pocket, and puts it in her hand. She instantly clutches it tight, and rises to her feet with a croaking laugh of satisfaction.

"Bless ye! Hark'ee, dear genl'mn. What's your Chris'en name?"

"Edwin."

"Edwin, Edwin, Edwin," she repeats, trailing off into a drowsy repetition of the word; and then she asks suddenly: "Is the short of that name Eddy?"

"It is sometimes called so," he replies, with the colour starting to his face.

"Don't sweethearts call it so?" she asks, pondering.

"How should I know?"

"Haven't you a sweetheart, upon your soul?"

"None."

She is moving away, with another "Bless ye, and thank'ee, deary!" when he adds: "You were to tell me something; you may as well do so."

"So I was, so I was. Well, then. Whisper. You be thankful that your name ain't Ned."

He looks at her quite steadily, as he asks: "Why?"

"Because it's a bad name to have just now."

"How a bad name?"

"A threatened name. A dangerous name."

"The proverb says that threatened men live long," he tells her, lightly.

"Then Ned—so threatened is he, wherever he may be while I am a-talking to you, deary—should live to all eternity!" replies the woman.

She has leaned forward to say it in his ear, with her forefinger shaking before his eyes, and now huddles herself together, and with another "Bless ye, and thank'ee!" goes away in the direction of the Traveller's Lodging House.

This is not an inspiriting close to a dull day. Alone, in a sequestered place, surrounded by vestiges of old time and decay, it rather has a tendency to call a shudder into being. He makes for the better-lighted streets, and resolves as he walks on to say nothing of this to-night, but to mention it to Jack (who alone calls him Ned) as an odd coincidence, to-morrow; of course only as a coincidence, and not as anything better worth remembering.

Still it holds to him, as many things much better worth remembering never did. He has another mile or so, to linger out before the dinner-hour; and, when he walks over the bridge and by the river, the woman's words are in the rising wind, in the angry sky, in the troubled water, in the flickering lights. There is some solemn echo of them even in the Cathedral chime, which strikes a sudden surprise to his heart as he turns in under the archway of the gatehouse.

And so *he* goes up the postern stair.

John Jasper passes a more agreeable and cheerful day than either of his guests. Having no music-lessons to give in the holiday season, his time is his own, but for the Cathedral services. He is early among the shopkeepers, ordering little table luxuries that his nephew likes. His nephew will not be with him long, he tells his provision-dealers, and so must be petted and made much of. While out on his hospitable preparations, he looks in on Mr. Sapsea; and mentions that dear Ned, and that inflammable young spark of Mr. Crisparkle's, are to dine at the gatehouse to-day, and make up their difference. Mr. Sapsea is by no means friendly towards the inflammable young spark. He says that his complexion is "un-English." And when Mr. Sapsea has once declared anything to be un-English he considers that thing everlastingly sunk in the bottomless pit.

Mr. Jasper is in beautiful voice this day. In the pathetic supplication to have his heart inclined to keep this law, he quite astonishes his fellows by his melodious power. He has never sung difficult music with such skill and harmony, as in this day's Anthem. His nervous temperament is occasionally prone to take difficult music a little too quickly; to-day, his time is perfect.

These results are probably attained through a grand composure of the spirits. The mere mechanism of his throat is a little tender, for he wears, both with his singing-robe and with his ordinary dress, a large black scarf of strong close-woven silk, slung loosely round his neck. But his composure is so noticeable, that Mr. Crisparkle speaks of it as they come out from Vespers.

"I must thank you, Jasper, for the pleasure with which I have heard you to-day. Beautiful! Delightful! You could not have so outdone yourself, I hope, without being wonderfully well.

"I *am* wonderfully well."

"Nothing unequal," says the Minor Canon, with a smooth motion of his hand: "nothing unsteady, nothing forced, nothing avoided; all thoroughly done in a masterly manner, with perfect self-command."

"Thank you. I hope so, if it is not too much to say."

"One would think, Jasper, you had been trying a new medicine for that occasional indisposition of yours."

"No, really? That's well observed; for I have."

"Then stick to it, my good fellow," says Mr. Crisparkle, clapping him on the shoulder with friendly encouragement, "stick to it."

"I will."

"I congratulate you," Mr. Crisparkle pursues, as they come out of the Cathedral, "on all accounts."

"Thank you again. I will walk round to the corner with you, if you don't object; I have plenty of time before my company come; and I want to say a word to you, which I think you will not be displeased to hear."

"What is it?"

"Well. We were speaking, the other evening, of my black humours."

Mr. Crisparkle's face falls, and he shakes his head deploringly.

"I said, you know, that I should make you an antidote to those black humours; and you said you hoped I would consign them to the flames."

"And I still hope so, Jasper."

"With the best reason in the world! I mean to burn this year's Diary at the year's end."

"It does me good," cries Mr. Crisparkle, "to hear you say it!"

"A man leading a monotonous life," Jasper proceeds, "and getting his nerves, or his stomach, out of order, dwells upon an idea until it loses its proportions. That was my case with the idea in question. So I shall burn the evidence of my case, when the book is full, and begin the next volume with a clearer vision."

"This is better," says Mr. Crisparkle, stopping at the steps of his own door to shake hands, "than I could have hoped."

"Why, naturally," returns Jasper. "You had but little reason to hope that I should become more like yourself. You are always training yourself to be, mind and body, as clear as crystal, and you always are, and never change; whereas I am a muddy, solitary, moping weed. However, I have got over that mope. Shall I wait, while you ask if Mr. Neville has left for my place? If not, he and I may walk round together."

"I think," says Mr. Crisparkle, opening the entrance-door with his key, "that he left some time ago; at least I know he left, and I think he has not come back. But I'll inquire. You won't come in."

"My company wait," said Jasper, with a smile.

The Minor Canon disappears, and in a few moments returns. As he thought, Mr. Neville has not come back; indeed, as he remembers now, Mr. Neville said he would probably go straight to the gatehouse.

"Bad manners in a host!" says Jasper. "My company will be there before me! What will you bet that I don't find my company embracing?"

"I will bet—or I would, if ever I did bet," returns Mr. Crisparkle, "that your company will have a gay entertainer this evening."

Jasper nods, and laughs good-night!

He retraces his steps to the Cathedral door, and turns down past it to the gatehouse. He sings, in a low voice and with delicate expression, as he walks along. It still seems as if a false note were not within his power to-night, and as if nothing could hurry or retard him. Arriving thus under the arched entrance of his dwelling, he pauses for an instant in the shelter to pull off that great black scarf, and hang it in a loop upon his arm. For that brief time, his face is knitted and stern. But it immediately clears, as he resumes his singing, and his way.

And so *he* goes up the postern stair.

The red light burns steadily all the evening in the lighthouse on the margin of the tide of busy life. Softened sounds and hum of traffic pass it and flow on irregularly into the lonely Precincts; but very little else goes by, save violent rushes of wind. It comes on to blow a boisterous gale.

The Precincts are never particularly well lighted; but the strong blasts of wind blowing out many of the lamps (in some instances shattering the frames too, and bringing the glass rattling to the ground), they are unusually dark to-night. The darkness is augmented and confused, by flying dust from the earth, dry twigs from the trees, and great ragged fragments from the rooks' nests up in the tower. The trees themselves so toss and creak, as this tangible part of the darkness madly whirls about, that they seem in peril of being torn out of the earth: while ever and again a crack, and a rushing fall, denote that some large branch has yielded to the storm.

Not such power of wind has blown for many a winter night. Chimneys topple in the streets, and people hold to posts and corners, and to one another, to keep themselves upon their feet. The violent rushes abate not, but increase in frequency and fury until at midnight, when the streets are empty, the storm goes thundering along them, rattling at all the latches, and tearing at all the shutters, as if warning the people to get up and fly with it, rather than have the roofs brought down upon their brains.

Still, the red light burns steadily. Nothing is steady but the red light.

All through the night the wind blows, and abates not. But early in the morning, when there is barely enough light in the east to dim the stars, it begins to lull. From that time, with occasional wild charges, like a wounded monster dying, it drops and sinks; and at full daylight it is dead.

It is then seen that the hands of the Cathedral clock are torn off; that lead from the roof has been stripped away, rolled up, and blown into the Close; and that some stones have been displaced upon the summit of the great tower. Christmas morning though it be, it is necessary to send up workmen to ascertain the extent of the damage done. These, led by Durdles, go aloft; while Mr. Tope and a crowd of early idlers gather down in Minor Canon Corner, shading their eyes and watching for their appearance up there.

This cluster is suddenly broken and put aside by the hand of Mr. Jasper; all the gazing eyes are brought down to the earth by his loudly inquiring of Mr. Crisparkle, at an open window:

"Where is my nephew?"

"He has not been here. Is he not with you?"

"No. He went down to the river last night, with Mr. Neville, to look at the storm, and has not been back. Call Mr. Neville!"

"He left this morning, early."

"Left this morning early? Let me in! let me in!"

There is no more looking up at the tower, now. All the assembled eyes are turned on Mr. Jasper, white, half-dressed, panting, and clinging to the rail before the Minor Canon's House.

From *The Mystery of Edwin Drood*

FAMOUS CHRISTMAS DAYS

NO GREETINGS FOR KING JOHN

THE Christmas of 1214 is memorable in English history as the festival at which the barons demanded from King John that document which as the foundation of our English liberties is known to us by the name of *Magna Charta*. John's tyranny and lawlessness had become intolerable, and the people's hope hung on the fortunes of the French campaign in which he was then engaged. His defeat at the battle of Bouvines, fought on 27th July 1214, gave strength to his opponents; and after his return to England the barons secretly met at St. Edmondsbury and swore to demand from him, if needful by force of arms, the restoration of their liberties by charter under the king's seal. Having agreed to assemble at the Court for this purpose during the approaching festival of Christmas they separated. When Christmas Day arrived John was at Worcester, attended only by a few of his immediate retainers and some foreign mercenaries. None of his great vassals came, as was customary at Christmas, to offer their congratulations. His attendants tried in vain to assume an appearance of cheerfulness and festivity; but John, alarmed at the absence of the barons, hastily rode to London and there shut himself up in the house of the Knights Templars. On the Feast of the Epiphany the barons assembled in great force at London and presenting themselves in arms before the King formally demanded his confirmation of the laws of Edward the Confessor and Henry I.

W. F. DAWSON, *Christmas, its Origin and Associations*

HENRY VIII MAKES MERRY, 1512

In this yeare the king kept his Christmasse at Greenewich, where was such abundance of viands served to all comers of anie honest behaviour, as hath beene few times seene. And against New Yeeres night was made in the hall a castell, gates, towers, and dungeon, garnished with artillerie and weapon, after the most warlike fashion: and on the front of the castell was written *Le fortresse dangereux,* and, within the castell were six ladies cloathed in russet satin, laid all over with leaves of gold, and everie one knit with laces of blew silke and gold. On their heads, coifs and caps all of gold. After this castell had beene caried about the hall, and the queene had beheld it, in came the king with five other, apparelled in coats, the one halfe of russet sattin, the other halfe of rich cloth of gold; on their heads caps of russet sattin embroidered with works of fine gold bullion.

These six assaulted the castell. The ladies seeing them so lustie and couragious, were content to solace with them, and upon further communication to yeeld the castell, and so they came downe and dansed a long space. And after, the ladies led the knights into the castell, and then the castell suddenlie vanished out of their sights. On the daie of the Epiphanie at night, the king, with eleven other, were disguised, after the manner of Italie; called a maske, a thing not seene before, in England; they were apparelled in garments long and broad, wrought all with gold, with visors and caps of gold. And, after the banket done, these maskers came in, with six gentlemen disguised in silke, bearing staffe torches, and desired the ladies to danse: some were content, and some refused. And, after they had dansed, and communed togither, as the fashion of the maske is, they tooke their leave and departed, and so did the queene and all the ladies.

Edward Hall's Chronicle

WITH THE PILGRIM FATHERS, PLYMOUTH ROCK, 1620

Munday, the 25 Day, we went on shore, some to fell tymber, some to saw, some to riue, and some to carry, so that no man rested all that day, but towards night, some, as they were at worke, heard a noyse of some Indians, which caused vs all to goe to our Muskets, but we heard no further, so we came aboord againe, and left some twentie to keepe the court of gard; that night we had a sore storme of winde and raine.

Munday the 25 being Christmas day, we began to drinke water aboord, but at night, the Master caused vs to have some Beere, and so on board we had diverse times now and then some Beere, but on shore none at all.

One ye day called Christmas-day, ye Gov'r caled them out to worke (as was used), but ye most of this new company excused themselves, and said it went against their consciences to worke on ye day. So ye Gov'r tould them that if they made it a mater of conscience, he would spare them till they were better informed. So he led away ye rest, and left them: but when they came home at noone from their worke, he found them in ye streete at play, openly; some pitching ye barr, and some at stoole ball, and such like sports. So he went to them and tooke away their implements, and told them it was against his conscience that they should play, and others worke. If they made ye keeping of it matter of devotion, let them kepe their houses, but there should be no gameing or revelling in ye streets. Since which time nothing hath been attempted that way, at least, openly.

WILLIAM BRADFORD'S *Journal*

ABOLITION OF CHRISTMAS

The House spent much Time this Day about the businesse of the Navie, for settling the Affairs at Sea, and before they rose, were presented with a terrible Remonstrance against Christmas-day, grounded upon divine Scriptures: 2 Cor. v. 16; 1 Cor. xv. 14, 17; and in honour of the Lord's-day, grounded on these Scriptures: John xx. 1; Rev. i. 10; Psalms cxviii. 24; Lev. xxiii. 7, 11; Mark xv. 8; Psalms lxxxiv. 10; in which Christmas is called Anti-Christ's-masse, and those Massemongers and Papists who observe it, &c.

In consequence of which, Parliament spent some Time in Consultation about the Abolition of Christmas-day, pass'd Orders to that Effect, and resolv'd to sit on the following Day, which was commonly called Christmas-day.

The Flying Eagle, London;
24th December 1652.

MOURNFULLEST DAY, 1655

25 Dec. There was no more notice taken of Christmas day in Churches. I went to London, where Dr. Wild preached the funeral sermon of Preaching, this being the last day; after which, Cromwell's proclamation was to take place, that none of the Church of England should dare either to preach, or administer Sacraments, teach school, etc., on pain of imprisonment or exile. So this was the mournfullest day that in my life I had seen, or the Church of England herself, since the Reformation; to the great rejoicing of both Papist and Presbyter. So pathetic was his discourse that it drew many tears from the auditory. Myself, wife, and some of our family received the Communion: God make me thankful, who hath hitherto provided for us the food of our souls as well as bodies! The Lord Jesus pity our distressed Church, and bring back the captivity of Zion!

JOHN EVELYN, *Diary*

MUSKETS AT THE ALTAR, 1657

25 Dec. I went to London with my wife, to celebrate Christmas-day, Mr. Gunning preaching in Exeter-Chapell, on 7 Micah 2. Sermon ended, as he was giving us the holy sacrament, the chapell was surrounded with souldiers, and all the communicants and assembly surpriz'd and kept prisoner by them, some in the house, others carried away. It fell to my share to be confin'd to a room in the house, where yet I was permitted to dine with the master of it, the Countess of Dorset, Lady Hatton, and some others of quality who invited me. In the afternoone came Col. Whaly, Goffe, and others, from White-hall, to examine us one by one; some they committed to the Marshall, some to prison. When I came before them they took my name and abode, examin'd me why, contrarie to an ordinance made that none should any longer observe the superstitious time of the Nativity (so esteem'd by them) I durst offend, and particularly be at Common Prayers,

which they told me was but the Masse in English, and particularly pray for Charles Steuart, for which we had no Scripture. I told them we did not pray for Cha. Steuart, but for all Christian Kings, Princes, and Governours. They replied, in so doing we praid for the K. of Spaine too, who was their enemie and a papist, with other frivolous and insnaring questions and much threatning: and finding no colour to detaine me, they dismiss'd me with much pitty of my ignorance. These were men of high flight and above ordinances, and spake spiteful things of our Lord's Nativity. As we went up to receive the sacrament the miscreants held their musketts against us as if they would have shot us at the altar, but yet suffering us to finish the office of Communion, as perhaps not having instructions what to do in case they found us in that action. So I got home late the next day, blessed be God.

JOHN EVELYN, *Diary*

HOW MR. PEPYS SPENT CHRISTMAS

1662 Christmas Day. Up pretty early, leaving my wife not well in bed, and with my boy walked, it being a most brave cold and dry frosty morning, and had a pleasant walk to White Hall, where I intended to have received the Communion with the family, but I came a little too late. So I walked up into the house and spent my time looking over pictures, particularly the ships in King Henry the VIIIth's Voyage to Bullen; marking the great difference between their build then and now. By and by down to the chappell again where Bishopp Morley preached upon the song of the Angels, "Glory to God on high, on earth peace, and good will toward men." The sermon done, a good anthem with vialls. Dined by my wife's bed-side with a great content, having a mess of brave plum-porridge and a roasted pullet for dinner, and I sent for a mince-pie abroad, my wife not being well to make any herself yet.

1664 Christmas Eve. This evening I being informed did look and saw the Comet which is now, whether worn away or no I know not, but appears not with a tail, but only is larger and duller than any other star, and is come to rise betimes and to make a great arch.

1665 Christmas Day. To church in the morning and there saw a wedding in the church, which I have not seen many a day; and the young people so merry one with another. And strange to see what delight we married people have to see these poor fools decoyed into our condition, every man and woman gazing and smiling at them.

1666 Christmas Day. Lay pretty long in bed, and then rose, leaving my wife desirous to sleep, having sat up until four this morning seeing her mayds make mince-pies. I to church, where our parson Mills made a good sermon. Then home, and dined well on some good ribbs of beef roasted and mince pies, and plenty of good wine of my owne, and my heart full of true joy and thanks to God Almighty for the goodness of my condition at this day. After dinner I began to teach my wife and Barker (the maid) my song, "It is decreed," which pleases me mightily. Then out and walked alone on foot to the Temple, it being a fine post, and so back home.

1668 Christmas Day. So home and to dinner alone with my wife, who, poor wretch! sat undressed all day till ten at night, altering and lacing of a noble petticoat. While I by her, making the boy read to me the Life of Julius Caesar, and Des Cartes book of Musick, the latter of which I understand not, nor think he did well that writ it, though a most learned man. Then after supper I made the boy play up on his lute—and so, my mind in mighty content, we to bed.

From *The Diary*

SIR ROGER DE COVERLEY

Sir Roger, after the laudable Custom of his Ancestors, always keeps open House at Christmas. I learned from him that he had killed eight Fat Hogs for this Season, that he had dealt about his Chines very liberally amongst his Neighbours, and that in particular he had sent a String of Hogs'-puddings with a Pack of Cards to every poor Family in the Parish. I have often thought, says Sir Roger, it happens very well that Christmas should fall out in the Middle of Winter. It is the most dead uncomfortable Time of the Year, when the poor People would suffer very much from their Poverty and Cold, if they had not good Chear, warm Fires, and Christmas Gambols to support them. I love to rejoice their poor Hearts at this season, and to see the whole Village merry in my great Hall. I allow a double Quantity of Malt to my Small Beer, and set it a-running for twelve Days to every one that calls for it. I have always a Piece of Cold Beef and Mince-pye upon the Table, and am wonderfully pleased to see my Tenants pass away a whole Evening in playing their innocent Tricks, and smutting one another. Our Friend Will Wimble is as merry as any of them, and shows a thousand Roguish Tricks upon these Occasions.

I was very much delighted with the Reflexion of my old Friend, which carried so much Goodness with it. He then launched out into the Praise of the late Act of Parliament for securing the Church of England, and told me with great Satisfaction, that he believed it already began to take Effect, for that a rigid Dissenter who chanced to dine at his House on Christmas-day, had been observed to eat away very plentifully of his Plumb-porridge.

JOSEPH ADDISON

THERE'LL ALWAYS BE A CHRISTMAS

THE CHRISTMAS OF THE FUTURE

By Frank Sullivan

THERE is every reason to believe that the old haphazard and unscientific methods of celebrating Christmas are slowly dying out and that the Christmas of the future will be observed with a maximum of efficiency and a minimum loss of energy.

In the past, Christmas as a holiday has often been fraught with danger to life and limb, but science is making rapid strides in the direction of making the Yuletide safe for democracy. An example of this: I heard only the other day of the admirable work a prominent inventor is doing to combat the holly menace. There are few of us who at one time or another have not received flesh wounds—not serious, to be sure, but none the less painful—as a result of sitting unawares on barbed holly left in chairs by frenzied Christmas-tree trimmers. Such lesions will soon be a thing of the past. I am not authorized to give details but I understand that within the year this inventor I speak of will have a serviceable and cheap rubber holly on the market, guaranteed not to puncture.

Other time-honoured Christmas features seem to have outlived their day. You no longer find Christmas trees festooned with ropes of popcorn. Those of us who are in our forties can remember when days were spent popping corn and stringing it into yards of trimming for the Christmas tree. By the time the tree was taken down at Twelfth Night the popcorn had hung long enough to acquire an attractively gamey tang, with a flavour of tinsel dust, lint, and dried evergreen needles. It was considered quite a delicacy by the small fry of those times. For years hot buttered popcorn seemed quite tame to me by comparison. This eating of mummified popcorn and the wholesale consumption by tots of Christmas-tree candles were probably, with the recent depression, the main factors in producing the dyspepsia which is so marked a characteristic of the generation of the present writer.

Popcorn and wax candles have joined the dodo and the Yule log. The children of to-day must find some other means of acquiring acute indigestion. They are resourceful and ingenious, and will no doubt have little trouble doing so.

Another Christmas reform impends. I am told that within a year or two science will have stripped the kiss under the mistletoe of its terrors. For some time past experiments have been proceeding with a new automatic antiseptic mistletoe. The leaves are of sterilized green satin and the berries are made of indurated milk. It will function on the principle of the automatic sprinkler, in this manner: Two kissers approach the mistletoe in a spirit of holiday lust. As they square off under the mistletoe the heat generated by their fondness for each other releases hundreds of tiny sprinklers concealed in the mistletoe "berries" and a spray of healing formaldehyde sifts gently down upon them like a benison, destroying all coryza, grippe, influenza, pneumonia, or tetanus germs that may be lurking about the kissers' kissers.

O course, the antiseptic mistletoe is only a temporary measure. Eventually the kiss under the mistletoe must go, bag and baggage. It is unhygienic, sloppy, and sentimental; and it breeds unscientific thinking. It has no place in our modern life.

The Christmas of the future will be a triumph of science over waste. Energy now frittered away in futile holiday pursuits will be conserved for more constructive purposes. For one thing, Christmas will be made to end immediately after dinner on Christmas Day, thus eliminating the demoralizing Christmas afternoon, the most depressing few hours in the Christian calendar. I refer to the period from about three o'clock on, when reaction from the hysteria of trimming the tree and opening the presents has set in and all the world seems dark and dreary; when the fruit cake is irrevocably inside the celebrant and has made unmistakably clear its determination not to merge with the port wine, walnuts, oyster stuffing, cranberry sauce, and the rest of the Christmas viands. It is the time when the kiddies begin to do battle for the possession of the few toys that remain unbroken; and it is the time when daddy, called upon to fix the electric train, trips over the track—or the baby—and plunges headlong into the Christmas tree, ripping off the electrical trimmings and causing a short circuit. Christmas afternoon must go.

In the Christmas of the future the gift problem, with its associated problems of shopping, mailing, wrapping, exchanging, etc., will cease to be the *bête noire* it is to-day. Every one will co-operate. Christmas cards will be mailed earlier and earlier until the bulk of them will have been delivered about the time the second income-tax instalments begin to clog the mails. Parcels will be wrapped more and more securely as the years go by until he will be a fast worker indeed who gets his presents all unwrapped by the second Sunday after Epiphany.

Shopping will not be the bedlam it is to-day. It will be controlled. The energies of women will be harnessed. There will be national leagues of shoppers. Teams from stores will compete with each other in shopping bouts under the rules now governing wrestling. It will be no time at all before controlled Christmas shopping has developed a hardy, buxom race of woman shoppers which might well serve as a first line of national defence in case of emergency. Perhaps it may eventually be said of the democratic countries that our victories were won on the counters of Wanamaker's or Selfridge's.

One of the worst psychological effects of Christmas on people is the rage that follows when a person gives a friend a gift and the friend fails to reciprocate. This will be eliminated in the Christmas of the future by the Declaration of Gift. This will simply be a public notice of every citizen's Christmas intentions. Early in the fall every one will be required by law to file a list with the Collector of Internal Revenue of the persons to whom he proposes to give Christmas presents, with the nature and the planned cost of each gift.

These lists will be tacked up at the post office and department stores of each city for public scrutiny. Each person can examine the lists, find out what his friends are doing, and act accordingly. If I have you on my list for a necktie or a compact and I find from the public list that you have not put me down for anything, I can just cross you off my list. Or, if a citizen thinks he has a right to expect a present from a friend who has failed to declare to that effect, the injured party shall have the legal right to apply to the courts for a writ of mandamus compelling the defendant, or recalcitrant donor, to show cause why the aforesaid present should not be given to the plaintiff, or piqued donee.

Two people who find that they are giving each other presents of equal value can pair off like senators voting at Washington and cancel both gifts, taking the will for the deed. This practice will be called phantom giving.

As Christmas becomes more and more scientific and less encumbered with sentimental flubdub children will play less and less part in its celebration. The heaviest burden of the Christmas celebration has always fallen on the tots, for it is the season of the year when parents have to be coddled and humoured more than at any other time. The child has to simulate an unfelt curiosity in mysterious packages that arrive during December and are whisked furtively to the attic. Children have to compose letters to Santa Claus to placate Christmas-crazed parents, and they are hauled off to department stores, where they are expected to display glee at the sight of a Santa Claus in palpably fake whiskers.

All this is too much of a strain on their little libidos. It fills their subconsciousnesses with impressions that pop out twenty or thirty years later in the most blood-curdling manifestations. In the future it is probable that Santa Claus will be required to be clean-shaven and that only disciples of Dr. Freud will be allowed to continue wearing a beard.

So it will go. As we progress scientifically we shall slough off the antiquated customs and leave off saying "Merry Christmas" or drinking wassail (of slight nutritive value and totally lacking in the essential vitamins). The celebration of Christmas will become more and more efficient until it will at last be so efficient that it will become unnecessary to keep Christmas at all.

THE HAND OF HEROD

By Heywood Broun

A NEWS dispatch from Paris says that the authorities have decided that midnight Masses may not be celebrated in any of the churches of the city during the Christmas season. It is explained that it would be impossible to keep the light from filtering out through the great stained glass windows of a cathedral. A candle by a shrine sheds a beam which is too broad for the warring world in which we live. If the figure of the Christ child were illuminated it might serve as a beacon for the way of wise flying men from out of the East. And their gifts would not be gold and frankincense and myrrh.

Once again the hand of Herod is raised for the slaughter of the innocents. But those things which were are with us now. I have seen men and women moved by devotion into such a mood that they felt themselves not only followers but contemporaries in the life of Jesus. To them His death was a present tragedy and Easter morning marked a literal triumph. And to those who are like-minded there lies reassurance in the revelation of the past. Herod was a ruler who for a little time had might and power vested in himself. His word was absolute and his will was cruel. As captain over thousands he commanded his messengers to find and kill the newborn king. An army was set in motion against an infant in a manger.

But though the hand of Herod fell heavily upon Bethlehem and all the coasts thereof, Joseph, the young child and his mother escaped into Egypt. "In Rama was there a voice heard, lamentation and weeping and great mourning, Rachel weeping for her children, and would not be consoled, because they are not." The blood of the young was spilled upon the ground even as it is being shed today. And it may well have seemed, some two thousand years ago, that there was no force which could stay the ravages of the monarch and his minions.

Around the child there stood on guard only Joseph and Mary, three wise men and shepherds from the field who had followed the course set for them by a bright star. Death came to Herod, and the bright star was a portent of the perfect light which was to save the world from darkness. The light of the world was not extinguished then, and it lives today and will again transfix the eyes of men with its brilliance.

In the dark streets of Paris on Christmas Eve, even as in the little town of Bethlehem, a star will animate the gloom. The call comes once more to kings and shepherds to journey to the manger and worship at the shrine of the Prince of Peace. Quite truly the civil authorities of Paris have said that it is impossible to blackout the light which shines from the altar.

And if I were in France I would go at midnight to the little island on the Seine and stand before Notre Dame de Paris. At first the towers of that great Gothic structure might seem to be lost in the blackness of the night. And it has been ruled that no congregation shall raise its voice to welcome the tidings of great joy. But then I think all the windows will take on magnificence, and that the air will resound with the message which has been given to the sons of men and will be offered again to the fellowship of all mankind. "Glory to God in the highest and on earth peace, good will toward men." And that choral cry will rise above the hum of Herod's grim messengers. It will be much louder than the crash of guns and the roar of cannon. No hymn of hate can prevail if we will only heed the eternal cadence of the Christmas carol.

PEACE UNDER EARTH

By Beatrice Warde (Paul Beaujon)

History seldom catches up so quickly with fantasy as in the case of the following. It first appeared in December 1937, as a Christmas Book privately printed for the author's friends. Part of it at once reached a wider audience through its inclusion in Mr. Arthur Stanley's anthology, "The Golden Road." It was based upon a seemingly fantas-

tic assumption going underground as the only method of preserving from destruction a city-focussed civilization. Before the year was out, the Crisis of September 1938 had thrust this "fantastic assumption" into the realm of human probability. The Great Dig had begun. The public lawns of London were furrowed with trenches. When "Peace Under Earth" appeared for the second time as a Christmas Book— this time in a limited edition—it was clear that this torn turf, still stacked beside the surface-excavations, would never be replaced. The dream of a strange future had become the immediate problem of a practical present one of Getting Down to Earth, the sixty feet of earth over which it does not pay to drop bombs. To these dialogues, events had lent prophetic interest.

In 1939, an American edition appeared; and now, to a new audience, its original text reproduced without any alteration, "Peace Under Earth" appears in a Christmas Book. In a wartime world, upon whose surface there seems no good-will anywhere, the spirit of man once more takes refuge in the deep shelter of the heart. This is not the first time faith has gone underground. In times dark as these, Christians found the Comforter in the catacombs. In this war of nerves there is one shelter always open: shelter in Bedlem. Into that safety the troubled spirit enters for refuge from the crowding fears of time.

"They were safe, safe, for that whole night and for long afterwards. . . . Will you remember that, whatever happens? That there was safety where They were? Will you remember it whenever Christmas comes?" And the child repeats, as one traces by daylight a path he must tread in the dark: "Safety where They were . . . Yes, I'll remember . . . Whenever Christmas comes . . ."

M.L.B.

I. EVENING, ABOVEGROUND

DECEMBER 24TH, 6 P. M.

Hallo, Uncle. Are you staying with us tonight?
Yes. My Shelter's not quite finished.

Then you'll be fined, won't you?

Oh, it's safe enough. Only I wasn't satisfied with the Air Conditioning system, and the Sun-ray lamps haven't arrived yet, so your Daddy's arranged for me to stay here over Christmas.

Ours is finished, and it's grand. Smells like the seaside.

That's the extra ozone. You keep using the same air, you know, so it has to be washed and . . .

Yes, I know. And, Uncle, we've got imitation windows in ours, with Sun-rays coming through: you can get sunburnt. It's much nicer than above-ground. Only it's awfully quiet when the radio's not on. No traffic noises.

Ah, but nobody *does* turn off the radio any more. It's against the law. How would we know when the Warning came? The new 1947-model sets haven't any "power off" switch. You just tune in to "Silence," or "Street Noises," or "Lullaby Music," if you don't want programmes.

Uncle, why are they making us spend tonight and tomorrow in the Shelters? Are you SURE *it's only a Rehearsal?*

Good gracious, yes. That's why they chose Christmas Eve and Christmas Day—so people wouldn't worry. No war would ever really start then.

But why not?

Don't you know? Why, it's simple. There are fewer people out in the streets, and more people at home, within quick reach of shelter, than on any other day of the year. So don't you worry. This will only be a way of reminding people about Safety. Tomorrow, when we're all being cosy underground, they're going to bomb the old Battersea Power Station. You'll see it televised, but don't imagine they're doing anything but practising on a big, easy target. The real power stations are safe underground, along with the hospitals and banks. Soon we'll have tunnelled all the new streets, with their shops and theatres; then we can wipe out all the old Built London and let the forest come back overhead. But you can't do that overnight. It takes propaganda. That's why they've brought out the new posters.

What do they mean? "The Foxes Have Their Lairs?"

That means "Be foxy; stop building from the ground up." You see, the whole point of a city has always been that it's a walled place where people can find safety long enough to be civilized. Civil-ized: city-fied. And Built Cities were finished as soon as they invented the airplane. But people are so sentimental. For thousands of years they've thought of a House as a Building. To them a Roof is Shelter, though it's only thick enough to keep off rain and snow. Why, as late as 1940 we were still dependent on the Battersea Power Station, and that's only a few years ago. No wonder the Government uses posters. "There is no Peace on Earth"—people have got to stop saying "ON earth" as if that meant Everywhere. They have to be made Lair-minded.

That poster goes on "—and no Good Will Anywhere."

Oh, that's only to educate the old people who still think that wars ought to be "declared"—out of sheer kindness, I suppose, so that the other side can nip in first.

But what does "Will" mean?

It's what makes you want to do things, or not do things.

But that's Glands, and how you were brought up.

No; "Will" is more than that.

You mean it's like Astrology, or something?

I shouldn't bother about it. The scientists·don't. They stick to things they can find out about. All they mean by "Good Will" on that poster is an Attitude that Hampers the Air Ministry. What they used to call Faith in Human Nature. Anybody that still has *that* needs educating.

So you don't think it's really going to start tonight?

No, we're as safe as hou . . . as safe as Shelters tonight.

I'm choosing some toys to take down. I'll want my model garage. Isn't it nice? Look at the little motor van.

Jolly good. D'you know, I can remember when people turned and looked when a real motor van went by.

Didn't they have vans when you were little?

They didn't have motors—any kind of motor car.

But how did they get about?

They used horses. You've seen pictures of horses, haven't you?

Yes. It must have been fun. Like the Wild West.

Oh, people didn't just ride on horses. They hitched them on to carts and things. Haven't you seen horse-drawn vehicles out in the country?

No, we go to the seaside. . . . It must have looked funny to see a car with an animal trotting in front of it. Was it only horses they used? Not cows? I saw a cow once.

They used something like a cow, once, for hauling heavy loads. A thing called an Ox.

How silly. Why didn't they invent motor cars?

I don't know. But I can show you an old picture of an Ox. It would be somewhere in that picture-book you have there.

Where? Oh, that's not a picture-book. That's Great Art Masterpieces. Pictures are when you can tell what it's about. When there's a story.

But here's one that has a story. Look, here's that animal I told you about. That's an Ox; this other one is an Ass. Don't you know this story?

It's religious, isn't it? I'm not s'posed to have religion yet. There's so much else I have to learn first.

Well, can you guess what's going on in this picture?

Let me look. . . . Is it a Zoo? Those animals are too big to be pets.

No. Look, the Ox was used as a *hauler,* so you could say he's really an old-fashioned kind of *tractor*—the word means the same thing. And they used an Ass the way we'd use a run-about. That stuff on the floor is called hay.

It looks like the stuff that was round the lampshade when it came. What did they use it for?

Fuel. Only it didn't smell beastly, like petrol. Now do you see what sort of place it is?

Why, it's a sort of garage!—Then what are the people in fancy costume doing there?

That's not fancy-costume, my lad. That was modern dress when this picture was painted, in the fourteenth century.

Is that when this story happened?

No, it happened long before that. Only, people have always liked to pretend, with this story, that *they* came into it too. You see, it's about a time when we were all taken by surprise, and most of us were made to look very hard-hearted and stupid. So people like to act as if it were happening again, only as if this time they knew, and could go and find the place. So they didn't paint these people in historical costume. That would make it harder to find the Stable.

This isn't a STABLE, *is it, Uncle? People aren't allowed in stables, Daddy says. They'd find out too much.*

Not a racing stable, silly! Still, if that's all the word means to you, we'll have to call it an Animal Garage, or you'll miss the point. At least you know what sort of place a garage is.

It's a nice place! There's one behind the hotel next door, and they let me play there.

Yes, but it's not a dignified place. It's not a suitable place for a baby to be born in. You wouldn't think much of a town where they let that happen. And if you knew some people were sleeping in that garage down the street you'd want to run out and help them, wouldn't you?

Tell the story. And pretend we come into it somewhere. Only make it about a REAL *garage, not that queer sort of a place with animals. There wouldn't be any such places near here. You said it didn't have to be fancy-dress.*

I don't know if it would work out the same way. For one thing, there's the hay. It's poor, cheap stuff for a baby's bed, but at least it's sweet and warm. The story doesn't say they were miserable, the way they'd be in a garage, with nothing soft to lie on. Still, they'd send out some blankets from the hotel, I suppose, nowadays.

Pretend I left my coat there. They could make a pillow of it.

All right, I'll remember that.

. . . Why were they there? Were they terribly poor?

Oh no. The man was a respectable master craftsman. He was a carpenter.

What's that?

Well . . . those bookshelves must have been built by a carpenter, a wood-worker.

They're not wood, they're steel painted to look like wood. Anybody can put them up—so THEY *say. Daddy started to: only he smashed his thumb, and then he rang up a man.*

Ah, now that man was a carpenter. So was this man. He worked somewhere else, but his family came from this town, and so did his wife's. That's why they'd gone there, just for a few days. It was something like a census. The town was all full of transients. They tried to get a room in the hotel, but it was full.

Maybe the hotel didn't want them. Were they Jews?

Yes, both of them! But that wasn't the reason. There really wasn't a room left. It was a shame, because . . . well, you see, the woman was very young, and tired, and she was going to have a baby.

Then they'd have gone to the hospital. I . . . I hoped they'd come and find that coat. . . .

Well, the story only says that there was no room at the hotel. But you could easily account for the hospital being full too. There might have been an air raid. Even an explosion in the poison-gas factory could crowd out the hospital. The point is they had to come to this strange, poor, unsuitable sort of place.

Why didn't the man knock at a door? Anybody would have taken them in, if they'd only known.

H'm. . . . Do you remember that man who came and put up the bookshelves? What did he do?

He looked at Daddy's thumb, and smiled, and fixed the shelves.

Precisely. This man, too, was used to having people come to *him* for help when things went wrong. And his wife must have felt the same. She wasn't frightened. She wasn't asking people to be sorry for her. She was being sorry for them. She must have known how they'd feel afterwards. But she knew it would do them good to feel that way—afterwards.

What way?

Well, that's part of the story. This town was already a Famous Birthplace. Now suppose you'd been a Town Councillor, and it had been predicted that a still greater person would be born in that town. You'd try to guess how and where, wouldn't you? You'd want the tourists to be able to say "What a fine, noble, appropriate Birthplace! What a credit to the town!" But how would you go about it?

See that all the Great Families had fine houses. . . . No, that wouldn't be making sure.

No, let's say they were cleverer than that. Suppose they said "No citizen of this town is to live in a slum. *Every* mother in this town is to be treated handsomely."

Then they'd be making sure, wouldn't they?

Think it over.

"No citizen of this . . ." Oh, I see! They didn't think about the Outsiders just passing through the Town. But why didn't they? I guessed.

Ah, that's the curious thing about the town of Bedlem.

Bedlam? I thought that was where everybody makes a noise.

No, there was a hospital named after this town, and you're thinking of the hospital. But in either place they badly needed help, because there was something wrong with the way they thought. People in Bedlem don't really believe there *is* any Outside. When it's very bad they're called Idiots—that's from a Greek word, and it means that nothing outside yourself is real. Ordinary Bedlemites are just people who say "everybody" when they mean "us." They're always being taken by surprise, and they hate it. Only a few years ago it happened with the Pint of Milk.

What was that?

The doctors said "EVERY growing child MUST have at least a pint of milk a day." So everybody agreed: only they decided that it only applied to *real* children. The others, the ones whose parents couldn't afford so much milk, were only Offspring (they said) and didn't really exist. We'd still be saying that if the Recruiting Campaign hadn't come along. Then all those Outsiders began to count, and it turned out that their children *were* real after all. But it was a shock. It made all those Retired Colonels feel silly to have to turn around and vote for universal free milk. People in Bedlem like to feel cosy, and they'll always tell you that Outsiders don't count—don't really exist. And when they've locked themselves in for the night they're sure of it.

This story is partly about one of those shocks. Think how they felt when three different International Celebrities came hurrying to this town, sent there by the Leader himself, and they had to be taken past all the fine buildings and shown into a poor, bare garage. "So this is how you received those people," the visitors would say: "Well, leave it just as it was; don't try to tidy it up and beautify it *now*." Why, even today you can make a rich man, or a professor, or any very important person feel stupid and small by showing him how the Bedlemites didn't quite guess.

At all events, I think that man and his wife decided on the . . . the garage. The hotel clerk would have seen that they were fairly comfortable. But still they looked around to see if perhaps somebody had left a coat there. . . .

And they found mine! Oh, I'm glad they did. They really needed it, didn't they? They weren't just pretending?

Yes, they really needed it, and they found it. I don't think they were frightened or upset at being in that place. The carpenter would know how to make some sort of bed, out of the draught, in between a . . . a motor van and a runabout, let's say. So then the night wore on, and the hotel lights went out, and all the town's lights went out one by one, and everything was very quiet. . . .

I'll tell you the rest some other time. You must have your supper now, and get ready to go down to the Shelter. Run along now.

Wait, Uncle. Do you think those people will be safe tonight? Will they be near a Shelter?

The story says they found a Shelter, so don't worry about that.

II. MIDNIGHT, IN SHELTER

Uncle, was that the Warning?

Hullo, you awake? No, that wasn't the Warning. Just part of the Rehearsal. The radio sounds so much louder down here. Go back to sleep. It's midnight.

I'm not sleepy. I . . . don't go, Uncle. Come and tell me a story. Tell me the rest of that story. . . . Do you think we're perfectly safe down here?

Of course we are. All sorts of things could happen Outside, up above, and we'd still be safe. Don't think about Outside at all.

It's a little like Bedlem, isn't it? We're locking ourselves in. . . . What happened next in the story?

The next part is about what happened to some people in the Outskirts of the town. You know what it's like just outside a small city?

Yes. There'd be factories.

Well, let's say there were . . . woollen factories. They were closed for the night, and they were being guarded by their night watchmen.

It's lonesome work, being a night-watchman, you know. They have too much time to think, and they have to watch the town lights going out one by one, and know that an Important Person would be at home asleep. I think they even blacked-out all the street lamps finally; so they had only the stars to look at. And you can't feel the same way about a star as you can about a lighted window. You can't feel sorry for a star, or wonder what's keeping it up so late. It just looks at you, and twinkles.

So there they were, with nobody but themselves to feel sorry for. . . . And only a minute later they were racing down the hill, leaving those factories unguarded, and thinking "What luck that we were awake!"

Because they'd seen a light in the sky, and heard a sound. . . .

Oh, Uncle, please don't have an air raid in this story. I don't like it. Even when they're all shot down in flames, I don't like it. PLEASE.

What makes you think it was an air raid?

What else would it be, that time of night, up in the sky?

Nonsense, this was a Voice speaking to them.

Oh. . . . But they don't allow Magnavox Advertising after nine o'clock.

Look, you're right as far as you go. A man-made noise in the sky at night would, naturally, be either an air raid or advertising. But this wasn't in the natural order of things, this Voice. You could tell that by what it said.

What did it say?

Well, tell me first what you'd expect it to say, if it were a plane with a Magnavox. That could only be an Air Patrol plane at that time of night. And their only reason for using it would be to wake people up to the danger of sleeping aboveground, by pretending to be an air raid and then shouting their Slogans.

I know. The ones on the posters.

That would be the natural thing, wouldn't it? But this story isn't all about perfectly natural things; and what happened at this point was . . . well, *above*-natural. Think of everything you know about, or could ever find out about, and call that the World, the World you're *inside*. Well, it has an Outside, too. And this Voice came from Outside. It wasn't a natural sort of thing: you could tell from what it said.

What did it say?

It said *"Don't* be frightened." It said that a Baby had just been born, and that would be the way out of all the horror and fear. And they were to go and see for themselves. Then there was a great sound of voices saying something you wouldn't know about, because you haven't been taught the words. But they went on to say "Peace on Earth, to men of Good Will."

It made those poor creatures feel that they had wills after all—even *good* wills. It was the first time that anybody had asked them to go and see for themselves, except in their own jobs. They'd always been expected to read books, or newspapers, and take what they were told, and trust the people that told them—because nobody cares much what night-watchmen think.

So they raced down the hill and into the town. It was very quiet. I expect only the poorest, least important people were sleeping aboveground anyway. They found the garage. They opened the door, stepping very softly.

And there was the Baby, lying in its Mother's arms.

Could you pretend we came in too, while the door was open? Would she mind? If we came very softly?

I think she'd want us to come. It wouldn't be like a King or a rich man showing himself off to the Best People, and trying to impress them. This was a helpless little Baby.

Wasn't there anything we could do?

All a baby needs is his Mother. But the Mother would need us— would need our Good Will. She would want to know that we'd already realized that this Baby was very precious. We could tell her that without saying a word—just by the way we looked and acted. . . . All the thousands of us, crowding in on tiptoe.

Were there so many?

The way *we* came, thousands and thousands of others came. All sorts of queer people; there were rough farmhands that wouldn't have dared to walk into a fine house, even if it had been open, because they'd have felt shabby and out-of-place; there were timid, stupid people who flinched if you looked at them, and knew how weak they were. They found the courage to come in. Nobody could feel particularly out-of-place in a garage, because it's not meant to *be* a place for human beings. Nobody could feel shabby after he'd seen how *they'd* had to make do. Nobody could feel weak and frightened while he was looking at an absolutely helpless new-born baby. People could stay away out of Pride, but not out of Poor People's Pride.

They kept pouring through that door all night: they'd found their way through Time, forward or back. Each of them saw a different-looking place; to some it was the stable where they'd played as children, when there *were* stables; and if they lived in northern countries they saw snow falling outside. They recognized the night-watchmen as simple people from their own villages. Others—the city people of today and the coming centuries—could see the room only dimly, because they'd never seen a real stable or real shepherds; so they saw everything second-hand through pictures, or through those little models they put up in the churches to help people find their way back. Some of those invisible guests saw a Cave: the children who were born underground in hiding could plainly see it was a Cave, whether they called it a Catacomb or a Shelter. You saw a garage because you understand about garages, and . . . and nobody's ever told you this story so as to make it sound artistic and religious.

Some people even saw that Mother and her Baby with black skins—and came away and put their pictures in the window of a wonderful cathedral in France, because they didn't think it was wrong to be black.

But whether they came from near by or by the long journey through centuries, and whatever *sort* of a shabby building it looked like, they all saw what they had come to see.

Go on . . . Uncle. . . . What did we . . . ?

(Ssh!) They saw the same Baby, all of them.

III. AFTERNOON, THE NEXT DAY

Well, have you enjoyed your first Christmas underground?

Yes, rather. But Uncle, they didn't really smash the Battersea Power Station. They kept missing it. You could see on the screen.

Oh, one bomb landed, and that would have been quite enough.

They smashed a lot of little houses round about.

But the people were all safe below in the Shelters. The wreckers will clear everything up, and then they'll plant the first trees of the New Forest there.

Uncle, did you say that people had lived underground before?

Yes, thousands of them were driven underground once because they couldn't live on the surface without being smashed or burnt alive. That's really part of the story I was telling you. That Baby lived long enough to do and say a lot of disturbing things. All sorts of unimportant people like slaves, and women, began to act as if they were *real* people who counted; they even died like real people. So that upset the whole economic system. Because by the time the smashing and burning began it was too late. From the moment that those people escaped from that stable it was too late to lock the stable door.

What were they escaping from?

Well, the Dictator of that country heard what had happened, and of course he was furious.

Why?

Because his whole System was to see to it that his people should be jolly frightened by just the particular things that he could save them from. Germs: he'd have them quaking about germs because he had the antiseptics. Other races: he'd play up all their race-fears because he had a Majority. Foreigners: as long as he had more aircraft. He had amusements: so he made them absolutely terrified of being bored or sad. He kept showing them horrible dangers and then saving them. You can't run a country unless you're the Number One Saviour in it and everybody admits it. The fatal thing is to let them see any danger that you *can't* save them from.

But how could you stop them from seeing it?

It's generally done by changing the words for things. For instance, make them say "healthy or unhealthy" instead of "good or bad." That's the surest way; but they only discovered it recently.

In this case the main thing was to find out whether the thing that had happened really *was* the sort of thing that would get out of his control.

So he asked three very Important People to find that town and tell him what they'd seen. They were to take presents along—gifts that would stand for what they had to offer. The first one, I think, was a famous and wise International Financier, and he brought Gold.

Gold? What for?

Sorry, I mean Credit Facilities. And the second man brought a kind of . . . well, incense. Let's say he was in control of hundreds of newspapers and magazines, and he knew that nothing in the world smells as sweet to Important People as the printer's ink in their own press-cuttings. His flagon of printer's ink stood for what they call Recognition nowadays.

And the third man brought a bitter liquid that had cost years of research. It was the Perfect Germicide, and it stood for a most precious thing called Health.

Now the story says that these were wise men, not simply clever men. So it must be that these gifts stood for their whole lives' work, for the Best Thing that each of them knew. And they were wise enough to know that any one of those things was precious enough to be the Price of any ordinary man or woman.

They found the place—they were meant to find it. They heard the night-watchmen's story, and talked with the carpenter; and then they went in and saw the Baby.

Now remember, their careers depended on standing in well with the Leader, who was waiting impatiently for their report.

What happened was that they laid down their gifts, but not at all as if they were a Price; and came away quietly and never even left a message with the Leader. They simply went out of that country as fast as they could.

Why did they do that?

I don't think you'll know how they felt until you're grown up; and only then if you're unlucky enough to fall hopelessly in love with someone who just doesn't happen to *need* a single thing that you can buy, or make, or do for her. It's a horrible, desolate feeling. Lovers are desperately proud. They can't bear the thought that their gifts are taken only out of kindness.

It was love that made them lay those gifts down as if they were worthless. Because of course they were wise enough to see ahead, to see the Danger that the Leader couldn't save them from. They must have seen a great deal in that moment.

But they weren't meant to go away heartbroken, and ashamed of their presents. And they didn't have to; because they could see with their own eyes that there was a real need. This Baby wasn't just pretending to be helpless. He was in very real danger, and any sort of help at all . . . an old coat, a good wish, a promise never to hurt him . . . any gift at all was really and truly needed.

So they came away with their heads high.

What did the Leader do when he heard?

Oh, then he tried a sort of Post-Natal Birth Control scheme he'd thought of.

Goodness! It sounds horrid.

Oh, just an Emergency Measure. It was rather like modern warfare: he aimed at one Objective and missed it, and smashed a great many little children. Only it wasn't quite as bad: he had the children killed quickly and personally by experts. They weren't pinned under beams waiting for the flames to reach them. They didn't die of poison-gas, slowly. He was a humane man, as these things go. But the principle was the same: "Hew to the Line, let the Bombs fall where they may." Unfortunately for him, he missed his Objective. These people got clean away.

And what happened to the Baby?

The rest of the story couldn't be told this way—as if it had only happened yesterday to people we know. It wouldn't need to be told that way. It's only in this first part that people keep wanting to make the scene familiar: and for centuries they've been telling it and painting it and singing it as if it lay just round the corner—*their* corners. That's so people could know what sort of place it was, and find their way there on Christmas Eve.

Is this a specially Christmas story?

Why, it's the *reason* for Christmas!

Oh, nonsense, Uncle! Everybody knows the real reason for Christmas. It's in all the books. Christmas is really the Turn of the Year. They've been celebrating it ever since the beginning, when they worried about the days getting shorter. The Old Romans had it; they called it—uh—Saturdaylia. And then the Early Christians just took it over readymade, only they made it religious. And now we have it, and pretend it's Santa Claus coming.

But *why* do we make so much fuss about Santa Claus? Why do people give presents to little children particularly?

People don't, particularly. Mother's been half crazy trying to remember all the grown-up people who were likely to remember her. And Daddy says, it's the only time of the year he can send presents to his customers without its being Bribry and Cruption. Of course children get presents too. But . . . don't you read the ads? Haven't you seen Santa Claus lugging out cases of Whisky? Don't you see the Exmas Sales?

H'm. Well, let's start over again. Look, something happened as the result of this Baby's coming into the world. I can only tell you that people found something *worth* being afraid of; and that stopped them being afraid of anything else. They found—they were shown —a really worthy Enemy, not one that rich men can buy off, or clever men argue away: an enemy who would take as much trouble over a slave as over a master: more, when the slave was harder to frighten. The Leader had guessed the truth; they did find out the Greatest Danger, and it did upset his system: when he trotted out his own Dangers after that, and started saving them, people weren't properly grateful, because they hadn't been properly frightened. They'd seen the Worst Thing, and they'd seen the Way Out. This really happened, mind you; it's as much history as those other people's living in Shelters.

But what is the Greatest Danger?

Being locked in *without knowing you are.* Seeing a door and not knowing what it's for. Being inside something and not dreaming there really *is* any Outside. People who are in that state are on their way to going insane. There's a long word for it, but that's what it means.

Well, these people had heard the one sound that you *couldn't* mistake for some Inside noise, such as the hammering of your own heart. It was the sound of human knuckles rapping urgently. So they said to themselves: "That must have come from the Outside . . . if there *is* any." . . . So they leaned their ears against the walls of their World, and heard it more plainly. After that, it wasn't hard to find the door and slide back the bolt. But nothing could have saved them if they hadn't been able to believe that the Outsider was really there. And they couldn't have believed *that* if it hadn't sounded like a real person.

You mean a REAL person? Not like "Mother Nature" or . . .

No, not a figure of speech. Someone who'd taken the trouble to . . . well, to be born, for one thing. And to learn to talk with words. And to find out for himself how well-hidden the door is. In other words, someone real enough to have got into real Danger.

And that's why we keep going back to this First Birthday of that poor Baby.

You see, what these Wise Men and the rest of us saw was our Rescuer from the Outside—the one who was going to help us out of our trap—caught fast himself and as helpless as . . . as a new-born Baby. He'd become an Insider. He'd been walled in, like the rest of us; locked in.

And we knew what would happen in the end. He was going to be killed for not being a proper Insider.

Killed?

Yes. He was going to be handed over to the Local Authorities of a big Empire by the very Insiders he'd been brought up with. The people who'd wanted him to lead a Racial-National Revolt, and still hoped he would if his hand was forced. And the others who weren't ready for a Revolt just yet, and found all the rumours awkward, even if they weren't true. And still others who were only thinking about a popular Racketeer who'd be let off if this Man were killed instead. In other words, people like us: Nationalists, Internationalists, and Fools. That's the point to remember: the things that killed this Man were things that are very strong in all of us.

If it isn't one thing it's another. If it's not Patriotism it's Diplomacy—or misplaced Hero-worship. We know that; and it makes us feel horribly ashamed.

I tell you—it's like a drunken driver waking up to hear that *some* drunken driver has just killed a child. Or no, it's worse than that. The person killed would have to be somebody who was pushing a child to safety. *That's* how the rest of the Nationalists and Diplomats feel when they think about what happened to this Man. And the Plain Fools would think it too, if they could think. It's that sick feeling of "*I* could have done it."

So now you see why we pretend . . . if you want to call it pretending . . . that we can find our way back to the Beginning of the Story. It's because we want to pretend it's beginning over again, and the Baby is still safe. It's so that *we* can be the Outsiders, the strong ones, the sharp-eyed ones who can keep watch, the rich ones who can spare a coat for a pillow. We want it to be Not Too Late.

But it is too late, isn't it?

That's the queerest thing about this whole story. It's something that nobody can begin to understand.

You mean it keeps happening over and over?

No, that's the last thing you could say. It happened just once, and for ever; it wasn't the sort of thing that could happen even twice the same way. That's why the scientists have to say it's "outside" their line: they can only deal with things that keep happening the same way.

But the queer thing about the beginning of this story is that we *can*, in a sort of way, be there when it happened. Or at least people have always acted as if they could. As if they could go and see for themselves . . .

But why do they do it specially at Christmas? I mean why not just any time they like?

Well, so they can; but for most people it's much easier to go all together in a party, with the children running on ahead to call the way, so nobody can get lost. But to do that everybody has to agree on a day.

So I think they chose the turn-of-the-year time partly because it's rather like a charade, with the nights "drawing in" like a trap around the littlest day. And of course it was already a Holiday.

But they didn't just "take over" the Saturnalia. They didn't feel any need to get drunk, for one thing, and they'd already made a principle of treating slaves like Human Beings, so they couldn't take *that* over as a special Yuletide custom. . . . You haven't any call to act superior to the Early Christians nowadays, you know. They were working for Peace *on* Earth, you know, even when they were down *under* it. And they had the sense to see that point about Good Will. *We're* only trying to prove that Will doesn't exist—

except when we're busy willing that our bombers should get in first. The best of us are still in the Reprisal stage.

What's the Reprisal Stage?

It's wanting to send out bombers *after* you know what it's like to be bombed.

But people don't WANT *to do that. They're only . . . willing to.*

There. I told you how convenient it was to change the words! I'll bet you never realized that "willing" had any connection with "will." You're not supposed to know that. It's much easier for the Willers if you go on thinking that "willing" only means "not minding." They don't want you to know it has any meaning *outside* that.

Why? Do many words have outsides to them?

Lots. . . . Are you going to have Latin?

I don't think so. Daddy says it's no use.

Well, here's some Latin for you. *Fortis* means "strong," and *confortare* means . . . well, do you know what a comforter is?

A feather quilt?

I wish you'd look it up in the dictionary, and see what it used to mean.

We have the New Dictionary, and it doesn't say what words used to mean. There wouldn't be room; it has to put in all the different things that the same word means nowadays.

According to who's using it, to whom?

Yes. It's ever so many volumes, but there isn't any Latin in it. What's the use of Latin when you're talking about a feather quilt?

W-well . . . suppose you woke up and noticed what a Lump you'd been to imagine that "willing" only meant "not minding." As if you hadn't any strength of . . . of mind; as if your will didn't matter. You'd feel a fool, though you'd be past the Worst Danger anyway. You know, the Danger of not ever noticing.

Still, you'd feel horrid, and you'd need comfort. You'd feel—well, dis-spirited, and you'd need spirit. So you'd look around, and if you didn't care much what words meant you might reach for a feather quilt, and all sorts of harmful spirits.

But the people that first wrote down this story, they didn't have so many words as we do—or at least not so many different meanings for each word. And the Leaders hadn't yet invented the New Way with Words, because they still thought that smashing might work.

So when those people said that some Spirit had got into them that made them able to write it all down and read it off so it made sense—well, that's what they meant. But when they called that Spirit "the Comforter" they didn't a bit mean "the Soother."

The last thing you need is a Soother when you're being driven underground. It would be mean to start to *soothe* anybody who'd just found out he was in the Reprisal Stage. Because he'd be just beginning to realize that he'd probably gone and locked himself in with Danger. The more you soothed him, the less chance he'd have to . . . *Hark!* What's that?

It's the "All Clear" signal. It's six o'clock. We can go outside now. Come on, Uncle . . . that's right; now the outer door. . . . Oof! How smoky it smells. And how dark it is. . . .

They've been practising the Smoke Screen. Look, there come the street lights on again. Hullo, there's a building been hit down the street. What bad aiming! It's a mile away from the Objective. That Smoke Screen must have confused the Raiding Side. Lucky we didn't take any chances.

Oh, Uncle . . . it's our garage . . . the one where I left my coat. Oh, that's dreadful. . . .

No, no, no, there wasn't anyone in it. *Please* don't think They were there. They *couldn't* have been there. Don't try to think of the Place as a garage. It was a stable. It was long ago. There wasn't any Smoke Screen, and They were safe, *safe,* for that whole night and for long afterward. Will you remember that, whatever happens? That there was safety where They were? Will you remember it whenever Christmas comes?

Safety where They were. . . . Yes, I'll remember. . . . Whenever Christmas comes. . . .

RING OUT THE OLD

Ring out the old, ring in the new,
　　Ring, happy bells, across the snow;
　　The year is going, let him go;
Ring out the false, ring in the true.

Ring out the grief that saps the mind,
　　For those that here we see no more;
　　Ring out the feud of rich and poor,
Ring in redress to all mankind.

Ring out a slowly dying cause,
　　And ancient forms of party strife;
　　Ring in the nobler modes of life,
With sweeter manners, purer laws.

Ring out the want, the care, the sin,
　　The faithless coldness of the times;
　　Ring out, ring out my mournful rhymes,
But ring the fuller minstrel in.

Ring out false pride in place and blood,
　　The civic slander and the spite;
　　Ring in the love of truth and right,
Ring in the common love of good.

Ring out old shapes of foul disease;
　　Ring out the narrowing lust of gold;
　　Ring out the thousand wars of old,
Ring in the thousand years of peace.

Ring in the valiant man and free,
The larger heart, the kindlier hand;
Ring out the darkness of the land,
Ring in the Christ that is to be.

ALFRED TENNYSON

INDEX OF TITLES

INDEX OF FIRST LINES

742

INDEX OF AUTHORS AND SOURCES